Nobody's Perfect

Nobody's Perfect

WRITINGS FROM *THE NEW YORKER*

Anthony Lane

 ALFRED A. KNOPF · NEW YORK · 2002

This Is a Borzoi Book Published by Alfred A. Knopf

 Published in the United States by Alfred A. Knopf, a division of Random House, Inc., New York, and simultaneously in Canada by Random House of Canada Limited, Toronto. Distributed by Random House, Inc., New York.
www.aaknopf.com

All articles were originally published in *The New Yorker*.

Library of Congress Cataloging-in-Publication Data
Lane, Anthony, 1962–
Nobody's perfect / by Anthony Lane.— 1st ed.
p. cm.
ISBN 0-375-41448-7
1. Motion pictures—Reviews. I. Title.

PN1995 .L28 2002
791.43'75—dc21 2002020809

Manufactured in the United States of America
FIRST EDITION

For Allison

ALGERNON: I hope tomorrow will be a fine day, Lane.
LANE: It never is, sir.
ALGERNON: Lane, you are a perfect pessimist.
LANE: I do my best to give satisfaction, sir.

—*The Importance of Being Earnest*

"Nobody's perfect."

—Osgood Fielding III, in *Some Like It Hot*

CONTENTS

INTRODUCTION

You are holding a hunk of old journalism. The prospect is not immediately appealing. Who, like Oliver Twist, will have either the nerve or the appetite to ask for more? Yet Oliver *did* want more; he knew what would land on his plate, if the beadle consented to his request, but he asked anyway. Even gruel has its uses, and so, more alarmingly, does a half-forgotten film review. There is surprising nourishment to be had from revisiting earlier judgments, if only for the pleasure of reversing them, wondering what curious conditions led one to cast them in the first place, or serving them up with relish to those who are constitutionally doomed to disagree. If this book has any concrete effect, it will be, I hope, in a small back room in a country town, where a reader will suddenly jump up and down in unprecedented fury, enraged by my appraisal of *Speed* or *The Bridges of Madison County*, and bang his head on the ceiling.

The book contains a selection of work from *The New Yorker*, at which I arrived in 1993. That I have now been with the magazine for almost a decade means that, if all goes well, I can soon expect to outgrow the status of stumbling novice; beyond that lie the ranks of the merely bewildered, and, forty years down the line, a cherished post as an acceptable part of the scenery. As a rule, writers should be treated like rubber plants—lightly pruned, occasionally watered, but basically left to do their own thing in a corner, away from direct sunlight. Even now, people ask wonderingly how my original appointment came about. All I can say is that, at some point, there must have been a clerical error of such embarrassing proportions that the magazine has spent the last nine years trying to cover it up. I myself wonder whether there is another and far more qualified Anthony Lane living quietly with his frustrations in a distant land, still waiting for the call from Tina Brown; in that case, I am a kindred spirit of William Boot, the malleable hero of Evelyn Waugh's *Scoop*, who, after a mixup with the true Boot, was hired by the *Daily Beast* to cover a complex African war, when all he really knew about was voles.

The manner and protocol of my appointment, likewise, remain fogged in mystery. I was sitting in London when the call came from Tina's office; I think I actually *stood up* to receive it, much as I would if a letter had come from the Vatican. It transpired that Tina had dispatched her scouts and spies—her roving monsignors—on a mission to find a new film reviewer, and that some hapless soul, presumably under torture, had croaked the name of Lane. So I mailed a sheaf of smeared photocopies and followed them to America, where Tina had summoned me to a breakfast meeting. This was a brilliant move on her part, since she must have gathered from her sources that, like Bertie Wooster, I am congenitally unable to speak before ten in the morning, whereas she has always made it her business to be neck and neck with the lark. The plan, I imagined, was that she would make all the running while I would sit there, breathe my tea, and nod my jet-lagged assent. At stake was a deal of great pith and moment: she needed a movie critic, and I needed the French toast with maple syrup and a gathering of seasonal berries.

Things did not go as expected. For one thing, I got the job, which was hardly part of the blueprint. Second, and more important, I didn't eat. So brisk and genial was Tina that she was out of there and heading to the next meeting, a few sips of coffee the stronger, while I was still debating whether I should try to eat grilled bacon, never the quietest of foodstuffs, in the presence of a public figure. Time, I am happy to say, soothed this difficult etiquette, and I gradually became one of the few men in America who could order pancakes in her presence and stack 'em high. Quite why I failed to join in the paralyzing awe of Tina that prevailed elsewhere is hard to say; maybe because she offered better value as a friend, but mainly because all my fears were displaced on to the magazine itself.

Nowadays *The New Yorker* perches high in the Condé Nast building on a corner of Times Square, an unenjoyable comb of offices that is redeemed only by Frank Gehry's infamous pod of a lunchroom, where diners fight to suppress the sensation that they have wandered into an episode *of The Jetsons*. Along the ovoid barriers of its salad bunker and sandwich barricade we slouch, in varying degrees of disrepair, behind the flawless begetters of *Allure* and *Vogue*, the synchronized rise and fall of whose hemlines remains, for those frozen to their iMacs, the one reliable guide to the shifting seasons outside. Yet *The New Yorker* of Forty-third Street, its previous residence, was no less arctic; long, hard corridors, doors as thick as logs, and a whiteness of wall that struck me as close to medicinal. Working late at night, I would listen out for the squeak of an institutional sneaker, convinced that Nurse Ratched had marched out of the movie that bore her—*One Flew Over the Cuckoo's Nest*—and into the wards of *The New Yorker*. The intimidation had begun on my first day at the magazine, as I was courteously shown into a small office, which was to serve as my temporary base camp. The door swung shut behind me with a *gthunk*, as in a horror story, and I was left to inspect the contents of my space: a pad of paper, a pencil, and a phone. Was there someone of substance waiting to be interviewed on Line One, already giving off small, sighing belches of impatience? If so, would he mind holding a little longer while I learned shorthand? Was I supposed to create something, instantly and without prior research? Panicking, I cast my mind back to the opening of *Manhattan*, and to Woody Allen's floundering attempts to capture the savage city: "Chapter One: He adored New York . . ."

This is not to deny the warmth of the welcome that I received. Although there were sound reasons to view me as a disruptive interloper—a would-be McMurphy, and a Brit to boot—there were, as far as I can gather, relatively few moves to have me lobotomized. On the other hand, there was Harold Brodkey. He was then in his Indian summer—already sick, and writing with great fluency and irate pathos for the magazine. The trouble was that one of my final acts before leaving British journalism, where I had been stewing for four years, had been to write an unfavorable review of his vast and long-digested novel, *The Runaway Soul*. Now, Brodkey read everything, and I knew that he had read this churlish piece; more to the point, he knew that I knew that he knew who I was and what I had said. Obviously, I could never meet the guy; his sensitivity and height suggested someone who dealt with unappreciative critics by holding up their hearts, still beating, in front of their bulging eyes. "Please," I said to Alexander Chancellor, who was then editing "Talk of the Town," "whatever you do, don't introduce me to Harold Brodkey." Alexander's eyes gleamed, much as Don King's must gleam when a call comes through from Las Vegas. He waited no more than a day. "Anthony," he cried cheerily, "meet Harold." The great man advanced down the corridor and held out his hand. "What a pleasure to have you on board," he said. I gave a milky smile and tried to remember how Mowgli had managed on his first date with Shere Khan. From then on, Brodkey couldn't leave me alone. I would be sitting at my desk when the door would open a crack, to reveal a bony head. "How are you getting along?" It was magnificent. He was kindness itself, knowing that courtesy would keep me in the first, virginal blush of absolute fear. The review was never mentioned, which meant that it was never forgotten. If Harold had slugged me, the matter would have been closed; but it stayed open until the day he died.

* * *

Terror aside, the advantages of working at *The New Yorker* became apparent within days. Of the many reasons for quitting the squalling pit of London journalism, one of the most heartening was that I no longer felt the slightest compunction to bang the drum for British cinema, an activity only slightly more useful than arguing the case for a fleet of Swiss submarines.

I was also sprung free from the indignity of the picture byline—a bizarre English addiction, based on the surely unprovable theory that readers of newspapers will be more, not less, likely to admire a piece of prose when given the chance to inspect the face of the motheaten specimen who cobbled it together. Not so: any fragile support that I commanded among London moviegoers, for instance, was severely compromised by the fact that my column was topped by what appeared to be an unhappy reject from the Hitler Youth. All that sank beneath the waves as I shifted my allegiance to America, and to a magazine whose more diligent writers would, if stalked by a portrait photographer, take care to climb inside a passing weenie cart and wait till the peril had passed.

The editorial attention, too, was of a different order from anything that had prevailed in Britain, being prolonged and scrupulous; as for the noble legend of the *New Yorker* fact checkers, it turned out to be fact itself. What impressed me most was that they took the trouble to check not only real facts but unreal facts as well; a checker would carry my film review along to a screening and insure that my Sharon Stone quotation was on the money. I knew that litigation was a popular sport in America, but it had never crossed my mind that one might be sued by imaginary characters. If I got Godzilla's name wrong, he could take me to the cleaners, and only the fact checkers could keep me in the clear. Given the level of caution that was brought to a hokey movie, one could scarcely imagine the pressure in the checking department when something of genuine weight was at stake; when the page was full of war crimes, or misdemeanors in the White House. Needless to say, such mania for accuracy is a long way from the journalistic practice of England, where most newspapers are ideally read as a branch of experimental fiction.

The other thing that *The New Yorker* could offer was a full set of dimensions: length, breadth, and width. I remember being impressed, in my youth, by a publication that could offer Pauline Kael three thousand words to write about *Popeye*, and, although there has been a certain downsizing since then, I was still flattered, in my turn, by the chance not merely to review *Showgirls*, say, but to consider at leisure the lush philosophical landscape from which it sprang. At a time when, for many viewers, the value of a motion picture is indicated by the rotation of a chubby thumb through 180 degrees, one should remind them that, of all the duties required of the professional critic, perhaps the least important—certainly the least enduring—is the delivery of a verdict. I am always sorry to hear that readers were personally offended, even scandalized, that my opinion of a film diverged from theirs. I wish I could convince them that I am merely starting an argument, as everyone does over dinner, or in a crowded bar, after going to see a film, and that their freedom to disagree is part of the fun. The primary task of the critic, (and nobody has surpassed the late Ms. Kael in this regard), is the recreation of texture—not telling moviegoers what they should see, which is entirely their prerogative, but filing a sensory report on the kind of experience into which they will be wading, or plunging, should they decide to risk a ticket. You may object to the films of Krzysztof Kieślowski, but, with their heavy filtration and cloudbursts of sudden music, not to mention the wounded emotions that drift across the faces of their heroines, they could have been made by nobody else.

All of which is a way of saying that movies deserve journalism. This may sound obtuse, not to say indefensible, in the light of those unusual thinkers whose most fervid desire is to have their words reproduced on billboards across the land. Broadcasting from radio stations so local that the presenters might just as well ditch the microphones, stand on the roof, and shout, these superbly untroubled beings scorch the earth with indiscriminate goodwill. However hellish that Adam Sandler fiasco you just saw, don't worry; there'll be somebody in Delaware who is prepared to stand and tell the world, "Hands up for the flat-out funniest comedy since *Father of the Bride*! Adam Sandler is a laugh riot, hands down!" And there will be people at Universal who will plaster it on a wall; by an appealing coincidence, they will be the same people who flew the guy from Delaware to a junket in Atlantic City and then inquired gently for his assessment of Mr. Sandler as the new Jim Carrey. I once went to a junket and heard the assembled hacks complaining to each other about the water pressure in their hotel jacuzzis. I am as corrupt as the next man, but, I must admit, the notion that you could trim your critical opinions to accord with the fizzy water in which you recently dipped your ass had, until then, never occurred to me, and it still strikes me as impractical today.

Nevertheless, I repeat: movies deserve journalism. Both involve a quick turnover, an addiction to the sensational, and a potent, if easily exhausted, form of communal intensity; books written about film are often devout and scholarly, but, unlike journalism, they bear almost no stamp of what it actually feels like to go to the movies. A review should give off the authentic reek of the concession stand; it should become as handy as that finest of nocturnal inventions, the armrest-mounted soda holder. This holds especially true for readers who have every intention of staying in, cooking dinner, and skipping the film altogether. When people tell me, as they frequently do, that they can't be bothered to see a subtitled picture (because it's too much work) or the latest and loudest blockbuster (because they know in their bones that it will be junk), what happens to the role of the movie critic? It should by rights be diminished; in practice, the reading of reviews, like a careful tracking of the weekend's grosses, seems to be growing into a perverse substitute for the act of moviegoing itself. The sheer, overhanging mass of cultural offerings is now so forbidding that the essay—literally, the attempt, like the attempt that a climber makes on the north face of the Eiger—has, if anything, reasserted its claim to be the sanest and most proportionate response. I know that sanity is not the first quality that one associates with film critics—one thinks more readily of our Styrofoam complexions and, as for our hairstyle, Fie, 'tis an unweeded garden—but the fact remains that a reviewer who does his or her job, and who steers you away from bad art, is sane enough to save you eight bucks.

To enhance that illusion, the following maxims should be obeyed by anyone who, having tried and failed to gain respectable employment, has decided to throw in the sponge and become a movie critic instead:

1. Never read the publicity material. Much of this is taken up with unconvincing claims of the expertise acquired by the stars in the buildup to the shoot: "Not content with a ringside seat, he actually spent ten months preparing for the role by acting as sparring partner to seven professional boxers, and is now hoping to contend for the welterweight title of the world." Worse still, you get a synopsis of the story, and thus a false impression of coherence; the printed credits will tell you who is playing whom, whereas the regular viewer, deprived of such help, may struggle to grasp the identities of the characters for half an hour, and one should honor that confusion, for it may signal a genuine messiness in the movie. After all, a critic is just a regular viewer with a ballpoint pen, an overstocked memory, and an underpowered social life.

2. Whenever possible, see a film in the company of ordinary human beings. If Steven Spielberg has spent two years and $80 million getting a movie onto the screen, it seems only fair to react in kind—to surround yourself with a thousand thrillable souls, all of whom are snacking hard in anticipation and none of whom would dream of taking notes. My spirits sag whenever a screening is laid on in one of the specialist rooms off Times Square, which I always think

of as peep shows for movie buffs. Can one honestly promise a nimble response when the screen is the size of a parking space and the three critics hunched beside you, doggedly scratching down the word "joke" at the point where normal mortals would laugh, have already seen an Eddie Murphy comedy before lunch and a documentary about Swabian transsexuals in the early afternoon?

3. Try to keep up with documentaries about Swabian transsexuals. This is grim work, but somebody has to do it. If reviewers don't get out and proclaim the merits of this stuff, nobody else is going to, and the popular will to peek over the ramparts of popular cinema, into the briars and swamps that lie outside, is being sapped with every month. All those scenes in Woody Allen pictures which found him lining up with a date to see Von Stroheim or *The Sorrow and the Pity* were partly jokes about Woody the film nerd, but they also reflected a period when adventurous moviegoing was part of the agreed cultural duty, when the duty itself was more of a trip than a drag, and when a reviewer could, in the interests of cross-reference, mention the names "Dreyer" or "Vigo" without being accused of simply dropping them for show. To rely upon readers' familiarity with a dead star or a faded, foreign director was to flatter them with the assumption that they already knew their way around the byways and backwaters of cinema, and that, with a few helpful coordinates, they would desire to know more. That time has gone. The number of repertory houses available to the Manhattan moviegoer has withered since my arrival at *The New Yorker*, though not, I trust, as a direct result. I recall going to watch *My Man Godfrey*, one of the smoothest of Depression comedies, (try explaining *that* genre to your kids), down at St. Mark's and getting, for my money, a double helping of suspense: Would Carole Lombard unearth the truth about William Powell? And would the movie itself burn up before she had the chance? The projector rattled and hummed, and the projected image slid into an alcoholic blur, as if it knew the end was nigh; the film just about held it together, which is more than you can say for the theatre. The film revival house at St. Mark's closed its doors in 1994.

4. Whenever possible, pass sentence on a movie the day after it comes out. Otherwise, wait fifty years. Films are most plausibly assessed either in the heat of the moment or with the icy advantage of the long gaze; anything in between is hedging one's bets. Cinema is both news and history, but it takes a long while for one to ripen into the other. We have no idea how *Titanic* will settle—how it will

fare, or fester, on the junky seabed of old movies. My guess is that it will be viewed, not unfondly, as a necessary anachronism; in fact, as with a large percentage of the films discussed here, one cannot but hear the sharp, wistful intake of the last gasp. If pressed, I would stand by my account of James Cameron's film as the heavily salted farewell to a tradition that was inaugurated by D. W. Griffith and, many will argue, never surpassed; much as *Beyond the Clouds*, the work of an aging Michelangelo Antonioni, seems to raise a hand, or a glass, to the vanishing presumption that movies can reflect on the stubbornness of human dislocation, rather than minister to an unearned dream of our togetherness. (The difference between those two films, of course, is not merely one of manner; there is also the small matter of an audience. Cameron's picture took in a billion dollars worldwide, and legends grew of teenage girls stitching themselves to cinema seats or offering themselves as virgin sacrifices to the holy brat that was Leonardo DiCaprio. *Beyond the Clouds*, on the other hand, was seen by about half a dozen people in America, two of which were me.)

5. Try to avoid the Lane technique of summer moviegoing. On a broiling day, I ran to a screening of *Contact*, the Jodie Foster flick about messages from another galaxy. I made it for the opening credits, and, panting heavily—which, with all due respect, is not something that I find myself doing *that* often at Jodie Foster films—I started taking notes. These went "v. gloomy," "odd noir look for sci-fi," "creepy shadows in outdoor scene," and so on. Only after three-quarters of an hour did I remember to remove my dark glasses.

This book is split into three sections. The first is a bunch of film reviews, starting with *Indecent Proposal* (1993), in which a man is offered a million dollars for a night with his wife, and closing with *Together* (2001), in which a man loans his wife out without charging for her, in the interests of free love, and looks extremely miserable about it. One is an atrocious movie, the other is liberatingly good, but, as stories, neither makes any effort to keep its fingers out of cinema's deepest and most promising pockets, the wallet and the heart. Whatever humans do on film, they do for love or money.

So, what happened to movies in those eight years? One should always tread carefully when attempting to follow the footprints of a trend, not least because it is in the nature of filmgoing, as of the other arts, to presume, with a sad shrug of the shoulders, that the path goes ever downward. The rule is that golden ages are always a dot on the horizon, and that present conditions are always newly horrendous. I was much taken by a line by James Agee, who was lamenting, as critics will, the films that filled his days: "The whole business has been dying here, ten years or more. Last year, it seems to me, was the all-time low—so far." And that year would be? 1942. Ah yes, boring old '42, the year of *Now, Voyager*, *The Palm Beach Story*, and *Casablanca*. What a bummer *that* was. Let us hope that we, in our turn, will be proved shamefully wrong—that critics of the future will look back and snigger at the myopic men and women of 2001, who had *Pearl Harbor* dangled in front of their noses, and who refused to smell it out as the fragrant psalm that it so plainly was.

Nevertheless, it would be cowardly not to ask why so many movies of the last decade managed to seem at once more tired and more convulsive than those which came before. The thrillseeker's hunt for nervous satiety, for a Dionysian wipeout of the senses, grew as strong as the certainty that it would never be attained. This may be a vice that has bled from the practice of video games, which depend on racking your challenges up from one level to the next; excitement is guaranteed and is therefore, strictly speaking, no longer exciting, having been shorn of surprise. It also signals the further abasement of dramatic downtime; even experienced filmmakers are now obliged to invest such care, and so much cash, in the niceties of the uptime—the firefight, the kickbox, the heat of the chase—that the gaps between the highs have come to be treated with a sullen laziness. Compare *Black Hawk Down* (2001) with *Alien*, made over twenty years before, and you find the same director, Ridley Scott, actually growing less mature—or, sadder still, being given less leeway to presume on the maturity of his audience. The finest moments in *Alien* are not moments at all, but minutes: that cheerful lunch, around the white table, before John Hurt develops a cough, or Beauty, in the elongated person of Sigourney Weaver, moving with careful, deep-space politesse around her escape pod, as she realizes that the Beast is lying there and watching her undress. Cut to *Black Hawk Down*, and you find that the space allotted to the cultivation of characters, let alone their interaction, has become insultingly small—hey, this soldier sketches! That one makes the coffee! And look, an African praying!

The irony is that, when a moviegoer's memory wings back to its treasured domains, it is almost always upon the small, scruffy patches of downtime that it tends to alight. The review of *Braveheart*, included in this volume, ends on a note of uncontainable agitation, enough to suggest that the film would roam my mental highlands for seasons to come; instead of which, I find that I have retained not a sliver of its—admittedly mangled—historical narrative, and that what remains is a vague, if prissy, wish that Mel Gibson could have found the time to wash his face. And yet I cannot shake from my mind a single shot from Woody Allen's *Sweet and Lowdown*—the title alone is tempting—in which Sean Penn, couched at ease on a bed, noodles away on his guitar, while Samantha Morton fixes herself in the bathroom on the left. She is mute, but she is not deaf, and as yet she has never heard him play; and as she listens, not expecting much, her movements relax into rapture, caught in the doorway's frame like a Bonnard. And what of that astounding final scene in *Big Night*, filmed without a cut, and with barely a sound, as if to demonstrate the eternal verity that, when it comes to directing movies, you *can* make an omelette without breaking sweat?

Maybe that is why this book has to move on, in search of quietude. The second section is all books: reviews, intemperate tributes, and a number of other resources for washing those films right out of your hair. If you spend your life staring heatedly at movies, then the cooling relief you require is not to be found in newly published books, many of which are subject to the same tides of hype that flood the current cinema, but in the subtly disputable achievements of the dead. I once spent four years editing book reviews for a daily newspaper, and the frequency with which publishers called me to evangelize on behalf of "a new voice in English fiction" lay in direct proportion to my yearning for old, ancestral voices—for styles that had long been found worthy by the tribunal of history, and that, requiring no further advertisement, lay beyond the reach of the publicist. The criterion for entry into the literary canon that operates in this volume is, therefore, embarrassingly simple: unless you are lonely, sexually self-locking, artistically unswayable, and born before 1910, forget it. (André Gide, it is true, had more sex than the rest of my subjects put together—than the rest of *France* put together, if his African trips are to be believed—and yet, by investing his disloyalties with the air of private devotions, he just about makes the grade.) Certainly, the essays on T. S. Eliot, Edward Lear, and other experts in unhappiness were devised and written as a welcome release—practically a vacation—from the life of the chronic moviegoer. There *are* a couple of modern novelists in evidence, but one, Thomas Pynchon, has removed himself so assiduously from the court of literary conversation that, whatever the labyrinth of his residence, he might as well be speaking to us from an imaginary country, or from another age. He is, in short, a classic—as good as dead, one could almost say, though I wish him long life, and I pray for more books as entranced as *Mason & Dixon*. The other is W. G. Sebald, who died, far too young, in a car crash, in the winter of 2001: a savage absurdity, although the soulful body of work that he left behind is already acquiring the mass and patina of a monument, both graven and overgrown.

That process, as well as its opposite—the entertaining sight of a sure thing crumbling to dust—was the motive for the two long articles at the head of the "Books" section, written in 1994 and 1995 respectively. I ploughed through ranks of best-sellers, old and new; what had appeared to be a simple task of sifting gold from dross was nicely complicated by the discovery that some of the dross bore the enticing glint, not of fool's gold, but of the real thing. That was as close as I shall ever come to setting out my stall; I claimed to believe primarily in trash and classics, and, if this book makes people question, afresh or for the first time, their dependence on the stuff in between (costume dramas, issue movies, politely searching new novels), then so much the better. We are not here long, so, if there are curiosities to be satisfied, we might as well cleave to those varieties of art that can be guaranteed to detain us only briefly—hence the kick, the delicious sting, of the action movie, from which we recover with nothing worse than a racing heart. Either that, or we must place our trust in the hands of those works (so few of them films), which we ourselves can detain for no more than a lifetime—those which have a previous record of compelling assent, and important business to conduct with unborn generations. There is nothing like a slew of motion pictures, for instance, for heightening one's bliss and bafflement at the still variety, whose mysterious effect is to slow the heart of the gallery goer, and to trap him awhile in glassy contemplation. If you asked me what has stirred me most, since I came to *The New Yorker*, I would offer you not a checklist of movies (although I still bow down before the flawless conceit of *Groundhog Day*), but a tour of the Rothko show at the Museum of Modern Art, a full set of Rembrandt prints, including all states of his *Crucifixion*, at the British Museum, a production of Berg's *Wozzeck* in Berlin, a rare, pervert-haunted showing of Balthus at the Palazzo Grassi in Venice, and the Walker Evans exhibit at the Met.

Hence, you might say, the click of shutters that litters the last third of this book. I have labelled it "Profiles," which is one way of shepherding an unruly flock of subjects. There are photographers (notably Evans himself), a fashion designer, a committed surrealist, and a handful of guys—astronauts and antarctic explorers—whose feats leave most action movies looking no more purposeful, let alone perilous, than a game of Twister on a summer afternoon. What possible bond, you may ask, links the exploits of Ernest Shackleton, who was never more content than when there were three inches of snow on his eyebrows, and Alfred Hitchcock, whose idea of a strenuous workout was the walk from his chauffeured car to a table at

"21," with his T-bone already poised to hit the grill? Well, all one can offer, in each case, is the tale of a great escape. In the boy from the East End, who wound up as inscrutable Hollywood royalty, there was the same pang of creative impatience that set Sir Ernest on the impossible, wasteful trail of the South Pole; every time, in fact, that I try to interest myself in the consciously developed careers of my heroes, be they sedentary or manic, I find that my true focus of study has been the sloughing of dead selves.

Maybe, after all, it is movies that propel such concern. What startles the worshipful viewer, in the life of Charles Foster Kane, is not the thought of Rosebud, dragging him back through time to the snows of yester-year, but the distance that he travelled, for good or ill, in those years of insatiable reinvention. We are consoled to learn that the balding old tyrant was no more than a kid with a sled; the scene defrosts our fears of what America can ask of a man. But the consolation, as Orson Welles recognized, is brief and sentimental; for all the exquisitely staged exhortations of Steven Spielberg, an American childhood must always be left behind. The sadness of that sundering, and the verve of what comes next, are an irresistible lure to European imaginations, which tend to be helplessly schooled in the small joys and instructive catastrophes of the past. Whenever I lift off from Heathrow (and I estimate that I have crossed the Atlantic some 150 times in the last decade, without once daring to try the curried beef), it does indeed feel like a liftoff, as if the fate of England had dwindled to that of a launchpad, and as if eight hours in the belly of a 747 might be sufficient not merely to start a business trip, but to fly me to the moon. Not that New York could ever be confused with the Sea of Tranquillity, as Henry James, born in the city, admitted in 1903:

> My native land, which time, absence and change have, in a funny sort of way, made almost as romantic to me as "Europe," in dreams or in my earlier time here, used to be, the actual bristling (as fearfully bristling as you like) U.S.A. have the merit and the precious property that they meet and fit into my ("creative") preoccupations.

And again, from the thick of the action, in 1911:

> I have been spending some weeks in New York, which is a very extraordinary and terrific and yet amiable place, as to which my sentiment is a compound of an hourly impression of its violent impossibility and of a sneaking kindness for its pride and power (it's so clearly destined to be the great agglomeration of the world!).

It is a breathtaking passage, swept up in its own agglomeration of the senses, and behind it you hear the swish of a pendulum. Here is a man who had spent many chapters of his life in England, who would become a naturalized Englishman in his final year, and one of whose guiding principles was that anything, or anybody, covered in moss was by definition deserving of reverence. Yet here he was, still in the entrance hall of a new century, having the wit to wonder if his homeland would, after all, turn out to be what he would call the Great Good Place; if the same adventure in consciousness that drew Isabel Archer over the sea would lead others to make the return trip, unable to resist the temptations, the edifying screwups, of the moral hazard. His instincts, as ever, were correct, and people have spent the last ninety years or so in James's trembling wake; even if you remain on English soil and merely read your way into America, you are stepping westward. London subscribers to *The New York Review of Books*, for example, can spirit themselves out of English rain and rancor not just with a reading of that journal's excellent reviews, but with an even more careful scan of its personals column—perhaps the boldest and most tireless display of unconscious comedy in the civilized world.

That is why I remain grateful to Tina Brown for my breakfastless breakfast: she showed me a way to break the habit of England. I have crossed from one continent to the other ever since, mostly in coach, never in fear, and always in hope of an upgrade; of all the frequent flyers on the planet, I must be the one most vexed by the possibility of a *downgrade*—gripped by visions of myself crouched in the freezing hold with all the drugged chihuahuas, blinded by falling Samsonites, or clinging to the tail fin with a vapor trail streaming from my nose. Yet somehow I arrive intact, to be greeted by customs officials, and by the agreeable, mortifying ghost of Harold Brodkey. "Anthony—meet New York." What follows here, for a few hundred pages, is hardly a love letter to America; no book which pays such elaborate homage to Evelyn Waugh could in all honesty claim such a distinction. But it is no less ardently meant; think of it, instead, as one of those exit visas which Rick slips under the lid of Sam's piano, in *Casablanca*, away from the eyes of Captain Renault and his flunkies—just a dumb sheaf of paper, but stamped with the irrevocable permission to seek a world elsewhere. That world, to me as to Victor Laszlo, can only be America; then again, as Rick says to Ilsa on the runway, "We'll always have Paris." But that is another story.

Movies

INDECENT PROPOSAL

Indecent Proposal stars Woody Harrelson and Demi Moore as David and Diana Murphy, a young married couple living in California. He is an architect, she sells real estate, but times are hard; the film starts in a welter of voice-overs as they look back on better days. This is sad for them but great news for the audience, which gets to see Woody Harrelson trying to play a high school kid by wearing a shaggy wig: it's one of those preposterous, sublimely wrong moments that make you glad to be a moviegoer. As I watched these early scenes, I began to tremble with anticipation: this could be the great bad film of our time, a host to all its plagues. The omens were certainly good: the director is Adrian Lyne, the man who brought us *Flashdance* and *9½ Weeks*. On the other hand, his last movie was *Jacob's Ladder*—confused, maybe, but also genuinely sombre and scary, and played without show by a haunted Tim Robbins. Was that just an aberration, or was Lyne really turning thoughtful? Would *Indecent Proposal* punch us awake with a study in sexual envy worthy of Polanski? No need to worry. From the moment when David and Diana sink to the kitchen floor and start to deconstruct their underwear, and the pulse of a love song throbs into life on the soundtrack, you know that Adrian Lyne is back in form. And there's more to come: a yacht that cruises into the sunset, straight from a Bacardi rum ad, and a Las Vegas casino where the dice are shot in fun-size close-up, tumbling in slow motion over the baize.

You may have gathered that *Indecent Proposal* is a teeny bit obsessed with money. Amy Holden Jones wrote the script, which is vaguely propelled by a belief that money can't buy you love; but the rest of the movie doesn't want to know. It adores the stuff, and can only come up with feeble suggestions for doing without it. "We never had much money," Diana muses, looking back on their early years, "so David would show me architecture that moved him." Now, there's a fun day out: have Woody Harrelson take you around and point out buildings that move him. All in all, it's a relief when the two of them go to Vegas on a whim and win twenty-five thousand dollars in a single night. They then make love on top of all the crackling bills, with the camera right there, shifting its position in excitement and rising to a sudden fade. (I think the movie comes before they do.) John Updike pulled a similar stunt in *Rabbit Is Rich*, where Harry Angstrom screwed his wife amid a hoard of gold Krugerrands, but there you heard the clink of self-delusion as Rabbit lost a coin and scrabbled around for it in panic.

No such ironies are permitted here. Instead, the film bundles together all its desires and smelts them into one gleaming character: a billionaire named John Gage, played by Robert Redford. Gage thinks that money *can* buy you love—or, at any rate, the kind of sex that might, you know, sprout into love. So when he sees Diana in a Vegas boutique the wheels of lust start to grind, and before you can say junk bond he's asking her to kiss his dice and throw a seven. She wins, of course, whereupon he installs her and David—who have just lost all their cash—in an expensive suite. They look awed and pleased, although it's probably the nastiest hotel room ever seen on film: a steel-blue mess, rounded off with a delightful touch, at least in the print I saw—a microphone nodding from its boom at the top of the frame. Gage then makes his big offer: a million bucks for a night with Diana—no aftermath, no strings. "It's just my body," Diana explains. "It's not my mind." I was glad to have that cleared up, though it does raise an interesting question: How much would you pay for an evening with Demi Moore's mind?

I would happily give away the rest of the plot, except that you can guess it anyway. *Indecent Proposal* induces a strange power in the viewer, a glow of prophecy: you can see every kink in the plot minutes, even hours, before it happens. Looking back at my notes, I found a scribbled menu of predictions—"He'll buy the dress," "They're going to lose," and the eerily specific "He'll find the copter taking off as he arrives"—each of them followed by a gratified "Yup." There's nothing wrong with movies that run true to form; you could easily guess how *Now, Voyager* would pan out, yet still warm to the pattern of its melodrama. In those days, the studios treated weepies like thrillers—in the pursuit of love, Bette Davis had to skirt all the obstacles that fell into her path. Demi Moore wins her man back, too, and, unlike Davis, she gets him all to herself, forever; but the manner of the victory is so sluggish, with long pauses sagging between the lines, that it hardly seems worth the bother.

The whole thing needs a leading man with snap and vim, instead of which it gets Woody Harrelson. Admittedly, it's an awful part, which calls for little more than unfocussed emoting, but then Woody trying to emote looks like anyone else trying to go to sleep. At one point, he has to give a lecture on the inspiring joys of architecture, rising to the contention that "even a brick wants to be something." He should know. Harrelson has long been crucial to *Cheers*, which both mocks and somehow dignifies the dumb hick in him; this movie does the exact opposite, solemnly turning him into a total idiot, and could subtly dent your pleasure in the TV show from now on.

And what, you may ask, is Redford doing in all this? Doing a Robert Redford, that's what: a lot of shy smiling, a lot of looks that say, Hey, don't worry, things will work out fine. Whenever Demi Moore comes into view, he doesn't so much see her as glance in her direction, look away, then double-take back to her—and we're meant to like him for it, the old flirt. The fact that John Gage is a manipulating shyster appears not to have crossed Redford's mind—a shame, because if Redford ever decided to turn really sour we could be in for a fright. We've sensed that once, in *All the President's Men*, where the moral grime of the story, as well as Dustin Hoffman's sneakiness, rubbed off on him. None of that here: Lyne treats him like a male model, fluffing his hair and making him stand around in long shot so that we get an eyeful of his (mostly disgusting) suits. And the closer the camera comes the softer the lighting gets, as if loath to admit how crinkled and potato-chippy—how interesting, in other words—the golden boy's face has become.

The worst scene in *Indecent Proposal*—and there are plenty of contenders—shows John Gage going to school. Diana has taken "a second job, teaching citizenship," and just as she is telling a classroom of immigrant students about the United States, one of them looks outside and sees Gage's Rolls-Royce. Their interest is stirred, rising to outright adulation as the man himself strolls in and starts to woo their teacher. He's a messiah, smelling of fresh money, and the movie can only sit back and agree: no messing around—if you've come looking for America, this is the man you need to be. In its flailing attempt to elevate the poor, a scene like this only slaps them down; you watch it openmouthed at the loftiness of the insult. *Indecent Proposal* needs to be seen, if only to furnish proof that a whole movie, and not just individual performers, can be vain, and that real vanity doesn't just look in the mirror: it can turn around and damage others. There are many good films about the rich, but this one is dangerously cheap.

Of course, it's only entertainment, except that you can't conceive of anyone's watching *Indecent Proposal* and feeling entertained. You stare at Gage and think, How can anyone have so much money and so little fun?

How can a roomful of immigrants want to be like that? As for Demi Moore, she goes from looking wistful, glazed, and poor to looking wistful, glazed, and rich—out of the fridge and into the deep freeze. The only character turned on by Gage's offer is the Murphys' lawyer, Jeremy (Oliver Platt), who has one short, cynical scene that blows the movie apart. "How could you negotiate without me?" he yells at David, sniffing a big commission. You suddenly realize that *Indecent Proposal* could (and should) have been a comedy; it starts off with much the same plot as *Honeymoon in Vegas* and smothers it in mists and moodiness.

This gets unbearable once Lyne decides to pay homage. On board Gage's yacht, Diana comes up on deck and finds him standing there in a white suit, staring out over the water. We're meant to think of another Redford role—Gatsby, on the end of his dock. It's a horrible grab at cut-price longing and pathos, but worse is to come: Gage's mournful recollection of his ideal love, a girl glimpsed once on a train and never seen again. "That was thirty years ago. . . . And I don't think there's a day goes by when I don't think about her." Remind you of anything? Try the aging Bernstein in *Citizen Kane,* remembering a girl in a white dress getting off a ferry in 1896: "I only saw her for one second and she didn't see me at all—but I'll bet a month hasn't gone by since that I haven't thought of that girl." Orson Welles called it the best thing in the movie, and said once, "If I were in Hell and they gave me a day off and said, 'What part of any movie you ever made do you want to see?,' I'd see that scene." How times change; when Redford speaks the lines, the audience giggles. Everything that *Indecent Proposal* touches, it sullies. It's trash without zest, keeping a poker face when there's nothing to be serious about; as for the sex, you can see most of it in the trailer. The kitsch extravaganza that I'd been hoping for just lay down and died.

APRIL 26, 1993

UN COEUR EN HIVER

When I first heard about *Un Coeur en Hiver,* my heart sank. It sounded like a do-it-yourself French movie: rainy Paris, Ravel on the soundtrack, mousy acquaintances having a narrow squeak with love. It even had Daniel Auteuil and Emmanuelle Béart, last seen together in *Manon of the Spring.* Yet out of this weak and watery material Claude Sautet has fashioned something rich and strange. The wintry heart of the title belongs to Stéphane (Daniel Auteuil), and its frost spreads way beyond his rib cage—into the careful gestures, the buttoned-down shirts that match his feelings, the tiny black eyes like lumps of coal stuck on a snowman's face. Now and then, the eyes give the world a darting inspection, but that only confirms what a scary place it is: time for Stéphane to back down and resume his inward gaze. There was a hint of this in *Jean de Florette,* where Auteuil played the nervous half-wit, but there the mannerisms had to slot into the movie's rather pat emotional scheme. Now he's on his own, and that natural hesitancy can be taken to the limit; we see the puffy, rodent features, and the tidy burrow he has made of his life, and we wait for the movie to coax him out.

Stéphane makes and mends violins for a living, which is perfect—so close to music and yet so far from its passionate risks. His latest client, Camille (Emmanuelle Béart), is a young violinist currently involved with Stéphane's business partner, Maxime (André Dussollier). She is, in every sense, a coming attraction: sex and success rolled into one—the kind of creature who would normally make Stéphane emigrate to Greenland in sheer terror. But, despite himself—or because of a shred of living self left somewhere inside—he starts to fall in love with her. They go from instant dislike to a mild thaw, then from deep-seated yearning to standup row, then from parting to sweet sorrow; in other words, they go through all the motions of love except the making of it.

"Well," I heard one viewer say as we left the theatre, "it was different." To be gripped by anticlimax is an unusual sensation for the seasoned moviegoer. O.K., you think, I know how this will pan out. These two may not be getting it together yet, but it's all part of the plan, just wait. Maybe a little longer. Come on, the joke's over, get on with it. But they never do. *Un Coeur en Hiver* goes from soup to nuts but misses out on the main course, and it offends our melodramatic instincts—the old, weather-beaten belief that a guy will get his gal. It is, in short, a Jamesian film—not in the finesse of its manners but in its willingness to contemplate failure as a respectable destiny, somehow essential to the man who suffers it. Stéphane is a descendant of John Marcher in *The Beast in the Jungle*, the man "to whom nothing on earth was to have happened."

Given all this, it seems unlikely that Bruce Willis will be buying up the rights to a remake. But that doesn't mean there's anything prissy or wearisome about *Un Coeur en Hiver.* Although Sautet keeps his cool, he's tough on anything that smacks of vagueness. There's barely a whiff of that smoky poetry of the streets, the distant trace of Jacques Prévert, which you find in even the best French films. When it does creep in—"Music is dreams," Stéphane says hoarsely—you groan and wait for the moment to pass, and it always does. Many scenes surprise you with their curtness, their refusal to linger over a mood in case it starts dripping melancholy. Even the close-ups feel efficient—brief glances at Stéphane's trade as he glues a violin together and clamps it with wooden screws, or wedges a neck into place with a satisfying creak. You realize how long it's been since a movie actually taught you anything.

Nor does this economy stop when the music starts. *Un Coeur en Hiver* is an object lesson in how melodies can be worked into the fabric of a film. Sautet uses Ravel throughout but doesn't merely match the sound to what we see; on the contrary, he wants the two to exist in wary, difficult discord. Stéphane goes to watch Camille rehearsing the Sonata for Violin and Cello; she keeps getting it wrong until he leaves, as though his very presence were a third instrument, forcing her to miss a beat. Later on, she records another sonata, this time with piano; Stéphane stares at her through the studio window—as so often in the film, they are glassed off from each other, impeded by shifting reflections. This time, she makes no mistakes; by now, his presence is a comfort and a spur. But listen to the music—the skittering, faintly sarcastic sign-offs to the last two movements, which Ravel called "Blues" and "Perpetuum Mobile." Though Béart's playing was dubbed, she learned the fingering, and that is what you concentrate on in the fierce pizzicato; many strings are tugged at in this movie, but few of the heart variety.

Classical music gets well treated here, which makes a change; it's been more abused than any other kind, ever since *Brief Encounter* snivelled along to Rachmaninoff, and, with the demise of the great film score (where is our Max Steiner, let alone our Bernard Herrmann?), the abuse is getting worse. Composers are regularly hijacked to prettify a picture and give the audience a hot flush of high culture. Think of poor Samuel Barber, press-ganged into *Platoon*, or of this year's *Tous les Matins du Monde*. Some people fell for that movie's nicely arranged gloom; I thought it was like being locked into a costume museum after closing time and beaten unconscious with a viola da gamba. *Un Coeur en Hiver* will have none of this, whatever the temptation. Camille and two friends play the plaintive Piano Trio, and Stéphane leaves in the middle, walking out into the street to catch a bus, and fading from our sight as the music fades from our hearing. He may be too moved to hear any more, or aghast at how little he is moved, or simply in a hurry to get back to work.

With his motives sliding around like this, it becomes hard to focus any sympathy on Stéphane, and the film is not in the business of helping you. That's what I liked most: it doesn't reach out and beg to be liked. *Un Coeur en Hiver* has been hailed as fine, delicate, and so on—all the usual terms that make cinema sound like tea or silk—but it's more cunning and diffident than that: almost Stéphane-like, indeed, in its chilly gaze. Whether it's believable is another matter. Despite the bar, the café, and the bookshop, I still couldn't recognize this unnerving *quartier* of Paris, almost entirely populated by emotional cripples. Stéphane veers away from Camille as if she were Jean Harlow, but I thought they were well suited; she wears long skirts, ties her hair back, and hardly ever raises her voice. Each is like the dull, brainy member of a Hollywood screwball couple, waiting for the brighter half to come along. When he takes his jacket off to shelter her as they run through the rain, dodging cars, you suddenly think, This is the most exciting thing they have ever done. They should stick together.

If the movie had stayed with their story throughout, it could easily have glazed over. Béart, especially, gives so little away. Even in *La Belle Noiseuse*, which involved her stepping out of her clothes and standing there for nearly four hours, she seemed on her best behavior. Her beauty is most alarming in small doses, and Sautet rightly allows the plot to ripple away from her for a while. It made me wonder how interested in true love he really is—the movie sometimes feels happier with casual friendships and professional contracts. It's full of mentors: Stéphane likes to visit his old teacher, who has a tetchy, affectionate relationship with his housekeeper. As for Camille, she lives with her agent (surely a bad idea), an older woman who is clearly upset by her charge's need for Maxime and, later, for Stéphane. Nothing is made explicit, but the film is continually, lightly ruffled by homosexual envy. The two men, rivals for Camille, start and end the movie with a keener understanding of each other than anyone else can hope for. (When they change after a game of squash, they put on identical clothes without even noticing.) The central couple of *Un Coeur en Hiver* never fuse together, but other bonds are being tested and strengthened all the time. You won't believe me, but it's not a lonely film.

JUNE 7, 1993

SLEEPLESS IN SEATTLE

Sleepless in Seattle stars Tom Hanks and Meg Ryan, so it has to be worth seeing. On the other hand, it doesn't really star Tom Hanks *with* Meg Ryan, so don't get too excited. They spend the whole movie falling for each other but hardly ever meet in person. It's a horribly suitable idea for the nineties, the last word in romantic common sense—a couple who practice safe love. Ryan plays Annie Reed, bored in Baltimore and sliding into marriage as if it were a coma. Hanks plays Sam Baldwin, recently widowed and living in Seattle. The opening shot shows him looking mournful in a cemetery, with his eight-year-old son, Jonah (Ross Malinger), standing next to him. Comic leading man plus weepy backdrop plus kid sidekick—yes, it's a Nora Ephron movie. She wrote this one with David S. Ward and Jeff Arch, and directed it by herself.

On Christmas Eve, a lonely Jonah rings a radio talk show to tell the nation about his dad, who really needs a new wife. Sam then comes on the line and, with a little pushing, confirms his predicament: he could do with another love but doesn't give it a chance—lightning never strikes twice. This, however, is romantic comedy, the first principle of which is that lightning will do whatever you want it to; just pick your favorite conductor. Annie, for instance, is driving along when she hears Sam's voice on the car radio, and, darn it, she just knows that, whoever this guy is, he's the one. Unlike her fiancé, Walter (Bill Pullman), who is anything but the one. He may even qualify as a total nobody, for all the help that Ephron gives him. She's normally generous with her minor characters, but Walter is just a blank wall for Annie to bounce off. Why not smarten him up with a lick of charm, like Gig Young in *Teacher's Pet*? When he came between Clark Gable and Doris Day, their need for each other was sharpened by the competition.

But Ephron doesn't want rivalry, or any other human impediment.

There's a whole continent separating these two, and that's enough. *Sleepless in Seattle* is a gentle meditation on fate, on what must come to pass, but there's no hint of a genial God pulling strings from on high; it's up to the characters to plot their own course toward a triumphant union. Nothing ever goes wrong between Sam and Annie, because nothing goes on at all. The movie simply presumes that all will be well; it's too busy dreaming of perfection to dream of anything else. Sam is actually in the middle of saying the word "perfect" when he first catches sight of Annie, drifting silently by in virginal white. It's like Dante getting his first eyeful of Beatrice.

Ephron wants her movie to look the part, all rich and heady with promise. Enter Sven Nykvist as cameraman, who beefs up the colors with the same gusto that he brought to *Fanny and Alexander*; like Bergman's movie, *Sleepless in Seattle* has the plush feel of a story that has already happened and is now being recollected in tranquillity. What it gains in pleasure it loses in suspense, and awkward practicalities are glazed over with ease; the characters' flights across America are traced in glowing dots against a map of nocturnal blue. Trouble starts, however, when the story needs to snap out of that relaxation. On the street one day, Sam tries to prove to a friend—a jovial cameo from Rob Reiner—that he's still in good enough shape to woo the girls. Nykvist frames the whole scene in long shot, but he should have held it back for the clinching gag—Reiner leaning over solemnly to inspect Hanks's butt. Ephron wanted it kept simple, presumably, but her lack of trust in the camera, in its ability to snatch a laugh merely by changing position, tends to stanch the movie's flow.

It's the old story: the writer who wants to direct, who goes on thinking in words when there are images begging to help out. The last twenty minutes of *Sleepless in Seattle* make you weep with frustration. It's New York, the Empire State Building is beckoning, and Sam and Annie are approaching zero hour. And what does Ephron do? She stops to give Annie a final scene with Walter, who was forgettable to start with and certainly shouldn't be clogging up the action this late. But Ephron is so fond of a good line—and hers are some of the best around—that she can't bear to see it go to waste; you keep hoping she'll cut away and leave her scenes on a high, but they dawdle on like smoky parties that no one has the energy to leave.

Which brings us to the question: How funny is *Sleepless in Seattle*? There always seem to be jokes around the next bend, but somehow the movie doesn't need to get there; it's happy to glisten with charm rather than buzz with life, to make an audience feel cozy and concerned. I like my romantic comedies to wake me up, but this one put me to sleep with its sweet mooching reverie, much of it secondhand. Ephron is a magpie of useful tunes, all of them guaranteed to put lumps in throats. We may have expected Nat King Cole, but not "As Time Goes By" over the opening credits. Has the woman no shame? None at all, plainly, although she's clever enough to realize that we don't have any, either. We watch sympathetically as Annie and a friend burst into tears during a discussion of the old Cary Grant weepie *An Affair to Remember*. We even see a short clip for ourselves, which may not be a good idea. For one thing, any Cary Grant film always looks better than whatever you're watching. And, for another, what does it say about a movie that its funniest and most delicious moment comes from the fond remembrance of cinema? Maybe Ephron is so cushioned in celluloid that she can't conceive of any adventures still waiting out there in the fresh air.

Poor Meg Ryan feels the brunt of this. When Annie first learns about Sam on the radio, she sniffs away a few tears. Fair enough, this is an old-style dating movie—what can you expect? But then, much later, when the talk-show host plays highlights of the season and Sam's appeal is one of them, that old look crosses Annie's face all over again. Is Nora Ephron really so unsure of the emotions served up by this tale that she has to dole out second helpings? It's a mild insult to the audience (pay attention this time, children) and a gross one to Meg Ryan, hardly an actress who thrives on repetition. She's a one-off, once-only performer, with a breathtaking recovery rate; what I loved about the orgasm scene in *When Harry Met Sally . . .* was that when the howls of bliss died away, the smile clicked back on like a torch. When she's on a roll, the ditsiness flies off her without warning—she's no more prepared for it than anyone else is. *Sleepless in Seattle* takes off at the moment when Annie starts dunking a tea bag and trying to chatter at the same time. It's almost too much for her whirring brain. But the movie never gives Ryan enough to do, and her face often settles into moping; it takes on the sadness of a spoiled child, which doesn't suit her any more than her sensible plaits.

The best reason to see *Sleepless in Seattle* is Tom Hanks, but then he's always the best reason to see a movie. Only once has everything fallen into place around him: in Penny Marshall's *Big*, where he took the central conceit—a child's soul padlocked in an adult body—and turned it into a rhapsody, way beyond anything that Marshall could have expected. He played not just a part but a set of variations on the theme of being a person; he showed us how we meet the world head on and learn to ride the bumps, except that in his case two decades of adjustment were squeezed into a couple of hours—a time-lapse image of moral growth. What's more, he cut the real adults down to size: their sneers and ambitions suddenly seemed like ghosts of playground energy. No other actor could have kept this up; it would have sagged into sentimentality, a loving look at the child within. But Hanks gave us the child without, the surface fizz, and in *Sleepless in Seattle* the effervescence still hasn't died down. When Sam asks Jonah where Baltimore is on the map and gets no answer, he bursts like a firecracker—"*There's* Baltimore," hitting the word with a cowhand's wild yelp—and we feel a blast from his past, a funny little gale of impatience. It cracks the moodiness that Ephron is trying to lay over the whole movie, but, more important, it tells you that Sam is still boyish enough to get off on the shock of falling in love—he won't go all sensible and mature on us.

The looks help, of course. Hanks will never be a smoothie—how could he be, with that topping of sprung curls?—but he has the smoothie's ability to stop the clock; at present, he could pass for anything between twenty and forty. He still has the scalp-lifting grin and the rubbery frame, which can stretch with glee or crumple in distress—he could snap on a bow tie and wander into a Thurber cartoon, no questions asked. Together with Steve Martin, he is the best physical comedian of his generation, although both of them are left floundering by their directors. You have to go to the cheaper, crummier movies, where Hanks is left alone with his lunacy, to catch him at his most nimble; next time *The Money Pit* comes around on TV, stay with it until he climbs the disintegrating staircase, each step dying under his footfall. Needless to say, Nora Ephron is above this kind of thing. She prefers to have Tom Hanks stand still in the moonlight. Yet the old mobility hasn't vanished—it's just all gone to his face. There's a quickness there, a skirmish of unlikely feelings that ranges well beyond the farcical, toward the more searching comedy of weakness and doubt.

It's no surprise that he should play off so neatly against the children in this movie: they seem tuned in to his channels of thought. Malinger is persuasive as Jonah, but the real pro is Gaby Hoffmann, as Jonah's friend Jessica. I have mixed feelings about child stars, believing firmly, for instance, that Macaulay Culkin should be shut in a damp cellar until the end of the century; but Hoffmann, already so assured in Ephron's previous picture, *This Is My Life*, now finds a higher and unnerving level of sophistication. "H. and G.," she drawls at Sam, who doesn't get it. "Hi and goodbye." Ephron turns the wisdom of experience on its head: the Sams of this world are now confused and afraid, the Jessicas sassy and controlled. (If this is true, we're in deep trouble.) And most of the plot is orchestrated by Jonah; he's the sensible Cupid who brings the foolish couple together.

Hanks doesn't forget this when, in the final scene, he is suddenly presented with the love of his life. So far, it's been soul to soul; now they are face to face, and you can feel the threat of schmalz overhead. But it never comes, because Hanks doesn't melt: he flinches. It's a tiny, sideways swivel of the head, no more than a tic of disbelief, as if to say "Are you kidding?" But it's enough: here is the grownup side of him talking to the childish, to the Jonah-like, pointing out that life is not a movie, that destiny is a joke, that things like this don't happen to ordinary Americans. For half a second, he defies the laws of romantic comedy, refusing to play the game. Resistance, however, is useless, as it always will be; and, besides, Meg Ryan is waiting.

JULY 19, 1993

POETIC JUSTICE

Think of the worst possible reason that John Singleton might have had for calling his new movie *Poetic Justice.* Now make it worse. And again. You still won't be close to the truth, so here goes: the main character is named Justice, and she writes poetry. Get it? She's the pivot of this meandering movie, in which four young Los Angeles blacks drive to Oakland in a mail van. Besides Justice, there is her friend Iesha (Regina King), brought along by her boyfriend, Chicago (Joe Torry), and his fellow mail carrier Lucky (Tupac Shakur). It goes without saying that this turns into a journey of discovery, motoring from lassitude to love with a shortcut via confrontation. Why can't people in the movies just *drive*, like the rest of us?

Justice provides the first starring role for Janet Jackson. If it should prove to be the last, I doubt whether Hollywood would mourn; she struggles hard, but can't do much with the absurd demands placed upon her by the movie. At one point, she has to gaze into the mirror and canter through a range of expressions: mope, snicker, pout, and so forth, rounding off with a lonely teardrop. Now, it's possible for an actress to get away with this, but she has to be Liv Ullmann, and the movie has to be *Persona*; it's not fair to expect a novice to come through unscathed. Singleton helps her out with a series of jump cuts, so that she can merely switch moods instead of joining them all together, but it still doesn't work: he wants the scene to suggest a quest for identity, and it looks more like a cover shoot for Jackson's next album.

Justice works at a beauty salon in South Central Los Angeles run by a career woman named Jessie (Tyra Ferrell). The first shot of Jessie is a disgrace: a leer at her endless legs and micro skirt emerging from a car. Even if she wanted to be more than an armor-plated sex machine, the camera wouldn't let her. Singleton makes Jessie immune to love and failure, dead set on her lively desires: "A man ain't nothing but a tool; you got to know when to take him out of the box." The problem is that, as a fictional creation, she isn't much better herself: she's a type—a tool employed by Singleton to hammer home his appeal for self-fulfillment. All the characters contribute to this message: if Justice equals depth without confidence, Jessie is the other way around. This may sound neatly structured, but in practice it squeezes the air out of the film. Every figure stands for something, but can't stand up of his or her own accord and fight for dramatic life.

This is bad news, because *Poetic Justice* doesn't have much going for it except characters. The motto urged upon us by Singleton's last movie, *Boyz N the Hood*, was "Increase the Peace." Well, the peace has now been increased to the point where for long periods nothing happens. We have to make do with arguments, reconciliations, and shots of a mail van passing through pretty countryside. You feel that Singleton can hardly remember what action looks like. Little incidents emerge in a rush: toward the end, there's a shooting, but it takes some time to work out who the victim is, and there's a fashion show, which I couldn't place at all. If this is supposed to be a road movie, someone forgot to bring a map.

There is one scene of immense and rather worrying charm. Driving along, Lucky sees a sign saying "Johnson Family Reunion." None of them is a Johnson, but who cares? They turn in and discover a pastoral idyll: young and old strolling about in the sunshine while the soundtrack sings of togetherness. Lucky is amazed: "I ain't seen so many black folks in one spot that there's no fighting." Singleton is in his element, choreographing happiness for the benefit of his wandering camera: the peace has been increased to maximum. It all looks delightful, but it makes you realize what a deeply conventional filmmaker he is. *Boyz N the Hood* was a two-tone piece of work: there was the gangland saga, which felt edgy and wired, and then there was a father's campaign to stop the fighting and heal the wounds. All the life of the movie was in the first of these, and that should have been Singleton's takeoff point for *Poetic Justice*, but he went for the second—the domestic responsibility, the hope, the drama that dies on its feet.

Boyz N the Hood got itself a reputation, of course, when some screenings were followed by violence; it manufactured its own hype. Singleton was a producer's dream, and you can't help thinking that someone must have given him carte blanche to do what he liked next—always a recipe for disaster. It's as if the new movie were scared of making trouble again and wanted to atone for past excesses. But take away the menace and the inflammation, and there isn't much left. Opinion will always be divided on

Spike Lee's *Do the Right Thing*, but it remains a thrilling panorama of social crackup—a wide and worthy development of themes that Lee had been mulling over since *She's Gotta Have It.* He asked himself the big question: What if *everybody* had to have it? Can freedom spread like fire—too far, and too fast? John Singleton seemed to be following the same path of inquiry, but he has shied away from it, in favor of a more simpleminded option: Let's pack up our troubles and get out of town. Leaving South Central, the van passes a building wrecked and blackened in the 1992 riots, but that is soon forgotten. The emotional peak of *Poetic Justice* looks more like *The French Lieutenant's Woman:* Justice wraps herself in a blanket and stares out to sea.

Just occasionally, the movie flickers with the old frustration. Lucky has a child, whom he goes to visit; the mother is in bed with another man, and there's evidence that she's doing crack. Lucky gets mad, grabbing his little girl and kicking out. He wants to protect her from violence but can do so only with violence of his own; you see the cycle starting to turn, and Singleton spins it along with a darting handheld camera. It's a rare moment of fury for Lucky, who is by far the most interesting character in the movie. Tupac Shakur finds a cool fatigue in him that isn't there in his lines; Lucky's distrust of life goes so deep that it comes out as nonchalance. We see it in his eyes, and in the slothful contempt of his movements—more than in his banter with Justice, which is meant to have an angry comic hustle to it but soon descends into clockwork rant. A typical exchange goes: "Fuck you." "Fuck you, bitch." And so on, over and over—a loop tape of favorite oaths. The soundtrack raps home the argument "Niggers don't give a fuck."

This pitch of profanity needs editing to match; when Scorsese cut back and forth between the mobsters in *GoodFellas,* the kick of it woke us up—we caught the full blast of their foul mouths. Singleton seems to lag behind the beat; we soon get tired of the talkers, and beg them to stop. But when they do, that means it's time for a snatch of verse from Justice. There's no middle ground here, nothing between the coarse and the highfalutin. "You got a poem for me?" Jessie asks. "Lord knows I need one." It makes poetry sound like drink, or crack—something to be sold for the quenching of an immediate need. Maybe it's always been like this; maybe Londoners sidled up to Milton in the street and whispered, "Hey, John, give me some of that Paradise shit. You know, the stuff with no clothes?" At least, they got high-grade epic for their money. *Poetic Justice* proceeds on the dreary principle that the only possible cause of poetry is self-expression—the confessing of inward torment and the itch for better times. "Alone," Justice murmurs. "Lying, thinking. Last night. How to find my soul a home . . . I came up with one thing. And I don't believe I'm wrong." When I heard this, I thought that Singleton had made it up for the movie. Then I decided that it must be a bunch of old, unused lyrics that Jackson had borrowed from her brother Michael. At the end of the movie, however, I discovered that every single word of verse had been written by Maya Angelou. Whoops.

Unwittingly, in fact, the film suggests a new use for Angelou's collected works: set them all to music. There was a gust of giggling in the theatre when Justice put on her best speaking voice and intoned the lines:

> I'm a woman.
> Phenomenally.
> Phenomenal woman,
> That's me.

No, it isn't—not unless Janet finds a smoochy tune to fit the words, brings in Quincy Jones to beef up the orchestration, and sings the whole damn thing herself. Then we'd have a ballad to make us swoon, and a movie with real zip. After listening to Jackson's latest album, *janet.*, I decided that there was a stronger pulse of sexual determination in a single chorus of "This Time" than in the whole of her debut movie. According to Jackson, someone suggested that she should make a musical—stick with what she knows. "I listened carefully to this advice," she told an interviewer. "But my instincts said, 'This is not a way to grow.' " She sounds like a little girl measuring herself against the bedroom door. Why not carry on performing, and let growth take care of itself? No wonder *Poetic Justice* reeks of earnestness: Jackson, Angelou, and Singleton have bonded together into a growth team, and it's infectious. I could hardly get my soul through the door on the way out. Poetic Justice, indeed. I think her parents should have called her License.

AUGUST 2, 1993

THE FUGITIVE

The Fugitive is adapted from the old TV series, but, unlike similar projects—*Dragnet, The Addams Family*—it relies on the simple, nagging hook of the original plot. Wrongly accused of murder, a doctor named Richard Kimble goes on the run and fights to clear his name by nailing the true culprit. The leading role, which was taken in the series by David Janssen, goes to Harrison Ford. If that doesn't count as an improvement, nothing will. For one thing, it provides the extra dash of suspense that comes with every Harrison Ford picture: What will he do with his hair? Throughout *Star Wars*, you stared at Han Solo and wondered how a civilization advanced enough to wage war in space could still allow its heroes to wear their hair over their ears, like midcareer Beatles. Ford turned up in *Presumed Innocent* with an unexpected razor cut, and now, in *The Fugitive*, he has shaggy locks and a beard. They give him an ecclesiastical air; if he slipped on a robe and held up two fingers, he could pose for a Greek icon. As the movie progresses, he is forced to change his appearance: the beard has to go, the hair is darkened, old clothes are sloughed off in favor of new. It's an ideal Ford role, because it beckons us to the heart of his appeal: he is an old-style leading man, rock-steady and scornful of outward show, yet that reticence allows him to dissolve into a crowd. He is always Harrison Ford, but he could be anyone.

Kimble is a vascular surgeon who comes home one night to find that his beloved wife has been bludgeoned and shot; she dies in his arms. He tells the cops that he grappled with her attacker, a man with a prosthetic arm; they listen carefully to Kimble's story, then book him. He is found guilty and sentenced to death, and we still haven't reached the end of the credits. The director, Andrew Davis, is not a man to hang around and think things over; these opening minutes are an editor's dream, hopping sweetly between crime and punishment, from grainy flourishes of slow motion to the melancholy hues of courtroom and jail. If you're waiting for the movie to brighten up, forget it; one of the many likable things about *The Fugitive* is that most of it takes place in lousy weather. Under a warm sun, all this running around would seem a bit of a lark, but Harrison Ford is up against wet trees, dead leaves, and a sky the color of soapy water. You can smell the desperation condensing around him in the air.

Not that the movie feels sluggish; it comes studded with set pieces, more athletic than violent. Even the crash that allows Kimble to go free, involving a bus, a train, a hillside, and a brace of firearms, is there to make you gawk, and even applaud, rather than flinch. Davis isn't too worried about finding new stunts; he just wants to stage bigger, crunchier versions of your old favorites. When word comes that Kimble is heading for a dam, for example, you sit forward and lick your lips, in full confidence that someone will shortly be leaping into a large body of water without holding his nose. On the debit side, you can also be sure of hearing the line "Only one person in a million could survive that fall."

Despite the tight job that Davis does on the movie, a few of these clichés still leak in. Most damaging of all is the soundtrack, which was composed by James Newton Howard, and is even more mindless than the one he wrote for *The Prince of Tides.* It appears to be based on the principle that nothing is as scary as hitting a drum apart from hitting it harder; this reaches a lunatic level when Sam Gerard, the deputy United States marshal who is tracking Kimble, walks around the scene of the original crime. The music is so loud that we can barely hear ourselves think, so heaven knows what it must be like for him—especially since he's played by Tommy Lee Jones, one of the few actors who can give a convincing impersonation of deep thought. Gerard wants his man, and nothing—no dumb Chicago cops, no head-splitting composer—is going to get in his way.

Jones is the best supporting player in modern movies, and is cut from the same cloth as Harrison Ford; to call them tough guys is to remind oneself that toughness begins in the brain. The most basic action picture—and you can't get more basic than this—is charged and refined by the presence of men who know precisely what has propelled them into action. *The Fugitive* represents quite a jump for Andrew Davis; until now, his most successful work has starred Steven Seagal and Chuck Norris, both of whom look as if they only just discovered fire last week. Ford and Jones come from the other end of the evolutionary scale; you can see it in the amused horror that twitches across Kimble's face when a bunch of cops get into the elevator with him, or in Gerard's initial reaction to the train wreck. "My, my, my, my, my," he says. "What. A. Mess."

Any other actor would have run those three words together, and probably would have shaken his head as well, trying to look concerned. Jones, however, is unimpressed—indeed, faintly contemptuous, his intelligence rising lightly above the occasion. He tends to keep his lines back, count a beat, and then deliver them, so that the angle of his response to the world grows ever more oblique, and more entertaining. He even gets a laugh out of the phrase "Thank you." Sam Gerard is a pure pro, yet somewhere inside him there's the flicker of a dandy: a mind that delights in carving order out of chaos, with a grave, cunning joy in getting things to go his way, and the ability to hold still while everyone scuttles around him. At one point, he issues orders to his team without so much as looking their way. Soon, only one of them is left idle.

"What are you doing?"

"I'm thinking."

"Well, think me up a cup of coffee and one of those chocolate doughnuts with the little sprinkles on top."

Oddly, this was the moment when I first took *The Fugitive* seriously. Davis's previous work, *Under Siege*, in which Steven Seagal managed to save the world without disturbing his ponytail, was a machine-tooled slab of pulp, about as good as an old Bond movie. Leanness was all; there wasn't an ounce of ordinary experience in the film—no little sprinkles on the doughnut. So it's a relief now to see Gerard taking time out from the plot to feel hungry, and putting the thrills on hold for a couple of seconds; you feel the same way when Kimble, risking everything by sneaking into a hospital, pauses to make an emergency sandwich with a patient's scrambled egg. It makes you laugh, although it's not strictly a gag; it's more the comedy of impromptu wit, when life suddenly appears broader and more chancy than cinema would have us believe. *The Fugitive* warms up in the presence of flesh and blood, which is something very different from blood and guts. The tale may have been borrowed from TV, but there are people like Ford and Jones having to live through it, and their involvement strips the hoariness away.

We are left to relish the peculiar pleasures of the chase picture, where the bloodhound sniffs his way into the soul of his prey. That's happened already this summer, thanks to *In the Line of Fire* and the sneaky, brow-darkening rapport between Clint Eastwood and John Malkovich; add the new pairing of Ford and Jones, and we may have a small trend on our hands. If so, it's very welcome, a strong rebuff to the sentimental horrors of the buddy-buddy convention that has blighted cop films over recent years. You could call it the Friendly Foe movie: two people whose intense enmity leads them to a pitch of understanding, of private common ground, denied to those around them. They thrive on brainpower, and feed on rare scraps of each other's weakness; above all, they stay at arm's length, and only draw close at the end. In both movies, they finally come together in a crowded hotel, as if the intimacy between hunter and hunted were too weird to allow them to meet alone.

The Fugitive does go on too long, and Davis tends to snatch at incidents that don't fit. At one point, Gerard and his men go after *another* fugitive, which can only confuse the issue; there's no real preparation for the scene, and no followup, and it makes you wonder whether the movie is heading for a second major derailment. Davis recovers his nerve, though, and the film stays on track, pursuing its unusual course: sombre, and frightening, but never less than fun. Kimble looks genuinely harrowed, and there's something juicy and inspiring in the spectacle, because you know what he must do to relieve the pain. And the relief is all there in the final, gasping confrontation, although it's hard to suppress a twinge of unkind regret. Nothing, you feel, should be settled so easily. Richard Kimble is a fugitive to the core, a creature of flight; and, whatever the justice of his quest, you half hope that he will go on running forever, harried by Gerard, away into the dark.

AUGUST 16, 1993

TITO AND ME

Tito and Me, written and directed by Goran Marković, is set in Belgrade in 1954. The "me" in question is Zoran (Dimitrje Vojnov), only ten years old but already boasting a waistline that would flatter a lifelong glutton. He lives in a small apartment with far too many relatives—his parents, grandmother, aunt, and uncle, plus his poisonous young cousin, Svetlana. She labels him a degenerate—hardly your average playground banter, but then, this is old Yugoslavia, where every tongue is trained in the communist lingo. "My uncle said the same thing," Zoran says mournfully, "when he caught me eating the wall." And there he is, digging plaster out with a spoon and giving it a thoughtful chew. As the camera stands back to survey the telltale craters, you realize that Marković is not in the nostalgia business. Far from being a placid memoir of youth, *Tito and Me* buzzes with casual surrealism, with the grave, inexplicable gestures that compose the rites of a child.

Zoran is possibly the least mercurial boy in the history of movies. He is stubborn, solid, gullible, and about as elfin as a dump truck. The movie is a marvellous rebuff to the notion that all children are unfettered spirits, as yet untarred by prejudice; Zoran is the perfect petit bourgeois, set to swell into a *bourgeois énorme* as time goes by. As his parents fall onto their bed, we see him lying in the next room, plainly irritated by the noise of endearments, and reaching for cotton to plug his ears. And when he stands in the living room, squat and charmless, Marković films him from a slightly low angle, to emphasize his self-possession. Later on, in shorts and suspenders, he looks more a Bavarian burgomaster than a small boy. We laugh at the idea that he so rarely smiles, but his precocious solemnity also gives us the creeps, and the film finds an ideal focus for our unease: Zoran is gripped by hero worship, and the hero is Marshal Tito.

Tito's place in the world's memory seems unstable: for every historian who acclaims the hero of the wartime partisans and the best hope of the Allies, there will be another who is more concerned with the precise transgressions of his long rule. At present, while the country that he held together proceeds to disembowel itself, his standing may well have risen; according to an impassioned but rather deluded logic, anything—even dictatorship—would be better than this spilled blood. Odd though it may sound, *Tito and Me* makes a useful footnote to the debate, for it remains honestly undecided about the past. Although filming began just after the start of hostilities in 1991, the film shows no hint of the current conflict; it appears slender, and eager to charm. Yet that very gentleness, its light air of mockery, illuminates the old regime with surprising clarity where a glare of anguish might have been too fierce.

During the opening credits, and many times from then on, we see newsreel footage of the marshal enjoying the reverence of his people—standard propaganda, which would seem openly threatening if it were accompanied by a Wagnerian march or a strident patch of Richard Strauss. Instead, Marković backs it with a nippy little samba number, the kind of thing you hear in Doris Day films whenever Doris goes shopping. It's a lovely device; it suggests that those cheering crowds may indeed have been having a nice day out, but it also shrugs at the silly pretensions of power. As in all decent political satire, the sharpest digs make the best gags: when Zoran writes a prizewinning poem that ends with the line "I love Tito more than Mum and Dad," we cut to a shot of his desperate father lying in bed and reading Freud's *Psychopathology of Everyday Life.* It makes you feel for this careworn, cultivated man. How can he possibly have spawned such an ungrateful lump?

Zoran is not alone, of course, in his love for Tito; everyday life has indeed become psychopathic when millions of citizens are devoted to a man with orange-dyed hair whom they have never met. Marković, in his mild way, is posing the crucial question: Under repression, can we rely on the intimacy of friends and relatives to provide our last recourse to full humanity, or will a good dictator always find his way into our bloodstream, and even touch our hearts? Zoran's teacher, certainly, looks to be in the full flush of sexual excitement as she chants the liturgy of political myth: "The life of the young Tito wasn't easy at all. He had to get up very early and go to bed very late." Tears prick her eyes as she announces that Zoran, one of *her* pupils, has won a place on a two-week trek around the marshal's homeland. You can't help wondering what the runner-up will get. Three weeks, maybe.

Once the trek gets under way, unfortunately, the movie loses steam. Until now, Marković's camera has tended to prowl around Zoran's apartment, nosing out family feuds and incidental details—a whole bright basket of red peppers, a dead deer slumped in the bath. From here on, however, it moves outside for a merry jaunt, and the comedy grows broad and blatant. We get a pair of tedious government agents, who really belong in an old Inspector Clouseau movie, and we get Raja (Lazar Ristovski), the zealot who leads his band of apprentices across the country. He picks on the hapless Zoran; their confrontation forms the core of the movie's second half, and it forces our hero to see the error of his ways. But I preferred those ways—Zoran the victim looks like any other tearful child, whereas Zoran the miniature bigot was strangely endearing. He was lost in his own world, in the newsreels that spooled through his tiny mind.

Happily, this sense of the unexpected returns at the climax of the film. Zoran stands on a podium and publicly recants his earlier judgment, issuing a list of people whom he in fact prefers to Marshal Tito: "I would particularly like to point out that I prefer my friends to you." Also favored are his parents, the "local loony," and "the gypsy who repairs the casseroles." It's a wonderful scene, because, although political justice has been restored, the sheer *oddness* of childhood remains intact. That gypsy is the kind of person whom David Copperfield would have noticed, and liked, and commemorated with a sudden, spirit-lifting mention in the course of his narrative. Zoran is as bullheaded as ever; we may find him more sympathetic as a consequence of his plight, but we're no nearer to reaching him. By the time the hikers are invited to meet the great dictator himself, Zoran has lost interest; he wanders away to prod the sweets and cakes, while, back in the reception hall, Tito—with equal, chilling delectation—pushes a lock of hair away from the forehead of an awed young girl.

Tito and Me is too long and misshapen, but it stays with you, and makes you think back to all the children who have paraded across our screens. Cinema is such a sophisticated business—not just in its wealth or its patiently acquired skills but in its need to skirt the borders of cynicism in search of the right audience—that when faced with the promise of innocence it tends to lunge with embarrassing hunger, as though in need of redemption. That is why children have had such a raw deal: celluloid has enshrined them as incorruptibles. With *The Kid*, Chaplin set a tone that can still be heard in the repellent, larky violence of the *Home Alone* movies; it is that of a child who is mischievous but never bad, and whose purity of spirit, treasured in close-up, is seriously considered an example to us all. Chaplin didn't just befriend the kid; he modelled his entire career on the conviction that it was enough to be lovable, not least in the urchinlike speed and cunning with which he fled the demands of adult life. (Keaton, too, knew that those demands were absurd, but he stood and met them head on, and took intricate, beautiful initiatives to fulfill them with good grace.)

Not for a moment did Chaplin doubt that a man, having put away childish things, could (and should) get them back. Movies like *Stand by Me* and *Cinema Paradiso* continue in this presumption, discovering within it fresh supplies of charm. But there is another tradition, dark and difficult by comparison, which digs its heels in and spurns such easy consolation. *The 400 Blows* is still the best film made about childhood, because it resounds with a schoolboy's inky, shin-kicking enthusiasm and at the same time yearns to bust free from the prison of youth. As an adult, Truffaut stands outside the bars, peering in and trying to remember what life was like inside, and wondering why so much of it should smack of pain.

Tito and Me is caught between these two strains; it captures old pleasures with ease, but wisely refuses to patronize its peculiar hero—or, indeed, to understand his motives. Zoran's obsession is well under way as the film begins, and he didn't inherit it from his parents, so where on earth did it come from? One can only respect Marković for struggling against the temptations of cuteness, even though he doesn't always win. His movie takes its place alongside *Empire of the Sun*—Spielberg's most underrated work—as a portrait of innocence carried to uncomfortable lengths; the English boy who thrilled to the spectacle of Japanese pilots, all enmity brushed aside by wonder, would know just how the Yugoslavian boy feels, sitting in the dark and rehearsing the mannerisms of Marshal Tito. If the film reserves judgment on that epoch and the mania that it bred—well, there's nothing wrong with mixed feelings, not in a place where unmixed ones are firing men up to murder their neighbors. Zoran would be almost fifty by now, and much less fat, and probably dead.

SEPTEMBER 6, 1993

THE AGE OF INNOCENCE

Set in the New York of the 1870s, Edith Wharton's *The Age of Innocence* was published in 1920. She was clear and determined in her aims: "I *did* so want *The Age* to be taken not as a 'costume piece' but as a 'simple & grave' story of two people trying to live up to something that was still 'felt in the blood' at that time." For anyone attempting to film the book, the task of respecting Wharton's wishes is tougher than ever. For we live in the age of Merchant-Ivory, when the very idea of a "costume piece" is taken as a blessed relief, a breath of good taste amid the snarls and fumes of mainstream cinema. But to treat history as a shock absorber is a cowardly delusion, from which we need to be rescued. It was a pleasant surprise, therefore, to learn that *The Age of Innocence* would be directed by Martin Scorsese, a man ideally qualified to deliver the shock of the old.

The opening scene is a test case, a white-tie occasion at the opera. All the trimmings are in place, starting with the gardenia in the buttonhole of Newland Archer (Daniel Day-Lewis)—scion of one of the city's more distinguished families, and engaged to the equally favored May Welland (Winona Ryder), who sits demurely in a nearby box. Everyone around them is a picture of composure, which by the lights of this world means ripe for composition: the movie is filled with paintings of the period, of the well-bred turned into Tissots. But Scorsese has other ideas. Together with his longtime collaborators—Thelma Schoonmaker, as editor, and Michael Ballhaus, as director of photography—he breaks up the show. The camera glides with all the stateliness of a Max Ophuls shot, then stops short as other images punch in: the conductor glimpsed through a haze of footlights; the auditorium viewed, from the stage, as a mass of silk and shirtfronts, then, from overhead, as an orderly parade. There is an extraordinary moment when its ranks begin to shudder; Scorsese is shaking his camera at them as though it were a fist, as though it were the artist's duty to disturb the peace and poise of another age. This is *Raging Bull* in a china shop.

The movie is only a few minutes old, but already miles away from Merchant-Ivory, and closer than you might think to Edith Wharton. Her life was a tug-of-war between obedience and rebellion, and her novels take the strain of that contention: she is an Alice in the wonderland of letters, on her best behavior in the presence of the courtly, yet yearning all the while to yank the tablecloth and send them flying like cards. Scorsese, likewise, has spared no expense in furnishing his movie down to the last glove button, to the succulent sinking of knife into canvasback duck; but his eye is too shifty and quizzical to let the luxury rest. The first twinge of upset comes with the arrival—in the Wellands' box, no less—of the Countess Olenska (Michelle Pfeiffer), May's cousin and the lovely black sheep of the Mingott family, easy prey for the snob wolves of Fifth Avenue. Ellen Olenska strayed from the true path: she married not just a cad but a European cad, and has now fled his clutches and returned, so she hopes, to the embrace of New York. Fat chance. "I didn't think the Mingotts would try it on," muses old Sillerton Jackson (Alec McCowen), the society sage, tasting the subtle savor of the outrage and rolling it around his tongue like Burgundy. Archer is more fascinated than disapproving; Ellen's first words to him recall a childhood encounter—"You kissed me once behind a door"—and raise the delicious possibility of more kisses to come.

The countess has clearly made something of a splash, and the rest of the plot ripples out from here. She is spurned by Jackson and the oily Lawrence Lefferts (Richard E. Grant); accepted back by Henry van der Luyden (Michael Gough), high priest of all that is respectable; pursued by the showy and sinister Beaufort (Stuart Wilson); and championed by her grandmother, Mrs. Manson Mingott, a woman whose girth and good humor give an unexpected, almost Wodehousean fizz to Wharton's careful prose. The movie role is fleshed out with equal magnificence by Miriam Margolyes, as an upper-class, pet-smothered sequel to her twittery Flora Finching in *Little Dorrit.* All these satellite roles, in fact, are played with gusto and good spirits, and they need to be, because you can feel something going badly wrong—something humorless and vacant—as you approach the core of the film.

It has to do with Winona Ryder and Michelle Pfeiffer, neither of whom looks remotely at ease. They seem corseted into their roles, unable to breathe, as if under the impression that a woman who did not yet enjoy full liberation—any woman of the last century, for instance—could only be one of two things: wounded or scared. As a slice of social history, *The Age of Innocence* thus makes depressing viewing, untrue to the sense of moral fight that rises from the pages of Edith Wharton. No one is asking that the film be spotlessly true to the book—if anything, I think Scorsese should have messed it around more—but you might as well grab what you can get from it; May Welland, for instance, is a detailed portrait of a complete airhead, and Ryder could have dug into the comedy of the part instead of worrying whether her accent was posh enough. To be fair, she has one great scene, near the end, when her dark eyes glitter like a vampire's as she leans toward her husband, and the last veil of innocence drops away from the age.

Pfeiffer bears herself with too little grace (a touch more Catwoman would have helped), but her real problems start from the neck up. Her hair is a bonfire of glowing ringlets heaped on top of her head; this reminded me of someone, but it wasn't until halfway through the movie, in the middle of an especially poignant scene, that I stifled a yelp of recognition: Lucille Ball! Newland Archer loves Lucy! There's also a plaintive, faintly whining tone that eats into the appeal of Pfeiffer's performance, and cuts down on the sexiness—it's not a patch on her milk-skinned Mme. de Tourvel, in *Dangerous Liaisons,* who finally slipped out of her inhibitions as if they were tight shoes. Ellen Olenska was properly a part for Annette Bening, or even for Sigourney Weaver; here is a woman disdained by the grandees not because she knows too little of their world but because she knows too much of other ones. She has fed on the corruption of the Continent, and if there is nothing exotic in the threat she poses, then Archer's love for her—the torture that should rack the whole movie—seems more like a gentleman's folly, a crush on the side.

It is dismissed as such, of course, by those in the know; but Archer really does have the life crushed out of him. Just for a while, the countess opens another vista—an escape route from his perfect match with May, and from the burden of perfection that bows him down. Unlike Wharton, Scorsese skips the actual wedding, and rightly so; fans of *GoodFellas* may find this movie low on set pieces, more of a nocturne about anticipation and disappointment, but that only sharpens it up as a study of tribal customs. What's more, the big day doesn't matter to Archer, who had it coming anyway—marriage is just another nail in the coffin. With the wife, the wealth, and the wardrobe, his path of contentment is laid down, as if on rails, from here to the grave. However nicely cushioned, it is a kind of doom, and it fortifies the central grievance of the story: that such a society demands everything you have, provides everything you need, and means nothing at all. By some miracle, Daniel Day-Lewis brings all this together in his brilliant balancing act: outward show versus inward tribulation.

If the balance had slipped, *The Age of Innocence* would have collapsed; how easy it would have been, for example, to mock the gestures of the period, and rig the movie in favor of underlying passion. But Archer never makes the leap, and Day-Lewis honors the fear in him: the manners are never less than perfect, the desires tucked away behind an embroidered waistcoat or a precisely calibrated smile. If anything, he improves on Wharton's original, scraping away the traces of prig to reveal something hopeless and humble. Archer makes a tragic epilogue to Day-Lewis's previous incarnations—Tomas in *The Unbearable Lightness of Being*, and Hawkeye in *The Last of the Mohicans*. He is carnality defeated, nobility tamed and tired, although neither is surrendered without a struggle. At the farewell dinner party for the countess, he is seated next to her, and can only swap small talk; but there is a huge devastation in his eyes, which are wet not with tears but with pure pain, as if somebody were chewing his leg off under the table.

Scorsese has found his man, I think—his strongest hero since the great De Niro days, and his first wholly plausible romantic lead. In *New York, New York*, De Niro inspected the romance of the part as if he'd just taken it out of the fridge, sniffing it for weakness; Day-Lewis is no more sentimental, but he understands how a man can melt into extremes of need, all the more thrillingly because he hadn't known they were there. During a fireside scene with Michelle Pfeiffer, the camera glances back and forth between their faces—his filling one half of the frame, hers the other, as if to say: Look how we lock together, how happy we would be. Both are rapt and heated, but Day-Lewis appears not just to gaze at his beloved—"fainting with interest," as John Berryman once put it—but to peer into his own soul, marvelling that anyone could have stirred its surface, let alone its depths.

This may sound like narcissism, but there's an urgency in it that drives the movie on. Besides, any hint of vanity is squashed by a scene with May in a flower garden, when Day-Lewis can no longer take comfort in exquisite city fabrics, and instead has to stroll around in a monstrosity of pale checks, crowned with a curly-brimmed derby the color of peanut butter. Out with the boulevardier, in with the Stubby Kaye look from *Guys and Dolls*. Cinema normally reinforces our presumption that former generations looked much cooler than we do, so it's a joy to come across evidence to the contrary, however brief. Day-Lewis was probably thankful that the camera refused to stop and stare, although it has to be said that Scorsese is so fond of cutting on the move that a simple chat like this can leave you punch-drunk. Think of Jeanne Moreau's entrance in *Jules et Jim*, when Truffaut filmed her head from different angles in a series of speedy, referential mug shots—he couldn't get enough of her. The rest of the narrative obeyed more lyrical rhythms, which she alone could fracture. In *The Age of Innocence*, however, almost *every* scene looks like that. It's exhausting to watch.

But then Wharton is writing about an exhausted world; with hindsight, she realizes not only that its formalities were on the wane but that even in their prime they demanded a round-the-clock vigilance from anyone who thought them worth observing, and something close to sacrifice from anyone who didn't. Day-Lewis is crucial to the re-creation of this; his pitch of concentration somehow justifies the camera's busy habits. When Archer goes to visit Ellen, he pauses in the hall, and sees that Beaufort has turned up before him. We get this from a handful of close-ups, flashed before us like a card trick: hat, cane, monogram, gloves. Some people will argue that Scorsese is showing off; I would give him the benefit of the doubt, and call it a genuine search for a visual grammar that will match the era of Newland Archer. For better or for worse (probably for worse), a gentleman would flick his gaze over faces and clothes, and his judgment would be complete in three seconds. It is Ellen, of course, who forces Archer to slow down and look deeper, and as the movie draws to a close even the camera is shamed into calm by the slow burn of regret—tranquil, but intense for all that—in the face of Daniel Day-Lewis. (What a pity that Elmer Bernstein's raucous score couldn't make the change, too.)

The Age of Innocence reminds me of *Bram Stoker's Dracula:* in both cases, you sense a filmmaker desperate to end a bad streak of work, throwing every technique he knows at a tale of high emotion. Coppola blew it; Scorsese, against all odds, has come up with a serious film—something I never thought he would do again, not after the disgraceful fakery of *Cape Fear*, or *The Last Temptation of Christ.* That movie was wrecked less by heresy than by hysteria, and there are moments in *The Age of Innocence*, too, when you feel like begging the director to take it easy. To make matters worse, he stuffs our ears with voice-overs, carved from the novel and barely digested into a script. But there are pleasures abounding here, and they stay with you—the shuffling, slow-motion city throng; the hard pewter landscape where Archer pursues his love in winter; and a burst of abandon worthy of Michael Powell, as the whole screen flames into red like a wound, or into yellow like a rose. Archer is playing with fire, and Scorsese backs him up by painting with it: the picture's dominant image is of long shadows momentarily beaten back by the lighting of a cigar or a taper, or by the crackle of bright coals. The ending is all embers; you leave the theatre with your senses peeled, and your heart still rising and falling with Newland Archer, to the swell and fade of his hopes. True to Wharton's wishes, this movie is not a costume piece, or a museum exhibit; it's a wake-up call from the past, and proves how much can still be "felt in the blood"—even in this, the age of knowingness.

SEPTEMBER 13, 1993

DIVERTIMENTO

Jacques Rivette's *La Belle Noiseuse* came out in 1991, and lasted four hours. Now we have *Divertimento*, half the length, and a different beast altogether—constructed, indeed, from different takes. The bulk of the long version was taken up by an encounter between an artist and his model; the primary image was of a hand moving scratchily over paper, and the effect was hypnotic—you were never bored, but you almost wished you had been, so strenuous was the effort of matching the artist's concentration. These studio sessions have now been pared back, and you have to admire Rivette for performing such ruthless surgery on his own work; it makes a change from all the expanded "Special Editions" foisted on us by other directors—by Kevin Costner, for instance, whose recut of *Dances with Wolves* includes previously unseen footage of Kevin Costner.

The action, if you can call it that, takes place over a few days in the South of France. Together with his girlfriend, Marianne (Emmanuelle Béart), a young artist named Nicolas (David Bursztein) is invited to meet one of his heroes, Édouard Frenhofer (Michel Piccoli)—a celebrated painter, many years his senior, who lives and works in a large house near Montpellier. The house is almost the hero of this movie, sometimes hemming the characters in, at other times encouraging them to lounge with elegance. From the street, it resembles a church, with broad steps leading up to chunky double doors; at roof level, however, where Frenhofer has his studio, it feels more like the castle of some minor duke, complete with parapets and an airy panoramic view, to which the camera casually turns when the drama is getting too intense. Frenhofer's wife, Liz (Jane Birkin), shows her guests "the chimera room, my favourite, because it serves no purpose." The implications of that line throb through the movie. It has a kind of aimless, drowsy magic—people keep dropping into a light snooze at random times of day. Not a lot happens here, but almost anything *could* happen; chimeras are waiting around the corner.

Frenhofer is the Prospero of this domain, albeit a Prospero in the twilight of his powers, waving a broken wand. No wonder that Michel Piccoli should feast on the role with such relish, for it drips with his favorite moods: the magisterial and the glum. When the call goes out for a benign yet crusty patriarch, American cinema turns to Jason Robards or James Earl Jones, but let's be honest: the French still stock the best vintages—Philippe Noiret, Michel Serrault, and, above all, Piccoli. He enjoyed himself no end in Louis Malle's laid-back idyll, *May Fools*, stripped to the waist and feeling for crayfish with his bare hands; now, in *Divertimento*, he has the air of one who has passed beyond simple pleasures and stumbled into the complications of old age. The epicure's touch has not deserted him—we first see him holding a dead rabbit, which means dinner, and his hours of painting are nicely oiled by swigs of red wine—but his mind is elsewhere, nicked by doubt and self-scorn. He sags and shuffles, and bumps into invisible walls; it's a marvellous, slightly upsetting picture of a man refusing to mellow.

If Frenhofer were more lonely, this last stand might be suffused with heroism; but he's surrounded by fans, and the roughness rubs off on them and scars their admiration. Standing in his studio, he makes them anything but welcome: "Liz and I have achieved a state of peaceful stability, even happiness. You arrive, and unhappiness begins. . . . Nothing personal, but for all of us the irrevocable has happened. . . . You bring us trouble, upset. You, too, will be unhappy." He acts like Duncan, but he sounds like one of the three witches, and this bizarre speech tells us, unmistakably, that we have arrived in Jacques Rivette country. The generous foreboding, the vatic utterance that you hope will turn out to be a joke, the shaggy-dog story with extra bite—these have been his hallmarks ever since *Paris Belongs to Us* (1962), which jumbled up a conspiracy thriller with an ad-hoc production of *Pericles.* All the world was a stage, and vice versa. Most films like to expose the theatrical side of our nature, presuming that the grandiloquence of the politician, the sexual braggart, or the party host can only be a sham. It was *Citizen Kane* that first had the audacity to suggest the opposite: the Kane who thunders nonsense on the rostrum is no less true to himself—may even be more so—than the Kane who marries an heiress or feathers a furtive love nest. We look in vain for the man behind the mask, because it fits him better than his own face. Rivette is one of the few directors to have taken this to heart, and pushed it further; his films are like intimate games played to unstated rules, and it is the characters, rather than the actors, who pronounce their lines as if they only just learned them last night.

Under these volatile conditions you can hardly expect motivation, the engine of traditional plots, to run with any smoothness. *Divertimento* nudges you with unexplained events. At dinner on the first night (a stiff occasion that softens into giggles, like a child's birthday party), there's suddenly a frightening thump of skull on wood: Frenhofer's friend Porbus has blacked out. Only Liz reacts; everyone else looks spaced-out and helpless. Later on, having recovered, Porbus suggests to Frenhofer that he use Marianne as a model. He agrees, as does Nicolas, but when Marianne finds out she turns on her heel and stomps off into the night; she has been traded between men like a marble statue, or a slave. Come morning, however, she arrives bright and early at Frenhofer's house, and before long she is easing off a robe and standing there before him wearing nothing but a look of defiance. Her change of heart is never explained, but you don't think of it as capitulation; if anything, she is taking the fight to the enemy. Just for a second, he gazes at her dumbstruck, but she outstares him, and he gathers his wits and turns to his sketchbook. She is ravishing, but Frenhofer (like Rivette) is not in the business of being ravished. The game is on.

The object of the game is not art, I think, but power play—the tiny, often ridiculous transactions by which all of us, not just artists, seek the upper hand. "Turn around. . . . Stand up straight . . . as if you were stretched to the ceiling," Frenhofer commands. "It hurts," she complains. "That's good," he says, pressing on with the everyday cruelties of his trade. There are heart-freezing moments here as he pulls and straightens her reluctant limbs, like a murderer arranging a corpse for his fastidious pleasure. But, as the film progresses, the balance shifts: he may be forcing Marianne to her knees, but she is bending him to her needs, inspiring him to take up an old, unfinished painting, *La Belle Noiseuse*, named after a courtesan of the seventeenth century—"a troublemaker," says Marianne, sensing a role model. Frenhofer resumes the masterpiece that never was (and never will be), covering an old image of Liz with a fresh one of Marianne. Soon she is the one who drags the easel to its place and pulls up the mattress on which she must recline. By now, there is nothing timid in her nudity—she looks coolly, ferociously free, and expects to be painted accordingly. "I count in this, too!" she exclaims when Frenhofer threatens to give up.

Like his heroine, Rivette is not concerned by artist's block, because he knows all too well that the world itself is never blocked—it spews ideas and setups all the time. That is why his movies mosey on so long, daring us to nominate a conclusion. I once had a chance to see his 1971 film *Out 1*, and spurned it, on the pathetic ground that I didn't have thirteen hours to spare. In a way, he is not asking very much of us—simply that we admit to the messiness of life; on the other hand, even four hours is asking a lot of most audiences, and there are good reasons to try *Divertimento* instead. For a start, the drawings and paintings (by the French artist Bernard Dufour, whose hand we see) don't really bear prolonged inspection; nor do they affect the substance of the film. Far from being rare or high-flown, it feels picky and downbeat; anyone who goes to French movies for a quick fix of artiness will come out grumbling. Yet there is no doubting Rivette's intelligence, or the calmness of his eye. The camera patiently circles Marianne, keeping its distance; sometimes it will begin a scene with a minute shift to one side, like Frenhofer seeking the perfect angle. For a film about scrutiny, there are remarkably few close-ups; to Rivette, I suspect, they smack of emotional shorthand, which is not his style.

But one has to ask: Does *Divertimento* really deliver that style? For all its polish, doesn't it have a sweet tooth for gloom? Rivette was one of the leaders of the New Wave, with its sting and slap, and his best movies maintain an unyielding playfulness. *Céline and Julie Go Boating* (1974) has a high old time inside the labyrinth of memory: two young women visit a spooky house and relive the same story over and over, subtly deflecting it to their satisfaction. They are doing a Frenhofer, in other words, but the ritual solemnity is frilled with farce. Rivette may not thank me for the suggestion, but I think he should recut *La Belle Noiseuse* again, this time pointing it up as a comic roundelay. Less this time of Emmanuelle Béart, who strains the movie toward melodrama, and more of Jane Birkin, whose toothy blitheness makes it float. There are so many strands, after all, to be gathered up: we know that Porbus once loved Liz, who now loves Frenhofer, who depends on Marianne, who has offended Nicolas, who seems indecently pleased by the arrival, late in the movie, of his sister Julienne . . . The possibilities are rampant. Go for it, Jacques. Third time lucky.

SEPTEMBER 20, 1993

DAZED AND CONFUSED

The action of *Dazed and Confused* begins, we are told, on "May 28, 1976, 1:05 p.m.," and ends eighteen hours later. You might expect this level of precision from a tense international thriller, but hardly from a meandering memoir of dope-fogged teenage laziness. That's the first of many good jokes littering the movie, which keeps a cool head while all around it are losing theirs. Written and directed by Richard Linklater, it has scarcely any plot and no perceptible moral, apart from the injunction to "Eat More Pussy" scrawled on a high school wall. Even that is disregarded; sex may be in the air, but it sounds like hard work once you knuckle down to it, and who wants to work?

It's the bicentennial year, and the last day before summer vacation. Smartly, but with no sense of hurry, the movie homes in on different groups: Mike (Adam Goldberg) and Tony (Anthony Rapp), for example—sensitive types who may lack athletic prowess but more than make up for it in folly. Moving slightly further toward Cloud Nine, we find Slater (Rory Cochrane). With his tiny, scrunched-up face and endless hair, he looks like an otter that just chewed the wrong kind of river weed. Slater's problem is not that he's stoned all the time but that he presumes everyone else must be, too, and therefore limits all communication to some personal cosmic wavelength, writhing around in mid-speech as if trying to align the aerial inside his own head. His riff on the Washington household—Martha always had a bowl of grass waiting for George when he came home—rises to a majestic hippie logic: "Did you ever look at a dollar bill, man? There is some spooky stuff going on on a dollar bill, man. And it's *green.*" This makes a wonderful change from the standard anticapitalism rant: money is no longer the enemy; it's just another freaky friend.

Meanwhile, up at the tougher end of the scale, there are jocks like O'Bannion (Ben Affleck) and Randy "Pink" Floyd (Jason London). I was hoping that Pink might have friends called Larry "Black" Sabbath or Chris "Deep" Purple, but, sadly, not; still, it shows how quickly one warms to the spirit of the movie. The crucial surprise of *Dazed and Confused* is that it conjures up affection for a silly era even in the hearts of those who weren't there, or those whose memories tell a different story. I spent most of that summer, for instance, cowering in the library or serving double faults, but the movie almost persuaded me that I, too, heaved bowling balls out of fast-moving orange cars. What could have been a narrow, cultish little picture, a mere retro-trip, fans out into a broader study of longing and belonging.

Pink has two problems. First, he wants to play football next year, but that means signing an official pledge—no drink or drugs. To him that's like agreeing not to breathe. Second, he has promised Jodi Kramer (Michelle Burke) not to thrash the hide off her younger brother, Mitch (Wiley Wiggins). Fair enough, except that today is initiation day for those coming up from junior high. For boys, like Mitch, this means being hunted down, turned around, and whumped with wooden bats; for girls, like Sabrina (Christin Hinojosa), it's more a question of being smeared with mustard and ketchup and generally treated like human hot dogs. If all this smacks horribly of a Kenneth Anger movie, don't worry: there's nothing underground or murky about Linklater, who prefers to revel in the open air, where grievances heal rather than fester. Finally caught by his seniors, Mitch grimaces as the blows strike home—he reminds you of Malcolm McDowell in *If. . .*, his pain closely scrutinized by the lens—but Pink stays his hand at the last moment, like a high-school Abraham, and thereby honors his promise.

Gradually, the action slows down and modulates into a beer party, planned for somebody's house but switched to the middle of nowhere. As the evening lingers on, and the movie shows no sign of losing interest, you realize that *Dazed and Confused* is working from the blueprint of *American Graffiti*, cramming a whole generation into a few short hours. George Lucas, however, was besotted: he was scoring a hymn to lost youth, to the tune of everyone's greatest hits. Linklater is unmoved by that pop pathos: he remembers his school days as clearly as Lucas does, but he's not so sure what he thinks about them—the more honest course. If *American Graffiti* turned high jinks into epiphanies, *Dazed and Confused* moves in the opposite direction: fuelled by joints, the characters yearn for significant events that never quite arrive. Hence the great moment when a girl wanders boozily into a shot and simply falls over, as if she had something vital to announce but couldn't be bothered. The spirit of the occasion infects even Mike, who used to shun frivolity in favor of helping the world. Now he's having doubts. "You're not going to go to law school?" somebody asks. "What are you going to do?" Mike pauses, his features twisted with the struggle to come clean. "I want to *dance*."

The film is resplendent with seventies clutter, right down to the bulging typography of the opening titles. But there's nothing spacey or Slater-like in Linklater's instinct for composition; apart from a cheap shot of a car reflected in a convex mirror, *Dazed and Confused* dignifies the period with a measured fluency, sliding from one bunch of figures to the next. *American Graffiti* was lit like a school prom, glossy with neon but blessed with enough pockets of darkness for a backseat fumble. Linklater gives his picture a crisper, critical edge, on the assumption that the first duty of a director is to commemorate rather than seduce. He allows himself the occasional descant, a few seconds of lyrical release (look out for Sabrina and her friends cleaning up in a car wash), but even then the image can tremble with mixed feelings. The sight of Mitch awaiting his fate on a baseball field, marooned amid luminous green and unconsoled by a huge sign that cries "Happy Birthday America," is one of the most arresting visions of loneliness in recent cinema.

In its daffy way, *Dazed and Confused* breaks with Hollywood habits to find a fresh, hip momentum in the quaint old principle of charity. It seethes with has-beens and wanna-bes, with the lovesick and the laughable, but Linklater refuses to set them up for target practice. Only one character is remotely vicious, and his comeuppance is no more than a dash of slapstick—the other seniors drift away from it looking pleased but not triumphant. It can be hard to adjust to this level of light comedy; you keep expecting things to turn gloomy or brutish—by definition, the rites-of-passage movie should come loaded with portent—and Linklater keeps wiping the smile back onto your face. Although the screenplay is pitted with minor moral quandaries, he steps lightly around them instead of plunging in. When Mitch stays out all night, for instance, returning home at dawn to face his mother, you brace yourself for a family firestorm; but just this once she lets him off—he's had a great time, and the glow of it gets to her. If Linklater were using the scene to wrap the picture up cutely, it would count as sentimental spoon-feeding, and you'd gag on the taste; but the emotions feel hard-earned, and Mitch, like all the other characters, deserves a break.

This makes a change from Linklater's last movie, *Slacker*, which hardly used characters at all; the credits listed "Scooby-Doo philosopher" or "Guy who tosses typewriter" instead of names. The camera tagged along with each in turn, and the world that emerged was somewhere between a drifting shoal and a nutty conspiracy; it was fun, but also a bit of a pain.

Though *Dazed and Confused* is equally thronged, it is far less arch; Linklater has moved beyond the patterns that people make, and started to ask himself why they link up in the first place. He has a classy feel for the tempo of an ensemble movie, which fosters its own brand of suspense not with plotting but through the rotation of characters: just when you're getting into X, along comes Y to claim your attention, leaving you thirsty for more X later on, and already looking forward to Z. The touchstone of this method is *Meet Me in St. Louis*, which still seems as pointless and pleasurable as a dance. You sit there waiting for Minnelli to get going, for the story to find its proper focus, and gradually you see that its fleet, nonchalant rhythm, handing on happiness like a baton from one person to the next, is all it has to offer. Who could ask for anything more?

Dazed and Confused can't match that grace—no film featuring Alice Cooper on the soundtrack could hope to do so—but Linklater shares Minnelli's desire to swerve aside from the threat of melodrama. Maybe he decided there was enough of it in the sight of all those flared jeans without adding any more of his own. He doesn't so much direct the movie as host it, letting people do their own thing; as a result, the acting is like a riposte to James Dean—buoyant with throwaway gestures, and draining the anguish and spite out of teenage rebellion until it seems no more than a variant of basic freedom. This will annoy some people no end—particularly aging rockers—but it's hard not to get hooked on the gags and join the party. Only then will you get full value from the closing scenes, and Linklater's pin-sharp rendition of the morning after—all liquor drunk, all passion spent, everyone sick and hollow and lightheaded at having soldiered through the epic of the night. It's a kind of appalled joy, and you watch it on the faces of the characters as they screw their eyes up against the early sun. The film ends with one of the elementary shots of American cinema—the view through a windshield onto open road. Is that a bright future ahead of them, or a false dawn, or just a lousy hangover? They hardly care, still blissed out from the smiles of a summer night.

OCTOBER 4, 1993

IT'S ALL TRUE

It's All True is the title of an Orson Welles film that was started but never completed. Now unearthed and fleshed out with documentary, it is being shown for the first time. The result is a peculiar hybrid of travelogue and treachery, fable and dance, all jostling for attention, none quite gaining the upper hand: in short, an Orson Welles movie. He appears only fitfully onscreen, yet the spirit of the man, puckish but expansive, hovers above the whole enterprise. It was ever thus: with a handful of late scenes, and with no attempt to wrest control from Carol Reed, he somehow turned *The Third Man* into a Welles production, just as all Vienna fell under the spell of Harry Lime. Welles liked to slip a dose of his own wit into every picture he touched, as though it were being filmed through his eyes. Eight years after his death, the effect has not worn off; on the evidence of *It's All True*, it is more potent than ever.

The story is a tangled and unhappy one. In 1942, Welles was pulled off the final stages of *The Magnificent Ambersons* and sent flying down to Rio. His task was to foster good relations with Brazil, as part of a State Department drive to win Latin American support in the face of war. Welles was to be cultural ambassador and professional charmer—to work his magic on the Brazilians as he had already done on the American public. The movie calls it "a gesture of hemispheric solidarity," which sounds like a description of Welles's dramatic technique in later life. He was slated to make a three-part film for RKO; the studio was worried about dropping money on the picture, but the United States government guaranteed up to $300,000 against any losses. In retrospect, the mission seems more like a gamble: America was funding its young genius in his patriotic duty—to go south and have a good time. Things could only go wrong.

And so they did, in spectacular fashion. The fallout was so widespread that it has taken years to piece together what happened. In 1985, Bill

Krohn, the Hollywood correspondent for *Cahiers du Cinema*, announced that parts of *It's All True*—missing, presumed lost—had been found in studio archives. There was footage from all three sections of the movie: from "The Story of Samba," a hymn to the Rio carnival, some of it shot in Technicolor; from "My Friend Bonito," the tale of a boy and a bull, overseen by Welles but directed by his colleague Norman Foster; and from "Four Men on a Raft," the reenactment of a celebrated voyage to Rio. Krohn collaborated with Richard Wilson, an old friend of Welles's who had worked on the movie in Brazil; together with Myron Meisel, they assembled the film we see now.

You can only admire the inspired patience of the reconstruction—half sleuthing, half archeology—and the tracking down and interviewing of those connected with the original shoot. On the other hand, a movie audience is impatient of scholarship; it will swallow any number of tall tales, but small, hard facts tend to lodge in its craw. No one knew this better than Welles himself, and as *It's All True* gets under way you realize how absurd the title is. With Orson Welles, it's *never* all true. Everything about him, from movies to monologues to magic shows, lends weight to the principle that you cannot look truth straight in the face, and even if you could it wouldn't be worth trusting; it's like Rita Hayworth among the mirrors, just one of a thousand reflections. There is nothing more sly or joyous in *It's All True* than the opening scene: Welles talking to the camera, explaining his version of the prickly events that surrounded the film. He shows a crude drawing: "This is a voodoo witch doctor. I ran into him down in Brazil."

Here is the eager, restive, oddly casual tone that you find in one of Conrad's yarn spinners, and—quite unfairly—it shames the rest of the documentary, turning its precision into pedantry. The voice alone is enough to draw you on: where else can you hear the sombre measures of a funeral sermon mixed with the burr of consummate bullshit? Cinema has given us a choir of heavenly growlers, from Jimmy Stewart right down to Lauren Bacall, but there is a select group—Welles, Ralph Richardson, and the John Huston of *Chinatown*—that knows that the richness itself is very nearly a joke, that anything can be achieved, anyone gulled, by such a ridiculous sound. Welles rubs his lines against us like cat's fur: the roguish closing credits of *Ambersons*, for example ("I wrote the script and directed it. My name is Orson Welles"), or Kane softly hamming his way into sincerity as he recites his declaration of principles. When the voice-over of *It's All True* is given to somebody else, it begins to sound like any other documentary: "The plans were about to change—dramatically." After Welles, everything always seems a little flat.

Nowhere do you miss him more than in "Four Men on a Raft." This was the heart of *It's All True*, and with Welles as narrator its air of downbeat grandeur would have been complete; as things stand, we have to make do with newly recorded sound effects (slap of waves, thock of axe on wood), and a rather strenuous score by Jorge Arriagada. Welles based his story on the recent triumph of four *jangadeiros*, Brazilian fishermen who labored under a harsh system with no form of redress: they sailed 1,650 miles along the coast to plead their case before the President. The plot is pared to elementals: a marriage, a death, and then the journey itself. Welles had precious little film to work with, and the result has an uncanny speed and concentration, as if he were trying to honor the sparseness of the men's lives with his own style; the wistful ease of *Ambersons* seems a world away. There are moments in "Four Men on a Raft" that calmly beat Eisenstein at his own game: the funeral procession, for instance, where the camera cuts from the snaking line of mourners to the trudge of their feet, and from there to the grim poise of their expressions, as if tracing the source of their dignity.

Here is Welles at his least lordly and most inventive—making the best of a cheap job, learning and storing new tricks along the way. The close-up that becomes a daunting icon, bodies honestly flattered by the clean coastal light: without these images from Brazil, would Welles have dreamed of the randy, sweltering scenes on board ship in *The Lady from Shanghai*? Without "Four Men on a Raft," without its abstract arrangements of wood and canvas, its complex pattern of shadows thrown by a simple net, would he have arrived so neatly at the murders of Desdemona and Roderigo in *Othello*—one masked tight by a sheet, the other stabbed through the slats of a Turkish bath? All these movies delve into a ravishing range of monochrome tones; I like to think that Welles saw the Technicolor rushes from "The Story of Samba," realized that color could never hope to match the expressive timbre of black-and-white, and thus stayed away from it for more than twenty-five years.

Let's not kid ourselves, however: *It's All True* is not, and would never have been, a major picture. It has an innocence about it, a trusting breeziness that charms the eye; if Welles had been operating at full throttle, he would have laced it with corruption, with a touch of evil. But that was not his job; he was there in the interests of America, not of Orson Welles, although back at RKO the studio heads were beginning to wonder if he knew the difference. When they saw what he had shot, they panicked and tried to pull him off the project; he persevered, and they fired him. Just for good measure, *Ambersons* was hacked up and released in a version that bore little resemblance to his original plan. Even as one greets the long-awaited appearance of *It's All True*, there is a feeling that we are watching the prologue to a tragedy. Welles called the whole episode "the one key disaster in my story," adding, "It cost me many, many other pictures which I never made; and many years in which I couldn't work at all."

That is certainly the received wisdom: for once, Welles is not having us on. But we must treasure what we have, not what we lack, and it seems to me that his existing films, most of them masterpieces, move gracefully under the burden of his wretched experience with *It's All True*. Welles is unique among American directors, after all, in being a showman who is interested in failure. Movie history is stuffed with Barnums of every description, but not one—not even Fellini—has Welles's instinctive need to hang around and see the big top come down. If Griffith and De Mille believed in the power of spectacle, it took Welles to convince us that spectacle reveals its meaning, its full bloom, only at the moment when it rots and falls. That is why the figure of Falstaff swelled in his imagination, and why, in some bizarre way, we should be grateful for the farrago in Brazil. For the first time, the boy wonder heard the chimes at midnight, and from here on they would toll through his career, endlessly refining his romantic pessimism. His movies turn aside from happy endings not because he was a grouch—he virtually defined the *bon vivant*—but because he knew that the arc of human endeavor has to pass through happiness and out the other side. After *It's All True*, he became the *jangadeiro* of cinema—close to the wind, almost on the rocks, forever in search of a good deal. In the heroic tale of the fishermen and the sad story of the movie director we hear the same refrain: Expect the worst, and hope for the best. If in doubt, do the samba.

NOVEMBER 1, 1993

THE REMAINS OF THE DAY

The Remains of the Day is directed by James Ivory and adapted by his habitual screenwriter, Ruth Prawer Jhabvala, from the book by Kazuo Ishiguro. The film flashes back and forth between the 1930s, when Stevens (Anthony Hopkins) was butler to Lord Darlington (James Fox), and 1958, when he is given time off by Mr. Lewis (Christopher Reeve), the new, American owner of Darlington Hall, to take a motoring trip around the West Country. In Ishiguro's novel, Stevens borrows a Ford from his employer; for the movie, it is quietly upgraded to a Daimler. Only little people have Fords. It goes without saying that the car is an immaculate contraption, as is every other vehicle on the road; reckless driving is plainly a nasty invention of the 1960s, like mud and sex.

As he slams down into fifth, stomps on the gas, and leaves rubber on the Dorset tarmac, Stevens has time to ponder those distant and devoted days before the war. To all intents and purposes, he ran Darlington Hall, assisted by the housekeeper, Miss Kenton (Emma Thompson)—younger than he, but equally assiduous in insuring that the shirts upstairs were kept properly stuffed. The highlight of that period, when most of the movie takes place, is an international conference at the house: a good chance for the movie to herd in some lumbering stereotypes—the tetchy bearded Frenchman, the rich and ruddy American, the bawling Wagnerian blonde. The story has a double hook: first, Stevens cannot see the growing folly of Lord Darlington, who is trying not to be beastly to the Germans, and thus getting into all kinds of trouble; second, he cannot admit the possibility that Miss Kenton loves him, for fear of discovering mutual stirrings in his own heart. As a butler, Stevens can spot a dirty fish fork at twenty paces, but as a man he is blind.

A parable of excess control, of professional pride taken to dire extremes—that is what Ishiguro dreamed up, and the movie, in its clunky way, does him proud. I have an unfortunate and incurable problem with regard to this tale: having been drenched in P. G. Wodehouse from an early age, I find it impossible to take the master-slave relationship entirely seriously. It can't just sit there and stagnate, but needs to be enlivened by subtle transactions of power. Even Hegel knew that, and he never got to read Wodehouse, although you can't help wishing he had. How could any decent butler follow his leader to the bitter end, allowing him to be reviled as an appeaser, when Jeeves—a mere valet by comparison—won't even let Bertie pick his own spats? This giant, Day-Glo implausibility tends to outglare the gentle irony on which Ishiguro's plot is supposed to hang, and the movie only makes matters worse. The scene in which Stevens's father (Peter Vaughan), himself a former butler, proclaims his ideal of dignified service—something to do with a tiger under the dining-room table—is stretched out beyond endurance; he's telling a joke, of sorts, but Wodehouse would have made the same point in half a paragraph.

Movies are pretty uncomfortable with this kind of social lockjaw. Hollywood has long preferred to take the Wodehouse line, which may have led it into moments of crassness (the *Arthur* films, say) but has at least maintained a nimbleness of spirit. While reflecting on *The Remains of the Day*, I made the mistake of revisiting that natty subgenre, the butler picture, and immediately hit the jackpot with *Tovarich* and *My Man Godfrey*. In both cases, the butler (Charles Boyer and William Powell, respectively) is wittier and more accomplished than those he serves, the point being that you can never tell where a true gentleman is going to pop up next. This is a highly, though not exclusively, American point of view—Capra took it, but so did Dickens—and it unveils a mild, sophisticated anarchy, in which the social order, while never under serious threat, turns into a game of snakes and ladders. Basically, you climb a ladder and try not to marry a snake.

I am not saying that *The Remains of the Day* should have been a screwball comedy, although the vision of Stevens tanking up on highballs and accidentally ripping the back of a lady's ball gown is a tempting one. I'm just not convinced that a medium as slippery as cinema can stand so demure and obsequious a take on the world. There is always a spot of humor in Merchant-Ivory movies—in this case, Stevens trying to explain the facts of life by gibbering on about ducks and geese—but, like the man himself, it knows its limitations, and rarely leads to a disturbance of the peace. When a performer really does take hold of a Merchant-Ivory part and shake it (as Daniel Day-Lewis did in *A Room with a View*), the whole prissy structure begins to shudder. The movies are both saved and shamed by the onslaught of comedy; Emma Thompson lit up *Howards End* with her smart, inquisitive Margaret Schlegel, but you felt her patience being sorely tested by those fey goings-on—she belonged in a different, more vibrant film altogether.

No such luck for Thompson in *The Remains of the Day*. She's stuck fast in this one, with no way out. It's not that she looks too young to be a housekeeper—more that she doesn't look like a housekeeper at all. The Miss Kenton she gives us is quarrelsome rather than bossy, bristling with feeling and faintly bored; she could be one of the Mitford sisters taking charge, just for a lark, on the housekeeper's day off. The film shunts her into the sidings of the action, as if unsure what to do with such a woman; her principal duty is not to list the laundry or buff the silverware but to alert the audience to the enduring sadness that squats at the center of the film. "Why do you always have to hide what you feel?" she asks Stevens, as if we hadn't noticed what was wrong with him. To be fair, this same demand yields one touching scene, when she invades the butler's parlor and tries to find out what he's reading; Stevens shies away, hugging the book to his breast, as if it contained the code to his misery, or dirty snapshots of the parlormaid.

Anthony Hopkins should be in his element here. There is always so much to watch in a Hopkins performance, his whole frame quivering with thought and afterthought; if he is unlikely to join that high rank of actors in whose company we can relax, it is equally clear that he will never bore us. He seems fussy, but the fuss is less that of a ditherer than that of a pedant, pecking at the world to test its resilience (certainly not for crumbs of comfort), checking every emotion before he goes public with it. The courteous cocking of the head, the semiautomatic smile, the minute hiss of impatience as he turns to leave, is called back, and whips round to face a further request: all these Hopkins trademarks slip beautifully into place for *The Remains of the Day*. Why, then, is the performance so oddly unsatisfying? How is it that his Stevens leaves us cold, when we were so easily churned up by his much slighter role as Frederick Treves, in *The Elephant Man*? The answer lies with David Lynch, who left Hopkins to play the industrious gentleman, with surgical manners almost untouched, but filled the rest of the movie with everything that Treves was holding back—all the wild curiosity and wilder pity spinning about in that cool head.

James Ivory gets it exactly wrong; he makes a movie that is even more anal and starchy than his hero. It's the old problem: if you think British society is stiff with class consciousness, you should try British movies. This is true for toughs as well as toffs; I recently tried watching a season of sixties working-class dramas—*A Taste of Honey*, and so forth—and simply ground to a halt under the weight of shapeless grievance. The glossy tradition has lasted longer, however, and become desirable property. You could argue that *The Remains of the Day*—made by Columbia Pictures, and coproduced (though you'd never know it) by Mike Nichols—represents a slick new breed: the wanna-be British film. Darlington Hall is a composite of four different country houses, and the scene where the local hunt meets in front of the house is borrowed from *Brideshead Revisited* and guaranteed to flutter the heart of anyone who's ever shopped at Ralph Lauren. Here is the sly effect of the Merchant-Ivory potion: it suggests that any movie full of well-behaved people is by definition a delicate work of art, and, more crucially, that the audience is refined and bettered by the mere watching of it. We are offered social elevation in the hope that we will confuse it with the spiritual variety, long fixed as one of the noble ends of art. It's an easy mistake to make. In their quiet way, movies such as *The Remains of the Day* play a low trick with high culture, and reverse its purpose: they turn us into snobs.

I therefore propose that from now on the figure of Stevens should appear at the start of every Merchant-Ivory picture, offering the audience a glass of sherry, like the muscleman who thumps the gong for Rank Films, or the MGM lion. Stevens stands for good manners at any cost, a terror of offending, the tacit withdrawal from unseemly sights: all the qualities we have come to expect from Ivory's work. There is plenty to recommend them in life, but they make lousy guidelines to the art of cinema. There is not a single shot in *The Remains of the Day* of which the butler himself would disapprove; the most daring motion of the camera is a quick peep through the spyhole of a door—more a useful subterfuge than a flourish of style. But that is the secret of Ivory's films: they have no style, no real signature. What they do have, in abundance, is an accumulation of good taste masquerading as style; needless to say, it is more reliable than style, shorn of embarrassing tics and obsessive longueurs. No wonder that the audience for these movies, almost butlerish in loyalty, keeps on coming back for more. The Ivory trade is here to stay.

NOVEMBER 15, 1993

THREE COLORS: BLUE

Fellini is dead, Tarkovsky is dead, Bergman sticks to theatre, and Godard is out to lunch. All of which leaves European cinema wandering around like a lost kid. Rescue has come in the unlikely shape of the Polish director Krzysztof Kieślowski—unlikely because a résumé of his early career, most of it in documentaries, barely hints at the glories to come. The man who made *The Principles of Safety and Hygiene in a Copper Mine*, fine work though that undoubtedly was, had a long path to tread before he arrived at *A Short Film About Killing*, one of the least hygienic movies ever made, let alone at *The Double Life of Véronique*, one of the most baffling and beautiful. His latest film, *Blue*, is the first in a trilogy whose titles refer to the French tricolor, and to the declared aims of the Revolution—"Blue" for liberty, "White" for equality, "Red" for fraternity. It sounds like a pasty mix of the pompous and the schematic, but don't worry: Kieślowski couldn't make a predictable movie if he tried.

Blue is indeed about liberty, but if you're hoping for Gérard Depardieu to come bursting out of the Bastille with a ripped shirt, tough luck. Kieślowski is merely curious about the fate of a noble ideal: what has it dwindled into, two centuries on? He deals with an ironic and very particular sort of freedom—the sort that comes from having your family wiped out in a car wreck. Julie (Juliette Binoche) is travelling with her husband, a celebrated composer, and their young daughter, Anna, when their Alfa Romeo hits a tree. The violence of the event is not exhausted: some of it spills over into Julie, and one of her first actions on waking up in the hospital is to carry on the bad work by smashing a window. Kieślowski's movies are often touched by grief, but you never get the sense of a peaceful aftermath, of anything—or, indeed, anyone—being laid to rest. Current wisdom may urge the bereaved to pick up the pieces and start gluing, but Julie couldn't give a damn about rebuilding her old life; she wants a new one, and fast.

For a start, the family home in the country is to be cleared out and sold. "Why are you crying?" Julie asks the housekeeper. "Because you're not" comes the reply. Julie calls a friend, Olivier (Benoit Régent), asks him to come around, tells him to undress, sleeps with him, and says goodbye: "I'm like any other woman. I sweat. I cough. I have cavities. You won't miss me." It's a great speech, and a false hope: Julie is about as forgettable as Cleopatra, and however fiercely she dreams of a clean slate, the past will always return to scrawl unwanted messages all over it. She moves into an apartment in Paris, for instance, and reverts to her maiden name, but Olivier tracks her down. She throws the score of her husband's unfinished concerto into a garbage truck, but somebody has already made a copy, and anyway there are rumors that she herself composed it, and could thus complete the work in her own time. Lastly, she discovers that he had a mistress, who is now carrying his child.

Whether all these incidents amount to a plot is debatable. Yet the film presses on as if there were a race to be run, or a great wrong avenged. As Julie struggles to pull away from the world, it yanks her back, and the tension between them hums like a wire. Sometimes, the edge of the frame is darkly filtered—you can sense fate coming down like a fog—but elsewhere Kieślowski switches to a handheld camera, running it along behind his characters as if he were still making documentaries and Paris were just another copper mine. Though anything less like a thriller would be hard to imagine, *Blue* is the only really frightening movie I've seen all year. One night, Julie looks down from her window and sees a man being beaten up in the street. He flees into her building and starts to bang on doors, working his way up toward her floor. You brace yourself for the knock, as she does; but Kieślowski makes you wait, and when it comes he turns the volume up full.

Moments like this blur the line between mainstream technique and the supposed concerns of art-house cinema—a boring distinction, in any case. Kieślowski is far more gutsy than cerebral: what you take away from *Blue* is not an intellectual pose but the slam of a piano lid, the scrape of knuckles against a stone wall, and the sight of Julie plunging into a deserted swimming pool—as echoing and scary as the one in Jacques Tourneur's *Cat People*, with shadows rippling on the walls. Above all, there is a series of shock blackouts, matched by thunderous orchestral chords, attacking the screen out of nowhere. These can happen anyplace—in the pool, in a café, in the midst of a conversation—and when they are over, the camera returns to exactly where it was, as if time had stopped dead to allow for a rush of memory.

The movie hardly leaves Juliette Binoche alone for a minute, but she thrives on the attention. That round, milky face is so pure and serious, so thrifty with its shows of feeling, that directors seem to grow impatient with it, and even resort to violence in an effort to force a reaction. In *Les Amants du Pont-Neuf* (a chaotic but remarkable movie by Léos Carax), she was ravaged by eye disease; and in her previous—and worst—picture, *Damage*, she had her head banged against the floor by Jeremy Irons. It was typical of that movie's crass erotic chic that she was supposed to enjoy this; Louis Malle put her through soulless routines, like a sex doll, and in return he got a blankly bored performance. In *Blue*, too, she starts off bruised and black-eyed, stiff in a neck brace, but slowly the movie brings her back to life, and she comes up fighting.

There's nothing very grand about this. Being a Kieślowski heroine, Julie tends to drop things and make snap decisions, and she's easily distracted by trivia—but then so is Kieślowski himself, almost all the time. He is taken aback by the vagaries of human nature, and if there is an urgency about his films it comes from the need to get that surprise across. The result is an odd marriage of brooding and slapstick, unique to Kieślowski but also alarmingly true to the on-off rhythms by which most of us live. I have seen *The Double Life of Véronique* four or five times now, and although there are plenty of things that don't make sense, I don't really mind—if anything, they become indispensable, like the maddening quirks of a friend. At key moments, both Julie and Véronique turn out their handbags, offering the private chaos of lipstick and photographs and candy wrappers as the clearest guide to the state of their souls. They could well be right.

All of which makes some people feel like Lady Bracknell: What on earth is all this fuss about handbags? Why doesn't this funny Polish guy just tell us what he means? But Kieślowski has spent long enough in a police state to acquire a thorough distrust of any movie, or poem, or play, that hustles its audience toward an agreed conclusion. His work radiates intensity, yet flickers with casual happenings; I feel more herded and browbeaten by Oliver Stone. Every moral that one tries to draw from *Blue* or *The Double Life of Véronique* seems an insult to the mysterious, often wordless procedures of Kieślowski's art. Not even in his *Decalogue*, a series of TV films shot in Warsaw, and based on the Ten Commandments, did he raise his voice. "We just treated the Commandments as a set of rules," he explained, "which allow us to survive from day to day without breaking each other's necks." Critics back in Poland have lamented this political indifference, but Kieślowski seems to me an exquisitely political artist, precisely because of his refusal to be sententious and his curiosity about everything that eludes political control. No wonder his movies are so sexy, so blue: the bed is a free country.

DECEMBER 13, 1993

NAKED

Mike Leigh's *Naked* may be the first British movie in a long while that is actually worth paying money to see. The reason is very simple: in Johnny, the main figure, Leigh has not so much created a character as let loose a force of nature—one of those misshapen, self-propelled centrifuges which occasionally spin across cinema screens, knocking aside everyone in their unrepeatable path and, in the process, outstripping the reach of the director. Jack Nicholson did it in *Five Easy Pieces* and *One Flew Over the Cuckoo's Nest;* Cagney did it in *White Heat;* the young Gérard Depardieu threatened to do it all the time. Here the honors go to the British actor David Thewlis; with his long, poky face and its desolate scrubland of beard, he looks like one of the Phiz engravings that used to decorate Dickens—a penniless clerk, perhaps, or a gravedigger soiled by his calling.

Johnny is a good-for-nothing from Manchester, and nothing is what he does all day, with infinite zeal and attack: "Whatever else you can say about me, I'm not fucking bored." This gives him an advantage over the camera, which seems to have run out of steam. When Johnny first comes down to London, and stands literally at a crossroads, it circles lazily around him, waiting for him to do something, to make the first move. So he rough-talks his way into an apartment, and into the affections of Sophie (Katrin Cartlidge). From here on, he hops and stumbles from one woman to the next: from the drinker who can hardly undress to the waitress who seldom speaks, from the spaced-out Sophie to the sad-faced Louise (Lesley Sharp), a former girlfriend. He asks how she is. "Peachy creamy," she replies, in the dead tone of one whose life went moldy years ago. You get a twinge of the problem that will gradually rack the whole movie: with a hero who burns so bright, everything around him starts to look dour and damp. Other people, especially women, seem consumed by helplessness, slipping weepily away to the margins of their own existence.

Some viewers will find this procedure too close to misogyny for comfort. But it goes wider than that: I think it's the latest segment in Mike Leigh's long career of sourness. Much has been made of his penchant for improvisation—slowly developing a script with his performers—on the assumption that it will open up a movie, roughen the moral texture until it feels convincing to the touch. But the plan keeps going awry: more often than not, a Leigh character seems to be cornered and pinned down, reduced to a battery of tics. When you laughed at Timothy Spall's slob chef in *Life Is Sweet*, the laugh was halfway to a grimace: you could sense that the film had already got the better of him before it began—the poor guy had no history, no hinterland still to be explored. *Naked*, too, has its fair share of human cartoons: the shrewish Sandra (Claire Skinner), with her semaphore gestures of impatience, and a yuppie called Jeremy (Greg Cruttwell), who nearly wrecks the film. If Leigh honestly thinks that real-estate agents still romp around with Porsches and champagne, he hasn't been to London for five years. Here are the true unfortunates of the movie: not those who have nothing but those who don't exist.

If Leigh is an uncharitable artist, however, David Thewlis is a model of attention; somehow, he redeems a sick picture, washing away its nasty taste. There is something not wholly English about the character he constructs: the bum who steals paperbacks, who quotes the Book of Revelation and settles down to read James Gleick's *Chaos*, who says he can't be "homerphobic," because he likes the *Iliad*—such literate despair is more of a European specialty, and Johnny would thrive in the pages of Sartre or in the voluble bitterness of Knut Hamsun's *Hunger*. As you listen to the little splutters that precede his jokes, fuelled by mockery and smoke-blackened lungs, and the eager predictions of apocalypse that tumble from his lips, you realize that this man is orbiting close to madness. Someone asks him whether he has ever seen a dead body. "Only my own," comes the reply. He is indeed a prowler in the underworld, pausing to look up and snicker at an unreliable God—"the monkey with the beard and the crap ideas." Sometimes, hesitantly, the camera draws close and stares at him, as if wondering how long such an unquiet soul can survive; he would die if he stopped talking, and even though he gets on our nerves, we don't mind having him there. Johnny expects us to hate him, and never asks for anything else; and, because of that, he becomes the first person in the work of Mike Leigh to earn our reluctant love.

JANUARY 17, 1994

HEAVEN AND EARTH

Heaven and Earth is the third, and last, part of Oliver Stone's trilogy on the Vietnam War. At least, I hope it's the last; being Oliver Stone, he may yet try to explode the whole politico-numerical myth of "trilogy," and whack us over the head with a couple more installments. One hardly dares think what those would be like, since, for all its surface excitements, the trend of the trilogy has been steadily downward. *Platoon*, which focussed on the frightened grunts, was hysterical but gripping; *Born on the Fourth of July*, a study of rebellious aftermath, was hysterical and high-minded; and now we have *Heaven and Earth*, which follows the Vietnamese side of the story and can barely summon the energy to get hysterical at all.

The hub of the movie is Le Ly, a Vietnamese villager whose placid life is messed up by a succession of disasters. Helpfully, she provides a voice-over to keep us up to date: "One day in the summer of 1953, the French came," or "Then, in 1963, the peasant countryside changed forever." These pointers are meant to clarify the action, but the effect is the opposite; you come away from the movie with a vague impression of tedium, mysticism, and distress, all stirred up together. It has to be said that the problem starts with Hiep Thi Le, an actress who was plucked from obscurity to play Le Ly. As plucking goes, this was cruel and optimistic: it's unfair to expect an actress of no previous experience to play a woman who ends up with more experience than she would care to remember. Hiep Thi Le appears in almost every scene, and soon exhausts her range of available expressions—sad, pert, then back to sad. You can't really blame her—I'd feel pretty sad if I had to speak lines like "Me and men, we have bad karma"—but neither can you safely predict a shining screen career for her. She and movies, they have bad camera.

The film also stars Tommy Lee Jones, only it doesn't. With an hour gone, he still hasn't made his appearance, and you wonder whether his name on the billboards was just a desperate ploy to get people into the picture. When he finally does turn up, playing a United States marine named Steve Butler, you cross your fingers and pray he's not too late to save the show. After all, he popped the inflated ideals of *JFK* with his weary, dandyish Clay Shaw; but Stone isn't going to let him get away with it again. He puts Jones through a rigmarole of booze and weeping and dream sequences, turning the character into a kind of military Jim Morrison. It's a perfect demonstration of how not to use Tommy Lee Jones. Here is an actor who lives on damage control; in every part he plays you sense both a grievous bruising of the spirit and a determination to cover it up and carry on. There's something hip and laconic in that effort; you need to go back to Bogart to find a man so amusingly pained. Both have an enticing ugliness that upsets the romantic habits of an audience: you look at them and want to learn more, to find out what went wrong, but they narrow their eyes, curl their lips, and silently tell you to back off. This interior struggle is the core of their attraction—the mystery of proud souls chewed up by self-loathing—but it has to be kept at the right temperature. Needless to say, Howard Hawks played it cool, but when Oliver Stone takes charge everything comes to a boil. Jones has to untie his emotions and scatter them over a wide area, until there are no secrets left for us to guess at.

Steve Butler walks into Le Ly's life and urges her to swap it for a new one back in his own country. There she gets to gape at the gleaming fridge, the Warholian ranks of supermarket soups, and broiled steaks the size of her own torso. Steve is so all-American that his mother is played by Debbie Reynolds, who, according to a press release, "returns to the movie screen for the first time in 20 years." It's an interesting choice—rather like waiting at a road junction for three hours and finally moving out into the path of a cement truck. Mind you, everyone gets squashed by *Heaven and Earth*. As Le Ly's long-suffering mother, Joan Chen hardly registers, and the harrowed gravity that Haing S. Ngor displayed in *The Killing Fields* is exchanged here for an embarrassing goatee and a nice line in pointless advice. The moment when he calls Le Ly "my little peach blossom" marks the point where most viewers will give up, and there's more of the same once our heroine arrives in California, which appears to be infested with Buddhist priests. "The future, the past are all the same," one of them tells her. After an hour of this film, you know just how he felt.

Heaven and Earth comes across as a deeply unappealing mixture of fuzziness and brutality; each betrays Stone's reluctance, despite his pretensions as a purveyor of true grit, to face up to his subject. When he chooses to convey the tranquillity of the village by having a couple of sage figures nod through the paddy fields in saffron robes and matching umbrellas, he must know how the image strikes the eye, how irredeemably it recalls a hundred airline commercials. This visual glaze never cracks; if anything, it hardens, lending a ghastly slickness to scenes that could only have worked through tact and restraint. When Le Ly is arrested, accused of aiding the Vietcong, then bound to a chair and given electric shocks, her head is haloed in a luscious blur of light, and the camera catches every drop of sweat whipped off her face by the jolts. In other words, a movie that preaches the need for self-respect is openly turned on by the prospect of humiliation, by a sneaky belief that violence is a pretty sight. *Heaven and Earth* is intended to make us muse afresh on the plight of the Vietnamese, and, in an unlikely way, it succeeds. First, they had colonial rule, then the Vietcong, then napalm, and now Oliver Stone trying to be nice to them. Haven't these poor people suffered enough?

JANUARY 17, 1994

THIRTY TWO SHORT FILMS ABOUT GLENN GOULD

The Canadian pianist Glenn Gould was born in 1932, read music before he could read words, gave his first public recital at the age of twelve and his last at the age of thirty-one, and died in 1982. In his later years, he took to the recording studio as an invalid takes to his bed, or, in the view of his admirers, as a bird takes to the air. Gould's capacity to inspire and to estrange, to aggravate and to soothe, has yet to die down, and is unlikely to do so as long as people keep listening to Bach. His peculiar genius has now been accorded a suitable memorial—a movie that lies somewhere between an act of homage and a public inquiry. *Thirty Two Short Films About Glenn Gould* is exactly what it sounds like. Some of the films run for forty-five seconds or so; none last longer than a few minutes; and the whole enterprise takes just over an hour and a half.

Directed by François Girard, the movie is a ragbag of styles, coming at its subject from every angle. It offers, among other things, interviews, animation, voice-overs, X-rays, rocket footage, a screen crammed with colorful drugs, and a screen buzzing with some kind of electrical pulse. (Wisely, it steers clear of the one thing most people know about Gould—his tendency while playing to hum like a stoned bee.) The overall effect is about as far from traditional biopic as you could want, although its needs are much the same: call it a biolyric. The man himself is not seen until the end of the final credits, when that long, Neanderthal jaw and wary, scrunched-up posture come into view. For the purposes of the movie, which dramatizes scenes from his life and excerpts from his prose, he is played by the Canadian actor Colm Feore—no great look-alike but a fair stab at the unmanageable bundle of qualities, ranging from the courteous to the stubbornly fervid, that were said to make up Glenn Gould.

The first image is one of limitless white: the freezing expanses of Canada, with a black dot approaching the camera like a wintry version of

Omar Sharif in *Lawrence of Arabia*—a kind of snow sheikh. It is Gould, wrapped in his favorite clothes, lost in his favorite landscape. The flat cap became a trademark, and his throat was forever guarded by scarves; the gloves came off indoors, though at one point in the movie he wears fingerless gray mittens—the supreme accessory, surely, for the concert pianist with a penchant for cold weather. Girard returns to the theme later on with shots of wet, desolate roads and a chilly German lake, and with a passage from Gould's radio broadcast "The Idea of North"; the point is not simply that Gould found beautiful and bracing what others would consider bleak but that, like Edvard Munch, he gave a good knock to our hand-me-down belief that artistic intensity is somehow the prerogative of the warm south. It is Bach, needless to say, that plays in this opening scene, contending with the wind and the creak of Gould's footsteps in the snow.

The next thing we hear, however, is the Prelude to *Tristan and Isolde.* That is the movie's constant tactic, its means of getting into the slipstream of Glenn Gould and following his example: it makes us think again. Who would have put him down for a Wagnerian? But there he is as a young boy, rapt beside a radio, listening to Toscanini, with his proud mother looking on; he might almost be the young Charles Foster Kane. The movie looks set to proceed through Gould's life chronologically; instead, it jumps straight to the grown man, then darts around from one anecdote to the next—Gould the pill-popper, Gould the unrequited lover, Gould playing Scriabin and Hindemith and, triumphantly, the Toronto stock market. Yet there remains something driven about Girard's film: however playful it seems, there is a rush of obsessions keeping it on track, and a gathering gloom in the air. You can sense the end coming, as Gould himself did. The astounding sequence of a pianist filmed in X-ray—spectral feet tapping at the pedals, finger bones flying, skull nodding along in time—is both a guide to the wonders of the human machine and a pitch-black joke about its eventual breakdown.

Thirty Two Short Films About Glenn Gould adds up to the best movie made about music in a long while, but that's not saying much. More than any other breed of human being, composers have suffered at the hands of cinema, and the classical repertoire may never get over the abuse it took from Ken Russell. It's hard to forget the sight of Richard Chamberlain in *The Music Lovers* slamming away at the keyboard, face muscles twitching as if hooked up to the strings, although some viewers felt that in a perverse way it actually restored their moral, if not their musical, faith in Tchaikovsky: however mad he was, they argued, he couldn't have been *that* mad. But the entire form of the music movie is itchy with embarrassment—all those tricky creative urges to be dramatized, all that performing wizardry to be faked. Whatever the skill of the actors, and the slickness of the cutting, you just know they're putting it on—pretty much like screen sex, but without any helpful sheets to cover their tracks.

Girard gets around this with a simple rule: nobody is seen playing a piano. It is Gould that we hear, but Feore never tries to mimic him; instead, we watch him listening to a playback and conducting wildly (rather too wildly, I suspect), or sitting in a chair, listening patiently, and shutting his eyes at the restful close of the piece. The sense of complications that unfurl and flourish at a rate we can barely keep up with, only to resolve themselves with an ease that we could never have foreseen: that is what Gould sought and clarified in Bach, and what threw him out of step with other musicians and critics, who were uneasy with the notion that these complications could be bound up with difficulties of feeling. Girard tends to leave the controversy alone, preferring to let his camera speak for itself. During the *Tristan* sequence, it stares steadily through the trees at Lake Simcoe, the Gould family's summer home, and moves only when the music has settled majestically into a resolving chord, as if touched off by the release of tension. This is what keeps the movie fresh: Girard doesn't try to illustrate a score (always a vain hope); he peels away from it, lightly and obliquely, to pursue his own melodic line of images.

Even that level of subtlety, on the other hand, might have been too much for Gould himself, who wrote, "There are musical moments of such grandeur that no screen can represent or interpret them adequately and for which the only appropriate visual response is abstraction, test pattern, or post-test-pattern snow." Girard takes him at his word, reducing parts of the movie to arrangements of pure shape; at one point, the camera travels inside Gould's own Steinway to observe the headlong parade of hammers during a prelude from "The Well-Tempered Clavier." This is dangerously hypnotic to watch, and, like so many of the sections, it's pruned well back; what could have been portentous or art-schoolish is brought up short by the presence of Bach. The one exception is a cartoon, by Norman McLaren: entitled "Spheres," and made in 1969, it can be honestly described as a load of balls, which zoom around in swirling outer space. Not even Bach can do much with this stuff; it merits a pretty bad-tempered clavier, and I hope that Girard included it only as a historical gag, to remind us of those far-off days when people took *2001: A Space Odyssey* seriously.

The best scene in the movie starts with a sick-looking Gould pacing a hotel room in Hamburg. There is a knock at the door, and a parcel is delivered; he opens it and pulls out a record. Until now, you haven't really noticed the chambermaid pottering about in the background; nor, do you think, has Gould. But now he asks her to stay, and sits her down while he puts the record on the phonograph. She protests a little, then gives in and smiles nervously, as well she might: just what does this lanky Canadian weirdo want from her? The music begins: Beethoven at his briskest, almost Bach-like—the Allegro from Sonata No. 13. In spite of herself, the maid is caught up in it, and her smile broadens; she gets up, looks at the cover of the record, and realizes who is playing. As the movement ends, she turns to Gould and says simply, "*Danke schön.*"

You get a fine hint here, as elsewhere, of lives crossing and sparking; the movie is rife with small-scale memories, each of them bearing full-grown emotions tucked away inside. The Beethoven sounds wonderful, but Gould's playing of it is only the start: we need to see how it spills outward—into the ears of the maid, into the look that she gives him. Girard is careful to show what happens on either side of music: the members of a string quartet murmuring among themselves as they lay down their instruments, or the ominous sight of Gould steeping his hands in hot water before venturing out onstage—for a split second, you think of slashed wrists. These details are perfectly judged, for it is Gould's achievement to engage us not only with the demeanor of his performances but with their suggestion of larger virtues beyond the piano—of a living temperament, a limber philosophical stance, unlocked by its keys. His writings, used frequently and freely by Girard, set him apart as the most learned and literate of modern musicians, matched only by Stravinsky. Gould was a solitary, but not an eccentric; rather, he made himself central, and drew people in. He was one of a band of impassioned ascetics thrown up by our century, all of them immune to intellectual half measures; this means that Gould groupies are a scary lot, who tend to read Wittgenstein and Walter Benjamin and Simone Weil, although it's probably safe to say that Gould was the only one with a taste for tomato ketchup and Petula Clark. Girard chose the right guy.

Why thirty-two short films about Glenn Gould? Partly, of course, as a tribute to the Goldberg Variations, which Gould recorded twice, once in youth and again at the end of his life. But what counts here is the spirit of profusion; the more films the merrier, I would say, including the melancholic ones. It's a change to find a filmmaker who has followed his wits and broken his allotted ninety minutes or so into appropriate lumps. If you'd asked Donald Barthelme to write a movie, this is the kind of thing he would have come up with. In its hip, ironic musings, it rescues Gould from the tag of gifted madman to bring him, more or less, down to earth. It also makes you realize just how tamely the art of cinema, which began in a flurry of formal experiment, has nestled down into a cozy narrative niche; with its skittish and searching manner, *Thirty Two Short Films About Glenn Gould* suggests a way forward. Gould himself would have approved, I think. It might even have made him hum.

APRIL 18, 1994

THE BLUE KITE

The Blue Kite begins with a sad scene. The year is 1953, the place is a communal courtyard in Beijing, and the residents are huddled around the radio, listening to the terrible news: Stalin has died, ergo all China is in mourning. Well, nearly all. One old lady asks, "Who's this Stalin person?" Ten days later, everyone has cheered up: two new arrivals, Chen Shujuan and Lin Shaolong, are getting married. At the height of the celebrations, the couple stand and sing a hymn of worship to their motherland, backed up by the assembled company. "Life gets better every day," they chant. But the camera refuses to join in the fun. It sneaks aside and cuts to a little clay horse, a wedding gift from a relation. As the music swells, the head drops off.

These early sequences offer a sip of the movie's singular method; everything feels homey enough, but there's a shock in the aftertaste, something sharp and stringent. Written by Xiao Mao, and directed by Tian Zhuangzhuang, *The Blue Kite* is one long sleight of hand. Looking back on it, you think of a family saga, of dull days peppered with minor squabbles; but in its demure way the film has the reach, if not the extravagance, of epic. The action runs from 1953 to 1967, a stretch of history plastered with the slogans of Maoist ambition—the Rectification Movement, the Great Leap Forward, the book-burning bonanza of the Cultural Revolution. I particularly relished the scene where someone rushes in and cries "The Neighborhood Committee wants to talk to you about collectivization!" with all the excitement of a scalper waving a handful of Streisand tickets. It brings back the old, unanswerable question: With five hundred million people to choose from, how come Mao couldn't find a decent copywriter?

Trotting along on the verge of this mass movement are Chen Shujuan (Lu Liping) and her young son, Tietou; in the course of the movie, she goes through three husbands, so that whenever we jump to the next stage of Tietou's youth the poor kid always seems to be acquiring a new father. First up is Lin Shaolong, a quiet librarian who wouldn't hurt a fly, and is all the more easily swatted by the establishment; crisis comes when he tiptoes out of a library meeting to use the men's room, and returns to find himself denounced as a right-wing menace and sentenced to a labor camp. The moral is clear: Hold your tongue *and* your bladder, and you might just survive in Beijing. Watching these pathetic pratfalls, we don't know whether to laugh or weep; a little comic stumble, and the movie trips headlong into the slough of despond. Lin's exile is sketched with minimum fuss: we see a train steaming across a snowy plain, and, later on, the marker of his unvisited grave.

After a seemly interval, Lin is replaced in Chen's affections by the hapless colleague who, without really meaning to, betrayed him. Chen forgives the guy, a placid sort named Li Guodong, and marries him. But her luck runs out again, when *he* sickens and dies, leaving her one final shot at happiness; this time, she goes upmarket and marries Wu Leisheng—slim and unsmiling, blessed with a car and a swanky house. In a way, Wu is the most interesting husband of all; the two others, jittery with apologies and ailments, were easy to like, but this one looks freeze-dried—offer him sympathy and he'll crunch it underfoot. Mealtimes chez Wu are not exactly a feast of fun, and Tietou's response is to overturn a bowl of rice and run out of the room. You can sense the movie's eagerness to set itself increasingly tough challenges: if it can get us to worry about the fate of someone like Wu, it can do anything. And that, of course, is what happens; he falls foul of the Red Guards, and offers to divorce Chen to save her any trouble. In the end, we learn, he has a heart attack, and she is once again stranded on her own: three strikes and out.

The Blue Kite is not the movie to see if you're in a Busby Berkeley mood. It goes about its business with patience and refinement; one of the camera's more charming habits is to begin a scene by observing people through a doorway and then slowly to advance, as if seeking a formal introduction. The whole enterprise looks like an antidote to *Farewell My Concubine*, a draught of clear style after that dizzying brew of opera and opiate. Not that Tian Zhuangzhuang is afraid of visual flourishes; he merely prefers to ration them to moments of intensity. The movie is full of strange flarings, portents that arrive when you least expect them. The idea that Li Guodong might be in love with Chen never crosses your mind until, one day, we see him digging outside her window, with the sun flashing behind him; just for a second, he looks like a bringer of hope. Then there is Tietou's uncle, a pilot with failing sight, hardly a credit to his nation; at one point, as the doors of a darkened hangar slide open, the light outside starts to blaze and blur in front of his hopeless eyes—rather like the paper lantern that Tietou begs for at the New Year, only to have it catch fire and burn to a blackened wreck.

As with so much in the film, you can't pin these sequences down symbolically; they hint at the rise and fall of personal fortune, but no more than that. Tian is not in the business of loading his images, of using them to score points; to do so would be to slide into precisely the kind of ham-handed, banner-waving methods of his opponents. *The Blue Kite* makes formidable political drama because it dares to suggest that the simple act of getting on with your life, with its cluster of silly mistakes and small acts of charity, is in itself a kind of rebellion: that the grand folly of Maoism was to presume not only that people could be whipped into line behind a political program but that they would always be interested in themselves as political animals—as opposed to good mothers, for instance, or loving fathers, or makers of perfect dumplings. There is not much brutality on show here, but what there is seems to be powered by an especially primitive fury; the soldiers who come to arrest Wu Leisheng are not so much punishing a deed as venting their anger at the man for being who he is.

This is the last word in the denial of freedom, and it's no coincidence that now, for the first and last time, Chen and her son take action. They have come to defend Wu, and they pay the price: Chen is dragged away, and when Tietou snatches up a brick and whacks a soldier over the head, he himself gets battered to the ground. It's the hot, frantic conclusion to feelings that have simmered throughout the film, yet it turns into slow motion, into a daydream of violence, as if a heavy, intolerable life were being gently eased from his young shoulders. As played by three actors of varying ages, Tietou is a case study in stubborn boyhood, kicking his heels, mimicking the grownups—all of it ideal preparation for the fiery spirit that he shows in the final scene. He's never cute, but he lightens the movie, and rescues it from the temptations of solemnity. He and the director share the same quizzical, unsurprised gaze; *The Blue Kite* is both deeply sophisticated and oddly naïve, with Tian Zhuangzhuang staring around like a child at the country that bore and bred him, and wondering how on earth it came to be run by these potent, ridiculous creatures.

Needless to say, this hasn't made Tian the flavor of the year with the Chinese authorities. So far, they haven't clubbed him with staves or anything, but it could be some while before they put his head on a stamp. They first got wind of *The Blue Kite*, or at least of its unhealthy attitudes, after it had finished shooting, but they still had plenty of opportunity to mess around with the plans for postproduction—getting the film processed, for a start—and in the end it had to be completed abroad, using smuggled footage and Tian's detailed notes. But that wasn't the end of the affair; when the movie was shown at the Tokyo Film Festival in 1993, and collared the Grand Prix, the entire Chinese delegation walked out and quit Japan that evening. I bet everyone was *really* sorry to see them go—you know, missing out on one last crazy night on the town. Finally, the master stroke: at the start of this month, the Ministry of Radio, Film, and Broadcasting banned Tian Zhuangzhuang from making any more movies. He doesn't have to leave China; he simply has to sit there and fester—do anything, in fact, apart from what he wants to do. None of his countrymen, meanwhile, have seen *The Blue Kite*—or, if they have, they're not allowed to say so. Decades after the Great Leap Forward, China is busy taking a whole bunch of little leaps back.

MAY 2, 1994

SPEED

Speed is set in Los Angeles. Most of it takes place on a bus. It is a film full of explosions but bare of emotional development. Its characters are no more than sketches. It addresses no social concerns. It is morally inert. It's the movie of the year.

The action begins in an elevator. There is a loud bang, the first of many; this is a movie that makes sweet music out of loud bangs. Everyone is stuck, and suitably scared, and the LAPD is called in. Jack Traven (Keanu Reeves) and Harry Temple (Jeff Daniels) are the two cops sent to check out the scene. They have to get the passengers off the elevator before it does any plummeting, and then go look for the guy who caused the bang. He is a vengeful madman with a sick sense of humor—played by Dennis Hopper, of course. He's also a bomb buff, who is happy to go on blowing things up until the city gives him a very serious amount of money. For his next trick, therefore, he wires a device to a bus full of passengers, which is peacefully travelling downtown on a sunny morning. And it better keep travelling, because here's the thing: if it drops below fifty miles per hour, it explodes.

When I first got wind of this plot, some time ago, I laughed for about a week. It's so clean and daft and promising: everything I want from an action movie. But could *Speed* live up to that promise? Could Jan De Bont, who has never directed a film before, make this one stick? I needn't have worried. Not only does he get full value out of the plot, he actually treats it as a guiding light. The movie, in other words, is like the bus—if it ever slowed down, it would crack up and fall apart. But it doesn't; it simply goes faster and faster, and takes more and more risks, and starts to enjoy the ride. Just when you think you've got the measure of it, everything pulls away from you and peels off in another direction. When a woman is seen ahead of the bus, for instance, pushing a baby carriage directly into its path, you say to yourself: Oh, come on, *that* old number—give us a break. And a break is what you get. The bus doesn't swerve aside, as it has done in a hundred other movies; it whacks the carriage head on, sending it sailing through the air, and leaves you flat on your back, ready for the final twist. There's no point in fighting this stuff, so you might as well give up.

Unless, that is, you happen to be Keanu Reeves. I was confident that the Reeves image would recover from *Little Buddha*, but I didn't know it would happen so soon. You could argue that *Speed* is not a response to the Bertolucci picture but a continuation: the Holy One attaining a new and even cooler level of being, stepping lightly from his place beneath a tree onto a fast-moving bus. It's hard to say whether Jack Traven is wholly at peace with the world, especially when the vehicle hangs a sharp right on two wheels, but he looked pretty damn fulfilled to me. Close-cropped and tuned up, Reeves makes an even better tough guy than you'd expect, and SWAT gear really suits him; he should wear it more often. So what if he's never going to be John Gielgud? Delivery isn't an issue here, because he doesn't have speeches—he doesn't have time for speeches. He has *lines*. In his muted way, Reeves is blessed with perfect pitch: aroused by the hazards thrown up by the plot, but not so smart that he forgets to be frightened by them; strong enough to carry the film, but never trying to swamp it with his presence. There's only one star vehicle here, and it's making hay on the freeway.

Jack never drives the bus himself; he merely leaps aboard from a passing Jaguar. The wheel is taken by one of the passengers, Annie (Sandra Bullock), who soon gets into the swing of things ("It's just like driving a really big Pinto"), merrily clipping the flanks of a dozen vehicles as she veers onto a side road, saying "Sorry, sorry!" as if she were running a shopping cart over someone's toe. And when a gaggle of children threaten to stream across the road, she yells out to them, "Why aren't you at *school*?" Bullock comes across as Julia Roberts with guts, an unbeatable combination. She doesn't lighten the movie, because she doesn't need to; she draws out the lightness that is already there—the sense of play that keeps it aloft and away from brutality. "You felt you needed another challenge or something?" she asks Jack, as he confesses to having punctured the gas tank in a moment of panic. She's ribbing him for playing the game, for wanting to be one of the boys, although the game wouldn't be half as much fun without the girl; update Claudette Colbert to the age of hard rock, and you'll get the idea.

Dennis Hopper, meanwhile, just lies back and looks on. I thought I was getting tired of his psycho act, but *Speed* spruces it up. He is given an evil laugh, a loopy speech about beauty and becoming which appears to be lifted from Heidegger, and a chance to taunt Keanu Reeves: "Do not attempt to grow a brain." Standard stuff, but it stays with you, seeping through the fabric of the film: Hopper is doing to Reeves what Jan De Bont is doing to us—toying with our nerves, staying one move ahead, raising our expectations but never waiting around long enough to meet them. Like the hero of any action movie, Jack is in fact *re*active, far too busy with the demands of a crisis to be troubled by its niceties; that is more the prerogative of the villain, who likes to have time as well as blood on his hands, and of the director, who is paid to ponder such things. When De Bont films the two great explosions in the movie, he shows us the rising fireballs, then cuts away to the reflection of the flames: once in the chrome front of a pay phone, and later in the windows of a bus—another bus, full of people knocked backward by the rush and glow of the blast.

De Bont used to be a cameraman; he photographed *Black Rain*, *Lethal Weapon 3*, and five movies for Paul Verhoeven, including *Basic Instinct.* He seems to have come away from the experience in ideal shape—his head crackling with images, but his taste intact. What makes Verhoeven's work so violent is not just the foulness of the deeds but the pride and pleasure that he obviously takes in grossing us out. He puts us through an ordeal, not an adventure. *Speed* is never so pleased with itself; from the second that Jack's police car soars in at the top of the frame—it must have hit a bump or something, but it looks like a spaceship coming in to land—we feel flattered by a surfeit of sensation. The whole film is a flier. De Bont crowds in with his cameras to catch the bus from every conceivable angle: a ground-level shot, gazing up past the windshield at a 747 taking off; a flawless, unshaken aerial view, taken from directly above the freeway, obscured for an instant by the smooth passage of a chopper. He's digging into the visual possibilities and rooting out everything he can. The result is loud and bright, but it doesn't annoy you—it cheers you up. And the tension gathers so steadily that, in some extraordinary way, you find yourself relaxing into it, like a tightrope walker pausing for a cigarette.

Speed is the kind of thing that Hollywood does best right now, although that's not saying much. Action movies make convenient showcases for the advances in special effects, but they also seem to suck in what's left of the old Hollywood virtues—the dregs of irony, the last remaining gags, the high style. *Speed* joins a select crew of pictures that have fought to lay their powers of invention at the feet of an audience; I'm thinking of the first *Die Hard*, the first *Terminator*; and, my favorite, *Aliens.* Jan De Bont's work is, if anything, leaner than all of them. There are no endangered loved ones here, no risk to the planet, no private traumas to be scoured out of existence: just one cop and various forms of public transportation. What makes it all so disciplined, what lends authority to its kick, is the refusal to slow down for sentiment; as Annie so crisply puts it, "you're not going to get mushy on me, are you?" Spoken like a Hawks heroine. There's one scene early on, when Jack and Harry get maudlin in a bar, but it soon passes, and you wipe it from your mind. You wait for the screenplay to spend a little quality time with each passenger on the bus, teasing out this man's history, setting this woman up for a pat payoff at the end; but that is an old habit, bred by disaster movies, and it won't wash here. *Speed* isn't a disaster movie; it's a stamina test, a survival riff, a victory roll.

And then something happens. Jack and Annie go through hell and come out the other side. "Are you all right?" he asks. "No," she says, and stifles a sob. And, just for a moment, I joined her. I went mushy. Huh? What was going on here? I am not, by nature or training, a weeper; I didn't cry at *Bambi* or *Ghost*, or even at *Camille*. But here I was, choking on a film about a bus. It wasn't sadness, of course—just the inevitable aftershock of excitement, but even so. And the fun part was, the movie wasn't done with me; it had half an hour still to run, and plenty more rounds in its clip. It was *Aliens* all over again. Is this what they mean by "pure cinema"? The phrase sometimes hovers around people like Tarkovsky and Ozu, and with good cause, but Hollywood occasionally throws a punch so clean that it breaks through to the same hallowed sanctum. It goes without saying that *Speed* is mindless trash, but a mind would only have got in the way, like the carriage in front of the bus; it is precisely because De Bont refuses to beg for our feelings that we give them so freely in the end. As our heroes hurtle out of darkness and into the light—the old, mythic journey, completed in pulp style—we feel wiped out with delirium and relief. The movie comes home in triumph, and we go home in shreds. It was never a contest; we're just not up to *Speed*.

JUNE 13, 1994

WOLF

Moonlight in Vermont, and the snow is gusting lightly across the road. Will Randall, the senior editor at an old-fashioned New York publishing house, has been visiting with an author and is now heading home. But the night is not yet through with him. There's a wolf in the way. He drives straight into it, then walks over to inspect the body. The wolf opens one cunning yellow eye, bites him on the hand, and runs off. The damage is done; from now on, to the accompaniment of bristling hairs and a growing taste for blood, the mild-mannered Will Randall is destined to change, inexorably and horrifyingly, into Jack Nicholson.

Written by Wesley Strick and Jim Harrison and directed by Mike Nichols, *Wolf* works far better as a literate black comedy than as a horror movie. For half an hour or so, it hits a beautiful balance; audiences may well have forgotten the joys to be had from this brand of sophisticated confection, rich and dark, laced with bitter little jokes. The environment through which Will Randall moves is clubbable and low-key, a place of polished wood and wrought-iron elevator cages—constructed for the safety of a gentleman, that is, not for the isolation of a beast. Will dresses like a professor, and the patter that bounces around his office is as entertaining as anything in the film. This is no accident: if you cast Eileen Atkins as a secretary, it means you want your dialogue, however light, to punch its weight. And David Hyde Pierce does a fine turn as Will's devoted assistant, Roy. "Are you sick?" he asks. "A wolf bit me." Roy shrugs. "I just asked," he says. It's hard to pin down the pleasure of moments like these, but there's a thirties touch about them; the characters are defined by their instinctive feel for one another's moods, and this gives them a rare chance to underreact. Feelings are there to play with, not to pour out.

Also in the offing is Stewart (James Spader), the young blood of the company, who, like Roy, professes undying loyalty to Will. Whether he means it is another matter. This is Spader's best movie to date; fresh-faced and soft-spoken, he has always been a weirdly smooth actor, a sort of yuppie Peter Lorre, and now he plunges the charm in up to the hilt, offering discreet but unarguable proof that Uriah Heep is alive and well and working in Manhattan. Stewart is in league with Raymond Alden (Christopher Plummer), another creep with oil in his veins, who owns the publishing company and would probably acquire the rest of the planet if he could only find time. One evening, at a low-lit reception, Alden goes for a walk with Will, fires him, and replaces him with Stewart. The old Will would have taken this lying down; the new one gives it some thought, then decides to take it on all fours with a howl of disagreement and a tongue dripping foam.

Wolf may be the first movie to merge lycanthropy and capitalism into a joint venture, but the novelty is rather too much for it, and the argument grows strained. To begin with, the bite of the wolf seems to enhance all that is decent and uncorrupted in Will, all that has yet to be sullied by the encroachments of modern life. This sounds promising, if a bit Robert Bly-ish, but it soon makes way for a more obvious image: the corporate wolf. Will outwits the fiendish Stewart with some devilry of his own, and joins Alden as another slavering boardroom carnivore. To compound the confusion, he goes to get advice from a cliché—from an old Indian sage, to be exact, who tells him that "life is mystical," that the wolf itself is not evil, and that "not all who are bitten change—there must be something wild within." Just for a second, I fancied that I heard the frantic hedging of bets. Shortly afterward, Will wanders through Central Park and mauls a mugger: an unforgivable scene, implying that with a dash more animal courage America could repel the advance of disorder—white wolves versus urban blacks.

Wolf is a broken-backed, ill-fitting piece of work, which only makes sense—only comes together, really—in the person of its star. This is not a great performance by Nicholson, but it's courageous and astute, because it forces into the open all the tensions that keep him wired and insure his potency as a star: his "agreeable and affable personality, his acute intelligence and his nice-mindedness on the one hand, and his completely unbridled instinctual life on the other." The words come from the conclusion to Freud's *From the History of an Infantile Neurosis*, otherwise known as "The Case of the Wolf-Man." Will Randall is the part that Jack was born to play. Freud calls the wolf an "anxiety-animal," one of many hideouts for a wandering phobia—just the kind of casual, unforced symbol in which cinema (a hopeless medium for confronting psychoanalysis head-on) can usefully trade. High-class performers tend to sneer at the monster movie, but it's their loss; as Boris Karloff discovered, there are terrible stores of pathos and frustration to be released. Surely, this is Nicholson territory, too; think of the inward turnings and lashes of rage, the hobo lyricism of *Five Easy Pieces*, or the stony control of his Eugene O'Neill in *Reds*. He was a wolfman long before this picture was ever conceived.

It's come only just in time. In recent years, Nicholson connoisseurs have watched in dismay as he has eased himself into a series of chuckling, expansive, shit-eating parts, from *The Shining* to *The Witches of Eastwick* and *Batman*. The grin is intact, and getting wider by the week, but it's the grin of a Cheshire cat who got the cream. The emotional sinews, the bulk and stretch of his more troubled roles, seem to have vanished from view. His Joker, in *Batman*, was delicious vaudeville, but it paid him millions and cost him nothing, whereas his McMurphy, in *One Flew Over the Cuckoo's Nest*, displaying a sanity so untrammelled that it had to be locked up, took all his wit and strength. The young Nicholson looked badly displeased with the world, and the pain of it led him into muss-haired madness; the older man looks pleased with himself. He's flying nowhere; he's sitting right there in the cuckoo's nest.

Wolf is like a one-movie retrospective of this schizoid career. It shows the relaxed pro turning into Jack the lad, although neither phase is free of the other. Even in the opening scene, with his features grimacing through the windshield, he strikes you as suspiciously feral, just as Jeff Goldblum clearly looked bug-eyed and jumpy at the beginning of *The Fly*. It's asking a lot of Nicholson that he should grow younger as the movie proceeds, and I didn't quite fall for his ability to outrun a forest fawn, but it's easy to believe that something is stirring in his lupine loins. Any other actor would have waited until the plot gave him license to get horny. Nicholson starts early, when he's still sighing and sweaty and pooped. Who else would dare to suggest that it's sexy to be long in the tooth? He transfers his affections from his wife (Kate Nelligan, a wonderful actress wasted in a plaintive part) to Alden's rebellious daughter, Laura (Michelle Pfeiffer). "What are you, the last civilized man?" she asks when they meet. It's a great line, facing two ways, both of them arousing: either a compliment or a taunt to bring his dirty appetites out of the undergrowth. "Old guy, huh?" she says. "Yeah. Old guy," he admits. This sounds like a declaration of amity, almost of indifference; in truth, it's more like Kim Novak encountering the graying Jimmy Stewart in *Vertigo*—a first hint that the oddest couples can sometimes take the plunge.

But *Wolf* is all hints; once they develop into plots, the fire goes out of them. The love story, too wimpish to be intense, is not helped by the sight of Will and Laura bonding gently in front of a lake at sunset; and the sex, so heavily prepared for, simply fails to happen. Will uses his teeth to tug at the cord of his wife's robe; his new admirer finds him alone in a hotel bedroom with a pair of police handcuffs. Let's face it, the guy can sniff out stray hormones from two valleys away, but what do we get? One of those paltry postcoital scenes where the camera picks its way demurely through a trail of discarded socks and silks. How can Mike Nichols, the maker of *Carnal Knowledge*, fob us off with this kind of carnal innocence? How can he take on a movie about the transmission of subhuman lusts, get his leading lovers together, and then fade from view like a footman? The strongest sexual current in the whole film flows across a kitchen table, where Will tells Laura that, beneath her beauty, she's not a very interesting person, merely sullen and withdrawn. It's an extraordinary speech—rude, true, and hurtfully seductive, the most naked dose of Nicholson since that time in *Carnal Knowledge* when he snarled his way through a slide show of old girlfriends. Pfeiffer's character—and her otherwise controlled performance—never really recovers from this broadside. The last civilized man is a bastard.

The climax of *Wolf* is supposed to be exciting, the fruition of all these violent, unhealthy passions, as the wolf within Will starts to go whole hog. In fact, it's the most boring sequence in the movie. I was waiting for some juicy transformation scene, and was surprised to see him sporting nothing worse than a set of flourishing side-whiskers. The movie sets off in bookish style, but does it really have to climax with our hero taking on the appearance of William Gladstone? The special-effects master is Rick Baker, who did such astonishing work on *An American Werewolf in London*, scraping our senses with the creak of burgeoning bones and the rustle of fresh pelt; I remember my jaw dropping as the hero's grew. But his effects in *Wolf* aren't half as cool; give me ten minutes in front of a mirror with a handful of cheek wadding, some amber contact lenses, and a strip of hairy doormat taped to each side of my face, and I, too, can look like a creature of the night.

It's not Baker's fault; Mike Nichols doesn't have the same spirited, pop take on the genre as John Landis, and he probably thinks himself above schlock tricks, although what he puts in their place is much worse. From *The Graduate* onward, he has relished the spectacle of Americans at one another's throats, but this is the first time that he has introduced sharp teeth and long claws into the process, and it's not really his field. He can't summon the tones for it; the interiors of the movie are warm and dangerous, but the outside scenes come across as plastic and false. The glades through which Will first scampers by night are not wild at all; they're a rich man's pleasure park—the grounds of Alden's estate. Even the passing of a werewolf causes no commotion, for Nichols, confronted by bodies that move fast, tranquillizes them with slow motion. Will hunting prey, Will scrapping to the death with a rival, Will pushed down onto a bed: all this takes place in a dozy, largo dream. "The Animal Is Out," say the posters for this movie, but the truth is more worrying still. Jack Nicholson bares his fangs and fights to break free, but the movie won't run with him; the animal is safe in its cage.

JULY 11, 1994

FORREST GUMP

Robert Zemeckis, the man who directed the *Back to the Future* trilogy, has now come up with *Forrest Gump*, a goofy, indolent wander through the past. The title is the name of the hero, a simple soul who sits at a bus stop and takes various kindly interlocutors through the story of his life: from the pastoral peace of his childhood in Greenbow, Alabama, to the great days of college football and the rainy nights in Vietnam. Gump, it becomes clear, is not just an idiot savant but an idiot triumphant—the extraordinary Joe who was everywhere, sprinkling American virtues into every rut of history.

This movie is so insistently heartwarming that it chilled me to the marrow. There are no moral crosswinds here, not a breath of doubt or unease to ruffle the Gump image. Woody Allen's *Zelig* was a narrow conceit, but Allen at least had the decency to make his hero resolutely unheroic, somewhere between a cipher and a creep; the only way to survive the century, he suggested, was to be the man without qualities. Forrest Gump, on the other hand, is pumped so full of qualities that he is able to deflect the march of time; his neighborly phone call sets off the Watergate inquiry, his prowess at Ping-Pong cements Sino-American relations, his appearance on *Dick Cavett* prompts another guest, John Lennon, to invent the lyrics of "Imagine" right there on the show. The patching of Gump into these visual backgrounds is snappy and seamless, and it's a pity that no one paid equal attention to the sound; new voice-overs simply dub Kennedy, or Lennon, with the required words, whether they match the lip movements or not. This nonchalance gives the game away; Zemeckis is happy to stack up the sight gags, but the small matter of their dramatic purpose seems no more than an afterthought. When Gump inadvertently supplies the slogan "Shit Happens" to a guy who dreams up bumper stickers, the audience thrills and giggles with recognition, but the joke comes out of nowhere and leaves no trace, apart from a faint stink of self-congratulation.

Gump is played by Tom Hanks, and the movie is a bit hard on him, because it's too easy. With his puppet-jerk motions and slow, yodelling Alabama vowels, Gump is the kind of technical exercise that Hanks thrives on, but it doesn't take him anywhere—it doesn't send him. Innocence comes naturally to Hanks, loosening him up with the prospect of fun; the Gump variety, however, feels more like a straitjacket, replacing his usual gummy grin with a stiff flicker of a smile. I can imagine the movie's being devised by people who kept hearing that Hanks was the Jimmy Stewart of his generation and thought they'd better do something about it. And so they clothed him in decency, stitching a character together from offcuts of George Bailey and Mr. Smith and Elwood P. Dowd, carefully ignoring all the perplexity in Stewart and all the mania in Hanks. In their different ways, both actors have proved their mettle by resisting the onslaught of sentimentality even when it threatened them from all sides. *Forrest Gump* is just such a test; at once mazy and tight-assed, it foists upon us the myth that we can know better, and do better, by being dumb. Tom Hanks is too smart to swallow that.

JULY 25, 1994

PULP FICTION

Everybody knows the old E. M. Forster distinction between story and plot: "The king died and then the queen died" is a story. "The king died and then the queen died of grief" is a plot. Fair enough, but what Forster failed to foresee was the emergence of a third category, the Quentin Tarantino plot, which goes something like this: "The king died while having sex on the hood of a lime-green Corvette, and the queen died of contaminated crack borrowed from the court jester, with whom she was enjoying a conversation about the relative merits of Tab and Diet Pepsi as they sat and surveyed the bleeding remains of the lords and ladies whom she had just blown away with a stolen .45 in a fit of grief." It is hard to know what Forster would have made of Tarantino's new movie, *Pulp Fiction.* I suspect he would have run gibbering into his study, locked the door, and hidden behind the bookshelves. Not just because of the bloodshed—all that brain matter suddenly appearing on the outsides of people's skulls, instead of working quietly within, where it belongs—but because of the equal violence done to narrative form.

Pulp Fiction contains at least three plots, but it's not a portmanteau movie, like *Dead of Night* or *Tales of Manhattan;* the whole purpose of the different threads is to cross-weave, tangle up with each other, and fray at the ends. The first involves Vincent (John Travolta) and Jules (Samuel L. Jackson), a pair of tough guys sent to fetch a briefcase from some preppy crooks and deliver the appropriate punishment. There may be some gunfire involved, but that doesn't bother Vince; what bothers Vince is that his boss, Marsellus (Ving Rhames), is going out of town and leaving his young wife, Mia (Uma Thurman), in Vince's care and protection. Events prove that he was right to worry. The second strand involves Butch (Bruce Willis), a boxer paid by Marsellus to lose a fight. Not only does he not lose—he actually kills his opponent, and then prepares to flee with his girlfriend, Fabienne (Maria de Medeiros). The final strand returns us to Vince and Jules, who now have a new problem, a car full of blood. This calls for serious valeting, so they bring in The Wolf (Harvey Keitel), who makes the problem disappear. Then everyone goes off to have breakfast.

The film sounds simple enough; but the various components seldom behave as they should, and there are roles for Tim Roth, Amanda Plummer, Eric Stoltz, and Rosanna Arquette that are almost too complicated to explain. For Tarantino, chronology exists to be messed around with, to be looped and spliced. A main character dies, but before we can mourn his passing we find ourselves flipping back to a time when he was still in one piece. Tarantino is playing an old Godard game, plugging our emotions just as we're about to let them flow. It may be a cold and cunning way to cut a movie, but it's urged on by a serious desire to stop any schmalz creeping through the cracks in the script. Elsewhere, though, he seems to be playing around for no reason at all, revelling in the sheer dictatorial power of the filmmaker, and forgetting that there are people out in the theatre who want to get on with the show. Butch, the boxer, has a lucky watch that he treasures, a family heirloom; most directors would want us to take that on trust, but Tarantino has to shut the entire plot down for a while in order to prove it. We have to sit through a childhood flashback and a deadpan cameo from Christopher Walken, who explains that Butch's father stashed the watch up his ass for five years. It's a joke, but hardly a good joke; and, having written it, Tarantino has to shoehorn the damn thing into his picture whether it fits or not. The enfant terrible of Hollywood can sometimes be a real kid.

The architecture of *Pulp Fiction* may look skewed and strained, but the decoration is a lot of fun. I loved the little curls of suspense that kept us waiting for fresh characters, the details pondered by the camera in advance of a full-face shot: the feet of Uma Thurman, the Band-Aid on the back of Ving Rhames's neck, and the smooth tuxedo of Harvey Keitel, who appears, rather stylishly, to be throwing a party at eight-thirty in the morning. The whole movie, all two and a half hours, is studded with teases and alibis: hit men stop to argue when they should be getting on with the job, and thus raise the level of threat. Even the plots are more like subplots, seamy sidelines into which Tarantino is poking his nose—somewhere, you tell yourself, up above this gutter life the main event is going on. It's a bizarre trick; imagine erasing the hero from *King Lear*, leaving nothing but squabbling brothers and sisters and an old guy strapped to a chair, scared of losing his eyes. Tarantino is ready to romp in vile jelly; you can hear him snickering at his own brand of Petit Guignol, and inviting us to join in. When Butch needs a weapon, he picks up a hammer, then a baseball bat, then a chainsaw, and finally, to his vast satisfaction, a curved Japanese sword; and when Mia needs a jab of adrenaline through the sternum, the horror is held at bay as long as possible, while Vince brandishes a needle that looks like a prop from *Moby-Dick*.

But these are the preludes to violence; as Marsellus so delightfully promises, "I'm gonna get medieval on your ass." What about the stuff itself? *Pulp Fiction* arrives with a reputation for being almost unwatchable, which is a publicist's scheme for getting everyone to watch it. At the risk of being a killjoy, I have to say that Tarantino is not quite the Pied Piper of mayhem—the joykill, so to speak—that he wants to be. Like *Reservoir Dogs*, the new picture feels more violent than it actually is. You could say the same of *The Big Heat;* but Lang's movie was a moral furnace, stoked with such guilt and vengefulness that nobody could come near the action without getting burned. Tarantino functions in a moral vacuum where the brutality is mostly verbal, where sticks and stones can break my bones but words can *really* hurt me. (The most violent movie he could make would have no violence at all, just talk: gangsta rap meets Ivy Compton-Burnett.) People queue up to attack a passing idea, the punier and more trivial the better: hamburgers, milkshakes, great coffee—all of them fast food for thought. The effect should be mock-heroic, but it pushes beyond that; think of Andy Warhol, who realized that if you blew a plain image up to absurd proportions, or reproduced it often enough, you were not sneering at its ordinariness but somehow gilding it with a glamour and pathos of its own. Tarantino is less an ironist than a chronic fetishist; he has cooked up a world where hamburgers matter, and nothing else.

Despite its title, the movie owes far more to the pop artists of the fifties and sixties than to the pulp writers of previous decades. The brackish streams of mood and motive that flowed beneath the work of James M. Cain and David Goodis may not have run deep, but they never ran dry; and the low-lit Los Angeles of Chandler is continents away from the garish, spasmodic town of Tarantino's fancy. Their only common currency is the knowledge that life is cheap; as Chandler wrote, "It is not funny that a man should be killed, but it is sometimes funny that he should be killed for so little, and that his death should be the coin of what we call civilization." But Chandler smiled at the joke, his rueful prose no broader than Bogart's smile; Tarantino laughs out loud. The idea of putting a man of honor on the mean streets, if only for dramatic contrast, would never occur to him. That is why, for all the wild things that happen on them, the streets of *Pulp Fiction* stay as flat as a map.

If anyone holds this movie together, it isn't Tarantino—it's John Travolta. He strolls through it without a wink of vanity, having long since relinquished the oily posing of *Saturday Night Fever* in favor of the first law of cool: Don't try to be cool. The very title, *Pulp Fiction*, sounds like a description of his face—luscious but squashy, easily bruised, the look of a former pretty boy who can still inspire tall tales. While Tarantino clamors for our attention, Travolta knows that he has it and isn't going to lose it in a hurry. He can afford to rumple and fatten his character, turning Vince into a slob and a patsy, driving the picture beyond the regulation hipness of *Reservoir Dogs* into a shabbier territory, where a man is known not just by his suit or his ruthlessness but by his hits of bliss and his flashes of panic, the big mistakes he can make as he tries to correct the little ones. What stays with you after *Pulp Fiction* has ended (and amazingly little *does* stay with you) is the close-up of Vince's slow, drugged smile as he drives through the darkness to meet Mia, or the rather endearing shots of him sitting on the toilet reading *Modesty Blaise*. Travolta has the nerve, in the midst of what feels like an action movie, to remind us of the pleasures of inactivity, the deep need to hang out.

My favorite scene comes at Jack Rabbit Slim's. This is Tarantino heaven, a movie-prop diner where you can order a Douglas Sirk steak from a Buddy Holly look-alike. Vince is eating with Mia, and trying hard not to fall for her. When she asks him to dance, he refuses, then yields. You brace yourself for a big Travolta moment. Will he nip to the men's room and come back in a white suit and black shirt? Will he roll his hands and point at the glitter ball? No way; the two of them take to the floor and quietly twist, while the camera stands to one side, snatches a couple of close-ups, then fades them out halfway through. It's a triumph of discretion, the only one in the movie, and you can't help feeling that Travolta and Thurman have calmed the director down. Tarantino is an artist mad for affect, terrified that his audience may be bored or moved (the same thing, as far as he's concerned). But his actors are ahead of the game; people like Samuel L. Jackson and Maria de Medeiros, and even a nicely troubled Bruce Willis, fight to flesh the movie out with warm-blooded gestures of feeling. That is what makes *Pulp Fiction* such an intriguing spectacle: not the acrylic brightness of its design, or even the funny filth of its patter, but the tension between the manic skills of its inventor and the refusal of his subjects to be treated like cartoons. It may well be that in thirty years the Tarantino landscape will look as bleached and dated as Antonioni's; that the blank morality and wicked accoutrements of *Pulp Fiction* and *Reservoir Dogs*—leather and chains, Madonna talk, sodomy in a dark corner—will have no more purchase on our imagination than do the rolling nudes and long, soporific takes of *Red Desert*. If the work does survive and prosper, it will owe a lot to the performers who flocked to Tarantino and confronted his ceaseless energy with their own. You catch a hint of the conflict to come, I think, in the climactic speech of *Pulp Fiction*, magnificently delivered by Jackson. "You're the weak, and I'm the tyranny of evil men," he declaims. "But I'm trying, Ringo, I'm trying real hard to be the shepherd." Will Quentin Tarantino try as hard? My guess is that he'll be too busy roasting the lambs.

OCTOBER 10, 1994

THE LAST SEDUCTION

John Dahl's *The Last Seduction* is a worthy successor to his previous movie, *Red Rock West.* The action has moved from dusty Wyoming to upstate New York, but the story is the same cat's cradle of cheats and lies. When a bad director repeats himself, we call it boring—the sure sign of a dried-up imagination. When someone like Dahl does it, we call it consistency—the evolution of a style. We like it that the people in his pictures behave in a reliably rancorous way; we want them to carry on like that and, if possible, to get worse; we even believe that they could slip quietly from one picture to the next, through a warp in the plot, and still find a place to make trouble. Like the crew of the starship *Enterprise,* who looked permanently and pleasantly surprised to arrive on a new planet and find its atmosphere breathable, the inhabitants of film noir can set down anywhere—the nineties, the forties, the big smoke or a clean-living small town—and always count on suckers and sex. Their obsessions rub off on Dahl, as they did on Joseph H. Lewis, say, or Robert Siodmak; a world as dark as this is not to be taken lightly.

The Last Seduction stars Linda Fiorentino as Bridget Gregory, living in Manhattan with her husband, a seedy doctor named Clay (Bill Pullman). Bridget's view of marriage is quite clear: those whom God hath joined together let seven hundred thousand dollars put asunder. She skips town—really skips, with a proud bounce in her step as she quits their apartment building carrying the laundered cash that she and Clay have just raised from a drug deal, and leaving him to the bone-breaking mercies of a loan shark "whose first and last names end in vowels." After a long drive, Bridget stops for gas in a nothing town called Beston, goes into a bar, picks up a guy, screws him, gets a job, changes her name, screws the guy some more, asks him to kill a couple of other guys, does a little killing herself with the help of a windshield, and generally has a good time. Then she turns *really* nasty.

Fiorentino is not one of the world's more expressive actresses, but that doesn't matter; if anything, it's an advantage, because an inch more range could have ruined the character. Her flattish delivery and bored, unpretty looks—cold and set, as if she spent half the time lying in a freezer—are ideal for a woman who knows that integrity, even more than beauty, is only skin deep. In an age when movies (and movie stars, in their plaintive memoirs) require villainy, like unhappiness, to have terrible roots, Fiorentino provides a gorgeous, unfashionable portrait of malice without a cause. Psychology is for wimps. With her thigh-high stockings and ground-level morals, Bridget rarely dresses in anything but black and white—living proof that a person can be as noir as a film. Her hard shell is there not to protect her true inward nature but to advertise the fact that she doesn't have one, which leaves her free to pick over the soft meat of other people's feelings. The rule that governs *The Last Seduction*, as it did *Mildred Pierce* and *Out of the Past*, is that a private history can only be a source of shame, to be dug up and exploited by those who have had the wit to erase their own. These movies lie at the darkest end of light entertainment, acid correctives to the Western and the musical; they laugh at the American legend of self-improvement, at the vaunted virtue of the fresh start. When the fine citizens of Beston say "Good morning" to Bridget, she rolls her eyes and goes to sit in the car.

Not that Dahl's work is depressing. It's tight and swift, eased along by an unbothered jazz score, and the spectacle of Bridget's progress is scandalously good fun. You cheer on her intellectual trumping of stupid men, and try not to flinch at the hyped-up physical relish that Fiorentino brings to the role; she doesn't smile much, but she licks money, and chews gum as if trying to bite through wire, and sniffs her fingers after feeling up a man. The dope in question is Mike (Peter Berg), whose efforts to be civilized, let alone affectionate, are not always a complete success. "You're not from around here?" he asks politely. "Fuck off," Bridget replies. He tells her about his job as a claims adjuster. "It's intimate," he says. "It's boring," she snaps, although when he starts mentioning some of the deaths he deals with, her expression changes, and the camera makes a wonderfully slow move toward her, watching her wickedness unfurl. That's about as flashy as the movie gets; the events are so lurid and lustful that Dahl wisely decides to compose them with visual calm. His trademark is the detail that flares in the gloom: at night, he picks out a plume of car exhaust, or the light receding along telephone wires. No wonder Bridget prospers here; this is a world for bright sparks.

You could argue that Steve Barancik's screenplay suffers from modernity, from too broad a license; the characters of fifties noir used to sweat not with desire but with the frustration—even sexier—of being forbidden to fulfill that desire in front of us, and the economical bitchiness of their dialogue was forced upon them by the fact that they couldn't swear, whereas Bridget can have Mike ("my designated fuck") as loudly and as openly as she wants. If *The Last Seduction* remains a shocking movie, that has nothing to do with the sex—Bridget hanging grimly onto a chain-link fence, banging the roof of her car, you name it—or with the occasional crunches of violence; it's because Dahl has kept his nerve and bred that rare and unsettling creature, the anti-love story. At one moment, Bridget seems to soften and relent, telling Mike that she has suffered, confessing shyly, "Maybe I could love you." Pause. She looks up. "Will that do?" I've seen the film twice now, and on both occasions the audience, schooled in sentimental repentance, gasped at this line as if kicked in the stomach. The true femme fatale would rather die than fake an orgasm, but she does a damn good imitation of the human heart.

OCTOBER 24, 1994

BULLETS OVER BROADWAY

Hollywood doesn't need great movies right now. It needs good movies. Nobody can legislate for genius, or train it, let alone predict it; but you can foster a culture in which competent, entertaining pictures are produced on a regular basis (and from which genius may spring without warning). The saddest thing about the industry at present is not that we lack masterpieces but that the staples—the romantic comedies, the thrillers—are, for the most part, so weak and illiterate. We need a dozen steady genre-nuts like John Dahl to plug away at their obsessions, and we depend on senior directors like Woody Allen to keep on producing the goods, the lighter the better. His new picture, *Bullets Over Broadway*, is so genial and well oiled, so exactly what is required, that it leaves you with a quite disproportionate sense of good cheer. It's set in the New York of the roaring twenties, although Allen has the good sense to go easy on the roars. He prefers the squealing, yearning, hamming, two-timing twenties; the movie is exuberant, and never less than fun, but, unlike *The Cotton Club*, it doesn't try to sell us the myth that an entire age can be consumed by nonstop exuberance. There are whooping showgirls, but their dancing ends quickly, and they matter less than the people watching them: the stubborn and the confused, the hopers, the no-hopers—all the regulars who troop through Allen's imagination.

First in line is David Shayne (John Cusack), an intense young playwright who believes that art can change the world—a pure conviction soiled only by the fact that his own view of the world stretches no farther than Greenwich Village. David's new offering is a soul-scouring drama, of which, mercifully, we hear only brief snatches; his leading lady, Helen Sinclair (a braying Dianne Wiest), offers to introduce him to Eugene O'Neill. "He's heard your work is morbid and depressing, and he's dying to meet you," she breathes. The production is funded by a mobster named

Nick Valenti (Joe Viterelli). With his pitted, sagging features and his unstoppable habits of destruction, Nick is a kind of human lava flow, and he's not about to let a little thing like artistic integrity get in his way. The play can only go ahead if it includes a part for his floozy, Olive Neal (Jennifer Tilly), who likes to wear a pink feather boa and slippers the size of Pekinese. Olive is duly cast as a psychiatrist, presumably on the ground that it is easier to investigate other people's minds if you aren't weighed down with one of your own.

Olive turns up with a bodyguard in tow. To begin with, he's not much more than a hat, a dark suit, and an attitude, but slowly he rouses himself into a character. His name is Cheech (Chazz Palminteri), and he knows more about life, and the various ways of ending it, than David will ever learn. At an indefinable point, you realize that what could have been a bitty little period piece, a stamp-album movie like *Radio Days*, is becoming something far more intricate—a soul-swap comedy. Distracted by his sentimental education, the playwright turns aside from drama, leaving the burden of his art to the moody Cheech, who beefs up the dialogue, shifts the structure, and takes care of a little casting glitch. Allen has always found hoods funny—decades ago he was writing about Albert "The Logical Positivist" Corillo—but this is his neatest invention yet: the aesthete who packs heat. Palminteri comes fresh from *A Bronx Tale*, and I imagine him pausing for a second before accepting the role of Cheech; after all, it gathers up and laughs at everything he treated so seriously in that film. But I'm glad he took the part, because he walks away with the picture. He tempers the edge of hysteria in some of the other performances, phasing himself into your attention until, by the end, you can't direct it anywhere else. It would have been easy to ascend from brutish to cute, but Palminteri makes things harder for himself, and more rewarding, by never dropping his guard, never relinquishing the swarthy and sinister side of Cheech's nature; he is as frightening in his defense of artistic autonomy as he was in the footsteps of his boss.

Allen respects that point of view, I think, more than he would admit. *Bullets Over Broadway* openly recommends love, of course, and its hero—deliberately or otherwise—grows into an alarming Allen clone, right down to the muted tweeds and the gulping patterns of speech, but you can't miss a sneaking admiration for the single-minded Cheech. Carlo Di Palma shoots the movie with his usual vigor, in saturated tones of taxicab yellow and fall gold, yet the scene that stays in your head is a peaceful one of Cheech and David perched at a bar, sipping beer and mulling over the play, with David inquiring gently into the perils of life beyond the stage: it feels like Allen having a conversation with himself. The last few years saw

Woody dragged through perils of his own—the press ambush, the bull-ring of the courts—with such force that you expected him to disappear forever, to grub a hole in the sand and stay there. And if he did come back, people asked, what kind of pictures would he make? Ibsen on the Hudson? A new Oresteia, only less funny? But, no, we get *Manhattan Murder Mystery* and *Bullets Over Broadway:* airy, unimportant, very slightly mad movies, neither bulging with gags nor straining on tiptoe to grab moral philosophy off the top shelf. They are the best—in retrospect, the only—reply he could have made. We thought Woody Allen had lost touch with the entire world, not to mention his audience; instead, he seems to be levelling with us, to be contenting himself with our pleasure, more keenly than ever before. Make 'em laugh.

OCTOBER 24, 1994

THREE COLORS: RED

Red is the conclusion to Krzysztof Kieślowski's commanding "Three Colors" trilogy, a companion piece to *Blue* and *White*. It is also, so he says, the last film that he will ever make. This may or may not turn out to be the case; for the moment, however, he is going off to smoke cigarettes, chop wood, and generally do whatever retired Polish film directors do. The new movie certainly feels like a late work, even a posthumous one; it is about many things—a man of magisterial but moribund powers, a shipwreck, near-magic, and the pairing of young lovers. In short, it is Kieślowski's *Tempest*, suffused with valediction, with something sharp and autumnal settling over the simplest action. When just the sight of a car pulling around a bend above Lake Geneva at dusk makes you reach for your handkerchief, you know you're in trouble.

Most of the film is set in Geneva, and the plot is essentially a two-hander. Other hands join in from time to time, but their gestures merely direct us to the main couple. The heroine, Valentine (Irène Jacob), is a model—the only false note in the movie, since she looks too short to be a model, and too hesitant, and definitely too beautiful. She lives alone in her apartment, trading awkwardness over the phone with a distant boyfriend, whom we never see. Driving home at night, she hits a dog—one of many accidents in the movie, ranging from a tiny stumble on the catwalk to a full-scale disaster. The dog is a German shepherd named Rita, whose role in life, it becomes clear, is to be a kind of furry Emma Woodhouse, yanking together those who might otherwise never meet. Valentine goes to the address on Rita's collar, and after passing through what appear to be the early stages of a horror movie—iron gate, gloomy house, the door unlocked and creaking—she finds the owner (Jean-Louis Trintignant) completely indifferent to the dog's fate. Days later, Rita leads her back to the same place, as if to insist that some good will come of the encounter.

This time, Valentine approaches in sunshine, with no cause to be afraid; but, inside, the owner hunches in a darkness of his own, tuning a radio so that he can spy on the telephone talk of his neighbors. "It's disgusting," she says. "Yes," he replies, "and, what's more, it's illegal." He seems to like it that way.

This perverse old man, it turns out, is a retired judge, although he could equally be an ex-con, the wreck of that impenetrable killer played by Trintignant in *The Conformist*. He is called Joseph Kern—a Kafka name, ideal for a person of his singular, selective tastes—but we don't find that out until halfway through the movie; Kieślowski delights in feeding us information drop by drop, not just because of his own instinctive reticence but because of the halting, half-assed comedy of human acquaintance that he sees around him. Kern and Valentine square off against each other, their repulsion overcome by the simple wish to learn more; like Hannibal Lecter without the appetite, he cross-examines Valentine as if she, and not he, had committed a crime, guessing her family problems—her brother is a junkie—and predicting her future. As the movie proceeds, she turns the tables, and draws from him a confession of heartbreak, of the betrayal that bled him dry and led him toward the secluded passion of the voyeur. "Maybe you're the woman I never met," he tells Valentine. This being a Kieślowski movie, the grand unburdening of Kern's soul is slightly interrupted by someone who asks if either of them has seen a cleaning woman carrying a bucket.

That is what Kieślowski groupies come to love in his work: not the mocking of tragedy but the gentle reminder that tragedy should never expect to have the stage to itself. Normal life keeps poking up through the trapdoor. The core of *Red* lies in two or three long, mournful exchanges between Valentine and Kern, and a plain account of the film would make it sound talk-heavy (like that other discursive Trintignant picture *My Night at Maud's*); yet you never feel lectured at, and you come away from it not with an earful of lines but with a head full of all the images that punched holes in the dialogue. The movie is almost radioactive; objects and expressions are hot with meanings that you can't quite tease out, and that resist the tedium of a symbolic reading. Even the color red—haunting the story in every shape, from a knot of ribbon to a gigantic poster—will not stay still, flickering from passion to wrath or warmth. What the central characters say to each other is less important than the leathery, bookish darkness of the room where they say it, or the shocking whiteout when Kern replaces a bare bulb in a lamp, or the stones hurled through his windows and then arranged on top of the piano. They were thrown by enraged neighbors, who have discovered his creepy pastime; in their place, he says, he would do exactly the same. At such a moment, you feel the whole movie revolving around Kern; he sucks the action into himself, until you can't tell whether he is pushing the other characters to and fro like toys or helplessly watching them slide toward his own brand of Hell.

This is Trintignant's picture—one of the great crusty-old-guy performances, putting him alongside Victor Sjöström in *Wild Strawberries*, although Trintignant seems even more resistant to mellowing. Grizzled and gray, his jaw as stubbled as a tramp's, old clothes hung on his bony frame, he seems a lifetime away from the sleek young paramour of *A Man and a Woman.* But then Trintignant was never a wholly convincing heart-throb; you could hear his brain throbbing as well, the hum of his mental radar as he scanned a swooning romance for danger signals. He had the intensity of a lover but the suspicious gaze of a private eye; his performance dried the tears of a wet movie, and made it more interesting than it had any right to be. In 1986, Trintignant and Anouk Aimée teamed up to shoot a sequel—an unwise move, needless to say, but also an unnecessary move, because the true aftermath, the only one that makes any sense, is *Red.* When the judge tells of being cuckolded, you can't help imagining Anouk Aimée packing her bags and sneaking out at dawn. Joseph Kern has arrived at such a pitch of disillusionment that you wonder at the strength of the illusions he started out with. The old man is unsteady on his feet, hobbling out with a stick as Valentine comes to his gate, but the steadiness is still there in his eyes, in the crisp manner of his speech. Exasperated by his reluctance to engage with life, Valentine snaps. "Then stop breathing," she says. Kern considers for a second. "Good idea," he replies, sounding rather chipper at this sensible suggestion.

It would have been easy to set up *Red* as a clash of styles—the aging complainer versus the spirit of youth. But Kieślowski keeps blurring the division: Kern starts to come off his leash, unwrapping a bottle of eau-de-vie and taking his tanklike Mercedes out for a spin, while Valentine, in turn, seems old for her years, at least in the full tide of emotions that floods across her face. Irène Jacob was discovered by Kieślowski, who saw her playing a short role in Louis Malle's *Au Revoir les Enfants* and realized (goodness knows how) that she was the one; she has worked with him only twice—in *The Double Life of Véronique* and now in *Red*—but she seems to gather up and project everything that his movies are about, as Catherine Deneuve did with Buñuel. Her performances are wonderfully exhausting. Watch Valentine accepting a refill of eau-de-vie; from the tangle of dread and delight in her expression, you might think that it really *was* the elixir of life. When Kern asks her to smile for him, she obeys, as she does when a photographer instructs her to "be sad"; but in both cases the look that follows is entirely her own, stronger than either man would have expected, or even wished. Jacob is at the mercy of her moods, yet somehow they give her definition (it would be fascinating to see her play light comedy); she is both fated and free, a one-woman demonstration of Kieślowski's abiding theme.

The climax of *Red* is a bit of a gamble, twisting events in order to tie the trilogy up. Valentine at last meets the man for whom she has been destined throughout: a young lawyer, a Kern-in-waiting, who shares many of the judge's attributes, right down to his suspenders and his pen. (Whether he will be luckier in love is anyone's guess.) With them are the main characters of *Blue* and *White;* when I first saw the picture, this struck me as little more than an in-joke, a nod to the director's fans and a mystery to everyone else. The second time around, I didn't mind it so much: the mystery felt lighter, a pleasing final flourish of the great Kieślowski principle that movies have no need to explain themselves. As the judge says to Valentine, "deciding what is true and what isn't now seems to me—" He stops, searching for the proper phrase, and finds it: "a lack of modesty." At the end, when he stands in his garden, amid icy sunlight and dripping trees, he could be a filmmaker ruminating on the dramatic storm that he has cooked up, and wondering whether it was ever really under his control. If Krzysztof Kieślowski is serious about giving up movies, that only proves he was serious about making them, and seriously modest about what they could achieve.

NOVEMBER 28, 1994

TOM AND VIV

Tom and Viv begins in 1915, with a young T. S. Eliot (Willem Dafoe) attending a philosophy tutorial at Oxford. His teacher is a little man with curious white hair, like the whipped cream that comes out of aerosols; from this we are meant to understand that he is none other than Bertrand Russell. In fact, Russell taught Eliot at *Harvard* (finding him "very silent"), but that is not the kind of distinction to trouble the director of this movie, Brian Gilbert. His interests lie elsewhere—to be precise, with Vivienne Haigh-Wood (Miranda Richardson), a woman in white cavorting about on the grass. Eliot goggles from an upstairs window, neglecting the charms of symbolic logic, and decides that she is the one for him. Before you know it, he is taking her out for a punt, thus allowing the camera to focus in slow motion on his pole as he plunges it, dripping, into the idling river. Guess what *this* guy has in mind. He leans her back and lays out his agenda. "I want to live in Europe and write poetry." Clear enough. But there's more. "I love you," he says. "I love you more than life itself. I'd do anything for you." This is *T. S. Eliot*? He sounds like Ashley Wilkes.

Tom and Viv is based on Michael Hastings's stage play, which, in turn, was based on almost nothing at all, apart from a smattering of blind prejudice and a thick ear for English verse, although it purported to tell the true story of the poet's first marriage. The film plods politely through this distressing tale. We get the seaside honeymoon, with the poet stalking glumly along the shoreline and his wife back at the hotel washing blood off the sheets; we get her brother, Maurice (Tim Dutton), making every effort to remain jolly, and her parents (Rosemary Harris and Philip Locke) looking pained and tense, unable to decide which is worse—a daughter who is diagnosed as suffering from "moral insanity," or a son-in-law without even the common decency to write in heroic couplets; we get Vivienne pouring chocolate through the mail slot of his offices at Faber & Faber, then threatening Virginia Woolf with a knife—examples of her growing lunacy, apparently. Eventually, a distraught Eliot has her committed to an asylum for the rest of her life. (Since the movie was made, a letter has been published in which Maurice informs Eliot that Vivienne has been committed. He didn't even know.)

I am glad to report that the film, written by Hastings and Adrian Hodges, loses none of the rich nonsense of the original play, although I was sorry not to hear the interesting line in which Vivienne reports that her husband "adores the Fascists." A daring little slander, not least because it was Vivienne herself who joined the British Union of Fascists, in 1934. That would not suit the playwright's plan—wronged woman versus cold fish—so he made the switch. By way of compensation, there is plenty of new nonsense; try as I might, I just couldn't get my brain around the idea of T. S. Eliot hugging the Bishop of Oxford, resting his weary head against the reverend waistband. Nobody minds liberties being taken with the facts, but one doesn't expect those liberties to be pressed into the service of a hardline willfulness; the film is more intolerant than the man whom it surveys with such distaste. When you see Eliot being baptized into the Anglican communion, for instance, with choirs carolling all around and the camera swooning, you can't help thinking of the quiet Cotswolds church where the real ceremony took place; the movie resents Eliot's need for seclusion and ritual and is set on disturbing his peace. Miranda Richardson certainly launches into this task with a vengeance, offering a performance so crazed with mannerism that in some terrible, backdoor way it does lead us to the heart of the matter; if Vivienne really *was* this annoying, it was big of Eliot to stick with her as long as he did. As for Willem Dafoe, he looked much happier charging about on rooftops in *Clear and Present Danger*, where, although under fire from drug barons, he could at least speak in his own voice. It is true that Eliot's accent, hovering between two worlds, grew very odd with age, but not even his recorded readings can prepare you for the soft, strangled delivery of Dafoe, who sounds like an Afrikaner telling a bedtime story.

Tom and Viv is a deeply unappetizing mixture: the snob section of the movie industry meets the sleazy end of the biography trade. Hastings has a high old time with stuffed-shirt, philistine England, which he thinks of as the ideal refuge for his trussed-up hero; the director, unfortunately, has rather a weakness for the trappings of that refuge. The props are straight Merchant-Ivory: parping old motors, garden parties, acres of white linen and black tie, a bunch of flowers thrown carelessly—ah, happy days!—into the air. But the motives that fuel the film are nowhere near as clean as the suits; it is a dramatization of envy, raising the dismal prospect that our age has become offended by genius. *Tom and Viv* carefully draws Eliot's creative sting, leaving him an average melancholic, no better than the rest of us, quite possibly worse, who just happened to possess a gift for poetry and wrote to relieve a psychological itch, aided by a companion who did most of the scratching. "I did so want to help you with your poetry," says Vivienne. "You will," Eliot replies. "You do. You're in every line. I can't do it without you." We see him looking blocked in front of the typewriter; Vivienne, by contrast, glances at a line of *The Waste Land* and rattles off a new suggestion, which he gratefully accepts. If you start to ask yourself who really wrote the stuff, then the film has got you exactly where it wants. Eliot is ripe for such treatment, of course, having been foolish enough, in modern eyes, to announce a discreet distance between the work of art and the life of its creator. As he wrote in 1929, "I have always found that the less I knew about the poet and his work, before I began to read it, the better." To prove him wrong has been the joy of biographers, and is now the delight of a moviemaker. No one can deny that if his marriage had been other than it was we would not have *The Waste Land* in its present form; but more than that we cannot say.

So what is the point of this movie? Who could possibly want to see it? Devotees of the poet will learn nothing new, and will leave the theatre in suitably controlled fury; he is now so unfashionable that the act of reading him has itself become a monastic, Eliot-like operation, and the film can only drive us deeper underground. Other, more disinterested parties will wonder vaguely what all the fuss is about, and may simply find the whole experience rather exhausting. If you think some of Eliot's plays were tough to sit through, just try *Tom and Viv;* it makes *The Elder Statesman* look like *The Wild Bunch.* You could argue that the dullness is appropriate, that it locks neatly into Eliot's own penchant for regularity; but it is dullness of a more pernicious variety—a tedium born of incurable histrionics, where every line and every gesture is decked out with self-importance. At the end of the film, we see Willem Dafoe standing in the cage of an elevator, doing his familiar impersonation of a dyspeptic sphinx; the camera stares back at him, and then returns for one last close-up, just to hammer home the point that Eliot was a prisoner of his own self. The effect, of course, is to lull us into superiority; we've seen through this guy, we know why he wrote, we know how he treated others, and, frankly, we're not surprised that he got on better with cats. The movie is not just lacklustre but irresponsible, because it will foster more Eliot haters than there are Eliot readers; people will come away knowing for certain why they dislike him, without feeling the need to discover whether they like his work. In "East Coker" he wrote, "The poetry does not matter"—a sombre, ruminative caution that gradually turned into a prediction. With *Tom and Viv,* it has finally come true.

DECEMBER 12, 1994

MRS. PARKER AND THE VICIOUS CIRCLE

Mrs. Parker and the Vicious Circle is more fun than *Tom and Viv*, but only in the sense that a clean razor blade is more fun than a rusty one. It's another movie about writers, and a damn sight sharper. The director is the moody and subtle Alan Rudolph, which makes a change from the galumphing Brian Gilbert; but you still end up asking yourself, What's the point? Why be surprised that writers are good only for writing, and some of them not even for that? The movie is determined to demythologize, and therefore proceeds on the assumption that there is still a myth worth eroding; but that simply isn't true. The celebrated wit and panache of the Round Table crowd, Rudolph tells us, concealed an undergrowth of alcohol and spite. Well, so what? Put any bunch of writers together, and the fur will start to fly. If this particular bunch could be furrier and funnier than most, good for them; but nobody still believes that the Algonquin was a laugh-a-minute carnival of joy, and we don't need a laugh-an-hour movie to put us straight.

Things begin in a drunken haze; you expect it to burn off as the movie warms up, but it never really lifts. The movie is more about drinking than about writing, which allows Rudolph to practice his fluid, dreamlike technique; there are plenty of smoky close-ups and smooth flashbacks, and I loved the way in which overlapping dialogue—a trick that Rudolph inherited from Robert Altman—acquires a moral edge, uncovering a breed of people whose principal desire is not to mesh their voices in harmony but to shout each other down. Most of the casting works fine: Matthew Broderick—a broader actor than audiences expect him to be—has a good, seductive shot at Charles "Baby Vomit" MacArthur, and I was pleasantly surprised by Jean-Michael Henry's cameo as Harpo Marx, but Sam Robards's Harold Ross is another matter. It is more than mere loyalty that compels me to ask whether the editor of *The New Yorker* really resembled the hero of *Eraserhead.*

Dorothy Parker herself is played by Jennifer Jason Leigh, who is starting to remind me of the young Robert De Niro in her strange, shocking ability not only to pick the lock of a character and slip inside but to breathe more easily once she is there. I have no idea what Jason Leigh is like, but she rapidly hardens the illusion that I know what Mrs. Parker was like. The portrait may or may not be true, but it coheres: the booze and the lethargy click into place as you watch Jason Leigh drawling the one-liners out of a thin mouth, like an invalid dribbling soup. That she has no qualms about turning this woman into a bore shows an alarming honesty, proving beyond reasonable doubt that the main problem with any movie about Dorothy Parker is Dorothy Parker—or, to break Mrs. Parker down into her constituent elements, a double shot of self-pity topped up with fizz. Over the years, her prose and her poetry alike have turned sour; it gets harder and harder to feel sympathy for a writer who reserved her tenderest emotions for the mirror. The film has a curious epilogue, in which, while the credits roll, our heroine proclaims her loathing of racial segregation and her passionate involvement in the Spanish Civil War; but this last-gasp attempt to save her from solipsism feels like a token gesture—as if Rudolph had only just thought of it, or had suddenly felt guilty about exposing Mrs. Parker—and it comes far too late. She was a solipsist, and there's an end on it. I can still laugh at the Constant Reader reviews in *The New Yorker*, but the laugh curls into a wince when I come across, say, her 1927 piece on the diary of Katherine Mansfield: "Only her dark, sad eyes should have read its words. I closed it with a little murmur to her portrait on the cover. 'Please forgive me,' I said."

This mating cry from one sentimentalist to another is as bad as any of the mashed-banana prose that Dorothy Parker found and berated in A. A. Milne; moreover, it is not so much a departure from her standard wit as its flip side. She was forever on the lookout for anything that could make her suffer in style, be it a faithless lover or a lousy play. Rudolph is right to let the bons mots fall flat (even if it means disappointing his audience), because Parker lacked the courage of the true aphorist; she unleashed ridicule, and it could be very smart, but it never crossed her mind to be comic at her own expense—her own misery was beyond a joke. The crucial comparison is with Thurber, who had just as much, if not more, to be sorry about, but who knew that it was his duty to be funny about it first. Honesty led him into self-doubt, and sometimes into a kind of decorous rage, but never into moping; I would happily give up the whole of *The Portable Dorothy Parker* for that single moment in Thurber when he catches himself standing foam-faced in the bathroom with his ear bleeding and his hands full of wet needles. The Parker equivalent would be the bathroom scene in Rudolph's movie where she decides to slash her wrists. This is filmed with typical assurance—we get the hard little thump of blade on flesh, and an astonishing close-up of Jason Leigh's eyes, with only the lashes in focus and the rest of her features curving away in a blur—but the mess of motives that swept Mrs. Parker to this crisis remains essentially boring. That she was sincere in these stabs at annihilation is no guarantee that we will find her interesting; it is more than possible to be melodramatic to the bitter end. Self-pity is just vanity with a poker face, and it kills any writer long before suicide gets there.

DECEMBER 12, 1994

THE MADNESS OF KING GEORGE

Movies made from plays are creeping back into fashion. What's more, the plays in question are not of the cheap, *Everybody Comes to Rick's* variety, trash waiting to be transmuted into gold, but works that have already scored onstage. The loyal theatregoer, of course, is scornful of such a process, afraid that Hollywood will mill the gold straight back into trash; but there's no need to worry. If anything, Louis Malle's version of *Uncle Vanya* was fresher than most stage productions, blowing away that dusty, fallen-leaf feeling that has settled onto the playing of Chekhov. Now we have Nicholas Hytner's *The Madness of King George*, adapted from Alan Bennett's *The Madness of George III*, which was a big hit in London when it opened, in 1991—so big that two years later it even came and played in Brooklyn for a few nights. The people at Goldwyn thought that Bennett's original title sounded like a sequel, so they changed it. Why not call the movie *Mad George III: Beyond Thunderdome*, and bring in Tina Turner to play the Prince of Wales? Happily, the basic data of the piece remain unaltered: the year is 1788, and the sovereign's urine is turning blue. These two facts are not logically connected, although you catch a vague sense that the disturbance of the royal mind may have been touched off by trouble in the body politic; the entire work is a sort of extended pun on the word "constitution." As if the rumbles from France were not bad enough, there is the matter of America—"the place we mustn't mention," as George puts it. When a man loses his colonies, the film implies, his wits will not be far behind.

The story opens and closes with the King (Nigel Hawthorne) in rude health: jovial, decorous, pink of face and warm of temper, alarmingly well informed about an alarming number of his subjects—in short, just right for the job. In between, however, he stammers, drivels, fouls himself, and besmirches the reputations of others: having spent his life rising above humanity, he becomes its lowest common denominator. This causes great distress to his wife, the homely and Teutonic Queen Charlotte (Helen Mirren); great excitement among his doctors, who between them cover the full range of human incompetence; deep concern to his prime minister, Pitt (Julian Wadham), who sees his own authority coming under siege; and barely concealed glee in those who think their time has come—Fox (Jim Carter), the Leader of the Opposition, and the Prince of Wales (Rupert Everett, who has either put on weight or else stuffed a duvet up his waistcoat). "To be Prince of Wales is not a position. It is a predicament," he complains. It's a neat line, glancing quite brazenly at the present British monarchy; the neatness is also more Wildean than anything we have come to expect of Bennett, its intelligence more sealed and rounded than his usual open curiosity. It is a line to declaim, not to exchange in conversation; in the theatre, you would get a kick out of it, but film is more impatient and tends to stumble over glossy witticism. *The Madness of King George* is more civilized and literate than most current movies, but at the same time—or, perhaps, for that very reason—it feels rather dead-ended. What with all the courtiers and politicians madly furthering their own interests, it should have been a riot, and Hytner certainly stirs them up with the swinging and scurrying of his camera; yet an odd stasis settles on the proceedings. It is not only the King's son but the King himself who is dramatically becalmed; his madness, too, is a predicament. It is not a plot.

Nigel Hawthorne played the same role onstage, and has now made it his own. He blusters beautifully, although it means leaving behind the deceitful satin tones that he patented elsewhere, whether in *Yes, Minister* or as the villain of *Demolition Man;* he is a natural Jeeves, as it were, who has transformed himself into a Wooster. None of the scenes at court, or in the chamber of the Commons, can match the head-to-head duel between the King and Dr. Willis (Ian Holm, as fierce and compelling as ever), the little Lincolnshire physician who finally stares him down and tames him into health. The play made it clear that the royal disease sorted itself out, that the formidable methods of Willis—strapping a man accustomed to a throne into what looks horribly like an electric chair—were to no possible avail; oddly, the film chooses to fudge this, leaving us with the suspicion that he *did* do some good. It's a pretty reactionary idea, madness as a complication of misbehavior, but then Hytner has come up with a surprisingly reactionary film. Bennett himself is of two minds, if not more, about most of the grand English traditions, including the monarchical; if you want to see that balance sustained, try the TV movies of his *An Englishman Abroad* and *A Question of Attribution*—both of them infinitely sharper than *The*

Madness of King George, which resounds too often to the cheer of the crowd. The smartly choreographed ironies of the opening sequence, in which a footman gives a quick spit and polish to the crown before it is lowered onto the king's head, are all but lost in pomp by the end; the Bennett tones are muffled, like the soft focus that Hytner brings to the crisp blue air around Windsor Castle. The monarch even comes round to the idea of America: Hail the special relationship.

The best reason to see this movie is a single scene, perhaps the simplest of all. (The studio, I am informed, fought to have it dropped. Nice.) George sits outside in a balmy garden, wearing a straw hat; he invites his Lord Chancellor and an obliging equerry to join him in a reading of *King Lear*—that unbearable moment when the hero awakes from his own ravings and sees Cordelia afresh. Bennett and Hytner do not need to force the parallel; the King has spotted it himself (much to the chagrin of Willis, who has never read Shakespeare and hasn't a clue what the play is about). This is anything but reactionary; it is, in fact, as touchingly radical as you could hope for, having the nerve to propose that art—neither quackery nor dreadful discipline but the consolations of poetry—will finally draw the fever from the lunatic. One King is purged by the ordeal of another, and the sight of that weird release, the idea that you can drop away from the wheel of fire into a pleasant summer afternoon, is more acutely English than any of the ceremonial palaver. "I've always been myself, even when I was ill," says George. "Only now I *seem* myself. And that's the important thing: I have remembered how to seem." This guy should be in pictures.

JANUARY 16, 1995

BEFORE SUNRISE

Before Sunrise starts with strangers on a train. One is Jesse (Ethan Hawke), a young American kicking around the Continent on a Eurailpass; the other is Céline (Julie Delpy), a French student making her way back to Paris. They start talking as the train hums toward Vienna, where Jesse is due to disembark—a foolish, not to say tragic, plan, since it involves never seeing Céline again. True, he has only just met her, but already he has spotted her copy of Georges Bataille, and if there is one rule that governs the life of the seasoned traveller it is: Once you find a French blonde reading Georges Bataille of her own free will, don't let her out of your sight. Hang in there like a limpet. But how can Jesse work it? What should he do before the lady vanishes? He does the right thing, of course: he proposes that they get off the train together, mosey around Vienna all night, then continue their respective journeys in the morning. This fine suggestion flatters Céline by assuming that she is as footloose and wacky as Jesse is; more important, it beckons the audience into a similar state of mind. The fact is that most of us would never have struck up the conversation in the first place, for fear of being arrested by the conductor and stashed in the freight car, but the director, Richard Linklater, is so adept at building up a mood of shrugging, petty-picaresque adventure that we kid ourselves that Jesse is doing the obvious thing, that cool comes naturally to all.

So he and Céline dump their bags at the station and set off into the unknown—the deep unknown, if you go by the standard of Linklater's earlier pictures, *Slacker* and *Dazed and Confused.* Both were set in Texas, which seems a long way from the Ringstrasse, but so swiftly did they establish what it was to be a Linklater character—flexible, late-rising, eagerly bemused, struck rather than tortured by doubt, extremely unlikely to wear a suit—that it comes as no surprise when his new heroes, dropped into foreign territory, are able to pick themselves up and get strolling without a qualm. Against the odds, Vienna turns out to be ideal for Linklater's purposes; he could have called the movie *Schlacker.* A more fashionable, closely packed city, like Prague, would not have given him the physical leeway he needs for his peculiar brand of near-aimlessness. He can let his characters loose across broad streets and patches of park, or keep the camera running on them as they talk away a long, dawdling trip in the back of a tram. The really smart thing about this style is the way it fends off cheap temptations. The very mention of Europe—or, worse, of Middle Europe—sends some directors into an expressionist jag (see Woody Allen's *Shadows and Fog,* or Steven Soderbergh's *Kafka*), the implication being that everybody living east of Munich is personally related to Dr. Caligari. How much more tolerant, and closer to the spirit of Renoir, is Linklater's suspicion that the knack of hanging out is pretty much the same wherever you go, and that it is best practiced not among angular shadows but in the calm light of day. In a neat riposte to *The Third Man,* he puts Céline and Jesse in one of the pods of a Ferris wheel, high above the city; it was here that Harry Lime looked down on the insect swarm of citizens, and spoke so witheringly of cuckoo clocks. It remains the most stirring hymn to misanthropy in all cinema, and Linklater answers in the only way he can, by hitting us with the movie's first kiss.

This has been a long time coming; but then the romantic rhythm of the picture goes through some fairly unusual variations. Think of the erotic clockwork that drives most Hollywood love stories: the initial meeting, maybe a couple more, then into the slushy kiss, the quick cut to discarded stockings lying on a bedroom floor, the camera travelling up to survey either the postcoital hug or the midcoital yelp. Now try the Linklater version: the long talk on a train, more talk in the city, another helping of talk, then a wonderful scene in the cramped listening booth of a record store, where both parties are aching to embrace but can't quite dredge up the courage, contenting themselves with looking terribly serious and swallowing hard, like fliers trying to adjust to high altitude—which, in a sense, is what they are. Still no kiss. Finally, it happens, up in the Ferris wheel, followed by *more talk.* Unbelievable, really, although only in terms of film formulas; in terms of human behavior, I believed every minute of it. "I think I decided to sleep with you when we got off the train," Céline says. "Now that we've talked so much, I'm not sure anymore." When did you last hear such an honest jumble of head and heart? Later, out on the grass, armed with a bottle of wine and stolen glasses, they do make love, but it doesn't strike you as a fortissimo conclusion to their tale—it's more like taking the next step, hitting the right note.

It should be clear by now that *Before Sunrise* is a very odd movie. It disobeys all kinds of rules; it consists mostly of two people wandering around getting to know each other, which sounds very close to boring; and the other figures who turn up—geeky actors, a poet, a belly dancer, even a fortune-teller—are borderline bohemian, which sounds very close to embarrassing. But Linklater, together with his cowriter, Kim Krizan, seems to relish these risks, and he never tries to conceal the fact that Jesse and Céline (particularly Céline) are at an age when it is de rigueur to spout equal quantities of bullshit and good sense. You prepare to wince, but the essential good humor of the movie gets there just in time. What's more, the performers are both so high on it, so tuned in to Linklater's requirements, that you can scarcely begrudge them an occasional flash of loopiness.

That open, unsmoothed feel of the piece—it comes across as improvised, but I imagine that every rough patch was planned and choreographed in advance—pushes both stars into the strongest work of their careers. *Before Sunrise* finally exorcises the ghost of *The Dead Poets Society*, a smug and pernicious movie that burdened Ethan Hawke with more angst than any young actor deserves. Something had to bring him down from that high, mournful sensitivity, and back from the grunge pose of *Reality Bites*. Jesse is just the role, and, like the movie itself, Hawke takes care to annoy us from time to time, insuring that we don't gag on undiluted charm. Then, there is the matter of Julie Delpy, a stern reminder that the first duty of a film critic—the sole qualification, to be honest—is to fall regularly, and pointlessly, in love with the people onscreen. Once this stops happening, you might as well give up and get a proper job. I was trying to work out why 1994 had been such a lousy year for cinema, and suddenly realized that it was at least six months before anyone made me spill my Sprite. Well, this year looks much more promising, because it's only January and my heart already belongs to another. Delpy did appear in boring old 1994, in *White* and *Killing Zoe*, but she may not have fully registered with the audience, not least because those films were—understandably—in such awe of her pallid, thin-armed Cranach looks that, without really wanting to, they raised her to the level of an ideal. Linklater makes her scruffier and more profane; if she's the girl of your dreams, it's only because the dreams are a big joke, and she knows it. "It's like some male fantasy," she tells Jesse. "Meet some French girl on a train, fuck her, and never see her again." She even has a murky past, and she chats merrily about a recent boyfriend, and the rumor that she was going to kill him. As she mentions the police, you can see Jesse flinching, asking himself, "What am I *doing* with this person? Is this her favorite hobby—meet some American guy on a train, knife him, and make sure nobody sees him again?"

There are plenty of moments like this, when the easy, unperplexed swing of the picture trips over ridges of threat. None of them come to anything, and that's why they lurk at the side of your mind: the Vienna night feels all the fresher and more enchanted for the storm warnings that brew and veer away. Céline and Jesse visit a small cemetery dotted with the graves of unknowns: vagrants and visitors, the odd Viennese without a name—"Maybe just a first name, I don't know," Céline says. All at once, you sniff a plot: they will die tonight, somewhere in the city, stripped of their belongings—maybe even of their first names. The story will come to rest in this same graveyard, the camera welcoming a pair of new arrivals.

It doesn't happen, of course. They have a great evening, suffer no harm, and promise to do it again—to meet in a year's time, on June 16th. Jesse mentions the date in passing, and no more is said, but it can hardly be an accident: they have had a happy Bloomsday. How are you supposed to take this hint? If you think it's a flashy little name-drop, buying into Joyce for the sake of intellectual glamour, fair enough; but I think it answers another, more respectable need. The point is not that Linklater has his head in his books—he'd never let them cramp his style—but that his movie is about people with books in their heads. Hollywood is so illiterate these days that when directors grapple with literature they either molest it brutally or, worse, freeze up in its presence. Martin Scorsese's *The Age of Innocence* was lush and honorable, but you couldn't help noticing how he backed away from disturbing the sanctity of the text; his diplomacy was preserved in Joanne Woodward's voice-overs, which soothed our ears with passages of pure Wharton, as if to reassure us of the film's credentials.

Richard Linklater does the opposite: he relaxes in the presence of literature—tossing in references for fun, never trying to load them with significance. They circle around in the discursive air of the movie, the kinds of things that Jesse might or might not know, that he could have picked up in the course of his rail-bound reading. At one point, he quotes Auden—or, rather, he imitates Dylan Thomas declaiming Auden. It's mainly a joke for Céline's benefit, but it feels right for the dopey, unforgettable dawn that has just come up on them, and you can't help recalling that the aged Auden lived out the dregs of his life a few miles away from where they sprawl; and then you think of Auden's great lyric about staying out all night, with its homage to "the sexy airs of summer." The poem seems not only to describe the movie but, as it were, to sponsor it; what Linklater has managed to do is to pull us back into that wordy, pleasantly confused moment of youth when people have the nerve—the pretension, maybe, but also the wit—to envisage their lives as a kind of literature, to imagine themselves sauntering gaily, or grimly, through one short story after another. That is why the glance at *Ulysses* works so beautifully: it doesn't try to argue that its hero is like Stephen Dedalus, or that Vienna is Nighttown, or anything so vain—it simply tells us that just once, for a single day, Jesse and Céline have given life the sort of shape and charge that until now they have found only in fiction, and may never find again. The movie ends, as did *Dazed and Confused*, early in the morning, the characters smarting with sleeplessness. Linklater is fast making this his time of day, as surely as John Cheever colonized the cocktail hour. Jesse and Céline are seen going their separate ways, smiling, and you wonder whether they dreamed, or fancied, the whole thing. Maybe they caught sight of each other on the train, began to make a move, thought better of it, and quietly went back to their books.

JANUARY 30, 1995

SHALLOW GRAVE

Shallow Grave, directed by Danny Boyle, is a smart new shocker from Scotland—too smart, at times, for its own good. John Hodge's close-fitting screenplay presents us with four main characters. Alex (Ewan McGregor), a journalist, shares an apartment with Juliet (Kerry Fox), a doctor, and David (Christopher Eccleston), a bespectacled accountant. The three of them get into trouble. The fourth character *is* the trouble. Played by the sublimely unpleasant Keith Allen, who makes you feel that the human face is destined to evolve into a sneer, he turns up when the roommates advertise for a new lodger. Allen recently took, or embodied, the role of the wife-battering Jonas in a new BBC production of *Martin Chuzzlewit*, and he still seems to be wrapped in a mist of Dickensian malice. In *Shallow Grave* he is mixed up in drugs, and has both the gall to die of an overdose in the spare bedroom and the decency to leave a suitcase bulging with money under the bed.

Alex and the others burst in and find him. They play it cool, but the camera is even cooler: like a Renaissance artist preparing an anatomical sketch, it travels carefully around the corpse, which is splayed in artful nakedness. The effect is heightened by the Titian blue of the walls, which glows ever more strongly as the days pass and the rigorous flesh turns purple-gray. This visual suavity is the great strength of *Shallow Grave:* after the first whippy travelling shot through Edinburgh streets, the formality of Boyle's framing lowers the temperature of the melodrama, and the color scheme—swaths of mint green and beef red, each room of the apartment like a different season—suggests that shades of feeling, too, are heading for a clash. Danny Boyle can't afford to paint the town red, so he settles for a door; if most of your movie is set inside an apartment, you may as well practice your interior decoration. Still, it's not healthy to stay in *all* the time. Everybody should get out now and again, so why not make a night of it—you know, seal a dead man in plastic, take him out to the countryside, chop off a few cold cuts, and bury the rest?

Shallow Grave is a new twist on that old Hitchcock teaser: How do you get rid of a body without losing your mind? Like *Rope* and *The Trouble with Harry*, it seems more of an exercise in logic than a chiller; it fights to keep a straight face while the three leads bicker and snap over the loot. As the body count climbs, Hodge's script plunges onward without remorse—bright with intelligence but also frosted over with something inhuman. The giveaway comes in the bit parts. Look at the pair of ludicrous police detectives who perch on the sofa as they deliver their dumb lines—these aren't people, they're props. Even the central characters have to work hard to convince us that they *are* characters. Kerry Fox, sad to say, has the weakest part of all, and the frowning emotional conviction that pulled her so truthfully through *An Angel at My Table* has nothing to hook onto here. If anyone carries the movie, it's Christopher Eccleston, who digs around in his role and comes up with a shining conceit: the young man who decides to steal money and slice up human flesh in order to convince himself that he is something more than a dull-hearted accountant, and then hoards the cash with precisely the kind of pedantic pains that made him such a good accountant in the first place. Crouched in a locked loft, watching tenderly over his treasure like Gollum guarding the ring of Middle Earth, he fulfills rather than betrays himself in crime.

The film needs more of this density, another layer of moral (as opposed to practical) unease, although, to be fair, you don't feel that need until you're well outside the theatre. While it's running, *Shallow Grave* is a thoroughly modern movie: quick, tortuous, greased with fine style, and enjoyably excessive. In Britain, it has already been greeted as the savior of the national film industry—a poisoned chalice if ever there was one, and a burden that Danny Boyle could do without. If he has had the intuition to make a film of the moment, we should pause to consider what the moment looks like. There was a point in *Shallow Grave* at which I saw, branching out ahead, the many possible paths available to the plot. It could take any of them, which is a tribute to the inventiveness of Hodge and Boyle, but it didn't *matter* which it took. I really didn't care—they were all the same to me. This is something new in movies: thrilled indifference, without even the corniest of sympathies to sway us in either direction. The only certainty is that of violence; by fair means or foul, preferably foul, we are led into battle. Audiences have changed utterly since the days of Hitchcock; they no longer tremble at the prospect of bloodshed but laugh out loud as the trickle swells to a flood. The idea that it could be withheld for the purposes of suspense wouldn't occur to them—or, if it did, would strike them as pure bad faith on the director's part. *Shallow Grave* pulls back slightly for the handsaw scenes, but not to worry; Boyle is reserving his forces for the grand finale. As the story reached the last twist of the knife, I looked around me and saw people having a great time—smiling, unshockable, Tarantino-trained. Everything is comedy now, or ripe for comic attack. What will it take to make us look away?

FEBRUARY 13, 1995

PRIEST

Priest is destined, and designed, to get people hot under the collar. Any kind of collar, regular as well as dog. The movie lashes out with such wounded scorn that no one in the audience can hope to escape untouched. The devout will be incensed; the faithless will be furious; newspaper columnists will feel an itching at their fingertips; many gay-rights advocates will be driven round the bend; and those who were molested as children will find their memories starting to flood. Anyone not covered by the above will need a stiff drink.

The movie, directed by Antonia Bird, is set in Liverpool, which remains one of the strongholds of English Catholicism, not least because it has been fortified by a continuing influx of Irish Catholics. Whether you could call the city a rock of the true faith is another matter; communities in England have a habit of soldiering on and protecting their own long after the beliefs that fired and molded them have fallen away. What you end up with looks solid but rings hollow, and this is the sorry situation that greets young Father Greg Pilkington (Linus Roache) when he arrives in Liverpool, aflame with zeal. He is unyielding in his views, and declaims them to a suspicious congregation. As a priest, he says, he must be concerned with the soiling and cleansing of the particular soul, not with the scapegoat of "that mythical beast called society."

Even as he speaks, the movie is preparing to set the poor guy up. You just know he's going to get butted by the scapegoat. Antonia Bird's camera is all too keen to inspect the social conditions that have failed to move Father Greg—in the tower blocks, for instance, where he tries to spread the word, only to have doors slammed in his face. Greg's stiff-backed reserve contrasts unfavorably with the shaggy manner of his fellow priest Father Matthew (Tom Wilkinson). The two share a house: Greg is seen eating alone and reading the London *Times;* Matthew takes the more liberal *Guardian*, bawls his way through karaoke night with the locals, and sleeps with the housekeeper.

Greg doesn't sleep with anyone, not at first. But you can tell what's coming, and with whom. One evening, he hangs up his ecclesiastical garb and reaches to the back of the closet for another uniform—a leather jacket. Soon he is cruising downtown on his bicycle, hitting a gay bar, picking up a man named Graham, and having breathy sex under soft light. Well, don't be so shocked. What did you expect? If the left-winger happily screws the housekeeper, it follows that the doctrinal conservative, the emotional miser, must be a repressed homosexual. The film is so good at snaring you in its convictions that you don't think twice about the logic of this—you hardly think once. In fact, it isn't logic at all; it's merely prejudice, stitching its sly patterns. How much more interesting if Father Matthew had been the one with the guilty secret, with a little closed door at the back of his open mind, and if Greg had fallen in love with the housekeeper, or else—and this would have been the sharpest shock of all—if he really had been celibate.

You might think that *Priest* is already brimming over with issues, but there's more: on top of urban decay and gay clergy we get child abuse. (Don't expect a repeat of *The Boys of St. Vincent*, though; these priests aren't *that* bad.) A young girl comes for confession and tells Father Greg that she is being raped regularly, and secretly, by her father. Our hero is thus imprisoned in the oldest and clammiest of priestly dilemmas, the one that got Montgomery Clift in such a pickle in *I Confess:* How can you see justice done while preserving the sanctity and confidentiality of the confessional? In this case, things aren't exactly helped when the tampering parent himself (William Pugh) turns up to menace Greg. "Keep your nose out of my business," he says, before elaborating on his obsession: "Incest is human. It's the most natural thing in the world. It's the one thing we'd all like to do." Oh, great, precisely what we need: not just a molester but a molestation *expert*, an incest wonk. Pugh is wonderfully cast: his moon-round face might once have been kindly, you suspect, and that's why it now looks so piggish with lust. The movie needed only to glance at the man in order to convey the bafflement and the brutality that drive such furtive deeds; but it has to give him a cause, and a big speech.

The writer of *Priest* is Jimmy McGovern, who comes to movies fresh from a lively stretch in British television: he wrote *Cracker*, a series about a police psychologist, and a secondary-school drama called *Hearts and Minds.* If they were more talked about than anything else on TV, that's because, short of buying a pair of earmuffs, you couldn't escape the sensation of being talked *at.* McGovern raises hectoring to the level of an art, though not a fine art; the result sounds like Brecht with good jokes, which makes a change from Brecht. Antonia Bird stuffs all the McGovern themes into less than two hours and wads them tight: the characters fight the system—the Catholic Church, the dysfunctional family—with muscles so clenched and quivering that you start to wonder what the system did to deserve all this. The sole purpose of its existence, apparently, is to hang there like a punching bag and get pummelled. McGovern certainly doesn't provide any real characters to argue the case for the system: once Greg's homosexuality becomes public knowledge, his clerical opponents include a scowling throwback who condemns him over the dinner table in Latin and a bishop who hisses, "The best way for you to serve God is to piss off out of my diocese."

Father Matthew will have none of it. "Bugger the bishop," he says to Greg, adding, "Don't take that literally." This keeps on happening: just when the movie is straining too hard and testing your patience, it wins you back with a nice low gag. Tom Wilkinson is exactly right for these moments; large and loping, he turns Matthew's textbook charity back into something recognizably human. McGovern and Bird want to make him stand for something, but he prefers to slob around, doing good in the way that other people get drunk. Wilkinson makes a great foil for Linus Roache, flesh to his bone; and you believe in this growing friendship, because the physical (and wholly unsexual) comedy of it suggests an ease and a tolerance lacking in the rest of the movie. Angular and brittle with worry, Roache's Greg is a hybrid of Stan Laurel and Cardinal Newman, and he needs a Hardy around—someone to annoy and trust in. He can tell Matthew, as he can tell nobody else, how useless it is to try to put things right with a little time and reflection. "I'm reconciled to my nature! Cue the uplifting music," he says. Fair enough, but there's one problem: time and again, the movie literally does cue the uplifting music, just one of the ways in which it keeps rigging the evidence. It does this so blatantly and forcefully that, against your better judgment, you feel yourself being swayed. (That may be one definition of a successful picture.) Greg attends a wake, and finds the smashed mourners singing "Great Balls of Fire" and collapsing into a weepy stupor. Why, I wondered, should we buy this gleaming portrait of working-class solidarity but not Greg's protestations of faith?

What you make of *Priest* will be decided by what you think of the prayer scene. This comes when Father Greg, aghast at his moral impotence in the case of the young girl, kneels by his bed and confronts the crucifix on the wall. "Do something—don't just hang there, you smug, idle bastard," he rants. I always thought that George Herbert had more or less covered the subject when he called prayer "the soul in paraphrase, heart in pilgrimage," "exalted manna, gladness of the best," and a dozen other things, but I now realize that he left out "shouting match" and "student agitprop." Greg warms to his theme, reading his Saviour's mind without a qualm: "You wouldn't give a damn about the Church, with its rules and regulations"—and so on, with the camera jockeying up and down to get the most acute angle on his exploding soul. Leaving aside the fact that some of those rules were laid down at the Last Supper, you can't help finding it odd that the mild-mannered Greg should now be addressing Christ in the style of a Liverpool soccer fan haranguing the referee. But this, I guess, is how *Priest* makes its mark: McGovern and Bird are prepared to sacrifice a little character in the interests of the plot, which must, at all costs, surge onward and knock the breath out of the audience. Their plan works, of course, and Greg's prayers appear to be answered: you leave the theatre winded and floundering, take time out, and then start to argue about what it all meant.

It doesn't mean much, apart from the obvious warning to keep away from institutions. That's down-to-earth advice, and you can hardly blame *Priest* for being a worldly film. Modern cinema is, let's face it, the most thoroughly secular medium in history—although anyone who argues that the universe is entirely random or entirely malign has yet to be introduced to the work of Audrey Hepburn. What bugged me about *Priest* was that it's a secular movie pretending to be a religious movie; it presumes to dramatize a range of religious emotions while refusing to take seriously, or even to notice, the beliefs that sponsored them. (This stubbornness, rather than any histrionic jeering at the Redeemer, pushes the work close to blasphemy, but, even so, I wouldn't want Rome to call down some thunderous Liverpudlian *fatwa* on the distributors.) McGovern seems to think that he's broken the code of spiritual need, that he's cracked this old-fashioned game; he ponders his characters psychologically, and often does so with dexterity and wit, but it seems never to have crossed his mind that the impulse toward faith may begin where psychology leaves off, and that the ensuing struggles may unfold far beyond its reach.

Priest feels less like a movie than like really good television; and, indeed, it was originally written to be a four-part series for the BBC. Its punches are thrown with passion but no style: you long for more grace notes, for breathing space, for the depth of detail that could help you to inhabit the priestly world. Whatever Greg says, a few *more* rules and regulations would have come in handy. Even in a film like *True Confessions*, whose careful blankness was no match for the intensity of *Priest*, the camera studied De Niro going about his ritual business as if it were genuinely curious about him, about the motors of his devotion; whereas Antonia Bird just follows the path laid down by the screenplay, which starts with the assumption that we understand Father Greg only too well and that all we need to do is track his folly to its close. But it's one hell of a close: an all-out wrencher, the kind that leaves the popcorn actually embedded in your palms. It happens during a celebration of Mass; even the director must have been overwhelmed, since she doesn't give us a simple establishing shot to clarify what's going on, which is that nobody is lining up to receive the Host from Father Greg. Finally, one person finds the courage to act, and thus the two central victims of the film are reconciled. Only afterward, as you walk away, do you realize what a weird form the reconciliation has taken: a *hug*. What ever happened to kneeling?

MARCH 27, 1995

DON JUAN DEMARCO

Don Juan DeMarco begins with a ritual that reeks of vanity and gallantry. Perfume is sprayed on male wrists, hands are eased into thick leather gauntlets, impossibly fine features are hidden away behind a black mask. We seem to have stumbled into the world of Rudolph Valentino and Douglas Fairbanks, that lost age when a masked man meant seduction rather than stalk-and-slash; but, just as we're adjusting ourselves to the climate of a costume picture, our man wanders out into the streets of modern New York, where a long, flowing cape counts as dressing down. People barely give him a second look. So who is he? Is he a jerk or a superhero? Neither, in fact, and that's the load-bearing joke of the movie: he is exactly what he seems to be—Don Juan. Entering a hotel dining room, he sits down opposite a lone woman, schmoozes her, whisks her upstairs and into paradise, returns her to the table before her date arrives, and quits the scene. The date finally makes it, saying, "I hope you started without me."

Surveying this opening gambit, you wonder how long the fun can last; maybe the whole film will be a repeat performance, trekking doggedly from one sated body to the next until the audience dozes off under the influence of Warholian gross-out. But no, all this was a swan song. "Now I must die," Juan declares, and he climbs to the top of a billboard. He is calmed and brought down by a psychiatrist, Dr. Mickler, who has him committed to a mental hospital for temporary observation. Here, you think, the delusion should unravel at the seams: the Latin Lover will lose his touch, the boy wonder will dwindle back into a boy. It doesn't happen. Asked why he believes himself to be Don Juan, the patient, in turn, asks the shrink why *he* persists in "this fantasy that you are some Dr. Mickler." And that is the nub of the movie, the source of its charm: you can be perfectly aware of the difference between real and imagined lives and still find the imagined irresistible—not just liberating but actually more coherent.

Juan is the least disturbed person on the premises; he is wholly confident of his powers, and quickly turns the female staff into jitterbugs of desire. The hospital chief is soon complaining that "there are more nurses on Valium than patients."

The writer and director of *Don Juan DeMarco* is Jeremy Leven, who, together with the producer Francis Ford Coppola, has taken the flimsiest of ideas—no more than a skit, really—and somehow stretched it out to full length. The movie is sweet and simple, yet the simplicity is not so much retarded as unfussy, and that's quite an achievement these days. The plot requires, needless to say, that the psychiatrist be rejuvenated by the example of the lively spirit in his care; but Leven handles the transfusion of joie de vivre cleanly and—most important of all—treats it as a basically comic exchange. This is a blessed relief; remember the high school portentousness with which *Equus* nagged us about the enviable energy of the mad? And *Awakenings*, in its snuffling way, wasn't much better; movies have a terrible habit of assuming that the only purpose of affliction is to juice up the souls of those deputed to cure it. *Don Juan DeMarco* has no time for such loftiness; it just wants everyone to have a good time.

That demand is met in full, thanks to the presence of Marlon Brando. The movie is mostly kind enough to frame him in half length; when you eventually catch him in full figure, you can't help gasping—it's a long shot, but even at a distance Brando bulges outward like a man seen through a spyhole. He plays Dr. Mickler to Johnny Depp's Juan, and between them they toy with the rather placid script—there aren't that many big laughs in the picture—and flick it up to a level of grave playfulness that Leven can scarcely have envisaged. His film wasn't written with either star in mind, but it makes perfect sense as an extended riff on the fact that at least half the human race already finds Johnny Depp completely adorable. Once his hand has slipped into Juan's glove, he's snug in the role, and too smart to try and squeeze us for extra sympathy. If anything, he holds back, calmly taking Mickler through an erotic inventory of Juan's dream world as though he were running through a list of the week's groceries: in flashback we see the Don's idyllic boyhood in Mexico, the loss of his virginity at the bosom of a tutor (Talisa Soto, no actress but almost illegally gorgeous), his two-year stopover in an Arab harem, and so on. And all the while Brando sits there, nodding along, permitting himself the odd smile of fellow feeling, as if to say: Great story, kid, but you should have seen *me* in the old days.

One of the hazards of being Brando is that his deep-running talent for introspection, not to mention his capacity for stealing scenes even when he doesn't especially covet them, tends to pin him to the spotlight and elbow other performers into the wings. We think of *The Godfather* as a miracle of ensemble playing, but the fever of suspicion within it is so high that the men turn into monads, suits full of solitude, each of them desperate not to intrude upon the loneliness of the patriarch. Don Corleone was a cautionary triumph for Brando, reminding us how antisocial his genius can be, how he resists the democratic pairings which grace the skills of his peers. Bogart was a loner, too, but he reached out for Bacall and also, in passing, for Claude Rains and Walter Huston; no one, however, came out of *The Missouri Breaks* and thought, What a team—Brando and Nicholson. Brando took charge of that venture and made it sing to the tune of his lethal, self-entertaining jester. This was nothing new; he had been centrifugal from the start, even before he arrived in pictures—maybe even before he studied with Stella Adler. There is real madness in his Method, and the movies that respect that and lend it scope will be his legacy. His greatest and most frightening achievement remains *Last Tango in Paris*, an anti-love story which proved that the only sort of *amour* Brando could manage was *propre.* The whole career needs redefining; his work with Kazan has already begun to fade, for nothing dates more quickly or corrosively than strenuous lunges at realism. I saw *A Streetcar Named Desire* again last year, outdoors in Bryant Park, and around me people were giggling at its sweaty contrivance; the movie didn't need a giant screen—it was overblown to begin with.

Mild fantasy, on the other hand, appears to have a quite unwarranted staying power. (This may tell us something not altogether flattering about the nature of movies.) Nobody could mistake *Don Juan DeMarco* for a distinguished picture: the tanned and toasted look that Leven summons for his romantic sequences seems painfully obvious; the climax is badly flunked; and the Bryan Adams song during the closing credits drives you whimpering from the theatre. Yet the film does have something, a kind of weightless grace. When Mickler, starting to feel the effects of Juan's good will, wanders into the hospital with a bunch of tulips, presents a flower to his grouchy boss, and strolls down the corridor murmuring "*Fantástico,*" you sense Brando himself beginning to bloom. Maybe this is what he needs—not the hothouse of melodrama but the fresh air of light comedy. There's a touch of affectionate jousting in his scenes with Depp and with Faye Dunaway, who plays Mickler's wife. As the movie proceeds, Mickler borrows some of Juan's glory and seduces her afresh; they even share a bedroom scene, which is pretty heroic of them. It's the only movie I've ever seen in which the man pulls the sheets farther over his chest than the woman does; Dunaway has the kind of excited, awed look on her face that Ahab must have had when he drew alongside the white whale. At such moments, the film does what more ponderous projects have never quite been able to bring off: it lights up Brando and makes him take an interest in other people. Finally, in the dusk of his career, he becomes a credible hulk.

At the end of the credits, Leven has the nerve to claim that the character of his hero "is based in part on *Don Juan* by Lord Byron." This is pushing it; *Don Juan DeMarco* has no satirical bite to speak of, and Leven never dares, as Byron does, to mock the very exploits that he honors. When the movie tells us that Juan has taken to metaphysics, he is seen perched by a stream, struggling to look pensive. In a voice-over, he even quotes a scrap of the Byron poem, although he stops short of the poet's own proviso:

> If you think 'twas philosophy that this did,
> I can't help thinking puberty assisted.

If any of that worldliness finds its way into the movie, it does so via Brando, who has long cultivated a Byronic knack for cutting fantasy down to size. The delivery of his lines—lisping, chewy, privately amused—has some of the casual scorn with which *Don Juan* cracks the whip of its final couplets. Byron never took the poem to the end of Juan's life: "I had not quite fixed whether to make him end in Hell, or in an unhappy marriage, not knowing which would be the severest," he wrote in a letter. In its silly way, *Don Juan DeMarco* suggests a third option, less severe, but still in keeping with Byron's cheerful disillusion. How about this? Don Juan grows old and eccentric, swells into a butter mountain, has a troublesome protégé, and, every now and then, tries his hand at his old skills. He discovers, to his delight, that he still has the fire in his belly—more smolder than flare, true, but better than ash. And that, in turn, ignites a steady sadness, casting Don Juan back to a time when he, like Don Corleone—like Marlon Brando—was the best and most beautiful of all.

APRIL 10, 1995

BURNT BY THE SUN

This year's Academy Awards ceremony was, even by the standards of recent years, a real stiff. It takes a great wave of money and effort to create that kind of style-free zone. The one bright spot in a gloomy, graceless evening came with the arrival onstage of a large Russian gentleman with a wide smile, an even wider mustache, and a very small daughter. His name was Nikita Mikhalkov, and he was there to accept the award for Best Foreign Language Film for his latest picture, *Burnt by the Sun*. The little girl at his side was eight-year-old Nadia, and she appeared to be less fazed by the occasion than anyone else in the building. She stared out at the stars with equanimity, presumably asking herself what a Gump was and why everyone kept talking about it. The terrible thing about Oscar Night is that the true emotions sound even phonier than the phony ones, and this particular show was no exception. Award winners trotted up, gripped their statuettes, and proceeded to speed-thank their entire family tree: parents, grandparents, godparents, babies yet to be born, cave-dwelling ancestors on the Kalahari plains, DNA spirals. In the midst of all this, it was stirring to find a man who had brought his daughter with him for the very good reason that she was also his leading lady. At the end of his speech, Mikhalkov hauled her up with one hand and threw her onto his shoulder like a sack of potatoes. I'm only sorry that Quincy Jones didn't try the same thing with Oprah Winfrey.

What most of the audience couldn't have known was that this nonchalant gesture was a visual quotation from *Burnt by the Sun*, in which Mikhalkov happily performs the same hoist. Not only did he direct the movie and collaborate on the screenplay, with Rustam Ibragimbekov; he also plays the hero, a Red Army colonel named Sergei Kotov. Nadia Mikhalkov plays Kotov's daughter—also called Nadia, just to confuse the issue. She first appears naked, squatting like a jockey on her father's bare back and whipping him lightly with a brush of birch branches. There are probably people who have this sort of image delivered to them in a plain brown wrapper through the mail, but don't worry: it is a fine summer's day in 1936, and the Kotov family are merely enjoying a healthful steam in a rural hut. Kotov's young wife, Marusya (Ingeborga Dapkunaite), is there, too, half naked and smiling. Everything is just dandy: God's in his Heaven—or, at any rate, Stalin's in his Kremlin, which comes to the same thing—and all's right with the world.

The movie's charm, which runs pretty deep, arises from this unfashionable view of pleasure as something bountiful, close at hand, and casually attained. What makes the tale more than charming, and gives it real heft, is Mikhalkov's willingness to show that same pleasure dying in front of your eyes—to watch the poison of a political system creeping into the characters' veins. He has tried the trick twice before, in *A Slave of Love* and *Dark Eyes*, but this is the first time it has come off; for once, the bliss and the menace seem to flow from a single source. The plot of *Dark Eyes* rambled from Italy to Russia, and offered a turn-of-the-century period elegance that stretched and bulged into kitsch; the whole of *Burnt by the Sun*—apart from a short Moscow prologue and epilogue—is set in and around a single dacha on a single day, and the languor is curbed and compacted until it feels like a well-mannered offshoot of surrealism. There are still plenty of folk wandering around in soft white suits, but by the end they strike you as victims not of style but of history—inmates in a vast national asylum. The fact that the villain, Mitya (Oleg Menchikov), dresses like a dapper English cricketer somehow makes him even more lethal.

Kotov shares the house with his wife and daughter, plus a selection of elderly creatures whom I couldn't quite work out. There's nothing vague about this—just a pleasing sensation of surplus, which fits the movie nicely. (It's an action-packed picture, if by "action" you mean such violent pursuits as teacup-trembling, woodland soccer, and jumping fully clothed off river jetties.) I counted at least three grandma contenders in the Kotov home, but they could well have been aunts; there's also a friendly, fleshy maid, who starts to cry when her dusting prowess is called into question, and a relaxed old sport named Vsevolod who spends most of his time reading the paper, and whose immaculate apathy prompts an inspired gibe from one of the women. "You're like *Switzerland*," she says. Then, there is Kirik (Vladimir Ilyine), an uncle of sorts, whose role in life, if he has one, is almost as ill-defined as his sexuality. He minces, rides a bicycle in to breakfast, wears a hairnet, and kisses Mitya on the cheek—a bad move, by any measure. On the other hand, he also makes eyes at a visiting young woman, takes her to his bedroom, and makes her hold a soccer ball while he leeringly pumps it up.

Ilyine's performance is oversized and very nearly bad: a cadenza of pouts and frowns, of grimaces directed at nobody and provoked by nothing in particular. But Mikhalkov must have let him run, and the risk pays off: the acting mocks the trim-fitting politesse that tends to constrain this kind of production, roughing it up into bagginess. The movie is much less tasteful than it could have been, and all the more likable as a result. The master of this method, of course, was Jean Renoir: he would violate the strolling naturalism of his scenes by encouraging his players—Michel Simon, above all—to go for big, vaudeville gestures. This near-caricature works best in a pastoral setting, perhaps because it calls up memories, or myths, of lascivious satyrs: Boudu tumbles back into his element, the gliding Seine; the skinny young lecher in *Une Partie de Campagne* dances after his matronly prey with a panpipe, and twirls his mustache with a ridiculous flourish. (Kotov, in *Burnt by the Sun*, twirls his the same way.) Mikhalkov has none of Renoir's economy—his movie is over three times as long as *Une Partie de Campagne*, and rather more confused—but he has inherited some of Renoir's imaginative frankness. He openly confronts our expectations, saying, Yes, my character *is* larger than life, but that is your fault for finding life too small—there should be room for everyone, for everything under the sun.

And the sun is Stalin. It is his presence that reddens the movie with fear and apprehension. At one point, a giant balloon rises over a wheat field; hanging beneath it is a banner of the great leader himself—borne aloft by hot air into a clear sky, from which he can survey and scorch his people. Stalin's representative on earth is Mitya, the smooth young man who drops in to visit the Kotov family. At first, all is sweetness and light: Mitya knows something about everyone, something innocent and silly—you would think he had files on them all. He charms the elderly, delights the young, and casually smolders at his old flame, Marusya. The erotic play between these two is the best thing in the film: as Mitya continues his banter off-camera, Marusya stands backlit, with the sun shining through her dress, and listens, sapped of everything but the will to hear more. She falls into a sort of private slow motion, at once dozy and turned on, while life continues around her at normal speed; she tries to fill a glass from the tap, and the water wells smoothly over the rim. When she's drinking it, she gulps and swallows as if she were trying to fill herself up, or put out a fire.

This central section of the story shows Mikhalkov working at an extraordinary, intuitive pitch. He specializes in averted melodrama: a shard of broken bottle lies in wait for bare feet, but the feet keep missing it by an inch; Mitya plays the piano in the nude, but only Marusya sees the show—he's just out of our line of sight, and anyway what matters is the indignant giggle on her face. Whenever important events curve into view, Mikhalkov's attention wanders elsewhere, as if he were following up a rumor or tracing a whisper in the next room. You could accuse him of simply rehashing Chekhov, who specialized in offstage drama, in stories that unfolded at arm's length, but Mikhalkov has done something new: he has taken that technique and applied it to a political bad dream. To exist under Stalin was indeed to be heard by ears pressed to the wall—to do your own thing while someone else, close by, finalized plans to start doing it for you. When it emerges that Mitya is a member of Stalin's secret police, come to arrest Kotov on ludicrous charges, we are not remotely surprised; in the Soviet Union in 1936, there was not much difference between lover and spy.

Burnt by the Sun covers a lot of ground. As the long, lovely day descends into talk of treachery, and from there into boozing and bloody faces, we seem to leave Chekhov a thousand miles behind. "It's the aroma, the taste of life that has vanished," Vsevolod says. What touches you most is not the individual fates of the characters but a feeling that the nostalgic style has been found wanting—that, while Mikhalkov has disinterred the graceful past, a delicate shroud has fallen away and exposed something wormy and decayed. All of which makes the movie sound about as cheery as a game of strip chess with Uncle Joe himself, yet, oddly, it *is* good for the spirits. It may have been the serpentine Mitya who tried to seduce Marusya, but it is Sergei who picks up the scent of arousal: husband and wife have great afternoon sex in the loft—all the spicier for a pinch of jealousy. As the happiness starts to flicker, Mikhalkov keeps an eye out for signs of life, and he finds them in unlikely places. Many of them come from Nadia Mikhalkov, who gives one of those penetrating, absolutely uncute performances with which children sometimes startle the most grownup of movies: "You're eating because you've been drinking," Nadia says to Kirik, an accusation against which there is no defense. When a long black car arrives to collect her father—and, in so doing, to pluck her life clean of all joy—she goes out to greet it, studies her reflection in the headlight, and tidies her hair. She is sweetly serious, and she makes the murderous types in the car look like infant goons. They drive Kotov away, warning him not to do anything stupid. "Like what?" he asks. "I did the stupid things ages ago." Does he mean the mistakes he made or the fun he had? Sexy and involving, scrappy and laid-back, *Burnt by the Sun* is a wonderful reminder of the basic human right to do the wrong thing.

MAY 8, 1995

BRAVEHEART

There are many amazing things about *Braveheart.* There are Scotsmen with blue faces beating the crap out of wicked Brits. There are horses thundering into a thicket of extra-long, supersharp staves. There is every kind of mortal blow: one guy loses his head, another is stretched out like human chewing gum, a third has a leg whipped off by a single slash of a sword. This being the depths of the Middle Ages, there is a lot of shouting, and a lot of rain. There is everything the picture books tell you to expect: a flaming fort, a battering ram, a flood of boiling pitch. But, above all, two-thirds of the way through a film that lasts almost three hours, there is the sound of Mel Gibson speaking Latin.

That takes real courage, but Gibson has already proved his commitment in the world beyond. The obsequies seem to go on forever: the bodies are buried at a Christian ceremony, after which a little girl comes shyly up to William and gives him a *thistle.* I thought, I'm out of here. Then it's off to a memorial service, conducted at night amid artfully lit fog and skirling music, plus running commentary from William's gnarled uncle (Brian Cox). "The pipes are saying goodbye in their own way," he explains. So why stop there? If the pipes get to say goodbye, why not have the shaggy Highland cattle do a flypast or something? The movie is so eager to cover all the bases, to sprawl and scatter its way into epic, that you wonder whether it will ever find its focus.

Not to worry. William is taken away for a few years of education (that's how he picks up the Latin). As his father once told him, "It's our wits that make us men." This, of course, is the well-established movie code for "Let me teach you how to swing a spiky ball on the end of a long chain." By the time we next see the lad, he has turned—bingo!—into Mel Gibson. Whatever they were putting in his porridge, it did the trick, for this is where the movie kicks into life. Now a solid young man, Wallace goes to a wedding, where he makes friends with his former playmate Hamish (Brendan Gleeson) and makes eyes at the thistle giver, who has grown into a beauty named Murron (Catherine McCormack). The ceremony is interrupted by a local lord, who has come to claim his feudal right: to sleep with the new wife. The protesting husband is held back as the bride (Julie Austin) glides serenely toward her fate in a kind of stricken trance, her half smile telling the assembled company that she can sail above this dirty squabble and survive. It's an extraordinary sight, the first hint of something beyond historical schlock. You see it in Catherine McCormack, too, in her broad Bruegel face. As Murron, she has little to do except fall in love with the hero, but she reinforces the sense that the women in the movie are wiser than the men, and that their dignity shames not just the malice of the villains but the compulsive bravado of Wallace himself. McCormack's final close-up, as she looks up and weeps with a knife at her throat, is one of the great swooning death shots, not far off Falconetti in *The Passion of Joan of Arc.*

Until this point, Wallace has claimed to be a peaceful soul. You don't actually believe him, but you realize that it will take something serious to ignite the man; hence the murder of his beloved Murron, at the hands of the English. We don't actually see Wallace's reaction to the news—we skip to the next stage, when he has had time to settle his nerves and prepare for action. There's a fearsome, long-lens image of Gibson riding through flames into the village where the English are encamped; then we get a brief pause, a cruel minute or two in which to savor the tension; finally, just as we're giving up hope, all Mel breaks loose. Gibson has always thrived on pent-up sensation, and when you see him hurling his sword like a tomahawk or advancing upon Murron's killer with pure retribution in his face, you can understand why he coiled the movie up so tight before letting it go. The strongest speech in the whole film consists simply of Wallace roaring "Hold! . . . Hold!" to his men as they face an oncoming charge, and it strikes you as the ideal motto for Gibson, both as director and as star. Ever since *Gallipoli,* his calm has been primed with something explosive: you can feel it in his quick snake eyes, which glance around for trouble, and in the cheeky snap of his line readings, invariably a little faster than you expect. From its title, *Braveheart* sounds more like a charity than like a movie, and you sometimes catch Gibson struggling to keep a straight face as he surges from one fine, upstanding deed to the next. At one point, he even has to rear his horse and wave, like the Lone Ranger; it's the medieval equivalent of doing a wheelie on your first motorbike. He would fain be cool.

* * *

Once Murron is dead and avenged, the film gathers pace, following what sounds like a plot but is in fact an anger-management session attended by approximately ten thousand people. The Scots are angry because the British are tyrannical, and the British are angry because the Scots are mischievous and unwashed—in short, not British. The two sides work out their differences with a variety of lethal weapons, but at least the violence onscreen is spasmodic, whereas the assault on the audience, as we sit there getting whacked over the head with cultural stereotypes, is pretty well unstoppable. Patrick McGoohan tries to work some calculation, some mental seasoning, into his playing of the English king, but the film is concerned only with broad strokes. The monarch is a monster, "a cruel pagan known as Edward Longshanks"; his son is a precious blond, married to a sex-starved French princess (Sophie Marceau); his noblemen sit on their horses (wearing bright orange, like traffic cops) and sneer at the opposing side. Over there, meanwhile, the talk is of freedom and justice; the Scots bare their genitals, rumps, and souls to anyone who will watch. The anti-British feeling is rampant in this film, as it was in the recent *Rob Roy:* British blood, especially of the true-blue taint, exists only to be shed. Ireland used to be Hollywood's arena for such sentiments, but the current cease-fire in Ulster makes it vaguely unsuitable; I'm not even sure that *Far and Away* or *The Crying Game* could get made at the moment. Celtic fervor has been shifted over to Scotland; the British are still bastards, but now they swivel north, not west, to confront their enemy. There's a lovely, quiet joke near the end of the movie, after the princess has at long last found herself a real man: bending low, murmuring into the ear of the dying Longshanks, she makes it clear that the entire line of English kings will henceforth spring from the seed of William Wallace. One up to Scotland.

Our hero's finest hour, therefore, takes place in bed, although to me it looked more like a finest minute, the briefest of Highland flings; what really turns him on is a nice, long bloodbath. The battle sequences are easily the best reason to see this film. They are thronged and unashamed, among the most ebullient since Olivier led out his men in *Henry V.* Everyone remembers the dense, thrumming arrow showers that flocked through the air of Agincourt like iron starlings; Gibson tries a different trick—he closes the camera in on each volley, until you can see individual arrows in flight and hear their soft whistle. Where Olivier went for the grand sweep, Gibson deals in vicious impressionism, a frenzy of sharpened details. His editor is Steven Rosenblum, who worked on *Glory,* a movie that felt suspiciously gracious even at its most frantic. For *Braveheart,* though, Rosenblum has accelerated the rhythm of the fighting until there's simply no time for poignancy or polish; he matches the hacking

Scotsmen, cut for cut. The fun thing is that if you turn green and shut your eyes the mayhem will actually get worse, because the *sound* of flesh under siege has been cranked up to abattoir levels. I would pay a lot of money to see this movie with a vegetarian.

What brings Wallace low, in the end, is not swordplay but duplicity. He is bored and impatient with political intrigue, and the movie shares his problem. It wakes up for warfare, but gets bogged down in bickering nobles and stumbles unerringly into Monty Python land. "Excuse me, Sire, but there's a very urgent message from York," a royal messenger declares. It's hard to work out what makes that line so deliciously wrong; maybe it's the wild historical gesture of "Sire" in the middle of a perfectly normal office conversation. The anachronisms pile up; and with them a feeling that Gibson's only reason for pillaging the past is to find fodder for an action movie. The result is the opposite of *Rob Roy*, which was all about the means—sometimes honorable, sometimes sly—of avoiding action. It, too, twisted the facts, but, unlike *Braveheart*, it somehow felt true to its time, with a salty, literate script that opened up foul mouths and hot appetites in every social class. It was much the better film, twenty times as intelligent and moody; and yet, looking back, I have to admit that *Braveheart* offers something that *Rob Roy* lacks. Gibson's picture, in its very want of taste, in its willingness to go all out and strive for effect, answers the craving for vulgarity that lurks in every moviegoer. Watching it, we come closer than ever to grasping just what it was that drove our parents to watch Victor Mature films. What is most thrilling about *Braveheart* remains inextricable from all that is most ridiculous. When you hear the battlefield cry of "Take out their archers!" you start to laugh. Then you think, Go on, guys, take 'em out. Faster, Pussycat! Kilt! Kilt!

JUNE 5, 1995

THE BRIDGES OF MADISON COUNTY

When I first heard that *The Bridges of Madison County* was being turned into a movie, I was overjoyed. Here, finally, was something sure and true, a rock of reliability in an uncertain world. Whatever else happened in the pictures this year, *The Bridges of Madison County* would not let us down. It *had* to be a turkey—proud and preening, right at the center of the farmyard. Other films would sicken and stun, and divide public opinion. Not this one: it would bind our wounds, bring us together in a common act of mockery. The novel it is based on, written by Robert James Waller, was the worst book in living memory; if the movie had any integrity, any guts, it would honor that achievement. And now look what happens. The film comes out, and guess what? *It's really not bad.*

The trouble started when they gave the project to Clint Eastwood, a man whose bullshit detector has been turned up to maximum for thirty years. (He both stars and directs.) Things didn't get much better when Meryl Streep was cast opposite him: she is quoted in the publicity material as saying, "I was blind to the book's power," which may be a polite way of saying she took one sip of Waller's prose and had to call for a stomach pump. The task of turning that prose into a script—into clear English, for a start—went to Richard LaGravenese, who wrote *The Fisher King*, *The Ref*, and *A Little Princess*. Plenty of quirkiness there, but none of the jello-headed schmalz that Waller fans would be praying for when their sacred text became a motion picture. Who could be trusted to keep the flame alive? It was easy to see how you could maintain the novel's clean, classical grasp of action—"She rose and dropped dumplings into boiling water"—but what about the potency of its hero, Robert Kincaid? "I am the highway and a peregrine and all the sails that ever went to sea," he says modestly, and how can a mere movie convey all that? There was only one flicker of hope: In the novel, Kincaid drives a truck that he calls Harry, and, what with those hours on the Iowa back roads, Harry gets dirty. Didn't the Eastwood fellow already make a film about that?

The plot is simple enough. A nice lady named Francesca Johnson (Meryl Streep) lived in Madison County with her husband, Richard (Jim Haynie), and their two children. One fine day, she was left alone while the rest of the family went off to do something with a cow at the state fair. They were gone four whole days, but Francesca was never bored, because during that time she looked after the house, went shopping, and committed adultery. A tall man by the name of Kincaid (Clint Eastwood) dropped by to ask directions. He was a photographer, and she accompanied him when he went to shoot the famous covered bridges that so enhance this lovely corner of America. (During their visit, the weather went from gray to bright very quickly, and the continuity person was sent to bed without any supper.) Kincaid seemed nice, just like Francesca, and soon she had him scraping carrots at the sink. The next evening, they made love, and Kincaid made her see that she had been trapped in lifeless erotic stagnation—and stultifying bourgeois complacency, too! Soon the tall, nice sex machine had to be on his way, and he asked the stagnant lady to come along, but she decided to stay. Richard and the children came back with great news: their steer had won first prize. Francesca was very pleased, and lived happily in stultifying bourgeois complacency ever after.

There are two ways to treat this tale. Either you can puff it up into something lush and operatic, as Waller did, and run the risk of portentousness, or you can nail it down into something tight and desperate, as Eastwood does, and incur the wrath of the people who preferred the other option. The first indication that his good taste—or, at any rate, his natural leaning toward the downbeat—may see him through the nonsense comes in the opening credits. I was expecting a fat, violin-fed score to start drooling all over us, but we don't hear a note. The uneventful landscape looks more ominous than inviting, and it makes you wonder what events will unroll here. If you didn't know Waller's story, you might think that the picture was heading for *In Cold Blood* territory, on the brink of some random, rustic bloodletting.

The suspicion lingers during the early scenes in Francesca's house. The production designer, Jeannine Oppewall, has done something cunning with the place, clammed up its heart. You can sense this in the rat browns and other drab colors, and also in the looming of the walls: the rooms appear to have been constructed one size too small, so that everyone within looks pinched and squeezed. The first people we see here are

Francesca's grown-up children, Carolyn (Annie Corley) and Michael (Victor Slezak), who have arrived to set matters straight after their mother's death. The central love story will evolve in flashback as they root through her letters, diaries, photographs, and other suspiciously well-organized junk. They are shocked by an old photograph of their mother in middle age; Michael's wife, looking over their shoulders, says, "She's not wearing a bra." The audience, meanwhile, is in even deeper shock; here we are, watching an adaptation of a Robert James Waller novel, and there are *jokes* in it. Carolyn's indignation slowly sharpens to a point: "Now I find out that in between bake sales my mother was Anaïs Nin."

The flashbacks present their mother as a sensitive, suffering soul—so sensitive that she is, in fact, Italian. In the novel, Francesca has "the smallest trace of an accent." Not here she doesn't. Let's face it: if Meryl Streep gets a sniff of the word "accent," she's not going to turn up her nose and walk away. She's going to take a deep breath and pounce. Please welcome the winner of the Madison County Anna Magnani Imitation Contest, 1965. The impression is rounded out with an appetite for grand opera and with hefty hips and a maternal bust; contrary to the report, one thing that Francesca is definitely wearing is a bra, and there's all manner of cladding built into the superstructure. Mind you, anyone can trot off to makeup and get fleshed out; only Streep could develop the perfect walk to match her new figure—a swinging stroll that tells both of rank boredom and of half-forgotten voluptuousness. Even better is her trick of dabbing strands of hair away from the side of her face with a flick of the hand; the camera catches her doing this as she gazes away from the breakfast table, where her family is pigging out in silence. At the end of her tether, she finds grace.

I have always been scared of Meryl Streep. She's brilliant, but the shine is that of an Ice Queen. One reason it's so hard to warm to her is that she visibly refuses to stop thinking about her performances; the recent escapes into high adventure *(The River Wild)* and broad comedy *(Death Becomes Her)* were intended as a change of gear, but you could still see the engine whirring away in her head. The big question, in fact, is whether *life* becomes her. Middle-period De Niro made you feel the same way; observing the two of them in *Falling in Love*, as they went through the precisely calibrated motions, was like watching Karpov versus Kasparov. *The Bridges of Madison County*, in its early stages, looks like another showcase for Streep and her Amazing Technical Command, but something weird happens. She and Eastwood get it together—they very nearly get down. They hit a steady, smiling rhythm; the movie is dreary when it comes to the main act of sex (though not as dull as the "orgasms of the mind" invoked by Waller), but the warmup routines—the flirting, the aimless joshing around the kitchen—feel not only skilled but sincere. Big news, I guess: Clint and Meryl melt. I'm surprised the bridges didn't get washed away.

Eastwood is the last great monolith, but even monoliths should let other people chip away at them; it does not reflect well on the Eastwood image that his most popular sidekick was covered with orange hair and ate a lot of fruit. Streep is his first real equal in a long time; you have to go back to 1984, to Geneviève Bujold in *Tightrope*, to track down the last strong woman in an Eastwood movie. (Maybe Wolfgang Petersen's *In the Line of Fire* loosened him up—the patter with Rene Russo, the hot line to John Malkovich.) On the other hand, there is an air of lonely sacrifice about *The Bridges of Madison County:* Clint has to clench his fists and spout garbage. He can't afford to lose the entire Waller vote at the box office, and therefore, while he and his screenwriter have surgically removed most of the horrors that grew in the original text, a few have been left more or less intact. For all you Kincaid wanna-bes out there, Mr. Eastwood has kindly agreed to say a few lines.

Here are some of your favorites: "I'm a citizen of the world." "I love people. I'd like to meet 'em all." And the vastly surprising "Good stuff, Yeats." (If only he were addressing an Irish sheriff or something, but no. He really is talking about poetry.) There's a hunk of baloney devoted to Africa, all about "the cohabitation of man and beast," but worse is to come: at one point, taking Waller at his word, Clint Eastwood wears a pair of *sandals.* What ever for? You don't see the Dalai Lama packing a .44 Magnum. The footwear was a bad omen; I could feel the spirit of Waller wafting into the proceedings like tear gas, and recalled his description of Kincaid as "half-man, half-something-else creature." Look out! Suddenly, without warning, Francesca starts to deliver her own voice-overs: she lies in the bathtub, stares at the drip on the rim of the shower head, and reels off a meditation about how "intensely erotic" the guy downstairs is. I think we had already gathered that, but thanks anyway. Then there's an endless dinner scene, in which the lovers thrash out the question of whether Francesca will or, alternatively, will not leave her husband. Make up your damn minds, people. If Kincaid is such a citizen of the world, why doesn't he just stash her in the trunk of dirty Harry and take off?

It's worth sticking around for their final, speechless encounter, a wonderfully shot sequence of trucks passing in the rain. Most of *The Bridges of Madison County* has a nicely curbed poignancy; if Spielberg had taken the helm, as he once threatened to do, you would have found a box of ten-ply tissues under your seat. What you remember about the movie, looking back, has nothing to do with love. It's the seam of anger running through it, the unexpected sneer in Francesca's diatribe against Iowa: "I'm supposed to say it's quiet and people are nice." Later, when she turns on Kincaid and labels him a hypocrite and a phony, you realize what Streep and Eastwood are doing. They aren't concealing Robert James Waller, or carrying on despite him, or pretending he isn't there. They're at war with him. *The Bridges of Madison County* is a half-good, half-something-else film, but it's a bold one, because it slights what it was meant to esteem. It shrugs at that whole strain of dumb pastoral folly and at the ten million suckers who fell for it. It drops the dumpling.

JUNE 19, 1995

FIRST KNIGHT

First Knight is set in Arthurian times, but the plot is far more recent. A proud beauty is torn by her desire for two men: the father figure who will never fail her and the tricky loner who will turn her heart to mush. In other words, Columbia Pictures presents *Casablanca* in shining armor. The lady is Guinevere (Julia Ormond), who is slated to wed King Arthur (Sean Connery), the Christian ruler whose moral rectitude is as deep as a moat. But the marriage is threatened by Lancelot, the lover boy (Richard Gere), who is neurotically insistent on rescuing Guinevere whenever she gets into trouble. This happens practically all the time, thanks to the foul intentions of Prince Malagant (Ben Cross), the Major Strasser of merry England.

With all this regular kidnapping, Julia Ormond never has a chance to try her hand at the standard activities of courtly heroines. She never has to plait bullrushes, pick herbs for monks, hand-rear forest fawns, or anything stupid like that. What she does find time for is a game of soccer—or, at any rate, an early version of soccer, which consists of booting an inflated bit of pig into a hole. She treats Richard Gere in much the same way when he turns up in her life, and you can't blame her. Lancelot finds Guinevere being hunted by Malagant's men, saves her maidenhood, and then has the gall to make a move on her, as if the maidenhood weren't worth much in the first place. She, being a trainee queen, gives him a topspin slap. "I can tell when a woman wants me," he croons, holding steady for a major close-up. You can see what Gere is up to. He isn't even bothering to behave or think in period; he's simply transferring his usual act—the slim-eyed supercreep, calm as marble—to an ancient landscape, and trusting that everyone will fall for it. It's a new take on Lancelot: Arthurian Gigolo.

If you think about it, this makes a kind of sly sense. Barely a scrap of Malory or Tennyson has survived in Hollywood's rehashes of the Camelot myth, and in the case of *First Knight* the bones of the story are barer than ever; but one aspect that strikes home to modern viewers is a suspicion that Lancelot's devotion to Guinevere is only a whisker away from self-obsession. I know that ceaseless worship of a lady was part of the ten-point plan for knightly perfection, but in severe cases the love was so consuming that the lady didn't really matter. Guinevere could have picked up her soccer ball and gone to the beach for a week, and Lancelot wouldn't have noticed. The oiled and pensive cool of Richard Gere may be laughable, but it's not so misguided as to wreck the movie. The whole production, in fact, lies just this side of ridiculous. It is heaped with anachronisms—I was especially keen on the pulley-powered speedboat rigged up by Malagant's men—but the director, Jerry Zucker, and his screenwriter, William Nicholson, are smart enough to see that Camelot was an anachronism to begin with. Squashed under the myth, the historical facts are so slender and uncertain that you might as well go with the myth, and shake it up to suit your fancy. Even Malory's *Le Morte d'Arthur*, the grandest tour of the Round Table, was a medieval expansion of old, inherited tales; John Boorman felt free to refashion them as a Wagnerian saga in *Excalibur*; and if Jerry Zucker now chooses to interpret *Le Morte d'Arthur* by having his villain ride in and shout, "Nobody move or Arthur dies!"—well, good luck to him.

I must confess I was worried about this movie. I had *First Knight* nerves. Zucker is a well-known parody addict, having worked on *Airplane!* and the *Naked Gun* series, and there was a moment, as the lights went down, when I found myself praying that *First Knight* would turn out to be a spoof after all. Maybe we had been duped by a watertight publicity campaign into thinking that Zucker was making a serious movie, whereas all along he had been secretly shooting footage of Priscilla Presley as the Lady of the Lake. But it was foolish of me to expect a distinction between spoof and serious, since any decent movie about King Arthur has to be both. When Guinevere is first welcomed to Camelot, the knights form diagonal, intersecting lines, then part in front of her like the Red Sea to reveal their king. Heaven knows who dreamed up this ersatz ceremony, but it's impressively silly, and Julia Ormond manages to keep a straight face as she processes through the ranks. The same goes for the armor: the knights cover their forearms in silver tin cans that could hardly fend off a barbecue skewer, let alone a broadsword. But it lends an air of general spiffiness, and that's what counts. For his part, Sean Connery has to walk around with a bright, polished mini-shield strapped to one shoulder. It looks like a pet bidet.

King Arthur should have been a stroll for Connery, but the movie gives him a surprisingly rough ride. It's not just the bidet—it's the fact that the bidet is all he needs. In the big battle scene, Arthur hangs back and surveys the action, too slow and senior to pitch in. In Connery's previous pictures, his age was seldom referred to; like his unchanging accent, his years served only to toughen his leathery appeal. But *First Knight* plays up the gap between Arthur and Guinevere: he was a friend of her father, who once asked, "Do all fathers think their daughters are so beautiful?" It's a line that Arthur quotes approvingly to his beloved, thus snaring the movie in an Electra complex. The plot demands that he be cuckolded and humiliated, enfeebled by love and unable to arouse Guinevere, whose hormones are stampeding in another direction; in the end, he relinquishes everything he holds dear. The sight of Connery contemplating his own weakness is disconcerting; you're so used to watching his features stiffen with authority or curl into that canny half smile that when they suddenly grow crumpled and thunderous you're not sure how to react. I was reminded of *Ghost*, in which the same director encouraged Patrick Swayze to become a cauldron of grief. True, the result looked like a man teetering for all eternity on the brink of a giant sneeze, but Zucker is obviously skilled at luring actors onto unfamiliar ground.

First Knight is busy and unpretentious, and firmly resistant to the strain of mysticism that seems to infect any movie set before the year 1500. As usual, there are too many table-thumping speeches designed to publicize freedom, truth, blood loyalty, and so on, although I guess they come in handy when the movie needs to change pace. They insure that for a few minutes, at least, we won't have to watch milk-white stallions in meadows or happy peasants preparing to get happier still. ("There'll be some feasting today, I tell you!") As pageant pictures go, *First Knight* obeys a peculiar rhythm: the driving forces of the plot—Guinevere's tug of love, Malagant's killer crewcut—are established so swiftly that, from there on, the players just circle round fulfilling their essential natures over and over again. It's hard to pinpoint the climaxes even after they've happened (which may also be Guinevere's problem with Arthur). Zucker bravely decided to stage his biggest battle at night—you can't really see what's going on, and you're not meant to. It swells into a confusing clatter of darkness, with the only light provided by fiery arrows and blades reflecting the moon. In one sublime long shot, from a high vantage point, the struggle for the soul of England looks like an uprising in a cutlery drawer.

This is far more beautiful than exciting; for a movie dedicated to valor, in fact, *First Knight* fights fairly shy of thrills. It was designed by John Box, who worked on *Lawrence of Arabia* and other David Lean epics, and, as with Lean, the decorum is so finely thought through that every now and then you long for something—a minor character, a stray line—to bust out and disturb the pattern. I loved the look of Malagant's stronghold, a jagged slate horror sliced by Piranesi shadows; but Camelot is annoyingly spruce, and the recurring overhead views of the Round Table itself, epicenter of all human virtue, tended to prompt heretical thoughts of Vanna White. *First Knight* is perhaps too solid and foursquare to be thoroughly entertaining; what the whole enterprise lacks—what makes it melt from the mind—is the kind of breeziness that graced the costume hokum of earlier years. When Jacques Tourneur or Raoul Walsh made a swashbuckler, or when Michael Curtiz found a way for Errol Flynn to misbehave without going to jail, you felt that everyone concerned was enjoying the trip. I'm sure that Jerry Zucker loves those movies; he's just unfortunate enough to be living in an age that likes its heroes to be introspective and its values to be hammered home. When Julia Ormond flings a marauding thug out of her carriage so that he smacks face first into a tree, you cheer like crazy; when Richard Gere sits and broods in the rain, you wish that the Dark Ages would lighten up.

JULY 17, 1995

NINE MONTHS

What is the worst thing that Hugh Grant has ever had to do? There's a long list to consider, starting with his early movies: Grant taking the unlikely role of Chopin in the 1989 picture *Impromptu*, and Grant undergoing the ritual humiliation, borne by many young English actors, of starring in a Ken Russell film. In Hugh's case, it was *The Lair of the White Worm*, which cast him opposite Amanda Donohoe. She played a blue-skinned, bloodsucking fiend whose idea of fun was snapping her fangs shut during fellatio. Grant's character survived the movie, and, amazingly, so did his career, but then he had to suffer the terrible embarrassment of seeing *Four Weddings and a Funeral* become a worldwide hit. Bear in mind that this guy is English, and that he is therefore liable to be embarrassed by things that most Americans would regard as pleasurable: success, sunshine, public acclaim. Public mockery is somehow easier to bear; it seems more morally fitting—the proper cost of self-exposure. Take that little encounter with Divine Brown on Sunset Boulevard last month. I don't know that we can call it one of the worst things. Until the cops turned up, it was probably one of the best. No fangs, but still one of the best.

All in all, the most fearful event in the life of Hugh Grant came last week, on Monday evening, when he resurfaced on the *Tonight Show*. For almost half an hour, we sat and watched Jay Leno grinding out his powdery jokes; finally, the moment arrived. "Hugh Grant!" the host announced. The audience clamored. The band began to rock. It was midnight by now, the witching hour, when unquiet souls patrol the earth, and here was one of them. Out of the wings, blinking with shock, like the Mole hitting daylight at the start of *The Wind in the Willows*, came a bundle of nerves doing a bad impression of a movie star. This was Hugh? This was the man at the hub of a nation's jokes? The one who drives a rented

BMW with extra headroom? It seemed unlikely. Peering out in horror at the hooting fans, he had the look of a small boy checking for beasties behind the nursery door before he goes to bed. Just for a second, you thought that Grant was going to duck back into the darkness and retire into private life. But the voice of Twentieth Century Fox whispered in his ear, and he walked on to meet his fate.

And all for a Chris Columbus film. That's the really galling part. To sacrifice your safety and dignity for a noble cause is itself proof of nobility, but to lay down your life so that others may watch you braining a fluffy dinosaur with a plastic baseball bat—one has to ask, Is it worth it? The movie in question is *Nine Months*, which is roughly how long America will take to exhaust its store of Hugh Grant hooker stories. Grant plays a child psychologist named Samuel Faulkner, who, with his girlfriend, Rebecca (Julianne Moore), leads a perfect, unwedded, childless life. When Rebecca gets pregnant, they are thrown into chaos, only to rise to a new, improved perfection when they marry and have the child. It doesn't pay to think too hard about the politics of this movie, which revolves around an entirely male neurosis—the terror of selling your Porsche and buying a stroller—and leaves the women characters drifting and redundant. Having given the most radiant female performance of the past year, in *Vanya on 42nd Street*, Julianne Moore now has nothing to do except put on weight at the front and lose it in her head. "I know that it's fashionable and PC to be a strong single mother," Rebecca says. "But I want this baby to have a mother and a father." You can just imagine the Speaker of the House easing back in his seat and sighing with relief. Here is the movie that the right has been longing for: *The Contractions with America*.

It's alarming to see how devotedly the picture takes its cue from Hugh. Even he must have winced when he saw all the trimmings that were snipped off *Four Weddings and a Funeral* and pasted onto a different story. For one thing, he gets married in morning dress, an outfit that has become to Hugh Grant what a rubberized breastplate is to Batman. Then, there are the snapshots that show up during the credits to sweeten our departure. And don't forget the verbal wreckage. In *Four Weddings*, it was the priest who fumbled his words. Here it's a Russian obstetrician, played by a frantic Robin Williams: "You don't want natural childbirth? You want Anastasia?" In both movies, the malapropisms are worked in as a foil to Grant's own delivery. Williams can get the lines out all right, but he can't control the direction they head off in; Grant has a more basic problem, in that he can hardly get them out of his mouth. Maybe Divine Brown could help.

Chris Columbus is the man who made *Mrs. Doubtfire*, which was tear-smeared dreck from start to finish, as false and padded as the bosom of its hero. Before that, he directed the *Home Alone* films, which, in their vision of a smirking child getting high on adult pain, seemed to me to inflict on the culture the kind of damage that some people associate with *Natural Born Killers.* So when I first heard that Columbus was making a movie about babies my reaction was to turn purple, kick my feet, scream all night, and dribble my lunch down someone else's shirt. What if some hitherto underexposed member of the Culkin family was hired to play the fetus? In the event, *Nine Months* has the streamlined feel of a comfortable summer hit. The last twenty minutes or so, which could have easily softened into *Natural Born Fathers,* quicken into spirited slapstick, with Grant, Williams, and Tom Arnold pratfalling around the delivery room. The drawback is that, ever since the trademark scream shots of *Home Alone,* Columbus has forgotten how to stand back from his leading men. He plants his camera right in Grant's face, and tells the face to mug and pull and stretch, so that what appeared charming in *Four Weddings* grows oddly oppressive, the oh-my-gosh tics of doubt broadening into a crazy-guy grimace.

Not that different, in fact, from the face of the white worm we saw on the *Tonight Show.* The Grant smile was still functioning, and the lovable stammer chugged away like an outboard motor, but he looked as if he were ready to throw up into his coffee cup at any moment. Hugh was funny, modest, perky with self-censure, and closer to imploding with distress than anyone I have ever seen on network television. I didn't know whether to keep watching or call Amnesty International to report a torture. What American viewers should understand is that for a certain brand of Englishman social defenses will always be the last thing to go; they can never be dropped in the interests of an emerging truth, and, anyway, they are likely to be twice as telling as any actual revelations. The *Post* followed up on the Leno show by asking members of the public, "Star's sorrow: Was it just an act?" But in the case of Hugh Grant that isn't a fair question: sorrow can be an act and still be genuinely ghastly—even more so, because of the effort required to keep it up. The only good question so far has been Leno's opening shot. "What the hell were you thinking?" he asked. Boringly, Hugh took this to mean "How could you do such a thing?" and offered another gracious mea culpa. If only he had taken it literally—"What were you thinking about *during* that blow job off Sunset Boulevard?"—we might have got some fascinating replies. "Chocolate-chip ice cream," for instance, or "Liz Hurley," or "Her Majesty the Queen." We'll never know.

* * *

Two days later, going head to head on *Larry King Live*, Grant was a different man. No jacket, no tie, no audience to spook him. Even the hair was back on form, flopping into its traditional spaniel-after-a-rubdown mode, as opposed to the curiously molded look pioneered for *Nine Months*, a style suggesting that Grant had arrived on the set via a wind tunnel. Prodded by King toward self-examination, he scorned the need for psychotherapy—a source of vast bemusement to his host, who failed to realize that Englishmen have devised a cheap alternative to shrinks. The technical term for this alternative is "a cup of tea." Failing that, "a good book." Hugh put it this way: "If you read enough good books, you're kind of sorted out in life"—a claim that will have the good citizens of Hollywood rushing to call their friends, desperate to know what these book things are and how to get hold of them. Just to drive home the point, Hugh added that his behavior had been "disloyal, shabby, and goatish," a fine turn of phrase that is only a beat away from sounding like a line of Robert Lowell. On Leno, the goat had been right at the end of its tether; on Larry King, it was stroked like a pet. Hugh was home free; his confessions were so winning that it was becoming hard to remember the original sin.

One of the perils of being a sweet guy, or a jolly nice chap, is the feeling of being caged in the role, but even worse is the premonition that you might start to enjoy it—that you'll lock yourself in and swallow the key. Some say that Hugh went in search of his dark side that night in L.A.; if so, all he found was a cop's flashlight and the hot glare of maximum publicity. And that was that. The niceness kicked in again. A couple of talk shows, and he was back on the path of redemption—the Englishman Who Went Down Sunset and Came Up Again. In England, where press intrusion is a kind of compulsory colonic irrigation, he will have to squirm a little longer; he will already have opened his London *News of the World* and found Divine Brown dressed as the Julia Roberts figure in *Pretty Woman.* In America, however, all is going according to plan. Grant's lawyer has pleaded no contest; Elizabeth Hurley turned up at his side for the premiere of *Nine Months*; and the public seems to be both prurient enough and forgiving enough to see the movie for itself. The only problem is that the great finale of American scandal—contrition, acceptance, mass love—may be a punishment even more disabling for Grant than the crime. The temptation will be to rip off the microphone, repeat the first six words of *Four Weddings and a Funeral*—"Oh, fuck, fuck, fuck, fuck, fuck!"—on live TV, and never be seen again. But Hugh Grant, I suspect, will always play the game. He is doomed to keep smiling through. As he said on Leno's show, "I've never been one to blow my own trumpet." Maybe he should have learned. It could have saved him an awful lot of trouble.

JULY 24, 1995

THE USUAL SUSPECTS

The Usual Suspects begins in the dark, with the sound of rich, rippling water, and music to match. Up come the words "San Pedro, California—Last Night." You think, It's all so romantic. Surely that's love in the air? Well, no. As a matter of fact, that's gunfire in the air, followed shortly by a giant fireball blooming upward from an exploding boat. Twenty-seven people are killed. A cargo of cocaine worth ninety-one million dollars is missing, presumed burned. One roasted passenger survives, and he lies in the hospital, babbling about a figure of incomparable evil whom he claims to have sighted at the scene. From here on, the story wades into a swamp of thievery and power plays and low language—it stinks like a fish. *So* romantic.

The movie now jumps back six weeks to New York. The police are investigating a robbery, and a detective named Kujan (Chazz Palminteri) pulls in five suspects for a lineup: Hockney (Kevin Pollak), McManus (Stephen Baldwin), Fenster (Benicio Del Toro), Keaton (Gabriel Byrne), and Kint, nicknamed Verbal (Kevin Spacey). It's a large helping of characters to serve up at once, and the film works hard to bind them into the plot while maintaining them as distinct entities. Keaton, for example, is the suave ex-cop who turned to crime, and Verbal is a creep with a limp, an amateur among pros. As for Fenster, it can be only a matter of time before a spaceship lands to take him back home. Del Toro gives one of the oddest performances seen in American movies in a long while. He doesn't have many speeches, but each gets a spooked laugh out of the audience; it's as if he had learned his lines and then been filmed at the precise moment when he was starting to forget them. His voice has a high, sliding air, a tone that oozes both deep sleaze and complete indifference—perfect for Fenster, who is, after all, only one letter away from being a member of the Addams family.

Once the five leads are shut up in a room together, the movie really gets going. In other words, they can talk. None of them are charged with the robbery, but during the long hours in a holding cell they have time to get acquainted and plan *another* robbery; everything that follows springs from this brainstorm. *The Usual Suspects* is a violent picture, but it's not a brutal one, because violence is not its first love; violence is simply what happens when people run out of things to say. There are three main bursts of activity—a jewel heist, a shooting in an underground parking lot, and the conflagration on the water in San Pedro—and all of them feel skilled and speedy. But they are mere interruptions of the movie's chief business, which is the trading of lies, rumors, and threats. We soon see why Kint is nicknamed Verbal; as the only suspect who is still alive after the explosion, he is questioned at length about the four others, and much of the film is taken up with his interrogation. Kujan against Verbal, Palminteri versus Spacey: it's a close match, the solemn lawman looming over the gibbering squirmer.

The Usual Suspects, which opens next week, was written by Christopher McQuarrie and directed by Bryan Singer; it's their second collaboration, following the 1993 *Public Access*, and they've developed a fine feel for the exact degree of complexity that a movie can get away with. Time and again, the narrative folds in on itself, and so much is presented in second-hand reports that we gradually forget a golden rule: Never trust a flash-back. Just because something is said to have happened—just because it happens before our very eyes—is no guarantee that it did happen. Film noir has always reeked of flashback; pictures like *The Asphalt Jungle* and *The Killing* sought to peel off a central crime layer by layer, as if to show how tightly malice and misfortune were wrapped in fate. Now the tone has shifted: we have *Reservoir Dogs* and *The Usual Suspects*—films that get high, rather than morose, about such convolutions. The wrapping is now more important than the core. Bryan Singer drives his characters toward a definite doom, as John Huston did, but the spinning out of that damnation feels like fun.

The doom derives from one man. Not even from that, perhaps: from a name. "Keyser Söze," rasps the burn victim in the hospital, and the cops around him don't understand what he's saying. Slowly, the words begin to make sense: other people have heard of Söze—the Hungarian warlord who murdered his own children, who came to America, who murders anyone who displeases him, or anyone he pleases. Few have seen his face; nobody knows his mind. The five suspects go quiet whenever he is mentioned, and the cops aren't even sure that he exists. Söze reinforces your suspicion that everything about this movie is a MacGuffin. There are stolen emeralds that don't matter, drugs that can't be found, a villain who's either an alibi or a myth. The film is poised between the sturdy satisfactions of a whodunit—we have to guess which, if any, of the characters will turn out to be Keyser Söze—and the more light-fingered feeling that it's all a game. Crucial facts just wash away; halfway through the action, the theft that started it all—the crime that led to the original lineup—is solved and dismissed with a shrug. Even when Söze's henchman turns up, you don't believe in him. His name is Kobayashi, his complexion looks like a fake tan, his accent lurches between Bombay and South Wales, and he is played by Pete Postlethwaite, last seen as an Irishman in *In the Name of the Father.* All of which makes him absurd, yet in some infuriating way Kobayashi suits the swagger and conceit of *The Usual Suspects,* its wicked hint that the world is no more than an anthology of tall tales.

Singer's film can be expected to pick up the same audience that trooped to see *Reservoir Dogs.* Both works assault your ears, throw your expectations out of whack, glisten with the pleasures of ensemble playing, and demonstrate the useful art of standing your ground and firing two guns at once. *The Usual Suspects,* however, doesn't try to ape the Tarantino hipness, and that's probably a good thing. It's largely a nocturnal movie, lacking the splashy colors of *Reservoir Dogs* and *Pulp Fiction,* and it's much less cool; people don't saunter around in white shirts and skinny black ties. Singer's men look ugly and scruffy; if there's a weak link in the cast, it's Gabriel Byrne, who is just too fine-boned for this low-rent landscape. (The poor guy was all wrong in *Little Women,* too. Jo is supposed to find her soul mate in a plain, chubby scholar; instead, she hooked up with Lord Byron.) What beauty there is in the picture arises from destruction: there's the angelic blurring of light behind Keaton's head as it gets punched by a frustrated cop, and the weird chronology of the explosion at the docks—first, the orange glow of its reflection, and *then* the fireball itself. Most directors would have done it the other way around, but Singer is dealing with a universe where effect is more reliable than cause, and infinitely more seductive.

The movie finds its perfect pitch when McManus, assuming the role of lonely sharpshooter, gazes through his telescopic sight and makes a quiet count of his distant victims, all of whom will have to be picked off, under the veil of darkness, within a matter of seconds. "One, two, three, four, five, six, seven," he says to himself, like Snow White checking under her duvet for dwarfs. He pauses, gives a little snarl of a laugh, and adds, "Oswald was a fag." What's great about the line, apart from the fact that it will amuse plenty of people who would prefer to be offended by it, is that it feels like the product of energetic concision. You can imagine a whole speech being chopped down to this one, oblique phrase: the dirty wit of it forces the audience to fill in the gaps. McQuarrie's script stays one step ahead of us, or so we believe; in the closing minutes, it becomes clear that we have in fact been trailing ten miles behind. The more movies one watches, the easier it is to spot the planting of a twist; the joy of being outsmarted, therefore, grows more precious by the year. I fell for *The Usual Suspects*, as I did for Mamet's *House of Games*. I walked out feeling pleased, excited, and very, very stupid.

Singer is so proud of his final twist that he nearly blows it. At the point of revelation, someone drops a mug of coffee, and we see it smash three times (in slow motion, naturally). I'm sure that the director will think back on this and regret it: he doesn't *need* a flourish of style to signal the big moment—it can take care of itself. The movie's confidence sometimes tenses up like this when it could afford to remain casual; real style tends to stroll in unannounced. Still, the twist survives to haunt you, like the charred figure in the California hospital. The film traps its viewers so neatly that the temptation to give away the plot, to share the pain of that trap, is almost too much to bear. Suffice it to say that the dexterity with which the baddie pulls the wool over the eyes of his peers is a blueprint for the way in which the audience gets screwed by the movie. This may be a defining virtue of all good noir, one source of its reputation for infectious paranoia. The notion that we can "identify with" the predicaments of noir heroes is obviously tripe: when did you last perch on top of a rising elevator, kill the lights, and shoot two of its occupants through the brow before they had time to frown? But the currents that render these heroes helpless and suck them under seem to flow out of the screen and along the aisles.

Some people, of course, won't like the sensation at all; they may not want to be manhandled into a corner, to submit to the seedy, masculine bruising that passes for social relations in a movie like *The Usual Suspects*. Women can hardly be made out through its dank atmosphere. "I love you," Keaton's girlfriend (Suzy Amis) says to him. There is no reply. "I love you," she repeats, in case he didn't hear her the first time. He heard all right; he just didn't care. Anyone who has overdosed on film noir, however, will recognize the fact that lovelessness is part of the deal. Even the characters who try to make room for love discover that greed has got there first and made itself at home. You could argue, once the effect of *The Usual Suspects* has worn off, that you've seen it all before. That's like cutting your finger and saying you're bored by your own blood; in truth, some things never lose their sting. I certainly don't believe that only movie buffs will enjoy the show; rather, it will leave everyone feeling like a buff—feeling, in other words, that life has started to turn into a movie, and that our actions, whose freedom we take for granted, seem to be following someone else's script. I still haven't figured out exactly what happens in *The Usual Suspects*, and I need to see it again, but one thing I know for sure: Keyser Söze rules the world.

AUGUST 14, 1995

PERSUASION

"Five charming sisters on the gayest, merriest manhunt that ever snared a bewildered bachelor! Girls! Take a lesson from these husband hunters!" That is how MGM promoted *Pride and Prejudice* back in 1940. I guess the plug was written by someone at the studio, although I like to think that they brought Jane Austen out of retirement and flew her in to help with the publicity. After that, she went quiet for a while, probably got a house out in the Hollywood Hills. Now she's back, and this time it's huge. We have already had *Clueless*, a modernized spinoff from *Emma*, and a period version of the same book is on the way; in England, the BBC is about to screen its new *Pride and Prejudice;* and Ang Lee has a *Sense and Sensibility* in the offing. All in all, Austen mania is the most widely publicized media growth industry since the advent of rap. I eagerly await the day when Bob Dole lays into Emma Woodhouse for promoting sexual interest between young people—hardly more than children, some of them—without giving sufficient weight to her own family-building responsibilities. The only thing that could slow the craze down is the unfortunate fact that it will soon run out of source material. Then, presumably, it will be the turn of Mrs. Gaskell to get it in the neck.

It is hard to believe that the Jane Austen trend will throw up anything better than Roger Michell's *Persuasion*. Whether the trend will survive the movie is another matter: Michell, the young British director who made *The Buddha of Suburbia* (screened at the Public last winter), has made it his business to roughen and dampen the Austen world into a state of nervous desperation. The social order holds, but only on sufferance. When Sir Walter Elliot (Corin Redgrave) leaves his country estate, he passes blithely along a row of footmen. In a fleeting series of close-ups, we see their faces—immobile except for the eyes, which follow their master with a sturdy contempt. The tale that Michell tells is still a comedy, but not a light comedy; it is still a period picture, in which women's dresses run from neck to ankle, but for once you notice how the hems drag up mud on a ramble. And the heroine should really do something about her hair. For those reared on Merchant-Ivory films, it could come as a shock to realize that styling mousse was not available over the counter in 1814.

Jane Austen devotees, too, will probably take one look at this picture and drop the sugar tongs; but they will be missing the point of Michell's homage. If he wants his film of *Persuasion* to ruffle the habits of costume drama, that is because the novel does something comparable—it deepens and confuses our apprehension of Jane Austen. Her earlier work set such store by fine manners that it's alarming to find her not merely loosening her respect for them but hinting that they are popularly used as cover for emotional atrocities. Anyone who knows *Persuasion* tends to know it well, perhaps because it's all about the renewing of acquaintances, the stoking of old flames: it somehow sets an example to the reader, who comes back to the story in the hope of further bliss, as the hero does to his beloved. The plot is curiously post hoc, the exact opposite of the delicious anticipation that lifts *Pride and Prejudice:* you sense that everything vital about *Persuasion* has occurred in advance—hence the autumnal air that is draped over the whole proceedings, a suspicion that the hours of happiness are growing short. It wouldn't do to lay this gloom on too thick; given that the characters include three sisters in varying degrees of frustration, Michell must have been tempted to produce a kind of Regency *Cries and Whispers*, but he sensibly opts for the odd, glancing image of leaves being raked and burned, and of trees on the turn.

Eight years before the action begins, Anne Elliot (Amanda Root) fell in love with Frederick Wentworth (Ciaran Hinds), a captain in the British Navy. She was persuaded by her confidante, a family friend named Lady Russell (Susan Fleetwood), to give the captain up as a bad thing—an impoverished thing, in other words, a thing without connections. "A man who had nothing but himself to recommend him," Lady Russell says of Wentworth, failing triumphantly to understand that nothing else matters. And now the suitor is back, still looking rather stunned, and the upshot is that he and Anne are thrown together again. Even if you've never read the book, you will catch their drift: they must circle back to the passionate point that they reached so long ago, while trying not to hit too many of the obstacles in their path.

The obstacles include Louisa Musgrove (Emma Roberts), who fancies herself in love with Wentworth; William Elliot (Samuel West), a young swell who wears a good green tailcoat and claims to be in love with Anne;

and, offstage, Napoleon, whose war with England has made Wentworth a wealthy man (ships' captains used to claim the value of captured enemy vessels), and who may yet require his presence in a fresh fight. Then, there is Anne's father, whose monomania makes Bonaparte look like a wincing wallflower. Sir Walter has a connoisseur's nose for blue blood, for its vintage and finesse; he is the last word in snobbery—and Jane Austen's final say on the matter, too, for *Persuasion* was published only after her death. As if unshackled from custom by her illness, she no longer stands on ceremony with her creations, and spares no sympathy for Sir Walter on the simple ground that he shows none for Anne. He is a monster, and a gift to any actor. On hearing that Louisa Musgrove, who is related to him by marriage, was badly injured in an accident, Sir Walter looks amazed—offended, even—that anyone should think of troubling him with such news. "Oh," he sniffs. "Farmer's daughter."

For those attempting to dramatize Jane Austen or to play her characters onscreen, she can be embarrassingly generous—almost up to Dickens level—with her covert stage directions. (This could be a clue to her current popularity in Hollywood. It's not her small world that appeals; it's the big help that she offers you in fleshing it out. She's her own script editor, virtually her own director—and it's all free.) Indeed, Michell's *Persuasion* feels closer to David Lean's great Dickens movies than it does to the sedate chattiness of most Austen adaptations. It has something of Lean's willingness to skirt the brink of caricature and stop an inch short; something, too, of his suggestion that in a society driven by bluster virtue is most likely to reside in the tacit and the diligent. There are moments in *Persuasion*, surges of near-fatal feeling, when the world blanks out around Anne. At her first sight of Wentworth, for example, the conversation of others seems to flow around her and leave her stranded in silence. The camera moves in swiftly toward her face, as if to test for signs of life; all that stirs is her hand, curling around the back of a chair. The same thing happens during Louisa's fall; normal life is suspended, and the world softens to an ominous rustle. In each case, a woman is struck dumb: one by a crack on the head, the other by a blow to the heart.

At first, you scarcely notice Anne; she is a slip of a thing, a ghost at the back of the drawing room. Looking at her lankness and pallor, her aura of muted rebellion, you find yourself thinking of *The Piano*—and Michell appears to borrow from Jane Campion in the opening shot of his movie, when a boat's hull splits calm water. The rest of *Persuasion* gently pushes Anne to the forefront, but even then she looks discomforted by her prominence. All of which means that some viewers will find Amanda Root's performance just too shrunken and scared; they may prefer their

Jane Austen heroines to be quick on the draw, as clear and ringing as a wineglass. But Root is timing her act; she knows that Anne is destined to bloom late, and that there's no use forcing a miracle. Besides, she is as much a point of view as a source of strength; she exists to scan a scene while others clump and bray around it, and the fun of *Persuasion* lies in seeing the supporting actors turn up the throttle while Root is parked at the side. None is better than Sophie Thompson (sister of Emma), who plays Anne's sister Mary—a snapping wife, a useless mother, a ravenous hypochondriac ("I am *so ill*"), yet by no means a wicked woman. Whereas Anne is threatened by the dead hand of saintliness, Mary is alive with shortcomings; the movie makes room for both of them. There is more tolerance and fresh air in it than you might expect: people wander off on walks and skim stones at the seaside, and don't really give a damn that someone—someone morally clearheaded, like a sister or an author—is watching them with such care.

The narrative divides into clean segments. There is the family home, which Anne leaves in order to stay with Mary; then the sunlit interlude on the coast; and the town house rented by the Elliots in Bath, where the twin souls are finally glued together. Michell greets each setting with a defiant key shift in visual tone. The country smacks of low ceilings and lower light; when Anne stands contented in the internal dusk of a cottage, you are reminded of the cramped quarters of a ship—precisely where she dreams of ending up. Bath, on the other hand, is pure sci-fi: a nightmare of bright white walls, hard floors, idlers promenading like androids. Michell's camera, often handheld, never stops; he grabs at people on the move, or spies them through windows and doorways. When Anne, near the end, walks into a game of whist and waits for Frederick, the candles in the room seem to haze and roar; they look like hellfire, or like underwater flares, and, indeed, the crowd at the card tables, oblivious of the lovers' secret, smiles and gestures with sluggish, submarine grace. The world is not playing but drowning.

Occasionally, the movie goes too far. There are times when its clutching at modern sensibilities makes scant historical sense; if you're going to show Anne and Frederick kissing in the *street*—a street in *Bath*, of all places—you might as well go the whole hog and have them perform oral sex in the Pump Room. But the kiss is just a romantic sop; far more fraught, and more convincing, is Michell's overall reading of Jane Austen's mood—the skill with which his movie takes the moral temperature of the novel. You look at Amanda Root and you see how patience has shifted into neurosis, how niceties have condensed into suffocation; the battle of wits is now a fight to the death. Heaven knows what MGM would have made of Anne Elliot: "One smarting spinster with the longest, loneliest memory that ever snared a saddened sailor! Girls! Take a lesson from this party-hater!" We fancy ourselves perfectly placed to pick up the distress signals sent out by *Persuasion*, with its tartness and well-trimmed melancholy. That is how we take our Jane Austen these days. If we are wrong, we cannot help it; we cannot conceive that anyone as long-suffering as Jane Austen could also be so funny. Her balance is beyond us; however good a person we may think she was, she was better.

SEPTEMBER 25, 1995

SHOWGIRLS

Paul Verhoeven's *Showgirls* is something of a novelty. It represents the first occasion on which a major studio—in this case, United Artists—has consciously courted an NC-17 rating instead of battling the threat of one. It launches the screen career of Elizabeth Berkley, in perhaps the most unusual debut since that of Ingrid Boulting in *The Last Tycoon*. And it has the distinction of being the first movie about Las Vegas that is actually more vulgar than Las Vegas.

Berkley plays Nomi, a stripper-dancer-whatever who's hitchhiking her way to Las Vegas. Once there, she falls in with nice Molly (Gina Ravera) and gets a job at the Cheetah Club, a crummy joint where her duties involve shimmying in front of salivating jerks. But Nomi has dreams. She wants more, much more. She has her eyes on the Stardust, a plush arena where she can shimmy in front of salivating jerks with money in their wallets—where she can be *herself.* One day, she is spotted by Zack, the "entertainment director" of the Stardust. Zack is played by Kyle MacLachlan, a real actor, who, for the purposes of this movie, graciously sinks to the level of the other performers. Still, I got the feeling that he was trying to hide behind his long, curving forelock in the unactorly hope that he might not be recognized. But that's him all right—buck naked in the swimming pool with Nomi, sipping champagne beneath the quietly tasteful dolphin-shaped fountains.

You may be surprised to learn that what happens next constitutes the only complete sex act in the whole movie. Even so, I'm not sure that it *is* sex: at the crest of her pleasure, Nomi thrashes her head in and out of the water so repeatedly that she may in fact be road-testing a new conditioner. If you believed the hype, *Showgirls* was all set to flay us with honest sex, to embarrass the timidity of mainstream Hollywood by bringing us the full, perspiring reality. In fact, it is neither as brazenly carnal as its creators would like nor remotely as vile as its detractors feared. The movie's big discovery is lap-dancing, an erotic pastime that it presents as something of a revelation but which looked to me as if it had been going on, more or less unchanged, for the last three thousand years. To lap-dance, you undress, sit your client down, order him to stay still and fully clothed, then hover over him, making a motion that you have perfected by watching Mister Softee ice cream dispensers. Nomi does this to Zack, who has a high old time, but she is berated by one of her friends, the artistically minded James (Glenn Plummer). "You fuck 'em without fucking 'em," as he delicately puts it. If Verhoeven were really bold, he would have used that line on the poster. *Showgirls* is not about sex at all; it is about the business of sex, which is a different matter.

Mind you, what a business! The plot promotes Nomi from the Cheetah to the Stardust, where her Fonteyn-like skills soon threaten the crown of Cristal (Gina Gershon), the star attraction. Here's the twist: Cristal both fears *and* fancies Nomi, inviting her out to lunch and announcing, "I like nice tits. I always have." Nomi strikes back, as sharp as a tack. "I like having them," she says, as if they were friends who occasionally come to visit. But can the art of dance survive their love-hate pact? As the owner of the Stardust says, "The show must go on. The Stardust will never be dark—never has been. Not while I'm alive." These fresh, new-minted phrases spring from the script of Joe Eszterhas, who worked with Verhoeven on *Basic Instinct.* By now, it is possible to trace a rough map of their common interests: chicks with weapons, chicks with chicks, and chicks. Between them, Eszterhas and Verhoeven make it abundantly clear that the title of their new movie is not so much a noun as an imperative. They have a story to tell, even a moral to expound, but their deepest wish is to get the girls to show. When Tony (Alan Rachins), who runs the dances at the Stardust, auditions a line of hopefuls, picks three, says "Show me your tits," and hands one of them a helpful cluster of ice cubes, he is acting on behalf of the entire film. (I'm sure that the auditions for *Showgirls* itself were, of course, conducted in a spirit of absolute professionalism and deep respect.)

For the most part, this movie is a blank—a waxwork museum with moving parts. But I did find something rather touching, in the emotional rather than the lap-dancing sense, in Elizabeth Berkley. She can't act, but the sight of her *trying* to act, doing the sorts of things that acting is rumored to consist of, struck me as a far nobler struggle than the boring old I-know-I-can-make-it endeavors of her fictional character. She must have been told at the outset that Nomi is supposed to be a driven woman, because she takes care to invest the most fleeting of actions with a

Joan Crawford intensity; the simple act of shaking a ketchup bottle, for instance, is modelled on the jack-hammer technique of a road crew. *Showgirls* requires that Berkley spend at least half her time topless, and it could be argued, in the interest not of prurience but of pure dramatic method, that her breasts are more expressive than her face. Looking closely at her mouth, I saw to my surprise that even her lipstick was wearing lipstick, and the sheer weight of Revlon, or whatever, seems to restrict the free play of her feelings from the neck up.

The crucial question is: Should we pay this ridiculous movie the honor of being offended by it? I am not sure that I can be bothered to work up the steam. I would be more troubled by its depiction of women if I thought that any care had been lavished on its depiction of men; you can't accuse a movie of degrading half of humanity when it forgets to grade humanity in the first place. I have cordially loathed all of Verhoeven's earlier pictures, but this was the first one that I didn't object to. *Showgirls* unveils more flesh than *Basic Instinct* did, but it's less explicit in its cynicism: Verhoeven doesn't prod us into ogling, because—and this is bliss—his movie likes to suggest that all these bare-assed boys and girls and all these swirling, nipple-raising, ice-and-fire routines at the Stardust are really rather classy. There is not a whisper of satire in this picture; it ambles along like a two-and-a-quarter-hour special edition of *Models Inc.*, which may be why people were laughing so hard in the theatre. The language may be rougher than anything on TV, but after a while the nudity grows as humdrum as a suit. You sit there ready to be shocked, primed for the practically hard-core, and find yourself skidding on soap. Here's the dirty little secret of this movie: it's good clean fun.

OCTOBER 9, 1995

THE SCARLET LETTER

What is the point of Demi Moore? It's not that I don't get her; I simply can't see what's there for the getting. I suspect that people revere the sheer steely professionalism that has propelled her into the first rank of fame; they react to her strategic skills, in other words, rather than to any particular artistry. Like many veteran politicians, Demi Moore seems to have lost the fizz that made her ambition rise in the first place. The rasp of her voice used to remind me of Veronica Lake; now I just want to chuck throat lozenges at the screen. Demi was funny and sexy in *About Last Night . . .*, casually naked and snapping greedily at the David Mamet dialogue; these days, she looks a little glum—proof that celebrity is no laughing matter—and the sighting of her nudity has become a regular national event, like the launch of the space shuttle. If she completes a successful docking, so much the better.

Moore has now taken it upon herself to assume one of the canonical American Roles: she plays Hester Prynne in the new movie adaptation of *The Scarlet Letter.* Roland Joffé's film is, in the words of the opening credits, "freely adapted from the novel by Nathaniel Hawthorne," in the same way that methane is freely adapted from cows. So little of the book is left intact that you ask yourself why Joffé and his screenwriter, Douglas Day Stewart, didn't junk the whole thing and compose their own story from scratch. If you want your Puritan minister to go skinny-dipping, your heroine and her black maid to stand around dripping in bathtubs, your scalp-hungry Indians to attack in the final reel, your lovers to slake their desires on top of what appears to be a hundred-weight of granola, and your forest to resemble a commercial for toilet freshener, then what's the point of traducing poor old Hawthorne?

The casting is a catalogue of wrong calls. Gary Oldman plays the Reverend Arthur Dimmesdale with ink on his face, lust in his loins, and a wavering Scottish accent. Robert Duvall's Chillingworth has vocal problems of his own as he struggles to wrap his tongue around English vowels. Under a better director, Duvall could have been ideal for the "refined cruelty" and "dark and self-relying intelligence" that Hawthorne saw in the character, but, apart from one creepy moment in Hester's house, when he wipes her face with a tenderness that toughens into rage, he is given no opportunity to dig around in that darkness. To be fair, I did enjoy his open-air scenes among the Indians. Chillingworth is taken prisoner by the fearsome Tarrantine tribe, presumably ruled by Chief Reservoir Dog, and we are faced with the unusual sight of one of our most distinguished actors dancing about with a dead, disembowelled, and rather surprised-looking deer on his head. Keeps the ears warm, I guess.

What kind of movie did Roland Joffé have in mind? Does he think of *The Scarlet Letter* as a period piece at all? The dialogue is no help. At first, Hester impresses the elders with her scholarship. "Thou canst quote the Scriptures!" one of them says approvingly. Fair enough, but by the last reel everyone has sloughed off the archaisms to reveal a somewhat livelier vocabulary. Hester, defending herself from a rapist, grabs what looks like a sawed-off musket, points it at her attacker, and shouts, "You bastard—get out!" There's something equally charming in her exchanges with Dimmesdale: learned discussions of Milton's *Comus* ("Yes, I've read it") make way for the prime-time directness of "Arthur, thank God you're here!"

The irony is that the novel itself could have given Joffé what he wanted. Just think of its majestic opening: Hester on the scaffold, the crowd (and the reader) unaware that the minister addressing her is her former lover and that the strange figure on the fringe of the crowd is her husband, long believed dead. There is more suspense, more dramatic torque, in one page of Hawthorne's heart-racked ruminations on the Christian conscience than in all Demi Moore's woodland gallops and horizontal barn dancing. Thou hast to be kidding.

OCTOBER 30, 1995

FRENCH TWIST

Moved by the passing, late last month, of Dean Martin, I sat down, poured myself a drink, and thought about bad behavior. Martin's trick was to appear drunk even when he was not, and to look even when he *was* drunk as if he were only pretending to be drunk and were fully in command of the situation—as, of course, he was, even though drunk. It makes your head spin to try to unravel the niceties of such an act, which relied on Martin's own head's staying remarkably steady. What mattered more than Dean Martin's needs and failings was the fact that to the viewer's eye he was never wound up by them. While the young Brando was peeling his own soul like an orange, men such as Martin and Crosby could cruise through a picture as if it were merely a nice place to hang out. In *Bells Are Ringing*, Martin, in the role of a playwright, even sang at his *typewriter*—a heroically relaxed image of the creative soul.

There is almost nobody in today's movies who can match that relaxation—who knows how to maintain a devil-may-care approach without losing sight of the devil. But I did feel the spirit of Dean Martin tapping me on the shoulder and pointing as Victoria Abril wandered naked across the screen in *French Twist.* Her nude scenes are the most endearing since Annette Bening's in *The Grifters,* for the simple reason that neither Abril nor the audience seems to notice that she hasn't got any clothes on.

The film is set in the South of France, and clothes just get in the way, but there's more to it than fine weather: to exist au naturel becomes less a physical statement than a comic attitude, and what is really unfettered about Abril is not her body but the grin that tops it off, along with the amazingly dirty laugh that becomes its signature tune. When her character, Loli, is offered a joint—her first in years—she accepts it with the grave warning (and the hope) that she will not be held responsible for her actions. "Watch out, I might pull my panties over my head," she says.

Loli is the loving wife of Laurent (Alain Chabat). He is a no-good, philandering real-estate agent, if that isn't a tautology; when she welcomes him home with a hug, he glances over her shoulder at his watch, as Jane Fonda did with one of her clients in *Klute*. Loli, on the other hand, despite the air of high-grade wickedness that hangs about her, has been until now a loyal wife and mother. Then, one day, her child announces, "There's a man at the door," and her life begins to spin. The man is in fact a woman: a jovial, bullish lesbian of no fixed address named Marijo (Josiane Balasko), who fixes Loli's plumbing, stays for supper, and, before the night is out, winds up caressing her in the garden. Loli strolls back into the bedroom with a liquid, super-sated look in her eyes, as if she were made of warm wax. Without knowing it, she is getting her own back at her husband; the film is rapidly thickening into one huge casserole of hormones, with all manner of fatty lusts stirred into the pot.

Not content with butching it out as Marijo, Josiane Balasko also wrote and directed *French Twist*. Viewers may recall her as the frumpy lover of Gérard Depardieu in Bertrand Blier's *Trop Belle pour Toi*. Some of Blier's shamelessness has stuck to Balasko: her tenderly perverse triangle of characters is indebted to *Going Places* and *Ménage*, and she obeys all the demands of erotic geometry while ignoring those of good taste. (No film that starts with a disco remix of *A Whiter Shade of Pale* is heading for the high ground.) Her work is more sunlit than Blier's, though, and less skeptical; it counts as a respectable example of that otherwise mangy species, the sex comedy. The very words summon up leering English farces from the seventies, in which window cleaners perched ladders up against bathroom windows, but Balasko operates on the more sophisticated principle that sex itself is a comedy. In the movie's first scene, Laurent, who is sitting in a café with one of his pickups, is approached by a flower seller and offered a rose for the lady. "No, thanks, we've already fucked," he says. The line is so virulently antiromantic—so crisp and cruel in its view of fusty cinematic habits—that you jump back in your seat as if stung. A whole movie like this would make you break out in a rash. But there's something to follow: the scene is capped with an epilogue, in which Laurent goes after the flower seller and buys an armful of roses. The graces of courtship are rubbished, then restored.

The sequence works beautifully, but it also hints at the sort of compromise that will soften the second half of the film. Once the courting is over, Marijo moves in with her beloved, sharing her with the disgruntled Laurent; Loli sleeps with each of them three nights a week. ("On the seventh day we rest," she says.) The comedy of domestic patterns, however unorthodox, is duller than the rude intrusions that first threw the household into chaos; it's no surprise that the film begins to nestle up to the bourgeois habits that it once yearned to strip bare. Loli has a couple of implausible teary scenes in which she confesses to her guilt and her love for Laurent (I felt like weeping for poor Victoria Abril); the farce grows broad and bloated, with bicycles tipping into pig muck; and there's even an aging whore, who dispenses the wisdom of the heart to a pensive Laurent. Give me a break.

At its best, *French Twist* offers a blithe, randy, quick-witted demonstration of the fact that the heart is stupendously unwise; that it runs on a rush of blood and suffuses people with cravings that come out of nowhere. Balasko ends up handing us a bunch of roses, as it were, by telling us that we discover our true natures in bed. But she began with the sight of people losing themselves in lust. I know which version I believe. Everybody, as Dean Martin assured us, loves somebody sometime.

JANUARY 15, 1996

SGT. BILKO

As I marched into a screening of *Sgt. Bilko*, a question tugged gently at my mind: "Why bother?" Ninety minutes later, I lumbered out without having come close to getting an answer. Over the last decade, Hollywood has been jabbing its snout into the trough of old television shows, the fodder of the fifties and sixties and seventies, and the rummaging hasn't ended yet: this year promises *Mission: Impossible*, and a new version of *The Saint*, starring Val Kilmer, will begin shooting soon. Life is too short for anyone to get stressed about these updates. There is nothing holy about the TV of the past, and our remembered childish devotion to a classic should not render it untouchable; on the other hand, the decision to raid the tomb of *Sgt. Bilko* does look like a folly of the first order—not sacrilegious, just deeply unnecessary.

For one thing, let's get the name right: the original wasn't called *Sgt. Bilko;* it was called *The Phil Silvers Show*. It was a Silvers-tongued creation: it belonged to the guy, and to snatch it away from him now makes as much sense as trying to recast *I Love Lucy*. Love is not love that an altered Lucy finds.

The lucky winner of the Bilko role is Steve Martin. The fact that his gifts are actually more elastic and unfettered than those of Phil Silvers is, sadly, of limited assistance. From his first appearance in the movie—and the camera holds back from him for a while, ratcheting up the suspense—Martin makes it plain that there will be no attempt to do a Silvers. This is surely the right move: no Roman-senator pate, no black-rimmed spectacles with bottle-thick lenses, but merely Martin's standard bristled shock of bright white hair. The trouble is that, among other things, he makes an even less plausible soldier than the original Bilko did. You could just about imagine Silvers as the kind of worldly survivor who would find and feather his nest in a big, rather bloated peacetime Army; his passing resemblance to an accountant, or even to the trusted manager of a small rural bank, somehow strengthened the illusion, and made him even more of a threat to surrounding wallets.

But if *Sgt. Bilko* is a sorry sight, that has surprisingly little to do with Steve Martin. The movie looks kind of sorry for itself; you get the impression that it gave up hope even before it started. No one expected the writer (Andy Breckman), the director (Jonathan Lynn), and the producer (Brian Grazer) to put their hearts into the project, but they might have taken the trouble to put their heads together, or their pens to paper, and devise a respectable structure to support the central figure. As it is, the story line of this full-length *Bilko* would have barely passed muster as the subplot of a single TV episode; it's as thin as tissue paper, and you can't even blow your nose on it. There is the weak, chubby Colonel Hall (Dan Aykroyd), and there is the cruel Major Thorn (a dull Phil Hartman), an avenging angel looming out of Bilko's past, who tries to shut the base down and to steal Bilko's fiancée, Rita Robbins (Glenne Headly). Bilko foils him, as you might expect, but not with guileful patter—the only weapon that the character once required. Rather, Lynn, in his wisdom, has opted for a techno-joke: a newly developed, top-secret hovering tank, which Bilko alone can transform from a white elephant into a thundering success. Cue some remarkably low-grade special effects; as the tank wobbled and shimmied unconvincingly before my eyes, I felt the spirit of American comedy slip from its seat, lower its head in shame, and head for the exit.

In a way, the tank was useful: it targeted and brought into focus the hopeless indecision that tends to weaken these TV-imbued movies. Should cinema revel in the retro look, or should it modernize the details for the sake of an audience that is often too young to be in thrall to the ancient shows? In thirty years' time, when some hollow-headed executive decides to remake *NYPD Blue*, will he turn Sipowicz into a lean, whippy bastard with a laser-guided firearm, or will he jokily go with the old-style fat guy, as distant as Henry VIII? Don't ask the makers of *Sgt. Bilko* to help out on this one. They plump, on the one hand, for a smiling fifties innocence (Glenne Headly has to sport little white ankle socks, poor dear) and for TV-style wipes between scenes. On the other hand, there are mentions of Stormin' Norman and the Gulf War: "We still haven't gotten over being left out of Desert Storm," a rueful Bilko says. And the proposed closing of the base is a reference to current defense cuts in the aftermath of the cold war. But Bilko's heart was warmed by the gusts of the cold war. It was a time when the nation lifted its proud eyes and fixed them firmly on a common foe—a time when it should, of course, have been watching a certain motor pool all along. An unsupervised Bilko is a terrible thing.

He is the only character created in modern times whom Molière would have been proud of. There was nothing fantastical or electric in the words that rattled out of Bilko's mouth, and many of his lines were not in themselves especially funny, yet Silvers's delivery told of a man who could no more curb the excesses of his covetous core than a dog can disdain its supper dish. He tested and proved the Molière theorem that vice in small quantities—or a choice selection of minor vices—is wretched and sour, but that the clamorous gush of a single iniquity can be so pure and triumphal, so comically consuming of a man's soul, that it smashes any onlookers with the force of a heroic virtue. Silvers's manner was a quite unrepeatable blend of the crooning and the imperious; like Jack Benny, he panned and prospected for money, and knelt before its semi-sacred power, but he also went much further than Benny in pumping other people to cough the stuff up.

You get a fresh taste of this in an early scene of the film, when Steve Martin lifts his nose, savoring the air, and declares, "Can't you smell it? It's money." Martin has a fine touch for such delicate desires, and I couldn't help thinking of his fire chief in *Roxanne*, waving an adoring schnozz in the direction of Daryl Hannah. But such fluting, Osric-like idiocy strikes no more than a single sweet note in the full, orchestrated mania that Martin is known to be capable of. He is (or once admitted to being) a wild and crazy guy; the appalling certainty that nobody in the movie audience—or, even better, in his live audience—knew where he was heading next, or whether his brain and his body would be able to hammer out an agreement on the matter, was demonstrated in glorious form by the half-male, half-female walkabout in *All of Me*. Who else could have starred in a movie called *The Man with Two Brains* and made the title look like a libellous understatement? Some of the lines in that picture seem to burp out of Martin's mouth as if he were a medium, reluctantly receiving distress calls from a pissed-off ghost. Hence the trailing, somewhat lonely tone of his later work: from *Parenthood* onward, we have always known where Steve Martin is going. In the two execrable *Father of the Bride* movies, we have watched him slope in the direction of a heartfelt domestic peace; and now, in *Sgt. Bilko*, we see him glumly save his job and his sweetheart without ever pausing to take stock of the lunatic possibilities that used to flower around him.

Every now and then, something stirs. When Bilko plays dumb at a poker game, pretending to be a novice ("Oh, goody, I get to play cards!"), or when he takes the men to Las Vegas and cries at the sight of it ("It's just so beautiful"), you hear the certifiable strains of the Martin madness. Whether they are right for the character is another matter; where Silvers gave us a one-track obsessive, Martin hints at a freak who will always enjoy his lyrical riffs on the allure of money—or on love, for that matter—far more than the cash itself. His comedy has always been egged on by a warped and oddly uplifting romanticism, whereas the real Bilkos of this world leave us skinned and floundering with their ground-level ruthlessness. Maybe Jonathan Lynn and his team knew this all along; hence the embarrassing moments in the movie where minor characters, as if charged with the fruitless task of promoting what they know to be untrue, pay tribute to their leader: "He's like a God," "It's like watching a magician," and so on. Saddest of all is Bilko's own boast, trembling with desperation: "No wonder they call me a Master Sergeant." They do?

APRIL 8, 1996

STEALING BEAUTY

The good news about *Stealing Beauty*, the new movie from Bernardo Bertolucci, is that it is set in Italy. The bad news is that it is set in Tuscany. Seasoned Bertolucci watchers have been praying for some time that the director would stop the globe-trotting, cut down on the lusciousness of movies like *The Last Emperor*, and return to his homeland—the scene of his strongest work. So now the guy comes back, and what does he do? He heads straight for the Sienese countryside and introduces us to a pack of English-speaking intruders whose sole function is to discourage us from ever going near the place again. In other words, the man behind *The Conformist* and *1900*—films that felt as if they *had* to be made, as if the artist had a duty to dramatize his country's disease—has now decided, in his wisdom, to give us Italy without the Italians.

The intruders are a mixed bunch, though not quite mixed enough; they have no defining force of character, merely a shared boredom and bonelessness. There is Diana (Sinead Cusack), who lives in an isolated villa with her husband, a sculptor (Donal McCann). At least, I think he's her husband; I spent much of the film wondering who on earth most of the people were, how (or if) they were related to one another, and why I didn't care either way. I was positive that Richard (D. W. Moffett) was married to Miranda (Rachel Weisz), given the steady rattle of their bickering, until it turned out that he was married to someone else. As for the old guy played by Jean Marais, I never did place him, but still—Jean Marais! The pleasure of seeing the star of *La Belle et la Bête* alive and working was so intense that it almost overcame the groggy embarrassment of his actual performance; did Bertolucci deliberately encourage him to ham it up? The sadness is that *Stealing Beauty* is by and large a badly acted film; in aiming at liquid languor and a haze of emotional incest, it gives the performers almost nothing to bite on. Even Jeremy Irons, whose haughtiness can usually be relied upon to lend any movie a certain acidity, a dry chill of intelligence, shuffles to and fro looking lost; he plays a houseguest named Alex, a playwright within spitting distance of death, but the film's mania for sophistication makes his pain more precious than melancholic. Bertolucci does to Irons what Visconti did to the Dirk Bogarde of *Death in Venice:* he deadens the dying.

Into this merry setting comes Lucy (Liv Tyler), a family friend who flies in to stay at the villa and generally to ripen her soul: think Daisy Miller with jet lag. As the film proceeds, you realize that its title, *Stealing Beauty*, is in part a coy, rather eighteenth-century euphemism for the relieving of virginity. Lucy is nineteen and is still a pure American maiden—a highly unlikely combination, but out of it arises the whisper of a plot. Who will deflower the girl? Will it be one of her fellow-guests? And, if so, how can she be sure that it isn't her own father? Lucy's late mother, we gradually learn, was a poet, and a suspiciously close friend to some of those now staying at the villa, where Lucy believes herself to have been conceived; Alex remembers the mother "writing transporting little verses in between fashion shoots." I am sorry to say that this line is delivered with no more than a drop of irony; one basic problem with the film, which was written by Bertolucci and Susan Minot, is that only at rare intervals do the characters express themselves in ordinary human speech. There are jokes here, of a kind, but you can never swear that they are intentional. Everything is very slightly off-key, just enough to set your teeth on edge.

All of which may, of course, be the point of the picture. Bertolucci may simply be registering his disdain for our expectations of realism, and tuning his uneventful tale to the pitch of fantasy. It certainly looks like a half-waking dream, the sort of erotic pastoral that might filter through a boozy brain after a long lunch. No other living director can equal Bertolucci's devotion to texture, his mastery of the illusion that the very skin of film is sexy; *Stealing Beauty* is often about nothing more than the work and play of light and the supersaturation of burnt-earth colors. The camera that pursues Lucy as she dives into a pool and glides along the bottom has its own matching fluidity, a rhythm halted only by a cutaway shot to the near-naked figure by the side of the water—Miranda, lounging there like a Matisse odalisque.

The movie's gaze is surprisingly unlubricious, somehow managing to remain cool and classical in the heat; when Lucy spies a young couple smooching under a tree, the camera travels upward to a stone creature perched nearby on a wall, looking pretty severe. Again, the title brims with suggestion: the beauty of this scenery is so obvious, such a common aesthetic currency, that the only way to endow it with any novelty or thrill is to steal it—to grab it on the run and move on to something else. If you want a smart answer to the drooling manner in which *A Room with a View*, for example, lingered over the vistas around Florence, check out the chopped editing of Lucy's journey at the start of *Stealing Beauty:* Bertolucci leafs briskly through the landscape as though it were a book. If only he were able to keep that momentum; sadly, by the end of the picture we are back with lovers canoodling before a bargain sunset. Lucy has finally settled on her elected predator—the shiest in a series of sensationally unappealing local lads. The film honors her integrity in this matter and grants her instant bliss, never daring to suppose that she might, like the rest of the world's teenagers, merely stumble through the fumble and get it over with.

The actual ravishing is a dreary, pop-video affair; it plainly didn't cross Bertolucci's mind that the hippest (and most arousing) of options would have been to skip the climax altogether, to cut from chase to afterburn. The trouble with *Stealing Beauty* is not that it's dirty—it's not quite dirty enough, to be honest—but that its tastefulness and reverence for glamour soften the whole enterprise into what you might call the higher pornography. The movie is stuffed with horrible types whom the director alone seems to find worthy of our attention; it's like *Kids* with a tan. If these curious, moneyed creatures want to strip and gambol by the pool, fair enough; but as they continue to unveil and display an engorged set of feelings that seem bereft of all motive you sense that a peculiarly glossy fraud is being perpetrated. The film passes off in-jokes as velvety secrets and cheap gossip as philosophical rumination. When Alex turned on his heel, smacked his walking stick in fury, and strode away from Lucy, all because Diana had told Lucy that she, Diana, had heard from him, Alex, that she, Lucy, was still awaiting her first lover, I'm afraid that I gave up. "We don't mean you any harm," Alex tells Lucy later. "Up on this hill, the only thing we have to talk about is each other." So why not give it a rest?

There is one commanding reason to see this movie, and that is Liv Tyler. Not the performance of Liv Tyler: just Liv Tyler. I'm not really sure how good an actress she is; some of her line readings come out stiff and graceless, and she seems happiest when she's allowed to forget the daunting fact that she is taking part in a film—when she puts on a Walkman, for instance, and thrashes around her bedroom as if trying to flush the delights of Tuscany out of her skull with a tide of rock and roll. But there are extraordinary moments in *Stealing Beauty* which feel like hours—suspensions of normal time, as the indulgent frippery that surrounds Lucy just falls away and leaves her stranded, alone with the camera. It's as if Bertolucci were confessing, to himself as much as to us, that he has got the movie wrong, that it was never going to make the grade as an elegant comedy of manners—that its true subject, in short, is Tyler's face. Leaning over the lip of the bathtub, or posing—hair drawn back, one breast exposed—for the sculptor, she stares with disconcerting directness at the lens and dares it to look away. The whole drama of innocence and experience that Bertolucci planned but failed to achieve in his plot is there in these close-ups, as strong-boned and swollen-mouthed as those of Liv Ullmann in *Persona.* Bertolucci's movie—roasted, ravishing, and ridiculous—is a piece of toy cinema compared with Bergman's great interrogation of troubled spirits; the inhabitants of *Stealing Beauty* find life less a trouble than a drag. But only the most confident and contemplative of moviemakers have the nerve to peel their art back to essentials: lights, camera, countenance. As Alex says to Lucy when his wasted frame is being stretchered out of the house for the last time, "I've so enjoyed watching you."

JUNE 10, 1996

EMMA *and* KINGPIN

The philosopher Gilbert Ryle was once asked if he ever read novels. "Oh, yes," he replied. "All six of them, every year." To subsist on a diet of nothing but Jane Austen never did anyone any harm, and in Ryle's case it was decidedly beneficial. Goodness knows what he would have made of a year in which four of her six novels have been transformed, with varying degrees of violation, into movies. We have already had *Sense and Sensibility*, *Persuasion*, a television version of *Pride and Prejudice*, and, in the daffy shape of *Clueless*, a variation on the theme of *Emma*. Now we have the real thing—*Emma*, adapted and directed by Douglas McGrath.

First impressions, at least, suggest that it is real enough. The bones of the story remain unbroken: Emma (Gwyneth Paltrow) is still the perennial matchmaker—busybody or mastermind, according to your point of view—of Highbury. Her efforts to pair off the naïve Harriet Smith (Toni Collette) with the local clergyman, Mr. Elton (Alan Cumming); the shock to her system when the man of God bypasses Harriet with a proposal to Emma herself; the arrival of Frank Churchill, the near-legendary son of Mr. Weston (James Cosmo), who was himself recently hitched to Emma's governess (Greta Scacchi); and the looming presence of Mr. Knightley, older friend to Emma and the apparent source of nothing more than benevolent counsel: all these complications have made it safely from novel to film. They bring with them a trace of that extraordinary sensation—peculiar to Jane Austen and Tolstoy, and to almost no one else—of a narrative that moves like a dance. Immersed in the book, you can never say quite who is in control; Emma thinks that she is leading the way, of course, but it emerges that she is being handed gracefully from one error to the next, from deceit to self-deceit. McGrath certainly gets a measure of this grace into his movie; there are plenty of neat, light-fingered moments when he cuts from the climax of one conversation to the midst of another.

His bravado in editing Austen down is almost, though not quite, enough to make you forget his eagerness to bring her up to date. When Emma cries "Good God!," she sounds less like an elegant, Empire-line schemer and more like a busty Betjeman girl being whumped at tennis.

The fact that the movie doesn't always sound like Jane Austen, however, is unlikely to wreck your enjoyment. The more insistent problem is that it doesn't look like Jane Austen; the world that McGrath conjures up has its charms, but it bears only the patchiest relation to the Highbury that was inhabited by the novelist's imagination. The screen is filled with nooks and libraries and fireplaces, with bowers of suspiciously rosy apples, and with a gentle veil of Christmas snow that falls to the sound of "Deck the Hall with Boughs of Holly." The whole movie is decked to the hilt; it reminded me not of Austen but of the illustrations you might find on the lids of the cake tins purchased by a coachload of tourists on a day trip to Austen country. In a way, you feel sorry for McGrath and his designers; they have to decide on a tone and stick with it, whereas the atmosphere of the original resists any such definition. You can spend a lifetime reading Austen and still be unable to place her: Is she affectionate or flinty? Does her tolerance float free, or does it exist to peg back her anger? McGrath turns her into a proto-Dickensian—Emma's infuriating father, in particular, becomes a Mr. Pickwick figure, all plaintiveness melted into joviality—but there is an equally strong case for revering her as the last of the Johnsonians. No burden weighs more heavily on a writer's shoulders than that of being much loved, but something unreachable in Austen shrugs off the weight. Only a fraction of this ambivalence is available to a film like *Emma;* McGrath has opted to make things nice and snug, but in so doing he dooms us to sit through the movie sighing for the lost astringency of the book.

All of which could plausibly be dismissed as precious and Janeite—as the paranoid desire to protect a literary touchstone at all costs. But no such defensiveness was provoked by *Clueless*, which had the wit to hunt around for a modern equivalent of the codified social conditions that prevail in Highbury. Alighting, naturally enough, on Beverly Hills, it proceeded to enjoy its stay within those curious confines, flaunting a wry critical acceptance that took it much closer to the spirit of Jane Austen than anything in McGrath's *Emma*. His idea of social edge is to have Knightley proclaim a fondness for home—"It's cozy here"—and at the same time to swing the camera around so that behind Knightley we see the home in question. It's a great chunky pile of a place, and we're supposed to laugh at the absurdity of finding it cozy, but the gag denies us the chance to reach back to a time when those privileged enough to live in high style were also capable, in all sincerity, of feeling at ease there.

Having decided in advance that the hierarchies of Highbury life are a complete joke (they are actually, as Jane Austen realized, a dangerous half joke), the movie prods at them with sub-slapstick. Harriet, for instance, assists Emma on one of her visits to the needy and succeeds only in dropping food all over the floor. This dire bit of stage business obscures Emma's charity, which Austen took pains to emphasize, and merely adds Harriet Smith to the roster of the movie's buffoons—not difficult when Toni Collette (last seen as the heroine of *Muriel's Wedding*) has been encouraged throughout to portray the blushing ingenue as a bundle of toothy giggles. The film has the distinction of being miscast right across the board. Sophie Thompson, who did such great work as Anne Elliot's dreadful sister in *Persuasion*, is just as funny here, but she is far too young for the kindly, over-the-hill spinsterhood of Miss Bates. Even further under the hill is Jeremy Northam, who is glowering, glamorous, and apparently the same age as Emma. This misses the point of Mr. Knightley, who ought to be openly middle-aged—given the life expectancy of Austen's era, thirty-seven was pretty wrinkled—and avuncular in his attentions right up to the fourth quarter.

As for Gwyneth Paltrow, there is both bite and languor in her, a finesse that can turn scruffy at will. She can convey anything, in fact, except the moral bossiness of Emma Woodhouse. Her pivotal pang of ruefulness after she insults Miss Bates is beautifully done, and the Paltrow cheekbones would cut a swath through communities far plusher than Highbury, but I never really believed her capable of calculation. This is a serious shortfall, because the plot of *Emma* is artfully constructed around the ethics of plotting: it tells you all about the damage that ensues when natural solicitude shades into an unnatural desire to make short stories out of your friends. And the tale is nothing without that chill; so much of its force springs from a willingness to snatch comedy from the jaws of cruelty. Austen is not vicious and manipulative toward her creations, but she nearly is—and so is Emma, in dealing with her neighbors. Paltrow offers delight, as she should, but she gives it without demur: where is the brainy boredom that drove Miss Woodhouse to meddle?

It could be argued that people who have never read the fiction—the majority of the target audience—will not be bothered by the rights and wrongs of the cast, having nothing to compare it with. But it's worth being picky on their behalf, because they will be denied the available pleasures of the story, and will almost certainly catch a whiff of something rotten. To them, Knightley will so obviously be Emma's main man from the start that the eventual yielding of her heart will seem long overdue; whereas it should come as a genuine tremor, to us as much as to Emma herself. It is not that McGrath's movie makes no sense but that it makes such easy, do-it-yourself sense that you leave the cinema untested and unsurprised—entertained, for sure, but given little inkling of why this Austen dame was so special. The film of *Sense and Sensibility* was reduced, after a couple of viewings, to a similar thinness—to the pleasant sensation of romance. Cinema might fancy that it has trapped Jane Austen where it wants her, but she has got away again.

It was absolutely to be; every preparation was resumed; and very soon after the party repaired to ——— in expectation of a novel diversion.

"It must surely go off tolerably well," said Mr. Woodhouse. "Only, I would not catch cold; if the establishment is damp and dirty, my dear"—(this to his daughter)—"I would chuse not to attend the display; indeed, I cannot be entertained in a draught. I am decided; we shall go to-morrow."

"My dearest papa! I hear nothing but favourable report of the entertainment; it was devised, you know, by a pair of gentlemen—I know them to be gentlemen—a Mr. Farrelly, I believe, and—"

"A Mr. Farrelly again!" Emma was surprized to hear this ejaculation; that it came from the lips of Miss Bates was the cause of further astonishment.

"They are responsible—but what would I know of it—you are so much better advised of these matters than I, Miss Woodhouse; but I fancy that these same brothers—for they are brothers, I am quite sure of it!—pleased us only last year with Dumb—"

"And Dumber!" cried Mr. Elton. The consternation that greeted this addition to the exchange was the greatest yet. Mr. Elton confessed that he had taken a chaise to London with no other purpose than to extend his already large acquaintance with the achievements of those gentlemen; that he had observed Dumb, &c; and that an equal gratification was to be had from—

"Kingpin!" said Miss Bates, very fast. At least, she believed so—it was something like; at least, there were kings, and pins—or bobbins—

"Ah! Miss Bates is not mistaken," said Mr. Elton. "No doubt, Ma'am, you know also that Mr. Harrelson and Mr. Quaid—Mr. Randolph Quaid, I should say, rather than *his* brother—are the players."

The company was far from disinclined to hear more; and Mr. Elton, whose refinement of expression was complemented by a most unsullied cordiality, spoke to them of bowling with ten pins; of the misfortune that was visited upon Mr. Harrelson in the losing of his arm; and of the ardent and uncouth intentions on the part of Mr. William Murray to impede the happiness that was both prized and merited by the heroes of the piece.

"I own that the Picture is less diverting than I had hitherto heard tell," concluded he. "If the intent was to raise the humour of those present, the result was quite other—a lowering of the spirits, indeed, and a considerable measure of disgust; and yet, it is commonly said that the Picture wants nothing in its likeness of middle-America."

Emma could not resist. "And I declare it as common as anything I ever saw!" she said rather warmly. "That is—I have *not* seen it; and would not, Sir; and as for the Americas having a middle, why, I am scarce persuaded that they have a beginning or an end."

Mr. Elton was grieved; he was sensible of being the occasion of much mortification; but Emma demanded no apology. She was pondering upon the imminent event—and, it must be allowed, upon the presence of Mr. Knightley. Was it not that gentleman who had made her a gift of the Popcorn in a similar circumstance? Was it not he who had felt so nice a concern for her pleasure that he had shewn her the works of Mr. Ace Ventura himself?

AUGUST 5, 1996

BEYOND THE CLOUDS

In the fog of an Italian town, a handsome young man falls in love with a beautiful young woman. He tries to kiss her. When this fails, he tells her, "I'm a drainage-pump technician." Amazingly, this approach, too, is unsuccessful. They spend the night in the same hotel, but in separate rooms. She undresses and waits for him, in vain. In the morning, she is gone. A voice informs us, "They never met again." Two years later, they meet again. By chance, they attend the same movie. Afterward, she brings him up to date. "I've been wondering recently why I have such a need to hear words," she says. He feels differently. "I'm enslaved by your silence," he says. At last they go to bed, where his desire is so perfect that he cannot possibly spoil it by actually making love. He leaves. Whether they ever meet again is unclear. Only one thing is certain: we have been watching a Michelangelo Antonioni film.

Beyond the Clouds could well be Antonioni's final work. I hope that I'm wrong about this, but the man is turning eighty-four next week, and is not in the best of health, and the movie feels like a summation of his abiding concerns. More than a distillation, certainly: it's a long haul, not exactly rambling but taking its time to stroll through a number of separate plots, as if touring the soundstages of a favorite studio, and pausing every so often to enjoy the sights, most of which consist of women's legs. There are four stories in all, beginning with the drainage pumper (Kim Rossi-Stuart) and his beloved (Inès Sastre). The scene then switches from Ferrara to Portofino, where a movie director (John Malkovich) spies a woman (Sophie Marceau) in a shopwindow. When they finally meet, and even before they retire for the statutory coupling, she announces that she murdered her father. The third and most complicated section—the only one, at any rate, in which cause and effect, rather than dream logic, have a say in human conduct—takes place in Paris, where Roberto (Peter Weller) has a lengthy affair with Olga (Chiara Caselli), to the chagrin of his wife, Patrizia (Fanny Ardant). When Patrizia eventually walks out, she goes to rent an apartment and finds it occupied by a man (Jean Reno) who looks as beached and betrayed as herself. Guess what happens next. Finally, we get a joke—a playlet that depends on its punch line. Niccolo (Vincent Perez) follows yet another beautiful woman (Irène Jacob) to church, where he falls asleep. When he awakes, she is gone. He runs after her, sweet-talks her, and asks to see her the next day. Whereupon she turns at the door of her apartment and fires off the last word in put-downs: "Tomorrow I enter a convent." And she goes inside, without even bothering to stop and have sex. Extraordinary behavior.

Beyond the Clouds is not a misogynist picture, but Antonioni is so thoroughly conditioned by the habits of an Italian lifetime to revere women, and so keen to ascribe a grail-like fascination to their bodies and souls, that it might be easier for all concerned if he did dislike them. The entire film, in fact, is riddled with the shortcomings that have made irreverent moviegoers snort at Antonioni for so long: his own sense of humor, for one thing, lying withered and unused in the corner, not to mention his sententiousness, and the infuriating ease with which he foists his characters into a kind of spiritual gridlock before—or, to be precise, instead of—making any attempt to introduce them. Such loftiness, which was already sky-high when Antonioni made *L'Avventura* and *La Notte*, thirty years ago, has hardly succumbed to the gravity of the years; *Beyond the Clouds* is still, as you might guess from its title, way up there. On what ground, then, might one dare to argue that this is, despite everything, a pretty wonderful movie, and that you should find a ticket while you can?

Well, there is the small matter of loveliness. After a summer of movies whose directors could quite feasibly have been swapped around without either raising or lowering the quality of their respective pictures, there is an intense autumnal relief in coming upon a filmmaker who could never be mistaken for anyone else. Antonioni's movies beg for parody, but the true parodic instinct is by definition born of homage—it's a half-respectful reply to a style that demands attention. Antonioni brings his own spaces and silences; he shrouds the earth in his own weather—close to the lyrical gloom of Marcel Carné, but with an extra pearl-gray veiling, which, far from clinching lovers together, tends to keep them errant and apart. I recall Woody Allen's expressing admiration for the fog scene in *Identification of a Woman* and a corresponding desire to re-create it for one of his own productions; Woody's eyes should mist over at the sight of the new movie, which appears to deliver its dramatis personae from a netherworld of haze and rain. They could, you sense, be sucked back into it at any time;

it's as if every relationship on view here were distantly modelled on that of Orpheus and Eurydice, its urgency matched only by the undying threat of transience. The one trustworthy status is that of solitude—you can break out of it, launch brief raids into the lives of others, and then retreat to lick your wounds. Nothing in *Beyond the Clouds* is more uncluttered, or more evocative, than a shot of John Malkovich at the beach: he sits perfectly still on a swing, while the sand at his feet, whipped by the coastal wind, eddies and breaks like waves.

So much sadness seems to rise and radiate from this scene that, as often happens with Antonioni, you're amazed that he feels the need to enlarge upon it in the surrounding dialogue. Reading back through my notes on the movie, I was battered by the memory of bad lines: "Have you noticed nobody watches sunsets anymore?"; "I think that to be happy we should eliminate our thoughts"; "We always want to live in someone else's imagination." In the unlikely event that any of these remarks turned out to be true, they would still be marked by an indelible dramatic gaucheness; it's almost touching to think that an effortless visual maturity can coexist with such adolescent *tristesse*. Malkovich gets the worst of the deal; in the role of the movie director—Antonioni's representative on earth, so to speak—he is not only caught up in the Portofino chunk of the plot but charged with the Virgilian task of guiding us through the other parts. The film begins with his cinematic musings on an airplane, and he keeps popping up, as if to reassure us, just in case we've forgotten, that it *is* a film. Well, I never. At the end, when Irène Jacob slips into her apartment, leaving her admirer on the stairs, Malkovich is there on the street where she lives.

There is an odd naïveté to this pattern of appearances; Antonioni nudges us to theorize about his work—he condemns us to become film critics, you might say, instead of proper viewers—even though the landscapes of *Beyond the Clouds*, both human and geographical, can and should be left to speak passionately for themselves. No one has found such fired-up anger in Fanny Ardant before, or such creepy brooding in the skullish features of Peter Weller; nobody—not even Kieślowski—has looked so carefully at Irène Jacob and realized that her natural expression is a kind of pun, at once flirtatious and sweetly devotional. When he gets down to sex itself, of course, Antonioni is in his element; the close-ups of limbs and breasts have a certain chill to them—if we are honest about lovemaking, he suggests, does it really comprise more than the suave or fumbling rearrangement of body parts?—and yet the sheer intentness of the erotic scenes shows people at their most desperate to come alive. I used to balk at the Antonioni movies of the 1960s and 70s, at the insistence—the moral bigotry—with which alienation was urged upon us as the only available option. The director was serious in his purposes, but that very sincerity acquired a frill of chic; what is most moving about *Beyond the Clouds* is that, far from growing crusty or irascible in his old age, Antonioni has relaxed. The film is rife with images of discord and disquiet, but, possessed of a grace that I haven't seen in his work since the elegant early days of *Story of a Love Affair*, it has the good manners to offer its unhappiness less as a precondition than as a suggestion: take it or leave it.

Beyond the Clouds is many things, some of them more successful than others, but I take it to be, above all, an elegy for the art movie. I never quite thrilled to the battle that was pitched between mainstream and art cinema, but if low-level warfare has simmered for the last fifty years it has now been comprehensively won by Hollywood. The dedication to European cinema has, within a generation, sunk from a robust moviegoing habit to a buffs' charter. That is why there is such relief, and a breeze of nostalgia, in watching *Beyond the Clouds*. It even contains a brief, inconsequential skit that serves no purpose other than to provide cameos for Jeanne Moreau and Marcello Mastroianni—king and queen of the art house. I know perfectly well that there is something absurd in such crumbling Continental melancholy, in the concoction of ravishing women and reflex, virtually thoughtless philosophizing. But this weakness for profundity nevertheless signals, in retrospect, a certain strength of character—an eagerness to get something across, or at least to wrap us in a hypnotizing mood. I don't happen to believe that Antonioni's work *is* profound, but the illusion of profundity is so spooky, and so exquisitely managed, that it will do just as well. "There's a cure for everything," Jean Reno tells Fanny Ardant. "That's what concerns me," she replies. The world of Michelangelo Antonioni throngs with sick souls, and we may be slightly sick of them by now, but I really wouldn't want them to get better.

SEPTEMBER 30, 1996

THE ENGLISH PATIENT

"Would you kiss me?" "No, I'll get you some tea." These are almost the first words that we hear in *The English Patient*, but they offer a miniature version of the expansive pleasures to come. The man who wants kissing is a wounded Allied soldier. The bringer of tea is a French-Canadian nurse named Hana (Juliette Binoche), working on the Italian front near the end of the Second World War. The movie will travel high and wide, and its physical geography—caverns and churches, mountains of sand that rise overnight and cypresses that have stood forever—is almost as varied as its emotional scenery, but everything can be traced back to this early trade in tea and sympathy. Written and directed by Anthony Minghella, and based on the novel by Michael Ondaatje, the movie brims with people who have no option but to kiss each other, yet, unlike most love stories, it also shoulders the burden of a civilized life—the English patience—that determines when and why the kissing has to stop. It is, you might say, both storm and teacup.

It also has lots of plots, more than most directors would know what to do with. Two sappers, for instance, are seen checking a country road for hidden mines. A dazed Hana walks past, and they scream at her to stop. Since it's close to the start of the film, and we're still concentrating on Hana, we pay scant attention to the soldiers; much later, however, they will inch their way to the heart of the tale, as if combing it for any dusted-over treacheries. I tried to remember where I had encountered this odd rhythm of long-range surprise, and realized that it is in fact the pace at which most of us conduct our lives, or at which they annoyingly seem to conduct us. *The English Patient* is nothing if not dramatic, and yet the basic pulse of Minghella's work rids it of melodrama and draws it close to home.

With the end of the war in sight, Hana splits off from the other medics and retreats to an abandoned monastery on a Tuscan hillside. Her self-appointed mission is to take with her a single patient who needs constant care while his body, like the war that destroyed it, winds down. His skin was scorched and has now dried to a veined vellum; his lungs, or what remains of them, suck little gasps of air. Hana feeds him by chewing a morsel of plum and then slipping it into his mouth, where he champs it gently like a tortoise. He is, in his own whispered words, "a bit of toast"; he is said to be English, but he has no name, not much of a face, no past to speak of, and no hope for things to come. He has nothing, in fact, except a copy of Herodotus—one of the many books that Hana reads aloud in his bedroom to kill time. Gradually, in flashbacks, time stirs and returns to life. The English patient is, it turns out, a Hungarian count named Almásy (Ralph Fiennes), who in the late thirties was a member of the International Sand Club, a group of decent fellows who mapped the deserts of North Africa. Also in the club was Almásy's friend Madox (Julian Wadham). Madox knew a pilot called Geoffrey Clifton (Colin Firth), and asked him along. And Clifton brought a wife.

The love affair between Almásy and Katharine Clifton (Kristin Scott Thomas) reminds us that movies are really pretty good at love affairs. I, for one, had forgotten; nothing in recent cinema or in Minghella's previous films—*Truly, Madly, Deeply* and *Mr. Wonderful*—had prepared me for the palpitating shock of *The English Patient.* It works on the same principle that fuelled *Now, Voyager* and *Casablanca:* a true romantic movie knows in its bones that romance is fleshed with failure. Almásy and Katharine claw and cling to each other in the furious certainty that everything—the looming war, their betrayal of her husband, deserts of vast eternity—is destined to disentangle them. No wonder the movie feels so highly sexed; when they sneak away from a Christmas tea party at the British ambassador's residence in Cairo, they have only minutes to make love against the wall. It's a marvellous scene: soldiers chanting carols in the thick, swooning heat, the dependable Geoffrey sweating away in a Santa Claus suit while indoors his wife, in cool, removable silk, is biting her knuckles to stifle her screams. The contrast is intensely comic, and yet Minghella is not in the business of sneering at the Geoffreys of this world; his passionate film shows a quiet, unfashionable respect for those whose sense of duty has blocked their access to passion. As Almásy says of Madox, who has guessed what is going on, "He keeps talking about *Anna Karenina.* I think it's his idea of a man-to-man chat."

But that's only half of it, for we keep cutting from the desert to the Italian sickroom. The Herodotus is interleaved with notes jotted down by Katharine and Almásy; Hana reads these sibylline scraps, and somehow the flame of fixation is handed on to her. The bomb-disposal experts arrive at the monastery, and Hana falls in love with one of them, a Sikh named Kip (Naveen Andrews). Unlike Katharine and Almásy, they have nothing to thwart them, and yet their bond is equally frail. Kip, if he is not disposed of by a bomb, will return to India, and Hana has the itchy-footed look of a woman who will always veer away from happiness before the thought of losing it becomes unbearable. Binoche is quite extraordinary in this movie; her switchback moods have always kept audiences guessing, but here the tremors increase to the point where she seems to take *herself* by surprise. Even in the way she chops her hair or plays hopscotch in the dark, there is an arousing, pale-faced pride in her own volatility. If I were Kip, I wouldn't know whether to take Hana to bed or to clear the immediate area and defuse her.

When did you last see a movie that offered two great roles for women? Hana and Katharine never meet; or, at any rate, they meet only in the mind of the patient, and you can imagine him mulling over the pair of them, tasting his impressions like wine. Hana, dark and desperate, speaks English with a French accent, whereas Katharine, who wears white to set off her tan, is the last word in English blondes, with an air of self-possession that is barely ruffled by a vicious sandstorm. She and Almásy spend a night in the front seat of a truck, while the desert drifts and mounts against the windows. They remain polite, but you can feel their fate being sealed by the sand. Almásy whiles away the hours by telling her about winds: "There is a whirlwind from southern Morocco, the *aajej*, against which the fellahin defend themselves with knives. And there is the *ghibli* from Tunis. . . ." Katharine stops him. "The *ghibli*," she repeats in her crisp tones. There is a flash of the famous Scott Thomas smile, and it relieves the solemnity of the moment. Almásy's learned speech, complete with *aajej* and *ghibli*, comes near the start of Ondaatje's novel, but there it lacks Katharine's interruption. What Scott Thomas shows is that the movie—unlike the book, which was so finely written that I found it, to all intents and purposes, unreadable—can allow itself a certain lightness of touch as it climbs with both intent and purpose in the direction of tragedy. The most touching aspect of Fiennes's performance, too, is the birth of good humor that accompanies the demise of his body. With Katharine he could barely contain his anguish, but after his baptism by fire he lies there, horribly amused by the ironies of the world, and talks to Hana like a sort of mummified Noël Coward.

It was Coward, of course, who emerged from *Lawrence of Arabia* and said that if Peter O'Toole had been any prettier the film would have been called *Florence of Arabia*. I thought of that when I was watching Fiennes: he has the bright, avenging-angel eyes of O'Toole, but there is more meat and sternness to him, and, indeed, the whole of *The English Patient* proceeds with an inquisitive determination that is foreign to David Lean's glorious spectacle. Minghella burrows into his heat-struck characters, where the lordly Lean stood back and stared. What links the two movies is a willingness, almost a need, to be entranced by landscape, and Minghella summons his own scenes of uncluttered bliss—the Cliftons' bright-yellow plane appearing like a shock of sunlight against the thin blue air, and the view from the cockpit down to the creaminess of dunes. *The English Patient* is what you might call an International Sand Film; the characters materialize from all over, and the desert is their one common arena. Almásy is so elusive about where he comes from, and yet so direct about what he wants, that he sometimes appears to be spying on himself. Bismarck once said that you could trust any Englishman apart from one who spoke French, in which case the English patient is as slippery as they come; he's so English he isn't even English.

Minghella has not simply trimmed Ondaatje's book; he has reinvented the story with his eyes. There are a few lines that still sound a touch top-heavy, but, equally, there are scenes that revel in their own wordlessness. Kip takes Hana on his motorcycle to a local church, where he puts a flare in her hand and hoists her up on a pulley, so that distant frescoes are suddenly glowing in front of her nose. It's a rapturous sight, and the rapture hurts; breaking off so vividly from the war, slipping loose from gravity and gloom, only sharpens the pain of going back. To say that *The English Patient* is about the difficult relations between longing and belonging suggests the traditional terrain of the art movie, and yet there is nothing fogged or precious about Minghella's achievement. Together with the producer, Saul Zaentz, the composer, Gabriel Yared, and the director of photography, John Seale, he has made a clear and hard-edged epic, and the movie is splendidly unabashed by its old-style stirrings toward adventure. It runs for two hours and forty minutes and fills that time to overflowing; I have seen it twice now, and if I find myself rapidly growing obsessed with it that is because the people in the movie are infected with obsessions of their own. The chords that greet the lovers' final appearance—Almásy carrying Katharine in his arms, weeping in the middle of nowhere—are unmistakably Wagnerian, and for once the echo rings true. Man to man, this is awfully close to a masterpiece.

NOVEMBER 25, 1996

STAR TREK: FIRST CONTACT

What is it with *Star Trek*? Why can't it be like any other TV series and stay where it belongs? Imagine if every show were like this—breaking free of the small screen and boldly heading for the big one. We don't have to sit through *Roseanne IV: The Wrath of Dan* or *ER II: The Search for Doc*, so I can't really see the point of *Star Trek: First Contact*. It's not a terrible movie, but it's about as substantial as the hologram sequences that the captain of the *Enterprise* can summon at will. Still, I was impressed by the care that went into the design of the plot—the way in which it is both ordinary enough to bore the space-pants off a *Star Trek* devotee and abstruse enough to leave more agnostic members of the audience completely baffled. I grew up with the old ship and its trusty crew, and, while I quite understand that it was time to put Kirk and his buddies out to pasture before they succumbed to permanent phaser droop, I find it nearly impossible to get up to speed with Captain Jean-Luc Picard—the name alone makes me laugh every time I hear it—and his state-of-the-art gizmos. "We appear to be caught in a temporal wake!" one of the officers shouted at the beginning, and I thought, Join the club.

The hook of *First Contact*—number eight in the *Star Trek* series, if you can believe it—is that planet Earth is once again threatened with destruction, this time by the Borg. The Borg are the scariest folk in the universe; they are half organic, like supermarket granola; they have forearms left over from the *Terminator* films; and they suffer from troublesome scalp problems, not least a bunch of little hoses sprouting from the backs of their heads. We are told that they have "a collective consciousness," with no concept of individuals, although by that criterion our galaxy would have long ago been conquered by the Partridge Family. The Borg idea of a good day is to wipe out—or "assimilate," as the jargon sensitively puts it—anything that stands in their path. What bugs them about Earth is that in the year 2063 (ancient history, by *Star Trek* standards), human beings make contact with aliens for the first time. Being violently opposed to the intergalactic peace process, the Borg travel back in time to stymie the crucial meeting before it can happen. I have to say, I'm with the Borg a hundred percent on this one; anything that will allow fans of *Star Trek*, let alone of *The X-Files*, to turn around to the rest of us and crow "I told you so" is an intrinsically bad idea.

The film is directed by Jonathan Frakes, who also plays Riker, the most boring of the characters. The casting is something of an embarrassment; the people on the bridge of the *Enterprise* are no more exciting than their twenty-fourth-century drip-dry knitwear, whereas some of the supporting roles show distinct evidence of intelligent life. James Cromwell plays a rangy rocket nerd who invents the first warp-drive mechanism, in 2063; Alfre Woodard appears as his assistant, who develops a minor sweetness for Captain Picard. Above all, there is the Borg Queen, the *fons et origo* of this ruthless race: you would expect such a figure to bellow her orders, like Tina Turner, but—and this is a lovely conceit—she is a model of feline courtesy. I like to think that she took the trouble to oil herself with the good manners of advanced civilizations before reducing them to rubble. At first, the Queen is no more than a disembodied head and shoulders, which float down from the roof as if advertising a cybernetic shampoo. Even then, under all the gnarled tracery of her makeup, I began to recognize that smile, and the voice that poured out from it like cream. As the head clipped onto the body, I got it: this was the helplessly seductive Alice Krige. As Harold Abrahams's actress girlfriend, Krige woke up the somnolent *Chariots of Fire*, but somehow the full-blooded parts that should have followed never arrived. You might call it a shame that she has been reduced to playing semimetallic androids in Christmas sci-fi; I prefer to think that the lasting joy of ephemeral movies, the saving grace of crummy genres, is their bemusing ability to toss up great cameos and to flare with snap intensity. *First Contact* is drab and halting, and oddly glum to look at, but when Krige is onscreen, glistening with wickedness and bathing Picard's brains with her Joan Greenwood whisper, the movie beams itself up to a more rarefied level. It was frankly a disappointment that she and her fellow-Borg had to get it in the neck, but that's not the end of the affair. I came out of the eighth *Star Trek* already pondering the ninth, in which Jean-Luc *et ses amis* take on the angriest force ever to menace our existence: if you thought the Borg were bad, just wait till you meet the McEnroe.

DECEMBER 9, 1996

CRASH

People have been talking about *Crash* ever since the director David Cronenberg announced that he was planning to turn J. G. Ballard's notorious 1973 novel into a movie. One of the curious side effects of hype, of course, is that the longer and more loudly a work is discussed the less idea you have of what it is actually like. When I finally saw *Crash*, it was something of a relief to discover that this mythical picture really did exist. So what is it? A road movie, a blue movie, a black comedy, or a load of white noise about nothing? A dose of each, I would say, although the best account of the film comes from one of the characters, Catherine (Deborah Kara Unger), as she sits by a hospital bed and murmurs, "Not a lot of action here."

She is visiting her husband, James Ballard; I have a sneaking suspicion that the name is intended to ring a bell. Ballard is played by James Spader, who seems to accept only roles that will allow him to stray from the path of normal behavior. Ballard has injured his leg in a crash; he hit another vehicle and killed the driver, but the dead man's fellow-passenger and wife, a doctor named Helen Remington (Holly Hunter), survived. At least, I *think* she survived; she certainly bared her breast at Ballard while they were trapped in the wreckage. (In the world according to Cronenberg, such a gesture counts as formal etiquette, like dropping a curtsy at court.) By the end of *Crash*, however, I was wondering whether Ballard and Helen had in fact perished in the accident—whether the inhabitants of this movie, like the infected zombies in Cronenberg's *They Came from Within*, are drawn from the ranks of the undead.

All this is particularly bad news for Holly Hunter, who is forced to replace her natural chirrup and joie de vivre with a grim somnambulism. Clenched of jaw and flat of voice, she doesn't register much joie even when she's making love—as if love, indeed, were the dirty downside of sex, the part we don't mention. The problem is that Cronenberg gives her, like almost everyone else in the film, almost nothing to do *except* have sex. *Crash* isn't plotted, it's programmed, and instead of narrative flow we are treated to a series of artful tableaux, as in a Peter Greenaway movie. When Ballard and Helen leave the hospital, they get it on in his car—a model identical to the one that he totalled. Into the equation comes Vaughan (Elias Koteas), a weirdo who specializes in car crashes—the patterns they follow, the celebrities they squash, and so on. When he is not reenacting famous collisions for public consumption, he is using his car for equally brutal encounters—with an airport hooker, with Ballard's wife, and eventually with Ballard himself. Ballard, for his part, makes out with an unnamed assistant at work and with a crash victim wearing leg braces (Rosanna Arquette), who then clambers into Vaughan's Lincoln for a sedate cuddle with Helen. Most shocking of all, Ballard keeps making love to his wife. How square can you get? Catherine, meanwhile, has her own packed schedule: in the opening scene, she bends over, hitches up her skirt for the benefit of an airplane mechanic, and never, so to speak, looks back.

As you may gather, *Crash* is more or less *La Ronde* on wheels, although none of it is terribly sexy. There are moments that are nearly titillating, just as there are lines that are almost funny, but Cronenberg seems to have developed a disdain for the customary satisfactions of cinema. It is standard practice to jeer at the fakery of skin flicks, but *Crash* makes you nostalgic for the ersatz heartiness of porno performers; at least they're pretending, for the viewer's sake, to have a good time, whereas the characters in *Crash* are so unsmiling—so driven, in every sense—that they make you ashamed of ever having enjoyed yourself. They squirm around in the backseats of automobiles, doing what kids did in movies like *American Graffiti* but having none of the fun. That, I guess, is Cronenberg's point: he assumes that all the leisure and liberty have drained out of driving, and that we now live with the unglamorous reality of the car as monster—half weapon, half sex aid. I hate to introduce a note of common sense here, but if Cronenberg is literally suggesting that we are turned on by freeway pileups he's wrong: what arouses us is *not crashing*, otherwise known as speed. If, on the other hand, his movie is primarily a metaphor, all about the human race sliding into the thrall of its own machinery, then it's kind of obvious, and, anyway, Cronenberg has done it before. James Woods having a tape inserted into his abdomen in *Videodrome* is a better sick joke about biotechnology than James Spader fondling a steering column.

People are right to be shocked by *Crash*, but for the wrong reasons. What it shows you, even in scarred close-up, is only mildly nauseating compared to what it insists on telling you. Cronenberg has become, you might say, an autodidact, and we have to sit there while his characters lecture us on the meaning of carnal cars. The worst offender is Vaughan. "For the first time, there's a benevolent psychopathology that beckons us," he tells Ballard. "For the first time, the car crash is a fertilizing rather than a destructive event—a liberation of sexual energy that mediates the sexuality of those who died with an intensity impossible in any other form." The first thing to be said about these lines is that, as Jack Lemmon pointed out to Tony Curtis, nobody talks like that. The second thing is that they are a pose—the sort of rarefied aesthetic, daringly indifferent to suffering, that was already well established when André Gide reworked it as the *acte gratuit* in *Les Caves du Vatican.* Although *Crash* is every bit as explicit as the rumors suggested, it is not sexually explicit; it's bare-assed philosophy, and you may not want to watch.

Cronenberg addicts will argue that the film is beautiful, and there's no denying that, true to J. G. Ballard's book, it gleams with an awful, metallic loveliness. The camera presides with unhurried aplomb, coolly inspecting the ruins of bodywork; after a hundred minutes, however, such loftiness grows tiring to the eyes, and you gradually realize that *Crash* is using style to seal itself off from the mess—the truly accidental qualities—of the world beyond. The movie is a controlled experiment, in other words, and the characters are nothing but lab rats; cars outnumber people here, and there's an eerie lack of background noise. Yet, at the same time, Cronenberg the soothsayer needs to engage with the mechanized society—to tell us, or warn us, about our accelerated doom. Can he really have it both ways? He is usually such a cruel wit, and *Crash* could have been thrilling, nasty, and horribly alive; what threw it off the road and stopped it dead was the desire—the deep, ridiculous desperation—to be a work of art.

MARCH 31, 1997

THE SAINT

There is a scene in the middle of *The Saint* that may, in time, come to be viewed as a critical moment in American movies. The Saint (Val Kilmer) and his young, blond, beautiful, poetry-reading, world-changing-scientist sidekick Emma (Elisabeth Shue)—in short, his girl—are rushing through watery tunnels in the bowels of modern Moscow. Our man is in a fix: the exits are blocked, and there are Russian-mafia goons coming up behind. Salvation arrives in the shape of a young, dark, beautiful, beret-wearing, gun-toting Russian art dealer who appears from the shadows, ushers him and Emma into a secret chamber, and tries to sell them some icons. When this attempt fails, she offers to lead them underground to the sanctuary of the American embassy, pausing only to deliver an outrageous product placement for our hero's waterproof watch. As the action unfolded, I sat there with my jaw resting lightly on the floor, and I thought, This is it. This is what we have been heading for all these years. Here is a film that makes *no sense at all.*

That is no reason, of course, not to see it. On the contrary, there's something rather bracing in the thought that Paramount Pictures chose to offload enormous sums of money on what is essentially a dadaist experiment. I've eaten bowls of spaghetti that were more tightly structured than this picture; it's meant to be a thriller, but what wound up onscreen suggests that the writers, Jonathan Hensleigh and Wesley Strick, were encouraged to free-associate—to jot down random ideas and lines of bad dialogue, toss them in a bucket, and leave it for the director, Phillip Noyce, to play grab bag. Plainly, none of these guys retain much loyalty to *The Saint*, and you can't blame them. It's not as if the brand recognition were that strong. The old TV series, in which Roger Moore's smirk travelled the world in the fight against crime, boasted only a couple of gimmicks: first, the halo that appeared—*ding!*—above Roger's head at the start of each episode, and, second, the unalloyed joy of the fact that he drove a *Volvo.* Noyce's movie is tragically halo-free, and even the Volvo is a sporty red number; I was praying to see the Saint pull away in one of those station-wagon models from the seventies or eighties, built like a bus and stuffed with kids and Labradors.

To ascribe a plot to this film would be sycophancy; all one can say is that a few, unconnected events come to pass. An orphaned boy who calls himself Simon Templar is beaten by a Catholic priest. He grows up to be Val Kilmer—more punishment, I guess—and spends his days assuming various disguises. Although there is a flicker of continuing spiritual agony in the fact that his aliases are named after saints, Simon's main motive seems to be his Swiss bank account: "If I can just break fifty," he says, musing on his millions. He is commissioned to steal a microchip from a budding Russian dictator called Tretiak (Rade Serbedzija), who, in turn, asks him to pilfer a formula for cold-fusion technology from Emma the scientist. Just another job for the Saint, you say, but wait: Emma keeps the formula tucked in her bra. How can he pull off the heist without falling in love? What is the future of Mother Russia? And what about the other man in Emma's life, the poet Shelley? As she movingly puts it, "How can I love a man called Percy?"

These are dark waters, and Phillip Noyce, who once produced a work as crisp and efficient as *Dead Calm*, wastes no time in muddying them further. Like some of the worst Bond pictures, the film staggers between high tech and low-camp comedy. The first half is especially strange, as the Saint switches teeth, hair, clothes, and accents in an attempt to remain invisible—a noble ambition, stymied only by the fact that almost every incarnation looks like Jim Morrison. Kilmer's face always appears a little swollen, as if fresh from a fight; add the kiss-me-quick lips and you get a definite surge of alternating sexual current. At times, he is practically a drag queen, which is not a bad idea; given that the Saint is professionally and geographically promiscuous, why not make him a chameleon in the sack as well? The problem is that neither Kilmer nor Noyce can decide how funny these variations are supposed to be; you don't know where or whether to laugh, and you end up simply squirming. I finally had to cover my eyes when the Saint turned into a mournful South African artist with rolls of fifty-pound notes tucked down his leather pants. "I'm not very good with people," he murmured. You said it, Val. The trick with multiple roles, as Alec Guinness proved in *Kind Hearts and Coronets*, and as Chevy Chase didn't in *Fletch*, is not to show off. Kilmer has many qualities, but the wholesale abandonment of ego is not one of them.

Once Elisabeth Shue enters the equation, the weirdness rating of this movie jumps off the scale. Shue is vulnerability made flesh; it seems unlikely that she will ever really leave Las Vegas, and you have to ask whether someone whose eyes are such fathomless pools of pain would be able to hack it as an Oxford physicist. I suspect a sneaky joke on Noyce's part here: who would have imagined that cold fusion—going nuclear at room temperature—would be solved by a woman with a superheated soul? The film is so wildly miscast, and so indifferent to logic, that you can't help wondering whether Noyce's whole game plan is to mock the genre of the superhero and to jeer, rather unpleasantly, at our basic need to be drawn into the story. Maybe he's right: maybe, after duds like *The Shadow* and *The Phantom*, only a movie as messy and vapid as this one can bring people to their senses and stop the flow. "Who are you?" Emma asks the Saint. "No one has a clue," he replies. "Least of all me."

APRIL 14, 1997

CON AIR

Advance word on *Con Air* said that it was all about an airplane with an unusually dangerous and potentially lethal load. Big deal. You should try the lunches they serve out of Newark. Compared with the chicken napalm I ate on my last flight, the men in *Con Air* are about as harmful as balloons. Still, if you are determined to enjoy this picture you may as well make the effort to believe in its inhabitants, so here goes. On board the plane, in the care of the United States Marshals Service, is Cameron Poe (Nicolas Cage), a former Army Ranger—"With your military skills, you are a deadly weapon"—who is hitching a ride home to his wife and child after serving eight years for killing some punk by mistake. During his time in prison, Poe took care to educate himself, learning, among other things, to speak Spanish and to practice origami. He is, we are told, "a nobody," but the rest of the passenger list is stuffed with somebodies. There is Cyrus Grissom (John Malkovich), evil genius, with the accent on genius; Garland Greene (Steve Buscemi), evil genius, with the accent on evil; and Diamond Dog (Ving Rhames), black-liberation terrorist. Together with the odd rapist and drug baron, these boys are being flown to a new, high-security prison, "designed to warehouse the worst of the worst."

You always know that a movie is in trouble when half the dramatis personae are required to waste their time beefing up the reputations of the other half. "All those monsters on one plane!" a woman at ground control says. "They somehow managed to get every crook and freak in the universe on one plane," Poe says. "Makes the Manson family look like the Partridge Family," says a convict friend of Poe's. What the screenwriter, Scott Rosenberg, and the director, Simon West, fail to understand is that the more blatantly they broadcast such wickedness the less we believe in it: everyone talks with such awe about Garland Greene, about his extravagant appetite for homicide, that you can't help laughing when his restraining mask is finally unstrapped to reveal the endearing bozo features of Steve Buscemi—a man who could, if he was feeling especially mean, kill a couple of cold beers. The mask, of course, is a steal from *The Silence of the Lambs*, as is the sobriquet of Grissom—Cyrus the Virus. Oh, please. Jonathan Demme makes a respectable and coherent thriller, and six years later Hollywood screenwriters are still looting it for ideas. Couldn't they, you know, have some new ones?

Needless to say, the villains break loose, with the aid of some painfully concealed straight pins. From here on, their task is simple: land at Carson City, dump the low-grade prisoners, pick up a fresh batch of hard cases, fly to a deserted airstrip, switch planes, then leave American airspace and spend the rest of their lives doing raffia work, or whatever retired psychos do. Only Poe can foil their plans; with his origami training, for example, he is capable of pecking Diamond Dog to death with a small paper goose. Anyway, he and the rest of the cons reach Carson City in the middle of a sandstorm—"Perfect," says Cyrus, who is able to leave the plane in a protective hood and so pass for a guard. But what would have happened without the sandstorm? How was the master criminal going to disguise himself on a nice calm day? I'm not saying that *Con Air* should be realistic—a certain hokey implausibility comes with the territory—but a little touch of logic in the distribution of lucky breaks and bad calls would not have gone amiss. As it is, the picture runs mostly on atmospheric, or at least acoustic, principles: the sole criterion governing the Carson City scene appears to be the director's profound desire to play with his wind machines, and anyone approaching from a distance is automatically filmed in long shot through a wobbly heat haze. In the closing minutes, all motives are jettisoned in favor of Sturm und Drang: with the plane forced to make an emergency landing, the choice of runway is quickly whittled down to either (a) the Las Vegas strip or (b) the Las Vegas strip. Jackpot guaranteed.

All this is a way of saying that *Con Air* was produced by Jerry Bruckheimer. With his late partner, Don Simpson, Bruckheimer was responsible for *Top Gun*, *Beverly Hills Cop*, *Crimson Tide*, and a host of other quiet, Bergmanish delvings into the agon of a godless world. To watch those movies was to have your brains tossed like salad, but anyone who claimed to be wholly impervious to the bright crunch of the Bruckheimer style was either lying or dead. I would be more than happy to welcome *Con Air* into the fold, but it is not one of Bruckheimer's best. There's a great moment when the airborne Poe sends a message to the authorities by scrawling it on a dead body and mailing it into thin air, but the rest of the film rarely risks the blackness of such comedy. Unlike *Top Gun*, it doesn't quite have the courage of its own cheesiness, although the Wagnerian leitmotiv of the toy bunny that runs, or hops, through the entire plot, culminating in a slightly damp appearance at the climax, should bring comfort and joy to cynics everywhere. Simon West is making his directorial debut here; like Tony Scott, a Bruckheimer regular, he is an Englishman who found success in advertising. As the publicity notes remind us, "His Pepsi Innertube spot was voted the most popular commercial of the 1995 Superbowl in a *USA Today* poll." Scholars of the West oeuvre argue that this early work is still his best—that, if anything, he has had trouble moving on. *Con Air* failed to touch my inner tube, but by the end I was dying for a Pepsi.

A few days later, I found myself watching *Spartacus*—the only Kubrick film that I really like, with the cold pedantry of his manner properly offset by all that sweat and sand. In particular, I watched a brief scene in which a quartet of slaves walk toward an arena in which half of them will die; Kirk Douglas is given no special treatment by the camera—he is just part of the lineup, the idea being that the ensuing scenes will thrust our hero, through force of arms and of will, onto center stage. Compare the villains arriving at the plane in *Con Air*, and you see how crassly West's camera picks out each figure and goggles at it; how brutishness is indicated by a slow-motion close-up of a pair of boots clomping like thunder against the ground. You could say that it's merely one overblown shot, but it does provoke the pessimistic thought that movies—perhaps under the influence of commercials—have woefully mislaid the virtues of unadorned storytelling. Where Kubrick established a steady, ominous rhythm from and against which violence would suddenly break, West choreographs the simplest motions as if they themselves were inherently violent. So swiftly, in other words, does he debase the currency of action that his thriller is all but spent before it has even begun. *Con Air* may look turbulent and aggressive, even rather seditious, but in truth West is a slave to the Bruckheimer ethic; and, unlike Kirk Douglas, he will never revolt.

In one respect, *Con Air* should be able to hold its head high. Kubrick hired not just Douglas but Laurence Olivier, Jean Simmons, and Peter Ustinov; West has Nicolas Cage, John Malkovich, Steve Buscemi, and, in the earthbound role of a heroically flustered marshal, John Cusack. How can you make a bad film with a cast like that? Well, it's a tall order, but somehow West pulls it off. I felt sorry for Malkovich, who normally tastes the pleasure of cruel lines as though with a forked tongue. Here he is faced with the saddest sound of all—dialogue that really, really tries to be tough, like a teenager who can't quite handle a drink. Cyrus to the pilot: "If you say a word about this on the radio, the next wings you see will belong to the flies buzzing over your rotting corpse." Whooh! Only Nicolas Cage, in fact, emerges intact from the rubble of this picture; he has managed to pass from light comedian to heavy action hero while maintaining the air of someone who finds existence to be one long, weary joke. "On any other day, that might seem strange," he murmurs, as a silver Alfa Romeo flies through the sky on the end of a rope. What is truly brave about Poe is not that he stays on board and opts to fight Cyrus and his merry men but that he refuses to be impressed by the explosive superfluity of the proceedings. His is a valiant quest for irony in a movie that wants only to whack us into oblivion, and in his low-lidded eyes we see a reflection of our own ever-growing predicament: there is nothing so boring in life, let alone in cinema, as the boredom of being excited all the time.

JUNE 9, 1997

MEN IN BLACK, BATMAN & ROBIN, *and* SPEED 2

It's that time again. The studios roll out the summer blockbusters, and we all wait to see just how thoroughly they can bust our blocks off. Thus far, almost everything is running scared of *The Lost World:* it may be fun to watch soft-shelled humans being cracked by raptors, but it's even more enjoyable to watch movies that were a long time in the making—and longer still in the hyping—getting munched into little morsels by Spielberg. Now we have a new bunch of offerings on the menu, the tastiest of which is *Men in Black.* Written by Ed Solomon and directed by Barry Sonnenfeld, this picture is easy—indolent, confident, and shy of risks, but so relaxed that you can hardly be bothered to complain.

The Men in question are Agent K (Tommy Lee Jones) and Agent J (Will Smith), who dress like the Blues Brothers and spend their days policing the activities of resident aliens. It appears that at any time there are some fifteen thousand foreign bodies on the planet, most of them in Manhattan, and a few of them in your immediate circle of friends. One of the pleasures of Sonnenfeld's project, in fact, is his determination to make a solid and unabashed New York movie—not just in its locations but in the crackle of passing gags at the expense of Queens and Staten Island. (How all this will play in the all-important Far Eastern video market that movie distributors keep yakking on about is anybody's guess.) Most aliens, it appears, are law-abiding citizens, who like to keep all three noses clean, but there are a few rogue elements to be arrested and, when necessary, splattered. The plot requires our heroes to track down an outsize bug that lodges inside the body of a farmer (Vincent D'Onofrio), who travels to New York in order to destroy the entire planet and generally have a good time.

The story is perilously thin, close to ignorable. Maybe that's deliberate; as in his *Addams Family* movies, Sonnenfeld is far more concerned with wrapping us in texture. The title of the new film sounds like a scholarly study of his complete works; no other director is so enthralled by black as a color and a mood, so eager to stretch its possibilities. The fetishistic gleam of the men's car is spectrums away from the flat black of their suits, or from the sharp shadows in which they hunt their quarry, or from the funereal fug so beloved of Morticia Addams. Against it you have the blaring brightness of the men's headquarters and of the Guggenheim Museum, not to mention the daft white plastic pod in which Agent J is hunched when he first applies for the job. Thanks to a kind of double-jointed chronology, Sonnenfeld delivers a nineties take on a sixties idea of what the future—a nineties future, for instance—would be like. It's a hip way to cover your back; it saves you, for one thing, from the embarrassment of a picture like *2001: A Space Odyssey*, where the shuttle attendants sported beehive hats that simply screamed 1968.

The trouble with *Men in Black* is that whenever the camera wanders away from Smith and Jones your attention goes with it; even Linda Fiorentino, as a horny medical examiner, feels irrelevant to the action. At the other end of the personal-grooming scale, the monsters on show are moist, blubbery, and somehow rather obvious: the joke, like the fright, wears off fast. Agent K has a neat little gizmo, flashing and phallic, that erases the memory of people who have just witnessed alien activity, and you can't help wondering whether Sonnenfeld is using the same device on his audience; I, for one, could remember virtually nothing about *Men in Black* the day after I saw it. The plot and the special effects had slid from my brain, leaving only a vague conviction that Tommy Lee Jones was back in form and registering levels of cool that would cause most actors to snap in half. Will Smith is speedy and high-spirited, and he runs with the picture, but Jones does something more cussed—he trips it up, and stalls it for a second, and stares unsmilingly at its gunk-coated farce. There's a tremendous moment when Smith apprehends an alien and reports his findings to Jones: "He said the world was coming to an end." Jones, without a flicker: "Did he say when?" More than ever, we need men like Jones to come to the aid of the party. When movies grow as bendy as cartoons, it becomes a matter of honor, not just of style, that someone continue to play it straight.

Could Jones have saved *Batman & Robin*? He didn't manage it with *Batman Forever*—never was there a more ominous title—and it seems increasingly likely that the Batman pictures will swallow and regurgitate any actor who tries to get in their way. *Batman & Robin* is the fourth

Warner Bros. installment, but it feels like the forty-fourth. Is it really only two years since Chris O'Donnell tried to convince us, and himself, that he looked good in leather? He is one of the old hands in this movie; newcomers include George Clooney as Batman, Alicia Silverstone as Batgirl, and Arnold Schwarzenegger and Uma Thurman as a pair of fresh villains—Mr. Freeze and Poison Ivy. This is quite a lineup, boasting a broad choice of dramatic styles, and what lends the movie cohesion and integrity is the fact that all those involved have come up with their worst imaginable performances. Even Clooney's bedroom smile makes no impact; if anything, I suspect an imminent case of Caruso syndrome, which causes actors to quit well-written TV shows in favor of movies that are barely written at all. The guilty party in *Batman & Robin* is Akiva Goldsman, whose script is a magnificent anthology of duds. I was especially pleased to learn that Batgirl had attended "Oxbridge Academy." Would that be in Royal England?

The plot is all about our old friend global domination. "First Gotham, and then . . . the world!" cries Mr. Freeze, whose hobbies consist of blasting innocent people with his ice gun, exclaiming "Ha-ha-ha!," and, in his quieter moments, stealing diamonds, which he then plugs into himself as if they were batteries. In his quest for power, Mr. Freeze joins forces with Poison Ivy, a former research scientist, whose principal weapons of mass destruction are bad breath and bright-green pantyhose. Poor Uma Thurman; Goldsman wrote a few speeches for her but forgot to provide anyone she could address them to, so she wanders round delivering monologues in a void, stopping her sentences in odd. Places in order to. Make them. Sound strange and vol. Uptuous.

The action sequences, one of which is apparently modelled on *Starlight Express*, are choreographed with so little care that it's impossible to work out who is doing what to whom. You sit there feeling brain-damaged and praying for the mayhem to cease; when it finally does, along comes one of the quiet and thoughtful scenes, which are somehow even worse. It is tempting to dismiss *Batman & Robin* as simply inept, but the crassness goes deeper than that. I thought I smelled something truly corrupt in this film: its expectation of what we expect from movies is so low and snarling that you come out feeling not just swindled but mildly humiliated. In its blending of the humorless and the apocalyptic, in the intolerance that it borrows from its own bad guys, and in its strutting preference for superhuman grandeur over the small scale of human activity, *Batman & Robin* inches close to a fascist aesthetic. Also, the back projection looks crummy. And Alicia Silverstone should stop chewing her lip.

* * *

There is less to object to in *Speed 2: Cruise Control*, although I am thinking of suing Twentieth Century Fox for breach of contract, on the ground that most of the film is set on a boat. Not a wave-slapping powerboat, you understand, but a hulking great cruise liner that looks like a luxury fridge-freezer. It boasts many original features, including tacky shopping malls with matching customers, and an official madman in residence named Geiger (Willem Dafoe), who wants to ram the vessel into an oil tanker. But where, pray, is the speed? I can bicycle faster than this ship. I know people who can *swim* faster. If things carry on like this, we can look forward to *Speed 3* taking place on the back of a pony.

The day is saved by a loving young couple—Annie (Sandra Bullock), who hails from the first *Speed*, and a cop called Alex (Jason Patric), who doesn't. Their task is to try to get engaged during a Caribbean cruise, although they soon lay aside such frivolities and proceed with the serious business of thwarting Geiger. This could have proved gripping, but the director, Jan De Bont, has grown awfully casual since the rush-hour momentum and crisp compositions of the original movie; *Speed 2* has a plot with split ends and an unsuitable fondness for fidgety, handheld shots. Jan De Bont pretending to be John Cassavetes is not a pretty sight. It's worth sitting through the picture for the sake of a great closing stunt, when Alex has to harpoon a seaplane, but I still left the theatre drenched in disappointment and missing Keanu Reeves. What is Jason Patric, after all, but Keanu without the passion, fire, and intellect?

JULY 7, 1997

CONTACT

Contact is Robert Zemeckis's first film since *Forrest Gump*, which makes it some kind of occasion. Based on a novel by Carl Sagan, it tells the tale of Dr. Ellie Arroway, a scientist who spends her days listening for radio signals from alternative life-forms, rather like Kris Kristofferson tuning in to all those hairy truckers in *Convoy*. Ellie is an obsessive; she was practically born with a pair of headphones over her ears, and as a nine-year-old girl (a good, uncute performance from Jena Malone) she was encouraged in these pursuits by her widowed dad (David Morse). He then died, leaving her to grow up into Jodie Foster—twitchy and lonesome, wearing Bill Gates spectacles and with her hair scraped back as if she were preparing for an emergency face pack. Even among those who share her fascination with outer space, Ellie is thought to be spaced out, and when government sponsorship is withdrawn from her project, she goes into hyperdrive, warning that lack of funds could cause her to miss "the most profoundly impactful moment in human history."

We now approach the most resoundingly crunchful moment in the cinematic event. Equipped with money donated by a bald billionaire and all-purpose super-creep (John Hurt), Ellie is seen lounging one day in a field beside her car. It's a beautiful and rather witty shot, with Zemeckis summoning a kind of techno-pastoral: Foster strikes an Andrew Wyeth pose, but stretching away in the background is a daisy chain of enormous radio dishes. Ellie seems comfortable in such a landscape, and stays there while daylight fails; the next thing we see is a close-up of her eyes, tightly shut and filling the screen, and the next thing we hear is a thump. A gusting, thrumming, fizzy thump, not wholly unmusical—almost a gump. Then one more, then another, until there's no doubt about it: call waiting. Although we knew that this had to happen, the point at which Ellie's eyes open, the slow dawn of her realization, is still unquestionably thrilling, and the next twenty minutes or so, as her colleagues get to work, are the busiest and most stirring in what is otherwise a long and patience-stretching movie. Since *Apollo 13*, I have had a weakness for scientists reeling off streams of data at each other—the louder and more incomprehensible the better.

In one respect, Zemeckis improves upon Ron Howard's film: he arranges for the technical details to gather pace and fury and then slams them into the side of a sick joke. The signal from the stars is decoded into a visual image and played on a video monitor; it is fine-tuned, focussed, and turned on its side to reveal what appears to be a swastika. Pull back a little and you get the full picture: Adolf Hitler. It's an inspired, not to say unsettling, gag. We like to imagine other species as either kindly child-substitutes with eyes borrowed from Jean-Paul Sartre or as wet-fanged beasties who like their earthlings medium rare, but it never crossed our minds that they might be *Nazis*. Thoughts of some ghastly interstellar *Bierkeller* are, thankfully, soon swept aside; it just so happens that the Berlin Olympics of 1936 marked one of the first television broadcasts, and some channel-surfer near the star Vega picked up the ceremony and beamed it back to say hi. Zemeckis isn't breaking new ground here: Joe Dante made a bright and underrated comedy called *Explorers*, in which the aliens acquire all knowledge of us from TV transmissions—their first words of greeting are "Ehhh, what's up, Doc?" But Zemeckis twists the idea and pushes it further; the only sad thing is that this represents the final moment at which his movie makes contact with the forces of irony.

In a thin strip at the top of the Hitler footage is a message: thousands upon thousands of what appear to be instructions. It is eventually decided that these constitute a blueprint for building some sort of machine, although I still maintain that if they are really *that* baffling they are far more likely to be a new and advanced recipe for phyllo pastry. Anyway, various world powers club together to build the contraption, which is essentially a gyroscope the size of a cathedral. Nobody knows how or why it should work; the plans merely specify a pod, like a giant French *boule*, with enough space for one passenger and no luggage, which will drop into the spinning gyroscope and travel to distant worlds, provided that it leaves Earth before rush hour on a Friday.

A shortlist of suitable humans is drawn up, but Zemeckis, who by now is well into yearning mode, is not interested in taking us through the cast of candidates, as Philip Kaufman did so smartly in *The Right Stuff*. The only contenders we meet are David Drumlin (Tom Skerritt), who used to be Ellie's boss, and Ellie herself. Hang on, guys. You have a whole planet to pick from, and you choose Jodie Foster? I am a major Foster fan, but one thing is perfectly clear: Ellie does not need a long trip into space. She needs to get (1) a square meal inside her, (2) some rest, and (3) laid. As a matter of fact, she does get laid, early in the film, but only by Matthew McConaughey, and that doesn't count. It certainly has very little effect; he plays a thinker and author named Palmer Joss, nicknamed God's diplomat, who wanders through this hundred-million-dollar special-effects bonanza reminding us of the perils of technology. (Speaking of which, is he the same Joss who invented the stick?) I suspect that one of Ellie's reasons for wanting to reach out to creatures other than us is that, whatever happens, it can only be more fun than a one-night stand with Palmer Joss. In an act of uncharitable constriction, the movie roots her passion for things extraterrestrial in an orphan's traumatic inability to connect with terrestrial beings. "I feel more real," she says of her stargazing, thus instituting a new and expensive habit for worried Americans: galacto-therapy. The politic, unscrewy Drumlin fades from the picture, thanks to an accident on the launch pad, and Ellie gets her own pod; as the machine starts to turn, you can't tell whether her face is quivering from all the g-forces or because Jodie Foster is doing her trademark shudder, complete with staring eyes and lips pressed into a line. It's a look that we have watched before, as Hannibal Lecter quizzed her softly through the bars of his cage, but there the neurosis rang true and sharp, and we were moved by Clarice's determination to ride her sorrows and finish the job. Ellie, by contrast, never seems like a pro at all. The Ripley of *Alien* would shake her off like moondust and leave her for dead.

It comes as no surprise, then, when Ellie has an Experience. The pod burrows through a wormhole in space-time, which consists of a million groovy colors screaming past at the speed of light. I was fully expecting her to bump into Keir Dullea from *2001* and his boring white hotel room, but instead she arrives on a gently murmuring beach. So this is the lesson of *Contact:* you spend half a trillion dollars, you travel twenty-six light-years, and you wind up in Maui. The joke is on Ellie, of course, who forgot to pack her golf clubs. No wonder she makes such a quick turnaround and hightails it back to Earth. To those on the launch site, she was absent for no more than a matter of seconds; Ellie herself timed the journey at eighteen hours.

By the time of Ellie's return, I was dreading what would come next. She becomes a Cassandra, poor thing, with only Palmer Joss having the courage to believe her story, but even worse is the awful manner in which she is compelled to tell it. "I was given a vision of the universe that tells us how tiny and insignificant and precious we are," she explains at an official hearing. "In all our searching, the only thing that's made the emptiness bearable is each other." How a movie that began with the promise of such excitement can fritter itself away into these plaintive consolations, I have no idea. It's a kind of dumbing up, a desperately ill-advised ascent into musings that don't have the nerve to be openly religious; *Contact* is the antithesis of a picture like *Close Encounters of the Third Kind*, which resolved itself into an array of luminous images that hinted at all manner of annunciation but wisely stayed free of any attempt to put such awe into words. Zemeckis is an old friend of Spielberg's, and the creator of *Who Framed Roger Rabbit?* and the *Back to the Future* trilogy—so what happened? Does he honestly think that to forsake the snap of those early works for the drooling spiritual hunger of *Forrest Gump* and *Contact* means that he has grown up? I clambered from the sweaty pod of *Contact* no wiser than when I went in, but I have to confess that, as I sat there in the dark, Ellie's words to Palmer Joss spoke to me soul to soul: "What are we doing here?" Good question.

JULY 21, 1997

MRS. BROWN

Was there ever a time when the British Royal Family was not touched by scandal? Is it not, indeed, part of the mysterious function of monarchy to be as scandalous as possible—to gratify the baser appetites of the sovereign's subjects? Can you imagine anything duller than a king who behaves himself? Such idle thoughts were prompted by *Mrs. Brown*, the neat and satisfying new movie from the director John Madden. In this case, the monarch is a queen: specifically, Victoria, in her blue, or post-Albert, period. Our tale begins in 1864, when the Queen (Judi Dench) not only has plunged herself into deep mourning but is threatening to drag everyone else down with her. The first we see of her is the back of the royal head, which, with its unshakable stillness and severe bun, is more expressive than the front; when we finally look Her Majesty in the eye, there is no one at home.

Into this dead zone comes John Brown (Billy Connolly), who is basically a forest of dense hair with a large Scotsman hiding somewhere in the middle, traceable only by a faint mist of whiskey rising from the upper slopes. Once a devoted manservant to Prince Albert, Brown now transfers his loyalty to the widowed Queen. At first, this is considered a good thing; Brown pretty much blackmails her by standing outside and holding her horse by the bridle, braving all weathers, until she consents to venture out for a ride. Slowly, her health returns, although we must bear in mind that the Victorian lady's idea of health consisted of cantering sidesaddle and going for a swim dressed in inflatable bloomers. Whereas the rest of the known world treats the Queen like a goddess, Brown is more straightforward. "Lift your foot, woman," he commands as he adjusts her stirrup. The vexed question of whether Brown's concept of service did or did not extend to springy bouts in the heather provided nineteenth-century England with some of its most succulent gossip, and even, if *Mrs. Brown* is to be believed, gave rise to republican stirrings. The movie leaves us in no doubt that mistress and servant loved each other, but remains too delicate—some may think too cowardly—to offer any proof that such bonding ever went, as it were, beyond the kilt.

The whole movie is, in fact, a nicely measured brew of respect and scorn. It was produced in part by the BBC, and I was worried that it would emerge as one of those staid, slightly twee period pieces like *Enchanted April*—all forced languor and trailing skirts—which lurk on the frontier between TV and cinema. Somehow, Madden manages to escape that trap; *Mrs. Brown* is more tightly framed and paced than his previous effort, *Ethan Frome*, and, for the first half in particular, it feels graced by a drollery all its own. When the Queen's private secretary, Sir Henry Ponsonby (Geoffrey Palmer), refers to "her sentimental but deeply held view that all Highlanders are good for the health," we get the refreshing sense of a movie that is prepared to hold its central romance at arm's length and submit it to the gentle assaults of a lugubrious wit. In an admirable attempt to fend off tragedy, it suggests that the semi-ridiculous flutterings of the monarch's heart gave her subjects—above all, her prime minister—the chance to be amused.

Antony Sher has more fun with the role of Disraeli than you would believe possible, let alone proper: eyes rolling and glittering, brows arched in mock astonishment, lips pursing for the coming barb, he expands his performance until, like one of the Victorian caricaturists, he arrives at a comic—and horribly plausible—magnification of the truth. (Is this, you ask yourself, what Dickens's dramatized readings were like?) Sher's Disraeli is so perturbed by the Queen's new attachment, and by its implications for the country at large, that he has no option but to pretend that it is a source of trifling and unceasing entertainment; it also gives him a chance to sneer at Scotland for being "six hundred miles north of civilization," by which he means the comforting hellhole of London.

Mrs. Brown does not quite keep its balance; as the tale progresses, this brocade of irony grows worn, and we are left with an unadorned love story—affecting in its fashion but a little too mawkish and openhearted for those of more corrupted tastes. (Imagine what Alan Bennett would have made of it.) Even so, there is something to relish in the rueful outcome: as the Queen returns to life, she feels able to dispense with the round-the-clock attentions of the man who revived her. All of which is fertile ground for Judi Dench, who has always been able to delve behind her kindly demeanor and come up with something clipped and even cruel; the voice alone wavers between a consoling huskiness and a more ambitious rasp. Billy Connolly, meanwhile, is in his element. Connolly is not widely known here, whereas in Britain, and especially in his native Scotland, he is—or used to be—the best stand-up comedian of his time. He was doing stand-up, in fact, long before it became the fashionable and faintly gruesome industry that we know now, with its conveyor belt of nervous nerds and dreary shockers. The Connolly act was founded, years ahead of Seinfeld, on the intensive harvesting of previously unnoticed details: before Connolly, nobody had ever inquired out loud why all deposits of human vomit contain diced carrots. Recently, he has somewhat faded from view, and there was a moment, weirdly prophetic of *Mrs. Brown*, when he was revealed to be a friend of the Duke and Duchess of York. It was hard to know where his foul-mouthed, good-natured talents, at once politically innocent and wise to the broad communion of human foibles, would take him next, and his new role is a godsend: Brown is a big man let loose in a society that is controlled by the smallest gestures.

At one point, he drives Victoria to a workers' cottage on the Balmoral estate, where they are to drink and dine. The queen, anxious to help, offers to lay the table, and then pauses with the spoons in her hand: she has never laid a table in her life. Brown looks over and gives a brief nod to show where the spoons should go, and for that moment the whole world stands tipsily on its head. That the ruler of an empire should take advice on cutlery may be an outrage, but it also shows why the revolution, in England, at least, was never going to happen.

AUGUST 4, 1997

L.A. CONFIDENTIAL

Directed by Curtis Hanson, *L.A. Confidential* is set at the start of the 1950s. It centers on the Los Angeles Police Department, but the center cannot hold: scraps of plot keep breaking off and spinning away to form stories of their own, each of them a lead worth pursuing. The roster of policemen includes Jack Vincennes (Kevin Spacey)—"celebrity crime-stopper," adviser to the TV cop show *Badge of Honor*, and all-round Mr. Smooth. Jack's idea of a big night is to bust a rising star on a drug charge and haul him in front of the flashbulbs, so that Jack's pal Sid Hudgens (Danny DeVito), trash reporter for *Hush-Hush* magazine, can splay the arrest all over his pages. Then you have Bud White (Russell Crowe), a vengeful thug who, despite his relative youth, brims with fury sufficient to last him a lifetime. At the other end of the scale comes Ed Exley (Guy Pearce): a model officer, though his real problem is that he's an officer who looks like a model. There is a constant battle for finesse between Exley's sense of morality and his cheekbones. He wears spectacles and sails through every police exam. He is widely loathed. In charge of the whole crew is an Irishman, Lieutenant Dudley Smith (James Cromwell)—"Call me Dudley." He is strong, trusty, and very nearly comforting. Think mother hen with brass knuckles.

Such, at least, are one's first impressions. By the end of the film, they are long gone, smothered with fresh evidence and a caustic layer of doubt. Those characters who are lucky enough to survive the onslaught of events—and this is a tale that racks up the stiffs like a Jacobean tragedy—are smarting from their wounds and richly transformed by the purgatory of the plot. What makes *L.A. Confidential* so unusual—the reason that it shames most of the other thrillers we have to grind through these days—is that it doesn't feel as if it had been created from a software package. It must have been hell to pitch. How can you tag characters who won't stay still? Who would dare to suggest to a studio executive that a film adapted from a James Ellroy novel might be more about time than crime? True, it glistens with wrongdoing of every stripe—a gashed throat in a motel, a herd of cops on a Christmas rampage, a multiple slaying at the Nite Owl Café. There are hookers and hopheads, and some juicy political blackmail. Yet the film itself is not savage; it is formidable, and oddly delicate, and much of the blood is spilled long before we step in it. Curtis Hanson deals in rumor and aftermath; by the time we reach the scene of a crime, its cause and effect—what it means for those around it—are already starting to leak. You have to feel your way through the picture, as if by touch. Just when you're certain that Bud is an animal and Exley a good boy, they begin, ever so discreetly, to trade places.

Both are required, in any case, to unravel the Nite Owl massacre. Three frightened black suspects are pulled in; Exley interrogates them with feline skill, Bud White with a gun to the mouth. Everything points to a random kill, a robbery gone awry, but Exley and White sniff something artfully concocted; it is the quiet contention of this movie that all crime is organized—planned and lusted after, if only for a minute. As *L.A. Confidential* proceeds, the title comes to sound like a tautology: for all the open spread of its streets, the warm welcome of its air, the city is constructed from secrets. This was a given in the days—and especially the nights—of Philip Marlowe, and it both rattled and aroused Jake Gittes in *Chinatown*, but the sense of Los Angeles as a warren of lies, as a comically deep game, has been missing from our screens ever since. Hanson revives it in style; the citizens of this picture are fighting to flee the past, and the smart types pretend that they have none. "Why'd you become a cop?" asks Bud White. "I can't remember," says Vincennes. Lucky guy; everyone else is busy tamping down the rot. You can taste it as Bud drives to Brentwood to see a man named Pierce Patchett (David Strathairn). It is a clean Californian morning, calmed by the swish of sprinklers, bright with the greenery of money and lawns: the perfect morning on which to ask what polite Mr. Patchett does for a living. In the words of Sid Hudgens, "He's a twilight—he ain't queer and he ain't Red." One thing Pierce does is find girls who look like movie stars, send them to a hairdresser and a plastic surgeon to heighten the resemblance, and then pimp them to the filthy rich. If you want Rita Hayworth for a night, for a price, she's all yours: Hollywood made flesh.

Doubling for Veronica Lake is a woman called Lynn Bracken (Kim Basinger). Not even in the gluey shudders of passion could you honestly mistake her for Veronica Lake; Basinger has a hard, half-defeated face in this movie, with none of the requisite dreamy droop. But Lynn is still a magnet, drawing first White into her embrace and then the incorruptible Exley. The cautionary number that plays as he crosses Lynn's threshold—"They're singing songs of love, but not for me"—goes in one ear and out the other. Any hint of an icon, any chance to play out your life (or your death) as if you were living not in L.A. but in movies themselves, in the silvered product that L.A. pours out to the world, is enough to send the levelheaded into a spin. Most starstricken of all is Jack Vincennes; he seems wholly in control, but when his bosses transfer him from narcotics to vice and suspend him from *Badge of Honor* something dies behind his eyes. How could they snip his lifeline to fame? All this is fuel for Kevin Spacey, who cruises through *L.A. Confidential* with such frictionless ease that you wind up grinning at the sight of him, wondering what his next move will be. His *best* move comes when he goes to question a black boxer who may have information on the Nite Owl. The interview over, Vincennes pauses at the door of his car: "Keep it up," he says, and delivers an air punch, a friendly, rolling jab of the fists. It lasts only a couple of seconds, but it breathes an entire climate of condescension; if that should chill into outright cruelty, too bad.

See this movie again and you could probably start to unpack the technical baggage of Spacey's performance: the gaze that slides back and forth across a crowd while the smile remains still, or the voice that he runs at three-quarter speed—as if Vincennes had spent time down South, long enough to pick up the languor but not the accent. Even his jackets play a supporting role: the fine fifties cut doesn't bulk Spacey out, but it gives him width, a little more front to face down the world. Here is a guy who loves to rub shoulders; so what if they're not his own? This is where *L.A. Confidential* scores so highly, and so freely: it's a period piece, but it refuses to recognize the border where design ends and character begins. Hanson doesn't care whether we get an ironic kick from these postwar motifs; he wants to plunge us into those movie-mad years until they spill over and into our heads. (When Lynn and Bud watch *Roman Holiday* together, the sight of them is at once sweet, improbable, and true.) Nothing in Hanson's previous work or in that of his coscreenwriter, Brian Helgeland—who scripted the laughable *Conspiracy Theory*—suggested that they would come up with a film like *L.A. Confidential.* Works such as *The Hand That Rocks the Cradle* and *The River Wild* are neat examples of formula management, but they feel frozen next to this; the only recent thriller to compare with it is Michael Mann's *Heat*, another study in overlapping shadows. Hanson's picture is less portentous, and he has somehow filtered Ellroy's unstoppable karate prose, all chop and whoop—"He could muscle the money out of her, glom some pimp scuttlebutt, close out the Cathcart end and ask Dud to send him down to Darktown"—into the more fluent rhythms of the screen.

With the end in sight, Hanson throws in a dumbfounding twist, and then stirs up a storm of bullets and blood. It had to happen, I suppose, but I found it more exciting than cathartic: so exact is the mood of apprehension as Vincennes and White and Exley crawl toward the truth (sometimes literally, beneath the floor of a house) that you hardly want them to reach it. Corruption needs to be washed away, of course, but none of us want to live in a shining city for long. "You have the eye for human weakness, but not the stomach," Dudley Smith says to Exley, who spends the rest of the film trying to prove him wrong. *L.A. Confidential* has it all: the eye, the stomach, the ear for jiving dialogue, and a silken skein of nerves which helps you to relax into your own jitters. It even has a family of rats, who arrive with a shiver of string music; what more could you possibly want?

SEPTEMBER 22, 1997

TITANIC

After all the hullabaloo, James Cameron's *Titanic* will finally set sail on December 19th. Already, however, the film has moved away from the quayside, with a premiere in Tokyo and a public screening in London. The latter was attended by the Prince of Wales, and if any of us wondered whether His Royal Highness was well advised to lend his gracious presence to the tragedy of a sinking ship we were too polite to say. It was altogether a polite occasion; there is always something absurd about going to the movies in a tuxedo, even more so when the movie in question wastes no opportunity to laugh at stuffed shirts. If he really wanted to show solidarity with *Titanic*, Prince Charles should have rolled up in corduroy and old boots.

The hero of the tale is Jack Dawson (Leonardo DiCaprio), a freewheeling scruff—a skinny kindred spirit, perhaps, of his namesake Jack London—who wins a couple of steerage tickets in a poker game. Armed with little more than a sketchbook and an insolent grin, he leaps aboard the *Titanic* as she is about to cast off from Southampton on her maiden—and, as it turns out, her funeral—voyage. Jack thus joins the hundreds of other happy fools who believe that they are heading for a nice time; among them are the nervy and elegant Ruth DeWitt Bukater (Frances Fisher), the suspiciously moneyed Molly Brown (Kathy Bates), and Smith (Bernard Hill), the captain of the ship. The only glum face on view is that of Ruth's daughter Rose (Kate Winslet), a young first-class Philadelphian who has already foreseen her own demise—not in the form of a large lump of ice in the North Atlantic but, far more scarily, at the hands of her fiancé, Cal Hockley (Billy Zane), the man with a heart of absolute zero. Unless something happens, she will marry him, live comfortably, and suffer the long, slow death of the soul. The something is Jack, of course, who rescues a despairing Rose as she stands at the stern, red silk shoes on the railing, and prepares to jump. He hauls her back, they fall in love, he draws her nude, they make out in the cargo hold, and then the ship, in a touching display of erotic sympathy, rears up on end and goes down.

You might ask how such a simple story can take almost three and a half hours to tell. The answer lies in the skill with which Cameron has framed, decorated, and wrapped the love affair. The film has been hailed as a fresh departure for him—as a flight from the panting mayhem of his *Terminator* films—but both of those pictures were obsessed by the bending and shaping of time. It is only in retrospect, appropriately, that we can see how serious that obsession was, how swiftly it went beyond a technical trick, and how thoroughly it has crept into every cranny of *Titanic.* If you've heard nothing about the movie, it's a shock to see it open in a modern-day setting, with a deep-sea expedition to the wreck of the ship. Like the spacemen who cut into Ripley's lost craft in Cameron's *Aliens*, a bunch of scientists descend to the gray ghost of the *Titanic*, send robots through the fish-filled rooms, and retrieve a safe. Back on the surface, they pry it open, expecting jewels; instead, they find a drawing of a naked girl. A lady of a hundred and one sees the image on TV and phones the explorers. "Oh yes," she says calmly, "the woman in the picture is me."

This is the aged but still blooming Rose (Gloria Stuart), a survivor in every sense—"Wasn't I a dish?" she says, looking at the drawing. From here the story unfurls in flashback, as she recounts her distant experience. Cameron's achievement is to shrink that distance: as Rose peers into the video monitor that displays the wreck, you see her face reflected in the screen until past and present are no more than a breath apart. Even finer are those sequences where the *Titanic* is resurrected; rather than simply cut to the spring of 1912, Cameron sends his camera gliding along the decks and gangways of the encrusted vessel until, as if in fulfillment of a wish, she *melts* into life. This may be the most beautiful special effect ever seen; in its peculiar magic, at once decorous and delirious, it feels closer to the Cocteau of *La Belle et la Bête*, say, than to the tedious wizardry of recent blockbusters. Many moviegoers, and almost all critics, inveigh against special effects, but what rankles is the abuse of effects; Cameron has repeatedly shown that in the right hands they are as fertile and provocative as any other artistic resource. At best, indeed, they answer to our hopes and terrors of transfiguration: the metallic morphing of the T-1000 in *Terminator 2* offered the most succulent image of self-replenishing evil since *Dracula*, and, at the other extreme, the way in which sunshine imperceptibly breaks upon the drowned corpse of the *Titanic*, and in which passengers start to stroll again upon its gleaming decks, is as bracing a prospect of rebirth as you could hope to imagine.

No wonder Leonardo DiCaprio looks so chipper. His performance is indeed that of a youth who has been given a new lease, or even the freehold, on life. Some of Jack's lines are straight out of the Hobo's Handbook—"I've got ten bucks in my pocket, I've got nothing to offer you"—but he manages to conjure an age when both he and the twentieth century were still in their teens and it was not entirely fanciful to be fancy-free. There's an extraordinary moment, near the end, when Jack and Rose cling once more to the stern where they first met; now, however, they are right at the summit of the ship, which is vertical and poised to plunge. As it begins to slide like a sword into the waves, Jack shouts "This is it!" and you realize that, even in the face of death—or especially there, when their hearts are on overload—these two are having fun. Kate Winslet is in her element, and that element is water; given her bright, bedraggled Rose and her Ophelia in Kenneth Branagh's *Hamlet*, not to mention the bathtub scene in *Heavenly Creatures*, you could plausibly argue that Winslet is emerging, like a shell-borne Venus, as the Esther Williams *de nos jours*. Winslet's talent, however, extends beyond her gills, and from the opening scene, when the camera curves down to seek out Rose's proudly pale face beneath the brim of her hat, you catch the same air of principled unpredictability—more Jeanne Moreau than bathing beauty—that lit up Winslet's fiery, cigarette-waving heroine in last year's *Jude*. Isn't she a dish?

It took guts, and a certain generosity, for Cameron to cast his two leads like this. The movie is blissfully free of the middle-aged A-list that you would expect from a project of this magnitude, not to mention the B-minus-list that used to bedevil disaster flicks; I like both Mel Gibson and Harrison Ford, for instance, but imagine how ponderous and straightforward *Titanic* would have seemed under their influence. As for Shelley Winters, there would have been no need for the iceberg. The best performance in *Titanic* comes from Victor Garber, who plays Andrews, the Irish builder of the ship. It would have been easy to nudge the role toward hysteria as his beloved creation breaks up beneath him, but Andrews is never more civilized and kindly than when he is overseeing the progress of doom. "She is made of iron, and she will sink," he says firmly. Garber offers a wonderful portrait of a man who is stricken, but not by panic; as the *Titanic* tilts and sinks, Andrews stands by a mantelpiece with a drink and adjusts the clock by the time on his fob watch. Not only is he a model of conduct to the other passengers; he corrects and refines the movie's automatic satire. For much of the time, we are invited to scoff at the snobs as they bicker and dine, and to relax in the unbuttoned company of Jack and his ilk. At one postprandial point, the camera whirls around with Rose as she dances a Celtic reel belowdecks—a shot borrowed from

Whiskey Galore—and then cuts hard to Cal and his cronies talking politics through a fug of cigar. Later, amid the chaos, Rose tells him that half the people on the boat are going to die. "Not the better half," says Cal. Boo! Hiss!

I didn't object to the presence of this stage villain—he could walk into a one-reel melodrama from 1912, no questions asked—because he reinforced the growing sense that *Titanic* is, for all its narrative dexterity and the formidable modernity of its methods, an old-fashioned picture. The most radical thing about it is the version of the *Demoiselles d'Avignon* which Rose appears to have bought in Paris, and is presumably lost forever, together with the fifteen hundred dead. In both its emotional thrust and its social judgment, *Titanic* pursues a clear and often obvious route. Like *The English Patient*, it could be described as a long historical romance, and yet it boasts none of the intricate byways that darkened Minghella's movie. At the close of the century, Cameron is pushing at cinema much as D. W. Griffith did at the start—raising the stakes of the spectacular, outwitting the intellect, and heading straight for the guts. He piles on the astonishment as if he owed it to the nature of his medium; there are sights here that no other director would have the nerve to design and stage—an old couple embracing on their double bed while the water flows beneath it like Lethe, or the ice-whitened bodies of passengers bobbing in the endless darkness, as if on a battlefield of water.

Some viewers have confessed themselves disappointed by the computer-generated images of the *Titanic;* the daytime shots, in particular, are lightened by a strange haze, and there are times when this unrusting palace resembles not so much an actual ship as one of those splendid, stylized liners from travel posters of the 1920s. Yet even that, I found, was no shortcoming, for it drove home the *Titanic* as a dream—a fatal vision of efficient loveliness for those who sailed in her, and a kind of unreal, awesome trip for those of us watching her now. She went down, according to this movie, as a direct result of Rose and Jack, because the men in the crow's nest were too busy spying on the smooching couple to notice what was looming ahead. So now you know: the *Titanic* was lost for love. James Cameron's film is grand and wrenching rather than clever or subtle, and it floods your eyes; if you are going to spend two hundred million dollars on a movie, this is the way to do it.

DECEMBER 15, 1997

NIL BY MOUTH

The actor Gary Oldman has written and directed his first film and called it *Nil by Mouth*. Nominally, the title refers to a hospital patient who can only be fed intravenously. But the bulk of its meaning is ironic, since the movie revolves around a group of people for whom everything is by mouth. What goes in is booze: the opening shot finds Ray (Ray Winstone) at the bar of a pub, ordering beer and vodka—"oh, and a drop of Scotch." What comes out is a multitudinous sea of filth. The story is set in South London, and the patois of the place is for the most part doggedly obstetric and quite unprintable. Suffice it to say that "up the Gary" is not, contrary to what you might think, a coy attempt at self-promotion by the director.

It was a surprise to hear the English language, as spoken by the English, still punching its weight. Moviegoers take it for granted that the screen was long ago colonized by American slang; the Brits can be relied upon for rhetorical starch, but any notion that there was spit and vim in the vulgar tongue of old England was dispelled by those crummy Michael Caine pictures in the sixties. Gary Oldman, however, makes the tongue wag like crazy; in the first scene, we listen to—or listen in on—a long Rabelaisian riff by Mark (Jamie Foreman), as he spills the particulars of an orgy. I sensed a small shock wave running around the movie theatre, but then people broke through the shock and began to laugh. Ten minutes in, and the movie had kidnapped us: Mark and his friend Ray were plainly rough around the edges, and the air was blue with smoke and smut, but they had earned our affection and from now on would hold us in their thrall.

More fool us. The rest of *Nil by Mouth* demonstrates the dangers of giving these lads an ounce of trust. Val (Kathy Burke) did the same thing when she married Ray, and now look at her. Considering all the jokes that are flying around, Val's drooping, fleshy face doesn't crack a smile as often as it should: "Change the record, for fuck's sake," she tells her husband. "I'm thirty today, and I feel so fuckin' old." Ray has overrun her life, like a one-man army, and she—together with her mother, grandmother, and six-year-old daughter, Michelle—still looks haunted and shattered by the invasion. Almost nobody in this film has a job—Val's mother works, but most of her earnings disappear into the heroin habit of her son Billy (Charlie Creed-Miles)—and the plot, too, proceeds with an ambling and unemployed air. When Billy winds up in prison, or Ray assaults his pregnant wife, the horror feels at once darkly predestined and completely random. All of which leaves one question: What is the point of paying eight dollars to see a film whose impact could be compared to getting whacked over the head with a shovel?

Well, some shovels are sharper than others. I went to *Nil by Mouth* in despondent reluctance, because everyone kept telling me how raw and uncompromising it was. But this movie is something else. Its onslaught on the nerves is such that only afterward can you consider the care and attention with which it is constructed. There are brief, dour landscapes, with morning mists the color of concrete and a sickly nighttime rain that turns yellow and green under city lights, but Oldman's real point of focus is the wreckage of the human face. Billy's features are blank and beaky, though rendered slightly more expressive when Ray tries to chew his nose off. Even scarier is a small boy in a hooded jacket whom we see in passing as he leaves a playground: he turns around, and his face has the dire, misshapen look of evil that can hardly wait to grow up. He is a riposte to the girl in red who runs through *Schindler's List;* where Spielberg sees children as a flash of hope, Oldman fears for the future they will bring.

Then, there is Ray. It's some time since I saw an actor fill a film in this way; gazing at Winstone, you can't help thinking back to De Niro in his great Scorsese years. You warm to Ray, as you did to Jake La Motta, because his verbal delivery speaks of a man whose appetite for life has become a craving; as his hunger deepens, though, and he starts to bite into lives other than his own, you pull away. With his cropped and sweaty hair and the trademark sniff of the cokehead, Ray proves that a fine figure of a man can go to seed in a season; when he sits in a pub wearing a V-neck sweater without a shirt, you can see the sheer squat packing of flesh in his neck and shoulders, the ropy cords of muscle that have started to slacken in the blur of drink. He throws his wife to the floor, kicks her head, and stands there tugging at the waistband of his boxer shorts like a kid needing to pee; once the demons have rushed out of him, Ray is hollowed and unmanned. Think of a bear chained to nothing but itself.

The one weak moment comes when Ray sits and talks about his father.

"I don't remember one kiss, you know, one cuddle, nothing," he says. As psychological explanation, this rings perfectly true; *Nil by Mouth* unfolds in a world where, in Philip Larkin's words, man hands on misery to man. The trouble is that by this stage we don't want explanation; Oldman has shown himself so adept at dramatizing the fallout from an exploding individual that Ray's self-analysis feels beside the point—everything he laments was there in the eyes of that boy in the playground, and we glimpse it again in the final scene. This is staged as a happy ending, with all sins forgiven and the family back together, but I found it terrifying; when Ray rubs noses with his daughter Michelle, all I could think of was who long it would take for the milk of human kindness to go sour.

Nil by Mouth forced me to clarify everything that I dislike about Oldman's fellow-directors in Britain. His characters may rant their lungs out, but he himself, unlike Ken Loach, has no desire to hector us, and his film is too shapely and unskewed to strike political attitudes. And where Mike Leigh seems to be gripping each social class in a pair of tweezers and slyly holding his nose, Oldman faces his characters square on; he has a story to tell, and he doesn't flinch from no-go areas such as the notorious kinship of violence and sentimentality in the British working class—just look at the drunken Ray, mouthing "I love you" to a bare wall. It is a world kept alive and intact by women; no wonder that the amazing Kathy Burke, who won the award for best actress at Cannes, should loom larger as the film goes on. Val is a still point of decency and a rebuff to the self-pity of angry men.

Gary Oldman chose not to appear in his own film. Whether that is a declaration of intent I don't know, but his recent roles, like the hammy villain in *The Fifth Element*, suggested a weary contempt for the grand studio style. *Nil by Mouth* is the way out for Oldman, and a way forward. Ray may be stuck in the groove, but Gary has changed the record.

FEBRUARY 9, 1998

LOLITA

A little girl is sitting on her father's lap, with her back to him, reading the funnies. Both parties are wearing pajamas. She is giggling. Gradually, the giggles become gasps. She is catching her breath. The pajamas are not quite in place. The girl is no longer reading. The man is not her father.

This scene comes from Adrian Lyne's new movie of Vladimir Nabokov's *Lolita*, and may go some way toward explaining why the film is unlikely to be shown here. The issue depends on your definition of child pornography. Does it, for instance, mean "any visual depiction . . . of sexually explicit conduct, where"—and I quote, of course, from Subsection 8B of Section 2256 of Chapter 110 of Part I of Title 18, "Crimes and Criminal Procedure," of United States Code—"such visual depiction is, or appears to be, of a minor engaging in sexually explicit conduct"? That "appears to be" is the zinger, for the man in question is Humbert Humbert, played by Jeremy Irons, and the child is Dolores Haze, played by Dominique Swain, who at the time of filming was fourteen years old.

The irony is that the scene presents a witty sandwiching of Nabokov's themes: the sweat of semi-incest is not merely linked but synchronized with the innocent joy of trash culture. In France, needless to say, the coupling is on permanent view. In the city where Maurice Chevalier—creepier, in his bonhomous, tilt-hatted fashion, than any number of Humberts—publicly thanked heaven for little girls, *Lolita* can be viewed any day by anybody. Well, almost anybody: "Int.—12 Ans," say the movie listings, in unfortunate shorthand. The phrase sounds dirtier than anything onscreen, but it simply means that children under twelve are forbidden to see the movie. Quite right, too, although it is hard to imagine such children as the target audience for a story in which they themselves function generically as targets. One of the incidental benefits of Lyne's film is that it reminds us of the original fuss and flap of 1955, the year of the novel's publication, and of 1962, the year of Stanley Kubrick's adaptation; we pride ourselves on having got over those outrages, and it is salutary—even poignant—to rediscover an old shocker that still has the power to shock.

What surprises and shames us about Nabokov's masterpiece, however, is that we are so readily enchanted by matters that should properly repel us, and the new movie works the same trick. It is only a thin shadow of the novel—as any dramatization of the luminous *Lolita* is doomed to be—but it is by no means a travesty. The screenwriter, Stephen Schiff displays a careful, even loving, loyalty to the book; as familiar scenes and lines unroll before us—from the roaring icebox to the gum-like bubble of blood that swells and pops on the lips of the dying Quilty (Frank Langella)—we are reminded of the delicate art of non-transformation, of leaving well alone. In this respect, at least, Lyne's *Lolita*, of which I had heard little but dispraise, marks an advance upon the Kubrick version, which mangled the novelist's own screenplay and became, in his words, "a blurred skimpy glimpse of the marvellous picture I imagined."

On the other hand, so deftly did James Mason fit and expand our sense of what Humbert is, or should be, that it takes a brave actor to squeeze into what is inescapably a Mason-shaped role. Jeremy Irons is leaner and lankier, and, where Mason's slow grin was wide enough to melt both mother and daughter, the new Humbert seems more pained by the obligation to smile than by his duties in the marital bed of Charlotte (Melanie Griffith). One gift, of course, connects Mason and Irons: they boast two of the most beautiful voices in the history of cinema. The former gave us his Americanized Yorkshire with a faint serpentine hiss; the latter, a lonely drawl. Their only rivals, I think, would be Claude Rains and George Sanders—all of them exiled Englishmen who leave you with the abiding suspicion that there is something dangerous in the deracinated. And that is where Humbert comes in: with his dodgy French boyhood and his weakness for Baudelaire (himself no moral strongman), Humbert finds it not only convenient but arousing to take Lolita everywhere, for he is a man from nowhere. That Nabokov's novel is commonly thought to have ruptured a taboo is the least interesting thing about it; more crucial is the feeling that it waved farewell to romance—the last romantic hero in literature is a pervert, and how could he be anything else?—and, in particular, to the appeal of the cosmopolitan lover. One of Humbert's more insidious crimes is to make you wonder what his gentlemanly forefathers may have done to their daughters; with Isabel out of the way, for instance, what cracks might Gilbert Osmond have inflicted on the porcelain virtue of Pansy?

Jeremy Irons is right, and ripe, for these areas of promising moral rot.

Once you've got an Oscar for impersonating Claus von Bulow, the prospect of Humbert Humbert must seem like a day at the office. Irons's best moment in the movie comes as Lolita, on the point of leaving for summer camp, jumps from the car and sprints upstairs for a goodbye kiss. The camera backs away in a panicky rush from poor Humbert, who has no time to prepare for the crown (so far) of his foul career; Irons fusses and pats his pajamas like a schoolboy awaiting the headmaster, or a visit from his parents. It is a tiny hint of the role reversal that will form the basis of his accurate but disreputable plea: "It was she who seduced me."

No one buys Humbert's excuses; Humbert himself offers them as you would a bowl of plastic fruit. Still, it is hard not to wince at the moment, in both novel and film, when knowing Lo, resigned to her role as victim, begins to demand money for services rendered. If one frustrated pedophile feels himself vindicated by Lyne's *Lolita*, and thus works up the steam to ply his trade, then the film will have blood on its hands; the question is whether we should have our moviegoing (or our reading) curtailed by that freak possibility. There is a case for arguing that more corrosive damage was done to American morals by the widespread viewing of two earlier Adrian Lyne pictures, *Fatal Attraction* and *Indecent Proposal*, than could conceivably be caused by a brief art-house run of *Lolita*. A generation of men came out of those raucous hits in the vague belief that women were either mad harridans or gambling chips; Lyne shows far more respect for Dominique Swain than he ever did for Glenn Close or Demi Moore. Thankfully, the dreary erotic gag of her first appearance on the lawn—sprinklers spurting behind her behind—makes way for a more sober style. (Apparently, Miss Swain's mother attended the production in the role of on-set chaperone: a deliciously Charlotte-like deal.) The actress is too old for the part, but, with her leg-swinging boredom and the braces on her teeth, she is not too beautiful, and her untrammelled vitality, which makes Kubrick's Sue Lyon look comatose, allows Lolita to stand proud of Humbert's solipsism, to be more than the sum of his lusts.

None of these niceties, presumably, will dent the determination of the major studios, and it will take a bold (and probably minor) distributor to pick up the movie, much as the novel itself was first issued by a publishing house of known lubricity. It is all too easy, as a Nabokov lover, to forget that for many people out there, especially those who have never read it, *Lolita* remains a dirty book. What chance for the film, then, in a land still ruffled by the unsolved slaughter of a six-year-old beauty queen? The image of Dolores Haze, complete with smeary lipstick and a rocketing temperature, spreading her legs for her legal guardian would not, let us say, sit happily with that of a rouged and bejewelled JonBenet Ramsey. In the years since *Lolita* was written, child abuse has soared up the league of human vice until it is now viewed as worse than murder—understandably so, for it entails the violation of a soul.

In so febrile a climate, it might be prudent to pause before springing *Lolita* on American viewers uncut. Equally, it would be a pity to deny them a chance to make up their own minds, for there are lovely things here: Humbert hanging a sad sweater from a tree for target practice, or lighting a cigarette in a bone-white desert, with a backdrop of mountains already fired up. Apart from the gory *guignol* of Quilty's demise, Lyne has checked his natural hysteria and produced a slight, tender movie—not, I think, worth fighting a battle over, let alone bringing to trial. If anything, the film is not risky enough: it turns down the bright, rampant polyphony of Nabokov's creation until we are left with a tone of reedy regret. (The film is seldom funny; the novel is seldom anything but.) My overriding memory, as I left the cinema, was of Jeremy Irons quoting Humbert's reveries, in voice-over, to the sound of Ennio Morricone's wonderfully rueful score. Who would have thought that an infamous tale of underage rape would end up sounding like *Brideshead Revisited*? What Vladimir Nabokov, hunter of lost youth and scourge of nostalgia, would have made of it all, we can only guess.

FEBRUARY 23, 1998

TWILIGHT

In Robert Benton's *Twilight,* Paul Newman plays a man called Harry Ross. Harry is a cop turned private investigator turned handyman, and a drunk who's clinging to the wagon by his nails. The sight of someone as weathered as Newman sipping ginger ale out of those dinky little green bottles is certainly a sobering experience, rather like watching Steve McQueen on a tricycle. Everyone in *Twilight* appears to be giving something up. Catherine Ames (Susan Sarandon) wants to quit smoking, although this heroic ambition is slightly compromised by her belief that if someone else lights the cigarette for you it doesn't count. The moral implications of this principle strike me as endlessly fascinating. Nixon would have liked her.

Then, we have Catherine's husband, Jack (Gene Hackman), who is renouncing a pleasure even more scalding and elaborate than a good smoke. Jack is dying, and doing it fast. He will leave behind a wife whom he loves ever more fiercely as the prospect of losing her nears, and a daughter, Mel (Reese Witherspoon), whom he loves despite her tendency to scoot off and get laid in Mexico. He will also miss his old pal Harry, with whom he plays cards; their games of gin rummy are as practiced and benignly peevish as those of Judy Holliday and Broderick Crawford in *Born Yesterday.* Harry lodges in the Ames household in Los Angeles; they feel they owe him, perhaps, since he went to fetch the straying Mel and came back with a bullet in the groin, or thereabouts.

The word at police headquarters is that Harry was emasculated. Paul Newman as the world's first dickless dick? Cassidy without the Butch? Surely no major star could live with such a role, and, indeed, my interest flopped as Harry dutifully added to his list of errands by going to bed with Catherine. Compared with changing the motor on the tumble-dryer, this new task is definitely a step up and, if all goes well, unlikely to be blocked by lint; in the words of Jack, however, who soon finds out what happened, "I'm curious to know what kind of man fucks his dying best friend's wife." "Not a good one," Harry replies, without missing a beat. Newman isn't afraid to make Harry something of a sad case—weary and watchful, and none too impressed with himself. But the movie cuts him some slack: even before the opening credits, he is required to lower his shades and give us a flash of the Newman eyes, their sea blue all but undimmed.

Adultery is the least of Harry's worries. The most is that Jack gave him an address across town and asked him to deliver a package to a lady named Gloria Lamar. Harry looks a mite suspicious at this request, and you can't blame him; the first rule of being a private eye, working or retired, is to cancel all deliveries and head for the Yukon rather than meet up with anybody called Gloria. *Twilight* is a serious film, possibly too serious, yet there are times when it steps dangerously close to parody; it reeks of that throbbing, whiskey-sour climate that enveloped the later Chandler books, and some of Harry's lines, especially those in voice-over, replay the aimlessly vengeful riff of Marlowe's disappointment. "Before he was dead he was a very sick man," says Harry as he ponders the unfamiliar corpse—what else?—that lies fat and slumped in Gloria's apartment. From here, it is a slow trail through the buried, ruinous secrets of Jack and Catherine, the passions of young Mel, and the plans of the elusive Gloria (Margo Martindale), who winningly describes herself as "blond, big, mucho hair, mucho tits." Sounds like Schwarzenegger in *Red Sonja*, but there you go.

The plot of *Twilight* is suitably knotted, but I'm not sure that Robert Benton's heart is in it; like his fellow-director Alan Rudolph, he is more enthralled by the mood that rises from mysteries than by the mysteries themselves. You come to the end of the affair feeling more seduced than satisfied; it's the kind of film in which the sleuth traces the dame through the smell of her perfume. As the title suggests, it's about a time of day and a time of life—about the pinks and grays that fall upon you before the final noir. The director of photography is Piotr Sobocinski, who shot Kieślowski's *Three Colors: Red*, and he proves equally adept at taking the emotional temperature of L.A.—starting with a nude in a Hockneyish pool, dropping to still-warm sunsets, and quietly cooling to aquamarines. The movie is full of mirrors, and of glass that should clarify but seems only to confuse. Harry's friend Raymond Hope (the very name is half a joke), played by James Garner, lives in an aerie overlooking the city; its rooms, propped aloft by steel stanchions, jut out into nothingness, and the bravado of the design comes to strike you as mighty precarious. These are men who would prefer not to be reminded that they, too, are hanging over the void.

Twilight is a beautiful and annoying movie that doesn't quite click; its honorable attempts at a slow, pensive pace tend to veer into the sluggish, and I do wish that the characters would stop promising to be "right there" for one another. Given that its narrative would just about grace an average episode of *The Rockford Files*, the best reason to see Benton's film is, unsurprisingly, the smooth mesh of its performances. In their various exchanges, Newman, Hackman, and, best of all, Garner—whose name isn't even on the posters—set and sustain a rhythm that leaves the other performers stranded, and even embarrassed. Stockard Channing, buttoned into unflattering suits, looks out of sorts as a local police lieutenant, and Giancarlo Esposito takes the role of Reuben, a dope who wants to partner Harry, and tries to make it funny. Comic turns do not sit happily in the world of Robert Benton, whose sense of humor is as cautious as the half smile of his leading man.

One thing is for sure: Paramount has picked the right time to release a movie that showcases the skills of an older generation. Put *Twilight* next to the list of Oscar nominations for Best Actor, which includes Jack Nicholson, Peter Fonda, Robert Duvall, and Dustin Hoffman, and the whole thing starts to look like a campaign, or, at any rate, a cri de coeur, from Hollywood: Where have all the smoothies gone? What is lacking in the lusty youth of America? Instead of young Nicholsons and Hackmans, what we get nowadays is an almost indistinguishable roster of boys with big chins: Chris O'Donnell, Matthew McConaughey, Matt Damon. Matt Damon! Cary Grant would have tipped him five bucks for being a good bellhop. The biggest laugh I have had in the past couple of years came from a *Vanity Fair* cover story that hailed McConaughey as the next Paul Newman. As *Twilight* demonstrates, there isn't much wrong with the current one. I would love to think that in forty years' time, in the remake of *Twilight*, Matt and Chris will sit at a table and deal cards, or enjoy a craggy conversation about prostates and old peckers. But don't count on it.

MARCH 16, 1998

THE SPANISH PRISONER

Half an hour into *The Spanish Prisoner*, the heroine turns to the hero and asks, "Who is what they seem? Who in this world is what they seem?" Sadly, the answer to that question is "Almost everybody," but it is the privilege of movies to pretend otherwise—to baffle us with characters who change their identities as often as their underwear. One leading purveyor of such deceit is David Mamet, whose films tend to feel more elusive than his pumped-up work for the stage: his plays are bulls, but his movies slip through your fingers like eels.

The Spanish Prisoner is Mamet's fifth venture as writer and director, and it revisits the shadowlands that he traversed in *House of Games* and *Homicide*. Campbell Scott stars as Joe Ross, a young inventor who has come up with something called the Process. The nameless company that Joe works for will, by virtue of the Process, "control the global market," according to his colleague George Lang (Ricky Jay). All this is left deliberately grand and vague; the uncharitable view would be that Mamet hasn't bothered to research the fiefdoms of big business and industrial espionage, but my guess is that he wanted the background to hang heavy, like the looming institutions that bedevil a Kafka hero. When Joe is asked to predict how much profit the Process will make, he says, "A conservative projection is that we're going to generate for the company a windfall of something on the order of," and he writes a figure on the blackboard. We do not see that figure. Joe is like a gentleman who picks up the tab and refuses to let us glimpse the damage; money is a dirty secret, so the least one can do is act clean.

Not that *The Spanish Prisoner* is unfriendly to exactitude. Its attention, indeed, is skewed toward people of no apparent interest and objects of no particular worth: a pair of spectacles, a torn old book. When Joe's fellow-employee Susan (Rebecca Pidgeon) stops by with a bag of goodies from her local bakery, watches him prepare to cut them up, and remarks, "Nice knife," you fear the worst. It's like Janet Leigh saying how much she admires your bathroom fittings. And when Joe, on a working trip to the Caribbean, takes a photograph on the beach, a stranger named Jimmy Dell (Steve Martin) offers him a thousand dollars for his cheap plastic camera. Later, the two of them have a drink, and, shortly before Joe returns to New York, Jimmy asks him to deliver a package. It's precisely the sort of transaction—casual but suspect, with a trembling capacity for tipping the balance of power—that Mamet loves to drop into his plots; Joe is doing Jimmy a favor, simple as that, but he is also under the obligation to do it right.

From here on, needless to say, everything goes wrong, and the movie starts to sweat. Jimmy gets mad, apologizes, takes Joe out to dinner, questions him lightly about his job; Joe admits that he fears he will be inadequately rewarded for his invention; Jimmy offers to help. This is all aboveboard, but Mamet—a connoisseur of the great American con—gives the impression that there is fast work going on beneath the table. In *House of Games* he took us for a ride in the first half hour, and then encouraged us to believe that we couldn't, and wouldn't, fall for that kind of stunt again. Big mistake. There's no such double whammy in *The Spanish Prisoner*, which prefers the slow, choking buildup of paranoia: the certainty that all is not well creeps into the movie like a lick of smoke under your bedroom door. Helping Mamet stoke the fear are the composer Carter Burwell, whose ominous, exotic score has a thump as soft and rhythmical as a pulse, and the director of photography, Gabriel Beristain. In an interview for this month's *American Cinematographer* Beristain said that he used medium lenses to film the various faces: "We had thought about using 200-mm. and 300-mm. lenses for a lot of the closeups, but we were afraid that might provide clues about the characters' true natures." God forbid.

This intense desire to keep one's distance is at the core of Mamet's filmmaking. You don't sense it in his efficient, brazen scripts for pictures like *The Untouchables*, but, once he gets behind the camera, the people in front of it begin to hit the famous beat of Mamet-speak, with its unfazed continuo and its weirdly dogged repeats. Joe Mantegna was the most skillful soloist, but Rebecca Pidgeon—Mamet's wife—is becoming expert at the gnomic naïveté of his patter. "You never know who anybody is," Susan says, no fewer than three times, and the extent to which this bald announcement may or may not be true is far less interesting than the zombie stiffness with which she utters it. At first, I always tell myself that Mamet's films are badly acted, but, gradually, as the stories take hold, I find myself sliding, rather like the performers, into a cold, contagious trance.

Until last year, I had never properly registered Campbell Scott; he is one of those unfortunate stars who are condemned by their own good looks to play dullish leading men. And then, without warning, Scott gave us *Big Night*, which he codirected, with Stanley Tucci, and to which he contributed a pin-sharp cameo as a candy-sucking car salesman. Suddenly, Scott looked wry and astute, and it's slightly disappointing that *The Spanish Prisoner* has returned him to the doldrums. His Joe Ross is a dope and a dupe, and the film's conceit demands that he, the man who made the Process, should be stupid enough to tumble into a trap. To give Scott credit, he gets around this with an inspired reaction shot: as Joe finally gathers what has happened to him, he neither curses nor collapses but simply allows himself the light despair of a quarter-smile, as if turning his face to the sun. You can guess what he's thinking: I thought *I* was smart, but this . . .

The Spanish Prisoner is not Mamet's cleverest film, partly because his earlier work has schooled us in the art of foreseeing the twist. But it's the most seductive, summoning the audience to a place that resembles modern capitalist society yet feels and sounds more like a netherworld guided by shamanistic rites. (Spot the difference, Mamet would say.) It also has the knack of amusing us without ever being very funny: "Keep a sense of humor," an FBI agent says to the beleaguered Joe, more in hope than in expectation. This itchy sensation that comedy lies a fraction beyond our fingertips is ideal for Steve Martin. Jimmy Dell is a straight role, and Martin plays it straight, but you are nagged by the thought that Jimmy is fooling with Joe, and with the rest of us, not in the interests of profit but in the service of some vastly intricate joke. I have watched Martin in recent years, in shockers like *Sgt. Bilko* and *Father of the Bride*, and seen the dying fall of boredom behind his eyes. For David Mamet, he looks perky, mean, inquisitive, and as suave as a cat. Only a grouch would ask someone of Martin's genius to give up gags, but *The Spanish Prisoner* offers him the chance to hit a higher gear and to see where his watchful mania—the obsessiveness of the natural-born comic—will take him next. You never know who anybody is.

APRIL 13, 1998

DEEP IMPACT

The new DreamWorks picture, *Deep Impact*, stars Téa Leoni as Jenny Lerner, who discovers that everything we love and respect on this planet is about to be wiped out. Since Jenny is a TV reporter in Washington, you might have thought that this counted as company policy, but for some reason she looks dismayed, as does everyone around her. For heaven's sake, we're only talking about a 500-billion-ton comet heading straight toward us. It's not the end of the world.

The film was directed by Mimi Leder, who obviously decided after *The Peacemaker* that one-nuke movies were for wimps. She has now upgraded to a story so blast-happy that at one point an entire arsenal of Titan warheads is loosed off into space and she doesn't even bother to show it. The script was an unlikely collaboration between Michael Tolkin, who wrote *The Player*, and Bruce Joel Rubin, who was responsible for *Ghost*. At a wild guess, I would say that Tolkin had something to do with the chirpy stuff at the beginning and the end, and that Rubin filled in all the blubber in the middle.

The first half hour of *Deep Impact* certainly gives you a rush, from the moment a Virginia schoolboy named Leo Biederman (Elijah Wood) spots a nameless blur in the sky to the trail of lucky breaks which leads Jenny, one year later, to trip over the big bad secret. The world—played, in a bold piece of casting, by the United States of America—is facing an ELE, or Extinction Level Event. Various moves, announced by President Tom Beck (Morgan Freeman), are under way to counter the threat. First, a crew of astronauts will be sent to rendezvous with the comet, land on its surface, plug it with nukes, and jolt it off course; second, all Americans will be required by law to get in touch with their feelings or, failing that, their relatives; third, there is to be an immediate freeze on wages, prices, and anything that resembles a sense of humor.

This is a shame, because Leder has assembled a bunch of performers who are capable of rescuing any film from Extinction Level. Téa Leoni's jerky, hiccupping style is so fresh, and she looks so great in her natty Washington whites and pale blues, and her tendency to wear pearls in the face of impending catastrophe is just so *right* that you can't believe the film will be dumb enough to cramp her. Once Jenny has been promoted to anchorwoman, however, something freezes in her eyes, and she devotes her spare time to juggling the hangups of her divorced parents, played by Vanessa Redgrave and Maximilian Schell. This is in many ways a fine movie for senior citizens: the ripe, sagacious commander of the space mission is an easy ride for Robert Duvall, and I felt a surge of relief ripple through the audience at the mere appearance of Morgan Freeman.

On the other hand, the middle-aged will have good reason to feel aggrieved, for *Deep Impact* proposes that, with Western civilization on the point of finishing its coffee and asking for the check, a million Americans will be bused to Missouri and locked into limestone caves for two years, while the fatal dusty winter caused by the comet rages overhead. The deal is that, apart from specialists such as doctors, military personnel, and personal-injury lawyers, and not counting a selection of our choicest plants and animals, only people under fifty will be picked to enter the refuge. In short, you can take your flamingo but not your grandma. The worst part of this is that young Leo, who has earned himself a free pass to the caves, wastes a sizable chunk of the movie trying to get his boring girlfriend to come with him. Is he crazy? Here is his chance to spend two years dutifully propagating a new species, and all he wants to do is hold hands. But then this is a DreamWorks production, with Steven Spielberg as one of the executive producers, so making out is verboten.

Such puritan rigor is one of the reasons that *Deep Impact* becomes so glum to watch. It asks how we should script the penultimate chapters of our lives, yet refuses to countenance the possibility that, aside from those worthy souls who wish to heal their psychic wounds, there might be large sections of the population who would prefer to hold a toga party. The film is cashing in on millennial nerves, but in truth the only reliable guides to correct eschatological behavior are the Book of Ecclesiastes, which advocates at best a penitential caution, and the lighter Horatian or Catullian model, which involves packing in as many kisses as you decently can before the final hooter. Nobody in *Deep Impact* has much fun: we get a full hour of moping before a piece of comet rolls up and dives head first into the Atlantic. The splash causes a thousand-foot tidal wave that sweeps along at more than a hundred miles an hour; quite rightly, everyone in the theatre howls like a fiend when the water hits the Eastern Seaboard and thunders down Madison Avenue without staying clear of the bus lanes. But the special effects are like computer-generated De Mille—vast, roaring, and rather obvious, with a cardboardy grayness that whispers of VDU screens. Leder gives you buckets of grandeur without a speck of high-toned wackiness. As the wave rolls in, why not have a guy in a lemon-and-lime wetsuit perched on top of the Empire State Building with a big grin and a surfboard?

The trouble, I guess, is that the surfer would require a subplot to himself, and the film is already tearing itself apart trying to pay court to the many interest groups. Jenny has our attention for the first third of the picture, whereupon we switch to the exploits of the space crew; then it's back to lovey-dovey Leo and noble President Beck. All of them toil and sweat under sentence of death: there's too much of the higher vulgarity here, the kind that one recalls from Stanley Kramer's *On the Beach*, and not enough of the lower vulgarity, the kind that links *Deep Impact* to the cheesy disaster flicks of the 1950s and sixties. Does Leder not realize that the destruction of the world is a subject so engulfing that all it's good for is a cheap thrill—that the only thing to do with our appetite for the apocalyptic is to tease it, then feed it? I left *Deep Impact* feeling hungry for more, and what really intrigues me is the thought of Téa Leoni heading home after a long shoot to be with her husband, David Duchovny, who was busy making the *X-Files* movie at the time:

"Hi, honey. How was your day?"

"Oh, the usual. Aliens tried to suck my brains out through a straw. Yours?"

"So-so. A lump of flaming rock the size of Central Park fell out of the sky. You want to eat in?"

MAY 18, 1998

GODZILLA

How long is *Godzilla*? Well, the movie itself is a little over two hours, but we seem to have been living with it forever. Since the moment when Roland Emmerich and Dean Devlin—the director and the producer, respectively, of *Independence Day*—announced that they had thought of a new way to stomp all over America, and to test the mettle of its citizens, the beast from beneath the waves has been tapping its muzzle on our windowpanes. The marketing machine has been chugging away for months, its strategy being to seduce us with details—the wink of an eye, a cheeky tremor of foot. The true, overwhelming appearance of *le tout* Godzilla was left to our imaginations. As a friend of mine thoughtfully remarked, "But we know what it looks like. It looks like a big fucking lizard."

I am giving away no secrets when I say that my friend was right. All those who were covering their eyes in anticipation of some giggling, flesh-eating Barney are in for a letdown, although cultural critics will argue that our purple friend has already laid waste to larger areas of the commonweal than his green and horny cousin could ever dream of. Godzilla confines most of his pillaging to New York, and the most surprising aspect of the film is how soon he arrives here. The first half hour of the story charts his approach, beginning with the nuclear tests that were conducted during the 1960s in French Polynesia. Godzilla was apparently warped into existence by the radiation; what he's been up to for the intervening forty years is anyone's guess, although rumors persist that he studied for his baccalaureate in Paris and was about to embark on a doctorate in semantics when he began to feel hungry. The quest for food—his diet consists principally of fish, but he also likes to snack on crunchy character actors from halfway down the cast list—takes him from a canning ship in the South Pacific, which he treats like a tin of cat food, to a trio of trawlers off the Eastern

Seaboard. Finally, he makes it to the city, clearing immigration with suspicious ease.

Looking at my watch, I wondered what on earth Godzilla was going to do for the next ninety minutes. Once you've blown a few taxis down Madison Avenue just by breathing on them, how do you fill the time? The answer is too dreary for words: the filmmakers cut away to human interest. Everyone complains that Emmerich's movies tend to crush thought and emotion under the heel of special effects, but the fact is that his reliance on effects is now so skilled and automatic that when he does return to the vexed question of people—or "non-computer-generated-image complexes," as we must learn to call them—you rather wish he hadn't. In this case, the people are Nick (Matthew Broderick), a scientist who specializes in irradiated mutant species, and Audrey (Maria Pitillo), who used to go out with Nick many years ago; given that she describes him as her "college sweetie," I would say that he's well off without her, but the movie is determined to yank them together again. Audrey is an aspiring reporter for TV news—shades of the Téa Leoni character in *Deep Impact.* What is this curious new link between civic devastation and the career choices of young women? I wouldn't mind if we were talking Rosalind Russell in *His Girl Friday*, but Miss Pitillo is a lightly smiling blank; it's almost as if Emmerich had deliberately undercast his picture, to prove where the real interest lies.

Thankfully, he fails. Not because of Broderick, who is given scandalously little to do: too much of his time is spent staring with dropped jaw at the monster—or, actually, at nothing at all, since most of the monster shots were patched in later. Broderick is always likable, and to a generation of moviegoers the first half of *Ferris Bueller's Day Off* is tantamount to holy writ; but what strikes you about *Godzilla* is how disturbingly ageless this performer has become, as if a touch of Polynesian fallout had frozen him at Ferris stage for all eternity. The best reason to see the film is Jean Reno, who plays Philippe Roaché—supposedly an insurance agent, although one look at Reno hints at murkier purposes. What a face: rodent teeth and Salman Rushdie eyes, with a random allocation of stubble and a deep, shrugging weariness toward the world. Emmerich tries to patronize the character by giving him lame, funny-French lines about coffee and croissants, but Reno is way too good for him; I think we can all agree that he is officially the coolest actor now at work, and I find it inspiring that a man who could so easily be playing *Endgame* should be lending vital grace to a trashfest about the end of a giant reptile.

The plot of *Godzilla* boils down to a handful of chase sequences; in essence, Nick and Philippe go looking for the beast, and then, in a dramatic reversal, the beast comes looking for them. What happens in the middle, and all but cripples the movie, concerns a large quantity of free-range eggs; not wanting to spoil your viewing pleasure, I will simply say that Godzilla develops an unexpected child-care problem, and that Emmerich confronts the even bigger headache of trying not to rip off entire sequences from *Jurassic Park*. It is chastening to reflect just how swiftly we have been programmed to expect these artificial thrills, and how little they stir in the pit of our imaginings; all we want is the next big thing, and the only howl-worthy scene in the picture comes when our heroes, having been snapped up by Godzilla on the Brooklyn Bridge, manage to drive their yellow cab out of the creature's mouth. Huh. Twenty stories high, and it doesn't even swallow.

The grandest disappointment of *Godzilla* is Godzilla. The golden rule of monster movies was set down in 1933, when the stuttery, stop-action movements of King Kong touched even his violence with a panicky shyness, and Fay Wray drew tender inquiries from his crooning mouth and those yard-long eyebrows with a mind of their own. There are fleeting gestures toward personality in Godzilla; he and Nick go eyeball to eyeball a couple of times, and for one breathless instant I thought that Broderick was going to turn all Robert Redfordish and start whispering into the ear of the unhappy beast. For the most part, however, the villain has no character whatsoever. All we know for sure is that he suffers from poor table manners, prefers to take the subway, and has to have sex with himself. Basically, half the men in this town could have applied for the role. The only oddity in Godzilla's rather loutish behavior is his tendency to overrun famous landmarks; in the course of the story, as if to top the White House explosion in *Independence Day*, he puts paid to the Flatiron Building, the Chrysler Building, the Met-Life Building, and most of the Brooklyn Bridge. If I didn't know better, and if Emmerich and Devlin weren't so beholden to the makers of the original *Godzilla* series, I would say that the new movie is one long gag about the Japanese tourist from Hell.

I saw *Godzilla* twice last week, which must sound like going back to the dentist to have a filling removed. In the event, it got better. At the press screening, where I was surrounded by movie critics, the film felt at once drab and hysterical, but the following night, when I enjoyed the company of twelve thousand maniacs—real live people, without notebooks—at Madison Square Garden, everything fell into place.

The special effects started well before the movie did: as I opened the invitation, it gave out a furious roar that tailed off into an echoing, agonized moan. I listened to this for a while and seriously considered calling Random House and telling the editors to fit the same device to their new Norman Mailer anthology. Outside, in the evening sunlight, the luminaries swarmed; there were interviews with Mayor Giuliani and the Taco Bell Chihuahua. As we climbed to our seats, free popcorn was distributed in boxes that advertised Calvin Klein underwear, raising widespread fears among parents as to whether the humongous Godzilla would remain, you know, decent. As the time of the screening neared, we were counted down with booming heartbeats and were introduced to "the biggest premiere in motion-picture history" and "the heavyweight champion of the world"—a reference to the lizard, and something of a slight to Muhammad Ali, who was in the audience. Watching closely, I felt that Godzilla kept leaving himself open as he made a long-arm jab at the military's missile launchers, and that Ali would probably have had him down in the fifth.

What Madison Square Garden made clear was that *Godzilla* is not, strictly speaking, a movie. It is what the studios like to call a motion-picture event: a hard kernel of movie wrapped in brouhaha. You could see it in peace and quiet, or on video, and claw its credibility to shreds; but, to be fair to Roland Emmerich, his picture doesn't ask for peace and quiet, nor was it conceived with serious attention in mind. The atmosphere at the Garden was the closest that modern man will ever come to the feeding frenzy of the Roman circus: we sat there in the round, with a holiday air, and bayed for blood. Yet there was no catharsis in the experience: few in that crowd would have admitted to any terrors, let alone troubles, that required purgation, and what widened the eyes was the sheer levity with which we slaked our thirst for catastrophe. Afterward, we trooped outdoors to the party, on Thirty-first Street, where drinks were served under the canopies of United States Army tents, and where mortars were positioned wittily among the hot dogs. The only scare came as Matthew Broderick, who had survived a foot as big as a bus, was almost crumpled by the mob that surged toward the exits. Is this what all moviegoing will be like one day? I remembered Broderick's character in the film referring in awed tones to "the dawn of a new species, the first of its kind." Silly me. I thought he was talking about the monster.

JUNE 1, 1998

THE TRUMAN SHOW

The new Jim Carrey picture, *The Truman Show,* is set in a fictional town called Seahaven. Just how fictional the place is may be gathered from the weather or, rather, the lack of it; sunlight sugars the streets, not to mention the spotless whites and pastels of the houses, with the alarming benevolence of a laxative commercial. On those rare occasions when the climate falters, it does so with surprising accuracy. Take Truman Burbank (Jim Carrey), one of Seahaven's more congenial citizens. Married to the honey-blond Meryl (Laura Linney), Truman is a sweet guy who wouldn't hurt a fly, if there were any flies around to be hurt. One night, he finds himself caught in a downpour—to be specific, in a kind of stealth rain that falls on him alone, as if he were taking a shower, or as if God were trying to tell him something.

Into each life some rain must fall, of course, but Truman's life is not quite as each as he thinks. He is, in fact, the unwitting star of "the longest-running documentary soap opera in history," which is gulped down by billions of viewers. It began with Truman the fetus and will end, presumably, with his grand decomposition. He is as real as his first name suggests, but everything around him is fake. His parents are actors; his friends are actors; even Meryl is a performer, and for all we know she gets a bonus every time she has sex with her unbeloved husband. The sky above is the roof of a cavernous biodome in which Truman's world is enclosed; follow the horizon far enough, and you bump gently into the skin of the dome's synthetic wall. The good people of Seahaven are extras, with earpieces to feed them their lines; in one beautiful crane shot, we see them pause on the sparkling sidewalks and wait for instructions, with the movie freezing like a photograph and Truman just around the corner. You look at these folks and wonder, Did their hearts just stop, or their batteries?

The plot of *The Truman Show* hangs on Truman's dawning awareness that he is not as other men, and on his plan to do something about it. His fear that he is being watched is both paranoid and wholly justified: there are five thousand miniature cameras concealed throughout the town. "Have you ever felt like that—like your whole life has been building up to something?" he asks his friend Marlon (Noah Emmerich). "No," says Marlon. So Truman runs, and gets nowhere. Magical fires blaze up in his path, and he is manhandled back home. He lies low and then tries again, setting sail in search of a new world or, at any rate, a world without product placement. The director, Peter Weir, has taken us on this trip before; Mel Gibson didn't want to flee Jakarta in *The Year of Living Dangerously* any more than Harrison Ford wanted to forsake the Amish homestead in *Witness*, but, like Truman Burbank, each man knew that he couldn't stay forever. Truman has endured thirty years of living safely; now he craves a hit of risk, and the chance to play a bit part instead of a leading role.

Weir's touch is formidably sure; there is no living director who is more adept at convincing us that reverie need not be vague—that the dreamed can offer textures more crisp and unignorable than our drab quotidian rooms. His debut feature, *Picnic at Hanging Rock*, was always too acute and perplexing to merit its reputation as a petticoat piece. *The Truman Show* is the closest he has come to recapturing that radiant nightmare, but, for all the unfogged clarity of Weir's eye, I can't help thinking that the new movie is slightly too charmed by its own conceit. If you show off the deliberate falsity of your surfaces, isn't that merely rigging the evidence for your subsequent unveiling of what lies below? The dark underbelly of America hardly comes as a shock when the dorsal fin is so plainly made of plastic.

There is also the question of Jim Carrey. Amid the ecstasy that has greeted advance screenings of the movie, Carrey has been lauded for tamping down his instinctive mania in favor of a more lightly tortured soul. To me, the spectacle is admirable but painful: he looks like a drunk who is not only making do with Pellegrino but pretending that he likes the stuff. What is unclear is why on earth half the planet would want to watch a man like Truman. As the film proceeds, we cut away to viewers around the globe—in an American bar, say, or a Japanese living room—as they thrill to the highlights in his existence, but the fact remains that a universe as enamelled and orderly as Truman's is desperately low on dramatic heft. It has no highlights—not until he makes a break for freedom. Weir's movie is, among other things, a venomous satire on our entrapment by television, and yet Seahaven satisfies none of the alluring criteria of the small screen: it is at once too serenely sanitized for documentary grit and not blessed with enough narrative molding to work as soap opera. Nothing much happens, very nicely, over and over again; the cameras even turn blushingly away when Meryl takes Truman to bed. If we have become a nation of morally gelatinous Peeping Toms, would we honestly be happy to spend years of our lives failing to see Mr. Everyman getting laid? And what of his hemmed-in happiness? How could he spend three decades believing that nothing was up? With his belted and checkered fifties suits, and his jumpy half grin, Carrey is as likable as ever, but he's also too much the fool.

Weir and his screenwriter, Andrew Niccol, would presumably say that it is exactly the pressures of techno-pleasantry which have made Truman so dumb, and that the same would happen—already does happen, every time we switch on—to the rest of us. And it must be said that *The Truman Show* is as bright as hell and more smoothly provocative than the rest of the summer movies strung together. Nevertheless, it makes life too easy for itself, as it does for its hero, and I was intrigued to read an early draft of Niccol's script, which set Truman in the more testing and abrasive surroundings of New York. What murk there is in the finished film adheres to Christof (Ed Harris), the inventor and producer of Trumania. He sits in the control room, calling forth a storm or changing the baleful moon into a searchlight. "Cue the sun," he says as the hunt for the missing Truman gets under way. Harris's role here is the demonic mirror image of his mission chief in *Apollo 13:* instead of guiding the lost boys home, he urges his marooned doofus to stay in inner space, and by the end it is he, more than Carrey, who tenses the movie for its climax. "I am the creator," he declares, adding, "of a television show." In that pause, and in Harris's terrifying attempts at a paternal smile, you catch all the mirthless comedy of Christof's megalomania; his wire-rimmed spectacles and his beret show you what happens when a *poète maudit* is turned loose on television. As yet, America has made no Truman Burbanks, but we await the coming of Christof every day.

JUNE 15, 1998

OUT OF SIGHT

The most gratifying thing about the new George Clooney movie, *Out of Sight*, is that it turns out to be a good George Clooney movie. People were starting to talk. What with *One Fine Day* and *The Peacemaker*—not to mention *Batman & Robin*, which was as much fun as chewing black rubber—it was beginning to look as if Clooney couldn't punch his weight in the big ring. But from the opening scene of *Out of Sight*, when his character, Jack Foley, walks into a bank with no gun and walks out again with a brown envelope full of used bills, you can tell that everything's going to be all right. Who else could rob a bank with a fully loaded smile?

The film was adapted by Scott Frank from the Elmore Leonard novel, and he has done a beautiful job of it. That robbery sequence doesn't show up in the book for seventy pages, but it delivers such an obvious dramatic kick, and it's such a good chance to establish Jack as both amiable and culpable—to nudge him into the Leonard pantheon of good bad men—that Frank was right to promote it to the head of the picture. It also means that the director, Steven Soderbergh, gets to show his credentials: he's trying for an unpolished, raggedy look, and there are a couple of zooms inside the bank which bring back nervous memories of *Kojak*. This is more than ironic pastiche; Quentin Tarantino gave a hearty seventies spin to his own Leonard movie, *Jackie Brown*, and both directors seem to be using that awkwardness to thumb their noses at current Hollywood gloss, as if to say that the seamless fluency of a Joel Schumacher or a Ridley Scott would be shamed by the dialogue of Elmore Leonard. Listen to his cranky little solos for minor characters; how can a movie match up to all that jazz?

Out of Sight does better than most, because it refuses to be identified as either thriller or romance; I wound up tagging it as a comedy of errors. Jack Foley, for instance, is a successful thief, with more heists to his name than he can remember, but if he were a *real* success he wouldn't be on his third spell in prison. Jack is hardly a patient con: when some fellow-inmates dig a tunnel under the boundary fence, he goes along for the crawl. Waiting on the other side is his buddy, Buddy (Ving Rhames), with a getaway car. Also there—and this was not part of the plan—is U.S. Marshal Karen Cisco (Jennifer Lopez). She pulls a shotgun, but they relieve her of that burden, and she and Jack climb into the trunk of the car. Karen is a hostage of sorts, but, to be honest, Jack could use the company, having been starved of intelligent conversation. So they lie as tight as sardines and discuss movies. Karen wonders about Robert Redford and Faye Dunaway in *Three Days of the Condor*—"They got together so quick." She should talk.

It's not long before Karen gets away, but Lopez and Clooney have already brewed up enough chemistry—or, given their proximity, enough physics—to convince us that Karen will want to come back and find her man. The rest of the film is a sly and arousing *pas de deux*, or, rather, it would be if the other characters didn't get their dirty great *pas* all over the place. The cast is so strong that it's almost embarrassing: in addition to Ving Rhames we have Don Cheadle, as Snoopy, a cheating boxer, whose appetite for violence is as keen as Jack's distaste for it; Catherine Keener, reliably smart and gaudy as Jack's ex; Steve Zahn, the nineties answer to Michael J. Pollard, as a small-time crook and an even smaller-time human being named Glenn; and Albert Brooks as Ripley, an alarming ringer for Sgt. Bilko both in the sheen of his pate and in the finesse of his business methods. Ripley was briefly in jail with Glenn, Jack, and Snoopy; Glenn, who would be impressed by anyone who remembered to wake up in the morning, can hardly get over the fact that Ripley paid a fifty-million-dollar fine by check. Now Ripley is out, and living with his uncut diamonds in a house that reminds Jack of a prison. All the main characters roll up there for the finale, as if they were part of a Jacobean tragedy, or a bedroom farce.

It's easy to pick holes in *Out of Sight*. For one thing, there's a lot not to believe in. The movie confirms Jennifer Lopez's status as a qualified voluptuary, but she is not the *most* plausible U.S. marshal I have ever seen. The way she holds her shotgun during the jailbreak suggests someone trying to prod a spider with a broom handle. Still, in her belted leather coat she looks as lethal as Marlene Dietrich, and her beauty actually settles the rest of the picture. Without her help, Clooney would be stuck with the creaking myth of the tenderhearted felon; in the event, his partiality for nosing around high-risk areas in Miami and Detroit feels not just explicable but dutiful—how else can he be sure of seeing Karen again? They have one lovely scene together, when she sits with a bourbon by the dark window of a hotel bar, sees off a couple of suits who fancy their chances, and then catches the reflection of a third man in the glass. "This is not a game," Jack says, and Soderbergh comes closer than any previous director to gauging those barely visible lines, perfected by Elmore Leonard, where flirtation and foreplay—and this is a matter not just of sex but of life itself as something you toy with—are forced to stop.

The sex, of course, is a comedown. How can someone as sharp as Soderbergh sink back into the lumpen grammar of the traditional Hollywood lay? An alien watching modern movies would think that human intercourse consisted of nothing more than two faces approaching and docking in horizontal silhouette. Soderbergh throws in some jumpy freeze-frames to liven up the proceedings, but the same device works much better elsewhere in the movie—not least in the opening credits, where Jack rips off his necktie in a rage. It's the first time I have seen George Clooney in the grip of true anger, and *Out of Sight* is the first Elmore Leonard film that reaches to the difficult core of its hero: Jack grins with the criminal's disdain for what he perceives as regular life, but he also simmers with a suspicion that only regularity—a job, no jail, his own car—would have laid the groundwork for such luxuries as love. It is a terrible bind, and it leaves you with a prickly feeling that *Out of Sight*, for all its talents as a funny and pleasurable jive, is itself in sight of a more radical disquiet than Hollywood would like to contemplate. Soderbergh has done Elmore Leonard proud, but then just think what a director like Abraham Polonsky, blacklisted into oblivion, would have made of this stuff. And how could Jean-Pierre Melville, or even Godard, have learned of Jack's world and not warmed to its recklessness, to its deceitful sunshine and forgetful snow?

JULY 6, 1998

THE THIEF

The Thief begins with a woman giving birth, in back-bending torment, on a stretch of desolate road. She is unattended, and the sky above is the color of nothing. As if to drive home the point, the film closes, ninety minutes later, with the word "nothing," gravely intoned three times. All of which is a way of saying that *The Thief* is a Russian work. Written and directed by Pavel Chukhrai, and already festooned with awards and nominations, it stars Ekaterina Rednikova as Katya, the woman on the road, and Misha Philipchuk as Sanya, the boy who was born that day. Most of the movie takes place in 1952, when Sanya is six years old, and revolves around the peculiar predicament, or the acute imaginative luxuries, of being six.

Our first sight of Sanya is on a train, where he and his widowed mother play a torpid game of cards—a deft way of hinting that their journey, though it must have a destination, is an endless test of patience. A soldier (Vladimir Mashkov) turns up, resplendent in captain's uniform and high polished boots, and hoists his belongings onto the top bunk opposite them; in this moment Sanya's life changes tracks and sets off toward a different horizon. "Keep an eye on my stuff," the soldier says, and swings Sanya onto the bunk. Among the stuff is a revolver, snug in its buttoned holster, and in Sanya's face you detect not just fascination but a swelling of pride: he has been allotted a serious responsibility, and thus a sudden chance to grow up. This is what *The Thief* is about; only gradually do we grasp how corrupting such chances can be, and not merely for the boy. Does the soldier honestly wish to flatter Sanya; or is one glance enough to tell him that the child will be the quickest route to the woman?

If so, it works. Before long, the soldier is sliding his hand up Katya's stockings, on the clattering platform between carriages, and the next thing you know the three of them have become a sort of instant family. In voice-over, Sanya informs us, "We got off with Uncle Tolyan in some random city." That "Uncle" is the first of a hundred duplicities; for the sake of decorum, and in order to secure lodgings, Tolyan and Katya must pretend to be married, although the boy keeps having visions of a real father, whom he never knew. While that distant ideal remains intact, the truth about Tolyan starts to flake and fester. He and Katya are forced to share a room with Sanya, who sleeps across three chairs tied together, and who is woken and frightened by their lovemaking; when he later tries to join them in a dance, Tolyan pushes him away. The irony is, of course, that such spasms of misbehavior, with their flecks of wickedness and sex, serve only to pull the youngster in. It's the old story, the ugly comedy that was molding and firing children long before the invention of the dysfunctional family: they do not have to understand what they see, or even to like it, in order to give it their love. Uncle Tolyan may be a brute and a fraud, but he can roll a razor blade in his mouth and stamp on other guys' bicycles, and he sports a couple of mean tattoos—a panther on his shoulder and another maneater, Joseph Stalin, on the muscles of his chest. How can Sanya not treat him as a god?

At the back of this misguided worship, you can roughly make out the traces of allegory: Sanya is to Uncle Tolyan as the besotted, beleaguered nation is to Uncle Joe. But Chukhrai has too much sense to labor the suggestion, and, besides, his gift is not for the broad political stroke but for dabs of slippery human oddness. The place where Sanya and his so-called parents set down may be "random" but it bristles with specificity, and there is no disguising the relish with which Chukhrai's camera starts poking its nose into the drab apartment that, for a while, they call home. A number of other rooms are let out to fellow-citizens, and so telling are the snapshots of these unfortunates—the actress, the drunk, the lame girl, not to mention the dough-faced landlady—that you can barely suppress the sensation of having wandered into a book of short stories. Chukhrai has that determinedly Russian knack, which stretches back at least as far as Gogol (and to the Dostoyevsky who so treasured *Oliver Twist*), for creeping toward vertiginous caricature and then stopping with his foot on the brink. No one in *The Thief* is grotesque, and there are none of the visual tricks (wide angles, hectic crosscutting, and so on) by which grotesquerie tends to be built up; and yet the adult characters loom over Sanya and brand themselves on his eyes.

For some viewers, those eyes will be a problem. The moony face and wide blue gaze of Misha Philipchuk, who was eight when *The Thief* was made, may well bring on a nasty case of the cutes, but the movie staves off sweetness by refusing to endorse Sanya's natural talent for high hopes.

Even his thrills are fretted with disappointment; when he finds his surrogate father bundling other people's silverware into tablecloths and making off with bags of swag, he thinks both more and less of him. The child is then forced—and, to some extent, honored—to lend his diminutive services to the next nocturnal theft, but the exploit is also a sure sign that his childhood is dying. At first light, he and Katya are seen scrabbling in the dirt beside a railroad track, hunting for a pair of dropped earrings that might be used to bribe an officer of the law. What kind of dawn is that?

The Thief is a fine film, with more iron in its soul than you might expect. Mashkov, in particular, offers a full-blooded study in caddishness. Tolyan is an officer and a gentleman who turns out to be neither: at first, he resembles a billboard for Soviet manhood, but then licks of his brushed hair start to fall across his brow and give him the look of Picasso at maximum devilry. If there is a shortfall in Chukhrai's movie, it is one of ambition and scope; the picture works on you almost too neatly, risking little, trapping you in its tight emotional patterns. The inescapable way in which it invites literary comparison makes it both more solidly civilized than the rest of the summer movies and a little heavy on its feet; you come away absorbed by the sight of a young life in the making, or the marring, but there is something more dour going on here—a wound is being stanched, perhaps, or a case proved. To get the full measure of it, to discover whether it represents the fruit of a mature genre or the best of a bad lot, I suspect that we would have to watch a lot more Russian movies. Sadly, only a handful make it here every year, and, even then, there is no established etiquette for getting people to see them. "Hey, we should try this cool one about the search for a father figure in the lean years of postwar Stalinism!" You should indeed.

JULY 20, 1998

SAVING PRIVATE RYAN

The opening half hour of the new Steven Spielberg picture, *Saving Private Ryan*, provides what must be the most telling battle scenes ever made, largely because they tell you almost nothing. They just show. The time is around seven on the morning of June 6, 1944, and Captain John Miller (Tom Hanks) is hunkered down in a landing craft off the Normandy coast. His company of Rangers is poised to go ashore at Dog Green. When the ramp drops, the man at the front takes a bullet through the helmet, and from then on nothing goes according to plan; indeed, it is hard to conceive that there ever was a plan. Those Rangers who are not cut down in the first seconds bundle over the sides of the vessel; those who are not shot or drowned in the water wade and stagger to the sand; and those who are not killed or maimed on the beach, where there is no cover from enemy fire, aim for the seawall at the foot of the bluff. There are not many men at the wall. Miller shouts something at one of them, then turns away; when he turns back, the man has a hole where his face was. Somehow, the survivors must make it to the top of the bluff. Then they can start fighting.

One of the many historical sources for *Saving Private Ryan* was Stephen E. Ambrose's oral history of the invasion, *D-Day* (a work so engulfing that it demands to be read in real time, over a long day). You can't help noticing the wry lament that surfaces in veterans' recollections: the one thing to which D-Day bore no resemblance whatsoever, they insist, was a movie. According to Private Jack Keating, who fought with A Company of the 2nd Rangers, "It's not like in Hollywood. The actors jump into the water and in three seconds they're charging up the beach. Well, it isn't like that." You might say that Spielberg's objective in these opening minutes is to heed that admonition and, if possible, to make a film that doesn't look like a film—or, at least, to arrange his drama so carefully, and with such instinctive fidelity to the illusion of chaos, that people watching it will forget that they are sitting in a movie theatre.

Such dexterity is not unusual for Spielberg—there were times in *Jaws* and *E.T.* when he had you riding the rhythms of the picture with a kind of oblivious glee. Watching *Schindler's List*, you were never lost in quite the same way; unavoidably, its sense of historical duty weighed heavily on the body of the action. The Omaha Beach sequence, on the other hand, simply throws a barrage of detail at you and leaves you to work it out for yourself. Some hope. Caught between cold water and human beings on fire, this is as credible and confounding a vision of Hell as could be imagined: you see the water lapping red on the sand and (a sight confirmed as authentic by Ambrose's book) an armless man hunting dumbly for his lost limb. It's like high-speed Bosch. Some of the shots are miniature plots, complete with ironic resolution. One soldier feels a round clang off his helmet, which he then removes; dumbfounded, he strokes his untouched scalp, thanking his lucky stars, whereupon another bullet plugs him in the brow. No more stars.

The entire scene is, among other things, a rebuke to the controlling genius of a director like Sam Peckinpah. *The Wild Bunch* and *Cross of Iron*, his fine Second World War picture, went for the gut, as does *Saving Private Ryan*, but you could never shrug off the suspicion that Peckinpah took pleasure in exploring the wound. Spielberg cuts into violence and away again so swiftly that pleasure is forbidden to leak into the excitement; if nothing else, his film should insure that critics who dote on action movies will stop using the word "balletic" for a while. This is not to deny that Spielberg himself is ceaselessly artful; it's just that his art, at its best, is self-camouflaging. True, there are patches of slow motion in the early scenes of *Saving Private Ryan*, but they feel like the opposite of Peckinpah's infamous *tableaux mourants:* we see Miller grind to a crawl and hear the crackle and crump of German fire thicken into a slur of distant thunder. He is in danger of giving up; death is wafting toward him like chloroform, and it takes all his fortitude to shake free and start up again.

Spielberg had Janusz Kaminski, his cameraman on *Saving Private Ryan*, remove the coating from the lenses, so that the light grows dour and diffuse: think of Robert Capa's smudgy Omaha stills pasted together into a strip of film, and you'll get some idea. The colors of skin, soil, and uniform are as flat and drained as those on the translucent Stars and Stripes with which the film begins and ends. Best of all, Kaminski switches shutters in such a way that every activity gets a slight but infectious touch of the jitters. It is curious, to say the least, to watch a nineties film and catch a whiff of the panic and panache that used to litter silent movies. The first half hour of *Saving Private Ryan* is almost all noise, but none of it is dialogue. Those lines that do make it through are as basic as pre-talkie titles: "I'll see you on the beach," "Anywhere but here," and the straightforward radio communication "We do not hold the beach."

Once Miller and his men have taken and held their allotted territory, the camera wanders through the bodies left behind and comes upon a corpse face down at the sea's edge, with his name on the back of his pack: Ryan S. We now have a story on our hands. We know we have been watching a film—we have seen Tom Hanks going for broke, assisted by the formidable Tom Sizemore as his loyal sergeant, with whom he fought in Italy—but we have been sucked into the sheer plotlessness of the piece. The movie has been as crazed, and as scornful of expectations, as D-Day was to the Rangers themselves; now, like them, it has to pick itself up and do a prearranged job. You know that Spielberg has no option, but, even as the traditional thrusts of cinema (suspense, comic relief, character development) kick in, you can't suppress a twinge of disappointment. What would a movie consisting of nothing but close combat, of mess and fear and wordlessness, have felt like? Unwatchable, I guess. Now we will never know.

To be fair, I would prefer to have Spielberg follow a one-off mission than to sit through one of those character-packed but soulless epics that used to be thought appropriate for war; *The Longest Day* needed four directors and looked as if none of them had shown up. Spielberg concentrates on Miller and a group of men who, aided by the whey-faced interpreter Corporal Upham (Jeremy Davies), learn that Ryan was one of three brothers killed in action in various theatres of war; Mrs. Ryan received all three telegrams of notification on the same day. (This Sophoclean horror was actually perpetrated on the Niland family: half a paragraph of Ambrose's book provides the meat of Spielberg's movie.) The sole surviving brother, James Francis Ryan, dropped into France with the 101st Airborne; now he is somewhere in Normandy, and Miller's team, on the orders of George Marshall himself, has to find him and pull him out. They set off, and we are hauled through a series of wrenching episodes: the hidden sniper, the machine-gun emplacement, the crashed glider. These are, for the most part, staged with verve, and the speeches that fill the downtime are well written, by Robert Rodat, but there's the rub; they sound written, and are nicely placed, whereas so much of *Saving Private Ryan* feels grimly ridiculous or casually happened upon. Miller finally locates Ryan (Matt Damon) when the boy pops up in a field of high grass; the camera glances at him for a second and moves on by.

You perk up, in an awful way, as it becomes clear that the men are heading for another hopeless situation. A crucial bridge must be kept open for the Allies, and the Germans, who will get there first, must at all costs be held off. Ryan refuses to leave his post, so the Rangers stay with him and slug it out. In short, the last half hour of the picture is, if not a repeat of the first, at least a return to its air of flabbergasted extremity and reflex courage. Despite Spielberg's avowed intent to darken and coarsen the formulas of the war film, old moviegoing habits die hard: I was practically standing on my seat and yelling at Tom Hanks to kill more Germans, and then, when he had finished killing Germans, to kill more Germans. If anything, the heroism in *Saving Private Ryan* is all the more startling for not being rigged or haloed; it seems to bloom out of the shapeless dreck of fighting like a madman for your life.

This is welcome news; I was nervous about going to see any movie that might make me feel guilty—or, worse still, indifferent—about enjoying *Where Eagles Dare*, a work of art I revisit with the devout regularity that others reserve for the shrines of saints. Miller's company is shredded on the sands of northern France, whereas Richard Burton took a rockbound Bavarian fortress with the calmness that comes only to those who have previously stormed Elizabeth Taylor; still, I persist in believing that both kinds of picture are admissible, and even mixable. Abandoning the seesaw queasiness that saw him sway between high-fibre projects like *Amistad* and oversalted junk food like *The Lost World*, Spielberg has come up with a work that combines both functions—the tighter it grips, the more morally provocative it becomes. He really doesn't need the epilogue, in which one of the survivors revisits the graves of fallen comrades; this is a pilgrimage faithfully undertaken by veterans, but to a moviegoer it feels like arm-twisting, and it blocks the punch of the movie. How could any director knock us out with the Omaha Beach scene and still think that he needs to instruct us in the virtues of selfless conduct, or to woo us with the soaring choirs that wash over the final credits? (John Williams has done great work with Spielberg, but it may be time for an amicable split.) As *Schindler's List* suggested, Spielberg has forgotten how to end his movies; he wraps the action, then starts to preach.

All this is annoying, but it fades fast; if *Saving Private Ryan* has anything to offer the youth of today, it is a lesson in how to stick a mirror on the muzzle of your weapon with chewing gum, so that you can poke it out at an angle and spot the machine gun around the corner. There's a lovely moment when Tom Hanks rubs his mirror before holding it out again; you wonder how he could bother with such nicety in a world brimming with blood and sand, but that is precisely why he does it. Hanks, needless to say, doesn't put a foot wrong in this picture; no other movie star is so at ease in ensemble work, and that sense of fellow-feeling, of inborn democracy, gives you a hold on Captain Miller himself. Hanks gets solid support all around, especially from the ferrety and laconic Barry Pepper as Jackson, the company sharpshooter, who quotes from the Bible as he squeezes the trigger. At the shaken core of the movie is Jeremy Davies as the perplexed young interpreter, Upham. Devoid of combat experience, unable to interpret the lingua franca of mass slaughter, Upham is pitched into a firefight; all our moviegoing experience tells us that he will redeem himself, become a man, and save the day, but the cards don't cut like that. It is the most unromantic suggestion that I have come across in a Spielberg picture, and one of the most honest: heroes are not freshly forged in the furnace of high drama. They are trained, and they are lucky.

AUGUST 3, 1998

HALLOWEEN H2O

Who is Michael? What is he? I refer to Michael Myers: not the funny one from *Austin Powers: International Man of Mystery* but the other one—the local man of mystery who has made life so difficult for the residents of Haddonfield, Illinois. We first saw him as a six-year-old boy holding a knife, in the opening sequence of John Carpenter's *Halloween*. Michael, who had just slain his sister, was locked away for good. Needless to say, he escaped, and the movie caught up with him as he came back to town. Now a strapping lad in a white rubber mask, he spent the best part of ninety minutes trying to kill seventeen-year-old Laurie Strode (Jamie Lee Curtis). He failed, and returned to the chase in *Halloween 2*, in which we learned that Laurie was his other sister. Five sequels, of rapidly diminishing worth, made you wonder what exactly Michael's business strategy was. Now the man is here again, in *Halloween: H2o*, pitting himself against Laurie one last time.

Whether "man" is the right word is open to debate. In the credits of the original picture, he was listed as "The Shape"—a name that hinted at diabolical powers of transmutation, though to modern ears it makes him sound like a supermodel. ("Laurie wanted to kick Shape's ass," John Carpenter told me approvingly.) In the latest installment, our heroine summons Michael with the cry of "Psycho!," which is at once a nod to movie buffs and an indictment of his mental state. Dr. Sam Loomis (Donald Pleasence), who tried to treat Michael and ended up tracking him through the course of several films, had little truck with such delicate psychological terms. In the first movie he referred to his former patient as "the evil"; by the time of *Halloween 4*, he had narrowed this down to "evil on two legs."

The new picture, directed by Steve Miner, is subtitled "H2o" not because Michael has decided to slip something nasty into Haddonfield's water supply but simply because twenty years have passed since Carpenter's film. You could be forgiven for thinking that the *Halloween* franchise was dead and buried, but in 1996 Wes Craven's *Scream* raised it smartly from the grave. *Scream* climaxed with the villains' stabbing themselves for the sake of an alibi—an ideal image for the bewildering narcissism of the whole enterprise, in which a variety of clean-cut students either suffered or perpetrated violence through a tangle of movie references. Specifically, they were all worshippers of *Halloween*, and of the rigor with which it observes the rules of horror. One of the more unbendable rules states that, whenever the television is switched on in a scary film, another scary film will be playing; it's never golf or Home Shopping, although both have terrors of their own. During *Scream*, we kept seeing Jamie Lee Curtis's face flickering in the corner of the room; she was still there when Neve Campbell, with a nice easy follow-through, crunched the TV set onto the killer's head.

With a plug like that, it was inevitable that Michael and Laurie would be dusted down and brought out to play. It's a relief to see Curtis back in the series again, not just because she has been AWOL since *Halloween 2* but because she makes such a welcome change from all those kids. I find the teenagers of *Scream* wholly interchangeable; it is hard to be mortified by the demise of those who have given little evidence of living. Curtis was hardly more than a kid herself in *Halloween*, but there was always an uncommon gravity in those long-boned, elegant features: she was at once more virginal than the jocks and bimbos around her and more adult—less convinced by the notion of the world as a playground, especially after it turned into a charnel house. Now, in *H20*, she has grown into a single mother, a secret drinker, and (under an assumed name) the headmistress of a school in Summer Glen, California. The movie delves into her fraught relations with her son, who has reached the age that Laurie was in the first movie; her experience in Haddonfield was, as Curtis dryly put it to me recently, "not without its fallout." There is no mention in *H20* of Jamie, Laurie's little girl, whom the bogeyman pursued in *Halloween 4*. In the final shot of that picture, Jamie herself was gripped by demonic possession, clasping a long knife, just like her uncle Michael. What *is* it with this family?

There were two reasons why I did not see *Halloween* when it came out. First, I was not legally old enough to do so, and second, I wouldn't have been caught dead at a horror flick. When you are in the full flush of juvenile movie snobbery, you don't go and see films that excite you for an hour and a half; you go and see films that bore your socks off for three hours, on the medicinal principle that they must be good for you. Scornful of Illinois, I preferred movies that were set either north of Hamburg or east of Prague, and replaced orthodox narrative with at least three of the following: a dream sequence, a dwarf, a clown removing his makeup, a religious crisis, and a nude bathing scene. After three years and much huffing, however, I was persuaded to skip the new Tarkovsky and see *Halloween* instead. And that was that.

By now, I must have seen the movie twelve or thirteen times, but, on that first viewing, most of the in-jokes remained too in for me. I did not yet know that Jamie Lee Curtis was the daughter of Janet Leigh, or that Sam Loomis was named after the John Gavin character in *Psycho.* I got no sneaky countercultural thrill from the fact that *Halloween* had cost only three hundred thousand dollars. (It has since recouped that sum 150 times over.) I didn't even realize that Michael's headgear was a spare William Shatner mask from *Star Trek.* All I knew was that this guy Myers had parked in my head and was refusing to move on. I couldn't shake the four-note mantra of the score (composed by Carpenter himself) or the even less florid piano theme—a one-finger plink—that accompanies Michael's arrival at the head of the stairs. Indeed, the whole movie seemed to work in dotted crotchets: as you braced yourself for a fright, Carpenter would hold for an instant and *then* let fly, just as you were relaxing into the delusion that nothing was going to happen. It was a method inherited from Hitchcock, and it barely survives in today's movies, which tend to deliver their traumas right on time.

Best of all, there was Laurie's infamous slump and slide against a wall. The wall takes up half the screen—the other half is shadow, and we know that Michael will jump out of it. But he doesn't jump; he *fades* into view. The white face slowly glimmers out of the dark like a memory that you have struggled to recover, or like a ghost who is bashful of his own remorseless power to scare. The sound in the movie theatre at that moment was like nothing I had heard before: a rising siren moan, not unmixed with pleasure. Carpenter had taken an old and cloudy conceit—the maniac on the loose—and distilled it to something pure and clean. Tarkovsky would have wept.

Carpenter's achievement was to suggest that there was nothing exotic about horror; that it was more inbred than outlandish; and that it was best considered as the evil twin of what one might call the lyrical conservatism of American movies. "There's no place like home," intones Dorothy, and yet Oz is peopled with figures adapted from those whom she loved—and feared—in Kansas. And what of *Meet Me in St. Louis,* a rapturous hymn to the comforts of the known, which suddenly dispatches one of its elect, Tootie, into the awesome ritual of Halloween? Carpenter's film may be said to have sprung from Tootie's fevered dreams; I like to think that she grew up, married, and had a grandson named Michael.

That is why, after *Halloween*, small towns—not just in the movies—looked like paradises lost. If *Jaws* made us check the blue pleasure ground of the sea every time we dipped our toes in, *Halloween* made us wonder whether suburban houses, set back peacefully from the road, were quite the refuge that had always been promised. Laurie runs from one door to the next, trying to rouse sleepy householders with her howls; finally, she is alone with Michael in a single dark dwelling. When they grapple on the second floor and she pulls off his white rubber mask, the man underneath is more like a boy—a farmboy, almost, with broad, puffy features, who looks rather surprised to be exposed in this way. "Was it the bogeyman?" Laurie asks in the last lines of the movie. "As a matter of fact," says Loomis, "it was."

The good doctor is onto something: Michael Myers *is* a matter of fact. In the world proposed by the film, he is part of the landscape, or the furniture. Even when Loomis puts six bullets in him, he simply moves on. These days, such a beautifully smooth gear change into the supernatural would look like a cute setup for a sequel, but Carpenter had no such plan; he just wanted Michael to stay out there, biding his time. ("An O. Henry ending," the director calls it now.) That is why a movie that started with the pantherish glide of a Steadicam closes with still shots of all the places—the corners, the stairs—where Michael has been, and where he may yet come again. There's no place like home.

Freud, as usual, was on the case before movies got there. In his 1919 essay "The Uncanny," he demonstrated, via inspired linguistic sleuthing, that *heimlich* (homely) and *unheimlich* (uncanny) are on a collision course, and that at some point they mean the same thing. Both words whisper of secrecy and concealment, and they lead Freud toward what any moviegoer would recognize as the full robes and trappings of horror: the inanimate that dawns into life, the perplexing appearance of a double, the action that unnerves by repetition—all those occasions on which the familiar grows strange. The problem with horror flicks, of course, and the reason so many of them disappoint, is the speed with which the strange becomes not just familiar but a total drag. For every *Halloween*, with its effortless if unwitting dramatization of Freudian themes, there was a *Nightmare on Elm Street Part Four* or a *Friday the 13th: The Final Chapter*, which itself was swiftly followed—and, you might think, severely compromised—by *Friday the 13th Part V: A New Beginning.*

The presiding irony of horror is that, while no genre offers more imaginative license, few of the directors—or, indeed, the novelists—who turn to it have more than a thimbleful of imagination in the first place. (They have a sweet tooth for the fantastic and the glutinous, which is hardly the same thing.) When visionaries and obsessives deign to frighten us, on the other hand, the results can be spectacular: look at Murnau's *Nosferatu*, Dreyer's *Vampyr*, or the Karloff *Frankenstein* pictures (which redefined horror as a species of warped romance). Neither Fritz Lang nor Buñuel ever made a straight horror movie, and yet all their work is laced with the horrific; the Peter Lorre of *M* is both a serial killer and the cowering victim of his own monstrosity. As for Hitchcock and lesser masters such as Jacques Tourneur, the director of the original *Cat People*, their movies are mischievous and oddly puritan; Hitch sometimes feels like the torturer who tickles your soles with a feather while his poker warms in the fire. John Carpenter is best seen, I think, as the last of that breed; *Halloween* may have spawned some bastard children, but in fact it glances back longingly to the 1940s and 50s—to an age when it was enough to scare us as efficiently as possible. If people screamed loud enough, the deeper and more pungent fears would seep out. Now it is 1998, and what is there to be scared of?

I attended a sneak preview of *H20* at the Gotham on Third Avenue. I bought my gallon pail of Coke, took my seat, and stared around. It didn't really matter if the movie spooked me or not, because I was already terrified by the audience. It seemed unlikely that any of them had seen *Halloween* when it first came out, for the simple reason that none of them had been born yet. They made me feel seventy-five years old, a sensation enhanced by the opening credits. Janet Leigh has a cameo in the movie ("If I could be maternal for a moment," she says to Jamie Lee Curtis), but her name drew no response; when LL Cool J came up, on the other hand, the place exploded. You could argue that this was no more than an update of 1978, when Carpenter specialists had snickered at Sam Loomis; but the Gotham was not full of specialists. It was full of moviegoers, and what gave me the creeps was not what they knew, or what they didn't know, but what they didn't care to feel. To them, *H20* was a comedy—a little black round the edges, sure, but basically a scream.

Miner's movie is far bloodier than *Halloween*, whose severe lack of ketchup was a tribute not merely to its budget restrictions but also to Carpenter's feeling for the sore spot. (Blood is not frightening; what worries people is the uncertain certainty that it might yet be shed.) But the kids laughed at the gore, whooped at the shocks, and left the theatre in merriment. All those George Bush–period warnings about media desensitization suddenly seemed a little less crusty than before. One more layer of innocence had peeled away here: not the innocence of joy but the even more primal innocence that allows us to be terrified. It asks that we revisit, however briefly, the nightmares that first enfolded us in the nursery, when patterns on the wallpaper assumed shapes and rocking rhythms of their own. If you are seventeen in America today, however, with no serious bogeymen in your life, what could possibly be less cool than slipping back into infancy? Why bother to be scared out of your wits when wits are both your plumage and your claws?

In keeping with my newfound senescence, I *was* scared by *H2o.* It is plainly the only serious *Halloween* movie since Carpenter's original, and Miner stokes his tale into a kind of glowing dread. The script, like that of *Scream,* keeps winking at the audience, but Jamie Lee Curtis, to her immense credit, plays it with a straight and stricken face. *Halloween* was stripped to the bone and untroubled by motives, whereas *H2o* labors under the fleshy weight of the past. To put it crudely, Laurie is now as much of a head case as Michael himself, and you can feel the thunder in the air when they meet face to face. They gaze at each other through a small round window; it resembles a porthole, or a looking glass, and it brings sharply to mind what Freud said of the double—that it is "the uncanny harbinger of death." You realize that Michael has become, if not a mirror image of Laurie, then the other half of her being: he cannot live without her, and she cannot truly live until he dies.

No wonder, as the finale looms, that Laurie declines to flee; instead, she takes an axe and marches back to the fray. The camera rises high to watch her go, as if she were Gary Cooper in *High Noon.* Jamie Lee Curtis described this scene to me as "strapping on the guns." She went on, "By running, Laurie is never going to redeem her soul, but if she turns around and faces the person who took away *everything* that would have given her pleasure—her ability to trust, to love—then what she gains by that act is to get her soul back." This may sound heavy, but the moment itself is, as Curtis puts it, "weightless." With the end in sight, after all these years of Michael, "you feel high, on some level free." As a matter of fact, you do.

AUGUST 10, 1998

RONIN

As Robert De Niro stood up on the front seat of the speeding black Audi and poked the upper half of his body through the sunroof, the better to rest the rocket-launcher on his shoulder and aim it at the car in front, I arrived at the mature conclusion that *Ronin* was, all things considered, a rather enjoyable film. The lead vehicle duly explodes, flips over, and carries on travelling for a while; we are on the Côte d'Azur, along whose glamorously lethal curves Grace Kelly took the petrified Cary Grant for a spin in *To Catch a Thief*, and by those standards the occasional rocket attack feels like a cautious contribution to road safety. Rumor had it that *Ronin* contained one of the best car chases in recent years, but that is not strictly true: *Ronin* contains at least *three* of the best car chases in recent years. The most fruitful approach to John Frankenheimer's movie is, perhaps, to treat it as one long car chase, with occasional pit stops for the refuelling of character and plot.

Our story begins in Paris, in a Montmartre café; somnolent viewers will be shaken awake by the chewy and unusual sound of Robert De Niro speaking French. He plays Sam, an American who has left the CIA and now hawks his services elsewhere. With him in the café is a bunch of other freelance operatives: Spence (Sean Bean), who claims to be a British ex-soldier; Vincent (Jean Reno), a Frenchman so French that he still smokes those ozone-busting yellow cigarettes; Gregor (Stellan Skarsgård), the computer buff who, as in most Skarsgård performances, resembles a bank manager with submerged homicidal tendencies; and Larry (Skipp Sudduth), who likes to drive. None of them have met before; they have been brought together by Deirdre (Natascha McElhone), a young Irishwoman who wants them to steal a suitcase. Now, this is extremely good news: we have grown so weary of the inflated narrative device—the interplanetary wrecking ball that threatens the future of Earth, the leering villain who must sate his bottomless psychic needs—that McGuffin lovers everywhere will rise to applaud a film that depends on nothing more burdensome than the recovery of lost luggage.

Needless to say, the team itself takes the suitcase very seriously indeed, and not just because the financial rewards are high. When Sam and his colleagues sit in hotel rooms and plot their next move, *Ronin* takes on a quiet and purposeful air—not quite solemn, but never wholly free of the educated suspicion that, in so tense an enterprise, there will always be someone whose thoughts slide toward treason. Frankenheimer is still fond of the deep-focus shots that worked so well for him in *The Manchurian Candidate*, where faces loomed close to the camera, and he has finally found another tale to suit that bulging paranoia. "When there is any doubt, there's no doubt. That's the first thing they teach you," Sam says to Vincent. "Who taught you?" asks Vincent. "I forget. That's the second thing they teach you," Sam replies. Such doubts creep in near the start of the movie, in an extended sequence by the side of the Seine. The men have come under cover of darkness to buy weapons, yet even this shopping expedition turns into a miniature cold war. You could accuse Frankenheimer of overkill here, and of delaying the takeoff of his plot; but he is equally concerned, I think, to thicken the mood like mist, and to strengthen the ticking sense that something explosive is about to happen.

There is no better place for that squirm of unease than the quays of Paris, and *Ronin* nudged me back in the direction of gloomy delights like *Rififi* and Jacques Becker's *Touchez Pas au Grisbi*, in which Jean Gabin, like De Niro, was knotted in double crosses. It is certainly a vast relief to watch an American director taking command of territory and textures that he knows. After the grind of international thrillers like *Mission: Impossible*, *The Saint*, and *The Peacemaker*, all of which dropped in on locations because they looked pretty or sounded grim, *Ronin* feels properly grounded and travel-stained; apart from a few uninterested aerial shots of Nice and Arles (and a disastrous final voice-over about Ireland), Frankenheimer cleaves to the relaxing dramatic principle that the best way to infiltrate the spirit of a place is to have your characters go about their business there—visiting a garage, say, or sipping a cup of coffee. Frankenheimer speaks French, and has often worked in the country before; remember the tetchy Popeye Doyle in *French Connection II* and his lung-bursting run along the docks of Marseilles.

On the debit side, there was *Grand Prix*, in which Frankenheimer fell for the modish notion—very 1966—that motor-racing was viewed to best advantage on a split screen. Thankfully, that flashiness has died away, and when the motors of *Ronin* race they are filmed from a terrifying point of view just below the front fender; occasionally, the camera faces the other way and eats up a hundred yards of cobbles in two or three seconds. At one point, the participants accelerate down into a tunnel under the Seine; the last person to do that was Henri Paul, and you have to admire Frankenheimer for holding his nerve and sticking to his guns, or his gas pedal, while the Diana memorial industry was in full cry. Most people in *Ronin* get to show off their driving skills: Natascha McElhone jumps lanes and heads straight for the oncoming traffic, which may be the only sensible means of beating the Paris rush hour, while De Niro, with a shuddering face, locks and stiffens his arms to grip the wheel, slammed back into his seat as if by the sheer G-force of being Robert De Niro.

Ronin is full of stars, yet it is not a starry picture. For a thriller, it feels oddly democratic; De Niro's soft chestnut jacket is almost the only concession to color in a movie of dour monochrome, and nobody, even when the plot untwists at the end, seems to have the moral edge on anyone else. Maybe this is because Sam and his men are ronin—a Japanese term for former samurai, masterless and wandering. Some moviegoers will have heard the word before: "I am Kambei Shimada. I am only a ronin. I am not a samurai and I have no followers. . . . I've got nothing out of fighting. I'm alone in the world." Thus spoke the gently smiling sage in Kurosawa's *The Seven Samurai*, shortly before he beat the shit out of the bandits, and *Ronin* can be read as an act of homage to the Japanese director, who died recently. Like him, Frankenheimer uses his movie to break down some of that loneliness, and to nurture at least the temporary illusion of companionship. "I never walk into a place I can't walk out of," says De Niro, closely echoing the even more inward character he played in *Heat* ("Do not have anything in your life you are not willing to walk out on in thirty seconds flat"); yet he kisses Natascha McElhone to put off a passing police car, and offers no objection—he's not an idiot—when she considers for a moment and then turns her face to him for more. We never see them kiss again, let alone make love, and in most films that would count as a loose end; in the world of the ronin, however, a single smooch is all you can afford.

There *are* loose ends in *Ronin:* after the central shootout on the Riviera, the action switches confusingly back to Paris, and the all-important substitution of—wait for it—a second suitcase is performed so swiftly that you barely realize what's happened. But these are faults of urgency, not of laziness, and much of the script has a good laconic crunch to it: "You ever kill anybody?" "I once hurt somebody's feelings." The movie was written by J. D. Zeik and Richard Weisz; it came as no surprise to learn that the latter was a pseudonym for David Mamet, polisher extraordinaire, and I wonder whether he or Frankenheimer was behind the sadistic, can-you-watch scene in which Sam, without anesthetic, supervises an operation on his own punctured torso. *Ronin* is undoubtedly cruel at times: it makes no bones about the fact that bodies—whether those of the principals or of innocent bystanders, nicked by fenders and crossfire—are likely to be crushed in the fray. Yet even the grating shock of that violence appears weirdly honest beside the huge, harmless mayhem that we have come to expect from our blockbusters. In the sombre air of *Ronin*, a car crash is a car crash, not some funny fireball of special effects patched on at Industrial Light & Magic long after the scene was filmed. It's as if the 1980s had never existed: John Frankenheimer has made a fine return to form, not to mention the best Audi commercial of all time, but, more important, he makes you believe, for a couple of hours, that Simpson and Bruckheimer were nothing but a bad dream.

OCTOBER 5, 1998

LOVE IS THE DEVIL

In 1963, George Dyer fell in with Francis Bacon. The fall was literal: one night, like a bad annunciation, he crashed through the skylight of Bacon's studio and found himself among the tools of the painter's trade. Such is one of the Bacon legends, at any rate, and it forms the starting point of John Maybury's startling and viscous film *Love Is the Devil*, which follows their relationship through to Dyer's unfortunate, if unsurprising, death on a Paris lavatory, in 1971.

The part of the painter is taken by Derek Jacobi, and he takes it by force. Viewers possessed of a delicate sensibility may ask themselves whether one of the more distinguished knights of the British theatre should be seen kneeling against a bed in his underwear and awaiting the approach of another man, whose fist is bound with a creaking leather belt. But such was Bacon's cup of tea, so to speak, and Jacobi—whose squarish features somehow puff and crease into a remarkable likeness of the painter's full-moon face—is not in the business of eliding the less savory details of his subject's pugnacious life. The most enjoyable sequence in the film consists simply of Bacon preparing to go out in the evening. We see him brushing his teeth with bleach and touching up the sides of his hair with shoe polish, as if he were more domestic hardware than human being.

It sounds like mere narcissism, but the fact remains that, in its light euphemistic comedy, this scene is the movie's most persuasive demonstration of Bacon at work. We do see him drawing around the lid of a trash can and slinging paint at the resulting circle, but the Bacon estate decreed that none of his paintings could be shown onscreen, and John Maybury has done the wise thing and made the most of this galling restriction. Not for him the catastrophic decision taken by the Merchant-Ivory team, makers of *Surviving Picasso*, who tried to surmount a similar ban by having contemporary artists knock up a few ersatz Picassos. (That whole film, by extension, turned its face away from the brute fact of the artist's appetites, which is like forgetting to mention that King Kong was a little on the hairy side.) Only once in *Love Is the Devil* do we see a slice of a would-be Bacon, and that is strictly for the purpose of a visual gag: a drunken George (Daniel Craig) stumbles out of bed and relieves himself sleepily against a highly convincing painted lavatory. Given the open arms with which the artist famously greeted the assaults of chance, he may well have considered his lover's contribution to be an improvement.

What exactly George Dyer contributed to the larger life of Francis Bacon is a more prickly matter. "If they're getting on, then they're unhappy. That's what love means," one acquaintance says. The two men shared, or inventively forged, a set of sexual tastes, but beyond those the overlap was less secure. "Not much of a burglar, are you?" Bacon says when George first appears, and the truth is that Dyer was not much of anything. He was a minor criminal from the East End of London; in one scene we see him being warned by friends about the treacherous benefits of life in the West End. Bacon, on the other hand, hailed from a smart and wealthy Anglo-Irish family. His first carnal experiences, he claimed, came with the grooms in his father's stables, and there is nothing more tediously true to the pornographic tradition, homosexual or otherwise, than the gentleman who likes to trash his own gentility in the pursuit of low life; nevertheless, Bacon remained capable of behaving with ease and charm in the drawing rooms of his own social kind. None of this emerges from *Love Is the Devil*, which chooses to depict Bacon, as it were, with Dyer's hand. We see the two of them boozing, or attending a boxing match where a fighter's blood flies melodramatically into the painter's face; the movie director, like the lover, is delighted to gratify Bacon's desire to be roughed up.

It is not hard to see why Maybury took this course of action. Movie audiences, weaned on difficult heroes, should warm to the prospect of a self-taught painter whose studio resembles a bomb site; one wonders if the young, broad-headed Brando would have been tempted by such a role, or if Bertolucci had that match at the back of his mind when he rolled the opening credits of *Last Tango in Paris* beside a pair of Bacon's images. The love affair with Dyer, moreover, like the playwright Joe Orton's with Halliwell, seems to present an enviable distillation of the Bacon hell-brew—the daunting cocktail of artistic ferocity and prodigal nights that, for a variety of reasons, were doomed to remain sleepless. As it turns out, *Love Is the Devil* is an oddly lockjawed piece of work; it drops us directly into the affair and then just hangs around. Part of this is financial constraint: any movie that illustrates a trip to the United States not by going on location but by showing an American flag flapping behind one of the characters is operating on a limited budget, and Maybury can be excused for clinging loyally to his London setting. The downside is that we are forced to pay repeated visits to Soho, and especially to the Colony Room, a noisome joint where Bacon's cronies used to lap like beasts at a watering hole. Some Bacon fans maintain that the Colony was a rousing place to be, but I prefer to think of it as the only place that was actually more repellent than the refrigerated inferno of his art.

What redeems *Love Is the Devil* is its willingness to be infected by Bacon's bewildering mixture of the sly and the head-on. His figures may confront us unavoidably with their sexual gluttony and its congealed consequences, but they themselves tend to avert their gaze or glance aside, and Maybury has a knack for summoning that same air of secrecy. Transplanted into cinema, all the paraphernalia of the kinky—the long leather coat, the hand on the shoulder, the light from a bare bulb—suddenly shrugs off its naughtiness to reveal something more darkly dismaying, as if we were watching a spy being interrogated, or the cross-border hunt for a Graham Greene hero. While the film makes no effort to explain Bacon's paintings, it does gesture toward the conditions in which they began to swarm and breed. I am thinking of the drinkers filmed through the distending glass of a bottle, or of Jacobi stirring sticky paint, with the recording level so high that if you close your eyes you could be listening to the sound of a pastry chef or a midwife at work. Then there is the small, hinged mirror in Bacon's bathroom, which reflects his face in three separate panels. Bacon had completed his first major triptych, *Three Studies for Figures at the Base of a Crucifixion*, in 1944, but his fondness for that form was undimmed four decades later: how better to ponder its potential than to see yourself three times whenever you shave?

Such bold and casual suggestions are as much as movies can manage when it comes to paint. Beyond that, they resort to violence: Nick Nolte lashing out at the canvas in Scorsese's *Life Lessons*, or Tim Roth, as van Gogh, munching blue pigment off his knife in Altman's *Vincent and Theo*—much the same blue that Jacobi smears across one cheek in the new film. These are like furious denials of the peace and pedantry with which so many artists must, against all the rules of cinema, conduct themselves. Many viewers will recoil from the spasmodic impressionism of *Love Is the Devil*, but, although it plays loose with the facts of Bacon's life, it does not dishonor his memory. There are moments here of horrendous beauty—none more so than the recurrent shot of a bloody figure crouched at the end of a diving board and falling away. The wonderful twist is that the nightmare belongs not to Bacon but to George Dyer, the man lying twitching beside him. To feel and inherit the dreams, even the bad dreams, of another, and to mold his suffering into your art: is that not, in its perversity, a proof of love?

OCTOBER 12, 1998

GODS AND MONSTERS

Most of *Gods and Monsters* takes place at an unnamed time and location, but if I had to hazard a guess I would say we were looking at 788 South Amalfi Drive, Pacific Palisades, in the late spring of 1957. It was in that impeccable climate that James Whale, the director of *Frankenstein*, lived out his last days; and it was against the concrete bottom of the pool at 788 that he appears, quite purposefully, to have dashed his noble brow. He certainly drowned there on the morning of May 29th; it is the events leading up to that morning which interest Bill Condon, the writer and director of the movie. Condon plainly believes that Whale should be ranked, with the William Holden character in *Sunset Boulevard*, as one of the most illustrious floating corpses in California.

Gods and Monsters is based on *Father of Frankenstein*, the 1995 novel by Christopher Bram, though it depends, too, on the strenuous biographical endeavors of James Curtis, whose updated study of Whale was published earlier this year. Above all, what lowers over the movie—what drapes it like a shroud, despite the glittering sunlight of its setting—is the shadowed, angular landscape of Whale's own work. Whether he liked it or not, his fame rested on only a handful of his twenty full-length features; moviegoers tend to forget that he was responsible for *Showboat*, but the name of James Whale clings like a cobweb to *Frankenstein*, *Bride of Frankenstein*, and *The Invisible Man*. It is one of the satisfying ironies of Hollywood that to a surprising degree horror has been the preserve of gentlemen. The two Frankenstein movies are at their best when they are punctuated by monosyllabic grunts, but they were devised by a man whose idea of a relaxing day was to put on a three-piece suit, pour himself a cup of tea, and copy a Rembrandt.

Whale is a peach of a part for Ian McKellen; it isn't every day that you get a chance to deliver the line "My pajamas are all tailored." He directs us to the enervation of the perplexed dandy: the man who is primed to improve the world—the look of it, at least, rather than its sclerotic morals—but in whom the world is no longer interested. (*Showboat* was released in 1936, and in his final decade Whale found only fitful employment.) When McKellen lingers for a fraction of a second on his consonants—"*Wh*ale," "*p*ills"—you catch not just the intonations of the snob but also the mournfulness of someone with time hanging heavy on his hands. The blue eyes gaze around for anything that might serve as a cure for boredom, and, passing over his purse-lipped housekeeper (a very funny Lynn Redgrave), they alight on his new yardman, a drifter named Clayton Boone (Brendan Fraser) with a Marine tattoo on his arm.

The bulk of the film—most of which, like Boone himself, is fictitious—tells of the two men becoming friends, and of the incredible fact that friendship is as far as it goes. Whale sucks a hulking cigar in the direction of the younger man, but Boone is unfazed by this presidential overture. "You're a homosexual," he says to Whale over lunch, as if he had just identified an impossibly rare species: you're a narwhal; you're a quagga. Boone is straight and uncomplicated, although it is Whale's climactic achievement to twist and enrich him into something more disturbed. You wonder whether all movie directors treat their fellow-men like this—as scripts in need of development.

What guarantees the shrewd, precise grandeur of *Gods and Monsters* is the shape of Brendan Fraser's skull. The movie doesn't belabor the resemblance, but you know that Whale has finally found someone as levelheaded as the creature whom he electrified into existence in 1931. At one point, the ailing director has a Frankenstein dream, but it reverses the roles: it is the white-coated Boone who leans over the recumbent Whale and removes his brain. Who, we are meant to ask, is the monster now? There are a number of these fantastical episodes littering the film: not just clips from *Bride of Frankenstein* but a splendid sequence in which Whale's errant memory returns to the set of that picture—to his younger incarnation, complete with cigarette holder, and to Rosalind Ayres as a hair-raising double for Elsa Lanchester. Then there is Condon's cruel visual pun, in which the iron skies and blasted trees of *Frankenstein* merge into the unfaked Gothic of the trenches where Whale fought (and, according to the movie, fell in love) during the First World War. What matters, however, is not who he once was—a working-class English child—but what he chose to become. Like any good immigrant, he viewed America as a second chance—as a vast and radiant laboratory where he could play doctor to his own dead self and revivify it as an exquisite beast.

The movie's most radical suggestion is that Whale's own status as outcast—as a gay expatriate in need of love—somehow filtered through to the glazed loneliness in Boris Karloff's eyes. The problem is that, as his biographer makes clear, Whale was notably candid and content with his lecheries; *Frankenstein* was long gone before he started to feel the kick of frustration and the displeasure of Hollywood puritans. As often happens when a public figure is retrieved from oblivion and gilded as a sexual icon, *Gods and Monsters* overplays its hand: the campiness wafts outward from Whale into minor characters such as an obsequious young student (Jack Plotnick) who comes to interview him. Much better is the royal garden party at the home of George Cukor, where Whale bumps into some famous names: we see, in ascending order of horror, Elsa Lanchester, the elderly Boris Karloff, and Princess Margaret. You don't have to be a film buff to relish this portrait of Hollywood—to laugh at a world where the monsters, after a couple of martinis, are indistinguishable from the gods. Whale scoffed at the nonsense of the movies, yet he knew that they can strike our minds like lightning, and he adored his time as the creator who threw the switch. This picture does him proud, and its closing shot—one of the loveliest I have ever seen—shows Boone stalking through a rainstorm with stiffened legs and outstretched arms, in casual homage to the old British guy with the pool. It's alive!

NOVEMBER 9, 1998

CELEBRITY

Near the beginning of the new Woody Allen movie, *Celebrity*, a journalist named Lee (Kenneth Branagh), who specializes in writing about film, interviews a movie star named Nicole (Melanie Griffith). After a brief cautionary exchange with her press agent, Lee drives Nicole, in his own Aston Martin, to the house where she grew up. Sidling past the old lady who owns the place, they go upstairs to the bedroom. This, says Nicole, is where "I used to lie on my bed naked and watch my body develop." The journalist makes a move, which the star, who is married, gently rebuffs. Intercourse, she makes clear, is not in the cards. Then she unzips his pants.

There are many things to be said about this sequence, but you could not, with a clear conscience, call it cinéma vérité. *Celebrity* was shot in black and white by Ingmar Bergman's former cameraman, Sven Nykvist, but this is not one of those occasions on which monochrome denotes authenticity; if anything, the absence of color suggests, as it did in *Manhattan* and *Stardust Memories*, the lingering presence of a dream—in Allen's case, a fairly moist one. He must know what public relations consists of in the movie business; he must realize that someone of Lee's ilk would be lucky to snatch twenty minutes of Nicole's time, in the company of five other hacks and a vase of odorless flowers, in a ninth-floor hotel room that had been hired for the bleak monstrosity of a junket. Nicole would coyly concur when Lee, with outspoken audacity, asked whether her latest role had been one of her most challenging to date; but that would be it. Not only would she not go down on him; she would not even stand *up* for him. If he laid a finger on her, Nicole's publicist would spring out of the corner like a winged fury and ban him from seeing any motion picture, anywhere, ever again. So why does Woody Allen pretend otherwise?

Three possible reasons come to mind. First, Allen doesn't get out much, so the ways of the world are largely a matter of guesswork. (This presents a serious handicap to his movie, which purports to satirize certain excesses of the modern media; heaven knows, these are real enough, but Allen has to invent some more along the way. Would a TV interviewer really waft her microphone into Jean-Georges at lunchtime and grill the customers on air? Do book critics still wear bow ties?) Second, if the story is to show any muscle, Allen needs his hero to interact with famous people, rather than dawdle bashfully behind the red rope. Third—and this may be more of a concealed instinct than a conscious plan—the director needs to make it clear that, if we're going to compile league tables on the subject, Bill Clinton should rank as only the second-most-fellatio-fixated middle-aged male in the United States. Viewers of *Celebrity* may not know where to look as Bebe Neuwirth, playing a hooker, gives Judy Davis a practical in deep throat. Each woman has a banana, and Neuwirth chokes on hers. The scene struck me as rife with vengeance: Allen seems to be paying his female characters back for old, unspecified but rankling crimes. Would Annie Hall have submitted to such treatment?

There is, of course, a noble Swiftian tradition of men who grow wrathful and scurrilous with the years; the trouble is that offensiveness seems to jar Allen's artistry and throw it off track. *Celebrity* traces the doomed desires of Lee as he cannons from one woman to another—from Melanie Griffith to Charlize Theron (a supermodel) and on to Famke Janssen (a book editor, and more beautiful than the model) and Winona Ryder (an actress), and then to nobody at all. These are all smart dames, so one wonders why none of them turn to him and say, "What's with the bad Woody Allen impersonation?" Did Branagh do it deliberately, and, if so, why didn't Woody stop him? On the other side of the plot, we follow the upward curve of Lee's ex-wife, Robin (Judy Davis), who calms her quailing nerves and finds true love with Tony (Joe Mantegna). As ever, the cast has class, and is rounded off by a neat turn from Leonardo DiCaprio, who travels way out of character to play a feral, hotel-trashing movie brat. As ever, too, there is the pure dramatic economy with which Allen, more deftly than any of his peers, marks the passage of time: we sense the characters' spirits (not merely their fortunes) swell and crash like waves.

Yet *Celebrity* fails to collect itself—to gather to what I am reluctant to call a head. Robin finds happiness, Lee loses it, and the symmetry should satisfy; but this picture, like *Deconstructing Harry*, leaves you with an impression of bitty desperation, as if Allen had determined, with laudable honesty, to confront his demons, only to have them turn around and bite. "Ask not for whom the bell tolls or, to put it more accurately, for whom the toilet flushes," Lee says. It's a dirty joke and, by Allen's empyrean standard, not a very funny one; like everybody else—not just the famous—he is stricken by the prospect of life's going down the tubes, and he is taking that terror out on his own characters. *Celebrity* may be glamorous to look at, but it's not a pretty sight.

NOVEMBER 23, 1998

MEET JOE BLACK

I had heard vile rumors that *Meet Joe Black* ran for almost three hours. The rumors were true, but let's be fair: what matters is not how long a film is but how long it *seems*, and *Meet Joe Black* doesn't seem like a three-hour film at all. It seems like a ten-hour film.

Directed by Martin Brest, who, on the evidence of *Scent of a Woman*, has always liked it deep and slow, the new picture stars Brad Pitt as Death. This must be part of some secret educational venture, devised jointly by the leading Hollywood studios, in which their shiniest stars will assume the role of abstract nouns. Already in the pipeline are Demi Moore as Rationality, Jim Carrey as Peace, and Tom Cruise as Personal Growth. Pitt is not dead at the start of the film: he is a young man just arrived in New York, who meets Susan (Claire Forlani) in a coffee shop, falls in love with her, and steps into traffic, which serves him right for failing to get her phone number. What happens next—and follow me closely here—is that Pitt's body, still fresh, is adopted as a disguise by Death, who has come to claim the soul of Susan's dad, Bill (Anthony Hopkins). Why Death should choose this particular shell is unclear, unless he is a kind of spectral Pandarus who likes to bring pretty people together.

And, boy, are they pretty. Forlani has the almond eyes and catlike demeanor that in certain countries would cause religions to be established in her name, while Brad gazes out from the screen, undistracted by such fripperies as plot, in order to catch the personal attention of fifty million molten female viewers. I always imagined Death as a figure of suave ennui—an Alan Rickman type—but for some reason Pitt plays him as a jerky, robotic goof, who licks peanut butter off a spoon like Tigger eating Roo's breakfast malt. His suits droop off him as if the pockets were lined with lead, and you keep wanting him to puff his silly blond fringe out of the way; there is honest panic in his eyes as the big speeches approach, and he pronounces "Machiavellian" as if Machiavelli were one of tonight's specials. Mind you, all the performers are bowed down by the sort of dialogue which explains the popularity of document shredders. "I want you to levitate," Bill tells Susan, oblivious of the fact that they are both in a helicopter. "I want you to sing with rapture and dance like a dervish." Even more impractical are the wise words of his thrusting underling Drew (Jake Weber): "You can't unscramble scrambled eggs. The train's left the station and you're on board. . . . Wake up and smell the thorns." Smell? Thorns?

Bill is a widowed media magnate on the verge of sixty-five, with a house the size of Maine, but I fail to see how he made his billions: nobody who says "Forget your head and listen to your heart" has ever earned more than fifty grand a year. Hopkins has entered tycoon territory before, when he prowled the stage as the wolfish Lambert LeRoux in *Pravda*, but this is a new departure; Bill is a nice Rupert Murdoch, which is a contradiction in terms. He foils Drew's plans, he enjoys his final birthday party, and then he dies, taking rather longer over it than James Cameron took to sink a ship. Does Death allow everyone such a stylishly long goodbye, or does money punch its weight even in the afterlife? I have no idea what this movie is trying to tell us, or sell us, but, whatever it is, most people at the premiere were gaga for it, and I had a sudden prickle of dread: we could be in for another case of the Gumps. *Meet Joe Black* is endless, bewildering, starved of logic, and, if you stand back from it, something of a joke. In short, it feels like death.

NOVEMBER 23, 1998

RUSHMORE

Despite a diligent search, I have yet to meet anyone who has not enjoyed *Rushmore*. Wes Anderson's picture showed in September at the New York Film Festival, where tough-skinned viewers in black polo shirts were severely discomfited to find that they were having a good time. This was highly unorthodox: festival moviegoing is intended to be the cultural equivalent of polar exploration—grim, chilly, bad for the extremities, but just about worth it. Yet here was a film whose vital signs indicated the worrying presence of fun. It was short, smart, strange without being willful, and piled high with non-crusty jokes. The really amazing thing about *Rushmore*, however, is that even though it considers the unquenchable (if stubbornly unrequited) need for underage sex, it is produced by Disney.

The age in question is fifteen: junction time, with childhood finally clattering away into the distance. Max Fischer (Jason Schwartzman) is balanced weirdly—though, as far as he is concerned, far from uncomfortably—between the enthusiasms of youth and the rock-strewn responsibilities of the adult world. Like his namesake Bobby, he has more than a touch of the prodigy about him, although what makes Max prodigious is not that he excels at one thing but that he is contagiously moderate at a heap of things. When we first encounter him, Max is in the tenth grade at a pleasant, slightly down-at-heel private school named Rushmore Academy. To say that he attends Rushmore is like saying that the Holy Father hangs out at the Vatican: Rushmore *could* exist without Max, but there would be no point to the place. In a sprightly montage, we learn that he runs the fencing team, the debating team, the calligraphy society, and a host of other groups; he edits the school newspaper and keeps the school bees; above all, he is the leading light of the Max Fischer Players, which were founded by Max Fischer. Guess who writes the plays.

The sustaining joke of *Rushmore* is that, for a Renaissance man, Max is still stranded deep in the Dark Ages. He has a long, blockish head that's three sizes too big for the body below, with a face as expressive as a shoebox; his thick spectacles are like twin televisions, their hefty black rims nicely echoed by Groucho Marx eyebrows. (As far as I can gather, Max represents a new cinematic species: if he has a precursor, it is the sensible schoolboy in John Duigan's *Flirting*—the one who smoked an empty pipe and packed his best friend off to a sexual tryst with the words "Remember her needs as well as yours.") Max sports a blazer, naturally, with a row of pens clipped to the pocket, and—for that artistic touch—a very unwise red beret. All this should mark him as an ambassador from the Republic of Nerdia, but there is something in Schwartzman's careful and uncowed performance which makes him unexpectedly touching; to look at, Max is pure antihero, but you are charmed to discover, by the end of the film, that the "anti" has dropped off. True, he has been expelled from Rushmore, he has failed to get the girl he loved, and he has spent time in jail; but he is still recognizably Max Fischer, and his proud refusal to countenance the possibility of tragedy has seen him through. It's as if Othello were to put the pillow down, make his apologies, and go off for a drink with the boys.

The Desdemona in Max's life is Miss Cross, who teaches first grade. Played by Olivia Williams, who seems to have recovered splendidly from *The Postman*, Miss Cross is a traditional English rose, and she blooms very happily in the mysterious air of *Rushmore*. With a typical respect for secrets, the movie peeks politely into her heart but never reveals too much. She is a widow of the non-merry variety, and at some point in the film she acquires a handsome boyfriend; in the meantime, she is courted haplessly by Max, whose idea of romance is to climb through her bedroom window with his forehead covered in fake blood, and more successfully by Max's friend Mr. Blume (Bill Murray). Mr. Blume is the rich, miserably married father of two other Rushmore pupils, and, like Max, he envisages Miss Cross as a courtly ideal to be wooed and won. "What's your first name?" he makes so bold as to ask. "Rosemary," she says. "What's yours?" "Herman."

Now, that is in itself not an amusing line of dialogue, but we're talking Bill Murray here, so watch out. Those of us who worship Murray, who take him to be the exploding cigar in the complacent face of Hollywood, have been waiting years, ever since the unadulterated joys of *Groundhog Day*, for him to find another film that fits. Herman Blume is only a supporting role, but then so was Harry Lime. You can tell it's a great Murray movie because you find yourself wondering all over again. "How the hell did this guy ever become a star?" That gangling height, those scrunched and pocky features, the limbs that disobey and the hair that wants to retire: How can the same industry employ him and Brad Pitt? There are moments in *Rushmore* when the director must have thrown away his storyboards: a beaten-up Murray with two cigarettes in his mouth, a bored Murray not chipping but *tossing* golf balls into his swimming pool, a girl-shy Murray finishing a conversation and suddenly, for no discernible reason, hurtling away from the camera in one of his mad-puppet runs, no strings attached.

All credit to Wes Anderson, then, and to his cowriter, Owen Wilson, that the picture never veers out of control; they give Bill Murray free rein, but at the same time they delicately curl and bind his character into that of Max, until you can hardly imagine man and boy apart. "I'm in love with her," Blume says of Miss Cross; "I was in love with her first," protests Max. He is like an eight-year-old going on fifty, and Blume is the other way round; they arrive at the principle of deadpan from opposite directions. Bill Murray's glazed expression sees no cause for hope in the world, whereas Jason Schwartzman's level, myopic gaze sees nothing else. The two creeds collide beautifully at the barbershop: Max, ashamed of his origins amid his wealthy classmates, has always pretended that his father is a neurosurgeon, and it is not until late in the film that Blume learns otherwise. Max introduces him to the barber—"My father," he says. If you want to pick one shot from this year's movies, try the look on Bill Murray's face as he shakes hands with Fischer senior: puzzlement, disbelief, a speck of outrage, the quiet rush of truth, and, last of all, a gentle settling of kindness. The entire thing takes maybe four seconds: this is known as acting.

Rushmore is not without flaws. The scene where Max gets drunk and abusive at dinner seems too exotic for his tidy tastes, and I caught a definite slackness in the third quarter: the film is so indebted to Max's moods that, when his fortunes slump, everything else follows suit. For the most part, however, *Rushmore* is a model of economy; as if to rebuff the slacker generation, it goes about its appointed tasks with Max-like vigor and aplomb. Still, why should so small and parochial a comedy exert such a pull? Maybe it has to do with the two-tone color of the project: Anderson has made an up movie on a down theme. In truth, Blume is a dead soul and, at fifteen, Max is close to the verge of failure—he even lives next to a graveyard. But the two of them kick out like true Americans, and the whole movie jumps with the buzz that you hear in the songs on the soundtrack. Best of all, there are the Max Fischer Players, who studiously mount the most elaborate school productions ever witnessed. Max's version of *Serpico* looked pretty good, but his Vietnam play, complete with real dynamite, looked even better. As he stood there onstage in full *Deer Hunter* makeup, blazing away with a flamethrower, I thought, This kid is something else. He should be in pictures.

DECEMBER 7, 1998

THE THIN RED LINE

It has been twenty years since Terrence Malick last honored us, or beguiled us, with a movie. *Badlands* came out in 1973, *Days of Heaven* in 1978, and that was it: Malick went to ground, and the rumor industry, which loves a no-show, went to town. Now the man is back, bringing neither a masterpiece nor a catastrophe but something so ravishingly strange that only he could have made it.

The Thin Red Line is adapted from James Jones's novel of that name, although, as you listen to the moony monologues that resound through nearly three hours of film, you could be forgiven for thinking that when Malick sat down to write the screenplay he slapped a copy of Emerson on top of the Jones. "What's keeping us from reaching out, touching the glory?" one character muses toward the end. What's keeping him is the small matter of Guadalcanal: the picture centers on an Army Rifle company that runs ashore, fights its way up a green hill, takes out a village, rests up, and leaves. Comparisons will inevitably be made with *Saving Private Ryan*, but in truth the battlegrounds are barely on the same planet: Spielberg's men drive forward not just on a particular mission but in pursuit of a greater good, whereas Malick turns soldiers into wanderers. They seem to have drifted into the service of a random destiny, and they leave the island with the air of men who have given their all to a near-nothing. *The Thin Red Line* is scarcely a war movie, because there is no Second World War to be seen—just the quick chill of death and patches of sun-warmed fatigue.

Malick's climate control, in fact, seems more coherent than his grasp of character. D-Day, as Spielberg reminded us, lurched into life on nauseating seas, but there is something far more ominous in the low, clear-gold light that gilds the ships near the start of *The Thin Red Line*, and the velvety swell of water at their bows. This illusion of blessedness stays with the men as they storm the beaches and find nothing but lustrous, travel-brochure sand. They are here to clobber the Japs, and the Japs refuse to play. Malick stretches the suspense for as long as he dares, sending his camera out to prowl at grass-top level and to stare at the local wildlife, which, for the remainder of the movie, stares right back. (To signal the Japanese presence with a shot of upside-down fruit bats is not, shall we say, the most diplomatic use of montage in the history of cinema.) At last, the company comes under fire from the top of the slope, and we in turn have to duck in our seats beneath a barrage of dramatis personae. Who are these people? Their names are sawed-off single syllables: Fife (Adrien Brody), Welsh (Sean Penn), Witt (Jim Caviezel), Bell (Ben Chaplin), Gaff (John Cusack), Keck (Woody Harrelson), Storm (John C. Reilly), and Tall (Nick Nolte).

There are tremendous actors in that long list, but some of them have to carve a character out of nothing more than a set-piece speech and a couple of smokes. Cusack, looking wise and seasoned with grime, pops up out of nowhere, leads a thrilling assault on the bunker, and then disappears; Nolte, as his superior officer, confides that he views him as a son, but we see no evidence of their relationship. John Savage staggers around in full crack-up mode, reinforcing our embarrassed sense that we are watching a preemptive Vietnam film, and there are meaningless cameos for George Clooney and John Travolta, the latter sensibly taking cover behind a ridge of mustache.

You could argue, of course, that the movie's lack of a core—of a single soldier whom we can hook up with—is true to the chaos of the occasion, and that the lopsided narrative (the frontal attack is followed by an hour of cleanup operations and hanging around) reflects the rhythms of wartime soldiering, with its tedium pockmarked by panic. But *The Thin Red Line* is an infuriating film, which keeps grabbing and then brushing off your interest. There are signs that Malick genuinely wanted to engage our sympathies; Private Bell, for instance, is a fine part for Chaplin, who is fuller of face these days, with a heavy sadness about him. The pastoral flashbacks that besiege him—summer foreplay with his wife back home—are both a nod to devotees of *Days of Heaven* and, in some weirdly believable way, the reason for his lunatic bravery on the hill. Bell tells his beloved that if he dies, "I'll wait for you, on the other side of the dark waters." Like the best of Malick, this stirring line is an inch short of pretentious; it deals in what you might call the Homeric demotic, and who else has the nerve to conjure that?

Needless to say, Bell speaks the words inside his head. Malick has always had a fondness for voice-over, but while Sissy Spacek's ruminations in *Badlands* struck you with their scary moral numbness, the ramblings in *The Thin Red Line* offer the more undisciplined suggestion of a trip. What a gonzo world the movie constructs: intense physicality on the battlefield, helpless poetry on the brain, and nothing in between. (Even Nick Nolte's bellowing rants to the troops sound like messages to himself.) The trigger for these yearnings is the opening sequence, in which Witt and a fellow rifleman, who have gone AWOL, sport with the native Melanesians. The boys among whom they gambol in the waves have amazing orange hair, like miniature Dennis Rodmans, but Witt sees in them the promise of earthly peace; by the end, to no one's surprise, they have grown fretful and pustular. "Look at the things you have made," we are told, and the plaintive accusation confirms that we have been watching the world's first Rousseauist combat movie. It is only incidentally concerned with America versus Japan: Malick directs us instead to the wrestling of man with man, and to the irredeemable spoliation of virgin hearts and skins. You may not buy that vision, and if I were a veteran of Guadalcanal I would be tempted to take it as an insult. But, a week after seeing *The Thin Red Line*, I am starting to be spooked by it, and already I need to see it again.

DECEMBER 28, 1998

THE PRINCE OF EGYPT

> The power is real. The story is forever. The time is now.
>
> —BILLBOARD SLOGAN FOR *The Prince of Egypt*

The time is then. The place is Egypt. The boy is born. The prognostication is dodgy. The answer is bulrushes. The boy is launched. The boy is found. The adoption process is unimpeded by interference from government agencies. The dad is Pharaoh. The brother is Rameses. The stage is set.

The time is later. The kid is a hunk. The kid is a *prince.* The chariot-racing is extreme. The traffic is nonexistent. The living is easy. The problem is conscience. The workforce is enslaved. The suffering is Jewish. The prince is twitchy. The answer is Get Out Now. The desert is deserted. The tribe is welcoming. The prince is at peace. The prince is home. The chick is Tzipporah. The flirting is hot. The sex is not. (The studio is DreamWorks.) The day is dawning. The bush is burning. The bush is *talking.* ("I am what I am." The bush is *Popeye?*) The message is clear. The stage is set.

The prince is back. The pharaoh is Rameses. The rivalry is nonfriendly. The deadlock is grim. The answer is plagues. The Almighty is mad as hell, and he's not going to take it anymore. The attack is frog-based. The river is blood. The wind is death. Frankly, the place is a mess. The pharaoh is crumpled. The prince is tops, and the People is Let Go! The chase is on. The pharaoh is closing. The sea is in the way. Correction: the sea is not in the way. The sea is, like, whoompa-*whoosh.* The enemy is swamped. The Jews is through.

The picture is O.K. The picture is *fine.* The cast is packed. The prince is Kilmer. The brother is Fiennes. The squeeze is Pfeiffer. (The dance is hubba-hubba.) The trouble is scale. The trouble is bombast. The predecessor is De Mille. The mood is tumescent. The music is nuts. Look. The thing is this. The cutting-edge computer-generated imagery is white-hot new. The movie is old-fashioned. The story is forever. The movie is for the holidays. The choice is yours.

DECEMBER 28, 1998

LOCK, STOCK AND TWO SMOKING BARRELS

The new British gangster film, *Lock, Stock and Two Smoking Barrels*, has been a booming hit in its native land. I have a suspicion that it could take off here, too, and that, a year from now, sophisticated American travellers will be signing up for the full Smoking Barrels Mean Bastard Tour with Luxury Pub-Wrecking Option. Those with money to burn could even be offered a guided tour of Vinnie Jones. Vinnie plays a debt collector named Big Chris, and he is the best reason to see the picture. I find it difficult to describe the Jones face, with its almost unbroken line of eyebrow, although I feel confident that you could strap it to the front of a truck and use it to clear snow. *Two Smoking Barrels* is Vinnie's first film; until recently, he was a soccer player or, more accurately, a Visigoth in the cunning guise of a soccer player. He attained the status of Public Hero No. 1 back in 1988, when, awaiting a corner kick, he reached behind him and, without looking back, grabbed the private parts of Paul Gascoigne (his only rival as England's leading lout) and twisted hard. This touching moment was captured in a famous photograph; the people looked upon it and said, Surely this man could be a movie star. And, lo, it came to pass.

Two Smoking Barrels tells of Eddie (Nick Moran), Tom (Jason Flemyng), Bacon (Jason Statham), and Soap (Dexter Fletcher), a bunch of friends with a good idea. The lads send Eddie, an accomplished card-player, to an illegal game and wait for him to return in triumph; but the game is rigged, and they find themselves owing half a million pounds to Hatchet Harry (P. H. Moriarty), the employer of Big Chris. At this point, they overhear—as one so often does—a gang of uglies next door discussing a forthcoming drug heist. So our heroes get into place and duly rob the robbers. The story marches on toward a sanguine shootout, after which only a handful of the characters are left intact, and it closes on a cliffhanger—the most blatant what-happens-next setup since the teetering bus at the end of *The Italian Job*.

Not that all this should be mistaken for a proper movie. Rather, think of it as a carefully constructed entertainment for the benefit of people who really, really like beer commercials. The director, Guy Ritchie, has filmed a number of advertisements, and it shows in his style: when you can't decide what to do, swing the camera around the room like a cat, and—here's a nice one—try freezing the action for no reason and then have objects continue to move in slow motion. Add a gravy-brown filter for that scummy East End look and, voilà. As for the dialogue: given that Cockney rhyming slang was lurching out of date by the time Michael Caine made *Alfie*, in 1966, what hope for resonance now? And why do all the actors—apart from Vinnie Jones, whom I would not wish to upset—serve up these linguistic leftovers in such a numb, crawling tone? It's supposed to be a caper flick, not a deathbed scene. Listen to the street trader selling dodgy perfume in the opening shot; if he pattered that slowly in the London I know, he'd be out of business. Word has it that at a Los Angeles screening of *Lock, Stock and Two Smoking Barrels* no less a personage than Tom Cruise was heard to comment, "This film *rocks.*" I rest my case.

MARCH 8, 1999

THE DREAMLIFE OF ANGELS

The first thing you hear in *The Dreamlife of Angels*, before any images appear onscreen, is the scrape and shuffle of someone walking along, as if beneath a heavy load. The someone is Isa (Elodie Bouchez), who drifts around France in a T-shirt and baggy sweater, with all her worldly goods on her back, picking up odd jobs and even odder friendships. But she lacks the daze of the traditional drifter; her round eyes are dark with determination, as if she were aiming to meet a goal that had yet to be named. Far from being out of her head, Isa has a knack for shining a light into the tumbledown minds of others; no wonder she latches on to Marie (Natacha Régnier), whose spirit is as fierce and flustered as Isa's is serene. Put simply, Erick Zonca's film is a record of their acquaintance; it also happens to be one of the best French movies since Jules met Jim.

The two girls come together in a clothing factory in Lille. Isa, the newcomer, needs a place to sleep, so Marie takes her home. The apartment she's living in belongs to somebody else—to a friend who died in a car crash, and whose daughter, Sandrine, is still comatose in the hospital. Marie, who is flinchingly sensitive to her own troubles and half blind to those of others, has taken the opportunity to move in, but you sense the spectral presence of the previous owners—especially that of Sandrine, whose teenage journal, complete with the usual scramble of ecstasy and frustration, is found and studied by Isa. Zonca is endlessly alert to the lives that hover on the fringes of our own; he sinks us deep into the tale of the two girls, yet, even in the midst of one of their arguments, you hear someone practicing scales on the piano. And the final shot of the film moves calmly away from Isa along a row of unknown women, all of them hard at work, until it settles at random on a new face, as if to say: It could have been her.

It is this conviction—a quiet, democratic intensity, the highest virtue of

French cinema—that nudges the secondary characters onstage. Isa and Marie try to talk their way into a rock concert, but a pair of burly bouncers jeer at their efforts and send them packing. That might have been the end of it, but then they all bump into one another in a bar, and soon, without really trying, Charly (Patrick Mercado) and Fredo (Jo Prestia) are looming large—not difficult, since both of them are built and coiffed like yetis. In a moment of insane courage, Marie even goes to bed with Charly; people have won the Légion d'Honneur for lesser acts, although what stays with you from the scene is the hulking sweetness of the man. Graced with the semantic skill that is the birthright of every French citizen, Charly points out that fatness is purely a matter of vocabulary; and from here on he and Fredo, against all expectations, grow into the sanest and most reliable figures in the film.

At the other end of the evolutionary scale lies Chriss (Grégoire Colin)—playboy, restaurateur, and full-time worm. He gets Marie out of trouble when she is caught shoplifting, and then, as if he had earned a favor, sleeps with her. Their affair, if that is the right word for a few breathy writhings on corpse-white sheets, wrenches Marie away from her friends—Isa and the bouncers—and deludes her into a flickering belief that love is in the air. But Chriss is in love only with himself, and the close-up of Marie's eyes as she lies next to him is the loneliest shot in the film. The sex in Zonca's movie was strong enough to earn it an NC-17 rating, and he had to make additional cuts to bring it down to an R. This is no surprise; I stopped taking the Motion Picture Association of America Rating Board seriously when it demanded the removal, from a trailer for *Six Degrees of Separation*, of a glimpse of the naked Adam on the ceiling of the Sistine Chapel. (That Michelangelo—what a sleazebag *he* was.) The irony is that the bedroom scenes in *The Dreamlife of Angels* are among the most dramatically telling in the film: Chriss conquers Marie out of contempt, while she screws herself ever deeper into despair.

If that makes the movie sound like a drag, fear not. I have seen it three times, and even now I find it hard to take a reading of the tone: it has a lightness, a pace and buoyancy, that deters the tragic, and yet it knocks at the heart with an insistence that leaves comedy behind. Everything you need to know about *The Dreamlife of Angels* is there in the faces of the two actresses. They were joint winners of the best actress award at Cannes last year, and it would be invidious to try to separate them. Régnier is fair and reedy, with a volatility that not only sweeps her between moods, from flashes of warmth to wintry blasts of ire, but seems to change her physically: the Botticelli beauty, cheeks flushing with desire, can tighten within seconds into the pinched plainness of the spoiled brat. Bouchez is the epitome of toothy tolerance, with a smile that can encompass virtually anything—but not all—that experience can provide. She looks so *on* for everything: during the course of the film, we see Isa roller-skating, impersonating Madonna, and eating cold pizza from the fridge. When I saw Bouchez in films like *Clubbed to Death* (1995) and André Téchiné's *Wild Reeds* (1993), her dark hair was long; now it's cropped like a boy's, as if she were readying herself to play Peter Pan or Viola, and you can't help focussing on the tiny white scar that nicks her right eyebrow. Did Isa, of all people, get into a fight? Her history has certainly been rough enough, and yet such is her effusion of goodness that one shudders to think of a hand being raised against her.

The film feels so grounded, and the camera is so responsive to this pair of helplessly expressive creatures, that halfway through I began to wonder what the title was about. Only afterward did it strike me as true and fit: there is not a hint of moral tutorial in *The Dreamlife of Angels*, but it resounds with a kind of scruffy miraculous urgency. Isa writes in Sandrine's diary, as if bringing her up to date might bring her back to consciousness, and she spends a night of vigil in the hospital chapel—all this, remember, for a girl she does not know. Marie, on the other hand, is beyond even Isa's help, and there is a scene near the end which rocks you back with shock; it has been a long time since I heard an audience gasp in unison. Isa, we finally realize, is a full-fledged seraph, gusting through life on a wing and a prayer; Marie is a falling angel, and her descent is terrible to behold. One day—her only happy day—she goes to the coast with Chriss and runs along the sand, like the fugitive Antoine at the close of *The 400 Blows*. But he at least got to see the sea; Marie is all in a mist.

Looking back on such a scene, it's hard to tell where character ends and texture begins—so much of the movie seems to unfold next to the skin. Chriss is a thin-eyed monster, but I will remember him best by the glass of water that Marie slings in his face, and by the sharp, stinging slap that Isa delivers when he asks her to do his dirty work—to tell Marie that it's over. He is flush with money, while the girls are forced to scavenge on the margins of society, and yet all of them are strangely levelled by the flat northern light of Lille; for a film that could so easily have settled for the politically plaintive, or for a satirical snarl, *The Dreamlife of Angels* is startlingly fair, as if its prime duty were not to cast stones but to oversee the stumbling dance of its disparate souls. Like *Leaving Las Vegas*, which was equally attentive to individual faces, and to their terror of desolation, Zonca's film was shot on 16 mm, a process that—as his cinematographer,

Agnès Godard, has pointed out—creates its own form of intimacy. This eager simplicity, a rebuke to the blockbuster, appears to be hurrying back into style: *The Celebration*, which makes the same fervent demands on its performers, was shot on video and transferred to film. Neither work, it goes without saying, was nominated this year for an Academy Award: how can you hope to qualify for best foreign-language film if you fail to include a cute little kid in your script?

Not only is *The Dreamlife of Angels* resolutely unchildish; it is not even a young man's movie. Zonca has never made a full-length feature before, and he is forty-three; rising from his story is an unmistakable sense that, unlike some of the young guns making American pictures, he has kicked around, and he knows something of existence—of the world that matters—beyond the hothouse of cinema. *The Dreamlife of Angels* was more than three years in the writing, and Zonca shot enough footage for a three-hour film, before chopping it back to two. Hence, perhaps, its extraordinary rustle of discovery: most films we see these days seem wrapped, locked into place before they've even started, but you feel this one probing its way ahead, more than capable of twisting and trailing in a dozen directions. What began in the manner of a fogbound documentary ends up with the grave clarity of a requiem. In the meantime, we have grown as near to the characters as any audience could wish to: we hear the close-up crackle of Marie's cigarette, and we watch Isa's red, rubbed fingers resting on the smooth white hand of the unconscious Sandrine. We look at these people and think, Whose life is it anyway? It is theirs, and it is Erick Zonca's, and it is ours.

APRIL 5, 1999

THE MUMMY

I want my mummy. One shouldn't make a fuss about this, but, still, if I go to see a movie entitled *The Mummy* I feel that I have a democratic right to expect bandages. We know what happens in mummy pictures: a bunch of adventurers find a hidden burial site marked with a hieroglyphic inscription that reads "Do Not Disturb," and, having mistaken it for a sign saying "My Room Is Ready for Cleaning Now," they duly get their comeuppance from what appears to be a giant sports injury. This time, however, Universal has gone for something different: instead of a nice old musty package with Boris Karloff or Christopher Lee quietly suffocating inside, we get a skeletal computer-enhanced figure that stalks around with fragments of three-thousand-year-old flesh hanging off it. If you made a nourishing winter soup out of white beans and Terminator, this fellow is what you would find at the bottom of the pot.

As far as audacious genre deconstruction goes, that's about it. The writer and director of *The Mummy* is Stephen Sommers, who has practiced his refurbishment skills with live-action versions of *Huckleberry Finn* and *The Jungle Book*. There's only so much you can do with Egyptian revivification, however, and so the standard ingredients are hauled out of the cupboard. The dashing hero is Rick O'Connell (Brendan Fraser), who is blithely, though never ravenously, in quest of treasure; the heroine is Evelyn (Rachel Weisz), bespectacled yet bosomy, and never happier than when manacled to a plinth by the forces of darkness; and the twit is Evelyn's brother, Jonathan (John Hannah), whose cowardice is designed to heighten the already dazzling gleam of O'Connell's courage. These three are the nonexpendables; the remaining characters can all go hang, or go melt, or, in the most unfortunate cases, go without their vital organs, which are urgently required by the renascent mummy if he is to put on weight and rejoin polite society.

We start with a burnished prelude, set in 1290 B.C., during which the high priest Imhotep is buried alive with a hissing crowd of flesh-eating bugs, thus proving that ancient Egypt, notably ahead of its time in areas such as irrigation and civil bureaucracy, was also the home of the press conference. A quick jump brings us to the 1920s, and to O'Connell's obsession with the fabled city of Hamunaptra. The twenties are a good Brendan Fraser decade: he has the hale, self-mocking hulkingness that suits the artless journeying of those years. Fraser is on a roll just now, and *The Mummy* is the perfect follow-up to *Gods and Monsters*, a fresh and frantic twist on his likability. The joke is that he's never as dumb as you expect, or as his fictional foes would hope him to be; his broad shoulders lend him a touch of Johnny Weissmuller here, although, unlike Johnny, he seems confident that dialogue is the stuff that comes out of the hole at the top of your body.

I'm not so sure. Among the inventive tortures devised by Imhotep, none is quite so excruciating as being forced to speak Stephen Sommers's lines. "Lady, there's something out there," O'Connell solemnly tells Evelyn. "In a word, evil." You could excuse this as traditional hammy horror, but I found it depressing that Sommers should lean on that tradition as a prop for indolence; despite a Spielberg-like knack for nudging the recklessness of his action into hilarity, his script sounds like an early draft, and there are no first-class frights. The only whisper of menace comes when Imhotep sifts himself into sand and pours gently through a keyhole; I have a soft spot for changelings and shape-shifters, and it should be possible to equip them with a little moral alchemy for good measure, but *The Mummy* can't be bothered to pause for the consideration of character. This is partly the fault of the casting director; whoever asked John Hannah to play a yellow British buffoon, for example, was presumably blind to the fact that he is sly, slender, smart, and extremely Scottish. However much he was paid to shout the words "I say, bloody good show, chaps," it was not enough.

Finally, there is the Arab question. The Arab people have always had the roughest and most uncomprehending deal from Hollywood, but with the death of the cold war the stereotype has been granted even more wretched prominence. In *The Mummy*, I could scarcely believe what I was watching; as one character says that camels are dirty because they spit, the Arab riding behind him expectorates, right on cue. Later, an unfair complaint about the stink of the burial chambers is redirected toward the true source of the smell. Guess who. So here's a party game for any producers with a Middle Eastern setting in mind: try replacing one Semitic group with another—Jews instead of Arabs—and *then* listen for the laugh. One could argue that the racism of *The Mummy* is merely period detail, or that the gags zip by so quickly that they don't have a chance to stick; I find, however, that they hang around while the rest of the movie fades. It's a shame, because much of *The Mummy* is a blast, and you cheerfully root for Brendan Fraser; he promises such innocent fun, and yet the film teases the innocence away from him. Lady, there's something in this movie. In a word, ignorance.

MAY 10, 1999

THE PHANTOM MENACE

A long time ago, in a galaxy far, far away, people made movies with people in them, and some of those movies made sense. Then something happened, and the people started to vanish from the movies, along with most of the sense. For a while, the spectacle was fun to observe, but slowly the pictures tipped into insanity, or, at any rate, into the hypnotically bad. The joke was that the number of viewers willing to submit to such hypnosis went not down but through the roof. Historians of this phenomenon are now agreed that the change became irrevocable shortly before the end of the second millennium, with a George Lucas film entitled *Star Wars: Episode I—The Phantom Menace.*

As everyone in our own galaxy has been informed, this is the first of three prequels to the old *Star Wars* trilogy; the resultant sexalogy, if that's the word I'm groping for, will bring us the history of the Force from soup to nuts. The last person to try this tactic was J. R. R. Tolkien; after finishing *The Lord of the Rings* (whose Frodo and Gandalf are clear forerunners of Luke Skywalker and Obi-Wan Kenobi), he devoted his days to filling in the mythological back story of his epic. Lucas groupies—of whom one hears so much, but of whose acquaintance one never actually seems to have the pleasure—contend that *Star Wars* is all about good and evil, or the search for a father figure, or the struggle to find significance in the universe at large. This being so, the same admirers may be troubled by the surprising revelation that *The Phantom Menace* is all about taxes. Why Lucas didn't release it on April 15th is beyond my comprehension. The opening credits tell us that "The taxation of trade routes to outlying star systems is in dispute." There are young Americans whose hearts will leap like deer at this news; if so, they will be the first creatures to be inspired, as the direct consequence of an aesthetic experience, to plan a career in the IRS.

But that, after all, is the Lucas way. Geographically, the *Star Wars* series may be the most outlandish of sagas; in terms of its emotional politics, however, it remains the most shrinkingly conservative. Every time it sets sail for new worlds, it turns out to be landlocked by attitudes that would have sat snugly in a Western of the 1920s. The threat of the malformed and the rapacious is regularly defused by a body of tall white knights; Samuel L. Jackson plays a Jedi in the new movie, but he is fobbed off with a handful of lines and no determinable character. In the Lucas scheme of things, the token woman may be spunky, but she is still a token, and the idea of a female on the Jedi Council seems as pointless as a punk in a gentlemen's club. The warriors fronting *The Phantom Menace* are the young Obi-Wan Kenobi (Ewan McGregor) and his mentor, Qui-Gon Jinn (Liam Neeson), who are dispatched on urgent business to the planet Naboo—a peaceful spot, ruled by Queen Amidala (Natalie Portman) and threatened by a hostile-takeover bid from the Trade Federation. The Federation, the object of principled scorn throughout *The Phantom Menace*, is a massive corporate body that happily tramples over the protests of elected governments in its bid to expand, and will not rest until wearily compliant leaders sign on the dotted line; *The Phantom Menace*, on the other hand, is being distributed by Twentieth Century Fox, a charming family business that ventures only where it knows it will be welcome, and likes nothing better than to close a deal with a cup of coffee and a smile.

On Naboo, the Jedi do battle with tedious droids and run into Jar Jar Binks, whose name suggests a failed rap artist. He is, in fact, a gungan—a tall creature with ears like flippers, who makes his home in an underwater city. He is also, I regret to announce, the focus of the film's "comedy." This entails his getting caught in the stirrups of one lumbering beast, stepping in the excrement of another, and so on; Jar Jar has a squealing accent, apparently borrowed from Peter Sellers in his *Goon Show* era, and a weakness for malapropism. All in all, he is one of the unfunniest characters you could wish to encounter, and even the small children beside me stayed tight-mouthed through his gruelling antics. So did the heroes; like many of his fellow bit players, Jar Jar was added separately, by computer, so if Liam Neeson and Ewan McGregor look straight through him you can hardly blame them.

Taking a shortcut via Naboo's core, Obi-Wan and Qui-Gon arrive at its majestic capital, which combines the styles of myriad architectural periods and therefore resembles an overpriced Indian restaurant. Here they pick up the Queen and spirit her away, only to spring a busted hyperdrive in deep space—always a bummer on weekends. The nearest spare spacecraft parts can be found on Tatooine, a dusty crock of a planet on the Lower East Side of the galaxy. By chance—or, if you prefer, by the beneficent will of the Force—they bump into a kid named Anakin Skywalker (Jake

Lloyd), a slave who builds robots in his bedroom and lives with his mother. "There was no father," she says to Qui-Gon. "I carried him, I gave birth to him. . . . I can't explain what happened." Now, this is only a wild guess, but I suspect that we are in the presence of a Religious Parallel. Anakin has been sent to save those life-forms who have behaved themselves properly, and the Jedi are his evangelists. Here ends the lesson of *The Phantom Menace*, although Lucas has made it clear that everything will go haywire in future installments: Anakin will turn bad and become Darth Vader, if you please, but not before boffing Queen Amidala and fathering Luke and Leia. This is the hardest part to imagine: you look at the exquisite Natalie Portman and the cocky Jake Lloyd and think, She's going to go to bed with *that?* By then he will have been replaced by an older and less brattish actor, but the idea still gives me the creeps.

It is telling that Lucas, reticent and control-freakish in many respects, has been so liberal with his declarations of narrative intent. He seems to have lost all interest in suspense, either in this particular plot or within the larger saga; what he really doesn't want to give away is his special effects. I would dearly love to spoil them for you, but there's not that much to report, apart from an indistinguishable array of rubbery snouts. The one moment at which this moribund enterprise comes alive is during the high-speed pod race, in which Anakin pits his wits and his rusted, scrap-metal machine against those of the snouts. The sequence has a gutsy, Roman-circus buzz to it, unbothered by the mystical claptrap that prevails elsewhere, and it reminds you hearteningly of the Indiana Jones movies (which were partly devised by Lucas himself). But Spielberg has a gift for the swift sketching of character, whereas Lucas is so fatally gulled by the latest tricks of his trade that he abandons the actors to their fate; it's as though, unable digitally or animatronically to control their expressions, he had to shut them down altogether. (There's no Han Solo figure to mock the grandeur here, and that's a dangerous loss.) Natalie Portman, whose lightly worn radiance in *Beautiful Girls* is my fondest memory of moviegoing in the nineties, seems baffled and overawed; Liam Neeson has the sullen air of a man who would rather be three galaxies away; as for Ewan McGregor, what happened? He looks as if he just sat on the sharp end of his lightsabre. It must have taken some nerve to drain the charisma out of this cheerful Scotsman and force him to speak like Noël Coward. McGregor may well be laughed off the screen when the movie opens in Britain—an unthinkable turn of events. His first words in the film are "I have a bad feeling about this." Yes, laddie, and you've got two more episodes to go.

* * *

It is, of course, profoundly gratifying that *The Phantom Menace* should emerge as a work of almost unrelieved awfulness. It means, for one thing, that the laugh is on all those dweebs who have spent the last month camped out on the sidewalks beside movie theatres, waiting for the big day. You could argue that they will be so conditioned to enjoy themselves that they may not notice the awfulness; if so, they are getting the movie they deserve. There is nothing more off-putting about *The Phantom Menace*—more insulting, in the light of Lucas's democratically barnstorming credentials—than the feeling that it has been made solely to feed the habit of *Star Wars* junkies. For the first ten minutes you think, What the hell is going on?, and two hours later you want to cry out, "Is that *it*?" I dutifully thrilled to the earlier films, to their contrast of black-velvet skies and blinding white sands, but I was a little too old to worship them or study the variorum editions. Even in the late seventies, we had a suspicion that *Star Wars* was nerd territory—for boys who had the toys (rarely girls, who know junk when they see it), who were tuned in to Mos Eisley, womp rats, and Pizza the Hutt, or whatever his stupid name was. If you wanted cool new movies, you watched *Jaws* seventeen times, and, rather than rush to *The Empire Strikes Back*, you treated yourself to the grownup horrors of *Alien*. Lucas couldn't give us a human being to rival Sigourney Weaver's Ripley, let alone an android in the same league as the replicants of *Blade Runner*; and the mother ship in *Close Encounters of the Third Kind* could have blown a fleet of Imperial star cruisers out of the sky.

I wonder whether the prerelease fuss over *The Phantom Menace*, which has surely been greater than the sum of all the fusses that surrounded the earlier episodes, will prove to be nothing more than the last, ludicrous gasp of seventies retro-chic—*Boogie Nights* for the sci-fi crowd, with the prosthetics in different places. Trying to see the picture in advance was like asking the president if I could borrow his nuclear codes; no one would tell me the location of the screening until I presented myself in person at the Fox offices to collect my ticket. As I approached the theatre, I was expecting a full-body search, with employees snapping on rubber gloves and telling me to face the wall, and it was a relief merely to have my hand blue-stamped on entry, as in a teenage disco. This was all part of the monstrous amalgam of secrecy and publicity which has sealed the picture from the public gaze; the worst marketing ploy I have found so far is the *Star Wars Learning Fun Book*, for kids of kindergarten age. ("What is this? It is a Hutt. Say it out loud: Hutt.") *The Phantom Menace* raises the spectre of an industry where the parasitic arts of buildup and spinoff will outgrow and choke the product itself. In fact, the true masterstroke would have been *never* to release the film; Lucas could have milked the anticipation for as long as he pleased.

In truth, something like this has already happened. The most costly and influential installment of *Star Wars*, after all, failed to come to fruition. It was otherwise known as the Strategic Defense Initiative, but not until it acquired its enticing nickname was the interest of the public—and, more important, of the president—aroused. You cannot help thinking that it was images of Han, Luke, and Leia that spun round inside Ronald Reagan's head as he approved funding for the program—one of those rare occasions when he did not see eye to eye, or dream to dream, with the unfanciful Margaret Thatcher, who was not known as a moviegoer. (Another instance was the US invasion of Grenada—again, more of a bad war picture than a serious military undertaking.) One should not underestimate the effect, at once extravagant and insidious, of popular entertainment on the political imagination. It is only since *Star Wars*, after all, a work that displays the casual annihilation of planets but not a single drop of blood, that America has discovered its alarming and wholly impractical taste for the deathless war—a war in which, if we must have dying, it should always happen to the other side.

What the effect of *The Phantom Menace* will be on America, and on the wider world, I shiver to imagine. The Force is with this movie, whether we like it or not, and it will doubtless tap into our cloudy millennial disdain for the operations of reason. "Concentrate on the moment," Qui-Gon says to Anakin. "Feel. Don't think." This is an update of Alec Guinness's advice to Mark Hamill in the original *Star Wars:* "Let go your conscious self, and act on instinct." Wise words, Obi-Wan, but there has never been a less instinctive movie than *The Phantom Menace*. Its calculation glitters in every frame; the climax is hectically explosive, as you would expect, yet perplexingly uncathartic. None of the fans around me, not even the kids, were whooping or waving their fists in the approved manner, and I had the dismaying thought that Lucas may be doing it on purpose—that he may have held back from providing satisfaction because there are more courses still in the kitchen. *The Phantom Menace* is at once childishly unknowing and rotten with cynicism; I would call it the disappointment of the decade except that, along with many other people, I had a sneaking fear that it would turn out this way. What is this? Crap. Say it out loud: Crap. And will it make the magic billion dollars? You bet.

MAY 24, 1999

NOTTING HILL

The star of *Notting Hill,* in case you're wondering, is Notting Hill, a fashionable and multiracial patch of West London. Here it plays a distilled and disturbingly white-faced version of the real thing. In the same vein, Hugh Grant plays a hapless rendition of himself called William Thacker, who runs a small travel bookshop with a startling lack of profit. One day, Anna Scott (Julia Roberts) turns up to browse. We first see her as an unfocussed blur in the background; she then comes sharply into view and, from there, into the forefront of William's life. His opening move is to tip orange juice over her chest, paw weakly at the stain, and suggest that she change her T-shirt in his apartment across the road. In the first of many rousing implausibilities, Anna accepts his offer, not realizing that if you remove any item of clothing in the vicinity of an Englishman he will, regardless of his current status, become your love slave for eternity.

The joke is that Anna is a global movie star; now that I think of it, she reminded me slightly of Julia Roberts. Anna earns fifteen million dollars a picture but has forgotten how to confront the world without her sunglasses; she is so famous, and fame is now such a stockade, that it will take someone of lunatic determination to break down the gates. And that is the plot of *Notting Hill:* Anna and William fall for each other and try to establish whether you can commit to someone who is not demonstrably of the same species. When the princess sleeps with the frog, and the frog refuses to turn into a prince, what next? Can the princess be persuaded to jump into the pond?

In this tale of commoner meets royalty, the director, Roger Michell, and the writer, Richard Curtis, have found a neat hook for their movie—even neater than that of *Roman Holiday,* say, in which Audrey Hepburn jumped off her pedestal for Gregory Peck. (Note what half a century can do to an ideal; with Hollywood more rampant and secretive than ever, who would now look to actual royalty for the unattainable?) If anything, Michell has piled too much on his plate. As he showed in his punchy TV drama, *The Buddha of Suburbia*, and later in *Persuasion*—the most vibrant of the Jane Austen adaptations—he likes to color his romances with quick, caustic swipes at the society that surrounds and smirks at love, and I sensed in *Notting Hill* a half-thwarted need to lay into the whole business of celebrity, with its hell-brew of the inhuman and the sentimental. The film is at its most wondrous, yet also its most irate, during the opening credits, where flashlit glimpses of Julia Roberts are rocked and lauded by the sound of Elvis Costello belting out "She" with what you might call passion aggression. William boldly declares, "It's as if I've taken love heroin," but the film fails to back him up; it's all about people—and, to an extent, aimed at people—who are turned on by a single lick of the love popsicle.

Richard Curtis, for one, is too canny to let obsession spoil the show. As he made clear in *Four Weddings and a Funeral*, he is the acknowledged expert at fine-tuning a script to meet and flatter our expectations without bruising our assumptions. Anna's big speech rises to the simple announcement that "the fame thing isn't really real, you know," which I wish were true. She continues, "I'm just a girl standing in front of a boy asking him to love her," which must have been as tough to deliver as that James Stewart line in *The Philadelphia Story* about the "fires banked down" inside Katharine Hepburn. Curtis has been wise enough, and hopeful enough, to ally himself with a particular tradition of romantic comedy—with the heartfelt (if alkaline) conviction that everything is food for comedy except the romance itself. He honestly roots for Anna and William, and exhorts us to do the same.

From here on, it's a matter of taste. Many people will be wowed by the central pairing of *Notting Hill;* as time went by, however, I thought that William and Anna looked less and less like enraptured lovers and more and more like really good friends. Curtis might take that as a compliment; his constant demand is that, apart from a couple of walk-on stooges, everyone in his movies should get along handsomely. Much of the film is consumed with conversations—at dinner parties, in restaurants, in a car—between a bunch of William's pals. There is Max (Tim McInnerny), who is married to Bella (Gina McKee); there is Bernie (Hugh Bonneville), a useless stockbroker; and there is Honey (Emma Chambers). In an earlier version of the script, Honey was William's suitor; now she is his sister. Such is the amiable, deeply unthreatening world of *Notting Hill*, and no wonder Anna is made welcome.

The problem is that she spends a large chunk of the movie perfecting her impression of Bambi caught in the headlights. Everyone around her is terrified by the prospect of a superstar and then slowly softens; Julia Roberts, on the other hand, never really defrosts. When Anna asks William up to her room at the Ritz, her tone is fringed with desperation, as if what awaits them were not a downy bed but a session on a therapist's couch. The driving conceit of the story is that this woman should melt into normality and yield to the levelling of love; but the effulgence of the Roberts smile, and even her posture, have a curious fixity that forbid her to unwind. There's a morning-after scene when William and Anna lie in bed and talk, as one does, of breasts. "I mean, they're just breasts," she says. "You must have seen a thousand of them—what's the fuss about?" Needless to say, the sheet stays tucked securely around her upper half, and she gets out of bed off-camera; the dialogue is a hymn to openness, but you would have to pay Julia Roberts a lot more than fifteen million dollars to stroll naked across the room. (If she were ever going to do it, now would have been the moment.) It was easy to imagine Audrey Hepburn—always game for a good time—gaily spending the rest of her life with Gregory Peck. That made it all the more of a wrench when she had to return to duty at the end. But Anna and William as a married couple? We see him accompanying her to a premiere, and he wears the expression of a man who would rather be at home with a bowl of cereal.

To be fair, the need for peace and quiet is a major weapon in the Hugh Grant armory. In a recent interview—always a pleasure, since he has a more graceful turn of phrase than any other movie star—he called his acting range "sinisterly narrow," but, if so, it's a brilliant sliver. He gets at minor-league feelings that few performers can be bothered with: the hangdog, the casually stricken, the polite pointing out of clouds behind the silver lining. One sequence in *Notting Hill* finds him at a press junket, posing as a hack from *Horse & Hound* in an effort to see his beloved; he falls at every conceivable fence, and the full-length shot of him wandering haggardly down the corridor afterward is an unimprovable study in petty disaster. This makes him a suspect choice for happy endings, but there's no doubt that Grant suits—and even redeems—the peculiar, stop-go motion of Curtis's plot. Boy and girl hit it off, then lose it, then hit it off again, and so on, with gruesome snatches of soft rock covering the cracks in the narrative. There's a climactic car chase, but it's set in motion by nothing more than William's acquaintances soberly debating the justice of his conduct. Also, it stars only one car. Typical bloody England.

Notting Hill is the most cunning work of transatlantic fiction that I have seen in years; there is a dash of diluted Henry James in the way it lets each nationality feel subtly superior to the other. The English will snigger at the neuroses that appear to be draped like jewelry around the neck of the successful American, while viewers here will gaze down pityingly at the stuttering incompetence of the English; an entire scene, indeed, consists of William and his friends vying to be hailed as tragic losers. Michell and Curtis try to cast a spell over the streets of Notting Hill—wait for the overhead shot of a moonlit tryst in a private park—but the magic resolves itself into nostalgia, into an ill-defined hunger for an age when desire (not least the desire to go to the movies) had its own established decorum. Anyone expecting a rerun of *Four Weddings* will be bemused by the gently unfarcical air of *Notting Hill;* it turns on the charm, but the laughs are surprisingly sparse. Most of them are farmed out to Spike (Rhys Ifans), William's foul and gangling flatmate. "All that awaits me at home is a masturbating Welshman," William says sadly. Word has it that American preview audiences were much taken with Spike, even to the exclusion of the Hugh-and-Julia story. So much for romantic comedy. We live in troubling times.

JUNE 7, 1999

BOWFINGER

The good news about the new Steve Martin picture, *Bowfinger*, is that it's set in Los Angeles. After the clouded, low-pressure feeling of *The Out-of-Towners*, Martin is back in his own town, the one that he chastised so rhapsodically in *L.A. Story*. It must be said that *Bowfinger*, which Martin wrote himself, is not half as beautiful as the earlier work; the pace is too maddened to allow any of that sprinkler-hissing lushness to seep in at the edges. By way of compensation, we get Martin in centrifugal mood, with gags and bit parts flying off him like shrapnel, plus a sample of those strange little sounds—meaningless clusters of sticky consonants—that he tends to deliver under the influence of inspiration. The director is Frank Oz, who made *Little Shop of Horrors*, *Dirty Rotten Scoundrels*, and, lest we forget, *The Muppets Take Manhattan*, and there is something muppety, something inordinately gonzo, about his new movie that wipes out all resistance. Yet the premise could not be more depressed; Bowfinger (Martin again) is a deadbeat movie producer who lives in a dusty shack with a Greek portico stuck on the front door. The first ten minutes of the movie are telephone-bound—a flurry of calls and messages, most of them concerning a script that Bowfinger admires, but all of them racking up his levels of loneliness.

The script, entitled *Chubby Rain*, is by a genial accountant named Afrim, and Bowfinger wants it made; thanks to a well-rehearsed roster of deceptions—ripping the car phone out of a Mercedes, say, so that he can use it as a mobile in a restaurant—he gets an O.K. from a studio executive (Robert Downey, Jr.), who reads not only the first page but the last page, too. One small problem is that Bowfinger has to get Kit Ramsey (Eddie Murphy), the world's hottest, angriest, and most paranoid movie star, and the hero of *Explicit Endeavor*, to commit to the new film. Kit turns him down; undaunted, Bowfinger decides to shoot *Chubby Rain* anyway, with Kit in the leading role but without Kit's realizing that he *has* a role—

indeed, that he is in a movie at all. According to Bowfinger, this is standard practice: "Did you know Tom Cruise had no idea he was in that vampire movie until two years later?"

The farce factor of such a plot is off the chart, and Martin and Murphy barely miss a trick. Bowfinger claims that action heroes require no more than six proper scenes, the rest being filler, so those are what he films. His other performers—Christine Baranski as a drama queen, Heather Graham as a nice Ohio girl who sleeps her way through cast and crew ("I've never done it lying down before")—approach Kit and jolt him into the right reaction shots. Even better, Bowfinger's dog, Betsy (gutsily played by Mindy), has a pair of high heels strapped onto her front paws, so that she can trot through an underground parking lot and cause a terrified Kit to take off in his red Ferrari. In its storming silliness, *Bowfinger* does niggle at some Hollywood home truths—the enduring suspicion, for instance, that stars are never *not* acting, even to themselves, and that to catch them off-duty is your right as an American citizen, your privilege as an artist, and your personal introduction to what Bowfinger, in a pensive moment, calls "Cinema Nouveau."

In truth, *Bowfinger* is pretty solid *cinéma ancien*, and it stays alive through sheer width of wit: Martin refuses to narrow the range of his targets—stepping into ethnic territory, for example, that more timid writers would leave alone. We get a bunch of illegal Mexican immigrants who are lured through the gunfire of the border, hired as a film crew, and taught the ropes; by the end, they are reading *Cahiers du Cinema* and taking calls on their cell phones. We also get Eddie Murphy playing a second part as Kit's shy brother, Jiff, "an active renter at Blockbuster." Murphy seems happiest when, as in *The Nutty Professor*, he is given the opportunity to slip out of his jiving character and into someone less deafening; Bowfinger asks Jiff if he would mind cutting his hair for a screen role, and Jiff says he prefers to have someone else cut it for him. *Bowfinger* is that kind of picture; Oz and Martin understand that knocking Hollywood is easy money, so they settle into a headlong but sweet-natured surrealism, closer to *Roxanne* than to the hostility of a film like *The Player.* Such tolerance can be unhelpful to logic, and it does seem unlikely that *Chubby Rain*, with its overall costs of $2,184 and its fumbling zooms of Eddie Murphy in the back of a car, would premiere to such warm applause. Still, it is hard to begrudge the makers of *Bowfinger*, like those of *Chubby Rain*, their happy ending; after all, in its penchant for the rough and ready, in its scorn for the cheaply therapeutic, and, most important, in its induction of the backward car chase into world cinema, *Bowfinger* is a skit on happiness.

AUGUST 16, 1999

WEST BEIRUT

There is no disguising the fact that *West Beirut* is all about West Beirut. Either you have the guts to see a movie set in Lebanon in 1975 or you don't. To those who give it a chance, Ziad Doueiri's first feature should prove anything but a chore; it may even seem familiar—closer to the easygoing Baltimore pictures of Barry Levinson, say, than to some of the more chastening rigors of recent Arab cinema. Like Levinson, Doueiri realizes that if you make a film local enough the air of authenticity will be contagious, and the audience will end up feeling nostalgic for a place they never knew.

To point out that 1975 was not the quietest year in Lebanese history isn't saying a lot; the strangely calmative lesson of *West Beirut* is that, in some ways, 1975 was pretty much the same wherever you went. The story starts with a playground full of schoolchildren watching a dogfight between Israeli and Syrian jets overhead; at ground level, however, the kids are wearing floral shirts with Huggy Bear collars, and our hero, a teenager named Tarek (Rami Doueiri), wears jeans so flared that he appears to be travelling on a pair of small hovercraft. At one point, he goes to see his friend Omar (Mohamad Chamas); they smoke cigarettes in the bedroom, put on a record, and begin to dance. For a minute, I thought, Ah, yes, here we go: an ancient Arab litheness, peculiar to the rhythms of the region and requiring skills that will forever be impenetrable to the Western soul. Then I caught the tune on the turntable: "Rock Your Baby."

It is this dogfight between the known and the distant, between the consoling and the perilous, that gives Doueiri's film its snap. Tarek's last name is Noueiri, one letter away from his creator's, and he is played by the director's younger brother, so it would not be presumptuous to view this as an exercise in autobiography—a stack of things past, shuffled and dealt anew. Certainly there is a fierce warmth in the portrait of Tarek's parents—

Hala (Carmen Lebbos) and her languorous husband, Riad (Joseph Bou Nassar). Rites-of-passage movies tend to freeze the parents out or knock them down, but here they set all the right examples, even the sexual ones; she is crisp and bobbed, he is baggy-eyed and bent over a book, and they can hardly keep their hands off each other. Their test is to stick together while Beirut rips itself apart. Roadblocks go up between the Christian-controlled East and the western sector patrolled by Muslim militias. "There is no Beirut, today it's East and West," says a guard at the crossing point, and this division shuts down the livelihoods of Riad and Hala. She can't practice law and he can't farm, although, being Riad, he promises that the country they love will stay inviolate. "I'll prove it to you," he says, and, like a paramour in a poem, brings her strawberries in bed.

As far as Tarek is concerned, if this is the end of society he can't get enough of it. The whole trajectory of the film is touched off by the sly, demonic grin that appears when he first gathers that war means no more school. Most of what follows counts as free time; the best scenes come early on, and they jolt along with a roughness that verges on the haphazard. Beirut-watchers may be reminded of *Circle of Deceit*, Volker Schlöndorff's devastated love story, which he was crazy enough to film in the city in 1980, while the war was still going on. *West Beirut* is a lighter enterprise, but it's equally tricky to predict; although neither Doueiri nor his actors are improvising, the characters themselves, with the ricochet of luck and bad luck whining around them, seem forced to ad-lib their existence. One moment Tarek is staring up at a girl on a balcony, and the next he is strolling beside her as if the pickup itself were too slight to mention. Her name is May (Rola Al Amin), and she is a Christian; that alone makes you think of another balcony, in Verona, and of other young lovers stuck in the wrong tribes on the wrong side of town.

Such plot as there is concerns some home-movie footage shot by Tarek and Omar on Super-8; thankfully, Doueiri soft-pedals any hint of youthful creativity, preferring to stress the practical challenge of getting film developed during a civil war. The shop with the Kodak sign lies just beyond a checkpoint, and the boys, with May in tow, approach it with trepidation. Omar—small and gnomish, with a slippery wisdom beyond his years—takes hold of the crucifix around May's neck and tucks it under her sweater. It's a smart move, for within seconds they are lined up at gunpoint and accused of being Christian spies, and it takes much bowing and scraping on Omar's part, together with a peace offering of cigarettes, to pluck them out of trouble. *West Beirut* is a slender picture, and it scrapes against the sentimental, but scenes like that are amazingly adroit in their negotiation of mood; although Lebanon has been culturally colonized by France since the 1920s (and Doueiri duly supplies a very funny lampoon of French hauteur in Tarek's class at school), there remains the ironic likelihood that French cinema, more than any other, has shaped his style. It is men like Renoir and Truffaut, after all, who saw how accurately movies could measure changes in the wind, and how quickly the farcical could turn foul.

That is what happens at the rally. For fun, Tarek and Omar join a street demonstration and merrily chant the name of Kamal. "Who's Kamal?" asks Tarek. "No idea," Omar says with a shrug. In a flash—literally so, as a Molotov cocktail flares in front of them—the fun stops dead, and the two friends are separated. Tarek hides in a car, which, to his horror, passes the Kodak shop and heads for the forbidden territory of the East. Once there, he escapes and finds himself in an apartment stacked with guns. A lark has turned into a frenzy, which turns into a lark of a darker variety, and so on; suffice to say the switchback does not end there. The unforced surrealism of Beirut's plight keeps spewing images as if they were gags; we have much to learn, for instance, from the philosophical gentleman who runs errands for a brothel madam, and who thus passes unscathed across a sniper's alley with a bright-red bra tied to his car aerial. "If they see the bra," he says, "you live."

You could argue that such comedy is irresponsible, or, at any rate, morally frivolous. In April, 1975, Shimon Peres, then the Israeli defense minister, was asked how Israel would respond to the landing of PLO terrorists on the beaches of Tel Aviv: "We shall allow Lebanese internecine strife to retaliate for us," he said, and his prophetic confidence was amply repaid. In the same month, members of the Phalange, the paramilitary wing of the Maronite Christians, shot thirty-one civilians, mostly Muslim, on a bus in East Beirut. The ensuing fifteen months saw the death of thirty thousand people in Lebanon, 70 percent of them under the age of twenty. Twenty-five thousand children were orphaned. Kamal Jumblatt, to whom Tarek and Omar so kindly lend their support, was the leader of the left-of-center National Movement; he was murdered, by persons unknown, in March, 1977. How can you put a backdrop as stained as that behind a drama whose most heartfelt sequence involves a lanky youth trying to focus a cheap camera on the cleavage of his best friend's aunt, while the friend murmurs, "What a piece of lamb"?

The only answer must be: This is what it was like. Not everyone was caught in the blast; even in Lebanon, history is something that passes by, rattling the windows, and you simply have to pray that you're not at home when it finally breaks in. Only a few artists, of Tolstoyan omniscience, can meet the grand events head on; the rest must throw sidelong glances and hope for scraps. *West Beirut* is instructive in this regard; Doueiri does begin in high style, with the Phalangist attack on the bus, and it's the worst thing in the film. Blood bursts, an old woman tumbles in slow motion, and a soprano laments lustily on the soundtrack; everything about the scene looks false and puffy, and Doueiri takes the rest of the movie to reestablish his credentials as a director of dexterity and wit. What stays with you from *West Beirut*, in short, is not its immersion in political complexity but its homage to half-knowledge—to the state of randy innocence in which Tarek and Omar are suspended, and which saves them from the maturity of despair. When Omar warns that godless foreign pleasures will be frowned upon by the new fundamentalism, Tarek is appalled. "Is Paul Anka the work of Satan?" he asks.

Maybe it was the same spirit of curiosity that sent his alter ego, Doueiri, from Lebanon to the United States, where he wound up as a cameraman on *Reservoir Dogs*, *Pulp Fiction*, and *Jackie Brown* before turning, or returning, to *West Beirut*. From mass slaughter to Quentin Tarantino: I'm not sure that counts as progress, but Doueiri's movie, honestly tremulous in the face of guns and girls, is a rousing introduction to pulp fact.

SEPTEMBER 6, 1999

ANYWHERE BUT HERE

The latest Wayne Wang picture, *Anywhere but Here*, begins with Susan Sarandon driving a big car across a desert landscape. You think, Hey, didn't they motor off the cliff at the end of that movie? And where did Geena Davis go? The ghost of *Thelma and Louise* trails ahead of Wang's film, raising dust; we get the same impatience dressed up as yearning, and, from Sarandon, the same motormouthed determination to have her own way. This time she plays Adele August, who just quit her second husband; now she and her teenage daughter, Ann (Natalie Portman), are travelling from Wisconsin to Beverly Hills. In Adele's view, the road is pure yellow brick, and the Oz of Los Angeles will glitter with good jobs. In Ann's view, the whole thing stinks.

From here on, dangerously little happens. The two of them arrive safely, try the beds at the Beverly Hills Hotel, check into a Travelodge, and then into a succession of cruddy apartments. The rest of the film resounds to the lilting strains of domesticated crabbiness; mother and daughter spend so much time arguing that you know it can merely be a matter of time—almost two hours, in fact—before they will be snuffling the words "I love you" in an airport departure lounge. If movies are to be believed, airports are permanently knee-deep in tears. Fortunately, movies are not to be believed.

Anywhere but Here should by rights be unendurable. It suffers from puzzling gulfs of logic; one moment the lights in the apartment go off because Adele can't pay the bill, the next she and Ann are stacking up on Christmas gifts. Even more bewildering is the sex, or the tragic lack of it. Wang and his screenwriter, Alvin Sargent, are so busy supplying Susan Sarandon with scraps of sub-philosophy—"When life gets rough, and you only have a dime in your pocket, go out and get your shoes shined"—that they forget the lady has a voluptuous reputation to keep up. To make amends, she suddenly turns flirty and starts sucking olives at an orthodontist named Dr. Spritzer (Hart Bochner), who then flosses her off and breaks her heart. End of sex, at least until Ann decides to try it for herself. A friend called Peter (Corbin Allred) declares that he wants to kiss her. "What for?" Ann asks. He says he wants to part her lips with his tongue. "And then what?" she asks. "I don't know," he replies.

But she knows; or, rather, Natalie Portman gives a riveting impersonation of someone who badly wants to know. *Anywhere but Here* is Portman's movie, all the way; she aims to look sulky and straggle-haired, but in truth her beauty has now become so disabling that you should not attempt to drive or operate heavy machinery for twelve hours after viewing this picture. The most heinous crime ever perpetrated by George Lucas was to cast Portman in *The Phantom Menace* and then belabor her with that red robe, the geisha lipstick, and a couple of cow horns strapped to the side of her head. The poor girl looked deep-frozen, and it's a relief to watch her thaw under Wayne Wang's more benign attention. With the instinctive, weirdly innocent cruelty of adolescence, she toys with the movie's sentimentality and spurns it; the brisk hug that she administers to a beloved cousin—at the airport, of course—is chilly with suppressed adoration, and, when she finally locks lips with the hapless Peter, her eyes close more in needy perplexity than swoon.

Portman owes much to the director of photography, Roger Deakins, who is absolutely on her case; just as he leaves a California beach looking bleached and stranded, under sunlight as white as a bone, so he refuses to linger on Portman or lush her up. Her radiance, he sees, can take care of itself, so he lodges her in unlovely compositions; just wait for the image of Annie, garbed in funeral black for a Christmas party, lolling and kicking with indecision in an outdoor passageway, with a plastic Santa at the rim of the frame. It's an unimprovable snapshot of teen tension, and it stresses how strong American movies are these days when it comes to the no man's land (or, far richer territory, the no woman's land) between childhood and maturity; I would rather watch Portman and Anna Paquin and Christina Ricci, with their quick-change flips from kidding to gravity, than any of the more ripe and rooted stars. *Anywhere but Here* may be long and nagging, but Natalie Portman disproves the title; when she's onscreen, you want to be there and nowhere else.

NOVEMBER 15, 1999

THE WORLD IS NOT ENOUGH

Everybody loves James Bond. To be precise: what everybody loves is not so much Bond himself as looking forward to a Bond movie. Even in the mid-eighties, when rumor had it that dear old Roger Moore needed a stunt double for his acting scenes, people drooled at the prospect of yet more 007. That is why the opening sequence of a Bond film is by tradition the best and most arousing part of the picture. The problem is acute with the latest installment, *The World Is Not Enough*, whose opening is in fact three sequences—one in Bilbao and two in London. It erupts into a boat chase along the Thames, complete with torpedoes and an emergency dive button; at one point Bond adjusts his tie *while underwater.* After about fifteen minutes, the director, Michael Apted, finally remembers to roll the opening credits. When I saw the movie last week, everyone started clapping and whooping, and I thought, Why not end it there? It's been a great party, the best fifteen minutes of the year; let's go home.

Instead, we get an hour and a half of anticlimax. Only the numb of sense will fail to enjoy themselves, and yet, beneath the fireballs, there is a lowering niggle of sameness: once you've seen one attempt at global domination, you've seen them all. Bond (Pierce Brosnan) is required to save the world's oil reserves, or, at any rate, to forestall a monopoly on oil deliveries to the West. For a plot hook, this is resolutely unsexy; as telecommunications quicken in the next century, will Bond be the only agent still defending heavy industry? Must we expect entire episodes to center on smelting plants and pungent fish canneries? On Bond's side are M (Judi Dench), who gets a chance to leave the office; R (John Cleese), who is slated to replace Q; and Dr. Christmas Jones (Denise Richards), a nuclear-weapons inspector in atomically hot pants. Evil is represented by Renard (Robert Carlyle), a small madman with a hole in the head. Lurking in the middle is Elektra King (Sophie Marceau), an oil heiress in whispering silks with only half an ear. All the folks in this movie seem to be missing bits of themselves.

What Bond is missing—and it pains me to report this—is his defining sense of style. Brosnan looks trim, and the narrow lapels of his suits are a touching homage to early Connery, but the film allows him to order one martini and no more. There's no good food, no wine, no space in which his suavity can expand; if the producers can be bothered to show a Russian caviar supremo (Robbie Coltrane) floundering in his own oil-black product, surely they could give 007 a chance—it would take no more than a line—to prove that he knows his sevruga from his osetra? In a way, Brosnan has preempted himself; *The Thomas Crown Affair*, which came out this summer, was an investigation of human Bondage, inquiring lightly into the condition of the chronic thrill-seeker. Yet the world was plainly *not* enough for Crown, not unless it contained Rene Russo; there's little in the Bond flick to match that urgency, and even the musky Miss Marceau feels off the scent. Christmas Jones arrives too late in the panicky plot to have much effect, although Bond does get to round off the movie with the immortal words "Always wanted to have Christmas in Turkey."

It's a once-in-a-lifetime line, and I like to think that Apted and his screenwriters shifted the action to the banks of the Bosphorus purely for the pleasure of the joke. Brosnan's Bond is more geographically restless than ever, but somehow less worldly; he seems to be tossed into varying situations in the hope that a touch of personality will leak out. With its regular announcements of location—Baku, Azerbaijan, Kazakhstan—this movie should prove a nightmare to George W. Bush, and yet, apart from the initial river run and a contretemps on the ski slopes, *The World Is Not Enough* is starved of fresh air. My heart sank as I realized that the whole farrago would be grinding to its climax inside a submarine. Subs were at their peak in *The Spy Who Loved Me*, when the villain built a tanker that ate them, but these days they look *so* cold war, and viewers may be less than gripped by the sight of the dastardly Renard trying to insert what appears to be a giant ballpoint refill, packed with plutonium, into a small hole. This fiddly finale is miles away from the jubilant, throwaway commotion of the start, but no matter; just before we leave the theatre, the end titles soberly inform us that "James Bond Will Return." I can't wait.

NOVEMBER 29, 1999

LIBERTY HEIGHTS

The setting of the new Barry Levinson movie, *Liberty Heights*, could scarcely be more specific: "Baltimore, Fall 1954." To the inhabitants of this tiny world, even a trip beyond the Jewish quarter of the title is more daunting than space travel. One of our heroes, young Ben Kurtzman (Ben Foster), develops a longing—more knightly than lascivious—for Sylvia (Rebekah Johnson), a black girl in his class. He casually mentions to his mother, Ada (Bebe Neuwirth), that he finds Sylvia, who is arguably the most beautiful being in Maryland, not unattractive. Ada reels at the news. "Just kill me now," she says. "Just kill me now." (If ever a line begged for the slow, proud deadpan of Bebe Neuwirth, the woman with dry ice in her lungs, this is it.) But Ben persists, and takes a streetcar to Sylvia's neighborhood—a wealthy black suburb, and no place for a working-class Jewish boy. Sylvia has to hide him on the floor of her car, from where he can look up her skirt.

All of which should reassure Levinson fans that the man is back to his best. He has the most schizoid CV of any American director. There is the rancid corn, like *Rain Man*, *Disclosure*, and *Good Morning, Vietnam*, which is good for headlines and Academy Awards, and then there are the real movies, like *Diner* and *Tin Men*. The rough rule—buckled but not broken by *Avalon*, and settled by *Homicide: Life on the Street*—is that whenever Levinson goes home to Baltimore he comes alive. In *Liberty Heights*, the logistics alone show an artist at ease: he has to juggle the fortunes not just of Ada Kurtzman but of her husband, Nate (Joe Mantegna), who runs a numbers racket out of his burlesque theatre; not just of Ben but of his brother Van (Adrien Brody), who falls for an unreachable Gentile by the name of Dubbie (Carolyn Murphy); and not just of Van but of Van's friend Yussel (David Krumholtz), who gets the best Jewish gag in the movie. Casting a cold eye around an old-money house, lined with antiques and Persian rugs, he is unimpressed—"They couldn't get wall to wall?"

It would have been easy to light the fuse on this combustible material; one day, perhaps, Spike Lee and Barry Levinson could shoot an identical script and see what they come up with. The sign outside the local pool that reads "No Jews, Dogs, or Coloreds" is the earliest indication of what the youngsters face. By the end of the picture, we see them inside, sitting at the water's edge, pale and grinning; their moral victory, like most of the small successes in *Liberty Heights*, is no less worthy for being pulled off as a joke. "Burlesque is finished," Nate says, but the beauty of this movie is that, even as the stage darkens, the tradition of light farce seems to spill out through the wings and into the lives of ordinary citizens. Who but Ben, overwhelmed with desire, would cover the damp patch on his pants with an Eartha Kitt album? Who else, when driven home by his girlfriend's indignant father, would refuse to leave the car until the Sinatra track on the radio comes to an end? "You don't walk out on Frank, sir," he explains. "It would be too disrespectful."

Some people will find this film itself too softened with respect; when Van's rival in love turns into a friend, and when even a kidnapping is resolved with no harm done, it is tempting to dismiss the result as an unhelpful dream—easy listening for social historians. But there are little prods of pain throughout; the meltdown of the frosty Dubbie, cashmere and all, is not easy to watch. And Levinson's command of period is so assured that you follow him as loyally as Ben on that streetcar. If *Liberty Heights* wants to sell me a vision of ethnic strife as abrasion rather than revolution, as a smarting opportunity for nostalgia, then, for once, I'll buy it—just like Nate Kurtzman sidling out of synagogue to visit the automobile showroom, where he can worship the new '55 Cadillac in mist green.

NOVEMBER 29, 1999

THE TALENTED MR. RIPLEY

If your last movie was *The English Patient*, what do you do next? When half of your previous characters tended patiently to the pains of the dying, how do you snap out of it? Easy. You make a movie in which death is as swift, and as easily settled, as a hotel bill. And so Anthony Minghella has found his way into *The Talented Mr. Ripley*. He has adapted Patricia Highsmith's novel, whose perfume of disdain has barely dispelled since it was first published in 1955, and nudged the action forward a few years, toward the randy finale of the fifties—closer to the Fellini of *La Dolce Vita*, say, than to the wasp-waisted primness of *Roman Holiday*. There is almost no sex in Minghella's film, but there is hardly a scene that doesn't crackle with small jolts of desire or—this being Highsmith—with revulsion. What is it, after all, that sends Tom Ripley (Matt Damon) from New York to Italy, in search of Dickie Greenleaf (Jude Law)? Nominally, it is Dickie's father, Herbert (James Rebhorn), who needs to reclaim his prodigal son; Dickie is wasting his time and his Princeton education under the sun, in the company of a mystery blonde who goes by the unmysterious name of Marge (Gwyneth Paltrow). In truth, however, the good Mr. Greenleaf simply provides Tom with the excuse (plus the lavish expenses) to stretch his limbs and his elastic morality in the service of an ideal; Ripley wants to flee America, not to mention the person that America took him for, and to establish precisely how *dolce* the *vita* can get.

He is not the first pilgrim to tread this path. In the Highsmith novel, Mr. Greenleaf suggests that Tom read *The Ambassadors* before leaving on his trip, and it would not be fanciful to construe both book and film as the last gasps of the Jamesian experiment; when Minghella shows a classical bust doubling as an offensive weapon, the joke hits home. Lambert Strether was shocked to see his young charge out boating with a married woman, but that's nothing; on *his* boat trip, Tom beats Dickie to a pulp, and spends the rest of the story assuming the identity of his victim, down to the rings on his fingers. He must outwit not just the Italian police but the suspicions of Marge; he must maintain a dexterous intimacy with Meredith Logue (Cate Blanchett), who thought he was Dickie from the beginning; he must fend off the brutish inquiries of Freddie (Philip Seymour Hoffman); he must consort with Peter (Jack Davenport) but not come too close; above all, he must not go mad.

Crackup haunts this picture, right from the frame-slicing credits at the start. It is there in the maniacal leaps of musical mood; Minghella hurries us from Chet Baker to Bach like someone spinning the dial on a radio. And you see it in the twitchy, bespectacled features of Matt Damon, as he fights to overcome his own solidity; despite the cheek of his enormous smile, Damon basically carries and conducts himself like a regular guy (which is why Spielberg recruited him for Private Ryan), and he can no more slither into perversity than he could enjoy a night out in women's clothing. The intellectual hauteur of Ripley, who was a murderous Europhiliac snob when Dr. Lecter was still in med school, is planted in the sight of Tom reading Shakespeare or musing on the Forum at dusk, like Gibbon on the brink of a big idea; all the same, I see no calculation in Damon's eyes. I think *The Talented Mr. Ripley* is a struggle for him, if an intriguing one; the movie becomes the tale of a man looking for that talent, not using it. Damon's Ripley is more nervous neophyte than sociopathic pro; he kills Dickie in a taunted panic, and Minghella is careful to scotch any murmur of premeditation. What we get is a lush psychological thriller—a nineties take on Highsmith's novel, which was a philosophical handbook for vacant spirits. When Alain Delon played Ripley in *Plein Soleil*, the 1960 adaptation of the same work, his coolness was like a dazzling offshoot of Sartre; Damon, by comparison, is a bright boy on a dangerous dare—Bad Will Hunting.

In homage to the Highsmith principle that our personalities are as slippery as snakes, I would like to see *The Talented Mr. Ripley* reshot with the male leads reversed. Matt Damon could be the simple, unbookish Dickie, and Jude Law—the only current movie star handsome enough to have swung it as a heartthrob in the Hollywood of old—would be Ripley. Law is so bronzed and strolling, with his linen pants and his flattish porkpie hat stolen from the cover of *Come Fly with Me*, that poor Gwyneth Paltrow never really gets a grip on him; he seduces both men and women without even bothering to seduce them, all of which would be perfect for Ripley's lascivious horror of boredom. Highsmith was turned on by same-sex relations, and openly scornful of female characters, such as Marge, who were drab enough to love one man; the prototype for Ripley was Bruno in

Strangers on a Train, immortalized by Robert Walker in Hitchcock's film. Walker would have eaten Matt Damon alive, with a light dressing of virgin oil, but Jude Law might have given him pause—Bruno might have recognized a fellow-devil. That we could be as promiscuous with our souls as with our bodies was the guiding light of the Ripley books, and Minghella is perhaps too generous a romantic, too much the connoisseur of human sympathies, to embrace so chilling a proposal. The Italy of the novel felt rocky and crumbling, and you didn't want to be there while Ripley was around; the Italy of the film laps at you like warm waves, and you never want to leave.

In short, Anthony Minghella does a Jude Law on us. He lays siege to our sensibilities with jazz clubs, espresso machines, sidesaddle Vespa rides, and the Grand Canal; he glances at one man sitting on another man's knee and tying his tie, while the two of them glance at a passing girl; he dreams up the Cate Blanchett figure—far more alluring than the moaning Marge—and puts her in powder-blue coats and soft cream berets. He gives her a wonderful speech about having enough money to despise money, which cuts to the quick of the Ripley dream; at the end, she even reaches for a kiss from Tom himself, and makes you believe that he likes it. The movie is more cunningly planned than any of the crimes on display; you can't help yielding to the tranquil, slightly stoned gaze that it turns upon the world. At one point, the camera stalks slowly behind Tom as he approaches Marge; she has got hold of an incriminating clue, and he has an open razor in the pocket of his robe. There is a shudder of strings on the soundtrack, but what they snare you with is not so much fright as a succulent unease; we are lost in a Mediterranean *Vertigo*. Thank goodness for Philip Seymour Hoffman, who keeps his certainties while all around are losing theirs. He knocks back each of his scenes like a double brandy: "How's the peeping?" he yells from the stern of a yacht to Matt Damon, who is trying not to pry into sex belowdecks. The answer is that the peeping is just fine; I guess I miss the deep rot of Tom Ripley, but his beating of the odds remains as enviable as his unearned income, and the talented Mr. Minghella has forced us to confess, once again, that we like to watch.

DECEMBER 27, 1999

AMERICAN PSYCHO

The scariest thing about *American Psycho,* Mary Harron's steely adaptation of the Bret Easton Ellis novel, is not the film itself; it is the sight that confronted me as I left the theatre. There, at the end of a row, oblivious of the moviegoers stumbling past in varying states of shock, was a couple necking. Soon they would disconnect their lips and go to dinner—somewhere romantic, with a good steak tartare and a curranty Côte Rôtie. Such is the fate of satire: however strong you make it, there will always be people who like it spicier still—who barely notice that it was meant to be satire in the first place.

Consider Ellis's book, for instance: damned before it hit the stores, and all but flattened by the charge of pathological misogyny. Readers—men and women alike—seemed unsure whether to be numbed by the outrages committed in the text or outraged by the nullity of the telling. Now, at a distance, the book reads better than it did; it feels lit with a kind of cold hellfire, and Ellis has become our most assiduous tour guide—more solid than the excitable Tom Wolfe—to the netherworld of the 1980s. In fact, given the formations of excess that have since encrusted New York, he must be wondering, as satirists since Juvenal have wondered, whether he went far enough. The urge expressed by his hero, Patrick Bateman, to see the streets cleansed of low life is now civic policy; the means may be less fanatical, but Bateman, who extends zero tolerance into every crevice of his existence, would surely look on with approval. As for designer labels, the furor has spread like a rash; not even Bateman could have prophesied the second coming of Gucci.

So how do you pin the madness onto a screen? The first task is to hire a woman director; no man, I think, would be safe with this material. It lay for a while in the hands of Oliver Stone; he had replaced Mary Harron, who subsequently returned to the project. Let us give thanks for this merciful escape. Stone's choice of leading man for Bateman—murderer, moneymaker, and galloping clotheshorse—was Leonardo DiCaprio, who is good at victims but too sweet for the practice of monstrosity. Harron went with Christian Bale—a Brit, though you wouldn't know it. His accent is as perfect as his pectorals, and his face is smooth and carved, almost sanded; that it gives so little away is proof not of hidden depths but of open shallows—there really is nothing to give. Near the start of the movie, Patrick takes us through his cleansing routine, itemizing his lotions and potions, and finally peeling away his exfoliating mask—a rubberized visor, ideal for the urban hoplite—to reveal the harder mask of his good looks. At the same time, he speaks in voice-over, explaining his drastic want of personality: "There is no real me." This is true, but I wish that Harron had trusted the grip of the image. The guy is shiny enough as it is; he needs no further gloss.

Elsewhere, thankfully, the gleam of the picture does the trick. Harron and her director of photography, Andrzej Sekula, have developed a weird plasticity for their creations; when Patrick and his cronies sit around with drinks, the light bounces off them as if they were mannequins, or cutouts from a magazine. Even their hair has a mirrored, deco sleekness; they could be the natty fall guys who roamed the comedies of the 1930s, and you sense, in their casual putdowns of women and Jews, the vengeful bite of talentless men who have suddenly seen their chance. Bateman is not a freak; he is a type taken to the limit, and, if his story did not offend us, then Ellis and Harron would not be doing their job. Satire demands that you hold your nerve; the hydrochloric horror of *A Modest Proposal*, in which Swift counselled the eating of children as a cure for famine, relied on his playing the joke straight, and the film of *American Psycho* is right not to pause for contemplation. The reductio ad absurdum of a mind that knows nothing save money is a desire to treat your fellow-citizens as commodities—things to be named, consumed, and then expelled as trash. "I'm into murders and executions," Bateman tells a blond woman in a club. "Most people who work in mergers and acquisitions don't really like it," she replies. Did she miss what he said, above the music, or did she get him all too well?

What Patrick does to earn his keep remains a mystery; at the office, he plugs wearily into his Walkman and makes dinner plans. He never stays late, and the film is itself too cool and lofty to inspect the work ethic that was one of the more enduring manias of the period. There is little plot here, no highs and lows; events descend calmly toward the uncontrolled. With a few swings of a chrome-plated axe, Bateman slaughters a friend named Paul Allen (Jared Leto) and takes over his apartment. There is no hint of a Ripley complex; Patrick simply needs a place where he can kill in peace. Were the movie to follow the mayhem of the novel in any detail, it would be unwatchable, but Mary Harron wants us to watch; we see the fallout of violence, and we catch the stink of approaching violence in the air, yet there is little actual violence to make us look away. As a result, the film, less savage than the book, is much creepier; when Bateman stands behind his assistant, Jean (Chloë Sevigny), with a nail gun pointed at her head, the whole cinema moans in fear. He doesn't do anything, though, and the scene winds up with a devastating string of double-entendres: "I don't think I can control myself," he says. "If you stay, something bad will happen. . . . You don't want to get hurt, do you?" Jean has no inkling of his designs; to her, these phrases ring with the panic of the obsequious admirer.

I was left uneasy by the casting of the women; Harron has filled the film with faces that are dangerously bare of expression—look at Cara Seymour, playing a hooker named Christie, or, indeed, at Sevigny herself. Even actresses as forceful as Reese Witherspoon and Samantha Mathis, as Bateman's fiancée and mistress, respectively, are seldom allowed off the leash. I can see the reasoning here; through Bateman's pitiless eyes, women have no character worth preserving. Or perhaps a larger feminist argument is at work; with men like Bateman around, no wonder women shut down their emotions. For all this, I wanted someone to fight back, to show a contrary spirit, if only to stop the movie from shrinking into Patrick's dramatic monologue. That is why the best moment comes when he returns to Paul's apartment and finds the blood wiped off the walls, the bathtubs emptied of flesh, and a real-estate agent showing clients around. "I think you should go now," she says. The question of what she knows is left beautifully suspended, and we realize that in the frenzy of the New York property market it might well be easier to cleanse your apartment of abomination and make a quick sell than to bother the authorities and see the value drop.

In the final twenty minutes, *American Psycho* is turned on its head. Bateman begins to self-destruct; Bale cracks up convincingly, but it dulls the razored edge of the film to find its Marlovian hero recast as a nutcase. I believed in him more as a cyborg, at least 50 percent machine, than as a damaged man, shedding real tears; the notion that his private abattoir was no worse than a dirty dream may be a nice twist of the narrative, but if writers or movie directors identify a malignancy—a psychosis at large in the world, not merely inside a single brain—they should pursue it to the death. Still, *American Psycho* is a fierce and timely piece of work, a bad brother to *American Beauty*. Like Sam Mendes's film, it makes you laugh in ways, and at times, that should hardly be funny at all. The Reagan-era trappings—the noisome rococo of nouvelle cuisine, the early cell phones as long as a shoe, and the rise of Phil Collins—are fair game, but that is just the start. When I saw the picture, the audience whooped with glee as Bateman, in mid-murder, discoursed eloquently on the significance of Huey Lewis and the News; it was as if musical taste this dire should be read as mitigating circumstance. How did we get to such a stage? When did the faculty of irony become so refined, and so rapacious, that all human transgression, even on the borders of inhumanity, could be corralled into the comic? Personally, I blame the eighties.

APRIL 17, 2000

GLADIATOR

The new Ridley Scott picture *Gladiator* begins in triumphant gloom. The date is 180 A.D., and the Roman general Maximus (Russell Crowe) is stuck in the mud and mists of Germania, on the northern flank of the Empire; his legions, fanatically faithful to their leader, are ranged against a tribe of Germans so aggressively hairy that even a soldier as war-wise as Maximus is uncertain whether to harass them with cavalry from the rear or simply shave them to death. Maximus is followed into battle by his fearsome dog. "At my signal, unleash hell," he says. Is that a battle cry, or is it time for a walk? At any rate, we are plunged into a melee of sprayed blood and breath that steams in the air; great tubs of fire are catapulted toward the enemy, and flaming arrows fly like shooting stars. Victory nears amid descending snow.

We have been here before. The date was 1964 A.D., and the movie director Anthony Mann was sticking to his guns, or his javelins, in *The Fall of the Roman Empire*. The most memorable scene in that overarching, undervalued movie is also set on a northerly plain, with lighted torches flaring in swirls of snow. I guess that Ridley Scott and his writers—David Franzoni, John Logan, and William Nicholson—are trusting the short memory of the moviegoing public, but I was touched to see them returning to the embrace of so wondrous an image. It seems to gather in all the fearful ambitions of an imperium; are we meant to imagine civilization blazing a trail through barbarous wastes, or the scorched-earth policies of unchecked power? Maximus himself is poised between the two: a good man meting out brutality. Crowe is stocky, sad, and stubbled, with a low Neanderthal brow and quick eyes, educated in suspicion; though shorter than most of the men around him, he has mastered the art of walking taller than any of them. Once or twice he tries a smile, and it practically cracks the lens.

The story is your basic three-act affair, the kind of thing that screenplay workshops teach as holy writ. After his German victory, Maximus is asked by the aging emperor Marcus Aurelius—played by a loose-haired Richard Harris, who is about as Roman as a pint of Guinness—to be his successor. Maximus goes away to stroke his chin and think about it, but before he can offer a response Marcus is smothered to death by his own son, Commodus (Joaquin Phoenix), who promptly declares that he, not some sweaty soldier, will be taking charge. Viewers new to the period may ask themselves how so sane and pensive a parent—Marcus wrote the *Meditations*, after all, a touchstone of the Stoic temperament—could have sired so rich a fruitcake. Digging around, I found a fourth-century historian who claimed that Commodus's mother fell for a gladiator and confessed her lust to Marcus; he, in turn, ordered not only that the gladiator should die but that his wife "should wash herself from beneath in his blood and in this state lie with her husband." That would explain a lot. Amazingly, it doesn't get into the film.

Maximus escapes death, goes home, finds his family slain, faints, wakes up on a slave train, and ends up being sold to Oliver Reed. What a life. Reed, who plays an ex-gladiator named Proximo, died during the making of the film—of drink, needless to say, the blood having long since passed from his alcohol-stream. Having cowered at his Bill Sykes in *Oliver!*, I thought he was a terrifying actor who never got his due; with his bullock's bulk and that soft, whispering sea-roar of a voice, he could have trodden the Burt Lancaster path. This last role is not quite meaty enough for a sendoff, but I liked the sight of his blue eyes, glazed with the tedium of daily massacre, opening a little wider as he first watches Maximus in the ring—gold dust glinting in the sand.

All plots lead to Rome, and Maximus, presumed dead, arrives incognito at the gates of the Colosseum, accompanied by his new best friend and fellow-slave Juba (Djimon Hounsou), plus a barrel load of computer-graphic imagery. *Gladiator* takes CGI about as far as it will currently go; much of the ancient city is a virtual re-creation, as is most of the throng that packs in to watch the games. It's hard to pin down, but your senses are never quite pricked with the sharpness of the real; you can see the air humming with bloodlust, but you can't smell it. Maybe that's a good thing, because if *Gladiator* were any more authentic the audience in the movie theatre might start spearing one another in the throat. You find yourself thrilling to acts of violence, but that, I guess, is the freakish strength of this picture: it shows you the tantalizing laws of cruelty, and it forces you to ask yourself just how speedily you, too, would slide from citizen to lout. At one point, Russell Crowe opens his forearms wide, with a blade in each fist;

then, with a swift, double-forehand jerk, he scissors a man's head off. My, how we cheered. If Jerry Springer ran the Super Bowl, this is how it would end up.

At the climax, Maximus even takes on Commodus himself; this may sound unlikely, but the young emperor was, indeed, a crazed amateur gladiator, who fought more than seven hundred times, once against an unarmed giraffe. So says Gibbon, at any rate, and if you want to prep yourself for this film skim through volume I of *Decline and Fall of the Roman Empire*. Note, in particular, the famous claim: "If a man were called to fix the period in the history of the world during which the condition of the human race was most happy and prosperous, he would, without hesitation, name that which elapsed from the death of Domitian to the accession of Commodus." In other words, Ridley Scott's movie—like Anthony Mann's, which had the same background, and most of the same characters—is positioned at the exact moment of paradise lost. "So much," says Marcus, with a weary pause, "for the glory of Rome." It's a wonderful line: is he dissing the fatherland or proudly recalling all the wars he has fought—"so much"—in the name of Pax Romana? The exhausted opening of the film already feels like an ending, and, with his mad gaze and milk-white armor, Joaquin Phoenix, who has fleshed out alarmingly since his gawky teens, is just the kind of bad angel who can ruin your peace and call it entertainment. Romans rise ecstatically to their feet, not knowing that he has brought them to their knees.

High politics wind through *Gladiator* in a tangle of constitutional announcements. "There was a dream that was Rome," we are told, and the echo of Dr. King bounces awkwardly off the sight of Juba, a near-naked black man, scrapping for the pleasure of the crowd. "Give power back to the people," Marcus tells Maximus, but nothing that ensues does much honor to popular virtue, and when Maximus complains to Commodus's elegant sister Lucilla (Connie Nielsen) that he has "the power only to amuse a mob" she replies curtly, "That *is* power." Maximus does not want to fight, but only by fighting can he avenge his family and salve the wounded state of Rome; on the other hand, he does rather enjoy himself out there, wearing a spiffy helmet, engaging hungry tigers in hand-to-paw combat, and making the charioteers wish they had fitted the optional airbag.

Gladiator, like its hero, is aroused by everything that it knows to be corrupt; why else would the musical score (by Hans Zimmer and Lisa Gerrard) march so doomily in the footsteps of Mars from Holst's *The Planets*? "I will give the people the greatest vision of their lives," Commodus says, and it is no accident that he sounds like a film director: D. W. Griffith, perhaps, or Leni Riefenstahl, one of those dangerous geniuses who remind you what menace a vision can bear. There are times when *Gladiator* appears to be not so much photographed as cast in iron: gray-blue skies, flesh as cold and colorless as the armor that protects it, and hardened profiles that you could stamp on a coin. I spent half the movie trying to work out what the computerized Rome reminded me of, and then I clicked; it was Albert Speer's designs for the great Berlin of the future. Scott's is hardly a fascist film, but it is insanely watchable in ways that set you fretting; like his own *Blade Runner*, it makes you desperate to know the worst—to see what extremes this poisoned world can stretch to. When one gladiator has another pinned on the ground like an insect, he asks the emperor to decide the fallen man's fate by the raising or lowering of a thumb. The mob does its best to sway his choice, which leaves us with the disconcerting spectacle of multiple, raving, Latin-speaking Siskels and Eberts—forty thousand thumbs *way* down. So that's what mass slaughter was like: just another trip to the movies.

MAY 8, 2000

MISSION: IMPOSSIBLE 2

The big problem with the new John Woo movie is not what it's about, or whether it adds lustre to the epistemological conundrum that is world cinema, but what we are supposed to call the damn thing. In my innocence, I had presumed that any sequel to Brian DePalma's *Mission: Impossible* would bear the title *Mission: Impossible II* or *Mission: Impossible—Just Got a Teeny Bit Harder*; but apparently the latest installment would prefer to be known as *M: i-2*, which looks almost as ugly as it sounds. It is an appellation fit only for a laptop, and, indeed, the whole film is strewn with magic Apples; none of the characters could conceivably go to the john without downloading the national sewage blueprints.

M: i-2 stars T.C.—Tom Cruise to you and me, although he would be happy with Top Cat. Once again, he plays Ethan Hunt, who, along with Luther Strickell (Ving Rhames), is the sole survivor of the crack espionage team that made such a hash of things in the first movie. (Not even the theme tune pulled through; the Lalo Schifrin original, the punchiest riff since *The Magnificent Seven*, has been hard-rocked out of all recognition.) This time, Ethan's mission, should he choose to write it down on a stickie and put it on the door of his fridge, is to save the world from a lethal virus called Chimera—a real virus, of the kind that makes your ears bleed, although you might think that Ethan would be more vulnerable to the kind that barbecues your hard drive. The first step toward saving the world, as always, is to recruit a slinky young thief wearing a tight lace dress and a Bulgari necklace down her cleavage. To this end, Ethan has to fly from Australia to Spain, or, rather, in the refreshing visual shorthand of *M: i-2*, from an aerial shot of the Sydney Opera House to a close-up of a flamenco dancer going clackety-clack-*clack*. It's the old rule of blockbusters: the more global a movie's ambitions, the more it flattens the globe into a pile of picture postcards.

The thief's name is Nyah (Thandie Newton), and if only she'd said it loud enough to Tom Cruise he might have gone away and left her alone. As it is, he lands her in the deepest of pickles. She is the ex of Sean Ambrose (Dougray Scott), a former associate of Ethan's who has gone to the bad; last seen jumping out of a 747 over the Rockies, he is suspected of stealing Chimera, and Nyah can confirm those suspicions only by showing up and pretending to be in love with him all over again. What we have, in short, is a reheated *Notorious*, with Newton in the two-timing Ingrid Bergman role; the screenwriter, Robert Towne, even supplies a long scene at the racetrack. Now, *Notorious*, being perhaps the most beguiling and heartsick thriller ever made, is not easy to keep up with, and I was hardly surprised to see *M: i-2* begin to pant and flag. It was when Nyah, silk scarf fluttering at her neck, took about ten minutes to walk the length of a jetty toward the waiting Ambrose that I felt the audience shift impatiently in their seats.

What they were experiencing was an entirely novel sensation: a boring John Woo picture. I know it sounds ridiculous; one might as well talk of a plodding Ernst Lubitsch or a flat-chested Fellini. But there were times when *M: i-2* seemed happy to neglect its Woovian duties. Working through the director's back catalogue, from the American hits like *Face/Off* and *Broken Arrow* to the purer anarchy of his Hong Kong flicks, I felt honored to be in the company of an artist who had such intense designs on my eyeballs and so minimal a claim on my brain. His beginnings are notably toothsome; after little more than ten minutes of *Hard Boiled*, for instance, Chow Yun Fat and his well-armed friends have whittled an entire restaurant down to the consistency of bean sprouts. The great Chow ends up with his face masked in white flour and iced with lines of blood; it could be some ancient, theatrical image of vengeance. By contrast, the new film is soft-boiled; true, we get a cliffhanger before the opening credits, but it consists simply of Tom Cruise hanging from a cliff. There is no plot on the move, and no other character in sight: nothing but pecs and peaks, and the first of a thousand close-ups. Chow's face told us what had happened; Tom's face tells us who he is.

The unpalatable truth about this new *Mission: Impossible* is that it is, to a mountainous degree, a Tom Cruise enterprise. He coproduced both movies, but this time you feel his touch on every frame. Early on, during the scenes in Seville, there is a shot of Ethan's profile as he walks away. It serves no dramatic purpose, apart from allowing us to muse on his slightly unwise choice of a rabbit-colored suede blouson; if there is a point, it is his hair, the indubitable star of this movie. Gone is the sharp, military crop of *Mission: Impossible*. In comes the long, floppy look, as pioneered by Ilie

Nastase in the early seventies. Whatever Ethan is doing in the story—tipping his motorcycle forward for an unprecedented front wheelie, taking his Porsche for a spin up against Nyah's Audi—the camera is there to record the ebb and flow of his locks. Until now, John Woo has used slow motion as a homage to the unbeatable lightness of being; not since Sam Peckinpah has anyone striven so tirelessly to show the human body rising to the occasion—all but soaring—while everything around it comes apart. The technique is a lie, of course, but a gracious one, and I was crestfallen to find it doing the work of a L'Oréal commercial. Why, I asked myself, should we pay good money to see Tom Cruise's coiffure bounce in creamy waves? Because he's worth it.

There is nothing new, and nothing especially damnable, in the notion of a vanity project. It's a tradition that has prospered ever since Dietrich gave instructions to her cinematographers on the best way to illuminate her cheekbones, and, if we are honest, our grasp of what we worship most hotly in Hollywood is inextricable from the splendor with which the actors' features, as tall as houses, fill our screens. But even von Sternberg, or the Hitchcock who lavished his ruthless love on Grace Kelly, knew that there were tales to be told, whereas the attention paid to Cruise—Cruise as icon, jaw pornographically ajar—actually interrupts the onward rush of events. It is not for me to comment on the extensive reshoots that were reputedly ordered on *M: i-2*, let alone on the question of who ordered them; suffice it to say that the film never finds its balance, jerking awkwardly as it does from the bone-bruising exhaustion of violence to slack romantic canoodlings. There was a hint of desire in the first *Mission: Impossible.* Cruise touched his cheek wistfully after a kiss from Emmanuelle Béart, but the rest of their relationship must have slipped to the cutting-room floor. The new film wants to be warmer, but, for all the glories of Thandie Newton, Cruise is close to unreachable; you can't imagine him giving way to her, and for some reason Towne—the man who wrote *The Last Detail* and *Chinatown*—can't find a crisp seductive patter for the two of them to share. After the shuddering car chase, her first words to Ethan are "What's your name?" She might as well be asking for his license. "Damn, you're beautiful," he says the next morning—perfectly true, but Cary Grant would have demanded a rewrite. And the reason Ethan hires her? "It takes a thief to catch a thief." I wonder who thought of that.

The final third of *M: i-2* works hard to make up for lost time. We get exploding fuel tanks, motorcycles locking horns like stags, and a sandy, sweat-lashed, slo-mo martial-arts demonstration in which Cruise spends so long in the air, getting his little legs ready for the killer kick, that his opponent could easily wander off, have a cup of coffee and a doughnut, and still make it back in time to get it in the neck. People laughed at the sight of this, and it was a generous laugh, gladdened by the thought that John Woo had, at the last gasp, recovered his comedy of excess. But it's too much, too late; Heaven knows, the first *Mission: Impossible* was a mess, but it respected the finicky teamwork of the TV series, whereas Cruise now has the air of a lone wolf. Apart from an uncredited cameo by Anthony Hopkins, there are no first-rank stars to obscure Cruise's glare; he is buoyed along by a Scot, an Englishwoman, and a couple of Aussies. Even then, half of them seem to have rubber Tom Cruise masks that they don and doff like hats. "The hardest part of being you is grinning idiotically," Ambrose says to Ethan—a nice touch, and all too credible. People switch identities in this film with bewildering ease, and there were moments when it felt like an extended denouement from an episode of *Scooby-Doo:* "Why, it's old Mr. Cruise from the fighter-pilot movie!" If I followed the island shoot-out correctly, Tom Cruise must have been carrying a spare Tom Cruise face in his backpack all along, just in case. Damn, he's beautiful. If you love the guy, this is your picture, but, if you like your thrills more evenly spread, here is the bad news: *M: i-2* is N: f-ing: G.

JUNE 5, 2000

TIME REGAINED

How do you film Proust? What would an accurate film of *In Search of Lost Time* look like? More to the point, what would it *smell* like? Here was a man who could be prompted, by the fleeting aroma of gasoline, to recall "cornflowers, poppies, and red clover"; short of pumping compound scents into the movie theatre, how do you honor a moment like that? The truth is that a true Proust movie would last for days, even months; the projectionist would need to switch nimbly from blazing CinemaScope to the thin, seedy viewing slots familiar to frequenters of peepshows; above all, we would require the revival of Sensurround—rustiest of gimmicks, long left to rot with the disaster flicks that it once adorned, but ideal, surely, for those quakes of jealousy and tidal surges of desire that the author, ever generous with his emotions, so wanted us to share.

But life is short, so we will have to make do with Raoul Ruiz's *Time Regained.* In the event, this is no hardship, since the film is mostly on target: serene but anxious, gallant but bitchy, quick to freeze and thaw with every shift in the social climate, and rife with equal measures of languor and fuss. *Time Regained* is the title of Proust's final volume, but one should be wary of presuming that Ruiz has simply—or, indeed, intricately—adapted it for the screen. If anything, the movie seems to be both a loose, silvery dramatization and a careful inquiry into what it might be like—what it might wring out of a man, especially a weakening one—to write such a book. We begin in the bedroom of a bearded Proust (Marcello Mazzarella), as he dictates a particularly dazzling sentence of *In Search of Lost Time* to his housekeeper and scribe, Céleste (Mathilde Seigner). As if to help us on our way, he also takes up a magnifying glass and inspects a sheaf of photographs, naming each of the forthcoming characters in turn: Odette (Catherine Deneuve), his parents, Robert de Saint-Loup (Pascal Greggory), and Gilberte (Emmanuelle Béart). These, along with others, will rotate and sway through the rest of his story, like the shapes of a child's mobile above a crib.

In the course of two hours and forty-five minutes, you will learn much about these people, perhaps more than they would like you to know; whether you will gather who they are is another matter. Confirmed Proustians should, you might think, have the advantage here; they will understand, for example, that Gilberte is the daughter of Odette and Swann (the hero, of sorts, of the earlier volumes, and thus conspicuous by his absence from these proceedings), and that Odette is mostly referred to in the film as Mme. de Forcheville—a reference to her later and lesser husband. And yet I cannot help feeling jealous of the novice. If you have never read the book, the movie will be a mystery, and that is exactly as it should be; Ruiz is never vague, but he tricks, entices, confuses, and overwhelms as if he were throwing a vast party, festooned with open secrets. You mingle with the movie, and eavesdrop on its conversations; you grasp nothing more than the half-life of these immaculate snobs and dupes, these fools for love, and thus you end up obeying the Proustian principle that nobody can be known, or loved, except in snatches—odd, unmatching offcuts from their real existence. Is Gilberte a flirt, or an ice maiden, or a worthy object of reverence? She is all three, depending on who you are, and what you want.

She is also Emmanuelle Béart, of course, which always helps. The first sight of her, clipping roses in a garden, is almost atrociously beautiful; you immediately see why men like Saint-Loup and the narrator would happily waste their lives on her behalf. It is appropriate that Béart should play the child of Deneuve, for both have the infuriating capacity—a defining French gift—of holding a movie together purely by gazing into the lens. You can imagine yourself looking forward to losing this Gilberte, and to the delicious pain of ruing that loss; she honors the perversity of the novel's nostalgia—a good thing, too, because, for all its other strengths, *Time Regained*, in its clawing back of the past, does not move you as fiercely as you might expect. The Combray of the narrator's boyhood, summoned so indelibly in the earlier volumes, is fading by the time the book draws to a close, and the movie skips through those childish treasures in favor of social richesse.

So we are left with concerts, soirées, and awkward encounters in the park. We have a fine funeral, at which Mme. Verdurin (Marie-France Pisier) ruptures the Gallic pomp by complaining of a dropped earring; as the mourners peer and poke at the sacred ground, we are reminded how briskly Proust could bring himself to violate the very decorum that earned his pedantic respect. Ruiz's film, for all its loveliness, is like an antidote to costume drama; why else would his arrangements of furniture and foliage glide and shove so weirdly within the frame, if not to puncture the settled plush of the genre, and to hint that the beau monde, like its favorite possessions, is little more than an elegant prop to be dragged in and out of the wings? Far from being inveigled into the hauteur of that world, we are encouraged to view its noble protagonists as poor players who strut and fret their hours—their whole lifetimes—upon the stage. When they strike attitudes, Ruiz holds them fast; early in the movie, a crowd of onlookers is suddenly stilled, with their faces caked in white powder, while they watch the young narrator at play—as if everyone present were preparing to be a statue in his imaginary museum. Watching the movie again, I wondered whether all of it unfolds within the cranium of the expiring Proust, whether his bedroom is as much a greenhouse of memory as Charles Foster Kane's, and whether Gilberte, like the other young girls in flower, is just one of his innumerable Rosebuds.

Time Regained may be a French production of the greatest of French novels, but somehow the Frenchness doesn't swamp you; the ludic Ruiz is a Chilean, his Proust is an Italian, and his Charlus is an American, John Malkovich. In fact, Proust has been served more widely and respectably by the movies than you would think—far more so than Henry James, say, who at first blush would seem to be twice as filmable. The German director Percy Adlon made *Céleste*, a dazzling sidelight on genius, with Eva Mattes as the author's devoted servant. Another German, Volker Schlöndorff, went to the front of the novel and came up with *Swann in Love:* hardly an unqualified success, but braced by the stiff, stricken glamour of Alain Delon. His Charlus makes for an alluring comparison with Malkovich's; the Frenchman is numb with tragedy, the American more amused and fetishistic—observing his fellow-diners with a mirror concealed inside his top hat, and refusing to allow his appetites, however jaded, to die in the mouth of time.

If Ruiz's Proust is not as wrenching as the original, it compensates with the elastic reach of its comedy, and its unpredictable patchwork of shadows. Non-Proustians, who may have been put off by the silken, somewhat feminine reputation of the book, will be surprised by the violence of the film. It is all there in Proust, but you tend to hear less about it: the air-raid sirens moaning over the restaurant, or the Croix de Guerre left on the floor of a male brothel, where the sheets are sauced with blood from a recent whipping. Why on earth, you might ask, should we bother with the scandals and satisfactions of this ruinous crowd, the kind of people who demand "strawberries in ether," when Ruiz shows us newsreel footage of the First World War, in which thousands were dying every day? It is not enough to claim that Ruiz brings Proust to life; rather, the film confirms our suspicion that Proust brings us back to life—that, in its son et lumière of minute sensations, *Time Regained* echoes the heed that he paid to the stage directions of ordinary existence. Listen for the rattle of Mme. Verdurin's jewelry (a little too much, like the rest of her), the tap of spoon on teacup, and the repellent sound of Saint-Loup, back from the front, chewing militantly through his steak. These are not the things that history will remember us by, if it remembers us at all; but the asthmatic Proust, forever short of breath, knew that we would remember them at our last gasp. He was not fond of the cinema; but if he, and not merely his work, were alive today, he might well change his mind.

JUNE 19, 2000

THE NUTTY PROFESSOR 2

I am not convinced that the world needs a sequel to Eddie Murphy's *The Nutty Professor*, which was itself a rehash of the Jerry Lewis version, of 1963. But there is money in Murphy, and that is why discerning *cinéastes* across America are being offered *The Klumps* for their viewing pleasure. As with the first installment, Murphy plays half a dozen characters, all of them members of the same family. There is Sherman Klump, the portly scientist, together with his brother, his father, and his wearily well-mannered mother; there is his leering grandma, with her false teeth and authentic libido; and there is Buddy Love, who is a kind of id savant to Sherman's milky, innocent ego. A few other actors sidle shyly into the frame, finding a little space to perform in the shadow of the Murphy circus: Janet Jackson is Sherman's beloved, and Larry Miller is his mean-mouthed boss, whose comeuppance involves being raped by a giant hamster. I find it hard to describe the texture of this movie; let us just say that comedy has moved on since the days of Noël Coward.

Grossness is certainly the chosen flavor of the new millennium; if you scan the credits of *The Klumps*, the names that spring out are not those of Peter Segal, the director, or even of Jerry Lewis, who is an executive producer, but those of Paul and Chris Weitz, who so recently charmed us with *American Pie*. The problem with the broad, below-the-waist farce of today is not that it will offend delicate sensibilities—remember them?—but that it's not offensive enough. The great scatologists, from Rabelais to Rowlandson, followed the logic of excess to its disgusting conclusions, in a bid to flush political and ecclesiastical toxins from the body politic; theirs was a physical assault on the mismanagement of souls. A film like *The Klumps* is a battalion of special effects in search of an enemy; the editing is almost unwatchably frantic, chopping back and forth between one Murphy incarnation and the next, as if the sheer fervor of silliness could persuade us, as the Marx Brothers used to do, that points are being scored. But nothing hits home; like Sherman, the movie is mostly wind.

Oddly enough, this was not the case with *The Nutty Professor*, in which Murphy made the canny decision to attack himself. The Klump clan was then a mere sideshow (and that is what it should have remained); the spotlight was on Buddy Love, who represented all the jive-talking, skirt-chasing disdain that had oiled the triumphal progress of the Murphy show, from the days of *48 Hrs.* and *Beverly Hills Cop*. You need wit and nerve, as well as a perverse narcissism, to turn on yourself in public, and *The Nutty Professor* pointed the way to Steve Martin's *Bowfinger*, where Murphy took an axe to his personality and cleaved it perfectly in two—the gentle goof and the raging star. This makes *The Klumps* an even more disconsolate experience—a seven-league backward step, in which Buddy Love barely registers, and which invites us to do nothing but acclaim Murphy and his variety act. The result is the polar opposite of a work such as *Kind Hearts and Coronets*, in which Alec Guinness played eight or nine roles—I always lose count, because he disappears into them like a magician's rabbit slipping back into its hat. Guinness was coldly grateful for the anonymity that was vouchsafed by a one-man crowd, whereas Murphy seems to say, Look at me, and me, and all the other me's—the thrill of the human six-pack.

There may, I regret to inform you, be worse to come; rumor has it that Robin Williams is to remake *Kind Hearts and Coronets*—a strange decision, given that there were no ailing children in the original. In their day, Williams and Murphy were the best stand-up comedians in the land; movies have stroked their vanity, loosened their jolting connection with an audience, and, in Murphy's case, coarsened the nimbleness of his posturing. *The Klumps* left me more uneasy than ever, as Papa Klump sat there at the dinner table singing out lines like "Hallelujah Yankee Doodle!" Murphy knows full well that he is toying with images of blackness, but he should also remember that postmodern games mean perilously little in the multiplex; there were people in the theatre roaring at sights that would have flattered the prejudices of their grandparents. Judging by this film, we have a good idea of what can occur to Murphy's body—baldness, belching, a Falstaffian ballooning of the gut—but what on earth is going on in his head? How does he think this eye-rolling, tongue-lolling parade of appetites will play in the gallery? Half of the strongest actors in Hollywood, starting with Morgan Freeman and Denzel Washington, happen to be black; does Murphy wonder what they will make of this minstreling? Peter Segal's picture is dimly plotted and horribly shot, and I tasted loathing in the whole endeavor; it is not impossible that Murphy is at once feeding us what we like and despising us for swallowing it. The bitterness doesn't stop there. *The Klumps* may be a vanity project, but it also bears the traces of a man who hates himself.

AUGUST 7, 2000

DANCER IN THE DARK

Offhand, I cannot think of many directors who would ask a leading lady to break into song as she is about to be hanged. Mel Brooks, at the apogee of his tastelessness, might have done it, as a nod to gallows humor; now we have Lars Von Trier, best known for *Breaking the Waves*, who chooses, in all solemnity, to entertain us with musical enchantment right up to the snapping of his heroine's neck. The work in question is *Dancer in the Dark*, a godsend to those of us who pray for divisive works of art, and who would support any federal measure that introduced legalized scuffling in cinemas; when the movie was shown at the Cannes Film Festival this year, the claque of viewers who sought madly for eggs and tomatoes to pitch at the screen was matched by the number who rose and cheered.

The cast is achingly hip: Catherine Deneuve; Jean-Marc Barr (star of *The Big Blue* and of Von Trier's hypnotizing *Europa*) as a factory foreman; Peter Stormare (a hit man in *Fargo*) as a nice guy; and, in her first acting role, Björk, the funny little Icelandic techno-sprite who has become a goddess to millions of rock fans you've never met. She wrote the songs for the new film, and she also stars as Selma, a Czech who lives in America with her young son, Gene (Vladica Kostic). Selma's eyesight is fast failing ("It's a family thing," she says). Her best friend at work, Kathy (Deneuve), guesses as much and helps out whenever she can; then, there are Selma's kindly neighbors, a cop named Bill (David Morse) and his free-spending wife, Linda (Cara Seymour). Bill has money worries, and, when he sees how much Selma keeps stashed behind the ironing board, he cannot fend off temptation. Discovery leads to agonizing, agony to bloodshed; Selma goes from courtroom to cell, and finally paces out the 107 steps to her appointed place of death.

She is a fall girl, and her story, with its gathering blindness and its fog of injustice, peers back not just to Warner Bros. weepies but to the classic predicaments of silent cinema and early cartoons; Björk's smiling heart-face is part of an elfish tradition that began with the Gish sisters, Mary Pickford, and Betty Boop. There is something of the mad professor in Von Trier's wild distillings of movie history; versed in innumerable genres, he nevertheless feels no compunction about shaking them into lurid compounds. Every week, Selma rehearses for an amateur production of *The Sound of Music*, and, as the film darkens, she keeps daydreaming her way into song and dance; anything can get her going—the slam and gasp of machinery, the tap of wire against a flagpole, scratchy pencils, or a needle hissing in a groove. Fred Astaire had the same, hypersensitive effect on his surroundings, but his world was sleek to start with; Selma is a single mother stuck in a trailer, and the film stock that glows and quickens for her musical reveries can revert, with a single cut, to the weary gray-and-beige schemes of her natural life. For the scene in which the whole factory twists and shouts, Von Trier ran a hundred fixed cameras simultaneously; back in the trailer, he switches to the anxious, handheld fidgeting of *The Idiots*, his previous exercise in shock.

Can you handle this? If you happen to remember Godard's homages to the Hollywood musical—*A Woman Is a Woman*, say, or Anna Karina skipping and chanting by the sea in *Pierrot le Fou*—you may not feel so alarmed, although Von Trier is a showoff to a degree that the more gnomic Godard would never have countenanced. Yet there is melancholy in the madness of this film; it was shot in Sweden (with his fear of flying, Von Trier has never visited America, and has no plans to do so), and, with its polyglot cast and nameless setting, it feels like an immigrant's haunted myth of the United States—at once more cruel, and more generous with its raptures, than the real thing. It is a country where you can still see Busby Berkeley pictures at your local theatre, where happy, leaping hoboes ride the railroad, and where hanging, not lethal injection, is the state's preferred means of execution. Selma's faith in the New World is both her prop and her tragedy; she thinks that Bill and Linda's house looks like a movie, and that "in a musical, nothing dreadful ever happens." But *Dancer in the Dark* is riven with dread, and there are moments when you don't know where to look—not merely in exasperation or embarrassment but because the pain of Selma's pitiable case is too exposed, too far from being soothed. As she reaches down to remove the spectacles from the eyes of her sleeping son—whose sight, unless corrected, will also decline—the grain of the image becomes a kind of gloaming, and the curt, unsentimental inventory of the condemned woman's cell (blanket, shelf, toothbrush) is a way of saying, "Do not kill her. These are signs of life." To maintain her sanity, in the blank silence of prison, Selma sings a fragment of "My Favorite Things." And then she won't feel so bad.

We are on the brink of frivolity here, though not, oddly enough, of the mawkish. If Björk were more artful in her registration of pain, the film would turn horribly cute; as it is, her flightiness—those fanciful swoops away from suffering and back again—seems inborn, and there is something unfeigned in her final bout of panic, when the black hood is yanked over Selma's head to block her useless gaze. As if quieted by such directness, Von Trier drops the trickery and simply tightens the screws; to watch Catherine Deneuve, the ice queen of modern cinema, thaw and howl with distress at her friend's undignified doom is a sight guaranteed to unnerve. The two friends in front of me came out steaming with derision; the woman behind me trailed away in tears, as if Björk's keening croon of a voice were still wailing around her head. Go and see this movie, even if you quit before the end; after all, Selma herself used to leave her favorite pictures "just after the next-to-last song." That way, she explains, "the film would go on forever."

SEPTEMBER 25, 2000

THE YARDS

The last James Gray picture, *Little Odessa,* was about a criminal coming back to his old neighborhood, comforting his ailing mother, and getting himself into trouble. The new James Gray picture, *The Yards,* is about a criminal coming back to his old neighborhood, comforting his ailing mother, and getting himself into trouble. Do not be fooled by this fleeting resemblance. The first movie was set in the Russian community of Brooklyn, whereas the second delves into the silky, glamorous world of spare parts and supply contracts in the New York subway system. More important, *Little Odessa,* for all its snowstruck beauty, was a piece of apprentice work, with a young director trying on a style. This time around, it fits.

Mark Wahlberg, last seen in *The Perfect Storm,* plays Leo Handler—long in the face, down in the mouth, and desperate to stay clean after serving sixteen months for auto theft. A welcoming party greets him on his return from jail, but the prodigal son sidles quietly through the door, as if wishing that none of them, least of all himself, had to be there. As the camera pokes around the room, casually introducing us to Leo's reception committee, you begin to see what a fine, layered collection of characters Gray has bolted together: there's Leo's mother, Val (Ellen Burstyn), her widowed sister Kitty (Faye Dunaway), and Kitty's daughter Erica (Charlize Theron), who seems strangely bowed down, though whether by mourning or by the burden of mascara it is hard to say.

Erica is dating Leo's best friend, Willie Gutierrez (Joaquin Phoenix), who has money to burn and every intention of drawing Leo to the flame. The clanging memory of *Gladiator* is such that it takes a while to forget Phoenix in a suit of armor and get used to him in just a suit; what hasn't changed is the tense, oddly compacted expression on his face, as if his head were caught in an invisible vise. Willie toils in the subway offices, hustling for contracts, greasing every palm he can find; Leo becomes his sidekick, to the disapproval of Frank Olchin (James Caan), who runs the legitimate (or, at least, the visible) end of the business. Frank is Leo's uncle by marriage, being Aunt Kitty's new husband, and he wants Leo to earn an honest trade. Confused? You should be. The family tree in this movie is so entangled that it ends up blocking its own light and sucking the sap from surrounding growths. It lacks the pontifical suavity of *The Godfather*, but Gray has inherited Coppola's dark central joke—a vision of amity and betrayal outgrowing one's immediate circle, rooting into the city and beyond.

In fact, if you have seen *The Godfather* recently, or, better still, Fritz Lang's *Human Desire* (the doomiest of train flicks), you will be nicely primed for *The Yards*. The problem for Gray is that most viewers now exist on a diet of *The Sopranos* and have come to enjoy their Mob melodrama with a coating of comedy, like bitter chocolate. *The Yards* has an old-fashioned heft to it, and it may strike you as perilously humorless; the only course of action, as you take your seat, is to switch off any wicked ironies at the same time as your cell phone and yield to the slow, Stygian pleasures that Gray has stirred up. Offhand, I can think of four great nocturnal scenes. First, the evening on which Willie takes Leo and a band of saboteurs to the yards, where they short out the circuitry installed by their rivals; Leo looks trapped by the dusty bronze glow of the rails, and, indeed, from here on he becomes a wanted man. Then, there are the nights with guns, all but drowned in a gray-green gauze of light: Leo in a hospital, sneaking up on a patient who must never be allowed to wake, or tracking a silent foe on the far side of his apartment wall, aiming where he thinks the head must be. Finally, the best and most fruitless fight I have seen in modern movies: a scrap between Leo and Willie, full of tugged shirts and blows that never connect, with the camera calmly pulling back to watch the old friends slug it out in the ruinous gold of the streetlamps.

That is Gray's way: an enriched realism, in which bodies shift and sweat with familiar human awkwardness but the world around them feels dreamed. Gray likes to paint scenes in watercolor before he shoots them, and it's a dangerous talent; the directors we value for their compositional care—men as different as David Lean and Michael Mann—are also those who have to fight hardest to prevent their characters from shrinking to figures in a landscape. Gray beats the trap, this time, by hiring a cast of dependables (you try sidelining Faye Dunaway) and, more cleverly still, by turning that very issue—the treatment of people as objects—into the meat of his plot. Look at Leo and Willie, near the beginning, striding into Borough Hall, with its blank white curves and its little knot of tough guys at the far end; how can the young pair hope to fill that space? Even between them, the balance tips; Leo is loved by Willie, then chased, then feared for what he might divulge. With fifteen minutes to go, *The Yards* could head in any number of directions: it could hang fire in indecisive gloom, or spout a Coppola bloodbath, or even rouse itself for a Capra-style trouncing of the villains and a promise to clean up the streets. I am not sure about Gray's eventual choice, but the rest of his film smells oily and authentic; if you can take the murk, and the grownup lack of special effects, it becomes both thrilling and dreadful to see these driven souls rattle, like subway cars, toward their destination.

OCTOBER 30, 2000

CHARLIE'S ANGELS

Who is responsible for *Charlie's Angels*? According to the credits, it was "directed by McG," thus raising the intriguing prospect of the world's first motion picture to be made by a hamburger. I would love to report that the film was shot with such distinctive grace and aplomb that the personality behind it comes searing through, but, tragically, this is not the case. After seeing the movie, I have even less grasp of McG than when I went in, although the evidence suggests that we have Thick Shake to thank for the screenplay, and that the impressive special effects were by Large Fries.

The spectacle of new films chewing hungrily on the entrails of old TV shows should no longer surprise us, but is it practical? On the small screen, with a running time well under the hour, you can get away with a skinny plot, but, writ large, the frailty is all too apparent. More than any other hit of the 1970s, the original *Charlie's Angels* survives not as remembered episodes but as flash-like images, or poster stills, and there is something unusually absurd about wrapping a vast studio project around the sight of keen young women striking and holding a karate pose.

The Angels still total three; you might expect the team to have been swollen by inflation, but what was good enough for Dumas's musketeers is good enough for Charlie's more fragrant task force. In descending order of height, it consists of Natalie (Cameron Diaz), Alex (Lucy Liu), and the misleadingly named Dylan (Drew Barrymore). The first is blond, the second dark, and the third a redhead, but they switch wigs, outfits, and, occasionally, languages with such reckless zeal that, were Wim Wenders directing this picture, I would call it a classic study of ontological meltdown and the disintegrating self. At one genuinely troubling moment, two of the three girls turn into guys, complete with suits and mustaches; I caught the sound of spluttering and zapping, and a quick look around the theatre confirmed that this innocent twist of plot had caused five hundred male sexual radars to implode simultaneously.

The purpose of the Angels' unremitting alchemy is to track down the villain, or villains, of the piece. May I gently refer the scriptwriters—Ryan Rowe, Ed Solomon, and John August—to a simple rule of cinematic math? If a is the number of obviously good people, and b is the number of darkly suspicious people, then the number of interesting characters in the movie should, whenever possible, be greater than $(a + b)$. Otherwise, the element of surprise, when it comes to the unmasking of evil, will be zero, and the audience will buy itself an ice cream for being cleverer than anyone onscreen. The Angels are blessed with such gifts that it pains me to think of them as dense; how else, though, can you explain their willingness to take on assignments that would set alarm bells clanging inside the heads of lightly educated sheep? If a techno-genius as creepy as Eric Knox (Sam Rockwell) wanted me to break into the mainframe of a rival company, I would at least ask to think about it until the following Tuesday, but the Angels just plow right ahead. Eric is accompanied by his colleague Vivian Wood (Kelly Lynch), who wears so much black leather in the course of the film that I ended up viewing her less as a woman and more as a giant foot. She, too, wins the Angels' instant trust.

To be honest, *Charlie's Angels* is not really a film at all. It is a collection of settings and happenings joined not by dramatic necessity but by a vague, nagging impression that the last scene has become boring and it might be fun to skip to the next one; anybody who has watched a small girl fool around with Barbie dolls, shunting them from horseback to kitchen to dance floor, or hooking them up with the smooth-crotched Ken, will feel utterly at home in the molded plasticity of this movie. Even weirder is its giggling, pubescent approach to the mythical world of sex. Like Barbie, it is bedecked with the glittering insignia of physical attraction, yet at the same time it has no wish to grapple with what those signs portend. Although Drew Barrymore wakes up in guys' beds a couple of times, her face betrays not the molten memory of orgasm but the chirpy, what's-for-breakfast excitement that follows a successful sleepover. That's Drew for you, I guess; the more she whips her top off in public and alludes to the jungly excesses of her adolescence, the more we love her as an ingenue—the button-bright, kiss-me-quick sort that she played in *The Wedding Singer*, and that arcs back directly to her scene-stealing Gertie in *E.T.*

There is one sequence in *Charlie's Angels* that dices with erotic threat. Dylan has been captured and tied up in the desolate old tower where the nasty people live—it's that basic, I'm afraid—and there are now five strapping henchmen, dressed in black, advancing upon her. She spreads her legs and makes it clear that she will take on all of them at once. Of course, this involves knocking them out cold with her hands tied behind her back, but there is something queasy in the quick slip from rape fantasy to emasculation, and it reminds you, not altogether pleasantly, of the ambivalence that hovered over the TV series. Farrah Fawcett-Majors, as she was then known, and her sisters in crime prevention were allowed—indeed, obliged—to be ball-busters, but they also had to wear the kind of abbreviated clothing that would look lickable on bedroom walls. They got their own way, yet behind them was an unseen, controlling man. Girls wanted to be Angels, and every boy dreamed of being a Charlie.

Not much has changed, and Charlie remains little more than a crummy white speakerphone. The Angels' boss on the ground is Bosley—a role for Bill Murray, which is good news, but a shapeless one, which is a bust. Murray was put on this earth, in all his scrunched-up madness, to wreck any pretensions that encourage the rest of mankind to find purpose and steadiness in life; we stand on our dignity, and Murray ties our shoelaces together. Ideally, he should circle lethally among squares, spreading doubt and mischief; what he should not do is hang out with three young women who are not only cute and silly but perfectly happy about it. I think we are all agreed that, if there's one thing Cameron Diaz doesn't need, it's comic relief. She comes equipped with her own, and, if you truly wanted to crank up her luminosity even further, you would have to pair her with a total stiff.

Diaz's Natalie is the only good reason to see *Charlie's Angels.* Lucy Liu is game, too, but less relaxed, and Diaz represents something that we all revere: the good sport. To be that beautiful and not mind looking like a dog, as in *Being John Malkovich,* and to make a fool of yourself with a grin that betokens your faith in the power of folly: such things demand both ease and pluck, and Diaz, if she can keep up the pace, and if anyone feels like furnishing the dialogue, should be heading for Carole Lombard land. There is even a Monroeish moment when Natalie blithely tells a UPS delivery guy to "feel free to stick things in my slot"; she really, really doesn't get the joke, and that means more for us. What the audience enjoyed more than anything—more than the skydiving, the auto-racing, or the dreary spectacle of the Angels' office exploding—was Natalie's crush on a barman named Pete (Luke Wilson). Their rapport hardly stretches beyond the sweet, but, compared with the fakery that swirls around them, it boasts not just freshness but even a squeak of suspense; she keeps having to interrupt their cell-phone flirtation in order to fend off a kung-fu attack. The villains may expire, and the world may be a safer place, but who gives a damn, as long as Cameron Diaz gets her date?

NOVEMBER 13, 2000

CROUCHING TIGER, HIDDEN DRAGON

The opening fifteen minutes of *Crouching Tiger, Hidden Dragon* are difficult and tense. It is safe to say that the director, Ang Lee, is starting off in crouch mode. Everybody seems to be waiting for something to happen. We are in a large house, on the fringe of a peaceful lake, in the heart of an unspecified past. There is a rustle of excitement; up goes the cry "Master Li is here!" In strides Li Mu Bai (Chow Yun Fat), bearing a sword so rare that, like Excalibur, it has a name: Green Destiny. That it sounds more like a brand of herbal tea than like a lethal weapon is not a topic to be discussed in polite company, and the present company is more polite than most. Mu Bai is lofty, pensive, and ineffable; "I was surrounded by an endless sorrow," he says of his combat training. Even his pigtail seems to be under control, although, compared with Yu Shu Lien (Michelle Yeoh), the grave warrior woman to whom he entrusts the sword, he looks like a nervous wreck.

Shu Lien heads for Beijing, which, if we are to believe Lee's wondrous panoramic shot, is laid out on a grid system, like a clay-colored New York. Green Destiny is handed over for safekeeping and promptly stolen by night. At this point, the movie takes off. I don't mean just that it quickens up or starts to grip our interest; I mean that it *takes off*, with the main characters leading a concerted revolt against the forces of gravity. There is a moonlit moment when Shu Lien runs toward the robber, whose back is against a wall, and the robber simply turns and runs *up* the wall, with no more fuss or effort than someone rounding a corner. Nothing in the movie has pointed to this sudden change of gear, and what makes it so laughably exhilarating is that we accept it as perfectly natural; to leave earthly things behind seems like the obvious, perhaps the only, next step. Lee is counting on our ceaseless, all but unspoken, need for weightlessness, for letting go; it is as true, and as foolish, as the wish to become a child.

Being Lee, of course, he meshes this desire with other, more sophisticated emotions. You leave the film on air, but you can't decide whether you feel like a five-year-old coming out of *Peter Pan* or like a Cary Grant fan coming out of *To Catch a Thief*. Lee's fliers are not aloft all the time; just as they touch down fleetingly every few yards, like astronauts on speed, so the film has to ground itself regularly in the niceties of motive and plot. When Shu Lien dances across the rooftops, she is in hot pursuit, and none of the ensuing encounters are there for show; one person is always struggling to snatch the advantage from another, and it comes as no surprise to learn that the fight-and-flight choreography is by Yuen Wo Ping, the man who twirled a startled Keanu Reeves through *The Matrix*. The difference is that nobody here is required to sit through the Laurence Fishburne instruction course. If you're in this movie, you've already earned your wings.

This is especially true of Jade Fox, who is not, as you might think, a porno star but a slippery master criminal. Jade, whose gender is a matter of some debate, and who for purposes of multiple homicide favors an elegant combination of sickle and Frisbee, wants to find Green Destiny and slay Mu Bai into the bargain. Then, there is Jen (Zhang Ziyi), a young noblewoman with a fiancé she doesn't care for and a governess with whom she is in league; Jen befriends Shu Lien and treats her the way a young black kid would treat Michael Jordan—as a blend of role model, escape route, and god. Add to this Shu Lien's concealed passion for Mu Bai, and Jen's reverence for a ruffian who attacked her father's wagon train in the middle of the Chinese desert (not *quite* your average teenage crush), and you can see that Lee, who has been juggling a full set of loves and lusts ever since *The Wedding Banquet*, once again has his hands full. He has described this new project as "Bruce Lee meets Jane Austen," and, unless you are literally expecting Mr. Knightley to kick Mr. Elton in the head, the judgment stands. Yet what lends trouble and depth to the movie—the hidden dragon—is not so much wit, or the sustaining of ideals, but a mysterious acknowledgment of time. We cannot guess the date of the film's setting, and even the faces are strangely unreadable, as if the years had been stretched or stilled: Zhang Ziyi looks about fifteen in her formal costume, yet her character, as we gather from a prolonged and dusty flashback, has already taken a lifetime's dose of romance. As for Michelle Yeoh, those long almondy features speak of slow suffering rather than high kicks, and her soaring motions—a one-woman rebuke to *Charlie's Angels*—are, like the whole picture, the incarnation of pace without haste.

The career of Ang Lee—and its prospects—strikes me as the most interesting in Hollywood today. There are directors who are more surprising, more vainglorious or violent, more guaranteed to provoke; but none of them seem to share his patience or his range of curiosity. If Lee's passport is stamped with entries to Regency England, for *Sense and Sensibility*, to Civil War Missouri, for *Ride with the Devil*, and to the East Coast of the 1970s, for *The Ice Storm*, that is not because he wants to try his hand but because each new environment promises the chance of immersion. Lee works on the principle that if the physical conditions of his films punish or play on our senses with sufficient force, the rest of the period will follow. Of all the filmmakers who have delved into the seventies, he alone has not bothered with the era as a trove of retro kitsch; there is one good waterbed gag in *The Ice Storm*, but if you ask people what they remember of the movie they talk about Kevin Kline carrying Christina Ricci back home through the wood, with its shivering saplings and soft gray sleet. What a decade, you think: even the trees were shrunken. Contrast the extraordinary hand-to-hand, or bough-to-bough, combat in *Crouching Tiger, Hidden Dragon*, where Mu Bai and Jen cling to the trunks of full-leafed trees and *sway* at each other, blades at the ready. For viewers who associate the martial arts with a scruffy, stripped-to-the-waist, bone-cracking street fight, welcome to the green and whispering variety: the pastoral-arts flick.

This movie is not just the best of its kind; it seems on the verge of creating a new kind, surpassing and deflating the old Bruce Lee jamborees with the same dashing intelligence that allowed Michael Curtiz's *The Adventures of Robin Hood*, starring Errol Flynn, to outstrip the more basic bravado of Douglas Fairbanks. Curtiz, the director of *Casablanca* and *Yankee Doodle Dandy*, was born Mihaly Kertesz, in Budapest, and Ang Lee can be seen as a Curtiz for our times: the uncondescending outsider, reading the runes of the New World. Hollywood needs such men—civilized craftsmen with honor and humor—more than it needs the maverick or the self-igniting genius, and just now the need is acute. China and the Pacific Rim are delivering the liveliest and least cynical filmmaking in the world, and also the most uncowed. (Heaven knows, there is plenty to cow them, and Lee's native Taiwan is on permanent alert.) Is it too fanciful to suggest that the generation of Lee, Chen Kaige, Wong Kar-Wa, and Zhang Yimou, or perhaps the generation that follows them, might ride to the rescue—or, at any rate, the resuscitation—of American movies with some of the panache that marked the great Mitteleuropa immigration of the thirties and forties, itself an escape into the entertainment industry from a world of threat? Would Ernst Lubitsch, watching *The Wedding Banquet*, not have recognized the stirrings of a kindred spirit? To be fair, I should add that *Crouching Tiger, Hidden Dragon* is not strictly an American movie; it's in Chinese, with subtitles. I should also add, however, that I didn't even notice, and that I don't care. The crossover begins here.

DECEMBER 11, 2000

SNATCH

Only the clouded of vision, or the shrunken of soul, could fail to be enraptured by the latest Guy Ritchie extravaganza. Emboldened by his success with *Lock, Stock and Two Smoking Barrels*, the young British director has gone for the big one: Babylonian budget, sweeping locations, dazzling deployment of multiple cameras, tender use of a child character, and the near-religious radiance of a female icon.

Such, at any rate, was Mr. Ritchie's wedding to Madonna, which took place recently in the Scottish Highlands. By way of contrast, he has also taken time to deliver another of his snarling little faux-gangster sagas. This one goes by the charming, take-your-grandmother title of *Snatch*, and, once again, it features an assortment of feral men, each of them vying not merely to steal a giant diamond but to outdo his fellows in ungentlemanly conduct. We can tell that they are tough nuts, because few will admit to a normal name; we have Franky Four Fingers (Benicio Del Toro), Bullet Tooth Tony (Vinnie Jones), Brick Top (Alan Ford), Turkish (Jason Statham), and so on. The fashion for thick skins, and its matching contempt for regular feelings, is so pronounced in Ritchie's world that nothing could take its citizens by surprise, yet you can't help feeling that, were someone called Murray or Dave to show up, the whole place would go into shock.

Glancing off the jewel heist is another plot, founded on the fixing of boxing fights—bare-knuckled, needless to say. The secret weapon is Brad Pitt, who plays One Punch Mickey O'Neil. I think he is supposed to be Irish, or possibly a wild Romany, but no one can tell, since Pitt has wrapped himself in an accent as thick as a blanket. The other characters strain to catch his mumbling drift, as does the audience, and you begin to wonder if he is making sport of those rusty Cockney voices that left American ears bleeding in the wake of *Lock, Stock*. The presence of a superstar always throws minor films into awkward relief, and for once I was glad for the mismatch; everyone else in *Snatch* is trying so hard—not least Ritchie himself, with his split screens, his freeze-frames, his closed-circuit TV footage, and the tic of his heebie-jeebie editing—that to watch Pitt being funny and relaxed is a balm to the eyes. His character is supposed to lose, but, true to his fists, he just can't stop himself from winning. In years to come, this tricksy but obnoxious picture will be forgotten for its style but analyzed by college students for its allegorical intent: quiet American beats up loudmouthed Brits.

JANUARY 29, 2001

HANNIBAL

Hannibal Lecter doesn't want to eat you. He just wants to pick your brains. This is the reassuring message sent out by *Hannibal*, a full-blooded adaptation, scripted by David Mamet and Steven Zaillian, of Thomas Harris's novel. When the book was first delivered, it was called "The Morbidity of the Soul," a resounding title that would have reduced sales by 75 percent. A more accurate description would be "The Snobbery of the Soul," for what drives the good doctor to feast on humans—not his fellow humans, for he himself barely qualifies—is that he looks down on them like a diner gazing at his plate. "I forget your generation can't read," he once said to Clarice Starling when she was still a trainee with the FBI, and the new film finds Hannibal the bookworm, under the assumed name of Dr. Fell, munching his way through the Renaissance. Are we supposed to recall the dry little ditty by Thomas Brown, the seventeenth-century author of *Letters from the Dead to the Living*?

> I do not love thee, Dr Fell.
> The reason why I cannot tell;
> But this I know, and know full well,
> I do not love thee, Dr Fell.

No, indeed. Even in gregarious Italy this modern Fell looks ominously friendless. Much of the action is set in Florence, where he is applying for a position as the curator of a venerable library, and where every gesture—the licking of an envelope, the downing of an espresso—becomes a minor art. "What I want is a view" was the request of the imprisoned Lecter, in his Baltimore cell; now, exactly ten years after *The Silence of the Lambs*, in which he made his escape, the free Lecter has a Forsterian view to die for, or to kill for, and the rooms to go with it. The director is Ridley Scott, and nobody with an eye as readily seduced as his could be expected to forgo the pleasures of plashy fountains and dim, cooling colonnades. But you would get those in a Merchant-Ivory film, too; what you would not get is the *campo* of Scott's opening credits, shot in shivering black-and-white instead of the drenched colors that he adores. Nor would you get his flock of unsettled pigeons; seen from high above, they flap and fidget across the square to form, briefly and miraculously, the face of Hannibal Lecter.

In short, Lecter is everywhere. We know this from the pages of *Red Dragon*, *The Silence of the Lambs*, and, latterly, *Hannibal*, throughout which Harris dropped deftly into the historic present to indicate that the doctor, far from being locked in the security of the past tense, is somehow always with us: "Dr. Lecter has six fingers on his left hand," or "A brief silence, always, follows the name in any civilized gathering." Even behind bars, Lecter managed to roam across our minds as if they were open prairies. Hence the many problems of Harris's *Hannibal*, in which our hero was set literally at large, finally practicing all that he had preached. Big deal. When evil can do what it wants, the edge is taken off our fear and our sneaky sense of fun.

Here comes Anthony Hopkins, though, returning to the role, and determined afresh that all concerned should have a ball. He ups the camp factor, lightening Lecter's unearthly stillness—look how erect he stands, like a sentry or a statue, in a blade of Italian sunlight—with a series of winks and smiles (the half-second smile that never has time to reach his eyes), plus a peculiar predilection for the word "okey-dokey." This is said with relish, as if Hannibal were a chummy butcher in an Ealing comedy, while he prepares to unzip a man's belly and release the rope of his intestines. Yet I prefer Lecter in more solemn moments: the air of peacefulness, scented with something close to sorrow, that envelops him as he clamps a chloroformed handkerchief to a victim's nose, or the considerate tilt of the head which he gives when, for one reason or another, he is caught and bound, as if pitying those deluded creatures who think they can keep him captive for long—or, even more preposterously, bend his will to their own.

The truth is that Lecter alone prevails; his will is iron, and everyone around him is as breakable as bone. There is Mason Verger—played, somewhere far below his strata of prosthetics and makeup, by a famous actor, uncredited at the start, whose identity I will leave you to guess. Verger suffered at the hands of Lecter but survived, minus the traditional fittings of a face; now he lies, lapped in baronial splendor on the family estate in Maryland, and plots his rococo revenge. The trouble is that you can feel Scott, like Harris before him, cranking up the weird and the wicked until they hit the level of the laughable. The film does not require us to believe, as the book did, that Verger sips cocktails made from the chilled tears of children, but you still get a weary sense that the whole world has been Lecterized—ground down not merely by the burden of his perversions but by his donnish scorn for the ordinary. The FBI is no longer a trustable resource, as it was for Starling in *The Silence of the Lambs*, but a haven for misogynists. The Justice Department breeds creeps like Paul Krendler (Ray Liotta), who will shove Starling out of a job if he can't get into her pants. Dr. Lecter, as you can imagine, is keen to meet Mr. Krendler; he has a bone to pick with him.

Then there is Clarice herself; instead of Jodie Foster, who refused a reprise, we have Julianne Moore—at once more rarefied and more subdued, with a pallor that would do credit to the Lady of Shalott. Foster's Starling was a fighter, and Moore's calmer bearing makes her a less plausible product of the poor white South—"tornado bait," in Lecter's delightful phrase. On the other hand, it could be the calmness of shock; you suspect that Starling's heart has been anesthetized not only by a decade with the Feds but by her time apart from Hannibal. "I can't get him out of my mind," she says to Barney (Frankie R. Faison), who once guarded the doctor, and then asks, "What did he have to say about me?" The words could be those of a forsaken lover, and you can't help noticing the flush that fills her drained face when contact is renewed. Clarice's lead is a superior hand cream (this is a movie that swoons more over smells than tastes), faintly perceptible on a letter that Hannibal mails to her in an unwise spasm of sympathy. From FBI headquarters, Starling rings a senior police officer, Rinaldo Pazzi (Giancarlo Giannini), and warns him that Lecter will sniff out any pursuers, but the detective has ambitions of his own, aware that the doctor, like a tiger, is worth more if caught alive. Hannibal gives a lecture: "Avarice and hanging are linked in the medieval imagination," he declares, with the hapless Pazzi standing nearby. Try saying that name aloud.

Giannini is actually the best thing in the movie; he looks lived-in, as opposed to spaced-out, ruffled by recognizable lusts, and I could feel the audience reacting gratefully to a funny little scene involving nothing more than Pazzi, a pay phone, and the jangle of loose change. So much of the surrounding drama is drummed up rather than toned down; the composer, Hans Zimmer, keeps forgetting to hit the pause button on his choric chanting, and, while lifeblood streams from a slit throat, the camera looms, not once but twice, as if nerving itself to lap. When Jonathan Demme, the director of *The Silence of the Lambs*, showed us a dead body, he needed no more than a quick glance; what really gripped him was the flinching frown of Jodie Foster, as she saw the defilement done to another woman. Scott is more of a lingerer; without wishing to imply that he hangs out with serial murderers, I would say that he understands Hannibal better than he does Clarice. The brimming gore of the film is spilled not to upset or even spook us but purely in the spirit of aesthetic precision; that, at least, would gratify Dr. Lecter, and I wonder if both men might have been more at home not in the Florence of Dante but in the shadows of Caravaggio's Rome. To judge by Scott's record, he was the right man for Thomas Harris; they share an ability to fixate on disturbing detail while glossing over the frankly incredible. (Would an undisguised Lecter wander around a city teeming with American travellers? How do the FBI's Most Wanted pass through airports? Is Lecter really Clarice's Most Wanted, too?) If *Hannibal* falls short, that may be because Scott is still on a high from *Gladiator*, which was better fitted to the swagger of his method; the luscious locations of the new picture, like the enormity of Lecter's ego, have misled him to treat as grand opera what Demme recognized as chamber music—intimate, insidious, and high-strung.

Still, this is the movie that people will pay to see in the coming weeks. I would not recommend it for a hot date, and, for those who have recently ordered pork chops, I am obliged to refer you to a sequence involving vast, hungry hogs, which have been trained by Mason Verger's henchmen in what is technically known as multi-tusking. (Did Harris or Scott see a 1981 thriller called *Green Ice*, in which Ryan O'Neal watches a comrade being chomped to death by identical beasts?) It is followed shortly afterward by the interesting sight of Dr. Lecter at his most cerebral; I will add no more, except to say that chopped parsley gets a major supporting role. The result will make you either giggle or throw up; what it doesn't provide—what I missed in the entire, extravagant production—is the murmur of authentic dread. *The Silence of the Lambs*, in Harris's imaginings, was a matchless example of provocative pulp, showing how a lower genre can outwit the highbrow and make serious headway into our bad dreams. *Hannibal* may be richer fare, but only in passing does it taste like food for thought.

FEBRUARY 12, 2001

POLLOCK

Things are looking good for *Pollock*. Its director, Ed Harris, who also stars as Jackson Pollock, has received an Oscar nomination for Best Actor in a Leading Role; his costar, Marcia Gay Harden, who plays Lee Krasner, is up for Best Actress in a Supporting Role. Thus, the members of the Academy have allied themselves with their confrères in the world of American art. Now that the twentieth century has finished its run, to mixed reviews, many commentators would be happy to tip Pollock as Best Artist in a Leading Role, in which case Krasner—his wife and savior, whose own art was dimmed by her ferocious reverence for his—would be a shoo-in for her supporting act.

The movie is based on *Jackson Pollock: An American Saga*, which earned a Pulitzer in 1991 for its authors, Steven Naifeh and Gregory White Smith. A solid document, its prose was of that peculiar shade of purple which tends to win prizes: Judith Krantz for the gallery crowd. ("Beneath the boyish dimples and the tragi-comic drunken antics lurked this towering, inexplicable rage.") Things don't improve in the adaptation, which comes courtesy of another duo, Barbara Turner and Susan J. Emshwiller; to the end of my days, I will treasure the sight of poor Marcia Gay Harden wandering into the studio, staring at a painting, and saying, "This isn't really cubism, Jackson, 'cause you're not really breaking down the figure into multiple views." That isn't really drama, ladies, 'cause it doesn't really break down the meaning into speakable words. It is a measure of Harris's dedication that he transcends all this; like Pollock, he towers above his dimples.

After a couple of false starts, the film gets going in 1942, when Krasner presents herself at the apartment that Pollock shares with his brother and sister-in-law. It's an obvious point of takeoff; he wasn't floundering, but his drinking had run amok, and it was Krasner who made the effort to dry him out and set him on the true path. From here, we leap and lurch to the staging posts of his remaining fourteen years. We get Peggy Guggenheim (Amy Madigan in a fright wig) stomping up to his studio; she offers him first a contract and then her body—something of a coup, since it wasn't just anyone who got a contract with Peggy Guggenheim. We get reconstructions of the stills and documentary films that Hans Namuth took of the artist at work—an exposure so intimate that Pollock fled back to the comfort of the bottle. And we get Ruth Kligman (Jennifer Connelly), who became Pollock's squeeze in the final months; when you first see her, leaning over the side of his car in a summer dress, it does feel like a relief—the hint of an idyll after years of cyclonic marriage. Never mind the Pollocks, here's the sex kitten.

At regular intervals, the painter is seen hanging out with other painters; Willem de Kooning, for instance, is played by Val Kilmer, which suggests that casting, too, can be a form of abstract expressionism. Above all, there is Clement Greenberg (Jeffrey Tambor), who slides fleshily back and forth between his various duties to Pollock—as John the Baptist, Svengali, sounding board, and the guy who helps dry the dishes. Was there ever a closer, more contorted relation between creator and critic? I must admit, I fancy the idea; I'm determined to stroll into Universal Studios or wherever, take Mel Gibson aside while he's shooting *Lethal Weapon 9*, and say, "Mel, it's too . . . *muddy*. You're retreating into *images* again. Film is *film*, Mel. This is *mud*." He may throw his drink at me, but I know that he will listen.

No feature film about an artist is likely to tell us anything new about the artist. This is not to say that the genre is an unmitigated dud. Michelangelo scholars may hide their eyes at the very mention of *The Agony and the Ecstasy*, yet Charlton Heston scholars cite it as a major addition to the rocky myth of his invincibility, and the movie does contain one startling, Pollock-like scene when Chuck hurls red paint at a fresco. *Pollock* is far more careful than that; if a scent of kitsch remains in the air, it rises not from Ed Harris, who seems entirely honorable in his intentions toward his hero, but from the basic embarrassment of cinema when faced with art—with the nakedness of inspiration and the sweat of technique. Hence the Eureka moment, two-thirds of the way through, when Pollock, crouched in his Long Island studio, is pensively stirring his pot of paint. He removes the stick, a blurt of loose white falls onto the floorboards, and—*boom*—it's drip time!

The annoying thing is that this may not be moonshine. Pollock is a great, writhing test case for a movie, because, for once, so many of the ripest and cheesiest conventions of the Hollywood biopic turn out, disconcertingly, to be matters of fact. He really was a brow-clutcher and a hell-raiser, complete with dirty T-shirt and tied tongue; more than one onlooker compared him to Brando in *A Streetcar Named Desire*, and Harris, particularly from the back, has the bull neck and square Roman skull of a Kowalski clone. The loveliest sequence in the film shows him pacing like a lion in front of a daunting canvas, taller than he is and twenty feet long. It's blank, but not entirely blank; the artist's shadow softly looms and yawns across its surface, as if he were laying down a wash of himself. Suddenly, he stands up and paints, with lusty, aerobic arcs of his brush. You think, Come on, that isn't how paintings happen—tell me he ground it out over a couple of months. Go back to Naifeh and Smith, however, and it's all there; Pollock had been commissioned to provide a mural for Guggenheim's apartment, he was a day away from the deadline, and he painted the whole damn thing in fifteen hours without a break. "It was a stampede," he said later.

When the mural reached its destination, it was too long, and eight inches had to be chopped off one end. Marcel Duchamp said they weren't needed, and he was right; you feel that the painting has neither beginning nor end—it could be a slice of a loop, and you want it to go on forever, like a Bach chorale. ("How do you know when you've finished a painting?" Pollock is asked by an interviewer. "How do you know when you've finished making love?" he replies.) The irony of *Pollock* is that Ed Harris, in his debut as a director, is almost too fastidious in his own compositions; some shots are exquisitely framed, like the sight of Lee Krasner unbuttoning her dress at the end of a corridor, with a precoital Pollock looking worried in the foreground. (As well he might; before he met Krasner, his sex life was as much of a hit as his art.) Is this really the time and place for such finesse? If Pollock crammed every corner of his canvas, should a record of his life not seek to honor that? Is *Pollock* too muffled and mousy for the man who painted *Lavender Mist*?

On balance, we should give Harris the benefit of the doubt. Filmmakers who try to match the mania of artists, camera for brush, rarely pull it off; think of the woozy, pulsating sunflowers in Robert Altman's *Vincent and Theo*. Doggedness feels more honest, and, for all the hardcore Americanness of the subject (Pollock, bent on being one of the New Masters, never visited Europe to see the Old), I wonder if Harris borrowed his moderation from the French—from directors like Jacques Rivette, whose *La Belle Noiseuse* was a stubborn, four-hour lesson in visual patience. (After all, *Lavender Mist* itself, fifty years on, seems as reflective, in every sense, as one of Monet's lily ponds, and as intricate as the NASA photograph of a nocturnal, illuminated Earth.) There are plenty of raging meltdowns in

Harris's picture, which adheres to the rule that, whenever a drunkard overturns a table onscreen, it should always be laden with roast fowl and other festive trappings, for the purposes of maximum squelch; yet Harris, as a performer, is not one to let it all hang out, and what you remember from *Pollock* is a man fighting to hem it all in—riding a bicycle, say, with a cigarette in his mouth and a crate of beer on the handlebars. (When he crashes and spills his cargo, the roadway becomes a foaming work of art.) Even the climax, at which a boozy and bearded Pollock drives Ruth Kligman and her friend into the lethal night, is stilled into momentary hush; he looks peaceful and empty at the wheel, like a death mask. *Pollock* is a scrunched, unhappy movie; it finds contentment only in wordlessness, or in the passing flash of a flame-red overcoat or a painted stoop. To that extent, for all its loopholes, it does the painter proud.

MARCH 5, 2001

UNDER THE SAND

Charlotte Rampling addicts are a tenacious bunch, whose devotion to the cause is tested by the relatively small doses of her that they manage to obtain. In this country, at least, the supply is tightly rationed, although Her Serene Scariness tends to compensate by appearing in situations that are hard to forget. Just when you had spent a dozen years detoxing from the sight of Rampling in Nazi gear in *The Night Porter*, along came *Max Mon Amour*, in which, after careful consideration, she chose to make out with a chimp. Now we have *Under the Sand*, which overcomes its lack of fascists and primates by the unorthodox, if simple, tactic of being a very good film.

Rampling, appearing in pretty much every scene, plays Marie, who lectures in English at a college in Paris. She is, like Rampling herself, an Englishwoman who has all but shed the skin of her native land. Marie has been married to Jean (Bruno Cremer)—the ursine type, fond and slow—for more than twenty-five years. When we first see them, they are driving to their place in the country for a summer break. Anyone who is currently staggering through one of those moviemaking courses, in New York or wherever, should skip next week's class on How to Edit and watch the opening ten minutes of this movie instead. Note the way in which every detail, like the boiling of spaghetti or a hand brushing the bark of a tree, is allowed to register its quiet oddity but forbidden to outstay its welcome. Consider the dapper scissoring of one scene into the next and ask yourself about the rhythm of this couple's life. Is the fact that they barely speak an index of how instinctively they know and love one another, or is there a tiny bug of boredom scurrying around in the cracks?

On a fine day at the beach, Jean oils Marie's back and heads into the ocean for a swim. She never sees him again—not in the flesh, anyway, although much later on she stands over a slab of flesh that may or may not be Jean. ("We can't really call it a body at this point," the pathologist says.) The putrefaction, which we do not witness, means that Marie must strap a mask over her nose and mouth, and Rampling is forced to pack all her horror, the panic of disbelief, into her widening eyes. Throughout the film, she not only refuses to believe in her husband's death but continues, in the company of friends, to refer to him in the present tense. "Was this your husband's office?" asks a friend called Vincent (Jacques Nolot). "It is my husband's office," she says—not even stressing the "is," just correcting an error. Rampling makes you understand what it is to be beside yourself with grief; she is certainly not *inside* herself, and you feel that her soul has been shunted away to let her body go through the motions—the traditional French variety, such as shopping for ties and making love instead of lunch. The writer and director, François Ozon, is interested not so much in the trademark languor of the Rampling persona, the hawkeyed chill with which she surveys her territory, as in what kind of woman would feel the need for such intense control in the first place.

The result of this inquiry—it amounts practically to an interrogation—is that *Under the Sand* may come to stand as Rampling's best work; the possibility that it may also be the sexiest, given that she is now fifty-six, strikes me as cause for intercontinental celebration. It should provoke a tremor of envious unease in Hollywood, which, more than ever, seems rattled by the erotic requirements of anyone older than Kate Hudson. As Marie straddled a bemused Vincent and told him to stroke first her hips and then her breasts, I was almost too busy savoring the pathos of her instructions—the same ones, presumably, that Jean used to obey without even being asked—to fulfill my duty as a voyeur. At one point, the ghost of her husband, a hulking cuckold from beyond the grave, watches over her in bed with Vincent; she smiles at Jean as she comes. This is more tender than creepy, and, for all the formality of Ozon's approach, the film is wonderfully liquid; we see Marie dining behind an aquarium or standing before the iron-gray Atlantic, like a figure out of Casper David Friedrich, and she herself flows back and forth between youthfulness and the riptide of age, between what she dreams of and what she knows to be true. In the final shot, she runs hopefully toward a distant man on a beach. Some hope. Ozon, ruthless to the last, waits until she is almost there, then cuts her off.

MAY 21, 2001

PEARL HARBOR

The last Michael Bay film, *Armageddon*, was a handy guide to what you should do when an asteroid bumps into your planet. At the time, most critics scorned the picture as deafening and dumb; in retrospect, it feels like a mature, even witty, exercise in self-reference, considering that the effect of watching a Michael Bay film is indistinguishable from having a large, pointy lump of rock drop on your head. His new picture, *Pearl Harbor*, maintains the mood, pulsing with fervor as it tells a tale familiar to every child in America: how a great nation was attacked and humbled by the imperious pride of Ben Affleck.

He plays Rafe, a dyslexic Tennessee farmboy who has loved flying ever since he was old enough to crash. At least, I think he's from Tennessee; his accent takes a patriotic tour of several states, as if to indicate that the noble Rafe could have come from just about anywhere. His best buddy is Danny (Josh Hartnett); they join the Air Force together and play chicken in the skies over Long Island, much to the admiring wrath of Colonel Doolittle (Alec Baldwin), one of several real-life figures in the movie. Rafe is a young man of unusual courage. For one thing, he volunteers to be shipped to England to serve in the RAF. For another, he chooses the eve of his departure to inform his new girlfriend, an Air Force nurse named Evelyn (Kate Beckinsale), that he will not make love to her just now, on the ground that he wants to save something for later; this sacrifice, which leaves Evelyn looking a little huffy, makes Rafe unique in the annals of human warfare. She is posted to the heat of Pearl Harbor, where she sits and reads letters from a shivering Rafe. What a tribute to the forces of love: our hero's dyslexia, chronic though undiagnosed, cannot stop him writing to his beloved, or avidly reading the sheaves that come in return.

Life in Hawaii is sweet for Evelyn, as indicated by the large number of pineapples that are randomly distributed around the set. She has time to sit by the shore in natty little two-piece swimsuits, dreaming of Rafe and presumably trying not to notice Burt Lancaster and Deborah Kerr making out in the adjoining cove. Medical duties are light, composed mainly of soothing the scalded butts of zealous sunbathers and stitching the wounds of a young cook and boxer—another real-lifer, Dorie Miller (Cuba Gooding, Jr.), who becomes the first black sailor to be awarded the Navy Cross. (After his gotta-be-the-best diver in *Men of Honor*, Gooding is fast running out of water-based trailblazers.) This is one of those long but bitty movies in which actors get their characters handed out like parcels of rations—a nervous tic for you, a knot of frustration for him. Evelyn and the other nurses are delighted with a gang of fliers who are assigned to Pearl Harbor; we get Gooz (Michael Shannon), a fellow of few words and many bruises, Red (Ewen Bremner), who has a comedy stammer that you just know will kick in at a vital juncture, and, above all, Rafe's friend Danny. Uh-oh.

The moment he appeared, looking shy and sculpted, my radar picked up a large, aggressive plot twist steaming in from the northwest. When news arrived that Rafe was missing in action, presumed dead, after being shot down off the coast of England, I switched to full alert. Soon enough, Danny's attempts at consolation melt into drinks, illicit flights at dusk over the ocean, and the urge to do on a bed of parachutes what Rafe declined to do at a perfectly comfortable hotel in New York. And then, of course, Rafe turns up, back with his unit, alive and well and deeply pissed to see his friend and his girl going hula to hula. And then, to make matters worse, thousands of these Japanese guys turn up, although, as far as we know, few of them are driven by a specific wish to go out with Kate Beckinsale. In fact, observing this movie, I am not sure *what* they want; Michael Bay, whose passion for geopolitical history tends to be exceeded by his interest in fireballs, gives the enemy a dramatic shrift so short that even the most red-blooded American viewers may feel a trifle embarrassed. If your movie is three hours long, with minor characters packed like sardines into every nook, you should perhaps find space for a young Japanese pilot—a name to go with a face. And, if your budget is $135 million, you might consider something more sophisticated than a shot of the Japanese high command huddled over a small swimming pool, watching models of American ships being poked around with a rod.

To be fair, Bay does pay elaborate homage to the niceties of Japanese weaponry. Long before I saw *Pearl Harbor*, I was told to look out for the in-bomb camera, but that's not quite how it works; we don't perch on the nose so much as trail tightly behind, so that we can feel the whirring air and watch the looming target. Bay makes a fetish of the tiny propeller at the bomb's rear, gazing with kinky horror as it spins and then stops. He cuts away, holds for a microsecond, then delivers the bang and the boom. This blend of the minutely detailed and the enormously lurid is like the degraded fallout of a pop art sensibility; think of Lichtenstein and Rosenquist, of big pleading faces and fighter planes, then strip away the enamelling of irony, and you are left with the customized weirdness of the summer war movie, in which all strife is a blast.

Needless to say, *Pearl Harbor* works like a demon to pretend otherwise. We are offered regular sermons, notably from Alec Baldwin in his briefings and from Kate Beckinsale in a final voice-over, on the principles of combat and the lessons of loss; and our eyes are averted to Washington, D.C., where a staunch FDR (Jon Voight) urges his countrymen first to vigilance and then to arms. On the other hand, it must be said that a Washington in which Dan Aykroyd plays an expert in naval intelligence is not a Washington that would enjoy one's undivided confidence. Still, that is not Bay's field; his field is the buckling deck of the USS *Arizona*, her white-clad inhabitants blown through the air like exploding angels, and the vertiginous tilt when she groans over and starts to sink. As the men slid to the water, I realized that the model for *Pearl Harbor* was not other war films but James Cameron's *Titanic:* not the sober, battle-by-numbers approach of *Tora! Tora! Tora!* but the entwining of special effects and a love story that hopes, by sheer stamina, to grow special itself. To complain that the digital work in *Pearl Harbor* feels cold and gray is not saying much, given that the movie is about battleships; nevertheless, too much of the hardware—the toppling gantries, the Japanese Zeros that breed like rabbits in the air—is flattened by a matte dullness, like a kid's set of see-through stickers.

After the onslaught of false textures, it comes as a relief to take refuge in the look of the living, not least in the face of Kate Beckinsale, who is filmed with rapturous care. She comes on the heels of Nicole Kidman in *Moulin Rouge*, another alabaster goddess who calms a hectic film; staring at the pair of them, I get a pleasant, goosebumpy feeling that, if nothing else, mid-2001 will go down as the summer of skin. There is no doubt, of course, which of the boys will wind up with Evelyn, a woman at once so sexy and so saintly that she removes a stocking in the middle of the bombing raid to make an emergency tourniquet, causing me to wonder whether the patient's blood pressure is supposed to go up or down; what surprised me was how long it took for the winning lover to emerge. As Pearl Harbor lay smoldering, and the triumphant Japanese admiral uttered the words "I fear all we have done is to awaken a sleeping giant," I got up to leave. After all, that was pretty much the line that brought *Tora! Tora! Tora!* to a close. Then I glanced at my watch, sighed, and sat down again; forty-five minutes still to go, and we're off into an entirely new narrative, with Alec Baldwin recruiting the boys for yet another mission. "Do you know what top secret is?" he asks—the second-best question of the film, topped only when Evelyn finds Rafe packing a suitcase, and, quick as a flash, says, "Packing?" She is understandably distraught by her sudden change of fortunes. One moment she is trying to cope with two grown men scrapping over her like a couple of roosters, and the next, as she says in some exasperation, "All *this* happened." I am not absolutely sure what she means by "this," but I imagine that she is referring to the trifling matter of an enraged United States being hauled into a global conflict. I guess we should thank Michael Bay for so bold a revisionist take on the Second World War: no longer the clash of virtuous freedom and a malevolent tyranny but a terrible bummer when a girl is trying to get her dates straight.

What Rafe is setting off for—complete with Danny, a Silver Star, and a fresh head of highlights—is the Doolittle Raid on Tokyo, in the spring of 1942, when bombers were launched off the deck of a carrier. It's a great saga, and I applaud movies that take the trouble to sing the unsung, but it doesn't belong here, and the audience started to rustle with impatience—something I never expected to hear at a movie directed by Michael Bay and produced by Jerry Bruckheimer. Why did they go with this plan? Maybe Jerry sidled up to Michael halfway through the shoot and whispered, "Bad news. I just learned that this Hawaiian thing—with the planes and the ships, right?—well, it wasn't so great for us. Apparently, the Japs won. We *lost.*" So they tacked on another story, and went out on a high. *Pearl Harbor* may be stirring proof that right will prevail, but I hate to think what will happen when these guys get their hands on *King Lear.*

JUNE 4, 2001

APOCALYPSE NOW REDUX

So, the most hotly awaited movie of mid-2001 was made in the 1970s. Its only rival this summer is *Planet of the Apes*, the remake of a hairy hit from 1968. Is there nothing new under the sun? Where did all the ideas go? Whatever happened to the heroes? In the case of *Apocalypse Now*, you could argue that this one picture was so centripetal, that it sucked such a strange array of obsessions into its maw, that American movies took years to get over the shock. Think of a film like *Full Metal Jacket* and you start to wonder whether its mood—etiolated, vicious, vinegar-thin—flowed not from the coolness of Stanley Kubrick but from the plain, annoying fact that, eight years before, Francis Ford Coppola had called all the shots. Convention states that the primary lessons of Coppola's film were logistical: Do Not Waste Money. Finish Your Script Before You Start. Do Not Hire the Fat Man. And Don't Get Caught in the Storm. But the truth may be that other directors gazed at *Apocalypse Now* and quietly asked themselves, "Do I dare?" And, for the most part, they didn't. Instead, they took notes on *Star Wars*, with its nicely decorated vacuums, and proceeded from there.

Anyway, the horror is back, and this time it's even longer. A tantalizing recut entitled *Apocalypse Now Redux*, which Coppola showed to high acclaim at the Cannes Film Festival, in May, will shortly be screening across America. For the benefit of those lucky souls who are too young to know the movie, and who will thus be entering dark territory in a virginal state, it may be helpful to recap the twin, tangled stories of the original *Apocalypse Now*. The story inside the film, gingerly lifted from Conrad's *Heart of Darkness*, concerns a young intelligence officer, Captain Willard (Martin Sheen), who is ordered to take a boat upriver, into Cambodia, and terminate the command—and, while he's about it, the life—of Colonel Kurtz (Marlon Brando), who has exceeded his military brief by becoming, to all intents and purposes, a god. Wrapped around this mission is another story: the making of *Apocalypse Now*. As befits the tale of a man mythologized, the movie itself took root and bloomed into a legend; the shoot in the Philippines overran by eleven months, the production was plagued by everything from typhoons to a heart attack, and Coppola was scribbling down some of the dialogue as he went along. The cut you will see now runs to 196 minutes, but, if that sounds excessive, count yourself lucky; the total footage filmed ran to 370 hours.

I think it may be time to split these strands apart. The film has become mired in the history of its inception, like a child who has to stand there, stiff with shame, as his mother recites the saga of his birth. The separation could be painful, because there is still much to enjoy in the farrago of the Philippines; out of it sprang Peter Cowie's *The "Apocalypse Now" Book* as well as a documentary, *Hearts of Darkness*, which was itself based on *Notes: On the Making of "Apocalypse Now"*, the spry and instructive journal that was kept and published by Eleanor Coppola, the director's wife. But what matters is the result. Just as the players in a production of *Macbeth*, or an editor of the text, must at some point set aside variant readings and go with the version they prefer, so we should try to agree on what feels, for better or worse, like a finished product; and that is what *Apocalypse Now Redux* proclaims itself to be. To a kid of eighteen, standing on the sidewalk in midtown, poised to choose between *Jurassic Park III* and *Apocalypse Now Redux*, the question should be not "Did you know that Coppola sacked Harvey Keitel from the lead role after only three weeks?" or "Is it really true that Brando had to be lowered into position by crane?" but "Is this movie any good?"

The answer is yes, and, as far as the kid is concerned, it will be yes for a very specific reason: great helicopters. Better still, *real* helicopters. I cannot begin to describe the nostalgic pleasure of genuine hardware; when Colonel Kilgore (Robert Duvall) and his boys come clattering in over the beach and blitz the village, we know that they are riding actual choppers, not only because of the racket and the downdraft from the rotors but because, even if the digital skills had been on tap at the time, Kilgore was never a man to be fobbed off with the virtual. Is there a better cameo than Duvall's—a few short scenes, the last of them invisible, nothing but a barking bullhorn in the distance—in the history of cinema? Could even Orson Welles, casting his own limelight in *The Third Man*, vie with the spectacle of a shirtless Duvall in shades and cowboy hat, no more disturbed by a nearby explosion than he would be by the starting of a car? The trouble is, of course, that Duvall is almost too good; he forces the movie to peak and burn halfway through, but, more than that, he frightens the living doves out of us. *Apocalypse Now* was written by Coppola in conjunction with John Milius, and there are times—not just the maniacal minutes of Kilgore—when you can sense the director losing grip of his own political uncertainties and starting to quail before the sure, hawkish touch of the Milius talon. One reason for Kilgore to play Wagner from speakers on his gunships is to prime his troops for attack ("My boys love it"). Another, perhaps, is to remind the audience that we must reach back as far as Wagner himself to find so brazen an instance of that most radical of aesthetic effects: the conservative high.

The seasoned moviegoer might respond that such highs are everywhere, not least in the musicals of MGM. But those are light on their feet, whereas Coppola slows his pace and burrows into intensity. Just what the atmosphere of his movie is composed of—to what extent, if any, it was oxygenated by comedy, or by the merest breath of love—has become easier to gauge with the release of *Apocalypse Now Redux*. In this revised form, edited by Walter Murch, the movie contains forty-nine minutes of additional footage. Much of this has been known about and discussed by Coppola fans, who croon over every scrap of hearsay like relic hunters musing on the knucklebone of a saint, but, until now, little of it has been open to public viewing. Now we have it, and the rumor-mongers are out of business. There are several new sequences to take in: a dinner party for Captain Willard and his crew at a French plantation house upriver; the reappearance of the Playboy Bunnies, whom we last saw being airlifted into, and then out of, the fevered embrace of US troops; more of Kurtz, as he scornfully recites a passage from *Time* magazine to the imprisoned Willard; and, least obviously, but most affectingly, more time on the boat.

This is the coughing vessel—a descendant of the *African Queen* herself, maybe—in which Willard chugs toward his fate. I came away from the new cut with a much firmer grasp of the ship's company: Chef (Frederic Forrest), Lance (Sam Bottoms), Clean (Laurence Fishburne), and Chief (Albert Hall). The added material is nothing special, a few moments at the beginning of their voyage, but their companionship, and the resigned dignity of Hall in particular, feels like the last gesture of decency—even of pleasure, caught on the wing—before they get fouled up in barbarism. For a while, these folk remind you of the crew in *Jaws*—which had come out the summer before *Apocalypse Now* started shooting, and in which John Milius had a hand—and they make a more hopeful spectacle than anything in *Heart of Darkness*. The novella seems sour and sickly from the word go; Conrad was rummaging around in what he calls, with unforgettable nastiness, "the dead cats of civilization," and Coppola takes a little while to join him in feline hell. We still get Willard, wire-limbed and bendy with alcohol, punching the mirror in his Saigon hotel room, as if to destroy himself before the action gets under way; yet, throughout the revivified film, we feel Coppola and Murch exerting a slight, subtle pressure of the beautiful against the damned.

Hence the long sequence in the plantation house, where our heroes dine on French food and wine in the presence of French leftovers—a colonial family, who can no more flee Vietnam than a ghost can quit its nightly stage. (The diners could be cousins of Buñuel's stylish, paranoid snobs in *The Exterminating Angel.*) Willard ends the evening by sleeping with a young French widow (Aurore Clément), who offers him opium; indeed, the entire setup has the air of a pipe dream, as if the Americans were taking a magical history tour through the region. It goes on too long, and I have to agree with Murch's original account of the passage as an "ultimately indigestible lump of political information," yet somehow it belongs here, pushing the movie ever further from the terrain of the war film and closer to the tragic; we see more of what was lost, of what is yet to slide into these waters. And, if Coppola kept the plantation, he had to keep the Bunnies—a devastating new scene, as the boat draws up beside a medevac encampment, where the girls are lodged in refuge from the rain. Willard makes a trade. "Captain, are you giving away our fuel for the Playmate of the Month?" Chief asks. "No, Playmate of the Year." And that is how Lance and Chef get to make out with the Bunnies, inside a sodden, grounded helicopter at the ass-end of the world. Coppola finds a balance of tenderness and despair—the girls seem too drugged by the place, with its First World War desolation, to care about being manhandled—that he has never repeated elsewhere. Back home, to squire a centerfold was once the prerogative of swordsmen and billionaires: the wet dream of Middle America. Over in Vietnam, it's just wet, and even an Army cook with a drooping mustache can have his way. Welcome to Id Central.

And so to Brando's Kurtz, the superego, who has arrived at a place where even the unfettered lusts of others are his to command. We get a new slice of Brando here, and I like it not for what he says but for the light on him as he speaks; for the first and only time, it is daylight, and we get to observe that massive boulder of head, as steady with threat as any of the carved sculptures that encrust his temple. (The sister movie to this one, in its ritual dance around the totems of life and death, is *Last Tango in Paris;* that Brando was filmed, in both cases, by the Italian cinematographer Vittorio Storaro is no coincidence.) Kurtz in the shadows was pure mystery, but the visible Kurtz has a proud Roman madness, like something from the final volume of Gibbon, that harks back sadly to Brando's Mark Antony in *Julius Caesar*, and urges you to consider Coppola's movie less as a quest into the unknown and more as a meditation on the American imperium, and on its need to make itself—and its purposes, fair or fell—known beyond its shores. One wonders whether Coppola can taste the irony: he spent a year or so in a troublesome foreign land, and he wound up with a movie about home—about Willard, Chief, and the rest of the guys, and what they could turn into if cast adrift. That is why your heart breaks at the end, when Willard, having carved up the Colonel, finds the dazed and war-painted Lance, his sole fellow-survivor, takes him by the hand, and leads him away like a child.

The last minutes of *Apocalypse Now Redux* seem impossibly ripe and tense, graced not so much with Conradian gloom as with an odd, Jamesian sense of great matters being forced to hang fire. It is simply out of the question, these days, that a major studio would allow a director, of any stature, to close a big-budget picture by effectively leaving it open, with all manner of monstrosity still writhing around inside; indeed, I felt a small, vulgar desire—bred mostly, though not entirely, by sitting through the schlock of the eighties and nineties—to see the United States Cavalry sweep in, under a proud sun, and blow the heart right out of the darkness. As it happens, Coppola did film the destruction of Kurtz's stronghold, and you can see it in the DVD version released in 1999; for movie theatres, however, he has always preferred whimper to bang.

There is still plenty amiss with this picture; like Murch, I find stuff that is indigestible—sticky lumps of intellectual residue, like the general's big speech to Willard before the mission ("There's a conflict in every human heart between the rational and the irrational"), not to mention the perennial, uneasy suspicion that Kurtz's kingdom, run by Brando with Dennis Hopper as his Fool, is in fact nothing worse than a T. S. Eliot Study Group gone terribly wrong. But there is so much to set against that, beginning with the deep, *thugga-thugga* heartbeat of the choppers in the opening seconds; they fade in overhead, as if the audience were a restless river. (Murch got an Oscar for Best Sound on the picture, and his work remains unsurpassed; take a friend who is visually impaired to this movie, and I guarantee that he or she will get things out of it that you can barely imagine.) Twenty-two years on, the picture has aged better than we have; it both feeds our hunger for sensation and scorns our impatient need to have it all right now—apocalypse is, whatever the title claims, always waiting round the river bend. Many people will continue to find it incoherent; but, frankly, given the choice between a work so laden with ambition that it nearly breaks its back and the stiff, crowing blockbusters of today, too timid to stretch their wings, I know which I would take. If you have never watched *Apocalypse Now* in any form; if you know it well and wish to bend your Jesuitical attention to the latest addenda; if you have grown to love it on scumbled videotape but failed to catch it on the big screen; if you were out of your head during a pre-dawn college showing, duly noted the movie as a trip, and find yourself unable to remember whether the trip in question was Coppola's, America's, or yours; in short, however reverent or rocky your relations with this film—see it now.

AUGUST 6, 2001

TOGETHER

Just when I was starting to despair of ever finding a decent movie about life in a Swedish hippie colony in the mid-1970s, along comes a perfect example. Lukas Moodysson's *Together*, which opens in New York on August 24th, is the hopelessly endearing tale of a household in the chilly suburbs of Stockholm, crammed with endearing types who are themselves, you will be relieved to learn, completely hopeless. Take Göran (Gustav Hammarsten), a sort of Thor Heyerdahl without the spirit of adventure: rusty of beard, long of face, and so gentle of demeanor that you could run him over and he would apologize for getting in the way of your Volvo. He has a girlfriend, Lena (Anja Lundqvist), but this is a commune, and thus, unfortunately for Göran, she is at liberty to be everyone else's girlfriend as well. At one point, craving company of any description, she bares her bosom to a fourteen-year-old boy, who assumes the taut, stunned expression of someone who has been given the biggest toy in the store but no instruction manual. "I think I'm in love," he declares. Later, she tries to kiss him, and he immediately retracts his declaration: "I'm not in love with Lena anymore." Breasts are one thing, but kissing, well, yecch.

This is one of many splendid inversions in *Together*, which, taking its cue from the insubordination of the hippie movement—the principle that enjoins all members to moon the earthbound rituals of the bourgeoisie—itself refuses to play by the rules. When Göran's sister Elisabeth (Lisa Lindgren), a plump blonde with a cut lip, seeks refuge in the community for herself and her two children, our contempt is aimed squarely at the husband who struck her—Rolf (Michael Nyqvist), a boozer left kneeling in his own fumes on the floor of their apartment. Rolf resembles the wolfish Vladimir Putin with an added pelt of stubble: beat that for unlovely. So who could predict, from these grim beginnings, that Rolf, far from being left behind, would gradually claw his way back not only onto the grid of the narrative but, more implausibly still, into our wary affections? And which, of the many women in the story, would you mark down as the final target of Anna (Jessica Liedberg), the smiling in-house lesbian? I like her basic pickup line: "Have you ever tried meditating?" That's one word for it.

Moodysson is no stranger to same-sex attraction; his debut feature, *Show Me Love*, managed the near-impossible task of dramatizing a crush between two Swedish schoolgirls without getting itself steamed up—without, in fact, showing any love being made at all. I remember rising to leave the movie theatre and seeing an elderly gentleman in a hat and coat, who had obviously turned up expecting great things and was now sitting there dumbstruck with disappointment. In fact, *Show Me Love* was a great thing, in its sonata-like economy, and Moodysson has now rescored its companionable scruffiness for a small orchestra of characters. What *Together* shares with the best low-budget movies of the past year, such as *Memento* and *Under the Sand*, is a startling ability to hit the ground running; within ten minutes of the opening credits, we know exactly who all the commune's inhabitants are and what their problems are likely to be. We know Lasse (Ola Norell), Anna's estranged husband, who still lives there, with his devil's grin and his angelic son, Tet (named, needless to say, after the Offensive). We know the pair of hard-core, humorless utopians who will eventually quit the house and move "to Mother Earth," presumably asking directions along the route. We know Erik (Olle Sarri), the son of a banker and a devotee of the "Communist Marxist Leninist Revolutionary League," who agrees to fornicate with Lena on condition that they can talk about the iniquity of the profit motive immediately afterward. And we know Klas (Shanti Roney), who says that he would "love to be a housewife," and whose urgent quest for a man to share his bed is unduly hampered by his eerie, preemptive resemblance to Garth of *Wayne's World*. Party on, Klas.

Then, there are the children. If you want an unsentimental view of what an infected marriage can do to those conceived within it, try this film. Elisabeth's thirteen-year-old daughter, Eva (Emma Samuelsson), accompanied by her squashy-faced little brother, Stefan (Sam Kessel), seems too bruised to heal the wounds of others; she goes and sits outside in the hippie van, listening to Abba on her chunky portable tape deck through—and this is my idea of true period detail—one of those wiry white earpieces that we used to plug into the side of our heads. It's as if the title of the film (which is also the name of the colony) represented not a benign fact but a stubborn ambition—as if harmony of any kind had to be fought for in the face of competing solitudes. The best scene in the picture, the one that almost fells you with distress, shows young Stefan going to visit Rolf, who is living numbly on his own. The boy rings the bell, and his father, sprawled in booze, jumps to attention; he yanks on a shirt, sweeps up the empty bottles, and eventually makes it to the door. Too late: Stefan has already given up and gone. In happy homes, kids tidy up their mess before their dads come in the room; here it's the other way around, and it heralds a growing sense that kids of this era—of any era, maybe—were wise to life with a straightforwardness that their elders (you could hardly call them betters) could not dare to match. The irony bites even deeper, for it was precisely a desire to recapture the bliss of infancy, a moral and social stainlessness, that drove so many adults to drop out. And here are the kids themselves: impure as mud, watching TV, playing with toy pistols, and marching around the kitchen table bearing banners with the slogan "We Want Meat." If *Together* has a message for the disenchanted of the third millennium, it is this: man cannot live by chickpea alone.

The result, strange to say, is not a wacky movie. It is a flawless study of wackhood, right down to Göran's magnificent speech on the symbolic beauty of oatmeal and the flower painted on the telephone receiver, but the film itself could not be more clearheaded, and Moodysson has erased all traces of spiritual fug; he carefully closes the oatmeal scene with the distinctive slap—*schlumpf*—of porridge hitting plate. On the other hand, he is anything but a clinician; he is not on some smirking reactionary mission to slice these people up. Instead, by a sleight of hand that, even after a couple of viewings, I cannot begin to solve, he exposes the inner workings of the hippies' folly and still manages, as though unable to repress a natural charity, to convince us that they are, without exception, respectable souls. At some level, he agrees with their dreams, while reserving the right to find them hilarious, and that makes *Together* a comedy—not as much of a comedy for Anglophones, perhaps, as it was for the audience of Swedes with whom I first saw it, and who hooted permanently at the trickle of in-jokes, but a comedy nonetheless. All those zoom shots, pulsing in and out on Moodysson's hapless creations, are not just a clever tribute to the favored technical fad of the seventies; they are a means of restating the claim, made most eloquently by Robert Altman in *Nashville* and much obscured by the cinema of the intervening decades, that it is both our solemn privilege to imagine ourselves as being center stage and our comic destiny to be lost in space, stranded in the wings, on a nose-freezing night in Stockholm.

The ending of Moodysson's film is heavenly—an impromptu soccer game in the snow—yet the players have reached that goal, you feel, only after a hard training in pain. This is a winter's tale wrapped in crappy knitwear, and fleshed with casual nudity, and told to the sound of unforgettable songs that you would prefer to forget. I am normally allergic to heartwarming movies, but this one applies the heat with such tactical skill that none but the most iced-over cynics will wish to resist; both in the reach of its tolerance and in its re-creation of an epoch when the will to tolerate was most nakedly put to the test, this is, I would guess, the movie that *Almost Famous* longed to be. As Göran discovers, there has never been any such thing as free love; on the contrary, the purpose of *Together* is to demonstrate that love costs, or, rather, as Nazareth crisply informs us on the soundtrack, love hurts. On the evidence of this picture, however, and if you're prepared to swing a little, it's worth the effort.

AUGUST 20, 2001

Books

BEST-SELLERS I

Gore Vidal once wrote a celebrated essay with a very plain title: "The Top Ten Best Sellers According to the Sunday *New York Times* as of January 7, 1973." He had a high old time. He got to read Mary Renault, which he loved, and Solzhenitsyn, which he did not. He dropped a brace of Vidal smart bombs—phrases such as "I once wrote the screenplay" and "when my father was in the Administration." And he argued that the art of fiction was thoroughly, and perhaps irreparably, infected by the art of film. People were writing novels to remind us of old movies, and structuring them along the sleek lines of a good script. Within a few years of Vidal's essay, Hollywood proved his point, turning several of the books that he had pondered—*The Eiger Sanction*, *The Odessa File*, *Semi-Tough*—into motion pictures: back to the womb, as it were, from which they sprang. There was even a birdbrained screen version of *Jonathan Livingston Seagull*, which a friend of mine, ignoring all warnings, paid to see. A fortnight later, he was sitting up and back on solids, but it was a close thing.

And now it is Sunday, May 15, 1994. What is the news from the front line of the bookstores? Two decades after the Vidal survey, has anything changed? Well, Solzhenitsyn has gone back to Russia, and Mary Renault has died, and Frederick Forsyth is no longer in the top ten. He is, in fact, at No. 14, with a novel unwisely named *The Fist of God*. When he devised the title, it must have sounded crunchy and apocalyptic. Now it sounds like a club down in the West Village that you can't get into without a dog collar. I was grateful not to find Forsyth on my list, and nearly cried with relief on discovering that I had beaten the publication of the new John Grisham by a mere eleven days. There were some contenders, however, whom I was sorry to lose—steady players who had tasted the big time for a while and then dropped out. Spare a thought for Dave Wolverton, author of *The Courtship of Princess Leia*, the latest supernovel in the *Star*

Wars sequence. "His special talent is creating fully realized characters who live in worlds utterly different from our own," the blurb says, adding helpfully, "He lives with his family in Utah." May the force be with you, Dave.

There are sound reasons for musing on this stuff. It is easy to brush aside best-seller charts as the product of hype and habit, but they are a real presence in the land of letters, generating as much interest as they reflect. And if they do, to an extent, represent the lowest common denominator of the print culture, this only strengthens our need to pay attention, since where else is that culture common at all? 'Twas ever thus: anyone who imagines that a hundred years ago Americans were rushing out to buy the new Henry James is kidding himself. The editors of the *Times Book Review* would like to believe that they bring readers together beneath an umbrella of civilized discourse; but outside it is raining Danielle Steel. This is nothing to be ashamed of; it is a proper corrective to our historical arrogance, the conviction that the best writings of our time will, shored up by our plaudits, both outlive us and represent us in centuries to come. But they won't; we may not even have clocked the real thing when it passed before our eyes. That is why the ideal literary diet consists of trash and classics: all that has survived, and all that has no reason to survive—books you can read without thinking, and books you have to read if you want to think at all. In between is the twilight zone, the marshes of the middlebrow, where serious novelists lumber around with too many ideas on their back, ignoring the calls of the auditory imagination. I am not trying to be difficult when I say that, sentence for sentence, there is more going on in a page of George Higgins or Thomas Harris than in a whole chapter of, say, Margaret Drabble. They have a better ear for what we say, or try to say, or don't notice we're saying—for the small ways in which the mind works and stumbles. They have fun with the truth. There is no excuse for a boring pulp novelist, but a good one somehow plugs into the grid of our speech, into the power surge of ordinary fantasies, with a jolt that would knock more delicate writers across the room. That is why we should turn to the *Times* list every Sunday morning. If the language is still alive down at this end of the market—if there is juice running through the art of basic narrative—then we have no cause to be downhearted. Conversely, if the list is crammed with John Grisham, then we can all go out to brunch and rue the decline of the West.

A place on the list, in any case, brings many things: honor and glory, and buckets of cash, and the burden of responsibility. How do the chosen few shape up? First in line, at No. 10, is *Like Water for Chocolate*, by the Mexican author Laura Esquivel, which has been on the best-seller list for fifty-seven weeks. According to the Vidal theory, such wondrous staying power might be explained by the success of the accompanying movie. But the film is a far slighter piece of work, and its appeal has certainly died down by now, while the book is still going strong. It is set on a ranch run by women, among them the luscious Tita, who, condemned to a life of spinsterhood, sees her only love married off to an elder sister. The saving grace of this otherwise callow book, the spring that keeps it tense, is that it becomes both a study in frustration and a compendium of pleasures. Forced underground, physical desire keeps welling up elsewhere, most notably in the kitchen: the novel steams with elaborate foods, and Esquivel, in her sharpest coup, prefaces each chapter with a different recipe. Mexican readers fell on this book avidly, it seems, although its subsequent global triumph should surely give them pause; the main effect, after all, has been to perpetuate the myth of their homeland as lust-ridden, superstitious, and amusingly spicy. Whether you like the book depends largely on your appetite for second-generation magic realism: the shocking inspirations of, say, García Márquez reduced to familiar trappings—a river of tears, an imperious ghost, a bedspread that covers three hectares. Esquivel takes a shortcut to the magic without going via the real, and it's too easy a ride. The cream fritters sounded pretty good, though.

And so to No. 9, *Disclosure*, by Michael Crichton. This is what might be called an issue novel, something of a Crichton specialty. In his last two books, *Jurassic Park* and *Rising Sun*, the issues raised were, respectively, "Look out! Raptors!" and "Look out! Japs!" The new one is intended as a thoughtful, provocative, and altogether serious investigation of sexual harassment. In other words: "Look out! Women!" You can almost hear the *ping* inside the Crichton brain as the bright idea came to him: not just sexual harassment but sexual harassment with a twist, where the harassing is done by—you guessed it—a woman. Enter Meredith Johnson, the new vice president of DigiCom, hard drive incarnate: "We are talking about platform-independent RISC processors supported by 32-bit color active-matrix displays and portable hard copy at 1200 DPI and wireless networking in both LAN and WAN configurations." By the end of her first day, she has invited her old flame Tom Sanders up to her office. ("You still partial to dry chardonnay?") Before he knows what hit him, she has his pants open and is preparing to do it in both LAN and WAN configurations. Tom runs scared, her wrath still ringing in his ears. Game on.

Disclosure is Jacqueline Susann dressed up as modern sexual politics. No doubt Crichton decided that by reversing the roles (a dicey move in itself, implying that harassment by women is not just morally but statistically equivalent to harassment by men) he would be freshening the debate. In the event, it merely makes you wonder what turns him on: whether he just enjoys writing about women like Meredith Johnson—T. rex in slingbacks. The book, full of its own bravado, muscles into some crowded ethical areas, but there's something timid and square about the whole enterprise. How's this for a hot couch scene: "He had the feeling as he lay on his back that he was somehow agreeing to a situation that he did not understand fully"? Classic Crichton—human desire expressed in the language of the memo—and a fair summary of his own predicament. The novel comes alive only twice: once for legal sparring, once for a trip on a virtual-reality headset. It should look spiffy on the big screen.

A word of advice for Michael Crichton: Try reading Judith Krantz. She's just ahead of you on the best-seller list, at No. 8, and she's everything you're not. *Lovers* is a know-nothing, fly-anywhere kind of book, and after the stale air of *Disclosure* it's like a breath of fresh Chanel. In her glitzy way, Krantz is actually more honest and up-front about the give-and-take of sexual power play than the earnestly troubled Crichton. The characters make poor old Meredith Johnson look like St. Teresa of Avila; they insist on enjoying themselves, and each other, with a gluttony that one can hardly begrudge them, although I was a little worried about our heroine, Gigi Orsini, as she lay in bed at the start of chapter 4, "whiffing up the complicated infusion, the utterly satisfactory soup of masculinity that was particular to Zach." I hate to think what she did with his croutons. But Zach, whose name suggests he would be happier in a Dave Wolverton novel, is merely the warmup act for the next big attraction, David: "David smiled for the first time and now plunged freely, over and over, the diver liberated from judgment, immersed himself in the living depths of her until he quickly pounded to his own superb release." Always nice to see two young people getting on well.

This was my first visit to Krantzland, and I relished the occasion. Things were looking good right from the inside flap, where the novel is described as a "distillation of purest Krantz." I liked the sound of this. Just imagine all the Krantz motifs boiled down to one essential haiku:

A millionaire
Smiling at a girl with bra-
Less breasts and jet lag.

Sadly, it was not to be. Once La Krantz gets the bit between her teeth, she's impossible to halt, and 470 foam-flecked pages later I was lying there wiped out. The astonishing thing is that, with seven breakneck novels already behind her, this woman should still be in such a *hurry*. Characters are tumbled in and out of bed without a qualm, of course, yet the haste goes beyond that; no other writer could leave the plot on hold for two complete chapters, take a detour through the erotic history of a minor character, then swing back into line as if nothing had happened. But Krantz gets away with it. She takes us to the heart of trash appeal: she gives people space, and credit, for their preposterous dreams. She is perfectly at ease with the manner in which her heroine chooses to live, and this in turn allows readers a clear, conscience-free view of their own cravings in action; more artful novelists tend to be less generous—their disenchantment spreads like a stain, and the public feels dirty for desiring. The prose of Anita Brookner, for instance, as sad and tidy as a suitcase on a single bed, tells you that ideals are there to be missed; Judith Krantz springs the catch and brings out everything you could possibly want, and more. Hence her game efforts to squeeze twice as much information into a single sentence as it was designed to bear: "Did his cousin Billy Winthrop also take a pair of bodyguards with her wherever she went, Ben Winthrop asked himself in mild surprise as he leaned out of his car to give his name to the guard at the gatehouse that stood squarely at the driveway entrance to Billy's estate in Holmby Hills." Well, did she? Sometimes the strain is simply too much, and the syntax wilts before your eyes; take, for example, the woman who could reach her apartment "without seeing anybody or being seen, except by a stray unspeaking neighbor, all of whom were far older than she." The story of *Lovers* (fashion, film stars, Venice: the usual) is of no consequence; what matters here, and what keeps Judith Krantz at the peak of her profession, is her ability to celebrate an impossible way of life in prose that never fails to be radiantly, exultantly bad.

No. 7 poses a problem. *The Alienist*, by Caleb Carr, is a good book. A *really* good book, swift and dense—popular entertainment that brushes important questions with its fingertips. The problem, therefore, concerns the best-seller list itself: there must be people who go out and buy these books *because* they are on the list—who get the Michael Crichton and the new John Grisham as well as the Caleb Carr. If so, don't they notice the difference? Maybe it doesn't work like that; maybe *The Alienist* has nourished a clique of discerning admirers all by itself. It deserves them.

The time is 1890, the horse urine is freezing on the streets of New York, and the police commissioner is Theodore Roosevelt. Right from the start, Carr—a military and political historian by trade—shuffles real figures into his fictional deck. The presiding genius of the novel, Dr. Laszlo Kreizler, is an invention, but not pure invention; when we learn that he was the preferred intellectual sparring partner of William James, he comes alive in our hands. Kreizler is a forensic psychologist, or, as such men were called at the time, an alienist. Carr knows just how suggestive the word is;

it feeds into his brilliant apprehension of the city—brash, stinking, and secretive New York, afraid to confront itself as it turns the corner of the century. There is a killer at work, scooping the eyes from young boys. Kreizler is on the case, hindered by authority but helped by our eager narrator, John Moore. The book is openly indebted to Conan Doyle, of course, and also to *The Silence of the Lambs*, but it breathes a clammy atmosphere of its own making, a compound of the scholarly and the macabre: "It is, I believe, the preserved remnants of a human heart." The characters are present at the infancy of useful sciences—dactyloscopy, say, otherwise known as fingerprinting—but they also, in a wonderful touch, get excited by duds: the notion, for instance, that the eyes of a dead man preserve his final sight. Caleb Carr has done his homework, and, more crucially, he has galvanized it to create a drama. I could have done with one more twist at the end, but that's just greed. *The Alienist* makes you hungry for more.

No. 6, on the other hand, leaves you pleading for less. *The Day After Tomorrow*, by Allan Folsom, is a new recruit to a genre that I hoped had become extinct. How come tales of international right-wing conspiracy always manage to be hugely complicated and dismally small-minded at the same time? The plot is only a few pages old when we find ourselves knee-deep in used body parts: a head without a torso, seven torsos without heads, a cop without a clue. And the book itself appears to be constructed from bits of other books: where would Allan Folsom be without the snowy, faceless corpses at the start of *Gorky Park*, or the mad-scientist/Nazi-menace combo pioneered by Ira Levin in *The Boys from Brazil*? Above all, could he have done it without James Michener? The patent Michener process consists of gathering more research than any book could possibly need, then refusing to jettison a particle of it for the sake of dramatic form. The result, in the case of *The Day After Tomorrow*, is not so much a novel as a six-hundred-page fact sheet with occasional breaks for violence, cunningly arranged to give readers the illusion that they are in the holy presence of truth. Hence my favorite moment in the book, the most exquisitely boring clause to be found anywhere in the best-sellers: "Two hundred European cities have bus links with Frankfurt."

The odd thing about pedantry, however, is that it can't be trusted. Many of the writers on this list are under the impression that if they do the factual spadework, the fiction will dig itself in and hunker down, solid and secure. The effect, unfortunately, is quite the opposite. It suggests that the writers are hanging on for grim life to what they know for fear of unleashing what they don't know; they are frightened, in other words, of their own imagination. And they are right to be: they are up against one of the basic conditions of pulp. When Flaubert studied ancient Carthage for

Salammbô, or the particulars of medieval falconry for *The Legend of St. Julien Hospitalier*, he was furnishing and feathering a world that had already taken shape within his mind; when Allan Folsom looks at bus timetables, his book just gets a little longer. You start to feel sorry for his hero, Osborn, who can barely move without barking a shin on his creator's filing cabinet of general knowledge. Thus, before Osborn is allowed to jab succinylcholine into the buttocks of his father's killer, we are taken aside and given a full page on the drug's unique properties, just in case we can't accept its effect on the poor punctured villain. It makes you want to sit Mr. Folsom down and say, It's O.K., we *believe* you. Not that he needs consoling; the advance for this novel, including film and foreign rights, came to $5,300,000. Talk about a conspiracy.

No. 5 on the list is *Inca Gold*, by Clive Cussler. The plot is some farrago about buried treasure in the Andes, and the characters, though intended to be as tough as old boots, are not quite tough enough to curse properly. "Those fornicating baboons" is about as close as they get. The fruitful comparison here is with Judith Krantz, who I thought would be partial to soft-core euphemisms like "manhood" and "moistness" but never hesitates to call a fuck a fuck. The only point of interest in *Inca Gold*, in fact, is Cussler's attempt to out-Folsom Allan Folsom, sometimes in the most unsuitable places: "The underwater blast came like the eruption of a huge depth charge as a seething column of white froth and green slime burst out of the sinkhole, splattering everyone and everything standing within 20 meters (66 feet) of the edge." I love that parenthesis more than I can say. Someone should ask Mr. Cussler to edit an anthology of English verse. He could start with Robert Frost:

> And miles (multiples of 1.6 kilometres)
> to go before I sleep.
> And miles (multiples of 1.6 kilometres)
> to go before I sleep.

The Cussler hero, Dirk Pitt, is equally formal; he even has a trademark logo next to his name on the cover, although it's hard to see why anyone would want to steal it. I have yet to spot the commercial spinoffs—"A double McDirk with medium fries, please"—but they could only be an improvement on the book.

Which brings us to No. 4, *The Bridges of Madison County*, by Robert James Waller. This unusual work has been on the best-seller list for ninety-two weeks running, and the print run already stands at 4,790,000 copies. But who are the satisfied buyers? I don't know anyone who has read the book; I don't know anyone who knows anyone who has read the book. Of course, this simply means that I move in small, crabby circles; but that in itself is an exciting proposition, because it is part of Waller's mission to break through crabbiness and make his readers pure again. As he explains in his heart-melting preface, "In an increasingly callous world, we all exist with our own carapaces of scabbed-over sensibilities. Where great passion leaves off and mawkishness begins, I'm not sure. But our tendency to scoff at the possibility of the former and to label genuine and profound feelings as maudlin makes it difficult to enter the realm of gentleness required to understand the story of Francesca Johnson and Robert Kincaid." This sounds peaceable enough, a plea for literary armistice, but in truth it's more of a preemptive strike. Readers are being stripped of their wits before they even have a chance to use them; any attempts to criticize the novel will be treated as symptoms of the ailing culture that it is designed to cure. Well, tough.

Set in 1965, *Bridges* tells of a love affair between Kincaid, a photographer, and Francesca, a farmer's wife. They meet, they get on fine, they put away a good vegetarian dinner, they meet again, they make out, and then he quits, forever. Just one of those shits that pass in the night, you might think; but, no, theirs is a passion that transcends time. All this could have been rather touching and graceful; unfortunately, Kincaid and Francesca are not so much the victims of fate as the puppets of an unyielding sentimentalist. Not all of us would agree with the French theoreticians who proclaim the disappearance of the author, but sometimes one can't help wishing that he would disappear a little more. Robert James Waller is the literary equivalent of Leatherface in *The Texas Chainsaw Massacre*—he won't leave his characters alone for a second, preferring to harry them through the landscape and whip them into line with his own point of view. Instead of a clean phrase like "he added," Waller opts for "he quickly tacked on his caveat"; this brand of overwriting is a sure sign of an author who believes himself to be in command of the language but is in fact utterly at its mercy. Robert Kincaid, for example, is not allowed to be an ordinary photographer. He has to be "one of the last cowboys," and a poet to boot: "He liked words and images. 'Blue' was one of his favorite words. . . . He liked other words, such as 'distant,' 'woodsmoke,' 'highway,' 'ancient,' 'passage,' 'voyageur,' and 'India' for how they sounded, how they tasted, and what they conjured up in his mind." *Voyageur*?

That list is a key to the Waller method—a kind of writing-by-numbers, with severe restrictions placed on the available vocabulary. If you added the word "Cheerios" or "horny," for instance, the whole thing would faint with shock. (No phrase has been admitted to the book which you could not imagine being sung by Karen Carpenter.) The high point comes when

Francesca ushers Kincaid into a cattle pasture and cautions him, "Watch out for their leavings." There is nothing wrong with precisely chosen diction, of course, but it needs to chime with the substance of the work—unless you have comic intentions, that is, and Waller most certainly does not. His fancy concocts these lean countryfolk, but his language turns them into wimps and snobs. "The world is getting organized, way too organized for me and some others," Kincaid complains. "Hierarchies of authority, spans of control, long-range plans, and budgets. Corporate power; in 'Bud' we trust." Well, hold on here; is this the same guy who has been drinking Bud throughout? *The Bridges of Madison County* sets its face against modern society, but, wittingly or otherwise, it plucks its images of an unblemished life straight from the world of advertising: "tall and thin and hard," Kincaid is the first non-meat-eating Marlboro man. I found all this cowardly and delusive, a vacation brochure pretending to be a vision. Somewhere at the back of it, you catch the faintest echo of Emerson and Thoreau, but that only makes it worse: to hear the accents of Transcendentalism corrupted in this fashion, their severe self-scrutiny softened into narcissism, is worse than not hearing them at all. The victorious sales of *The Bridges of Madison County* make it a more depressing index to the state of America than Beavis, Butt-head, and Snoop Doggy Dogg put together. I got my copy at an airport, behind a guy who was buying *Playboy's Book of Lingerie*, and I think he had the better deal. He certainly looked happy with his purchase, whereas I had to ask for a paper bag. This book is worse than embarrassing. It's a crock of leavings.

Good news at No. 3, though. You can brush away the Waller with a burst of Sue Grafton. *"K" Is for Killer* is part of her trudge through the alphabet, which began back in 1982, with *"A" Is for Alibi.* She could well have problems in the future; stand by for *"X" Is for Xenophobic Racism on the Rise in the Former Eastern Bloc with Murderous Consequences for the Ethnic Balance of Coastal California.* The books are all about Kinsey Millhone, which is not, as you might think, a large pharmaceutical company but the name of a spunky, industrious female private eye. She has a lousy haircut, no sex life, and a slight case of moral principles, though not enough to make her a prig. "The victims of unsolved homicides I think of as the unruly dead," she says on the opening page. This brought me up short; it is a rather beautiful sentence, all the more provocative for being mildly archaic, and it's not a freak. Every now and then, in the course of a fairly ordinary murder tale, Sue Grafton scores a direct hit: "She was strung out on something, throwing off that odd crackhead body odor. Her eyes kept sliding upward out of focus, like the roll on a TV picture." Saul Bellow wouldn't be ashamed to think of that.

You come away from the book with a keen and sweaty sense of Kinsey's nocturnal prowlings, not to mention her taste in wine. (Chardonnay again, as in Michael Crichton.) But the whodunnit isn't much—secretary doubles as hooker, ends up decomposed—and Grafton relies, like Crichton, on crucial conversations that just *happen* to have been taped. The one conundrum left unexplained is the strange endurance of the mystery genre itself; it's such a thin piece of ground, and it was worked so richly by a couple of early settlers, Hammett and Chandler, that everyone since, even as skilled a worker as Sue Grafton, has been doomed to turn over old soil. You can alter the setting all you like, and change the sex of your shamus, but that sour, sudden poetry will never be wholly your own. This could be the attraction, of course; readers may relish the very lack of originality, like smokers who refuse to switch brands. What could be more cozy than the spectacle of violent crimes, the deepest imprints of human malice, deciphered like crossword puzzles over and over again? (No wonder serial killers are so hot; private eyes are serial solvers, and they need the competition.) If fiction is the art of telling lies, then murder stories are the whitest of all. A couple of them will always be found sprawled across the best-seller lists—evidence not of the popular appetite for blood but of the popular readiness to wipe it up. They speak of chaos let loose, then controlled: the perennial seesaw plot, as pleasant as the rocking of a cradle.

And so to No. 2, *Remember Me*, by Mary Higgins Clark. Ms. Clark looks out from the back cover wearing a fine brocade jacket and the confident smile of a woman with eleven best-sellers already under her belt and plenty more where they came from. Her fictional formulas are nicely worn by now, and the new book flows along the grooves; it never changes course, or tries anything that might upset the fans. This was the Agatha Christie method, too, but in her case practice made perfect: she breezed past all the unsightly psychological stuff but took immense care to stash her clues away in unlikely crannies. Ms. Clark, on the other hand, is so eager not to offend that even her surprises aren't surprising. The plot will ring a few bells. Young married couple, storm at sea, wife in the water, grief, foul play suspected but hard to prove, whole thing turns on the ring from wife's finger. . . . *Sleeping with the Enemy*, anyone? The setting is modern Cape Cod, and people drink *that* wine again, but the author's habits are those of a nineteenth-century melodramatist, one of that hearty breed who used to knock out adventures in serial form, leaving the reader gawping on the cliff edge of each installment. *Remember Me* has 110 chapters, some no longer than a page, and they tend to close like this: "He knows more than he's telling, and I'm going to get to the bottom of it." Menaced by danger, or simply struck by a thought, the characters keep feeling their lips go dry or their throats seize up. At one point, somebody exclaims "Haunted!"—a cry I haven't heard since the golden years of *Scooby-Doo.* All this is oddly comforting. You can't imagine actually buying this neat, style-free book, but it's the kind of thing you would borrow from a friend, or find on the shelves of a country inn, and polish off by breakfast the next day. The admonitory title is, of course, to no avail; I came to the end of *Remember Me* and immediately forgot all about it.

And so we make our ascent to the summit, to *The Celestine Prophecy.* The No. 1 author is James Redfield, and he brings good tidings of great joy, which shall be to all people, especially those with no ear for English prose. "For half a century now, a new consciousness has been entering the human world, a new awareness that can only be called transcendent, spiritual." One would like to know what triggered this fresh start. To many people, after all, fifty years ago means a series of events in Central Europe that prompted them not to tighten their hold upon the spiritual but to question it with unaccustomed force. Mr. Redfield, however, is not one to let history get in his way. He has more important things in mind. He has plans. "Once we do understand what is happening, how to engage this allusive process and maximize its occurrence in our lives, human society will take a quantum leap into a whole new way of life." All this comes from the author's preface, and it immediately raises questions. (1) Does he really mean "allusive"? What is being alluded to? "Elusive" would do equally well, not that it matters. (2) Why does the coy introduction of semi-scientific terms like "maximize" and "quantum leap," presumably intended to make readers feel that they are in safe hands, have entirely the opposite effect? (3) What is this guy *on*?

The Celestine Prophecy is set mostly in Peru. I kept waiting for the characters to bump into their counterparts from *Inca Gold.* Dirk Pitt has more urgent things to attend to than "a complete explanation of our existence," though, and this lot can hardly think about anything else. They mosey around, escaping from government interference and skeptical scientists ("That guy must really be evil"), watching pink fields of energy grow on their friends, and slowly working their way through the Nine Insights. These are contained in an ancient manuscript, and they reveal a master plan for the survival of our race on this planet. Many of them are variations on the theme (expounded rather more gracefully in the Bible) of "Try and be nice to people," and they reach a sensational climax with No. 9: "The more we evolve, the higher we vibrate." Sounds like a job for Zach.

I was shocked to find this book at the top of the *Times* list, although I shouldn't have been. It's exactly the kind of work that thrives at a time when organized faith is in retreat, and when every variety of garbage—systematic garbage, with pretensions to establishing a homemade religion—floods in to fill the gap. It's nothing new, really: Madame Blavatsky for the nineties. More grievously, it's an insult to the novel. Redfield has no interest in form except as a trampoline for his bouncy ideas—none of which, incidentally, have any discernible meaning. When he does gather his wits and make a gesture toward conventional narrative, the results leave you slack-jawed: "Her name was Sarah Lorner and she was sandy-haired and blue-eyed and could have been described as girlish except for her serious demeanor." It's hard to know what to say. America is not, by and large, a nation of confused, gullible, and sexist hippies, so who is buying this book? In 1973, Gore Vidal claimed that novels had become little more than surrogate movies. If only that were the case. Books like *The Celestine Prophecy* and *The Bridges of Madison County* are something far more sinister: surrogate *non*-fiction. They are guides to life, how-to manuals with a little squirt of plot piped around the edge. It is the very worst fate that could have befallen literature; even Tolstoy, the unrepentant didact, would not have wanted it to end like this. The *Times* nonfiction list for May 15 contains essays on good and evil, a discussion of "love and relationships," and two accounts of near-death experiences. The fiction list, on the other hand, *is* a near-death experience.

Or almost. I went toward the light but pulled back from the brink. After all, I had *The Alienist* to cheer me up. I had discovered Sue Grafton. And the mighty Judith Krantz, with her firm grip on human anatomy: "His eyes had narrowed into two thin question marks." What's more, I had learned a whole bunch of stuff in the course of my reading. Everyone is drinking a lot of Chardonnay, for one thing. And if I ever need to get in and out of Frankfurt in a hurry, I'll know which mode of transport to use. No, I thought, fiction's O.K. The novel will live another day. And so I rose, put down my ten books, tacked on my caveat, engaged my allusive process, and quickly pounded to my own superb release.

JUNE 27, 1994

SEX BOOKS

How was it for you? Was it O.K.? Was it great? Were you extremely emotionally satisfied, or did emotional problems interfere with sex? Did your last sex event include an occurrence of receptive oral sex? Would you say you are Mexican, Puerto Rican, Cuban, or something else? If a man and a woman have sex relations before marriage, do you think it is always wrong, almost always wrong, wrong only sometimes, or not wrong at all? Do you understand the question? Where are you going? Do you sell postcards? Could you direct me to the nearest Bureau de Change?

Life has suddenly got a whole lot more complicated since the findings of the National Health and Social Life Survey (NHSLS) became known. They form the basis of a fat, sophisticated, and sperm-freezingly serious volume entitled *The Social Organization of Sexuality*. Written by a team of four—Edward O. Laumann, John H. Gagnon, Robert T. Michael, and Stuart Michaels—this is the most comprehensive tour of our bedrooms ever published, going way beyond Kinsey (1948) and Hite (1979), not to mention Bumpass and Sweet (1989), the enchantingly two-faced Janus and Janus (1993), or the sterling team effort of Catania, Turner, Pierce, Golden, Stocking, Binson, and Mast in the same year. The title makes it sound like a dating guide, or an index of useful clubs—places where young Republican transvestites, say, can meet up with other young Republican transvestites and have themselves a ball. But this book is not in the business of giving us a good time. It is in the business of asking 3,432 other people whether *they* had a good time, and exactly what they did to make it so good, and whether they needed to replace the batteries afterward. These are questions of great importance, but the authors are in no hurry to provide the answers. *The Social Organization of Sexuality* runs to more than seven hundred pages, many of which are graced with pie charts, dotted graphs, and other filth. If you want highlights, you could always try

Sex in America, a digest of the same research, which comes in at a nippy three hundred pages and tones down the professorial hauteur in favor of what I hesitate to call laymen's terms. Plumping for the shorter book is like ordering the *menu dégustation* when you can't be bothered to go à la carte, or buying *Magical Mystery Tour* instead of the full set of Beatles albums. Needless to say, it's much less fun, although the index does offer some unexpected pleasures: Clinton, Bill; Clinton, Hillary Rodham; clitoris; clubs; cluster analysis.

One of the great glories of sex is the difficulty of talking about it—no other human activity, not even love, is so resistant to the assaults of language. Talking *during* it has never been easy, either, especially if you were brought up not to speak with your mouth full, but nothing can quite match the verbal shortfall of erotic anticipation and remembrance; struggling to say what we feel, we plod from the lachrymose to the smutty via the obstetric, and never seem to get any nearer. Keats got fairly close with all those warm jewels and fragrant bodices, not to mention the soothing jellies, but such double-distilled innuendo is hard to pull off. Most modern writers see no need for it—why hint at something when you can wave it under the reader's nose? Poets and academics alike will do anything to avoid appearing craven or ignorant in the face of sex; the authors of *The Social Organization of Sexuality* frown severely at our reluctance to discuss our sex lives—a hangover, of course, from centuries of repression—and at the rubbish we spout in the attempt. "Sexual activity almost always occurs in private and is usually talked about in highly routine and nonrevealing ways," they say. To which the only possible reply is: Fuck off. It is precisely that private quality which sets the carnal life apart; remove the privacy, invade it or parade it, and you lose what made it interesting in the first place. You turn it, in fact, into what the sex surveyors really want, which is a social contract; time and again, they claim that our lusts are shaped and conditioned by social forces, and not—as previously thought—by one person's unique wish to clamber on top of another. And if our ways of talking about sex are "routine," so what? Why does that make them "nonrevealing"? Nothing is more revealing than routine; it is the height of melodrama (and the opposite of scholarship) to imagine that we betray our true nature only in flurries of aberration. You read the authors' preface to this book and think, O.K., let's see what *you* can do. Come on, reveal.

It turns out that the technical vocabulary of sexologists is no better suited to the experience of sex than anybody else's. "The conventional sex script still seems to terminate in vaginal intercourse in most sexual encounters (i.e., although postcoital petting may ensue, no other discrete genitally oriented acts occur)." I love it when these guys talk dirty. Their well-intentioned grab at a dry word like "terminate" goes terribly wrong, ruined by overtones of Amtrak and Arnold Schwarzenegger, and bears them still further away from the moist joys of their subject; as that distance increases, so the whole book asserts its claim to be one of the comic masterpieces of our age, its command of tone as flawless as that of *Gentlemen Prefer Blondes*—or, as we should now call it, *College-Educated Male Members of Median Birth Cohorts Express an 80 Percent Preference for Penetrative Sex with Type II Protestant White Female Partners, Thereby Inheriting an Above-Average Risk of Sexually Transmitted Infection.* A major player in these books, "cohort" seems to be the beefy, official word for a statistical grouping—as in "over half those formed in the youngest cohort are cohabitational unions"—but after five hundred pages I was still taken aback by its appearance, imagining phalanxes of Roman legionaries in fancy breastplates laying waste to the singles scene. The most touching moments in *The Social Organization of Sexuality* come when the authors hear a small voice that cries to them from their own bareassed, backseat past, and try to find room for it in their brave new world: "Of course, not all adolescents complete the entire program or, to use the especially apt euphemism, 'go all the way.' " Only those with the courage of their conventions can place their trust in a phrase like "complete the entire program," which makes teenagers sound like washing machines.

So, what's the latest from the nation's boudoirs? How many youngsters still go all the way, from prewash to spin cycle? Bad news, I'm afraid. It seems that you could round up all the studs in America, herd them into Paula Jones's closet, and still find room for Paula Jones. Even then, nothing would happen. *Sex in America* informs us that "36 percent of men age eighteen to twenty-four had no sex with a partner in the past year or had sex just a few times." Huh? Did Warren Beatty labor in vain? It makes you wonder what the hell everyone is *doing* out there. Buffing the Lexus, I guess, or bonding with baby, or asking the investment manager round for a wild evening of Evian. Anyone still hoping to dip his toes in group sex will find it hard to gather enough people to make up the group. There are several states in America that continue to outlaw oral and anal sex, but the libertarians who take issue with this are rapidly being outstripped, it appears, by those whose only offense is to nudge the speed limit as they tear home to a family dinner and fresh pajamas. Not only are people getting married in droves when they could still be buckling Italian countesses to the bedpost, they are also having the best—and sometimes the only—sex of their lives within those marriages. To cap it all, the NHSLS researchers discovered that "there was not a strong relationship between having orgasms and having a satisfying sexual life." Yeah, and it doesn't matter what's on your plate: just enjoy the meal.

These books went on sale shortly before the midterm elections. I doubt if they swayed the voting patterns, but they sure offered an accurate prediction. If their findings are true, something has gone amazingly wrong with the national morality: everyone is turning into Oliver North. "Americans, we find, are not having much partnered sex at all," the authors sadly report. When the NHSLS was first announced, and funding was being sought for a survey that would cover twenty thousand respondents, Jesse Helms swung into action with a blocking amendment, thus chopping the number to almost a sixth of what was required; but the research went ahead anyway, and, by a delicious irony, came up with a set of numbers to bring tears to Jesse's eyes. Minimal gay activity, certainly nothing like the "one in ten" figure first proposed by Kinsey; monogamy still pulling 'em in; Christian churchgoers likely to have fewer partners over the last five years than the damnable heathen—as he scanned all this, Helms must have wished he'd doubled the funding and paid for a billboard campaign. There remain a few common vices to disturb his sleep, although these can be counted on the fingers of one hand; the most common of all, indeed, is done *with* the fingers of one hand. America is still in love with itself in a big way. As Henry James wrote so memorably in *Washington Square*, "He wanted to abuse somebody, and he began, cautiously—for he was always cautious—with himself."

The net effect of sex surveys always used to be the same: they would steep the reader in shame and despair as he looked back on a life of laughable monkishness and compared it with the woodland rutting practiced by the rest of the population. Not this time. *The Social Organization of Sexuality* turns the whole thing on its head—the only spot of kinky technique in sight. As the statistics came and went, and the national continence deepened, I began to feel like Fatty Arbuckle. Soon, however, that flash of pride gave way to consternation, and I found myself scouting rather desperately through the pie charts for a slice of the American people to keep me company in my meagre history of transgressions. Help arrived in the form of Jewish lovers, who continue to fizz, so I learned, with an erotic excitement denied to those of other faiths, and whose recorded achievements returned me to a comforting state of Protestant inadequacy. The Jewish male is almost the only predator still roaming the prairie of intercourse, and his choicest mate—no surprise here—remains the Well-Read Girl. "Twice as many women who went to college have given or received oral sex as compared to those who did not finish high school and twice as many of these better-educated women had or received oral sex the last time they had sex." So says *Sex in America*, which goes on to propound all manner of sociohistorical reasons for such a merry upswing, while ignoring the obvious fact that women who go to college are more likely than anyone else to be forced to read Henry Fielding.

There is, however, one subcohort whose entire waking life is dedicated to the finer points of arousal. I refer, of course, to those hardy souls dispatched by the NHSLS to conduct the long, face-to-face interviews on which the two books were based. According to the authors, "they reported back to us that the participants enjoyed the interview, that they found it a rewarding and often illuminating experience to be gently led through their sex lives and attitudes about sex. In fact, they said it was an affirming event." I bet they did. None of the doings reported by the survey are remotely sexy, but the earnest account of its procedures left me weak with desire. (Maybe this is the future: maybe Americans will retreat from their own indulgence in sex in favor of the clean, secondhand sensation of other people's orgasms, and will find it even sweeter on the hormones. Looking at Hollywood, you could argue that this has happened already.) Both books reproduce the questionnaire carried by the surveyors, a document whose arid appearance is merely tinder for the inflamed curiosity of its instructions: "About how many partners was that? RECORD NUMBER. IF DON'T KNOW PROBE FOR BEST GUESS." With any relationship of this intensity, there is bound to be a measure of jousting, as each partner seeks to outwit the other in the quest for sexual domination. As the authors warn, "when we ask an opinion—Is oral sex very appealing, appealing, unappealing, or not at all appealing—there is more room for fuzziness." I wouldn't have phrased it quite like that, but you get the point.

Sex rears its behind on every page of *The Social Organization of Sexuality* and *Sex in America;* every possible variation comes under scrutiny, from happily married nonagenarians to anonymous troops of bathhouse desperadoes, from the first kiss to what the authors term "autoerotic sex aids—movies, magazines, phones, and dancing." And yet these books are not about sex. They are not even about dancing. They are about lying. They are constructed with admirable clarity, but they represent the ne plus ultra of fuzziness—the unalterable fuzz of our duplicity, the need to hide the truth from other people in the hope that we will cease to recognize it ourselves. Read a sentence such as "Men report that they experience fellatio at a far greater rate than women report providing it," and you find yourself glancing down a long, shady vista of self-delusion. This is not a question of inefficient research, or of culpable hypocrisy, or even of that much loved villain of the piece, the male boast; it is simply what T. S. Eliot called *bovarysme*, "the human will to see things as they are not," and throughout *The Social Organization of Sexuality* it never once failed to give me a good laugh.

I finished these books with that curious feeling you tend to get from statistically burdened prose—the feeling that you are learning everything yet nothing, and that if you want to learn about the erotic life you would be better off putting your ear to the wall of a hotel room, or reading a couple of Maupassant stories. The principal benefits will be in the areas of epidemiology and health care, and you can't argue with that; but the very sobriety of the project, which fortifies those benefits, makes it blissfully redundant as moral inquiry. It tells us more than we care to know about our sexual behavior but next to nothing about our sexual nature; this is hardly the fault of the editors—it was not in their brief—but it brings you up hard against the vanity of the belief that there really is such a thing as average human conduct. It was only after a lifetime of case histories, of picking away at particular neuroses, that Freud felt able to ruminate on the general conditions prevailing in our moral constitution. One result was *Civilization and Its Discontents*, which identified a tragic impasse: the constraints of civic life tamp down those impulses—notably the sexual—which would, if given their liberty, improve our chance of happiness; yet the very act of liberation, on any scale beyond the individual, would rock the structures of civilized life. We exist, in other words, only under a tyranny of our own devising. This has always struck me as unarguable, but it seems that Freud has had his day. The gloom of Vienna will not wash in modern America. "Happiness with partnered sex is linked to happiness with life," sings *Sex in America*, adding, "We cannot say which comes first—general happiness or a good sex life—but the correlations are clear and striking." And so to bed.

DECEMBER 19, 1994

EDWARD LEAR

On the evening of January 2, 1865, Edward Lear was escorted home by a couple of new acquaintances. "Nothing could exceed the genteel & intelligent expression of their countenances, except the urbanity of their deportment and the melancholy and oblivious sweetness of their voices," he wrote in a letter. They sound delightful, and it comes as no surprise to learn that the relationship did not end there: the well-bred pair dropped by to see him some days later, bringing with them their two eldest children, whom Lear put into the washbasin. Harsh treatment, you might think, although it's worth bearing in mind that the friends in question were, in fact, frogs. "They informed me," he wrote, "that they were the parents of nine and forty tadpoles of various ages and talents some of whom were expecting shortly to emigrate to Malvern and Mesopotamia."

The more we learn about Edward Lear, the less alarmed we should be by such unorthodox virtues as politeness in the presence of pond life. The barely schooled child became a full-time wanderer, perpetually unsatisfied, and, later, an elderly expert on disappointment. Poet, painter, friend of Tennyson; cat companion, composer, clergy-mocking liberal; longtime lover of Greece but not, it seems, of anyone else; purveyor of majestic canvases to the aristocracy and of utter nonsense to generations of children; epileptic, myopic, bronchitic, nostalgic Lear, born in 1812 and dying in 1888: how graciously he rises to greet us as the complete Victorian. This is not, one hastens to add, because he fulfilled all the era's aspirations but precisely because he left half of them unfulfilled, under the gentle pressure of doubt, the great counterenergy of the time. "Is there not a brutal balance to all satisfactions?" he once asked, already knowing the answer.

Something strange has happened to Lear's reputation in recent years: strands of it have split off and peeled away from the rest. Most people, if they know anything about him at all, think of Lear as the man who wrote

"The Owl and the Pussy-Cat" and scores of limericks—none of which are remotely dirty or, indeed, very funny, although they have a habit of getting their claws into your memory and never shaking free. In this view of things, Lear remains a crowd pleaser, and the crowd is composed almost entirely of children. I happen to agree with this view—or, at least, I reckon that it remains the best point from which to start your travels into the world of Lear, even if it eventually leads you into sobering and unquestionably adult terrain.

It is now considered rather simpleminded, however, to admire Lear the children's writer, for Lear the artist is riding high. These days, his oils and watercolors fetch alarming prices at auction, and Lear experts have followed the fashion. His formidable skills were self-taught: his professional training was limited to an abortive patch in 1850 at the Royal Academy, during which he supported himself on a five-hundred-pound bequest from a family friend. That was his only private income; in order to survive, a Victorian painter needed wealthy patrons. In his late teens, Lear was introduced to Lord Egremont, the admirer of Turner. To Lear he was less encouraging—"But where is all this going to lead to, Mr. Lear?" he inquired, and it remains a good question. Yet one lord led to another, as lords do, and in 1846 Lear dedicated his *Illustrated Excursions in Italy* to Lord Derby. When Queen Victoria saw the work, she requested a dozen drawing lessons from the author, and appeared both to enjoy his company and to copy his draftsman's style. Lear, in turn, was amazed by some of the Queen's treasures. "I say, where did you get these?" he asked her. "I inherited them, Mr. Lear," she replied. Although Lear knew plenty of posh people, he was seldom locked into their circle; they, in turn, were amused by his unwillingness to be poshed up, so to speak, by their example. You could hardly call him a social climber—nobody who could drop off the ladder and go to ground, as Lear did so readily, could be accused of self-advancement. His career followed not so much a trajectory as an itinerary; he rambled from one friend to the next, from Greece to Asia Minor, from painting to verse and back again.

In his new book, *Edward Lear: A Biography*, Peter Levi declares his priorities at the start: "Lear was professionally and, I think, essentially a painter." Ah yes, the essence: the grail of modern biography, a secret vial that, once uncorked and sniffed, will release the true nature of the subject. But with Lear, as with any great Victorian, we need to think in terms not of essence but of expanse. In his lifetime, he published five books of nonsense, seven of travel, and three of natural history. In all he did, it is true, there is a kind of sigh: a comic, domesticated version of the "melancholy, long, withdrawing roar" that the more high-minded Matthew Arnold heard on Dover Beach. But Lear did so much; he covered such a range of tones. For every murmur of Arnold, there is an alliterative glee that smacks of Gilbert & Sullivan. Wherever you look, in the poems and the letters, in the watercolors and the cartoons, you catch a familiar downcast wit—that truest form of wit, which, by an unfakable reflex of the imagination, sees the other side of everything. Not just the funny side: there can be something witty in the well-timed glance at mortality. "I can't decide in my mind," Lear wrote in Cannes in 1868, "if it is wiser to wait death in one spot, making the spot as pleasant as may be, and varying its monotony by such pleasant gleams of older life as can be obtained, or—to hurry on through constantly new and burningly bright scenes, and then dying all improviso as may happen." The indecision kept him on his toes; it was, you might say, a practical species of wit that led Lear to set off over the horizon with such regular obsessiveness. A simple chronology of his life is hectic with visits to Rome, Calabria, Corsica, Sicily, Sinai, Suez, Albania, Malta, Corfu, Crete, India, and Ceylon. He finally built a house in San Remo, and died there, with what he called "the pulled blue of the sea breaking beyond."

Peter Levi's book is only the latest attempt to sort through the strange case of Edward Lear. Levi should be the ideal sleuth: he is a classicist and a poet, he has travelled as widely as his subject did, and his former incarnations include Jesuit priest and Professor of Poetry at Oxford. All of which make it rather a pity that this new book proceeds in such an eager, ramshackle style—somewhere between a prance and a ramble, descending at times into a parody of dotty donnishness. In discussing the illustrated alphabets that Lear produced for children, Levi writes, "I have the impression that I have not described all the alphabets I ever saw. I do not think I ever saw Gertrude Lushington's (c. 1860) mounted in a rag-book, though it is at Harvard, but I do recollect one published by Rota in 1968 which I have lost or given away." You could argue, of course, that this hither-and-thither prose ("His Arabic, like mine, is far from perfect," he remarks of Lear in passing) has a fitting charm; that Lear, with his connoisseur's palate for oddity, would have appreciated the shameless way in which Levi arrives at afterthoughts without appearing to go via thoughts. But Lear courted surprise, and he knew early that vagueness is the enemy of nonsense; his lyrics and limericks obey rules—laws of unnature, as it were—that he alone seems to understand, but they are rules nonetheless. "It is a sine qua non in writing for children to keep what they have to read perfectly clear & bright, & incapable of any meaning but one of sheer nonsense," he wrote.

Levi's book is bright enough, but far from clear. He trips from fact to supposition without any principle to guide him, and there are moments when his prodigious knowledge sours into a kind of historical knowingness, a presumption that one can be chummy with the not so recent past. From there, it is only a short step to real blunders of taste: "Lady Waldegrave now had almost everything that as a Jewish musician's daughter she can ever have wanted," he writes, referring to the new wife of one of Lear's friends. You may have thought that such clubbable snobbery had vanished from English prose, and it is a nasty shock to find it still smirking in the corner. The shock is heightened by our certainty that Lear himself would never have conceived of a friend (Lady Waldegrave commissioned seven paintings from him) in such a way. He was never a snob or an anti-Semite or a xenophobe, and, although he journeyed to various extremes of empire, and stayed with high-ranking acquaintances, he made a hopeless imperialist. If there was anybody he looked down on, it was himself: "A dirty landscape-painter who hated his nose," as Auden put it in his poem "Edward Lear." (Of all later poets, it is Auden who most resembles Lear; thrown together on a distant shore, these two masters of the avuncular-sinister would have had a high old time.) The briefest immersion in Lear's verse and correspondence, or in the basic data of his life, is enough to convince you that he was far too deeply soaked in melancholy, in the sorrows that fate rained down upon him through the years, to dream of making things wretched for anyone else:

How pleasant to know Mr. Lear!
  Who has written such volumes of stuff!
Some think him ill-tempered and queer,
  But a few think him pleasant enough.

His mind is concrete and fastidious,
  His nose is remarkably big;
His visage is more or less hideous,
  His beard it resembles a wig.

He has ears, and two eyes, and ten fingers,
  Leastways if you reckon two thumbs,
Long ago he was one of the singers,
  But now he is one of the dumbs.

This is the opening of his poem "How Pleasant to Know Mr. Lear." Somewhere between memoir and apologia, it is a pitiless look in a mirror: it skirts both pride and self-pity to arrive at a form of comical auto-elegy whose honesty—whose simple accuracy—has rarely been equalled. It is the greatest poem of its kind since Swift's "Verses on the Death of Dr. Swift," and it convinces you, without stridency or strong-arming, that its title is perfectly true. It *would* have been pleasant to know him.

If you want to see Lear steadily and see him whole, your best plan is to leapfrog over Levi and turn to *Edward Lear: The Life of a Wanderer*, by Vivien Noakes, which was first published in 1968. Mrs. Noakes is the First Lady of Lear studies; in addition to the biography, still unsurpassed, she has edited a selection of the letters, has argued the case for the art in *The Painter Edward Lear* (1991), and contributed a meticulous text to the catalogue of a Lear exhibition at the Royal Academy in 1985. Wherever you turn in Lear land, she is there to guide you and offer Virgilian advice; she is as indispensable to devotees of Lear as Richard Ellmann was, and still is, to devotees of Joyce. Next to the preciousness of Levi's book, *Edward Lear: The Life of a Wanderer* feels calmer and more unassuming than ever. It amasses the evidence, probes a few sore secrets, and weighs the probabilities; the result is one of the saddest books I have ever read—no surprise, really, for the life it reveals is so swollen with sadness that it almost makes you laugh. That is how Lear survived it, I guess.

Edward Lear was the twentieth of twenty-one children. Two siblings were stillborn, five others died young; three of Lear's sisters were christened Sarah, his parents persevering until a Sarah survived. Whether the shadow of infant mortality stiffened the stoicism of Victorian families or weakened their will is impossible to know; can grief be common currency without becoming debased? Lear, for one, never staled in his response to human fragility. His upbringing was entrusted to a beloved sister, Ann, twenty-one years his senior; when she died, in 1861, he wrote in a letter, "I am all at sea:—and do not know my way an hour ahead." Like Dickens (a rival addict of the grotesque, also born in 1812), Lear had a father of unstable fortune; Levi says that the senior Lear went to a debtors' prison. The young Edward suffered bad health and worse eyesight; he devised names for the conditions that began to plague him. There were "the Morbids" or "morbidnesses," pits of depression, and then there was "the demon," his epilepsy, which began when he was five or six; Levi reports that the attacks came "up to ten or fifteen times a month, sometimes several times a day." (They are marked in Lear's journal by small crosses, like intimations of mortality.) From what is termed the aura epileptica, he could tell when they were coming, and would take appropriate action; for his entire life, Edward Lear—a sociable and popular man—continually melted away from company so as not to embarrass other people with his fits. The Dong with a luminous Nose, the Pobble who has no toes: he created a bestiary of misfits who would share his self-enforced solitude. No one outside his immediate family knew of Lear's affliction, which thus became encrusted with social anxiety and erotic dread.

Vivien Noakes politely suggests that he felt a sexual longing for a man named Franklin Lushington, with whom he toured Greece in 1849; they decorated their hats, coats, and horses with spring flowers as they went. But longing never bloomed: in Lear's mind, and in his awkward body, desires were something to be buried deep, stuffed down until they became a tangle of roots. At one point, he thought of proposing to a close friend named Gussie Bethell, but the demon drove him back. Noakes's plain account of the situation makes you weep: "She might refuse him which would be distressing, or accept him which could be worse, for he would have to tell her about his epilepsy—and then she might change her mind." And so, being Lear, he fled:

Down the slippery slopes of Myrtle,
Where the early pumpkins blow,
To the calm and silent sea
Fled the Yonghy-Bonghy-Bò.

It is tempting, of course, to peel away the humor and uncover the sexual confusion that writhes beneath it; a Freudian reader, having feasted on *Alice in Wonderland* to his heart's content (the rabbit hole, the prim young lady holding a flamingo), can turn with glee to the outsized appendages that litter the pages of another repressive. How pleasant to solve Mr. Lear! It takes no stretch of the imagination to decide that the Dong with the luminous Nose was dreamed up by a lonely bachelor with a nose for luminous dongs.

But Lear's own imagination did stretch, far beyond the mere displacement of lust, and we should try to go the distance with him. From our earliest encounters with his work, we sense something amiss, a certain squeezing and wringing of the spirit. Readers fresh to Lear—children, say, or parents reading to children—may pause for thought even at the most innocuous moments:

O was an oyster
Who lived in his shell
If you let him alone
He felt perfectly well.

This chant is so quick and slight that it's easy to miss the emotion that leaks between the lines. Who but Lear would have considered an oyster not as a food, an aphrodisiac, or a gritty producer of pearls but as the epitome of independence? His writings are ruffled by a continual suspicion that it would be interesting to be other than you are; that the life assigned to your present species is so intrinsically discomforting that, rather than try to improve it by human means, you would do better to slip into the skin and soul of another creature altogether. Here is Lear on the inhabitants of the moon:

> From the tip of their nose depends an elegant and affecting bunch of hair, sometimes extending to as much as 20 miles in length, & as it is considered sacrilegious to cut it, it is gradually wound round a silvergilt post firmly placed in the ground, but removable at a pleasure. . . . These remarkable people, so unlike ourselves, pass 18 months of their year (which consists of 22,) in the strictest seclusion,—suspended with their heads downwards, and held carefully in crimson silk bags,—which are severely suddenly shaken from time to time by select servants. Thus,—exempt from the futile fluctuating fatuity of fashion, these estimable creatures pass an indigenous life of indefinite duration surrounded by their admiring ancestors, & despised by their incipient posterity.

The tone is one of firsthand observation—pornographically precise, and undeniably covetous. Lear is not alone in his yearning. *Old Possum's Book of Practical Cats*, for all its charm, seems to me suffused with something close to genuine envy: "Macavity's not there," Eliot says, with the smiling desperation of a man who has had to spend his time *right here*. And you often feel that James Thurber would have enjoyed existence more as an adored dog than as a bewildered human being.

Like Thurber, Lear was doubly gifted, or cursed: he could both write down and draw the particulars of transformation. He had a monkish genius for marginalia, and, to the delight of his correspondents, he used to illustrate his own letters, often with self-portraits. The Lear whom we see there cuts an absurdly vulnerable figure: a bearded puffball, the shape of a sparrow in winter, graced with a putto's wings or tottering on twig legs, spectacles jumping with shock from his nose. In one instance, his tailcoat looks exactly like the hard shell of a bug; it would have stopped Kafka in his tracks. These, like the illustrations that enliven the limericks, are still the images by which he is best known, if no longer those for which he is most honored. The main thrust of recent Lear studies has been to turn our attention to the serious—or, at any rate, professional—art. Most of it was scenic; Lear ("the globular foolish Topographer" is how he once signed a letter) sketched incessantly on his travels through southern

Europe, the Middle East, and India, and there is a fine air of restraint, of beauty reached for but not quite remembered, in his pencil-and-wash landscapes. Even those which have been completed look unfinished, and that dashed-off quality appeals to modern tastes. What people see in his glossy, over-finished oils (some of them close to the thundering vistas of John Martin) I have never really grasped.

If I could own a single item of Lear's art, it would be an early drawing of a parrot—Lear used to visit the Zoological Society Gardens, and his first publication was *Illustrations of the Family of Psittacidæ, or Parrots*—that appears on a page of his sketchbook. An exquisitely rendered bird stares down at an unexpected visitor: a short, round, roughly drawn man with hands in pockets, who seems to have wandered in from a different picture, or from another world. It is Lear, staring back at the parrot. He directs his formidable skills to recording nature as it truly is, but, damn it all, something silly—nature as it shouldn't be, if it would only behave itself properly—keeps creeping in. Lear is a helpless victim of the aura fantastica. Who else (apart from Dickens, perhaps) could listen to the clacking bills of storks and fancy that he heard the sound of backgammon?

It is when I come across a detail like that—a brief, half-hallucinated flare of perceptions striking against one another—that I feel most at odds with Peter Levi's opening argument. Lear is *not* essentially a painter. His delicate draftsmanship answers to Victorian visual tastes, and refines them; but it lacks the vigorous complication of his nonsense writing, which challenges those tastes as much as it delights them, pulling them into squalls and doldrums of feeling where they would otherwise never go. The passage about life on the moon comes from a letter of 1882, written not to a child but to the Honorable Mrs. James Stuart-Wortley, who sounds about as respectable as it is possible to be, and who, indeed, was married to Palmerston's solicitor general; Lear flatters her by assuming that, far below the surface of her manners, she can still respond as a child, that for a few private minutes she can unlearn the lessons of her age. In the boldness of that assumption we glimpse an abiding truth: without Victorian nonsense, we cannot hope to understand Victorian sense—not just good sense or common sense but the mechanisms by which writers and travellers tried to make sense of the world, and the variety of prejudices that they disclosed in the attempt. *Through the Looking-Glass* is an outrageous companion piece to *The Voyage of the Beagle:* both books are egged on by the conviction that wonder is all very well but brisk inquisition is better. If Carroll takes a stand in the face of illogicality, Lear takes wing; he flies in the shadow of his old friend Tennyson. "I am aweary, aweary, / I would that I were dead," says Tennyson's Mariana, a refrain that filters through to Lear's Yonghy-Bonghy-Bò ("I'm a-weary of my life") and to the unbearable straightforwardness of an early limerick:

> There was an Old Man of Cape Horn,
> Who wished he had never been born;
> So he sat on a chair, till he died of despair,
> That dolorous Man of Cape Horn.

Lear set Tennyson's verse to music, and was commissioned to paint scenes from the poems, but what links the two men unbreakably is the *sound* of their common regret—the long, moaning vowels both of the Lotos-Eaters, who came to a land where it seemed always afternoon, and of the Jumblies, who went to sea in a sieve. Tennyson draws out the solemn euphony in Lear, and Lear, in turn, reminds us just how daringly the Laureate himself brushed against nonsense. "I really do believe that I enjoy hardly any one thing on earth while it is present: always looking back, or frettingly peering into the dim beyond." That is Lear talking, but it could equally be Tennyson, or the idyll of a dying king.

How angry was Edward Lear? Did he sometimes wish that, like Alice, he could grab hold of the starchy tablecloth and pull? I sense an immaculate balance in him: the horror of being abandoned with his single self versus a fear of losing it in the bustle of society. Like another dolorous man of the time, Edward FitzGerald, Lear was a loner who specialized in friends. After a trip to Mt. Athos, he expressed hearty disapproval of the "muttering, miserable, muttonhating, manavoiding, misogynic, morose, & merriment-marring, monotoning, many-Mule-making, mocking, mournful, minced-fish & marmalade masticating Monx." It's an endearing broadside; even his contempt is ringed with jollity, perhaps because he was scaring away the forces of misery and marring that prowled about his own life. He once wrote a story entitled "The History of the Seven Families of the Lake Pipple-popple," in which the heroes—a frog, a flea, and so on—return home "full of joy and respect, sympathy, satisfaction, and disgust." That was the brew, I suspect, that brimmed Lear's own heart; the disgust never drained away, but he was too shy to do much about it. In his whimsical fractures of social convention we see just how rigorous that convention must have been, how efficiently it could take the whimsy in its stride and leave it behind:

> There was an Old Man of Whitehaven,
> Who danced a quadrille with a Raven;

But they said—"It's absurd, to encourage this bird!"
So they smashed that Old Man of Whitehaven.

The violence of the final line brings you up short; the old man is treated like a piece of glass, as if people had seen through his motives and judged him guilty. (The bird, presumably, was an innocent, lured into his dance like a child.) Who are "they," though? "But they said" and "When they said": in these brief, recurrent phrases you hear the moral leitmotiv of the limericks. It is the ruthless, anonymous voice of public opinion, suspicious of novelty, reluctant to allow these bulbous, elastic eccentrics the one thing that they ask for, which is the privilege of being alone.

By the end, Lear enjoyed the privilege all too well. He died in San Remo in January of 1888, cared for by an Italian servant; only two English friends made it to the funeral. Foss, his companionable cat, had died two months earlier, so Lear had little to live for. He was smashed beyond repair. Peter Levi quotes the final diary entry: "A beefsteak mascherato. Good in its way but nasty more. I should try to get some sleep if possible, but I have no light or life left in me. And the flies are as horrible as ever." There was never a time when Lear was not bothered; he was granted the gift of making other people happy, both in person and in the buoyancy of his work, but was denied the chance to be happy himself. It is the lousiest of deals, and countless writers have signed up for it; all we can do to palliate their pain is to keep reading. Edward Lear, by his own admission, was one of the dumbs, and his biographers make it clear that he was the leading light of the sads. But now he is one of the singers again, and his voice grows stronger all the time.

MAY 29, 1995

BEST-SELLERS II

It is the summer of 1945. You are a young GI, though not as young as you were. You landed at Omaha Beach, perhaps, or came ashore at Anzio, and you have grown old pretty fast. The war has died in Europe, but it still has a few weeks to live in the East. You took a bullet in the final month, and now you find yourself lying in a hospital with a hole in your right thigh and time on your hands. You used to read everything: classics, trash, the latest thing. What would the latest look like now, after six years of the world on fire? Something covered with scorch marks, for sure: something hard. So it's a big deal when a package comes from your sister in New York. It took weeks to arrive. "I enclose a novel you might enjoy," she writes. "Everybody here is just crazy about it." Here it is, the latest thing, right here in your hands. And just look at that title: *A Lion Is in the Streets*. You can smell the cordite already. You open it at random: "Somewhere the evening damp was pulling perfume from out the jasmine and spreading it like a tangible thing."

Huh?

The *Times* best-seller list for July 1, 1945, is strong stuff. It could take on any current list and knock it cold. Running your eye down the twenty most popular novels of the day, you won't find many bantamweights; we're talking big hitters here—names like Steinbeck, Sinclair, Irving Stone, and A. J. Cronin. Men who don't consider a novel to be a novel unless you can use it to brain a horse. What ever happened to the wartime paper shortage? On the home front, if you looked up and saw the Germans coming across the Hudson you could hold up your copy of Lloyd C. Douglas's *The Robe*, eleventh on the list, and be sure of fending off small-arms fire. As for Ayn Rand's *The Fountainhead*, 754 pages of pure beef, it could stop a tank. From what I gather, Ayn Rand could stop a tank.

It's a far cry from today's best-seller list. Today's list is for wimps. We like reedy novellas, quick-solve murder stories, distillations of wisdom. At the moment, there are even a couple of good books—Anne Tyler, Jane Smiley. What the hell are they doing there? Good was not an issue for the readers of 1945. Good was bad news. What people needed was *long*. John Grisham and Robert Ludlum might have passed muster, but no one else. What people didn't need was a sense of humor. In the top ten books I found not a single joke; wartime fiction lived under a frivolity curfew, a gag blackout. There was also an easygoing acceptance of euphemism. Whenever sex reared its head, it had to keep its hat on. The strict erogenous-zoning laws of the time meant that physical response had to occur at least two limbs away from the intended center of operations, as in this sentence from *A Lion Is in the Streets:* "His finger moved faster, faster, back and forth in a small flipping motion on her ear lobe." But another, larger form of euphemism prevailed in these books. Only four of them took war for their subject, but most of them took it upon themselves to offer the kind of spiritual encouragement that war demands. This was laudable, but the poor authors kept tripping over their feet as they lunged at the telling detail. During a chase sequence set in sixteenth-century Spain, say, we suddenly find the word "jackboots." Aha! The Nazi Inquisition!

With news of the war filling your head every day, I guess it was tricky not to let your pen slip into topicality. Edmund Wilson saw it happening all around, and expounded his dejection to readers of this magazine in the March 3, 1945, issue. Reviewing a book by Glenway Wescott, he wrote, "In general, it has been disappointing to find so many writers of serious talent turning away from the study of behavior to reassure themselves and their readers with some immediate political program or some resuscitated religious system. . . . The result of this tendency is simply to land the writer in melodrama." In the case of unserious talent, of course, the loss was less grievous; most of the best-selling authors were up to their necks in melodrama to begin with. But the advent of war seems to have loaded them with a sense of responsibility, which is the last thing that melodrama needs. Hadn't these writers seen *Sullivan's Travels*? Didn't they realize that people require *more* fun, not less, when times are tough? Many of the books on the list are stirring and righteous, but only a couple actually bother to entertain.

One of them is at No. 10: *Forever Amber*, by Kathleen Winsor. People still know the title—a real hummer, giving off the permanent, enviable resonance of the truly meaningless—but they don't have a clue about the book. Only the very *best* best-sellers enjoy this special, two-tone gift: the ability both to entrance a generation and to be almost completely overlooked by the succeeding ones. A librarian of today, coming across *Forever Amber* in the fiction section, might assume that it was all about traffic lights and reshelve it under Urban Planning, next to *Gridlock: The Facts.*

It is, in fact, all about Restoration England. How do we know this? Because our heroine, Amber St. Clare, was born in 1644; because she grows up to become the mistress of Charles II; because people keep saying things like "Odsfish!" and "flopdoodles" to her; and because at one point we find her "sitting in a chair reading Dryden's new play." Apart from that, however, we could be witnessing any era in English history—or indeed, any middle-period episode of *Falcon Crest.* Among Amber's favorite boys of the bedchamber are Rex Morgan, Luke Channell, and—her all-time top toff—Bruce Carlton. The novel swaggers along in the confidence of its own high spirits; it is the purest known form of Romantic Fiction, which means it was read with a flashlight under the bedclothes by millions of teenage girls, who then spent the rest of their lives wondering why nothing under the bedclothes ever came close to Bruce Carlton.

The higher Amber scrabbles up the social mountain, the more lustrous the inhabitants she finds. By the time she reaches royalty, both she and her creator are pretty well falling to their knees, which, not to be indelicate about it, is just where the King likes them. Winston Churchill was said to be the last person in the Western world who believed in the divine right of kings, but I think he would have met his match in the very British author of *Forever Amber.* It could be because her own name misses sovereign status by a whisker, but, whenever Charles rolls up, Miss Winsor falls into one of her fits, raving over "his swarthy good-looks, the powerful grace of his body, the deep smooth gentle tones of his voice." Mind you, here is a writer whose dialogue includes those well-known seventeenth-century phrases "Thanks a million" and "Hey, just a minute!," so authenticity may not have been her driving motive. I was touched by the closing pages, in which Amber takes ship for Virginia: "In another hour she would be gone from England—gone from Whitehall and its plots and schemes forever." The real schemer here is Kathleen Winsor, of course, who winks knowingly at her American readers. Courtly old England was a scream, but for real liberty—if you're trying to win a world war, for instance—you need the New World.

And so to No. 9. I have a problem with No. 9. I cannot read it. God knows, I have tried. I have downed three straight whiskeys and then tried to read it. I have leapt clean and sober from a cold shower, grabbed the book, and, standing upright, started to read it out loud. But the same thing always happened: I buckled like a puppet and fell asleep. No matter where I looked, I kept hitting characters saying things like this: "I don't see why our Liberal politicians should make such an effort to avoid reminding the people of Quebec that they *are* a part of an organization which, whatever its faults, is still the only concrete example of the kind of international federation which we want to see existing all over the world." Hear that language sing, my people! Can't you just *taste* it—the raw tongue of Canada, lashing the art of fiction into a fresh new lather?

This tale of the north is called *Earth and High Heaven.* It was written, if "written" is the word, by Gwethalyn Graham. I admit, in retrospect, that I should have seen trouble coming. There's a P. G. Wodehouse story in which Bertie Wooster falls for a girl named Gwladys. His Aunt Dahlia is appalled. "No good can come of association with anything labelled Gwladys or Ysobel or Ethyl or Mabelle or Kathryn," she says. "But particularly Gwladys." I would second that, adding only that a novelist called Gwethalyn somehow constitutes the worst menace of all.

The place is Montreal. The date is June 1942. The woman is Erica Drake, who comes from wealthy Protestant stock. The man is Marc Reiser—Jewish, reflective, and, as if to compensate for all the cads around him, equipped with what seems to me a ridiculous quantity of compassion. ("Marc had got up to feed the undernourished pigeon.") The first time Erica sees him, she knows that he is the one. You can tell this from the sudden, mad zing in the prose: "Another thing that was interesting about him was the structure of his face." How can she resist it?

She can't. Unfortunately, her parents can. Charles Drake, her father, is revealed in all the polite, poisonous anti-Semitism of his age and class. The young lovers struggle against this prejudice for the better part of three hundred pages before finally breaking free; needless to say, they carry the author's best wishes with them at all times. You cannot fault the ethics of this book. It was published in 1944; the camps had not yet been liberated, but American readers were under no illusions about the attempt to obliterate the Jewish people in Europe, and any reminder of the tribulations undergone by Jews in the free world served a useful and chastening purpose. But the best intentions have a nasty habit of breeding the worst art, and *Earth and High Heaven* is so inept that it actually ends up corrupting its own sincerity. Some may find its clumsiness rather calming; however dire the conflicts that rage around the world, crummy books never change. While everyone else was doing their best to win a war, Gwethalyn was blithely doing her worst, by writing prose. I suspect she had some awful inkling that, what with all her social duties to the reader, she was neglecting her obligations as a novelist. Hence those delightful moments when the polemic stops and a tiny, hopeless scrap of stage business starts up, does its stuff, and dies. Here is Marc in full flow: "Even when people don't dislike you, even when they really like you, you still make them feel slightly self-conscious, I don't know why. Maybe it's just because they've been brought up to regard Jews as 'different.' Do you want a biscuit?"

On to No. 8: *Dragon Harvest*, by Upton Sinclair. This is the only one of the top ten books that tries to be up to the minute. The action gets going in the South of France in 1939, and runs out of steam just as Paris is falling to the Germans. And, wherever the action is, there is Lanny Budd. Lanny is all things to all men. To some he is a playboy and an art dealer, son of the beautiful Beauty Budd; to others he is a sympathetic ear, listening gently as his good friends Hitler and Chamberlain explain why they must or must not go to war; to a select few he is a secret agent, dispatched by America to bring her the truth. His good friend FDR is fervently pro-Lanny: "A man who knows Europe as you do, and yet keeps the democratic point of view, is truly useful to me," he says. If anything, the president is a little jealous: " 'Lanny,' he remarked, 'you must get a great kick out of your job, associating exclusively with the world's headliners. How on earth do you manage it?' "

I'll tell you how he manages it, Mr. President. He manages it by being a complete jerk. Right from the second page, when I learned that Lanny "permitted himself no vices," I knew I was going to loathe this man. O.K., he saves the world and all, but anything less than universal justice is beneath him; you wouldn't trust him to feed your cat over the weekend. Also, does he *have* to schmooze Adolf and the rest of the boys with quite such gusto? Lanny's pretense of enthusiasm is so thorough that even the author seems to be taken in. Here is Upton Sinclair, standard-bearer of anti-fascism, on the charms of *der Führer:* "To be near him was like living in the midst of a tornado, like being in a Vulcan forge where new universes were being wrought."

It's the old Miltonic story: when your hero is a wimp, the villain steals the scene. This is bad luck for Sinclair, because the only justification for *Dragon Harvest* is to dramatize Allied propaganda. The book is barely held together over seven hundred pages by a framework of spindly clichés. The myth of the gentleman spy, for instance, died peacefully after Buchan and Somerset Maugham, and with it went the dream that the world was anyone's oyster. If you were forced to live under fascism, the world was your rotting fish head, and you picked off what sustenance you could find. And if you were fighting fascism you weren't going to draw much comfort from a creep named Budd as he swanned through high society and claimed that it was work.

At No. 7 we find *The Fountainhead*, by Ayn Rand. Many people will remember this story, for in 1949 it was made into a movie, starring Gary Cooper. It was a very strange movie indeed, but it was nothing compared to the book. The book is nuts.

As the plot begins, we encounter our hero, Howard Roark, who wants to be an architect. To be precise, he wants to be a universal life force who happens to specialize in architecture. Just look at his student drawings: "The buildings were not Classical, they were not Gothic, they were not Renaissance. They were only Howard Roark." Odsfish! True to his leonine name, Roark considers himself king of his profession even before he has joined it, and fate bears him out. His gas station is like no other gas station, and his Temple of the Human Spirit is, in the words of one opponent, "an insolent 'No' flung in the face of history." Roark waits for commissions from the few who understand him, while all around him the rest of mankind—the compromisers, the journalists, the second-rate—hustles and lies its way into mediocrity.

I have a terrible feeling that Ayn Rand believed everything she wrote. When her prose swoons over hunky Howard, over "the strange, untouchable healthiness of his body," I see her crouched feverishly at her desk, dabbing her temples at the thought of her gorgeous creation. She even gives herself a mouthpiece: Dominique Francon, the ice-cold daughter of a rival architect. Dominique is raped by Roark and loves him forever. ("That was the degradation she had wanted and she hated him for it.") If it weren't such nonsense, this masochistic kitsch would be offensive, but it *is* nonsense—the Higher Nonsense, a sort of visceral naïveté that can be maintained only through an utter lack of shame. It is distantly related to D. H. Lawrence—Roark rolls around on the good earth like Birkin in *Women in Love*—and, further back, to the high-springing, athletic declamations of Whitman. Now, of course, it sounds richly ridiculous, and I am amazed that readers were prepared to tolerate it in 1945; maybe the Good War marked the last time in which irony could not prevail—in which a common effort of society, bracing itself against a readily identified evil, gave people an unembarrassed taste for abstractions, for talk of integrity and terror. When Rand writes of one character that "the oval of his chest and stomach sallied forth, flying the colors of his inner soul," what she means is "He was fat." But that would never do.

Reading *The Fountainhead* after *Dragon Harvest* put a fresh slant on Rand's achievement. What may have come across in wartime as single-minded striving now reads like a crash course in the Will to Power, and Roark, for all his steely modernist intentions, reminded me less of Mies van der Rohe than of Albert Speer—or, indeed, of the volcanic Führer who erupts into the imagination of Upton Sinclair. The more Rand insists that her hero is not like other men, that he barely notices them, the less suitable he appears as a role model for Roosevelt's America. It is only the fact of his "preposterous orange hair" that disqualifies him from becoming the perfect Aryan. "The world is perishing from an orgy of self-sacrificing," he announces at the end, having dynamited one of his own constructions. If the book were any better, he might have been genuinely disturbing; as it is, he dwindles into something of a lonely dickhead. Poor old Howard: an *Übermensch* adrift in an *Unterbuch*.

Howard Roark may be a pain in the buttress, but his loony ambitions force you to keep reading, whereas Janie Driscoll Cauder merely gets on your nerves. She is the heroine of the sixth book on the list, Taylor Caldwell's *The Wide House*, and she's as mad as hell: a bony Scottish widow, newly arrived on the shores of America in 1850. She has four loathsome children and a cousin named Stuart Coleman, who, like most of the men in this novel, greets any tense situation with a manly, Errol Flynn laugh. ("He bent double, almost collapsing in his mirth.") Janie and Stuart have got a standard-issue love-hate thing going. It never really boils over, thanks to the smothering effect of the surrounding prose: "They wallowed in their emotionalism." Hippo talk. Like Kathleen Winsor, Caldwell is never happier than when wallowing around in adjectival ooze. The town of Grandeville, New York, is described in one passage as raw, overgrown, boisterous, vital, and bustling, and in another as raw, uncouth, bustling, and riotous. Fair enough, except that the two descriptions are only twelve lines apart.

The only point of interest in *The Wide House* lies in the anti-German sentiments that Caldwell tries to sneak into the action. We have to sit through endless accounts of the Schnitzel family—hardworking German immigrants who have made good. There is Herr Schnitzel ("slaughterhouse owner . . . rumbling and snarling . . . enormously bloated . . . cruel and suspicious"). And there is Frau Schnitzel ("sulky swinishness . . . bristling manner . . . brutish and merciless . . . arrogant and insensible"). All that comes from two short paragraphs. And it makes you wonder about those fifth-generation Germans, long since transformed into good American citizens, who had to read this stuff in 1945. Maybe they never saw a copy. Maybe they were too busy fighting the Germans.

And so to No. 5, *The Ballad and the Source*, by Rosamond Lehmann. During the eighties, her work was officially recruited into the feminist canon;

so what endeared her to the American public of the 1940s? Having finished the book, I am none the wiser. *The Ballad and the Source*, Lehmann's fourth novel, is English to a fault. The prose veers between jolly, down-to-earth larks and languid, up-in-the-clouds metaphysics, sometimes within the space of a single sentence: "A megalomaniac certitude coursed through me like draughts of ginger beer." That is the voice of the narrator, Rebecca Landon, who is ten years old at the time of the story and plainly needs to go to the ladies' room as soon as possible. At the start, she and her sister are introduced to Mrs. Jardine, a sweet old dear who slowly metamorphoses into a gorgon: someone who has blighted the lives of others and has suffered her own share of betrayal, and is basically a health hazard to any impressionable child. Yet the counsel that she offers is a hundred percent affirmative: "The source, Rebecca! The fount of life—the source, the quick spring that rises in illimitable depths of darkness and flows through every living thing from generation to generation. It is what we feel mounting in us when we say: 'I know! I love! I *am*!' Do you understand me now?"

Well, as a matter of fact, no, but I know a man who *would* understand. Mrs. Jardine? Meet Howard Roark.

That speech about the source can itself be traced back, I think, to the great exhortation—"Live all you can"—delivered by Lambert Strether at the climax of *The Ambassadors.* Rosamond Lehmann is steeped in Henry James. *The Ballad and the Source* is haunted by *The Turn of the Screw* and, more naggingly, by *What Maisie Knew.* The unspoiled Rebecca is all ears, but what pours into them is corroding her innocence like acid. There are brilliant moments here, fraught with the solemnity of the fanciful child: "I went downstairs with my heartache, and it was so horrible and so enormous, that it was like carrying a bag of stones tied on to the bones of my chest." None of the other writers in the Top Ten can claim Lehmann's learning or equal her intelligence. So why does this book leave one with an impression of profound silliness?

It is, in a way, a question of bad luck: the profundity itself has turned silly. Lehmann couldn't have guessed that the manner in which she buttonholes the reader, like that in which Mrs. Jardine lectures Rebecca, would fade irretrievably into a mannerism. You try to immerse yourself in the moral quandaries stirred up within the book, which are genuine and dense, but the perfume rising off the prose sends you reeling back: "Mademoiselle flutingly announced that it was time for us to make our adieux." Translation: "Time to say goodbye."

* * *

And hello to No. 4—*Immortal Wife*, by Irving Stone. Stone is the man who made a career of dramatizing the lives of the famous. *Lust for Life*—Vincent van Gogh (1934). *The Agony and the Ecstasy*—Michelangelo (1961). *Immortal Wife*—er, Jessie Benton Fremont. I can't help thinking that the readers of 1945 were getting the fuzzy end of the lollipop. Jessie's main achievement is to stand by her husband, John Charles Fremont, as he marches from one arduous adventure to the next: the young lieutenant in the Topographical Corps becomes the most intrepid traveller of his generation, is court-martialled in 1847, goes to California, wins a seat in the Senate, loses a presidential election, wins the love of his troops in the Civil War, loses his fortune, and so on. In between heroics, they just about find time for the old standby, aural sex: Jessie "took his finger and touched it lightly to the tiny circle of white lobe which she left exposed." Fremont enjoyed an absurdly full nineteenth-century existence—it must have felt like a three-volume novel even as he was living it—and Stone doesn't need to do much apart from marshalling the facts, which is pretty much what Jessie herself does, preparing the records of her husband's journeys for publication. She had many gifts, but what she was really good at was subediting.

In all honesty, Irving Stone could have used some help from his heroine. He's an old hand at what you might call the logistics of his trade, but these should not be confused with the activity known as writing. Right at the beginning, when Jessie first encounters John, there's a dark note of premonition: "She sensed that words were not the sole measure of communication, nor perhaps even the best." Stone should know. *Immortal Wife* seems even more sluggish now than it did in 1945; with the recent rise in the creative status of biography, the biographical novel has slumped out of fashion. It strikes us as a waste of good research for Stone to have dug up so many truths about the Fremonts and then crammed their mouths with such blatant invention. John, for example, has a shattering family secret, but I'm not sure that he unveils it with quite the right élan: "I live in terror . . . of the day when someone . . . will call me a . . . bastard!" Jessie consoles him, then marries him, whereupon he scoots off to the Wild West and doesn't come back for six months. Bastard.

Right, then—No. 3. No messing around now. *Commodore Hornblower*, by C. S. Forester. Sound fellow, Forester. Haven't read him since my school days, when we were lined up and told to read *The Gun*. All about, as far as I recall, a gun. Gripping read. This one equally gripping. Year: 1812. Plot: Commodore Sir Horatio Hornblower now has command of his own ship during war against France. Sails to Baltic: damn chilly up there, Russkies in the offing. Meets Clausewitz, teaches the egghead a thing or two. Showers naked in front of crew. Crew not sure where to look. Hornblower notices bald spot on head and, even more frightening, new level of wisdom in soul. No fog in the prose, though: clear view from start to finish. Plenty of technical lingo to make the reader feel briny and wide awake: "Twice the paul slipped over the ratchet as they hauled in on the spring and swung the ketch round." That sort of thing. Plain, solid English, not like the foreign muck: "He peered at the ragged sheets and found himself, as usual, thinking what a barbaric language German was." Just like the buggers that speak it, eh? Good, straightforward propaganda, Bonaparte barely disguised as Hitler: "No continental nation yet had successfully opposed Bonaparte, although every single one had felt the violence of his attack; only England still withstood him." And who will lead England? Hornblower. Toward the end, finds himself alone on unfamiliar vessel: same rocking motion as ship, different smell. Legs instead of keel. Horse, that's it. Rides into action. Good team effort from England, Russkies lend a hand, Hornblower gives captain's performance. Saves civilization. Again. That's the stuff to give the troops. End of story.

So grab a rope and swing over to No. 2, Samuel Shellabarger's *Captain from Castile*—a boring title for an overstretched melee of swordfights and colonial conquests, set in an age when every knight bore himself erect and every wench tucked a purse of dirty money into her garter. I ate it up. Six hundred and thirty-three pages of this sunburned trash? Pah! A mere scrap, *por Dios*. Had it been a thousand pages long—nay, ten thousand—I would have finished it off and asked for more.

Our hero is Pedro de Vargas, who has everything going for him: a cool cavalier dad; a sister called Mercedes; a crush on the luscious Luisa, who appears to have been ordered direct from the Courtly Love catalogue ("The arch of her eyebrows, the bow of her lips, her pearl-white complexion, were perfect"); and a no-strings nobility clause in his character ("He spoke and loved as a hidalgo should"). Then his world starts to crumble: his family is pulled in by the Inquisition, and Pedro has to flee the country. Cut to Mexico, where he hangs out with Cortés and has a small problem with the Aztecs: "Doom! Doom! Doom! Doom! pulsed the great drum of the War God."

All of which has nothing to do with literature—for once you can actually forget about the prose—and everything to do with movies. By the end of the Second World War, Hollywood had essentially commandeered the art of narrative. Most of the books on the *Times* list trespass on typical movie territory—warring families, new frontiers, bust-thrusting corsets.

But none of the books can match the grace and economy with which a studio picture could waltz through a daft story and almost keep a straight face. The wrist-cracking saga novel tends to plow on for seven hundred pages not because it needs the space in which to bloom and flourish but because sheer bulk is the nearest it can get to that infuriating ease with which even the dumbest movies seem to create and decorate a world. Most of the top ten books of 1945 are bulging with envy, but they're not envious of Tolstoy, they're envious of *Gone with the Wind*—and not of Margaret Mitchell, either, but of David O. Selznick. And the only book that has the guts to confess this is *Captain from Castile.* It openly mimics the manners of a plush film, being far too brazen for authenticity but not so reckless that it shrieks with caricature. I was unsurprised to learn that it quickly became a Tyrone Power picture. All of the villains here cry out to be played by George Sanders. One of them murmurs, mystified by Pedro's latest escape, "You can't conceal a sword in your breeches." Now *there's* a good title.

And so to the No. 1 best-seller of July 1, 1945, *A Lion Is in the Streets*, by someone named Adria Locke Langley. Dear me: "In Nature's own way, her inner being began its years of lying quiescent, encased—not sending out into the various spokes of her life that indefinable quality which makes for significant and meaningful living." Oh, *that* quality.

The spokeswoman in question is named Verity. I would love to report that she is a lying bitch, but, sadly, she spends almost five hundred pages living up to her name. She is married to Hank Martin, who goes from being coarse, horny white trash to being the coarse, horny governor of the Magnolia State. The plot is a backwoods version of *Mr. Smith Goes to Washington*—the little guy made big—but the rubbery emotions bouncing around here are unique to Ms. Langley; she makes Frank Capra look like Mad Max. The book is a hymn to the power of justice, pummelling your ear and your conscience with such humorless zeal that poor old justice falls by the wayside, leaving power to stride on alone. The one diverting aspect of Hank's political strategy is that you can't quite tell whether he's leading with his beliefs or with his pants. Right from the first pages, when he's still a poor peddler, hiking from door to door with "Sizzle, his special cooking fat," you know that this guy is *hot.* The newly ravished Verity recalls the sound of her mattress under pressure: "the many small cracklings of a while ago, cracklings that had grown rhythmical as if they were tapping a million drums—little, secret, earthy drums." Doom! Doom! Hank embarks on married life by running down his carnal menu: "Me, I like my kissin' with laughin' after lovin', 'r I like it with teasin' afore lovin', 'r I like it in earnest with lovin'." I reckon Hank Martin missed his vocation. Why go into government when you could be writing lyrics for Dolly Parton?

This sweaty allure, naturally, takes him deep into Gary Hart land. His maid, Selah, explains, "De womens jes' plumb git dat lolly-gag look." I have to say I was less perturbed by the candidate's libido than by his racial attitudes. "Aw, niggers has a stuck-uppityness a' their own," says Hank, but as soon as one of them stops being uppity and starts calling him Mister Hank our hero is won over: "Y'know, Verity, I like the sound of that. We're gonna hafta git us a nigger." You could argue that this is an accurate dramatization of a rusty worldview, were it not for the backup that Langley offers in her casual asides: "A wide toothy grin shone from the black face," and "Moses rolled his eyes." It is vastly depressing to find these minstrel cartoons being hawked around in the guise of civilized fiction. But there's a twist in the tale: even as Adria Locke Langley was infecting America with her garbled transcription of black speech ("I was gwine ast y'all wuz usn nevah gwine correck dis chile lak Mistuh Hank"), an antidote was being offered by another writer. There, at No. 2 on the nonfiction list for the same week, is Richard Wright's *Black Boy.* Langley *wants* her blacks to sound unintelligible, to be other; Wright asks only that they be the same as anyone else, and he furthers his case with the clean, perfectly lucid dignity of his dialogue. Language becomes—it has to become—as clear-cut as the rights that it is fighting to assert. By this standard, Langley is shirking her duty. "Hank took pride in never wasting time on non-essentials such as becoming the perfect grammarian," she writes. Try telling that to Richard Wright.

Time has done its work. *Black Boy* has become a classic, whereas the copy of *A Lion Is in the Streets* that I found in a New York library hadn't been taken out since 1948. Most of the Top Ten have gone under the sea; C. S. Forester still rules the waves, and rightly so, but the world is not a sadder place without the work of Gwethalyn Graham. So what else has survived from 1945? Well, that summer Robert Lowell published his magnificently coiled poem "The Quaker Graveyard at Nantucket"; meanwhile, over in France, Samuel Beckett, who had worked both for the French Resistance and for the Irish Red Cross, was finishing his second novel, *Watt.* Both men were operating, as George Orwell would say, inside the whale: they knew that the literature that endures pays no obvious heed to the conditions under which it was produced (although it would be foolish to claim that under different conditions it would have turned out the same). The great novels *about* the Second World War were years, if not decades, away: *The Naked and the Dead* would be published in 1948, *Gravity's Rainbow* in 1973. Evelyn Waugh's *Sword of Honour* trilogy was not completed until 1961. His contribution to the war effort had been *Brideshead Revisited*, a far lesser work, but one cunningly attuned to the time. He admitted later that it had been written "with a kind of gluttony . . . which now with a full stomach I find distasteful." It had, however, served its purpose—to cheer up the dismal British readers of 1944, short on food and fun. Did American readers, less heavily rationed, not crave the same luxuries? Did they really have an appetite for *The Wide House* and *Immortal Wife*? Was it their *duty* to buy them—a sort of mental combat training? I have read these books, and, believe me, I would have had a nicer time chewing through a log.

Back to our GI. I suppose he was shipped home, finally, with his leg still bandaged. He rested up, and read the other novels on the list; his sister bought them all, just for a treat. The lucky stiff. He put down *A Lion Is in the Streets*, had a smoke, and decided to stay in the Army. Books could go to hell.

JUNE 26, 1995

VLADIMIR NABOKOV

Isbas, snoopy, chromo, frass. Morphos and gibus, levigate and chitinous. Olivaster ambuscade, viatic vivarium. Elytra calling to cobold. My beloved axilla, my long-lost acreana . . . Oh, fatidic pellicles! Ocellated racemes! Chiromantically cacological, porphyroferous djoys!

If you are finding your verbal acquaintances a little tired and plain, if you wish to make new friends in the dictionary, then what you need is *The Stories of Vladimir Nabokov.* All the words cited above are to be found scurrying along in the underbrush of Nabokov's tales; most of them are rare, though that does not imply that they require rescuing from extinction. "Frass," for example, is rare only because most of us, in our confoundedly narrow existence, seldom come across what the *Concise Oxford Dictionary* defines variously as "a fine powdery refuse left by insects boring" and "the excrement of insect larvae," whereas Nabokov, onetime research fellow in entomology and all-around bug nut, presumably spent most of his life trying not to step in the frass. "Djoys" is another matter entirely: not a real word at all, to be exact, but the name of the author of *Ulysses* as pronounced by a Russian character and cunningly transcribed by Nabokov. Innumerable readers have delighted in Joyce, but leave it to Nabokov to sneak his delight into a new-minted version of the man's name. It is a trick that demands not just perfect verbal pitch (which Nabokov appears to have enjoyed from the cradle) but a wicked nerve: with one pun, he steps neatly into the noble line of Joyce's heirs.

Whether he belongs there remains an open question. This grand new volume, all 655 pages, should help us decide. The earliest story dates from 1921, when the émigré author was twenty-one years old and studying at Cambridge, and the latest from 1951, when he was teaching at Cornell and slaving over the hot *Lolita.* There are sixty-five stories, thirteen of which have never before appeared in book form; they offer a startling, cloudless view of a writer's development. Instead of an artist following the expected path—starting with a precocious roughness and slowly rising to the heights of power—we discover a young man who is not only gifted, and serenely confident in that gift, but more than able to hold his own against the sage celebrity that he finally became. The two men are in the same game. The tyro who wrote in his mid-twenties "He exhaled a megaphone of smoke" is already in the slipstream of the middle-aged Nabokov, the one who noted the "solemn somersaults" performed by dolphins in the wake of a ship and the disruption of any attempt to read a book on deck: "The inquisitive breeze would join in the reading and roughly finger the pages so as to discover what was going to happen next."

A similar eagerness urged me on through *The Stories of Vladimir Nabokov:* this book is a breeze. I kept wanting to press ahead, all the while wondering why this impulse should be so strong, since for much of the time not a lot actually happens. The intricate trouble that Nabokov takes with his plots is exceeded only by the energy that he devotes to submerging them beneath the undulations of his prose. It is quite possible to arrive at the conclusion of one of his narratives without knowing precisely what has been concluded. One of my favorites, "Spring in Fialta" (1936), spins out a full-throated, halfhearted love story through so many offhand flashbacks that, if I were asked to justify my praise, I might not be able to say much more than that it is basically about spring in Fialta. An earlier tale, "Gods" (1923), spends three and a half pages wandering through a city—seeing the sights, shouting out visions, addressing an unspecified lover. Then, suddenly, we get this: "Oh, listen—here is something that happened in Paris, about 150 years ago. Early one morning . . ." It's a curious device: a fable, a historical footnote flung in our direction like a scrap of cheap gossip. No other writer revels like Nabokov in the unbalancing of traditional structures, in the freaky redistribution of details. The slumbering past is jerked awake by a slap of present tense. Major events flash by like telegraph poles seen from a train, while silly sub-trash is held in the hand and pondered with inordinate care: "Pebbles like cuckoo eggs, a piece of tile shaped like a pistol clip, a fragment of topaz-colored glass, something quite dry resembling a whisk of bast, my tears, a microscopic bead, an empty cigarette package with a yellow-bearded sailor in the center of a life buoy, a stone like a Pompeian's foot, some creature's small bone or a spatula, a kerosene can, a shiver of garnet-red glass, a nutshell, a nondescript rusty thingum related to nothing."

As for the way Nabokov begins his tales—well, where do you start? The opening of "The Wood-Sprite" is the first sentence of the book: "I was pensively penning the outline of the inkstand's circular, quivering shadow." That early alliteration is a little rich, a little pleased with itself, and it is a pleasure that will never wholly fade. "Quivering," however, is pure Nabokov: alert to motions that the rest of us barely register. Some other openings:

> When the curved tip of one ski crosses the other, you tumble forward.
>
> —"WINGSTROKE."

> The last streetcar was disappearing in the mirrorlike murk of the street and, along the wire above it, a spark of Bengal light, crackling and quivering, sped into the distance like a blue star.
>
> —'DETAILS OF A SUNSET."

> In front of the red-hued castle, amid luxuriant elms, there was a vividly green grass court.
>
> —"LA VENEZIANA."

> My charming, dear distant one, I presume you cannot have forgotten anything in the more than eight years of our separation, if you manage to remember even the gray-haired, azure-liveried watchman who did not bother us in the least when we would meet, skipping school, on a frosty Petersburg morning, in the Suvurov museum, so dusty, so small, so similar to a glorified snuffbox.
>
> —"A LETTER THAT NEVER REACHED RUSSIA."

> Actually his name was Frederic Dobson.
>
> —"THE POTATO ELF."

> In the second place, because he was possessed by a sudden mad hankering after Russia.
>
> —"THE CIRCLE."

> The growth of his power and fame was matched, in my imagination, by the degree of the punishment I would have liked to inflict on him.
>
> —"TYRANTS DESTROYED."

> Do you remember the day you and I were lunching (partaking of nourishment) a couple of years before your death?
>
> —"ULTIMA THULE."

> Dear V.—Among other things, this is to tell you that at last I am here, in the country whither so many sunsets have led.
>
> —"THAT IN ALEPPO ONCE . . ."

And there, in a scattering of nutshells, you have Vladimir Nabokov. It is, I think, impossible to read such sentences without experiencing a chronic desire to carry on. One reason that this collection marks a crucial move in the endless game of trying to fathom Nabokov—a reason that the book is far more than a handy compendium—is that it renews and clarifies his ability not to lull or enchant his readers but to shock. Again and again, with polite indifference, the stories drop us in medias res, and leave us to work out what on earth the res might be. Many of Nabokov's novels, it is true, hit the ground running (*Laughter in the Dark* recounts its own forthcoming plot in a couple of brisk, chilly sentences), but we soon grow accustomed to their stride. This book won't let us settle: it is forever switching tack and pace, daring us to catch up. A sentence such as "Actually his name was Frederic Dobson" presumes that we have been chatting like party guests with the narrator, that we have perhaps made an observation with which he disagrees, and that suddenly the rest of the room is listening. The effect is similar to that of a Browning monologue: civilized, sociable, and distinctly alarming.

But something else is going on in those beginnings—something that prevents Nabokov's shocks from felling us completely. The grass court, the spark of light, the morning in St. Petersburg: these are the trappings of an obsessive, and they quietly reassure us that we may yet feel at home here. Has any other modern author compiled such a faithful, eccentric, loft-cluttering list of loves? Tennis, trains, butterflies, bicycles, chess problems, ripening young women with unforgettable napes, dawns that chill the bone, Russia dead and gone, varying degrees of madness, infinite variations on the color blue—these props and predilections litter Nabokov's fiction, long and short, from start to finish. They may, indeed, be more than props; they may be what drove him to dramatize in the first place. If he were not so famously scornful of Freud, one might almost tag Nabokov with a repetition compulsion; the sequence of traumas that beset him in youth was, by any standard, so terrible that, even if none of his works could be described as therapeutic, it is equally the case that none escape the knowledge of that desolation. Even his brightness has the blues.

Nabokov was born in 1899 in St. Petersburg, the son of a liberal politician who was assassinated, in Berlin, in 1922. The family had fled in 1917. If a first-class sleeper bears you away from a secure and prosperous home to the Crimea, from which you then depart for a life of ceaseless exile, which will end in acclaim and in America for yourself but in a concentration camp for Sergey, your beloved younger brother, is it surprising that your stories will come to resound to the clatter of night trains, to the thrill and devastation of a one-way ticket in the dark? Nothing in the collected stories is more acute than the suffering of the dining-car attendant in "A Matter of Chance": a Russian émigré who misses his wife so badly that he plans and carries out his own death, unaware that earlier in the evening she was sitting less than a carriage away. He has a narrow escape from bliss. His creator would become known, in novels like *Ada*, as our most accomplished chronicler of happiness, but these early tales make you wonder what distillations of despair Nabokov had to taste in order to dream of djoys.

Vladimir was a student at Trinity College, Cambridge, from 1919 to 1922. After Cambridge, he joined his family in Berlin, and many of these stories were written there in the twenties and thirties, under the pseudonym of Sirin. The writer left Germany for Paris in 1937, and never returned. His first book written in English, *The Real Life of Sebastian Knight*, was not published until 1941; readers new to Nabokov—and this volume is a good place to kick off—may not realize that at least half his output was written in Russian. (Only ten of the stories gathered here were composed in English.) We are fortunate that the novelist himself, together with his son, Dmitri, and other collaborators, was able to translate his own work; on the other hand, many of the translations were not undertaken until the 1960s and '70s, some forty or fifty years after the tales were first written. For those of us slackers who can't be bothered to get off our butts and learn Russian, the mystery must therefore remain unsolved: was Nabokov the Berliner really so mellow in his constructions, or are we getting them filtered through a later suavity?

Perhaps we are wrong to worry. Nabokov argued that his native language was in fact better than his acquired one. "My private tragedy," he wrote, "is that I had to abandon my natural idiom, my untrammeled, rich, and infinitely docile Russian tongue for a second-rate brand of English." It's a first-rate sentence, of course; the tragic, as so often happens with Nabokov, backs into a lofty private joke. His detractors (and some of his admirers) would maintain that what he did was not learn but overlearn English. In *Nabokov Translated* (published in 1977, the year Nabokov died) the critic Jane Grayson undertakes a lengthy examination of Nabokov's forked tongue, and concludes, "Personally, I would tend to agree with Nabokov that his Russian is superior—if only because it is less uneven and, on the whole, less mannered than his English. However, whatever general view is held of Nabokov's English, it is undeniable that his command of the language has improved over the years and that with time he has evolved a polished and strikingly original prose style." Well done, Vladimir!

With another writer, such textual comparisons can easily become a grind; with Nabokov, they're part of the game. He has always been a hero to those of bibliographical bent. In his lifetime, he published four short-story collections, which have now been broken down and rearranged in chronological order. The notes at the back of the book are intended to clarify the provenance of each story, but they read like a pastiche of scholarly caution. Nabokov's own remarks on "The Return of Chorb," though perfectly accurate, nevertheless give off that distant, unmistakable odor of amused contrivance which he lent to even the most fleeting of literary tasks:

> First published in two issues of the Russian émigré *Rul'* (Berlin), November 12 and 13, 1925. Reprinted in the collection *Vozvrashchenie Chorba*, Slovo, Berlin, 1930.
> An English version by Gleb Struve ("The Return of Tchorb" by Vladimir Sirin) appeared in the anthology *This Quarter* (vol. 4, no. 4, June 1932), published in Paris by Edw. W. Titus.

This is useful stuff, but does the pedant not relish the wah-wah throb of "Edw. W." just a fraction too much? And that "Gleb Struve"—I mean, *really*. He must be a figment—a slithy word to gyre and gimble with, a melee of joke consonants. Struve was in fact a friend of Nabokov's, and one of the earliest champions of émigré-Russian writing, but the point is that he still *sounds* like one of the novelist's inventions—an anagram, perhaps, like the "Vivian Darkbloom" with which Nabokov scrambled and smuggled his own name into *Lolita*. Throughout his life, Nabokov strove to emphasize the need for precision—to take down the world's particulars and to stake his claim as one of the great noticers of modern literature—but there existed in him a contrary talent for burnishing the recorded facts until they gleamed like the alchemical products of the imagination. He is, you might say, a semiprecious writer: neither as bejewelled as his rapturous clauses (or his many imitators) initially suggest nor as epistemologically earthbound as he himself liked to pretend. The indefatigable Nabokov sought only what he saw and remembered as true, and yet his fiction leaves you with the appetizing suspicion that truth is overrated.

* * *

Like many people who first stumbled upon the genius of Vladimir Nabokov at an impressionable, not to say puttylike, age, I now enjoy slightly Nabokovian relations with his works. I look back to a cheerful period when I sat in his old college and read everything of his I could find: novels, novellas, interviews, the marvellous, maddening biography of Gogol. This, I remember thinking—this is *style.* Every word pulled its weight, did its bit for the common good of the sentence. How could you fault the guy? Later, I started to drift and doubt—to read authors who nod from time to time, whose paragraphs can slip a gear, but whose ambitious imperfections somehow reach beyond the flawlessness of Nabokov. In his *Lectures on Literature* Nabokov wrote that many Western readers will be bored by the agricultural sections of *Anna Karenina,* but those are my favorites; I love the wet grass seeds on the wheels of Levin's cart. And I know that one shouldn't question Nabokov's authority on Russian appellations, but when he suggested that Tolstoy's Prince Oblonsky should properly be addressed as "Steve," my devotion took a bad knock. Steve! What about Nabokov himself, the man who coolly pinned down his characters as he did his damned butterflies? How about Vlad the Impaler?

Well, I'm sorry that I wavered. Once more, I pledge my faith, and I admit that it took *The Stories of Vladimir Nabokov* to bring me back. Given that most of its contents have been readily available for the last twenty years, however, why should we celebrate their reappearance? For one thing, there is the unequalled pleasure of submitting to Nabokov in full flow, when his words boil like a witches' brew of music and sex:

> He poured a small mound of the powder on his thumbnail; greedily applied it to one nostril, then to the other; inhaled; with a flip of his tongue licked the sparkling dust off his nail; blinked hard a couple of times from the rubbery bitterness, and left the toilet, boozy and buoyant, his head filling with icy delicious air.

Who needs cocaine when thirty-five dollars' worth of good prose can hit you with highs like that? The effect of such felicities en masse is not only addictive; they point to the finesse of Nabokov's ear but, more crucial, to the extreme and unembarrassable weirdness of his invention, the flight plans of his fancy. This volume of stories offers, among other things, a Jamesian oddity in which characters slip in and out of a Renaissance oil painting; a secret acrostic, spelled out in the initial letters of the words in a story's final sentence and calculated to send a message from two of its characters, now dead; one tale about a dragon, another about a furry angel in a hotel room, a third about Elijah crashing his chariot; an elf, a sprite, a governess; hallucinated accounts of travel, both tropical and interplanetary; and a peculiarly vicious horror story in which a professor frightens his wife to death by slipping into her warm bed the cold skeleton of a hunchback. Even nastier, in a way, is the infant memory that flickers in "Terror":

> I raised my still sleepy eyes while pressing the back of my neck to my low pillow and saw, leaning toward me over the bed head, an incomprehensible face, noseless, with a hussar's black mustache just below its octopus eyes, and with teeth set in its forehead. I sat up with a shriek and immediately the mustache became eyebrows and the entire face was transformed into that of my mother, which I had glimpsed at first in an unwonted upside-down aspect.

Proust remembered with longing his mother's bedside kiss; Nabokov, a self-confessed Proustian, inverts that beatific moment and smothers love with fear. He adds, in a footnote, that the story was written "around 1926, one of the happiest years of my life." Is he being blithe or monstrous? Or is it more fun to be both?

For a long time, the image of Nabokov that held sway was one of arrogance and hardness of heart. More recently, critics such as Richard Rorty have warmed the writer up; they have chosen to stress his ferocious loathing of cruelty in all its guises, personal and political. Brian Boyd, in the introduction to his learned, faintly exhausting two-volume biography, sets out to rescue his subject from the charge of frivolous ingenuity. "In fact he was deeply serious as a thinker—an epistemologist, metaphysician, moral philosopher, and aesthetician," Boyd writes. Poor Professor Nabokov. It should be added that he also enjoyed sunbathing. A more nimble, less heavy-weather critic is required to do Nabokov justice—someone like Michael Wood, whose new study, *The Magician's Doubts: Nabokov and the Risks of Fiction*, is the best book yet written on the novelist. Wood concentrates on the American works: *Pnin*, *Lolita*, *Ada*, and the other successes that sprang from the second half of Nabokov's life. One of Wood's graceful ruminations concerns "Signs and Symbols," a 1948 tale in which an elderly immigrant couple pay a thwarted visit to their mentally unstable son. They are pestered, at the close, by a phone call; it may or may not be a wrong number. The narrative doesn't go anywhere: it tosses and turns in the worst, most ominous kind of waking dream. As Wood says, "What seems to me most striking about the story is its immense shadowy background of pain and frightening possibility; not its secret but its silence. It is full of things not said, fuller than Nabokov's writing often seems."

There is, I suspect, a prosaic reason for this: "Signs and Symbols" is a short story. It embodies the quite unexpected importance that accrues to *The Stories of Vladimir Nabokov.* I would not claim that all, or even many, of the tales are masterpieces of the order of "Signs and Symbols," but most freshen and redirect our notion of Nabokov by suggesting that his notorious skills—his reverence for the unrepeatable moment, his plucking of epiphanies out of nowhere, the rainbow of his sensory perceptions, the waste bin to which he consigns didactic purpose—were sometimes most gainfully employed in short fiction. Of course, the major novels will endure, but I like to think that Nabokov the sprinter will keep up with Nabokov the marathon man.

So why did he stop sprinting? The final story, "Lance," was completed in November of 1951, a year before the purported death of Humbert Humbert. This whole volume, in fact, rustles with premonitions of *Lolita;* when Humbert lies awake in a hotel, frozen with desire for the stepdaughter by his side, hearing the "gurgle and gush" of the "manly, energetic, deep-throated toilet" that flushes throughout the night, he is really listening to a long-distance echo of the water that "gulps and gurgles in its hidden pipes" in a Berlin paragraph of 1925. It would be wrong to think of the tales as preparatory, as mere target practice for the American hits so admired by Wood; but insofar as Nabokov's stories document and improvise on the first half of his split life, it seems only fitting that their edgy melodies should cease at a time when his second-act fame was beginning to swell, when material security was not far off, and when the perpetual wanderer had at last, against expectation, found himself a home. We have grown used to the ludic persona, rarefied as mountain air, that was projected by the older Nabokov, and it is good to be reminded of the young man who preceded him—the uprooted European, low on cash, who discovered that the punch and blaze of short stories were ideal for his purposes. In the pages of this new book, Nabokov seems less aloof than elsewhere: his talent for ecstasy becomes apprehensive, caught up in blue-rimmed, insomniac worries and in glimpses of a capricious afterlife. These stories are incantations, and they summon the strangest things. Vladimir Nabokov, of all people, finally falls under his own spell.

DECEMBER 4, 1995

COOKBOOKS

Ready? Ready. O.K., here we go. "Fold the wings akimbo, tucking the wing ends under the shoulders as shown here." Lovely. "Then, on the same side of the chicken where you came out from the second knee . . ." Umm. "Poke the needle through the upper arm of the wing." Wings with arms, like a bat's. Cool. "Catch the neck skin, if there . . ." Hang on. *If there?* If not there, where? Whose neck is this, anyway? ". . . and pin it to the backbone, and come out through the second wing." And go for a walk in the snow, and don't come back till next year.

This wing-stitching drill, as any cook will tell you, is from the celebrated "To Truss a Chicken" section of Julia Child's *The Way to Cook*. It's a pretty easy routine, really, as long as you take it slow, run through a batch of test poultry first, have a professional chef on hand to help you through the bad times, and feel no shame when you get arrested and charged with satanic drumstick abuse. Julia Child is a good woman, with no desire to faze or scald us; she genuinely wants us to bard that bird, to cook it, and to carve it. ("Fork-grab under the knee. . . . Soon you'll see the ball joint where the leg-thigh meets the small of the back.") Hell, she wouldn't mind if we went ahead and *ate* the damn thing.

I don't know what it is about cookbooks, but they really drain my giblets. I buy them, and use them, and study them with the micro-attentive care of a papyrologist, and still they make me feel that I am missing out. I follow instructions, and cook dinner for friends, and the friends are usually friends again by the next morning, but what they consume at my table bears no more than a fleeting, tragically half-assed resemblance to the dish that I read about in the recipe. Although I am not a good cook, I am not a dreadful one, either; I once had a go at *mouclade d'Aunis*, once made a brave fist of *cul de veau braisé Angevin*, and once came very close to buying a carp. Last summer, I did something difficult with monkfish tails; the dish took two days to prepare, a full nine minutes to eat, and three days to wash up after. But an hour in front of my cookbooks is enough to slash my ambitions to the bone—to convince me that in terms of culinary evolution I remain a scowling tree-dweller whose idea of haute cuisine is to grub for larvae under dead bark.

And we all know the name of the highly developed being standing tall at the other end of the scale. Super-skilled, free of fear, the last word in human efficiency, Martha Stewart is the woman who convinced a million Americans that they have the time, the means, the right, and—damn it—the *duty* to pipe a little squirt of soft cheese into the middle of a snow pea, and to continue piping until there are "fifty to sixty" stuffed peas raring to go. Never mind the taste; one glance at this woman's quantities is enough to spirit you into a different and a cleaner world. "I discovered a fantastic thing when preparing 1,500 potatoes for the Folk Art Show," Martha writes in her latest book. *The Martha Stewart Cookbook* is a magisterial compendium of nine previous books, and offers her fans another chance to sample Martha's wacky punch lines ("Tie securely with a single chive") and her naughtiest promises ("This hearty soup is simple to assemble"). So coolly thrown off, that last line, and you read right through it without picking up the outrageous implication. Since when did you "assemble" a soup? Even the ingredients are a fright. "Three pounds fish frames from flounder or fluke," Martha says brightly, sounding like Henry Higgins. To the rest of humanity, soup is something that involves five pans, two dented strainers, scattered bones that would baffle a forensic pathologist, and the unpleasant sensation of hot stock rising from the pot, condensing on your forehead, and running down into the pot again as lightly flavored sweat.

Martha does not perspire. There is not a squeak of panic in the woman's soul. She knows exactly where the two layers of cheesecloth can be found when the time comes to strain the stock. She assembles her fish chowder as if it were a model airplane. Moreover, she does so without appearing to spend any time in the kitchen. "One of the most important moments on which to expend extra effort is the beginning of a party, often an awkward time, when guests feel tentative and insecure," she says. The *guests* are insecure? How about the frigging cook? Believe me, Martha, I'm not handing round the phyllo triangles with lobster filling during that awkward time. I'm out back, holding on to the sink, finishing off the Côtes du Rhône that was supposed to go into the stew. But Martha Stewart is an idealist who has cunningly disguised herself as a helping hand; readers look up to her as a conservative angel who keeps the dream house tidy, radiant, ready for pals, and filled with family. "If I had to choose one essential element for the success of an Easter brunch, it would be children," she writes, as if preparing to grill the kids over a high flame.

Yet the conservative image won't quite fit. The Stewart paean to the joys of Thanksgiving ("To not cook and entertain on this day would seem tantamount to treason") is itself rather joyless in its zealotry; you keep hitting something sharp and steely in her writings—a demiglace intolerance of ordinary mortals. Her kitchen is bewitched, and she's Samantha. You won't see it on her TV shows, but I bet Martha Stewart can wiggle her nose and turn any chauvinist Darrin into crabmeat. If you're planning to fork-grab her under the knee, forget it. Was it the spirit of the season or a quiet celebration of dominant female power that led to the baked-ham recipe at the start of *Martha Stewart's Menus for Entertaining*? It looks succulent in the accompanying photograph, and I have long yearned to make it, but three factors have restrained me. First, it serves sixteen, and I don't know that many people who would be happy to munch ham at one another. Second, you need "one bunch chervil with flowers." (That's plain silly, if not quite as ridiculous as a recipe that I came across at the peak of nouvelle cuisine, in the 1980s—a recipe that demanded *thirty-four* chervil leaves.) Third, the ham must be baked for five and a half hours in a pan lined with fresh-cut grass. As in meadow. "Locate an area in advance with tender, young, organically grown grass that has not yet been cut," our guide advises. "It is best to cut it very early in the morning while the dew is still evident." I'm sorry, Martha, but it just won't do. I have inspected the grass in my backyard, and I am not prepared to serve Baked Ham with Cat Whiff and Chopped Worms.

There must be millions of other people who refuse to get up at dawn and mow the lawn for dinner. This fellow feeling should be a comfort to me, yet somehow it makes no difference. Cooking, for all the apple-cheeked, home-baked community spirit in which food writers try to enfold it, is essentially a solitary art—or, at least, a guarantee of lonely distress. When your hollandaise is starting to curdle and you've tried the miraculous ice-cube trick and you've tried beating a fresh egg yolk and folding in the curdled stuff and the result still looks like the climactic scene of a David Cronenberg picture, it doesn't really help to know that someone is having the very same problem in Pittsburgh. Your only friend, in fact, is that shelf of cookbooks just out of reach. Leaving the sauce to its own devices, you grab each volume in turn, frantic for advice, and make your fatal mistake: you start to read. Two yards away, the sauce is separating fast—the lemon is pursing its lips, the eggs are halfway back to the fridge—but you don't care. By now, determined to find out where you went wrong, and already dreaming of a perfect future sauce, you are deep into Georges Auguste Escoffier's recipe for hollandaise: "Remove the pan to the side of the stove or place it in a bain-marie." Well, which?

In that simple "or" reside both the delight and the frustration of the classic cookbook. It should ideally tell you almost everything but not all that you need to know, leaving a tiny crack of uncertainty that can become your own personal abyss. If any text counts as a classic, it is Escoffier's *Le Guide Culinaire*, which was published in 1903. Escoffier was a colleague of César Ritz, and a man of such pantry-stocking initiative that when Paris was besieged in the Franco-Prussian War he fed the starving troops on zoo animals and stray pets. I eagerly scanned the *Guide* for pan-seared hartebeest or poodle mousse à la Fifi sauvage, but all I could find was this unflinching recipe for clear turtle soup:

> To kill the turtle, lay it on its back at the edge of the table with the head hanging over the side. Take a double meat hook and place one hook into the upper jaw and suspend a sufficiently heavy weight in the hook at the other end so as to make the animal extend its neck. . . .

It goes without saying that the flippers should be blanched, and that "the green fat which is used for making the soup must be collected carefully." But where, exactly, does this green fat come from? The author doesn't tell us. Somewhere between the carapace and the plastron, presumably, but I'm not sure that I really want to know.

Whether cooks still use Escoffier—or Larousse, or Carême, or any of the other touchstones of French cuisine—is open to question. It is not just the encyclopedic spread of these Frenchmen's interests, their desire to chew on something that we would prefer to watch in a wildlife documentary, that feels out of date; it is also their unshakable conviction that we already know our worldly way around a kitchen, that they are merely grinding a little fresh information into our basic stock of knowledge. When Escoffier tells us to "stud the fattened pullet with pieces of truffle and poach it in the usual manner," he presumes that we habitually spend our weekends looking for pullets to fatten and that we can poach them in our sleep. Many readers are scared off by this assumption; I feel flattered and consoled by it, all the more so because I know it to be dead wrong. I am not a truffle stud, nor was meant to be. Yet I willingly dream myself into a time when you could "quickly fry 10 blackbirds in hot butter"—just because I relish the imaginative jump required to get there, not because I particularly want a blackbird-lettuce-and-tomato sandwich for my lunch.

In other words, the great cookbooks are more like novels than like home-improvement manuals. What these culinary bibles tell you to do is far less beguiling than the thought of a world in which such things might be done. A single line, for instance, from Benjamin Renaudet's *Secrets de la*

Bonne Table, published at the beginning of this century, effortlessly summons up the century that has just ended: "When the first partridges are shot in the early morning, send them down to the house." If that grabs you, take a look at *Culinary Jottings for Madras*, a collection of recipes by Deputy Assistant Quartermaster-General Arthur Robert Kenney-Herbert. First published in 1878, the book tells you more about the nature of imperial rule in India than any number of political histories. If you can feed a party of eight on snipe soup, fish fillets à la Peg Woffington, mutton cutlets à la Moscovite, oyster Kramouskys, braised capon, and a brace of wild ducks with bigarade sauce, if you can finish off with prune jelly, iced molded pudding with strawberries, and cheese, and if you can serve and eat all that when it's ninety-five degrees in the shade, then you can conquer any country you like. Nothing can stand up to Peg Woffington.

There is a pinch of snob nostalgia in reading this stuff, of course, but I don't think it ruins the flavor. What is attractive about cookbooks, after all—what prickles the glands like vinegar—is not luxury but otherness. I have a particular weakness for the chunky, old-style blockbusters that sit in every kitchen, offering reams of advice that is seldom taken, or even required. Endlessly updated with new editions, these masterworks are doomed never to be up to date. Craig Claiborne's *New York Times Cook Book*, which has slowly acquired the gravitas of Holy Writ, was first published in 1961. I found an early edition, and smiled at the hors-d'oeuvres suggestions that are arrayed for our delectation in the first section of the book: how to serve oysters on the half shell, how to serve caviar, how to serve foie gras. It was a time capsule of America in the late fifties and early sixties; it made me want to watch *Pillow Talk* all over again. With a sigh of regret, I turned to the latest edition. How would it start in the nineties? Char-grilled calamari with arugula and flat-leaf parsley? Stuffed snow peas à la Martha? Shiitake tarts? But no, there it was again: how to serve oysters on the half shell, etc. What was once an accurate index of national taste has now become a museum piece. It's the same story with Irma S. Rombauer and Marion Rombauer Becker's *The Joy of Cooking*, which began life in 1931 and reads as if it had never got past 1945. Social historians should head straight for the "Pies and Pastries" section and check out the crusty jokes: "No wonder pictures of leggy starlets are called cheesecake!" Ba-boom.

Down below caviar, even farther down than cheesecake, there is a place where the joy of cooking gives way to the joy of not bothering to cook at all. Yet even here, on the ocean floor of *cuisine en bas*, among such primitive life forms as the Fried Peanut Butter and Banana Sandwich, there is food for thought. To discover this sandwich in Brenda Arlene Butler's *Are*

You Hungry Tonight? Elvis' Favorite Recipes is to be transported, without warning, to an age of innocence. The book's final chapter offers readers the chance to re-create the giant six-tier wedding cake that Elvis and Priscilla cut together on that happy day in 1967: the words "Eleven pounds hydrogenated vegetable shortening (such as Sweetex or Crisco)" speak to me as directly, and as movingly, as the partridges that Renaudet called for in the early morning.

There are times when this need to look elsewhere—to reach into the ovens of another age, or another culture, and pull out whatever you can—grows from a well-fed fancy into a moral necessity. Hence the invaluable contribution of Elizabeth David, whose name remains as revered in England as that of M. F. K. Fisher in America. (Why do women make such great cookery writers? Partly, I suspect, because they realize that it is enough to be a great cook, whereas men, larded with pride in their own accomplishment, invariably go one step too far and try to be great *chefs*—a grander calling, though somehow less respectable, and certainly less responsive to human need.) Both David and Fisher were spurred to action by the Second World War: Fisher's *How to Cook a Wolf* was published in 1942, when food shortages were beginning to bite, and David's *A Book of Mediterranean Food* appeared in 1950, when England was still rationed, undernourished, and keen on suet.

Elizabeth David's mission was to find the modern equivalent of Renaudet's partridges, to resuscitate flagging and amnesiac palates with the prospect of unthinkable dishes. Such food had no need to be rich; it simply had to taste of something, to bear recognizable links to natural produce, and, most important, to be non-gray. Whether it ever saw the light of day, or the candlelight of evening, was beside the point; the mere promise of it, David herself confessed, was a form of nourishment. "Even if people could not very often make the dishes here described," she pointed out, "it was stimulating to think about them." And so on the first page of *A Book of Mediterranean Food* she kicked off with *soupe au pistou* and its accompanying dollop of *aïllade*. The garlicky stink of Nice hit England full in the face, and the nation—or, at any rate, the middle classes—came back to life.

Nowadays, the situation is reversed. We know too much about food. Your principal obligation when you sit down at a restaurant in New York is to play it cool. Black spaghettini with cuttlefish and fennel tops? Been there. *Soupe au pistou*? Wake me up when it's over. In the past year, I have eaten both reindeer (a fun Christmas dish) and ostrich (better baked in sand, I guess), but they hardly count as exotic anymore. Cookbooks have followed the lead of restaurants and delicatessens: specialist works abound, the narrower the better. I gave up reading Sara Slavin and Karl Petzke's *Champagne: The Spirit of Celebration*, a book devoted to cooking with and for champagne, at the point where it instructed me to "roll each cheese-coated grape in the garlic-almond mixture." Isn't there some kind of Grape Protection Society that should be fighting this stuff? As for *365 Ways to Cook Hamburger and Other Ground Meats*, by Rick Rodgers, what can I say? Welcome to the most disgusting book on earth. It's not the dishes themselves that I object to—not even Ed Debevic's Burnt Meatloaf, or the Transylvanian Pork and Sauerkraut Bake—but the gruelling way in which one recipe after another resounds with the same mournful litany: "One pound ground round." Remember the wise words of M. F. K. Fisher: "The first thing to know about ground round steak is that it should not be that at all."

Far more cheering and plausible is Nick Malgieri's *How to Bake*, which runs for 276 pages before it even gets to "Plain Cakes." Should you find the book a little too broad in scope, you could always play the sacred card and go for *The Secrets of Jesuit Breadmaking*, by Brother Rick Curry, S.J. This alternates clear spiritual homilies with yeasty advice about cooling racks. Sometimes, with a brilliant flourish, Brother Curry kneads his twin passions into one phrase: "As we begin the most austere week in Christianity, tasty rich biscuits remind us that Jesus is coming." I suspect that such highly sophisticated reasoning may have been the downfall of Gerard Manley Hopkins, poet and Jesuit, who suffered what was reputed to be one of the worst cases of constipation in the nineteenth century.

If you really intend to be the star of your own cookbook, you need to watch out. (The finest cooks, such as Escoffier, are godlike, everywhere in the text yet nowhere to be seen.) Brother Curry, schooled in humility, gets it about right: when he says that his Loyola Academy Buttermilk Bread "goes great with peanut butter," we instinctively believe that he's plugging a good idea rather than himself. The trouble starts with celebrity cookbooks and tie-ins; try as I might, I cannot conceive of a time when I will want to concoct a meal from the pages of *The Bubba Gump Shrimp Co. Cookbook* or its literate successor, *Forrest Gump: My Favorite Chocolate Recipes*. *Entertaining with Regis and Kathie Lee* is remarkable less for the quality of the cuisine than for the photographs of Kathie Lee, who seems to spend half her time with her mouth wide open, as if to catch any mouthfuls flying by. Then, there's Rosie Daley, whose food looks perfectly nice, but whose *In the Kitchen with Rosie* might not have reached the best-seller lists were she not employed as a cook by Oprah Winfrey. It's kind of hard to concentrate on the ingredients, what with Oprah's cheerleading ringing out at regular intervals. "I have thrived on pasta. I can eat it every day and practically do." You'd never guess.

Whether such works can be relied upon in the kitchen is of little consequence. Cookbooks, it should be stressed, do not belong in the kitchen at all. We keep them there for the sake of appearances; occasionally, we smear their pages together with vibrant green glazes or crimson compotes, in order to delude ourselves, and any passing browsers, that we are practicing cooks; but, in all honesty, a cookbook is something that you read in the living room, or in the bathroom, or in bed. The purpose is not to nurture nightmares of suckling pig, or to lull ourselves into a fantasy of trimly bearded oysters, but simply to baste our rested brains with common sense, and with the prospect of common pleasures to come. Take this romantic interlude from *'Tis the Season: A Vegetarian Christmas Cookbook*, by Nanette Blanchard: "Turn down the lights, light all the candles you can find, throw a log on the fire, turn up the music, and toast each other with a Sparkling Grape Goblet." Oh, oh, Nanette. On the other hand, what could be sweeter than to retire with *Smoke & Spice*, by Cheryl Alters Jamison and Bill Jamison, whose High Plains Jerky would be an ornament to any barbecue? Those in search of distant horizons could always caress their senses with *The Art of Polish Cooking*, in which Alina Zerańska offers her triumphant recipe for "Nothing" Soup *(Zupa "Nic")*, adding darkly, "This is an all-time children's favorite."

If I could share a Sparkling Grape Goblet with anyone—not just any cook but any person in recorded history—it might well be with Jean-Anthelme Brillat-Savarin. Magistrate, mayor, violinist, judge, and ravenous slayer of wild turkeys during his visit to America, Brillat-Savarin is now remembered for *The Physiology of Taste*, which was first published in 1825. There is a good paperback version, translated by Anne Drayton, but devotees may wish to seek out the translation by M. F. K. Fisher herself; it has now been reissued in a luxurious new edition, with illustrations by Wayne Thiebaud. To say that *The Physiology of Taste* is a cookbook is like saying that Turgenev's *Sportsman's Sketches* is a guide to hunting. "When I came to consider the pleasures of the table in all their aspects, I soon perceived that something better than a mere cookery book might be made of such a subject," Brillat-Savarin writes. It is a perception that few have shared; the closest modern equivalent, perhaps, is in the work of A. J. Liebling, a man whose delicately gluttonous writings on food keep wandering off (when he can tear himself away) into such equally pressing areas as Paris, boxing, and sex. Brillat-Savarin, like Liebling, gives few recipes, though he muses on innumerable dishes, on the scientific reasons for their effect on the metabolism, and on the glow of sociable well-being that is their ideal result. He sprinkles anecdotes like salt, and he defines and defends *gourmandisme* ("It shows implicit obedience to the commands of the Creator"), following it through the various stages of delight and surfeit to its logical conclusion. There is a chapter on "The Theory of Frying" and a wonderful disquisition on death, embellished with gloomy good cheer: "I would recall the words of the dying Fontenelle, who on being asked what he could feel, replied: 'Nothing but a certain difficulty in living.' "

The lasting achievement of Brillat-Savarin is that he endowed living with a certain ease. Intricately versed in the difficulties of existence, he came to the unorthodox conclusion that a cookbook—a bastard form, but a wealthy, happy bastard—could offer the widest and most tender range of remedies. I'm not sure whether he knew how to fold the wings of a chicken akimbo, and if you'd handed him a snow pea and told him to stuff it he would have responded in kind; but it takes someone like Brillat-Savarin to remind us that cooking need not be the fraught, perfectionist, slightly paranoid struggle that it has latterly become. His love of food is bound up with a taste for human error and indulgence, and that is why *The Physiology of Taste* is still the most civilized cookbook ever written. I suspect that Brillat-Savarin might have been bemused by Martha Stewart, but that he would have got on just fine with Ed Debevic and his Burnt Meatloaf.

I sure wish that he had been on hand for my terrine of sardines and potatoes. There I was—apron on, gin in hand, closely following the recipe of the French chef Raymond Blanc. All went well until I got to the harmless words "a piece of cardboard." Apparently, I needed cardboard to lay on the terrine mold; the cardboard then had to be covered with "evenly distributed weights" for twelve hours. Weights? Cardboard? Twelve hours? They weren't listed with the ingredients. I had my sardines; I had my twenty capers and my freshly grated nutmeg; but I had no cardboard. Frankly, it would have been easier to kill a turtle.

That's the trouble with cookbooks. Like sex education and nuclear physics, they are founded on an illusion. They bespeak order, but they end in tears.

DECEMBER 18, 1995

CYRIL CONNOLLY

Who was Cyril Connolly? What was he? Not a poet, for all his dablings ("The pernod at the violet hour"); not quite a novelist, despite *The Rock Pool*, the brief, overripe slice of fiction that he published in 1936; and not precisely a journalist, since the book reviews that he wrote in England for the *New Statesman* and the *Sunday Times* remain much too ruddy and vital to lie down and die, as hackwork should. He was three times a husband, but whether that made him a good husband is open to question. He *was* a good critic, the sagest of his period, and nobody who saw him launch his culture-powered magazine *Horizon* in 1939 and stand firm at its helm for ten years would deny that he was a great editor. As for Connolly himself, he knew what he was: "No opinions, no ideas, no real knowledge of anything, no ideals, no inspiration; a fat, slothful, querulous, greedy, impotent carcass; a stump, a decaying belly washed up on the shore." Anything I can do to help?

Connolly was born in Coventry, in 1903, an only child par excellence. His father, Matthew, was a soldier with a consuming passion for snails; I like the sound of his masterwork, "A Monographic Survey of South-African Non-Marine Mollusca." Young Cyril, who could never decide whether or not to retreat into his shell, spent parts of his sensation-soaked childhood in South Africa and in Ireland. He went to preparatory school, from there to Eton, and from there, on a scholarship, to Balliol College, Oxford—the cloudless peak of his achievement, after which, he liked to maintain, it was downhill all the way. That sad estimation is upheld by Clive Fisher's *Cyril Connolly: The Life and Times of England's Most Controversial Literary Critic.* The less preposterous subtitle of the English edition, *A Nostalgic Life*, chimed better with the rhapsodic tone of Connolly's own recollections in *Enemies of Promise* (1938), the volume of criticism and memoirs that made his name, yet we should be wary of treating him as a kind of English Alain-Fournier. Connolly was not a victim of nostalgia but its careful cultivator, and what really seduced his imagination was a nostalgia for what he had never known or for what had never been. "I regard the burning of the Alexandrian library as an inconsolable private grief," he wrote. The problem with long-distance yearners is that, more often than not, they have scant sympathy left over for troubles close to home.

Fisher's book is the first full-length biography of Connolly, but it will not be the last: a competing account, by Jeremy Lewis, will be published in the next year or so. It is hard to fathom why interest in Connolly, which flared up after his death, in 1974, and again with the publication of David Pryce-Jones's *Cyril Connolly: Journal and Memoir*, in 1983, should now begin to sputter and glow once more. Connolly is no longer widely read, and it is not the best efforts of biographers that restore an author to public favor but a slow, seismic heave of taste, which cannot be forced, and may not come to a head for generations. Perhaps Fisher and Lewis consider their man to be the deserving object of millennial scrutiny; after all, the appetite for gloom drew him more to the crepuscular end of things than to bright dawns, which invariably turned out to be false. (He would have thought it a vulgar disappointment if they hadn't.) Fisher quotes the last article that Connolly published in the *Sunday Times*. "As civilizations die they become incomprehensible; every language will one day be a dead language and we ourselves wear out," he wrote. "For this reason the poetry of mortality has the edge on the poetry of love."

All this is pleasant to chew on, and is quite possibly true, but anyone who picks up Fisher's biography expecting the pages to be black-edged with despair will be surprised to find them brimming over with parties. For an expert in low spirits, Connolly seems to have had a high old time; but then what is more effective in the disgorgement of illusions than the aftermath of fun?

Connolly came from solid rather than smart Anglo-Irish gentry, and he lost no opportunity to gild himself as he went along. The refining of his prose style, in the twenties and early thirties, matched the curve of his effortless social climbing. What irks the reader of Connolly's writings, or of his biography, is not the outright snobbery, which is doughy and obvious—"The hotel is a favorite with people like ourselves and so old friends keep popping up," he wrote of a Roman trip—but the fact that the poppers-up are so damn *famous*. If one hunts in vain through Connolly's essays for a prevailing attitude toward ordinary people, that may be because he simply didn't meet any. Reading Fisher, you learn to breeze through the intellectual big shots as if they were small towns on a motoring trip; after a hundred pages or so, I barely noticed when I passed a line such as "They continued to Salzburg, where they encountered Isaiah Berlin, Stuart Hampshire, and Elizabeth Bowen, who was particularly pleased to see them." Dear Elizabeth. Such a doll.

Clive Fisher's previous work was a biography of Noël Coward, and he is happy to let the gregarious side of Connolly—the glint of his conversation and the drink in his hand—shine through the new book as well. Fisher introduces us to people with names like Racy and Ran and Lys, and to the terrifying Barbara Skelton, a bohemian glamour girl who married Connolly in 1950; he lists the literary notables to whom advance copies of *Enemies of Promise* were sent, and those who duly responded with admiring reviews; and he seems unbothered by the strange pseudo-poverty of the well-bred. A paragraph chronicling Connolly's activities in 1953, a rather glum year in which he collected some of his *Horizon* pieces in *Ideas and Places*, tells us of his growing overdraft, of his telephone's being cut off, and of his need to borrow twenty pounds from a friend; and yet we read in that same paragraph, "A more exciting invitation led to his accompanying George Weidenfeld on a cultural programme organized by UNESCO and revolving around the musical festivals at Salzburg and Bayreuth, and while the two men went from opera to opera Barbara stayed with Farouk, now living in Rome since his abdication the previous year." Somebody, somewhere, could have paid the phone bill. The sharpest glance at this weird world comes not from Clive Fisher but from George Orwell, who had known Connolly since their schooldays. Commenting on *The Unquiet Grave* (1944), Connolly's feverish, quotation-stuffed musings on the loneliness of the long-suffering artist, Orwell wrote, "This book exhibits that queer product of capitalist democracy, an inferiority complex resulting from a private income."

What matters about Connolly is that when you read *The Unquiet Grave* the friends depart and the hubbub dies away. But *Cyril Connolly* locks its subject into place among his peers and influences, because that is how biographies tend to function. It is the only way. No biographer can afford to admit the unpalatable truth that people are likely to be more expressive in what (and whom) they deny themselves than in their gratifications—that the plunge pool of like-minded society can sometimes be less inspiring than a solitary supper and a hot bath. Connolly's talent unfurled despite his background, not because of it. Fisher's book produces the standard roll call of Oxford dandies and Chelsea exquisites, most of them spaced out on the deadening fug of belles-lettres: Harold Acton, Brian Howard, Francis (Sligger) Urquhart, Logan Pearsall Smith, Desmond MacCarthy, Maurice Bowra, and so on. Anyone concerned with the period will have stumbled across them a hundred times before; what needs to be made plain is that none of them really count, and that from the whole, seething cultural throng only two men—Cyril Connolly and Evelyn Waugh—stand out and compel our attention.

Connolly and Waugh circled each other cautiously for decades. They had much in common. For one thing, both were prey to an encroaching corpulence; each looked as if he were understudying the other for the leading role in *Toad of Toad Hall.* Connolly resembled the product of some perilous gene-splicing experiment involving human and pug. One of the photographs in the biography shows him in shades and loud shirt and casting his plump shadow along a beach; he may have found the location suitably haunting, but the image suggests Al Capone in Florida taking a breather between slayings. Like Waugh, Connolly found pleasure in creating a character, a minor myth, out of his own temperament and appearance, and both writers wielded a bluff satire that was half in love with what it mocked. "O the joy of lingering over port and brandy with men in red coats telling dirty stories while it snows outside," Connolly wrote. His theory of underachievement—that Eton and Balliol had spoiled him for anything else—does seem to be shored up by the example of Waugh, who went to a lesser school and a smaller college, and was therefore left with something to prove. Absurd, but that is how England (or a fraction of it) sometimes works. "Cyril is the most typical man of my generation," Waugh asserted. "He has the authentic lack of scholarship."

The Unquiet Grave is indeed unscholarly, but it is also bookish to a fault. Composed under the pseudonym Palinurus—the pilot of Aeneas's ship, who fell overboard, washed ashore, and was murdered by the locals—it now feels less like a chronicle of self-pity than like a perfectly pitched anthem of wartime, as true to its era as *Little Gidding*. Connolly's prose reeks of the ration book and the air-raid shelter, of pages thumbed by candlelight; and his indecision—that perpetual sway between the eighteenth century and the severities of modernism, between the comforts of England and the lure of France—speaks of an embattled figure who has almost, but not quite, had enough. To anyone paralyzed by the thought of moral alternatives, Connolly proves that the hedonist and the ascetic need not be sworn rivals—that they can easily be blood brothers or a couple of swells and, in fact, are most usefully twinned within a single soul. If it is the case that, as Proust said, the only true paradises are those we have lost, why not push the irony a little harder and try to convince yourself that the only *point* of paradise is the losing of it—that the succulent moment is made sweet by the prospect of rot? Armed with this delightful logic, you can be sure of enjoying yourself even when—especially when—there is nothing to enjoy. Take the following passage from *The Condemned Play-*

ground, Connolly's 1945 collection of articles, reviews, and suspect journal entries:

> Bad lunch on Dover boat and dreary crossing. Oh, the superb wretchedness of English food, how many foreigners has it daunted, and what a subtle glow of nationality one feels in ordering a dish that one knows will be bad and being able to eat it! The French do not understand cooking, only good cooking—this is where we score.

When I first read these words, some years ago, I knew instantly that Connolly was a Good Thing, but time spent with Fisher's biography has only fortified my suspicion that he could also be a Bad Man. His marriages, to Jean Bakewell, Barbara Skelton, and Deirdre Craven, seem mostly to have veered from tempest to doldrum without passing through contentment. Any accusations that you can level at Connolly—of inconstancy, say, or snobbery, or dilettantism—are worse than useless, for he long ago tortured himself with similar charges, and twisted the knife until the wound was well explored. The attempt to gauge precisely where his self-loathing backs into self-aggrandizement is likely to leave his readers in a unique state of itchiness. His closest kinsman in this respect is Henry Adams, another round-the-clock moocher, and you can't help noticing that both men were pressed by their perversities of spirit into fangling a new literary form: the *Education* tacks back and forth between the long historical vista and the lugubrious gaze into a mirror, while Connolly's three most important books—*Enemies of Promise*, *The Unquiet Grave*, and *The Condemned Playground*—are all Pyrrhic victories over the forces of fragmentation. Like a bored bright child, or an old man unable to sleep, Connolly slides restlessly from one topic to the next. Literary analysis jostles with autobiography, and the parody of current fads makes way for a daunting encomium to his idols. In *The Unquiet Grave* he writes:

> What are masterpieces? Let us name a few. The Odes and Epistles of Horace, the Eclogues and Georgics of Virgil, the Testament of Villon, the Essays of Montaigne, the Fables of La Fontaine, the Maxims of La Rochefoucauld and La Bruyère, the Fleurs du Mal and Intimate Journals of Baudelaire, the Poems of Pope and Leopardi, the Illuminations of Rimbaud, and Byron's Don Juan.

It is an impeccable catalogue of works that share what Connolly calls "the maximum of emotion compatible with a classical sense of form," but there is real cunning, too, in the social mixture: if he had thrown a dinner party for this little cluster of geniuses (which would have been his idea of Heaven), how would the wild boys have fared with the well-behaved? How could Villon not get up Virgil's nose? Connolly was tempted by both categories: more than once, he had to seek out a Maecenas who could support his literary ventures, but the desire to cut loose, sleep around, or simply sleep all day was equally acute. He allowed his eternally peckish hormones to range free, like chickens, and indulged his dreamy Francophilia to the hilt. (English fondness for France is normally a sort of neutron love: take away the people and leave the buildings standing. Connolly got it right: he worshipped Pascal and Montaigne, and proceeded from there.) I have long looked up to him as the patron saint of sluggards, of gentlemen in England now abed; he was forever on the lookout for reasons not to get things done, and, despite his own psychological probing of this vice, we shouldn't lose sight of the more prosaic possibility that, however fine a writer, he was even more content to be a reader.

I was not sure before I opened Clive Fisher's book that Cyril Connolly merited a long biography. Couldn't his life be covered by his own chosen medium, the extended essay? But Fisher argues his case well and without pretension—it's a dry, judicious, nicely turned piece of work—and he tunes in fast to Connolly's quixotic tastes, even managing to keep track of the innumerable mammals that scampered about the critic's home. Ferrets, lemurs, a mongoose, and a coatimundi: did they stare up at Cyril's puffy features and spot a kindred spirit? The party trick of one particular lemur was to rush out into mixed company and bite a selected man on the penis; I consider it a matter of lasting regret that the creature failed to perform when Evelyn Waugh came to tea. Fisher takes Connolly's lyrical reveries on his menagerie at face value, as he takes much else; his book is slightly flattened, in fact, by its lack of humor. "You can't be too serious," Connolly once observed, with magnificent ambivalence. Did he mean "The need to be serious is unending" or "Lighten up"? Fisher's book presumes the former, but there is plenty to laugh at in Connolly's emotionally scrambled life, not least because the man himself took such relish in its conditions. His prescription for happily married life, for instance, is fraught with implied drama: "Whenever you can, read at meals." Similarly, to those making new acquaintances on the African plains: "If attacked by a lion thrust your arm down his throat. This takes some practice."

The string of travel pieces that Connolly produced in his later years—he was a chronic wanderer, shifting from town to country and then to the

Continent—betray a light-headed enthusiasm that seems a world away from the heavy heart of *The Unquiet Grave.* Who would have thought that the grouchy skeptic would finally be tamed by wildlife? Or that the famously blocked writer would, in the end, leave behind a legacy of thirteen books? If Connolly was honestly straining after what he called "a supreme design for failure," then, as this biography demonstrates, he failed. *Horizon* was a weighty success by any standard: from the work of Auden, Betjeman, MacNeice, Spender, and Henry Moore that graced the first issue to the notorious soothsaying of the last ("It is closing time in the gardens of the West"), Connolly's brainchild managed to keep its brow high but its touch surprisingly light. The very manner in which Connolly describes the hangover of its end—"Contributions continued inexorably to be delivered, like a suicide's milk"—shows that the dying fall of a Connolly sentence will long hum in the ear of anyone foolish enough to be obsessed with English prose.

Not long before Connolly visited America in 1946, he was credited by Jacques Barzun, then professor of history at Columbia, with "a representative modern mind," which is a pretty mean thing to say about anybody. It's like calling someone a great lover or a snappy dresser: from then on, failure will set in like a frost. Connolly's mind, like his library or his diet, represented no more than a small chunk of England at a certain time. What makes him touching is a lifelong effort *not* to represent his class—to turn down invitations and resist the polite hint that literature lies somewhere between a hobby and an embarrassment. If you want Connolly without literature, try the memoirs of Barbara Skelton—they are gossip-ridden, impatient, and, in every sense, artless. But when we turn to her husband's meditations on Baudelaire, or rococo architecture, or "the stormy life of wine," we reach the safe haven of the balanced mind, as cool and well stocked as a cellar. Connolly would have seconded the opinion of his hero, Flaubert, who said, "Something read in a book moves me more than a real misfortune." To subscribe to such a view is in itself a misfortune—it will shrink and shrivel you—but it promises riches of its own, and Connolly is one of the last Englishmen who thought it worth the risk.

JANUARY 29, 1996

IAN FLEMING

Who reads James Bond these days? More to the point, who knows that it is possible to read James Bond at all? Watching Bond is easy enough, and imitating him is kind of fun, if you can take the vodka. But *reading* him—well, apart from anything else, it sounds so un-Bondish. You don't catch 007 settling down for an early night with a cup of tea and a Stendhal. He is known to be a big fan of *Scarne on Cards*, and he once consulted that noble volume for a full half hour before fleecing Sir Hugo Drax of fifteen thousand pounds at Blades, in St. James's, but that was work. Bond could no more immerse himself in a novel than he could feed a .45 slug into the chamber of a Colt Detective Special. And yet he was born in a book—*Casino Royale*, which appeared in 1953. His publisher boasted that one copy was sold every six and a half minutes. There were thirteen more Bond titles to follow, and they became an industry unto themselves. Soon after Kennedy was elected president, *Life* ran a list of his ten favorite books: there, at No. 9, stood *From Russia, with Love*. By the time the movie of that name was released, in 1963, there were more than ten million Bond paperbacks in print in America. They had brought glamour and, it was presumed, immortality to the names of James Bond and of his creator, Ian Fleming.

A few weeks ago, I traipsed around the bookstores of New York in search of Bond. Five times, I drew a blank: nothing under "Fleming," either in the fiction section or among the other thrillers. At the sixth attempt, I came across a hardback set of the novels that had been remaindered at less than four dollars a copy. Nobody, it appears, wants Bond on the page anymore, apart from the antiquarians. Here is a man whom SMERSH and SPECTRE would track to the ends of the earth, but the only readers who hunt him down these days are collectors of first editions, who will pay hundreds of dollars for a mint early Bond, unfoxed and preferably unread, with the dust jacket in perfect condition. You could argue that the decline of Bond coincided with the last rites of communism, from which he drew his staunchest foes, but the truth is that 007 is riding higher than ever in the cinemas, and therefore in the public mind—a ride that is pulling him ever further away from the mind that conceived him. Fleming's fiction, both in spirit and in detail, is now deemed to be so outdated that I should probably have looked for it on the history shelf. James Bond is doing just fine; it is Ian Fleming who needs help.

Here, to the rescue, comes Andrew Lycett, who has written a solid new biography, entitled *Ian Fleming: The Man Behind James Bond.* Lycett's task is to restore a reputation, and he begins in full flag-waving mode, declaring in his prologue that Fleming was "a chameleon-like showman who presented the side of his character he thought people wanted to see." This is unfair both to chameleons, who devote so much of their energy to not being seen, and to Fleming himself, who seems to have spent most of his time getting his own way and not giving a damn. Not only did he tell the steward on the *Twentieth Century* how to mix a martini, for example, but he did so all the way from New York to Albany. "Wonderful ideas and wrongheaded arguments, tremendous charm and occasional shocking manners; a very good mind which I fear will never expand to capacity owing to an unfortunate adroitness at short cuts and a gift for well-organized leisure": that was the steel-tipped verdict delivered by his wife, Ann, and it makes Fleming sound close to impossible—bereft of the stamina, courtesy, and strange tranquillity of Bond. Lycett also quotes an anonymous partygoer from the mid-fifties: "Ian Fleming. Writes terrible books. Handsome in an 'old shoe' kind of way. Very forward with the ladies. Loves black lingerie." That's more like it.

Ian Lancaster Fleming was born in Mayfair in 1908. His mother, Eve, was a terrifying mixture of the aesthetic and the formidable; his father, a banker and a Conservative MP, came of rich Scottish stock and died on the front line in 1917. True to his genes, the young Ian—indeed, the Ian of all ages—swerved back and forth between a chappish bluffness and a surprising, if slightly strained, weakness for more rarefied pursuits. Few schoolboys complement a precocious athletic success, as Fleming did at Eton, by publishing a magazine that contained a poem by Vita Sackville-West. (It also contained a sketch by Augustus John, with whom Ian's widowed mother conducted a lengthy affair.) There is a tradition in England which states, not always convincingly, that arty types are required to loathe their public schools, whereas the hearties must have a rousing time and barely drag themselves away. Fleming, needless to say, was reluctant to settle in either camp; when his friend Paul Gallico prefaced a Bond compendium with an essay on Fleming that referred to his "implacable distaste for Eton," Fleming took the manuscript and changed those first two words to "mysterious affection."

Within that tiny revision—a brilliant find by Lycett—you can spy not just the torn complications of Fleming himself but the even more thwarted temperament of his most distinguished offspring. There is no point, as this biography demonstrates, in trying to map Bond closely on Fleming's character, yet both men grew to be grand masters of distaste, struggling manfully to discover anything, or anyone, able to command and keep their mysterious affection. The Bond books are invariably chided for their snobbery, but I find that their most touching legacy, for it is born not of breeding but of fear: it is Bond's heart rather than his job which draws him away from too close an engagement with the world. His preferred rapport is not with the passing goddesses and their comedy names (Domino, Honeychile, the unmistakable Pussy), or even with Tracy, the wild child whom he marries and loses at the end of *On Her Majesty's Secret Service*, but with his fellow-professionals on the opposing side, those who have registered equal contempt for an ordinary existence. Tracy's embrace suits him less than the poisoned blade that slides from the toe cap of Rosa Klebb.

So what does Bond love? The same things as Fleming, I guess: England, or England as it was, or an idea of England; men without women in a London club, savoring their claret and losing their unearned money with good grace at the gaming tables; "grilled soles, oeufs cocotte and cold roast beef with potato salad." Fleming set similar limits to his taste: when he lured potential conquests back to his bachelor pad, it was always the same old menu—sausages or kedgeree, champagne, coffee, bed. How he could tell a sausage girl from a kedgeree girl is not recorded. There is something paranoid—joyless, indeed—in joys so precisely regimented, but such were the patterns by which Fleming measured out his days and nights in the London of the 1930s. After Eton, he devoted himself to the pursuit of loucheness: military training cut short by the clap, the polishing of his languages at the universities of Munich and Geneva, and a raffish spell with Reuters, where a typical assignment required him to act as navigator on the Alpine motor trials.

From Reuters it was a short, if mood-lowering, move across to the City, where Fleming became, according to a friend, one of the worst stockbrokers in existence. The book's account of the young rake going into business—"His most important contact was the autocratic Lancy Hugh

Smith, third son of Hugh Colin Smith, Governor of the Bank of England from 1897 to 1899," and so on—shows that Lycett is one of those awesome fact hogs who dig up details that were perfectly content to lie buried in eternal gloom. When Fleming has an affair with a certain Maud Russell, we immediately learn all about the backgrounds of the partners of her husband's merchant bank. Yet this tendency toward excess, which fattens *Ian Fleming* to the bursting point, is not really a cause for regret, because it provides a useful service: it can hardly help reminding you of the perpetual, enthralling overkill of Fleming's fiction. What Lycett does with bankers and big-chinned aristocrats, Fleming did with everything under the sun, and under the belt, and over the counter. If you sit down and read all the Bond books—especially if you read them in sequence, starting with *Casino Royale* and closing with *Octopussy*—they melt and mold together into one unending fetishist's dream:

> His two battered suitcases came and he unpacked leisurely and then ordered from Room Service a bottle of the Taittinger Blanc de Blancs that he had made his traditional drink at Royale. When the bottle, in its frosted silver bucket, came, he drank a quarter of it rather fast and then went into the bathroom and had an ice-cold shower and washed his hair with Pinaud Elixir, that prince among shampoos, to get the dust of the roads out of it. Then he slipped on his dark-blue tropical worsted trousers, white sea-island cotton shirt, socks and black casual shoes (he abhorred shoe-laces), and went and sat by the window and looked out across the promenade to the sea and wondered where he would have dinner and what he would choose to eat.

Readers who like to think that brand-name addiction arose with Bret Easton Ellis's *American Psycho* should get a load of this passage from *Thunderball.* It prompts several thoughts: that the author has yet to learn what part of speech "leisurely" is; that Bond could easily be gay; and that the recitation of material comforts, when it is taken to extremes, eventually acquires a surreal lyricism that is, indeed, somewhat comforting. Bond's need to stabilize his rocky moods with constant shots of luxury (and the notion that he can afford to do so on a midlevel government salary) is part of what you might call the Fleming theory of self-possession: pile up the possessions, and the self will begin to emerge.

There is another, more innocent pleasure to be had from the accoutrements that litter the Bond books. It is the pleasure of the time capsule.

Fleming was an obsessive notetaker wherever he went—it relieved him of the pressure to be creative, which was never his strong suit. The density of his research now pulls his readers effortlessly back into a distant, upbeat vision of the fifties and sixties, when luxury was no embarrassment and travel was a gas. Here is Bond starting his flight to America: "The chief steward announced over the loudspeaker that the next stop would be Shannon, where they would dine, and that the flying time would be one hour and fifty minutes, and the great double-decked Stratocruiser rolled slowly out to the east-west runway." *Where they would dine:* it's like reading Thackeray.

But the true spirit of the fiction, as opposed to the trimmings, can more fruitfully be traced to another era. Fleming had long nurtured his journalist's contacts in the world of spying, and in August of 1939 they paid off. Shedding with relief the tasks of the stockbroker, he became the assistant to the director of naval intelligence (DNI) in the Naval Intelligence Division (NID), assuming the rank of lieutenant. A month later, he was promoted, as Bond would be, to commander, a distinction commemorated in the three gold bands that were subsequently applied to his (and Bond's) handmade cigarettes; his standing order was for a smog-inducing four hundred a week. Fleming had what is technically known as a good war. He performed well, met women in uniform, and, above all, had the opportunity to write stuff like this:

1. Obtain from the Air Ministry an air-worthy German bomber.
2. Pick a tough crew of five, including a pilot, W/T operator and word-perfect German speaker. Dress them in German Air Force uniform, add blood and bandages to suit.
3. Crash plane in the Channel after making SOS to rescue service in P/L.
4. Once aboard rescue boat, shoot German crew, dump overboard, bring rescue boat back to English port.

Under any other circumstances, this fantasy—two parts rococo to one part macho—would have been dismissed as the sort of irresponsible junk that you expect from, say, a novelist. In the Britain of 1940 it was, albeit briefly, given serious consideration. Fleming even appended his idea of the ideal pilot for the mission: "Tough bachelor, able to swim." Who on earth could he have had in mind? The standard reading of Bond is that he was, in essence, a creature of the cold war, but that merely happened to be his setting. His itchy feet, his urge to spread abroad the stalwart values of home (the cover for Fleming's fictional Secret Service was a company named Universal Export), the comical lengths he would go to in flexing and finessing his courage, and the occasional twinge of anxiety that the sacrifice might not be worthwhile: all these were rooted in the Second World War. The novels tell us that Bond saw action in the Navy, but more crucial was Fleming's own inaction—the practice swings of his imagination, as it were, in which he dreamed up escapades for fit young men.

It was in room 39—his office at the Admiralty—that Fleming also nurtured his love of gadgetry, and the sensation of control that it provides. "I'm going to put this in simple terms and not fill you up with a lot of stuff about Nozzle Expansion Ratios, Exhaust Velocity, and the Keplerian Ellipse," says the rocket wonk in *Moonraker*, thus allowing Fleming to prove that he personally is filled with stuff right up to the brim. We take it for granted that the mid-period Bond movies, depressed by the departure of Sean Connery, became fixated on dumb gizmos and weak jokes; but is the Roger Moore version of *Moonraker*, in which Bond saves the world and expands his nozzle in zero-gravity orbit, really any worse than the plot of Fleming's book, which asks us to believe that Britain would hand over the construction and launch of its first nuclear deterrent to a private individual with millions in the bank and red whiskers on his face? Lord Beaverbrook, not a man to waste words, called the book a "thrilling story about the good secret service bloke and the bad bastard": an unimprovable piece of critical analysis, I think, in its awareness that what matters about the Bond novels is the central duel of wits between compulsives. This is the one element that has descended from Fleming to the more plaintive, downbeat world of John le Carré: no more kidnapping of nukes but an increasingly single-minded conflict between Smiley and Karla, recalling the great set pieces of Bond versus Blofeld, Bond versus Largo, Bond versus Drax.

In Lycett's hands, Fleming himself becomes a case study in casual megalomania. His friend Ernie Cunco (later immortalized, for what it was worth, as a cabdriver named Ernie Curco in *Diamonds Are Forever*) once sat on a train and listened to a standard reverie. "Know what I'd like if I could have anything I wanted?" Fleming asked. "I'd like to be the absolute ruler of a country where everybody was crazy about me. Imagine yourself waking up in the White House. Instantly, the radio would announce to a breathless country, 'He's awake.' Bulletins would follow. 'He's shaving.' 'He's dressing.' 'He's breakfasting.' 'He's reading the papers in the garden.' Finally, at ten-thirty: 'He's ordered the car.' And at eleven o'clock I'd pass out through the gates, tossing medals to deliriously happy hundreds of thousands. I'd like that. And so would they." It is the last line that kills the humor of the speech and sends it spinning toward madness. The clinching vanity of the control freak—be he Blofeld or Mussolini or a self-inflated Fleming—is to assume that world domination must logically involve the world loving you back.

In Fleming's case, the power kick was almost, but not entirely, harmless. We should be grateful that he became a writer, and never thought of going into politics—a calling that he loftily despised. After the war, he became foreign manager of Kemsley Newspapers, which in practice meant joining the editorial conference at the *Sunday Times* and keeping track of foreign correspondents by means of a world map covered with flashing lights—"a fair old load of bullshit," according to one observer. There is something vaguely pathetic in the image—in the delusions of influence that it suggests, in the echo of a need to live dangerously. The only real risk in Fleming's life at this time was his friendship with Ann Rothermere, the famously cultivated and well-connected wife of the proprietor of a rival newspaper; she married Ian in 1952, roughly a month after he embarked on the career that would bring him fame, wealth, and a steady drip of ridicule from his wife's friends. According to Lycett, "Ian used to say that he wrote *Casino Royale* in order to take his mind off the horrific prospect of matrimony."

By Fleming's standards, that remark counts as New Age compassion. Whatever else this biography achieves, it will stand as an unrivalled anthology of chauvinist zingers. Fleming once admitted that his perfect wife would be a Dresden shepherdess. Like his friend Evelyn Waugh, Fleming was one of those writers who are at their funniest when they're being most objectionable. But he had boreholes of resentment where Waugh was calmed by irony, and he invariably ends up as the victim of his own jokes. "In the old days I demanded or perhaps pleaded for three things in a wife. She should have enough money to buy her own clothes, she should be able to make incomparable Sauce Béarnaise, and she should be double-jointed. In the event I got none of these things," he said of Ann. What he did get was a willing partner in his sadomasochistic rites: "I am the chosen instrument of the Holy Man to whip some of the devil out of you," he wrote to her, "and I must do my duty however much pain it causes me. So be prepared to drink your cocktails standing for a few days."

Where Fleming acquired his whippy tastes is hard to say, but Lycett does mention that Ian's housemaster at Eton "enjoyed wielding the cane"; and I couldn't help noticing that the youthful Fleming had in rapid succession a mentor called Phyllis Bottome *and* a lover called Monique Panchaud de Bottomes. Where the predilection ended, of course, is far more predictable: with "a beautiful Arab mare who would only allow herself to be ridden by a horseman with steel thighs and velvet hands, and then only with curb and saw bit—and then only when he had broken her to bridle and saddle." That is the heroine of *Thunderball*, and the poor girl doesn't have a chance; what dooms her to nothingness is not just sexual submission but the certainty that Fleming's self-arousing prose will forbid her to slip the shackles of caricature and become a character. The last word in gender relations comes in my favorite passage from *Moonraker*, a locus classicus of the unhip:

> Hair: Auburn. Eyes: Blue. Height: 5 ft. 7. Weight: 9 stone. Hips: 38. Waist: 26. Bust: 38. Distinguishing marks: Mole on upper curvature of right breast.
>
> Hm! thought Bond.

All of which leads us to ask the question, Why should we bother with Ian Fleming, or even with Bond? Lycett's long, dry biography is nevertheless worth reading, because it convinces you that Fleming was one of those people who are ideally read about in books; you come away feeling relieved that you never had to encounter him in real life. And what of *his* books? It is hard to deny that many of them remain graceless and indolent; even the saving virtues of the cheap thriller are often beyond them. Pace? Try grinding your way through the start of *From Russia, with Love*, in which Bond doesn't so much as show his face until chapter 11. Plausibility? If anyone can tell me why a brainwashed Bond tries to squirt cyanide at M. at the beginning of *The Man with the Golden Gun*, thus giving his beloved boss a chance to use the new sliding glass screen in front of his desk, I'd be very grateful. Why didn't 007 make use of that excellent invention known as a gun?

And yet in recent weeks I have read little else. The pleasure of finishing one Bond story and immediately picking up the next becomes peculiar and intense. The overall effect veers toward that of Jacobean drama: there is something dark and nasty about slipping into the poisoned moral swamp of Fleming's tales while the bright, silly plots fade from view. (It is the precise opposite of watching the Bond movies.) Fleming's Bond is notoriously devoted to the good things in life, but not for a moment do they tempt him into the belief that life itself is a good thing. His devotion, in fact, seems to spring from a half-hidden disgust; Lycett thinks that Bond is an antidote to boredom, to what Mr. Big, in *Live and Let Die*, describes as "the deadly lethargy that envelops those who are sated, those who have no more desires," but I like to think that Bond himself has to fight off satiety as if it were sleep. He works up his desires and seeks out the likelihood of fresh kills purely to sustain his interest in the world and to play a role, however meaningless, in its functioning. There's a flare of true contempt in *From Russia, with Love*, when Bond surveys his younger self: "What would he think of Bond's present assignment? What would he think of the dashing secret agent who was off across the world in a new and most romantic role—to pimp for England?" Hm! Like Fleming, Bond has to pretend that drabness and decline aren't there—that they will go away if you sip enough champagne, sleep with enough women, keep your Bentley polished, and maintain sufficiently close links with the prince among shampoos. The strain of the pretense told on Fleming, who suffered a heart attack in 1961 and died three years later, at the age of fifty-six. James Bond, meanwhile, in his scarred and pernickety solitude, acquired a life of his own and made the most of his bitterness: he turned low spirits into high style. "As Bond's biographer," Fleming once said, "I am most anxious to see that he lives as long as possible." His wish was granted.

JUNE 24, 1996

T. S. ELIOT

One day in the early 1980s, someone handed me a sheaf of papers. It was explained that I should on no account copy them and pass them on to anyone else, so, of course, I had no choice but to copy them and pass them on to someone else. And thus the early poems of T. S. Eliot smoldered and spread, in unreliable samizdat versions of manuscripts held at the Berg Collection in the New York Public Library. Rumor had it that Eliot fanatics, deprived of writing instruments, had sat in the library, memorized chunks of the verse, strolled to the lavatory, scribbled the lines on toilet paper with a concealed pencil, and tucked the results into their shoes: a legend so completely untrue that I instantly believed it. As I slipped my modernist contraband back under the floorboards every night, it seemed only a matter of time before I would be hustled out of a student café by black-hooded library operatives from the notorious Bergmeister squad, taken to lonely woods, and interrogated as to what I knew about a man named Prufrock. Still, it was a risk worth taking, for the sake of stuff like this:

The lady of the porcelain department
Smiles at the world through a set of false teeth.
She is business-like and keeps a pencil in her hair

But behind her sharpened eyes take flight
The summer evenings in the park
And heated nights in second story dance halls.

Man's life is powerless and brief and dark
It is not possible for me to make her happy.

The poem itself takes flight, starting in a department store and alighting at last on grand statements. At any rate, they sound grand; so precociously did Eliot school and steel himself in irony that what he has to say about man's life may, like the lady's teeth, have the appearance of truth, and even the ring of confidence, but should not be taken for the real thing. And that payoff is a poser. Who is this "me" making a last-minute entrance? And who suggested that it was either his right or his duty to make the woman happy? Eliot, throughout his poetic career, rejoiced gloomily in the mock-gnomic: in lines that court sententiousness and then leave it bereft, sidestepping with infuriating ease into the genuinely mysterious. "Old men ought to be explorers," he wrote in "East Coker." So what should young men be doing with their time?

Now we know. *Inventions of the March Hare: Poems 1909–1917*, edited by Christopher Ricks, brings to light a trove of almost fifty poems that had seemed destined to stay in the dark. Eliot trackers, like students of government policy, have grown accustomed to the immanent presence of classified material. There are, for instance, the letters to his close friend Emily Hale, hundreds of which remain under embargo at Princeton until the year 2020. And there are, or were, the poems that appear in this volume: prior to its publication, scholars could consult them but were forbidden by the Eliot estate to quote even the merest sliver. After so long a wait, you could be forgiven for finding some of the verse a trifle underpowered:

> On every sultry afternoon
> Verandah customs have the call
> White flannel ceremonial
> With cakes and tea
> And guesses at eternal truths
> Sounding the depths with a silver spoon
> And dusty roses, crickets, sunlight on the sea
>   And all.

This could only be Eliot, and yet it isn't quite Eliot. Everything is in place, but he hasn't tightened the screws; there is a lingering vagueness in the verse—"so elegant / So intelligent," in the words of *The Waste Land*—which Eliot would soon dispel. "The vague is a more dangerous path for poetry than the arid," as he said with severity in 1917. Those "verandah customs," too, are surprisingly unpeopled: various figures drift through *Inventions of the March Hare*—dandies, marionettes, ladies of the night, and "ladies who are interested in Assyrian art," as opposed to Michelangelo—but few of them are very lively, or even alive. If one were forced to make a distinction between these rough drafts and the finer finish of *Prufrock and Other Observations* it would not be made on a strictly poetic basis: Eliot's ear was already as well tuned as the young Tennyson's, but what he had yet to acquire was the ability to dramatize—to play all the parts and direct the action as well.

If there are no undiscovered masterpieces in *Inventions of the March Hare*, so what? Eliot readers would not expect them, since it was part of his genius—a twinning of his arrogance and his modesty—to refrain from publishing his poems until and unless they were first-rate. It follows that anything left behind was not up to scratch, although Eliot's scratch level is exhaustingly high. Unlike Pound and Yeats, he didn't limber up with lightweight volumes of semi-archaic lyrics before going public with the heavy stuff; he kept his pastiches and his practice pieces to himself, and then, when the time was propitious, he calmly changed the plot of English literature. "Let us go then, you and I": the first line of the first poem in Eliot's first book.

Inventions of the March Hare is the title that Eliot inscribed—and later crossed out—on the flyleaf of a leather-covered notebook. The earliest poems inside are dated November 1909, when he had just turned twenty-one. An auspicious time, suited to stocktaking: the poet supplied an alternative title, *Complete Poems of T. S. Eliot*, which Ricks calls "sardonic." But it also bolsters the strange feeling that Eliot was always older than his actual age, and was draping himself with a gravitas that should have taken decades to acquire. Just as *Four Quartets* shakes with the regrets and pacifications that we associate with the elderly but was in fact completed by a man in his fifties, so "The Love Song of J. Alfred Prufrock" is, among other things, a pitch-perfect act of ventriloquism by a young tyro who wishes—or finds it convenient—to sound like one of Henry James's flustered bachelors. Though "Prufrock" was not published until 1915, Eliot was working on it by the summer of 1911. Meet it in the company of *Inventions of the March Hare* and you are hit by the unnerving thought that in terms of chronology, if of nothing else, it rates as juvenilia.

So how come "Prufrock" *feels* mature—as ripe as anything that Eliot, cheese lover extraordinary, ever sniffed? What Ricks's magnificent edition proves is that "Prufrock" was indeed no beginning but the end product of a short and concentrated period of rhythmic rehearsal. *Inventions of the March Hare* is a barrage of dummy runs. It perfects the fine art of hesitation, exclamation, and all the other nervy, stop-go thrusts of Prufrockian motion; there is even a chunk entitled "Prufrock's Pervigilium," most of which was cut from the poem like the fat that Ezra Pound later skimmed from *The Waste Land*. The weather that broods over the collection is heavily dusk-based, and you wonder whether any poet operating between

1890 and 1920 was *allowed* to get up before five o'clock in the evening; but, although Eliot borrows the Georgian poets' clock, he refuses to veil himself in their gray mood. Instead, he sifts through a landscape of unlovely junk:

A street-piano, garrulous and frail;
The yellow evening flung against the panes
Of dirty windows: and the distant strains
Of children's voices, ended in a wail.

Bottles and broken glass,
Trampled mud and grass;
A heap of broken barrows;
And a crowd of tattered sparrows
Delve in the gutter with sordid patience.
Oh, these minor considerations! . . . .

This poem, written in 1909, is called "First Caprice in North Cambridge"—Massachusetts, not England—and any Eliot groupies reading it for the first time will be crossing their legs with excitement. So much Eliot seems to be sprouting in these lines: the street-piano will chime with the same instrument, "mechanical and tired," in "Portrait of a Lady," a poem that fades, as if with weariness, into an "evening yellow and rose"; the sparrows and gutters will greet the early waker in "Preludes"; "The Hollow Men" will put "broken glass" under rats' feet; "a heap of broken barrows" will tumble into *The Waste Land*, which will replace "barrows" with the broader "images" and will, for good measure, find room for "voix d'enfants" instead of "children's voices"—sounds that will haunt Eliot's ear as far as a minor poem called "New Hampshire" in 1934, and perhaps even further, into "Little Gidding":

The voice of the hidden waterfall
And the children in the apple-tree.

If you find all that a bit rich, you should try the Ricks edition, which flatters "First Caprice in North Cambridge" with four solid pages of notes in small type. Forget the poems that it would subsequently father. What about those that were present at its birth? Influences mentioned by Ricks for this short poem alone include those of Verlaine, Hardy, Mallarmé, Tennyson, Shelley, Milton, Longfellow, Henri Bergson, William Dean Howells, and, of course, Jules Laforgue, the poet who most thoroughly soaks the work of the young Eliot. Only a few of them are certifiable sources for the poem; some are no more than gentle suggestions. What Ricks is doing in this volume—and I am not sure that it has ever been done for any poet in such careful density—is to re-create the literary conditions under which the poet labored. The air of 1909 was filled with noises; all that we can say is that Eliot listened harder than most, and all that Ricks can do is offer a précis of those sounds. Sometimes they are nothing *but* sounds: confronted by Eliot's freaky rhyme "Cassiopeia / Explained the Pure Idea," Ricks compares the proximity, in Tennyson's "The Princess," of the word "Cassiopeia" and the refrain "Ida, Ida, Ida"—Ida being the name of Tennyson's heroine. Many will scoff at the thought, but we should never undersell the happy misreading.

At first sight, *Inventions of the March Hare* looks out of whack: 80 pages of verse in a book of 428 pages. But Eliot can do with all the annotation he can get. Apart from *The Waste Land* and *Four Quartets*, none of his published poems are available in decently annotated texts. As for Eliot's critical essays, what a mess. We live with what might be called a Faberized Eliot: reams of the honored sage, morose and verging on the pontifical, and not enough of the nimble young reviewer with his well-stropped wit. You can buy *The Idea of a Christian Society*, and you can read his awkward public attempt to be gracious about Goethe ("I can't stand his stuff," Eliot admitted privately), but unless you have access to a research library the short, shocking pieces on Henry Adams or Turgenev, say, will remain a closed book.

No wonder, then, that Christopher Ricks should make the most of his opportunity. Here is a chance not so much to read anything new into Eliot as to read behind him—to wield a "vigilant but never theoretic intelligence," as Eliot himself said of Turgenev. Any fear that Ricks is ascribing unnatural powers of assimilation to the poet, reducing him to a memory bank in a suit, should be countered by the fact that this is T. S. Eliot we are talking about; however much you think he may have read, you're way short. Having said that Shakespeare got more out of Plutarch than most men would get out of the British Museum, Eliot hedged his bets by consuming vast areas of Plutarch *and* the British Museum. The immense scholarly apparatus at the back of *Inventions of the March Hare* cannot be said to make a mountain out of a molehill, for the simple reason that a good Eliot poem is, more often than not, a molehill made out of a mountain.

All of which explains why Ricks's edition is the best book ever written on Eliot. That it is not a critical study is no accident. Eliot once said, "The ordinary man's experience in chaotic, irregular, fragmentary. [He] falls in love, or reads Spinoza, and these two experiences have nothing to do with each other, or with the noise of the typewriter or the smell of cooking; in the mind of the poet these experiences are always forming new wholes." If we admire a poem, it is natural that we should wish to isolate those original components; equally, it is indisputable that we shall fail, if only because we can never know what was cooking in the next room when Eliot was trying to write. Likewise, his falling in love (or, if we are talking of his first wife, Vivienne, his falling out of love) is a matter of great interest but of even greater conjecture—"hints followed by guesses," to borrow a phrase from *Four Quartets*. The only firm ground is Spinoza country, or Laforgue land, or wherever Eliot was toiling at the time. These are the areas that can be mapped, without presumption, by editors and critics, and no one is more skilled than Ricks at covering the ground. Eliot said that the poems in *Inventions of the March Hare* were "unpublished and unpublishable," and it is a pleasure to see him, on both counts, proved wrong.

There are those, of course, who think that Eliot was wrong pretty much all the time. When *Inventions of the March Hare* came out in England last year, it made waves in some of the newspapers. Not because of a sudden surge in the public taste for vers libre but because of lines like this:

> Bolo's big black bastard queen
> Was *so* obscene
> She shocked the folk of Golder's Green.

Which shows what happens when vers becomes too libre for its own good. The rhyme, which manages in a short space to insult both blacks and Jews (Golders Green, a suburb of North London, has a strong Jewish community), forms part of Appendix A to Ricks's edition. He prints a selection of Eliot's dirty verses, none of them published in the poet's lifetime. "The editor is aware that such scabrous exuberances may lend themselves to either the wrong kind or the wrong amount of attention," Ricks writes. You bet they may. Poor Tom was a fogey, a bigot, a woman-hater, and an anti-Semite, but now it turns out that he laughed at blacks, too. How's that for a full house?

There is much in *Inventions of the March Hare* that will cause the poetry police to twitch their batons in anticipation. A poem called "The Love Song of St. Sebastian" contains the rhyme "strangled you" / "mangled you" and the sheer physical weirdness of

> I would come with a towel in my hand
> And bend your head beneath my knees;

which suggests, if not calculated sadism, a certain tinge of the bathhouse. You begin to wonder whether the courteous Eliot held back from publishing some of these verses for fear that they would turn weak stomachs:

> Do I know how I feel? Do I know how I think?
> There is something which should be firm
> but slips, just at my finger tips.
> There will be a smell of creolin and the
> sound of something that drips
> A black bag with a pointed beard and
> tobacco on his breath
> With chemicals and a knife
> Will investigate the cause of death that was
> also the cause of the life—

The poet who once attended a fancy-dress party in the guise of Dr. Crippen never lost his taste for the macabre, and this passage, in its pungent domestic horror, feels seriously nasty. The stink of it will filter through to "Sweeney Agonistes," but Eliot could scarcely improve on the hard metaphysical punch of that final line. It sets in train a long process of investigation, culminating with *The Waste Land* and "The Hollow Men," into the extent to which life itself can kill.

The ditty about the black queen, however, is of an entirely different order. To begin with, like most of the "exuberances," it is negligible as poetry; there is nothing to it except the sneer. What is more, we have seen it before. It appeared in a letter to James Joyce in 1921 and was published in 1988 in the first volume of the poet's letters, edited by his widow, Valerie Eliot. Little fuss was made then. Eliot scholars had long known of his weakness for the scurrilous and the racist: it was, however regrettable, part of the scenery. What changed everything was the appearance last year of *T. S. Eliot, Anti-Semitism, and Literary Form*, by Anthony Julius. At once urgent and scrupulous, Julius's book is powered by the contention that Eliot's attitude toward Jews *was* the scenery. Julius doesn't have much to go on, but it's enough. Exhibits include the scarcely believable moment in *After Strange Gods* when Eliot says that "reasons of race and religion combine to make any large number of free-thinking Jews undesirable," a passage from "Gerontion," and these lines from "Burbank with a Baedeker: Bleistein with a Cigar":

> The rats are underneath the piles.
> The jew is underneath the lot.
> Money in furs.

The lowercase "j" was quietly capitalized in later editions, as if the damage could be undone typographically. "Burbank" is not a dramatic monologue, so there is little point in trying to cloak the slur within the mind of a putative character, or in disputing the animosity that prevails. What needs to be measured is the extent of that animosity. Julius does something rather Ricks-like with it: he reaches behind a handful of instances to disclose an entire history of prejudice—a wide tradition of contempt that narrowed to Eliot's individual talent. One hardly knows how to plumb the irony of the fact that Eliot particularly enjoyed reading his poetry to the Young Men's Hebrew Association in New York. "A very good, responsive audience," he said.

Julius is a lawyer by trade; for those who enjoy the frisson of such things, he represented Princess Diana in her divorce case. *T. S. Eliot, Anti-Semitism, and Literary Form* is a barrister's book: it succeeds less as literary criticism than as tireless cross-examination and withering summation. There are times when he pushes too hard. If, following Julius, you charge Eliot with anti-Semitism on the ground that he disparaged Freud, what are you going to do with a writer like Nabokov, whose anti-Freudian mockery was far more relentless but who also had to be dissuaded from throwing someone out of his house for making an anti-Semitic remark? More disturbing still is Julius's basic terminology. Every time he uses an apparently unexceptional phrase such as "Eliot's anti-Semitic poetry," or when he says that "Gerontion" is "an anti-Semitic poem," he is making a scary aesthetic assumption. To be blunt, how much loathing of Jews, covert or explicit, does a work of art have to display before we label it anti-Semitic? For that matter, how much love do you need to make a love poem? The word "jew" appears only once in "Gerontion," but Julius would argue that the tone is vicious enough to stain the whole poem. This seems to me unworkable: in saying that a poem is anti-Semitic, Julius implies that its drive—its essential purpose—is the denigration of Jews, whereas "Gerontion," the curtain call of the dramatic monologue, is a poem that splinters with helpless images of crackup and dislocation. Among them is what Julius terms "that most fatigued of cultural clichés, the Wandering Jew," but it does not overwhelm the poem as a whole, unless you want it to do so. These are rueful matters: I have long considered "Gerontion" one of the greatest short poems in the language, comparable—in more ways than one—to Tennyson's "Tithonus," but now I feel I should read it under the bedclothes. Does my history of reverence for the poem make me a suspect, too?

It is entirely to the credit of Anthony Julius that he should prod us to ask such questions. He inspects and prosecutes the anti-Semitism while never maintaining that Eliot was anything but a great poet. Would that such equipoise had transferred itself to his readers. Since the book was published, they have lined up in battle—and, indeed, created battle where none should exist. The critic Hugh Kenner launched a blustery defense of the poet in the *National Review*, while writers such as Frederic Raphael, Will Self, and James Fenton have sprung to the attack. In a lecture, Fenton called Eliot "a scoundrel," as if planning to horsewhip the fellow on the steps of a London club.

One must admit that there is something about Eliot, beyond the fact of his political opinions, that seems to encourage such assaults. They are nothing new. In 1949, he was among the Fellows of the Library of Congress who gave the Bollingen Prize to Ezra Pound for *The Pisan Cantos.* Pound, who had been charged with treason after his wartime activities, was being held in an asylum, and the award met with outrage. According to Eliot's biographer Peter Ackroyd, "Although Eliot was only one member of a jury which included Robert Lowell, W. H. Auden, Conrad Aiken and Katherine Anne Porter, he was singled out for abuse: in fact, he seemed to receive more than Pound himself." The *Saturday Review* bemoaned the "intellectual neo-fascism" of "this rootless expatriate."

That last phrase cuts peculiarly deep: it evokes, after all, one of the traditional rallying cries of the anti-Semite. (How much self-loathing lay at the root of Eliot's anti-Semitism, given his own undeniable tendency to belong everywhere and nowhere—to wander like one of his own parodies of Jewishness—is a nicety that needs to be handled with care.) There were Americans who could not forgive Eliot for his Jamesian transplantation to the Old World; similarly, in the clamor of his current enemies I sense a mockery of his efforts to become an honorary Englishman. The comparison with Pound is fruitful: nobody complains much about Pound's anti-Semitism, because he flourished it so openly and madly—good old Ez, him and his loony tunes! But Eliot, the smoothy whose whole career was an inside job, demands to be unmasked: his Englishness should be torn aside, his courtesy revealed as cowardice, and, above all, the coolness and distance of his verse reread as a front for emotional torment and the hiss of racial spite. Anyone who announces, as Eliot did, that poetry is an escape from personality can expect, now more than ever, to have his personality ripped open like a fox. The trouble with *T. S. Eliot, Anti-Semitism, and Literary Form* is that by the time its delicate judgments trickle down into journalism—or, even worse, into colleges—they will have hardened into thirdhand dogma. Philip Larkin was the first to get this treatment—some students would rather think of him as a racist with a palate for pornography than read his poems—and there is every danger that Eliot is now in the process of being Larkinized. His anti-Semitism will become the pre-eminent symptom in his case history: Eliot was a hater, and therefore it is meet and right that we should hate him back.

This is, you may say, unsatisfactory. What is most depressing about the Eliot issue is the moral vanity that seems to have crept into our reading habits—the demand that authors confirm our own convictions. Is it too much to ask that we should entertain mixed feelings about a writer? I suspect that no other feelings are worth having; that a writer who arouses clean, uncomplicated feelings will, in the final reckoning, turn out to be unworthy of serious attention; and that Eliot offers us a strong opportunity to revive the ancient art of being of two minds. "I think of a man whom I held in respect and admiration, although some of his views were exasperating and some deplorable—but a great writer," Eliot once wrote, adding, "It is easy to criticize a man for not being another man than the man he was." This is a test case, because the man in question was Charles Maurras—a very nasty piece of work, fuel to the flame of the nationalist *L'Action Française* and, it has been claimed, of Eliot's own anti-Semitism. And yet Eliot's final judgment is clear: lousy in parts, but a great writer. Sounds reasonable to me.

If, on the other hand, such a distinction strikes you as evasive and naïve, you've got your work cut out. All literature lies before you, awaiting your pronouncements. Once we begin to chastise poets for what they believed, what they cried in public declarations or murmured in idle moments, who should 'scape whipping? Having surveyed the sins of the leading poets in the language, I have come to the unlikely conclusion that the only one who can be honored with impunity is George Herbert. If you refuse to read anyone you disapprove of, I should warn you that you'll end up spending an awful lot of time with *The Temple*—a wonderful work, but still. It may be wiser, or more practical, to operate on the principle that poets engage our attention not merely in spite of their vices, sexual and political, but precisely because of what they do with them: because of the dramatizing, or the alchemical transmutation, of deep flaw into yet profounder form. I am not sure that I would be interested—would really believe—in anything written by someone of blameless character. Give me fault lines any day:

> And last, the rending pain of re-enactment
>   Of all that you have done, and been; the shame
>   Of motives late revealed, and the awareness
> Of things ill done and done to others' harm

Which once you took for exercise of virtue.
Then fools' approval stings, and honour stains.

So runs the terza rima of "Little Gidding," prompting the suspicion that whatever charges we level at Eliot today are as nothing compared with the fierce mortifications that he inflicted on himself. The Dantean perfection of this verse, the tidal sway of its disclosure, should not blind us to the fact that it is both salt and wound. Even the reader who finds T. S. Eliot unforgivable will pause to hear such a confession. Eliot was known to friends in later life as the Possum, adept at playing dead, and sometimes as the Elephant: unable to forget. That may be a literary prerequisite, but to the private Eliot, guilty of ethnic prejudice and the only survivor of a shipwrecked marriage, a long memory probably felt like hell. After he died, in 1965, his ashes were taken to the church at East Coker, the home of his ancestors and the scene, or starting point, of the second of his *Four Quartets.* On a plaque are the words "Of your charity pray for the repose of the soul of Thomas Stearns Eliot, Poet." The Eliot whom we read today is changed, though not utterly, from the poet who was esteemed by previous generations. Yet the poetry remains as unquiet as ever, the souls that patrol it allowed only meagre repose; the more we learn of Eliot, indeed, and the more we try to read between the lines, the more desperate are the snatches of happiness that we glimpse there. The March Hare may have jumped, but not for joy.

MARCH 10, 1997

THOMAS PYNCHON

Thomas Pynchon published his first book, *V.*, in 1963, and to this day nobody is quite sure what, if anything, that lonely initial stands for. The title of his third, and grandest, work, *Gravity's Rainbow*, refers in part to the trajectory of a wartime rocket; but only in part. It may also, for instance, point to the inevitable earthbound arc that is described by our mortal life; or, again, if memory serves, to the curve of a stocking top as it loops up to and away from the clip of its restraining garter. Pynchon nuts, who in the league of nuts are outstripped only by Kennedy-assassination wonks, will therefore suffer a brutal shock when they discover that the fifth, and latest, Pynchon novel, *Mason & Dixon*, really is about Mason and Dixon. To be exact: it tells the tale of Charles Mason and Jeremiah Dixon, the pair of English astronomers who, in 1763, were dispatched to America in order to measure out and mark the line that bears their names. Some twenty years later, their exploits are recounted for us by the Reverend Cherrycoke, who accompanied—or says that he accompanied, Pynchon narrators being reliably unreliable—the twosome on their travels. "What we were doing out in that Country was brave, scientifick beyond my understanding, and ultimately meaningless," says the man of God. He sounds like a reader of Thomas Pynchon.

The novel runs, and dawdles, and doubles back, for an impressive 768 pages. There are times when, as you pause for breath in the midst of an overgrown patch, you tell yourself that Pynchon's heroes, who merely had to hack their way for four years along the border of Maryland and Pennsylvania, had it easy. That is unfair, for they *were* heroic, in a quietly dogged way, and you feel by the close that they deserve a medal for surviving not just the rigors of their professional task but the incalculable travails of Pynchon's fiction. Like Leopold Bloom, Mason and Dixon have to keep their heads down while brilliance rages around them and the erudition flies like hail, and both of them—sorrowing widower and bluff Quaker—emerge somehow as substantial, even affable beings. Their story is buoyant and briny with departures: the men are forever on the move, on the lookout for stars and signs, and, perhaps because of that gazing restlessness, the book itself seems like a fresh departure. Things happen here. If you try to find plots in Pynchon, they usually come out sounding like plots to steal something or like plots of earth that harbor the dead, but this new book has a narrative—a real, honest-to-God story. What in the world is going on?

Well, for one thing, *Mason & Dixon* is Pynchon's first thoroughgoing historical novel. There is plenty of history, heaven knows, in *V.* and in *Gravity's Rainbow*, but the action there tends to sprawl and leap across the decades; those books, like his second book, *The Crying of Lot 49*, are torn between the wish to make secret sense of a civilization and a fretful suspicion that nothing makes any sense at all. The new book, however, is set, if not fixed, in the latter half of the eighteenth century. It sounds and, more important, looks like a period novel; it comes bedecked with archaic spellings, complex punctuation, words like "Nebulosity," "Fescue," "pinguid," and "G–d"—all the linguistic finery of its chosen age. Here is Captain Smith, of the *Seahorse*, a British vessel bearing the astronomers:

> Far from any Extortion-scheme, it had rather been the Captain's own Expectation,—the fancy of a Heart unschool'd in Guile,—that they would of course all three be messing together, Day upon Day, the voyage long, in his Quarters, drinking Madeira, singing Catches, exchanging Sallies of Wit and theories about the Stars,—how else?—he being of such a philosophickal leaning, and so starv'd for Discourse, it never occur'd to him that other Arrangements were even possible.

This is hard to fault as pastiche, and yet it moves beyond pastiche, with none of the cramped self-amusement that usually attends the genre. What is more, it bears the signature—wholly unmistakable but written, as it were, in invisible ink—of Pynchon himself. He appears to breathe amply in this distant air—more easily, indeed, than he did in the smoggy modern atmosphere of his last novel, *Vineland.* Such is his relish for dead locutions that he is able to laugh them back into life: "She grabs both sides of the Garment and rips it in two, or, actually, twain." The author who used to capitalize nouns in order to crown them with occult potency—the Zone, the System—is now at liberty to strew capitals wherever he pleases without driving his reader into agonies of baffled inquiry. Even his weakness for silly names gets a fillip: you may choke on "Cherrycoke," but it has the true tang of the parsonical. As for Pynchon's love of afterthought, a love so loyally ardent that thought itself tends to get trampled underfoot in the rush, what era could be more welcoming than the 1760s? Much of the multivolume *Tristram Shandy* was published during the years of the Mason and Dixon exploit, and, if there is fellow feeling between the pitch and yaw of Sterne's cogitations and the natural sway of Pynchon's own prose, such kinship offers not so much a technical challenge—imitation alone does not concern him—as a genuine prospect of imaginative release.

It goes without saying that, from time to time, Homer nods; I'm not absolutely convinced that the eighteenth century was conversant with the term "sex industry" or the phrases "run up a Tab" or "he wants out." Faced with such effrontery, one might more usefully assume that Homer is in fact winking, and no Pynchon novel would be complete without its fair share of anachronistic digs; the shipboard scenes include an honorary mention of a sailor named Pat O'Brian, "the best Yarn-Spinner in all the Fleets," and the current president might allow himself a small smile at the advice on Indian hemp which is offered to Cherrycoke as he prepares to set sail: "If you must use the latter, do not inhale. Keep your memory working, young man!"

Whether Thomas Pynchon himself would heed this counsel is hard to decide. His memory seems, as ever, not only to have gorged itself on facts and figures but to have kept the whole lot down; some of the astronomical passages are dense with dark matter. On the other hand, this book could easily have been conceived in the fumes of inhalation: it has a dreamed quality, an eagerness to be haunted. Mason and Dixon sail first to the Cape of Good Hope; they record a Transit of Venus, which proves to have a suitably warping effect on the libidos of those observing it, and then proceed to St. Helena, where the shadow of acute weirdness strikes even Mason as a little disconcerting: "He already suspects that the Island enjoys a Dispensation not perhaps as relentlessly Newtonian as Southern England's." In other words, the rules are breaking down. The place is rising and ripening into Pynchonland: trickiest of terrains, home to the depraved and dispossessed, smothered by apocalyptically (and comically) bad luck. We crossed it in the burned-out Berlin of *Gravity's Rainbow* and in the genocidal German colony of *V.*—Pynchon is plainly obsessed by southern Africa as a perennial pit of bestial behavior—and now we find ourselves stumbling upon it all over again. Yet *Mason & Dixon* is more insidious than its predecessors. We still sense a world turned upside down, but there is no fantastical forcing of the issue. Rather, Pynchon gathers himself to deliver quietly thunderous orations against "the great Worm of Slavery," or to scatter drops of unease in his flowing accounts of landscape:

"The Stars wheel into the blackness of the broken steep Hills guarding the Mouth of the Valley. Fog begins to stir against the Day swelling near. Among the whiten'd Rock Walls of the House seethes a great Whisper of living Voice."

Another great whisper reaches Mason and Dixon when they return to England: rumors of a trip to America, where they will act essentially as surveyors—a word that Mason abhors. The journey itself is not described; our heroes disembark without ado at Philadelphia. Pynchon likes to nudge us with these reckless and highly Shandean imbalances: patient descriptions of meals and telescopes, nothing at all about a presumably eventful Atlantic crossing. And yet the book does move; there is little of that panicky sensation you get from *Gravity's Rainbow* of being snared in the filaments of an invisible story. Pynchon cannot, of course, resist the occasional excursus: the tale of a monstrous cheese that rolls downhill and nearly flattens poor Mason, or the six-page fairy tale about a couple of Chinese astronomers who are borne aloft by a giant kite—shades of Benjamin Franklin, who duly makes an eloquent appearance in tinted spectacles. (There are walk-ons, too, for George Washington, Dr. Johnson, and, most learned of all, a talking dog.) But these subplots are definite, detachable appendages; they do not shape the body of the novel, or impede the westering momentum of Mason and Dixon. The main story is at once a Franklin-like homage to resourceful pioneers and a murmured warning of how this endless new country could conceivably end up:

> Does Britannia, when she sleeps, dream? Is America her dream?—in which all that cannot pass in the metropolitan Wakefulness is allow'd Expression away in the restless Slumber of these Provinces, and on Westward, wherever 'tis not mapp'd, nor written down, nor ever, by the majority of Mankind, seen,—serving as a very Rubbish-Tip for subjunctive Hopes, for all that *may yet be true*,—Earthly Paradise, Fountain of Youth, Realms of Prester John, Christ's Kingdom, ever behind the sunset, safe till the next Territory to the West be seen and recorded, measur'd and tied in, back into the Net-Work of Points already known, that slowly triangulates its Way into the Continent, changing all from subjunctive to declarative, reducing Possibilities to Simplicities that serve the ends of Governments,—winning away from the realm of the Sacred, its Borderlands one by one, and assuming them unto the bare mortal World that is our home, and our Despair.

At moments like these, you feel that *Mason & Dixon*—and, for that matter, Mason and Dixon—could, or even should, go on forever. Like

Donald Barthelme, his fellow parodist and fabulist, Pynchon is engaged in something much tougher than whimsy: their wry, devout exercises in the mock-heroic—which in Barthelme are usually shorn to a few pages and in Pynchon stretch to the horizon—help both of them to arrive, quite unexpectedly, at revelation.

So who will read *Mason & Dixon*? *Gravity's Rainbow* felt like a book that the world had been waiting for, not least because Pynchon was determined to cram as much of the world as possible into every nook of his prose. I fell prey to Pynchon in college, and spent months with my head in his books; I chastised myself for failing to discern the deep patterns—social, sexual, scientific, or whatever—that were reputed to run through them. I never did crack his codes, but now I wonder whether my efforts may have been misplaced; I failed to take on board the fact that Pynchon was, in the fullest sense, an old hippie. He has the authentic, reflexive impatience with existing society; the trusty combo of sweet-toned utopianism and a taste for dirty talk; the nagging urge to tell the truth, or the Truths, because nobody else has the balls to speak up.

None of this has quenched my belief in him as a great writer, but it takes the experience of *Mason & Dixon*—his calmest and most considered work—to clear one's head. Since the rocket-powered riffs of *Gravity's Rainbow*, Pynchon has learned how to stop worrying about the Bomb. He has even started loving a little, extending an amused tenderness in all sorts of directions: to Mason and Dixon, above all, whose deadpan exchanges—learned in part, perhaps, from Mercier and Camier, the unflustered wanderers set in motion by Samuel Beckett—conceal a slow maturing of affection. The astronomers' companionship, like their assignment, is contagious. It's hard not to be touched by the sight of Harland, a farmer on the southerly tip of Philadelphia, who, ignoring the protests of his wife, Bets, allows the Englishmen to set up their observatory on his land and soon, despite himself, takes an interest:

> Here is Harland, among the Sunflowers, having Romantic thoughts for the first time. Bets notices it. He is chang'd,—he has been out running Lines, into the distance, when once Brandywine was far enough,—and now he wants the West. The meaning of Home is therefore chang'd for them as well. As if their own Fields had begun, with tremendous smooth indifference, to move, in a swell of Possibility.

Pynchon at full surge, in case anyone needed reminding, writes with quite ridiculous grace and an instinctive refusal to turn pretty. There is enormous relaxation in the way that he angles the slope of his sentences;

they shift from cropped to lush, swelling like the Harlands' yellow fields. *Mason & Dixon*, with its talk of Chinese Jesuits and Swedish Jacobites, its recording of conversations between magical clocks, is as tolerant and capacious as its creator would like an ideal America to be—"as if Gravity," he says, "is become locally less important than Rapture." The result is both the most open and the most mysterious book that Pynchon has produced. You don't have to scrabble away to unearth a buried purpose; you get what you are given. Despite the best efforts of his fans, Pynchon was never a sacred seer; but the look of his thinking—the curve of his moods and the sharp incline of his wit—can never be faked or forgotten. His liking for ellipses, for instance, confirms him as a master of the dying fall: "Bright green Vines with red trumpet-shap'd Flowers, brighter indeed than the Day really allows . . . no doorways of any kind . . . then Rain, salt from the Leagues of Vacant Ocean. . . ." You can follow *Mason & Dixon* as a strolling adventure, or else you can parse it as you would a passage of Auden, or some of Berryman's "Dream Songs"—not in a spirit of furrowed perplexity but with a willingness to bask in the beautifully intemperate climate of his language. Pynchon is furiously clever, but more crucial, and I suspect more durable, is his anatomy of melancholy, his conjuring of a doleful burlesque. He offers readers a trip as long and full of yearning as that of his heroes. Good luck, and G–dspeed.

MAY 12, 1997

BLOOM ON SHAKESPEARE

Just who does Harold Bloom think he is? At the start of his new book, *Shakespeare: The Invention of the Human*, he calls himself "a heretical transcendentalist." Five hundred pages later, that is helpfully revised to "a gnostic sect of one." I would very much like to know which of these descriptions is entered on Bloom's tax returns. He currently teaches at Yale and at New York University, and remains one of the few academics who could write a sentence such as "I do not trust the scholars on Shakespeare's politics," as if he himself were a gentleman amateur, or a ruminating Bottom. Somehow, treading water at the brink of the mainstream, Bloom has managed to produce twenty-two books, beginning with a study of Shelley in 1959. If he considers himself to be less than a scholar, his students and admirers certainly revere him as more than one—as the wand-waving Prospero of American criticism. Equally, his detractors prefer to view him as its baffled and superannuated Lear, and you certainly catch an authentic tone of sovereign crossness in some of the pronouncements that litter his latest work: "I suppose it is my own outrageousness that tells me . . ."; "With my characteristic temerity, I assert . . ." At one point, he even declares a personal interest in Barabas, Marlowe's Jew of Malta: "A wonderful monster, the only stage role I perpetually long to essay." You may like to know that Barabas poisons nuns.

Shakespeare: The Invention of the Human is proof of a lifelong loyalty to the Shakespearean cause. Its final sentence runs as follows: "When we are wholly human, and know ourselves, we become most like either Hamlet or Falstaff." This is a generous view of our lives, although it is hardly undemanding: what Bloom politely fails to address is the possibility that many of us, what with getting the kids to bed and switching on the TV, tend to put off self-knowledge until tomorrow, and that all we can hope for, as the years slide by, is to become like Shallow, or the hapless

Roderigo, or the Fool. Bloom himself, by his own admission, did not acquire a television until he was nearly forty, sometime around 1970—a triumph of American denial, although one can't help wondering whether a prolonged acquaintance with Lucille Ball might not have spiced his already lusty appetite for Beatrice, Rosalind, and the other Desi-levelling dames of Shakespeare's art. Still, those four decades gave Bloom the bedrock of reading that you sense immediately in the bullish confidence, the knowledgeable naïveté, of his writings. Will his generation be the last to attempt that Victorian solidity of learning and not to mind the calumny it brings?

As if in personal tribute to those whom he calls Shakespeare's "heroic vitalists," Bloom charges onward for 750 pages, working his way through each of the plays in turn; in practical terms, this makes the book a more amenable work than it might at first appear to be, since none of the essays are so firmly stirred into the main argument that they cannot be sampled with pleasure on their own. The chapter on *The Tempest*, for example, could be propped against the faucets during a long bath, and a few pages of Bloom on *Othello* would usefully fill that long wait for the subway, although such is the critic's hymn to the satanic potency of Iago that you might consider it less fun to board the train than to nudge your fellow-travellers onto the track—and, needless to say, blame somebody else for their fall. If there is one belief that pulses throughout Bloom's book, it is the full-blooded sense of a Shakespeare who exists to teach us—not, one hastens to add, that he can teach us facts, or teach us how to behave, let alone how to be better. All he can do is teach us to "think too well," to guide us through the innumerable ways in which life may be led and understood, and sensation be kept alive and alight; he can teach us fullness, even if it burns and blackens into the fullness of despair. The lesson is bound to be humbling: we tend to congratulate ourselves on the thought that our existence is peculiar to us, but, in Bloom's account, Shakespeare invariably got there first. He not only preempted our characters; he practically made them up:

> We are lived by drives we cannot command, and we are read by works we cannot resist. We need to exert ourselves and read Shakespeare as strenuously as we can, while knowing that his plays will read us more energetically still.

To those who have never bumped into Bloom's prose before, this will sound at worst willful and at best gorgeously obscure. But you soon get into the swing of his persuasions, and it becomes clear that Bloom, like

Emerson, gives himself helplessly to criticism as if it were poetry: *Shakespeare: The Invention of the Human* makes more sense as an enraptured, incantatory epic than as a courteous explication of the plays. Although Bloom's beef against feminist critics, for instance, grows wearisome and unjust, he has a point when he says that Shakespeare has long since enfolded their arguments, and that no reader can press the claims of women as lucidly and wittily as Rosalind herself does, in *As You Like It.* But if it's practical criticism you're after, forget it: this stuff is about as practical as a unicorn. Bloom has made it his business to thrash those theorists and ideologues who treat literature as the outcome of historical circumstances, yet his own approach is stranger still: literature seems to flow, under high pressure, from the barely controlled circumstances of the writer's urges and instincts, and from a vexed misapprehension of earlier writers. The act of ordinary reading, by comparison, is close to involuntary. Texts may be hard and stubborn, but they flow into us like oxygen or coffee, whether we like it or not:

> Can we conceive of ourselves without Shakespeare? By "ourselves" I do not mean only actors, directors, teachers, critics, but also you and everyone you know.

This is magnificent and heartening; whether it is true is, of course, another matter. Dispatch a team of statisticians to count the number of children reading Shakespeare in school, or—and this is the more telling test—of adults who continue to read him afterward, and you would be lucky to come across Shakespearean exertions of any sort. The plays are still performed and filmed, and in England, at least, the image of the bearded bard seems to crop up wherever you look, even on ATM cards; but, if you were to walk into a housing project in London or New York—or, even better, into a Giorgio Armani store—and ask people at random whether they could conceive of themselves without Shakespeare, they would probably call the cops.

That would not dismay Harold Bloom, however, for the simple reason that he does not expect us to go around citing or pondering Shakespeare all the time; thoughts of Shakespeare lie too deep for quotes. No one who has followed Bloom's tireless inquiries into the mechanisms of poetic tradition would expect the inheritors of Shakespeare to do anything as vulgar as actually speak lines of verse. The import of the plays bears down upon us in other, more insidious ways; for four hundred years, Shakespeare has gradually molded our apprehension of the world and, more especially, of other beings. Whenever we inspect the actions and moralities of our friends, or muse on the private crazes of our politicians, or fumble around in the maze of our own motives, we are doing things that scarcely existed before the advent of Shakespeare. So Bloom would have us believe, anyway, although you may find it easier to go the distance with him if you blank out whole swaths of previous writing. Bloom himself refers to Dante and to the Jesus of the Gospels, but, on a less forbidding level, people have been reading someone like Horace for two thousand years, on the assumption, or in the fond illusion, that they know the guy: balding, bibulous, touched with cowardice, torn between the pleasures of the country and the need to crawl at court. Catullus and Juvenal set patterns of longing and scorn that have never been erased, and, a century and a half before Shakespeare, Villon took jagged poetic honesty about as far as it would go. It is true that Shakespeare scored all these dying falls, and a hundred more, in his own music, but does that make him responsible for *The Invention of the Human*?

This question nags at Bloom's work and never goes away, not least because he never really stops to define what he means by "human." The word itself is dangerously anachronistic for his purposes: according to the *Oxford English Dictionary*, the first recorded use of "human" as a freestanding adjective was in 1727, and its first use as a noun—meaning more than simple membership in the human race—came from Elizabeth Barrett Browning, in 1841. As far as I'm concerned, it's been going to the dogs ever since; I've sat through enough Hollywood miniseries to know that when someone is described as "very human," and the word "warm" is somewhere in the vicinity, it's time to switch off. So what does Harold Bloom want with it? "The representation of human character and personality remains always the supreme literary value," he writes in his preface. "Falstaff and Hamlet are the invention of the human, the inauguration of personality as we have come to recognize it. . . . Personality, in our sense, is a Shakespearean invention." This sounds resplendent, but there is something murky and tremulous in the terminology. "Personality," too, is a word that has been rubbed and debased beyond repair, and even Bloom's selfless attempts to coin it afresh are compromised by its vagueness. In his chapter on *Hamlet* he declares, "Life must be true to Shakespeare if personality is to have value, is to *be* value." If you can tell me what, if anything, that sentence means, I'll buy you a drink. Bloomian humanity obviously has much to do with inwardness, with the progress of self-consciousness, but even that is insufficient: though Falstaff often soliloquizes, his spirit is centrifugal, a welcome corrective to Hamlet's frowning absorption. Bloom has been harping on these two men, with canine devotion, for some time—they take center stage in his chapter on Shakespeare in *The Western Canon* (1994) and in the Shakespeare lecture that was printed in *Ruin the Sacred Truths* (1989)—and together they suggest that what he really and most profoundly means by "human" can be summarized as follows: "Drinks a lot" and "Refuses to shut up." Rather like Shakespeare, I guess.

"The decisive theatrical experience of my life came half a century ago, in 1946, when I was sixteen, and watched Ralph Richardson play Falstaff." So Bloom tells us in a chapter on *Henry IV*, compounding the two parts into a single play. He was not the only young man to be won over. Kenneth Tynan saw the same production, and marvelled at the scene in the orchard, with Laurence Olivier's Shallow paying lazy court to Richardson's Falstaff. "If I had only half an hour more to spend in theatres, and could choose at large, no question but I would have these," Tynan wrote. Yet the experience sent the two of them in different directions: Tynan spent the rest of his life watching and writing about the theatre, as if in pursuit of that once-glimpsed Grail, whereas Bloom became a literary critic. Most of his remarks on performances of Shakespeare are caustic and dismissive, as if anything less than Richardson were not worth the ticket; it isn't so much that a bad production, like a foolish piece of criticism, is an insult to Shakespeare as that no production can do justice to the original. The theatre is a little room, as Bloom sees it, and thus no place for the great reckoning of Shakespeare.

As another disappointed playgoer, spoiled by movies, I am tempted to side with this prejudice, and yet at a literal level it is nonsense: Shakespeare, however poets may prefer to forget the fact, wrote for the theatre, and, even if a performance of *Hamlet* offers only paltry illumination of the work, that experience becomes part of the endlessly angled light that the play, like a jewel, invites. I am more convinced by Bloom's perpetual grievance against the theatre than I am by the logic that proceeds from it. He informs us that "the largest fault of every staging of *Twelfth Night* I've attended is that the pace is not fast enough," and, of the appearance of Barnardine toward the end of *Measure for Measure*, says that "I have never seen this delicious and profound outrageousness properly directed and acted." This reinforces the Bloomian suspicion that Shakespeare belongs to the study, not to the boards; it's rather like saying that the Holy Bible should be read only in bed, and never in church. But Bloom's high expectation, his quick grasp of the dramatic possibilities that surge and brim in these plays, only proves how thoroughly they were conceived in terms of action; if he finds every *Twelfth Night* too sluggish, that points to formidable powers of acceleration on Shakespeare's part, to his sheer technical genius for bringing people onstage, spinning them around, swapping their identities, and getting them off again. No one, not even A. C. Bradley, has traced the accommodating confines of Shakespearean character with quite such dedication as Bloom, but you can't help wondering if he has neglected the inextricable kinship, proposed first by Aristotle, between character and action—if, that is, the urge to pick Hamlet up with a pair of tweezers and slide him under a microscope has blinded Bloom to the fact that Hamlet is not alone, that he talks to a skull, falls in and out of love, stabs an old man, and even stages a play.

Given this intolerance for Shakespeare in the theatre, you might expect Bloom to fall back on close textual readings—to get his kicks from the skin and muscle of the verse. But that is not his way; ever since he wrote *The Anxiety of Influence*, in 1973, Bloom has awed his readers (or freaked them out) by implying that what matters in poetry, and in the fraught abysses between poems, is not the poetry itself. Rather, there appear to be strange subterranean tides at work, a voluble ebb and flow of competing experience. In *A Map of Misreading* (1975), one of his Freud-driven surveys of the continuous wrestling between generations of poets, Bloom wrote, "Poetic influence, in the sense I give to it, has almost nothing to do with the verbal resemblances between one poet and another." I can quite understand how some of his students might have fruitfully misread that sentence as a wonderful excuse not to read poetry at all; if verbal surfaces are no big deal, bang goes the Western canon.

This lofty disdain for textual engagement is alive and mischievous in *Shakespeare: The Invention of the Human.* To be sure, the book is crammed with generous helpings of Shakespeare; like Dr. Johnson and Hazlitt, his favored precursors, and also like T. S. Eliot, his bête noire, Bloom is a brilliant quoter—a sure sign of someone who has read pretty much everything. But, unless I've missed it, I'm fairly sure that there is no point in 750 pages where he deigns to tell his readers that Shakespeare wrote his plays in something called iambic pentameter. He can just about bring himself to mention the fact that *Richard II* is composed entirely in verse, but even then his emphasis is a giveaway: "There is no prose whatsoever in *Richard II*, partly because there is no Falstaff to speak it." Ah, so *that's* the reason. I think Bloom is genuinely saddened that Falstaff is not available to wander into any and all of the plays, like Bing and Bob walking onto the wrong set in the *Road* movies, and I find it hard to disagree with him: the spectacle of Sir John tucking into the baked head in *Titus Andronicus* and calling for a dab of Norwich mustard would have been most edifying. But we must learn to live with that lack, and also to listen for the terrible moment, at the close of *Henry IV, Part 2*, when Falstaff breaks his habit and greets the newly crowned Hal, his former rascal-in-arms, with a line of scannable verse: "My King! My Jove! I speak to thee, my heart!" It is a pathetic attempt to raise his game, but far too late in the day, and the King's reply is a murder of sorts, more heartbreaking than that of Desdemona: "I know thee not, old man. Fall to thy prayers." The old world of prose and cutpurses breathes its last.

It is always risky to criticize the critic for what he fails to do, or for those paths which he has chosen not to pursue. Nevertheless, Bloom's determined indifference to form and his passing nods to the matter of Shakespearean diction sit uneasily with his overarching design: how can you chart the progress of the greatest writer who ever lived, and make your case for that greatness, without reference to what he learned from and within his medium? You might as well show a succession of Rembrandt self-portraits and ignore the gathering freedom of the brushstrokes, which reached their ironic apogee when the flesh was almost dripping from the bones. Early in the book, Bloom castigates a speech from Richard III:

> What do I fear? Myself? There's none else by;
> Richard loves Richard, that is, I and I.
> Is there a murderer here? No. Yes, I am!
> Then fly. What, from myself? Great reason why,
> Lest I revenge.

"I cannot think of another passage," Bloom writes, "in which Shakespeare is so inept." Later—almost six hundred pages later—he quotes another set of questions, from *The Winter's Tale:*

> Is whispering nothing?
> Is leaning cheek to cheek? is meeting noses?
> Kissing with inside lip? stopping the career
> Of laughing with a sigh (a note infallible
> Of breaking honesty)? horsing foot on foot?
> Skulking in corners? wishing clocks more swift?

This time, Bloom comments, "Leontes's tonalities have a rising intensity matchless even in Shakespeare." But what makes the first speech inept and the second matchless? Bloom's criteria of personality and "circumference of consciousness" will not quite meet the case, for we are as readily convinced of Richard's spiderish villainy as of Leontes's self-grounding paranoia. It would not take much, you might think, for Bloom to point out the youthful Shakespeare's slightly unconfident fondness for rhyming his lines too sturdily, compared to the older man's delicate ability to vary his end-stopped lines with phrases that run on and over—that entertain the ear with a kisslike fluency as well as with the more striking rigor of a clock.

It is because of this reluctance to get down and dirty among the nuts and bolts of poetry, I think, that Bloom gravitates toward the higher ground. You can feel the whole book taking a deep breath as it heads for the summit of the tragedies and for the peaks of the major characters. Yet that is not where *Shakespeare: The Invention of the Human* is either most lively or most instructive. The view may be great from the high ground, but, boy, is it windy up there. Try this: "Inference in Hamlet's praxis is a sublime mode of surmise." Or this: "Shakespeare's uniqueness, his greatest originality, can be described either as a charismatic cognition, which comes from an individual before it enters group thinking, or as a cognitive charisma, which cannot be routinized." What a choice. The younger Harold Bloom devised a florid new vocabulary for his pushy new ideas: *The Anxiety of Influence* introduced us to the delights of Tessera, Apophrades, and Clinamen, which made the critic sound like a gardener with a filthy mind. Those mock-classical tags have dropped off, and I rather miss them now that they're gone; in their place we find words such as "aggressivity," "overgo," and "passional," none of which are wrong but all of which are just off-center enough to make the reader stumble.

Compare that knotted language with this, on *Measure for Measure:* "It is one of Shakespeare's most effective outrages that Isabella is his most sexually provocative female character, far more seductive even than Cleopatra, the professional seductress." That is true, and provocatively true, all the more so because of its simplicity; it exactly articulates my reaction to watching Kate Nelligan play Isabella on television—a performance that made me seriously contemplate renting a wimple and entering a convent, just in case. Bloom is tremendously clear and credible on *Measure for Measure* ("a comedy that destroys comedy"), as he is on *Love's Labor's Lost* and *Twelfth Night* ("Forces somewhat beyond the characters seem to be living their lives for them"); whatever his overt preferences, he is gripped and turned on by the comic, and by Shakespeare's tendency to wind up even the most silvery farce into a problem play.

You could hardly ask for a more capacious and beneficent work than *Shakespeare: The Invention of the Human.* There is even a ripe, Shylockian gusto to Bloom's diatribes against what he calls the School of Resentment—

basically, anyone who cannot forgive Shakespeare for being dead, white, male, and scandalously better than he had any right to be. I am not sure, though, that Bloom's own taste for the capacious always serves him well. His barnstorming mission to spread the word of bookishness results not just in largesse but in unfortunate repetitions—the book could have done with a close shave—and, while I relished the epigraph from Nietzsche at the start, I was somehow less moved by it after its fourth appearance in the body of the text. Bloom's beloved line of Hegel, too, about the Shakespeare who makes his characters "free artists of themselves," is a zinger, and crucial to the Bloomian thesis, but, having come across it in two of his previous books, I was less knocked out by it this time.

On the other hand, what is the use of an obsession if it fails to linger and kick, like the Fool at Lear's feet? "Explaining Shakespeare is an infinite exercise; you will become exhausted long before the plays are emptied out," Bloom writes in his calming coda. I was frequently maddened by his own exercises, but never exhausted or bored, and there is real exhilaration in the unfashionable suggestion that plowing through Shakespeare will leave us, while not altogether Falstaffied, at least larger or other than we were. If Harold Bloom continues to devote his life to the hopeful proposition that ordinary readers, as much as players and scholars, may become free artists of themselves, then good luck to him. He's only human.

OCTOBER 19, 1998

MATTHEW ARNOLD

What did Matthew Arnold do? The figure who emerges from Ian Hamilton's new book, *A Gift Imprisoned: The Poetic Life of Matthew Arnold*, is certainly a many-splendored thing: poet, critic, educationalist, connoisseur of the mournful cadence, and all-around harried conscience of the nineteenth century. Above all, he was the proud owner and manager of one of the most formidable sets of whiskers in Victorian England; whatever his other accomplishments, lyrical or polemical, he set a standard of personal shrubbery that few could hope to equal. Insofar as you can discern a face behind the hedge, the expression that you meet in most photographs of Arnold is a perfect balance of the severe and the serene: the chin is firm, leading from the front, but a low-lidded languor in the eyes hints at an irredeemable habit of reverie. Here is a gentleman who, you tell yourself, achieved much in life but also spent his idle hours, such as they were, wondering what those achievements were worth, and what other lives he might have striven to lead.

What kept Arnold from idleness, especially in his later years, was a solemn mission to spread the word. The word in question varied from "culture" and "perfection" to "civilization" and, on a good day, "God," but the refrain was constant: there were other and better lives that the general populace could, like the poet himself, strive to lead. In *Culture and Anarchy*, for example, first published in 1869, Arnold turned to the question of America. He had not yet been there, but that didn't stop him from knowing what was wrong with the place: "Earnest young men at schools and universities, instead of conceiving salvation as a harmonious perfection only to be won by unreservedly cultivating many sides in us, conceive of it in the old Puritan fashion, and fling themselves ardently upon it in the old, false ways." Only Arnold could manage to sound so Puritan in his cool dismissal of Puritan intensity. Yet, behind the frown, what he advocates here is a liberality of demeanor and faith; the word "unreservedly" could be read as the first step on the long road to multiculturalism. No wonder Arnold has become so crucial a witness in the case of America vs. America. If you happen to deplore the closing of the American mind, it may feel bracing to recruit an evangelizing classicist who can open it up again. The bulk of the United States, Arnold said, consisted of "a livelier sort of Philistine than ours . . . but left all the more to himself and to have his full swing." That sounds vicious, but by "Philistine" Arnold simply meant the middle class; if it could "add to its many and great virtues the spirit of delicacy," then all would be well. Whether delicacy could be funded out of the budget surplus, he declined to say.

All this seems a far cry from Laleham, on the river Thames, where Arnold was born in 1822. However, he was the eldest son of Dr. Thomas Arnold, and that explains a lot. Five years after Matthew was born, his father became the headmaster of Rugby School, and from there he proceeded straight into British mythology. He was the heroically terrifying instiller of virtue in *Tom Brown's Schooldays*, the most celebrated of all novels about life in an English public—that is, private—school, and he was unceremoniously struck from that pedestal by Lytton Strachey, in *Eminent Victorians*, the most poisonous of all English biographies. All the clichés that have, fairly or otherwise, clustered around Victorian life—manliness, emotional clampdown, suppression of unrighteousness both in one's own heart and on the borders of Empire, an unstated but nagging conviction that God must be an Englishman—seem to have cohered in the person of Dr. Arnold. He stoutly believed that children were not valuable souls in their own right but half-formed adults who needed to be molded (and, occasionally, whacked) into shape. Sin was not only original; it was the raw stuff that raged within a boy until he came to Rugby, whereupon it came face to face with the head of that establishment and, after a brief struggle, took early retirement.

And that was Matthew's father. As Ian Hamilton puts it, with his customary dryness, "School holidays could never quite be holidays from school." The educational gene was rampant in the Arnold clan (four of Thomas's sons, Matthew included, would at some time be involved with teaching), and by the age of five Matthew was learning French, Latin grammar, math, history, and geography, and taking a yeasty extract of Scripture every day. One year later, he moved on to Greek, German, and Italian, and by the age of ten the boy was really motoring: "I used to construe only Homer and Xenophon, but I have lately been put into Aeschylus." This may raise eyebrows among our young scholars of today, some of whom arrive at college barely able to inscribe the words "Homer Says

D'oh" on their own T-shirts, but it would be wrong to imagine that Matthew felt constrained, let alone persecuted, by the pressure of knowledge. The Victorians did not so much frighten as flatter their offspring with the assumption that junior brains will gather up almost anything that you care to cast at them. If anything, these early harvests were precisely what allowed Arnold to sow his enthusiasms so fruitfully later on; no one, least of all the author himself, has ever been able to decide what he means by the word "culture," but, if it is what the world requires in the effort to become civilized, then culture can perhaps be interpreted most safely as "What I learned at school." Or, more succinctly, "Me and my dad." What Thomas had in mind for Matthew, Matthew wanted for mankind.

He went to Rugby, of course, and from there to Balliol College, Oxford, which, being surpassingly dank, was the fungal breeding ground from which the mid-nineteenth-century British establishment—religious, literary, and administrative—would grow and spread. In the college debating society alone there were two embryonic archbishops, a future lord chief justice, and a couple of substantial poets—Arnold and Arthur Hugh Clough. Arnold himself won the Newdigate Prize (later victors would include Oscar Wilde), for a long and strenuous poem about Cromwell, and he deepened his friendship with Clough, whom he had known at Rugby and for whom—more than for Arnold—great things were foretold. "Eight years without a Fault" was Dr. Arnold's daunting verdict on Clough's time at school; in the event, both he and Arnold ended up with second-class degrees, which, by their standards, was like being caught cross-dressing or feasting on human flesh. Thomas Arnold had died of heart failure two years before; it was probably a mercy that he did not live to hear of his son's exam performance.

Still, Arnold secured a fellowship at Oriel College, and then, in 1847, what sounds like a dream job: private secretary to Henry Petty-Fitzmaurice, third Marquis of Lansdowne and full-time political fixer. In practice, this gave him time to write poetry, cultivate connections, travel through Europe, and sit staring out the window of his sumptuous offices in Berkeley Square. No one of Arnold's temperament would expect such a pleasant interlude to last (the whole point of pleasure, indeed, was to provide sustenance for rueful recollection in later life), and in 1851 he turned serious with a vengeance, marrying a pious Tory named Frances Lucy Wightman and becoming, through Lansdowne's instigation, an inspector of schools—a position that he would hold for the next thirty-five years. During that period, while fulfilling his professional duties with diligence and even passion, he would swell into his most enduring role, that of public moralist; Matthew's essays and lectures, with their varying recipes for the creation of a staunch yet refined Christian society, would at last turn him into a son who was worthy of his father. And the poems would dry up.

It is the damming of inspiration that interests Ian Hamilton. In his short and punchy book, which pretty much ends with Arnold in his mid-forties, Hamilton sets out to discover why the muse was sent packing. One of the more convincing answers is that she was not quite a lady—not the sort of influence who could be relied upon to say the right thing in polite society. Arnold had inherited an obligation to flex his mental muscles for the sake of the common good, and here he was writing stuff like this:

He hears nothing but the cry of the torrents,
And the beating of his own heart.
The air is thin, the veins swell,
The temples tighten and throb there—
Air! air!

He sounds like a man who can't wait to get out of the drawing room. That extract comes from "Empedocles on Etna," a lengthy formal complaint against the burden of existence. Arnold published the poem in 1852; what his young bride, after barely a year of marriage, made of his "ineffable longing for the life of life / Baffled for ever" is anyone's guess. A year later, in a new edition, he withdrew the poem, arguing that, although Empedocles represented an intriguing philosophical novelty—"the dialogue of the mind with itself has commenced . . . we hear already the doubts, we witness the discouragement, of Hamlet and of Faust"—such tangled morbidity was not healthy. It was not *useful.* Who could conceivably derive profit or enjoyment, Arnold asked, from a scene "in which the suffering finds no vent in action . . . in which there is everything to be endured, nothing to be done"?

Well, Matthew Arnold could, for one. In fact, he had been plucking that particular string since he learned what poetry was. My chief delight, as I trawled through Arnold's collected works, was to come upon these lines:

Land of my earlier, happier days I cannot love thee less,
Though here I bid adieu for aye to human happiness!

This is feeble stuff, but no matter; the point is that Arnold wrote it when he was *thirteen years old.* To someone steeped in Keats and early Tennyson, melancholy was the obvious mask to wear; what takes Arnold beyond the moodily chic, and closer to the pathological, is that the mask got stuck to his face. He dedicated one of his best early poems to "Fausta," a pseudonym for his sister Jane, and called it "Resignation"; at thirty, he claimed that he was "three parts iced over"; and he published his last masterpiece, "Growing Old," when he was in his mid-forties, with another twenty years or so ahead of him (although his father had, ominously, died at forty-six). All the fears of the intervening decades, all the educated premonitions of mortality, flow tidally into Matthew's most heartsick and most widely anthologized poem, "Dover Beach":

> Ah, love, let us be true
> To one another! for the world, which seems
> To lie before us like a land of dreams,
> So various, so beautiful, so new,
> Hath really neither joy, nor love, nor light,
> Nor certitude, nor peace, nor help for pain;
> And we are here as on a darkling plain
> Swept with confused alarms of struggle and flight,
> Where ignorant armies clash by night.

Those last lines cast something of a shadow over the earlier exhortation; what is the point of being true to one another when love is a lie, or a battleground? The poem, incidentally, is addressed to his wife; Dover is where the Arnolds spent the first few days of their honeymoon. That must have been fun.

The biggest shock in Hamilton's book is the discovery that, for much of the time, Matthew Arnold *was* fun. A disappointed Henry James once said that Tennyson, in person, was not Tennysonian; if so, then Arnold was anything but Arnoldian. In his youth, at least, he was known as something of a fop. "Matt is full of Parisianism," reported Clough with glee, when Arnold returned from a visit to France. The rest of the Arnolds took offense at his waggishness and his refusal to treat anything with due respect; even bearing in mind the extravagant levels of solemnity in his family, this is an astonishing claim. "Matt does not know what it is to work because he so little knows what it is to think," his father wrote, and you can't help thinking that Matthew's later life, which consisted of nothing *but* slog and rumination, was a loyal response to that challenge. Arnold never lost his sting, his talent for principled mockery, and he was by all accounts an adoring and unstuffy father to his own children; but the cloak of adult responsibility fell heavily on his shoulders, and, for no good reason, his image has been handed down to us as an archetype of the Victorian stiff.

Hamilton is clever and biting on the implications of this accelerated gloom—on the Arnold who so seldom smiled for the camera, as if amusement were unbecoming to a man of his character. Hamilton's whole book is smartly summed up in one paragraph of his preface:

> When Arnold got married and became an educationist, he also turned himself into a pedagogic neo-classicist; the age, he said, needed the kind of large-scale, objective, architectonic verse-constructions which he himself, he came to learn, had no real gift for. Or, to put it another way, what the age didn't need were more poems of the kind that Arnold did have a real gift for, and had indeed already written: lyric poems of the self, that Arnold self which, as he came to believe, had or should have had more important things to do than, well, write lyric poems.

This has a satisfying circularity; Hamilton has always relished the process of rotating irony by which life fails to work out. His earlier publications include biographies first of Robert Lowell, who was blessed with an Arnoldian profusion of gifts and an Arnoldian confusion of duties, and then of J. D. Salinger, whose impregnability made it impossible for Hamilton to write the book he had planned. And Hamilton himself writes quiet and sinewy verse. His *Fifty Poems* was published in 1988; this April, in London, Faber will issue an enlarged edition, entitled *Sixty Poems.* Ten new poems in eleven years: Arnold would be proud of him.

In the last decade, Arnold has been subject to, if not outright rehabilitation, at least a cheering resurgence. Nicholas Murray's *A Life of Matthew Arnold* was published in 1996; more important, the same year saw the arrival of the first volume of *The Letters of Matthew Arnold.* Three of the six projected volumes are now available, edited by the tireless and tactful Cecil Y. Lang, who has already brought order to the correspondence of Swinburne and (with Edgar Shannon) of Tennyson. The task is even heavier with Arnold, whose own disorder—not in his practical circumstances but in the doubts that prowled the fringes of his consciousness—was active from the start. "I am a reed, a very whoreson Bullrush," he wrote to Clough from Rugby. "But to be listless when you should be on Fire: to be full of headaches when you should slap your Thigh: to be rolling Paper Balls when you should be weaving fifty Spirits into one: to be raining when you had been better thundering," and so on; Arnold never actually brings the sentence to a close, and no wonder, for it is increasingly clear that these stirring admonitions are directed less at Clough than at himself. Eight years later, poor Clough is still getting it in the neck, and Arnold's confidence has grown even weaker, dwindling into sad shorthand: "You certainly do not seem to me sufficiently to desire and earnestly strive towards—assured knowledge—activity—happiness."

What emerges from Lang's majestic edition, as from the biographies, is that no accent is stronger, or more strangulated, than that of self-persuasion. We may regret (as Arnold did) the path that he hammered out for himself, but there is no denying his perseverance. At times, it acquires a comic tinge, as in these lines to his late father:

> Languor is not in your heart,
> Weakness is not in your word,
> Weariness not on your brow.
> Ye alight in our van! at your voice,
> Panic, despair, flee away.

Like hell they do. Was there ever a more desperate attempt to crank up one's courage by sheer dint of rhythm? Arnold, whose best poetry grows faint with the elaboration of weariness, tries occasionally to turn verse into a kind of forced march, and the result is a hoot. His natural bent—the gravitational pull of his imagination—is toward the dying fall, and a hard-won, compact repose that no other poet has been able to mimic or match:

> And there arrives a lull in the hot race
> Wherein he doth for ever chase
> That flying and elusive shadow, rest.
> An air of coolness plays upon his face,
> And an unwonted calm pervades his breast.
> And then he thinks he knows
> The hills where his life rose,
> And the sea where it goes.

That last diminuendo breaks your heart, and it partly answers the charge of J. A. Froude, the biographer of Carlyle, that Arnold "only knows the shady side of nature out of books. . . . I don't see what business he has to parade his calmness and lecture us on resignation when he has never known what a storm is." It is a fair point, but there are times when the calm is so tenderly drawn that, against our better judgment, we start to believe in the storm.

It is chastening to read Arnold and to think of what was being read and written on the other side of the English Channel, let alone of the Atlantic, during his lifetime. He was born a year after Baudelaire, and the majority of his verse was published in the same decade—the 1850s—as *Les Fleurs du Mal*, and yet the two poets seem generations apart. What is more, Nicholas Murray makes the point that Arnold compiled his first volume of *Essays in Criticism* in 1864, the same year that Dostoyevsky's *Notes from Underground* came out; both men cultivated a deep suspicion of material prosperity, and both hungered after a spiritual cure for that condition, but you tremble to think of them together in the same room. It is not a question of the debt-ridden gambler versus the schools inspector but of the modern anatomist, unafraid of desire and depravity, standing beside the upholder of classical values, which were even then wilting in his hands. Arnold wrote in some agony of "the hot prison of the present," yet he didn't really dare to break the lock or file through the bars. It would have taken only a small leap of faith, or of honest faithlessness, for him to realize that the raptures of uncertainty might be no longer a source of embarrassment but the deserving object of one's analysis, and that civilization, from here on, would not be open to elegant solutions, let alone salvation, but instead would be defined by its discontents. If Arnold looked, however, he never leaped.

That caution makes it hard for us, these days, to approach Arnold for instruction. He offers succor and sorrow in equal measure, but the strictures that were developed and propagated in the second half of his life feel more stubbornly rooted in Victorian ground. In the 1980s, there was a move to coopt Arnold into the culture wars: in 1994, Yale summarized this debate by issuing a new edition of *Culture and Anarchy*, with essays by Gerald Graff, Steven Marcus, Maurice Cowling, and Samuel Lipman—in other words, from right and left. Unexpectedly, there was a kind of sneaky joy in the book, as the reader watched Arnold wriggle around and slip free of all attempts to pin him down. He was raised as a Christian, for example, and he remained a churchgoer, but he once defined God as "the stream of tendency by which all things seek to fulfill the law of their being," which sounds to me like the beginnings of Belief Lite. He appeals to the right because of his Parnassian standards of learning and his reflex indignation at mob rule—at the thought of democracy running amok. On the other hand, he said that "the men of culture are the true apostles of equality," and his impatience with the aristocratic ideal grates rudely on reactionary ears. He appeals to the left because—like Voltaire, whom he admired—he scorns the humbug and harshness of religious ideologues, and turns up his nose at the stink of high capitalism. He even favors an *increase* in state intervention. On the other hand, he defines culture as "a pursuit of our total perfection by means of getting to know, on all the matters which most concern us, the best which has been thought and said in the world," which sounds like bad news for media studies and good news for red-blooded defenders of the canon. Basically, the guy is too quick for us.

Gerald Graff, a professor of English at the University of Chicago, takes Arnold to task on many counts. "Using ritualistically repeated slogans to conceal contradictions" is one of the more incisive; but Arnold was never a philosopher, nor did he claim to be, and Graff's words are a helpful reminder that *Culture and Anarchy*, *Literature and Dogma*, *The Function of Criticism at the Present Time*, and the other daunting titles on the Arnold shelf were written by a poet—an ex-poet, perhaps, but not a failed one. "Dover Beach," "Empedocles on Etna," and "The Scholar-Gipsy" are also full of contradictions and ritual repetitions, but that is a source of their incantatory strength. When Arnold urges the citizens of England, as he does on innumerable occasions, to aim for "sweetness and light" as a salve for social ills, it sounds touchingly impractical; one would have liked to see him venture into the East End of London on a smog-bound Saturday night and ask for more of the same. If *Culture and Anarchy* holds up, however, it is not as a political manifesto but as a long-range prose poem—the nimble effusion of a noble mind.

I do not quite buy Hamilton's argument that Arnold deliberately closed the poetic chapter of his life, and imprisoned—or sacrificed—his gift for the sake of work and family, and for the stolidness of prose. The transformations of his career feel not timid but fiercely true to the difficulties of being intelligent, industrious, and therefore thoroughly perplexed in the depths of the last century. "Fret not yourself to make my poems square in all their parts, but like what you can my darling," he wrote to his sister Jane. "The true reason why parts suit you while others do not is that my poems are fragments i.e. that I am fragments, while you are a whole. . . . Such a person stands firmly and knows what he is about while the poems stagger weakly & are at their wits end." He added, "I shall do better some day I hope." Both the hope and the staggering, the sweet culture and the sweat of anarchy, are what we should value in Arnold, now more than ever. If he was fragments, what does that make us?

FEBRUARY 1, 1999

ANDRÉ GIDE

In June 1940, André Gide—novelist, diarist, sometime communist, and a hub of French literary life for half a century—found himself in Vichy. It was a loaded place to be, and there were many things to keep a Frenchman awake at such a time, but for Gide the cause was specific:

> Through the open window of my room giving onto the end of the park, I heard, three times, a heart-rending cry: "Pierre! Pierre!" and almost went down to find the poor demented man who was uttering that call, desperately, in the night. And for a long time I could not go to sleep, ceaselessly imagining that distress.

Such are the helpless sympathies of the creative mind: the sound of a single voice suggests a story, or an auspicious predicament, and the writer is instantly condemned to a desire to know more. For Gide—not just a fervent homosexual but an avid connoisseur of longing in other men—the possibility that Pierre was not only lost but lusted after, like the faithless lover in a medieval lyric, provided the evening with further bewitchment. All of which must have made it something of a letdown when, the next morning, Gide learned that what he had listened to was the local night watchman, who had seen a lit window and was warning the occupant of the room to observe the wartime blackout: "*Lumière! Lumière!*"

You can't help admiring Gide for his honesty here; some writers, with a cautious eye cocked at posterity, might have kept Pierre and killed the light. But this incident arises in Gide's journals, which, more than any of his other works, are the test site for his politely explosive belief that, whatever else happens, we should aim for sincerity. As convictions go, this is seldom practicable and sometimes close to indefensible, especially when, as in Gide's case, other people get caught in the blast. But it feels alarmingly apposite to our own era, when a few insincere words to the press corps are almost enough to unseat a president, and Alan Sheridan can be proud of himself for producing *André Gide: A Life in the Present* with such an elegant sense of timing.

He is not alone in his endeavors. The French critic Claude Martin recently brought out *André Gide, or the Vocation of Happiness*, which has yet to be translated into English. Like Sheridan's book, it runs to well over six hundred pages, but it covers only half of the story; a second volume will appear later. Given that Martin founded the Association of the Friends of André Gide, in 1968, and that he has hitherto written or edited *twenty-two* books by or about Gide, I can understand that he has a fair amount to say. Then, there is Jonathan Fryer's *André & Oscar: The Literary Friendship of André Gide and Oscar Wilde*, and, on a less gossipy level, Naomi Segal's *André Gide: Pederasty and Pedagogy.* I make a point of trying to read one completely unreadable book every year, and Segal's study looked promising; sadly, it's brilliant stuff, expertly tracking the contrary motions of outpouring and restraint in Gide's unpolluted prose. But the larger question remains: Why the refreshed interest in Gide himself?

The last—and, for most of us, the only—time we were likely to have encountered the man was in high school, where novellas such as *Strait Is the Gate* and *The Pastoral Symphony* were used to prod us along the pathways of French style. Both are models of lucidity and stateliness, so much so that, as Sheridan tells us, one London publisher turned down *Strait Is the Gate* in the early 1920s "on the charming grounds that the French of the original was not difficult enough to justify a translation."

There may have been other grounds, more treacherous underfoot. Gide is actually quite hard to translate; beyond the curt simplicity of his sentences, which makes him a more formidable recorder of physical action than his reputation gives him credit for, there is what he called the gait of thought. The pacing of this passage from *The Vatican Cellars* cannot be faulted, but where, exactly, is the author directing its steps?

> They had no sooner settled in Rome than they arranged their private lives independently of each other—he on his side, she on hers; Veronica in the care of the household and in the pursuit of her devotions, Anthime in his scientific researches. In this way they lived beside each other, close to each other and just able to bear the contact by turning their backs to one another. Thanks to this there reigned a kind of harmony between them; a sort of semi-felicity settled down upon them; the virtue of each found its modest exercise in putting up with the faults of the other.

There is a punctilious courtesy in such prose that could stiffen into staidness, were it not for the sense that underneath the good stylistic manners, as under the life of Anthime and Veronica, lurk all kinds of animosity; to the seasoned ironist, indeed, propriety is the only possible outlet for the perverse. The young man who, in the same novel, passes his penknife over a flame, jabs it into his thigh, grimaces "in spite of himself," and then sprinkles drops of peppermint water on the wound, all in an effort to cool a fit of anger, is like a model of the novelist's method, and well-bred English readers of the 1920s could be forgiven for suspecting that there was something not quite nice about the unflappable M. Gide.

In the English-speaking world, in fact, the vogue for Gide started late and faded fast, without quite reaching the fist-clenching mania that attended Camus and *The Stranger*. Nevertheless, there was a time when to be seen with a copy of *The Immoralist*—Gide's sparse yet luxuriant tale of a man who, in the philosophical interests of liberty, tries to pig out on life—was de rigueur for young males of errant libido and unsound mind, otherwise known as students. It was not until 1926 that Gide dignified one of his works, *The Counterfeiters*, with the rank of "novel"; the rest of his output was a melee of travel writings, poems, plays, polemics, lectures, essays, neoclassical dialogues, studies in criminology, apologias both political and sexual, librettos, autobiographies in numerous guises, and what he liked to call *récits* and *soties*—respectively, simple first-person narratives and light-fingered literary games. Plowing through the Gidean landscape is a lengthy business, though seldom an arduous one, and it is more in awe than in ridicule that one pauses for breath to reflect that most of his working life was spent writing about André Gide, or, on more generous days, engaging in a heartfelt struggle not to write about André Gide.

He was born in 1869 and died in 1951. The dates alone hint at his extraordinary span: here was a man who befriended Wilde, visited the ailing Verlaine, and attended the legendary *mardis*—the tobacco-filled Tuesday discussions at the home of Stéphane Mallarmé—but who also lived long enough to observe the crushing of the Nazis, to fall in and out of favor with Soviet communism, to niggle over the newly fashionable Sartre ("I'm willing to be an Existentialist, provided I'm not aware of the fact"), and, at the age of seventy-eight, to get terribly excited by the Kinsey Report. In 1908, he helped found the *Nouvelle Revue Française*, which, first as a journal and later in its links to the publishing house of Gallimard, became one of the more efficient powerhouses of French culture. It is hard to recall an equivalent figure in the English-speaking world; Edmund Wilson had some of Gide's persistence in a multitude of literary forms, and each man showed a laudable determination to muscle his way through disapproval in the pursuit of what he held to be right, even if, in repeated instances, he turned out to be wrong for the right reasons. (Wilson, who once called Gide "the fairies' Dostoevsky," would not have welcomed the comparison.) But Gide had a head start on Wilson, by more than a quarter of a century, and even his briefest encounters suggest someone wandering between two worlds—a vigorous hedonist cloaked in the guise of an Edwardian man of letters. He could be found in Cannes in 1912 with the unlikely duo of Arnold Bennett and Pierre Bonnard, and during a trip to Calvi in 1930 he divided his time between open-air debauchery with naked Corsicans and Thomas Hardy's *The Woodlanders*.

Gide himself insisted that there was a dash of doubleness in his nature from the start. "You know how complicated I am," he wrote to a friend in 1902, "born of a crossing of races, situated at the crossroads of religions, sensing within me all the yearnings of Normans for the South, of Southerners for the North." In fact, as Sheridan points out, Gide was a foursquare northern Protestant, and you had to go back a few generations on his mother's side to stumble across any bona-fide Catholics. Nevertheless, he represents an intriguing case history in French Protestantism, with its stern sense of persecution; James Baldwin, in a shrewd essay on Gide, remarked that the Protestant faith "invested all of his work with the air of an endless winter." On Gide's first day of school, as he recounts in *If It Die*, his wonderful memoirs, he was asked "Are you a Cat or a Prot?" by the other boys in the yard. His own reading of this incident was that "all Frenchmen, of whatever age or class of society, have an innate need to take sides," a need that seems to have driven him not into sedition so much as toward a chronic—and, in France, far more dangerous—ability to approach any given issue from every direction.

The Protestant attitude to mortal cravings makes for an interesting feast. In Gide's case, it came ungarnished with guilt; in his more youthful projects, there is a blatant attempt to squeeze faith and sensuality onto the same plate. Given that his adoring parents had read him both the *Arabian Nights* and the Book of Job, what else could one expect? His 1897 publication *Fruits of the Earth*, a deliquescent prose poem that just about rouses itself to tell a story, became a bible to restless young pleasure-seekers, although thirty years later he strove to defend it as more than a glorification of desire. Citing "the doctrine of the Evangelist," Gide wrote of "finding in the forgetfulness of self the most perfect realization of self" and of a "limitless allowance of happiness." Whether St. John would have countenanced Gide's idea of an allowance is open to question. The writer himself remained unabashed by the attention he paid to his own body; *If It Die* contains a famous passage in which the young André is expelled from school for three months for "enjoying alternately my pleasure and my chocolates" beneath a classroom desk. His parents send him to the family doctor, who points to a row of Tuareg spearheads on the wall behind him and declares that such weapons are commonly used to operate on boys who persist in self-abuse. The lofty Gide is unimpressed: "This threat was really too thin for me to take it seriously."

It is this two-tone constitution—the hot blood in his veins and the icy ink in his pen—that makes Gide's egotism, which should be unbearable, close to captivating. No other writer could have so mournfully, almost liturgically, expressed "a regret not for having sinned, but for not having sinned more, for having let some opportunity for sinning slip by unused." Experience, he claimed, "is usually nothing but exhaustion, a repudiation of the best that one once had." His autobiography draws readers through a roster of enthusiasms, inquiring coolly, "In the name of what God or what ideal do you forbid me to live according to my nature?" There are many honorable answers to that question, but Gide, by the time he was twenty, was in any case living according to his Nietzsche: he had infiltrated literary Paris, and in 1891 he published *The Notebooks of André Walter*, forging a fictional hedonist who bore a marked resemblance to Gide himself. The book drips with symbolist languor and with dreams of "the softness of brown skins." The impressive thing is that instead of merely playing with this idea—under the desk, as it were—the adult Gide decided to quit town and hunt the real thing. He sailed for Africa.

From here on, Alan Sheridan's book grows crammed to the point of confusion. It is not really his fault: Gide was such a mover, travelling tirelessly between Africa and Europe, between France and her eastern neighbors, and between Paris and the family home at Cuverville, in Normandy, that there were times when I wondered whether Sheridan should have dumped the whole idea of a biography and simply provided a highly detailed map. You would need crisscrossing lines for routes, green spots for oases of creative tranquillity, and clusters of little red flashes for sites of carnal interest. In Tunisia, for example, at the end of 1893, Gide lost his virginity to a boy in Sousse and then, in the New Year, lost it again with a female prostitute in Biskra.

This sounds like a busy schedule, and Gide was true to his inconstancy; he would never relinquish his sweet tooth for young Arabs, or for teenagers of any race, but, on the other hand, he would marry his cousin

Madeleine in October 1895, and remain unhappily married until her death, in 1938. It was not even a question of keeping the two halves of his existence apart; on their honeymoon, in Africa, Gide left Madeleine and sought out willing companions from his earlier trip, and in 1898, in Rome, he would photograph young men on the Spanish Steps and invite them back to his apartment while his wife was out. Theirs was, as Sheridan says, a *mariage blanc*, forever unconsummated, and it was no coincidence that Gide's beloved mother—he was, of course, an only child—had died a little over two weeks before he announced his engagement. A few months later, he wrote in his journal, "How often when Madeleine is in the next room, I *forget* that she is not my mother!"

There was a moment when this wretched alliance reached critical mass: after more than twenty years of marriage, Madeleine told her husband that she had burned every one of his letters to her. It was her sole surge of insurrection; for the rest of her stay on earth, she was as quiet as a nun. Gide's reaction, predictably, was to call this lost correspondence—only a small portion of his twenty-five thousand letters—"the treasure of my life, the best of me," and to compare its destruction to the death of a child. He does not appear to have asked himself what deeds of his—or want of them—may have forced her to such a flamboyant gesture. Sheridan quotes Gide's idealistic claim that only a gay man "can give a creature that total love, divested of all physical desire" and that "I thought I had built the very temple of love." As Sheridan sharply adds, "This is not an intelligent man of 1998 speaking, but it doesn't sound like an intelligent man of 1919 either." In the one area where he had most need of it, Gide's dazzling willingness to see the other person's point of view deserted him. Only after Madeleine's death did it hit home; Gide was hollowed out with grief and remorse, and it served him right. There are limits to happiness, after all, and they transform his biography from an adventure, and a notable success story, into a cautionary tale.

A purist would argue that we must sift out the chaff, and that Gide's disloyalty does not corrupt his achievements on the page. The trouble is that, more than any other writer of his time, he kneaded his life and art together into an indistinguishable mass. This is partly an issue of his many romans à clef; it takes a minimum of biographical skill to turn the *clef* and discover the figures locked inside the novel—to see in the devout and spinsterly Alissa of *Strait Is the Gate*, say, not just a portrait of Madeleine Gide but a more subtly horrified pondering of what she might yet become. Beyond such identifications—always, by their nature, unsatisfying—there is a sense that Gide was conducting his life as if it were itself an art form. His embattled quest for spiritual peace, his tendency to plan a new trip as if it were the next chapter, his rhythmical frequenting of high literary society and low-rent hustlers on the streets: all these lent shape to his experience, and they give Sheridan's account of it a more juicy, Balzacian feel than the thin and bitter taste that sometimes stains the fictions of Gide himself. Even his longest and most intricate novels, *The Vatican Cellars* and *The Counterfeiters*, are inclined to sound shrill these days, with their shrewish lampoons of Catholic piety and their disappointingly bloodless stabs at the fantastical. *The Vatican Cellars* is best remembered for an incident in Book Five when one character pushes a total stranger out of a railroad compartment: the infamous *acte gratuit*, mean and motiveless. You can construe the scene as a contribution to the history of surrealism, as a deliberate affront to the laws of civilization, or as a pastiche of the thriller; at a distance, however, it feels more like the mischievous dream of an author whose writing desk, in his Normandy house, looked not outward into the countryside but directly into a mirror. As the murderer muses just before the deed, "It's not events that I'm curious about, but myself."

The same loyalty—to self rather than to others—was the mark of Gide's love life. His sexual capacities, fully and soberly explored in Naomi Segal's book, suggest that if the writing had failed him (which it rarely did) he could always have found employment in Hollywood, or in the old industries of Forty-second Street. His close friend Roger Martin du Gard wrote in 1921, after a technical discussion:

> Gide needs to empty himself out completely of sperm, and he reaches this state only after coming five, six, or even eight times in succession. I don't need to mention that there was no trace of bragging in his account. . . . First he comes twice, more or less at the same time, "like a singer," he said, "who takes a second breath. . . . The second orgasm," he went on, "seems to climb on the shoulders of the first." . . . The third one happens soon after. He can rarely come more than three times with the same person. When circumstances permit, he then finds himself a second person and comes the fourth and often fifth time. After that he is in a very special state.

I bet he is. Martin du Gard adds that the final flourish, No. 7 or 8, tends to take place at home, alone. The remarkable thing is that Gide found time to do anything else. A typical diary entry for 1922 lists three hours of piano practice, an hour of Shakespeare, an hour of Sainte-Beuve's criticism, two hours of correspondence, six hours of novel writing, and thirty minutes or more of exercise, so how he ever slotted in a couple of sexual partners I have no idea. No wonder Madeleine couldn't control him; she would have needed one of those Texans who fly in to cap oil rigs. Fortunately, she never learned of a day in 1922 when Gide, more or less as a favor, had sex with a friend named Elisabeth Van Rysselberghe; at his first attempt, he fathered a child—Catherine, who at the age of thirteen was told of her father's identity, and to whom he maintained a touching devotion.

This capacity to surprise never failed: Gide accepted the Nobel Prize in Literature in 1947, but he spurned the invitation to join the Académie Française, which, considering his eminence, was like a bishop refusing to go to church. Most impressive of all is the sheer stamina of the man—his mental powers competing with his physical ardor in a race to disprove the theory of human decline. Two impassioned nights in Tunis, for instance, with a fifteen-year-old known simply as "F." were treasured for their "joyful lyricism" and "amused frenzy"; the boy "seemed to care so little about my age that I came to forget it myself." Gide was seventy-two. Shortly afterward, plainly rejuvenated, he returned to the task of translating *Hamlet* into French.

The most unexciting but telling fact about Gide, apart from his devoutly regular reading of the Bible, is that he inherited a private income—not vast but big enough to cushion the blows. As often happens with the conscientiously wealthy, he was generous to others but increasingly parsimonious with himself; leaving a hotel, he tried to run back to his room to find and finish a half-smoked cigarette. He never had to work for a living; his most sustained bout of enterprise came during the First World War, when he devoted sixteen months to helping Belgian refugees. We should not begrudge him his leisure, but neither can we help wondering how he would have conducted his life without a safety net. The young Gide believed in *dénuement*, in stripping life down to its spiritual and sensory essentials (with a prose style to match). As Sheridan points out, there was "something ludicrous" about a man's "sitting in the luxury of the Hôtel Kühn at Saint-Moritz, on the first stage of a honeymoon that was to last seven months, preaching the virtues of *dénuement*."

Sheridan is never fooled by his subject, and often takes him to task. In the 1930s, for instance, Gide abandoned his evenhanded political skepticism and, in common with many Frenchmen of the age, stared longingly and uncomprehendingly at the Soviet Union, with its "unlimited promise of the future." To his credit, though, Gide did what other fellow-travellers never bothered to attempt: he went to the promised land and reported back. At first, the Russians lionized him; he stood next to Stalin and Molotov in Red Square. But Gide, who began by crediting a parade of Soviet youth with "perfect taste," quickly saw behind the showpieces, and on his return he wrote *Back from the U.S.S.R.* Reading it today, you will find it mild and compromised. But to French communists, who brought to their totalitarian faith the kind of exclusive rigor that was formerly the preserve of French Catholicism, it was blasphemy. Gide's collected works were banned in the Soviet Union, and one year after his death they were placed by the Vatican on the *Index librorum prohibitorum.* This is a fine double whammy: any author who is deemed wrong by so many people must be doing something right.

What Gide did right was perhaps not as simple as the version that he offered to the world on receiving the Nobel Prize. "If I have represented anything," he wrote, "it is, I believe, the spirit of free inquiry, independence, insubordination even." He was a rebel with innumerable causes, it is true, but his protests, like his more unseemly political affiliations, have faded from our hearing, leaving behind a calmer but still frighteningly acute tutorial in self-inspection. What prevents many of Gide's novels from taking on a life of their own is his desire to hire characters for the purpose of investigating his own life instead. One of the heroes of *The Counterfeiters*, Edouard, writes in his journal:

> If I were not there to make them acquainted, my morning's self would not recognize my evening's. Nothing could be more different from me than myself. . . . My heart beats only out of sympathy; I live only through others—by procuration, so to speak, and by espousals; and I never feel myself living so intensely as when I escape from myself to become no matter who.

This was published in 1926, when all but one volume of *Remembrance of Things Past* had already appeared, and it reads like a dark, metaphysical riff on the more benign Proustian discovery that social life disperses the self among other people—that it is only through the courtesy of friends and gossips that we somehow exist at all. Sheridan's biography certainly leaves you with just such a queasy sensation; the Gide who demonically harried his young prey is himself out of reach—one friend called him "ungraspable." If you think the pursuit worthwhile, you must supplement the new biography with the journals—the core of his creative burrowings, I think, and not just an addendum to the formal works. In French, they are best followed, or picked over, in the two-volume Pléiade edition; my copy of the first volume, according to a stamp on the title page, was withdrawn from the library of the Facultés Catholiques in Lyons—a proscription that

Gide, who lost one friend after another to the lure of Rome, might well have relished. In English, there is a four-volume translation of the journals by Justin O'Brien, which is now out of print, as is a one-volume rescension published by Penguin. Surely someone could hitch a ride on the Sheridan biography and release the unabridged journals again for American readers. Who can afford to miss this entry, from October 1940?

> Art inhabits temperate regions. And doubtless the greatest harm this war is doing to culture is to create a profusion of extreme passions which, by a sort of inflation, brings about a devaluation of all moderate sentiments. The dying anguish of Roland or the distress of a Lear stripped of power moves us by its exceptional quality but loses its special eloquence when reproduced simultaneously in several thousand copies. Isolated, it is a summit of suffering; in a collection, it becomes a plateau. . . . The artist does not know which way to turn, intellectually or emotionally. Solicited on all sides and unable to answer all appeals, he gives up, at a loss. He has no recourse but to seek refuge in himself or to find refuge in God. That is why war provides religion with easy conquests.

The logic—the brute truth—of such a passage feels hard and steely, and yet there is tenderness in its plea for moderation. Against all expectations, Gide can be as companionable as Montaigne; indeed, the two men could be read as bookends to the bold, compendious tradition of French self-interest that takes in such contrary spirits as Rousseau and the Baudelaire of *My Heart Laid Bare*—an interest so clear-eyed, so supple in the honor it does to the vagaries of mental mood, that by the end it hardly feels like vanity at all. Reading Gide at his best is like watching the skies—fogged by sadness, sharp as ice, or foully clouding over with doubt. "I love life passionately," he wrote, "but I don't trust it." His daily commentaries on both world wars—on the weak victory in the first (Gide had foreseen a "long, dark tunnel, full of blood"), which led to French capitulation in the second—work as a discomforting analysis of a people and also as a downcast reflection upon his own infirmities. We like to think that diaries are written in the wings—in the half-dark, away from the action and the spotlight. Since his death, however, Gide's journals have moved to center stage:

> I am not writing these Memoirs to defend myself. I am not called on to defend myself, since I am not accused. I am writing them before being accused. I am writing them in order to be accused.

This magnificent masochism is a ringing rebuff to our current mania—barely more than a tic—for the confessional mode. We are besieged by personal revelation on every side, and at first blush Gide looks like a useful antecedent. In fact, he set a standard of honesty—on the page, at least—that shames the new bunch of plaintiffs. He does not settle scores or start rumors; he refuses to cry vengeance or claim compensation. "It was in the very excess of their modesty," he wrote of Baudelaire and Dostoevsky, "that their pride sated itself." Strange to say, Gide, after a lifetime of looking in the mirror, was not in it for himself.

AUGUST 9, 1999

EVELYN WAUGH

In July 1956, Evelyn Waugh gave a dinner party for his daughter Teresa. In anticipation of the event, he wrote to a friend, Brian Franks, with a description of the menu, closing with the words "Non Vintage champagne for all but me." Rarely has an edict been issued with such a firm smack of the lips, yet nothing could be sadder. At Oxford in the 1920s, Waugh had chosen his friends on the basis of their ability to handle, or entertainingly mishandle, the effects of alcohol; "an excess of wine nauseated him and this made an insurmountable barrier between us," he wrote of one college acquaintance. Now, thirty years later, he would sit in solitude, grasping his glass, proud that there was nobody present who deserved to share a drop. The hint is clear enough: Waugh, and Waugh alone, was of vintage stuff.

The years since Waugh's death, in 1966—and, in particular, the past decade—have been marked by studious attempts to savor his achievements. We have had biographies in two volumes from Martin Stannard and in one volume from Selina Hastings; more recent, and more slender still, is David Wykes's *Evelyn Waugh: A Literary Life*, which bravely introduces us to the new adjective "Wavian"—helpful to scholars, perhaps, but unlikely to gain a wider currency. Best of all, we have a fresh gathering of primary material: *The Complete Stories of Evelyn Waugh*. The title is clear, although in the Waugh canon a short story is not easily defined. The unfinished yet gracefully rounded tale "Work Suspended," for instance, which consumes eighty-four pages of the present book, feels almost a match for *The Loved One*, *Helena*, and *The Ordeal of Gilbert Pinfold*—the brisk, peppery, death-haunted trio of novellas that Waugh produced in his riper years, and which are available only in individual volumes. He himself was a chronic bibliophile and a connoisseur of typography, who was admired in his youth for his capacity to illustrate rather than compose a text, and his fussing is contagious; as a rule, I am quite happy to read any cruddy old softback with splinters of wood pulp poking out of the pages, yet I treat my early edition of *Vile Bodies*, with its vibrantly woodblocked title page, like a frail and endangered pet. The craving for Waugh can come upon one without warning, especially when the tide of public folly or private slush rises to flood level, but I resent having to slake my need with an emergency Penguin. The new batch of short fiction is a necessary purchase, and you should be able to claim it against tax as an aid to professional sanity, but the IRS might frown at the luridly whimsical dust jacket offered by Little, Brown. The hushed grays of the English edition, published by Everyman, would stand you in better stead.

The choice, nevertheless, is instructive. Is Waugh in hock to the riots that he records, or does he purvey a more Apollonian calm? Is *Vile Bodies*, his Anglo-Saxon chronicle of the 1920s, the last word in madcap, or does it represent the lethally coherent findings of an onlooker? Max Beerbohm once labelled himself a "Tory Anarchist," a tag that George Orwell would later apply to Swift, and it hangs well on Waugh, too; his nostalgia for abandoned glories (largely of his own devising) was matched only by his relish for current catastrophe. It is never enough, whatever the temptation, to mock the age in which you live; the mockery must continue to peal, like an echoing bell, long after the objects of your scorn have been decently laid to rest. Take the cruise liner; now little more than a floating mall for the retired and the tan-crazy, it was once a decorous addition to the Grand Tour, tricked out with just enough raffishness and cultural ambition to lure the satirically minded. Waugh got a whole book, *Labels*, out of a Mediterranean cruise that he took in 1929, and, four years on, he distilled the swaying, semi-nauseated atmosphere of those days into six pages:

> so we had champagne for dinner and were jolly and they threw paper streamers and I threw mine before it was unrolled and hit Miss P. on the nose. Ha ha. So feeling matey I said to the steward isnt this fun and he said yes for them who hasnt got to clear it up goodness how Sad.

If you had to pick a single Waugh word—the syllable that registers his demeanor as reliably as the "Sir" of Dr. Johnson—it would be "so." Designed to establish a causal connection, it may equally gesture toward a run of events so fluid that cause and effect can be found giggling under the table. The hurler of paper streamers is a case in point; beneath the chirpiness, her emotional logic is on its last legs. The passage comes from "Cruise: Letters from a Young Lady of Leisure," and it skewers a small world as cleanly as anything in *Gentlemen Prefer Blondes;* you could argue that comic ventriloquists such as Waugh and Anita Loos are among the most zestful descendants of Joyce—at least, of the Joyce who spoke in the tongue of Molly Bloom. Waugh detested *Ulysses;* I once heard him, during a television interview, decry it as "gibberish" with a hard "g"; but, as many of the stories make clear, the caddish young novelist was not averse to pilfering any modernist techniques that could be of service. The cinematic clamor of competing voices in *Vile Bodies* bears traces of the pub talk in *The Waste Land;* you can still hear it in "Excursion in Reality," written in 1932, with its clicking exchange of dry-hearted lovers:

> "I say, was I beastly tonight?"
> "Lousy."
> "Well, I thought you were lousy too."
> "Never mind. See you sometime."
> "Aren't you afraid to go on talking?"
> "Can't, I'm afraid. I've got to do some work."
> "*Simon*, what *can* you mean?"

Note the absence of guidelines: no "he said," or "she replied." Note, moreover, how little you need them; never in a Waugh conversation do you have to backtrack and work out who is speaking. (Try this some day in the privacy of your own writing, and see how hard it is.) The tones are tethered tightly to character, yet at the same time they seem to float upward like a plainsong of fatigue.

The miracle of Evelyn Waugh is that withering cannot age him. The *Complete Stories* comprises nearly six hundred pages of weariness, withdrawal, disappointment, tweediness, harrumphing snobbery, and flashes of red-faced rage; by rights, the book should grind you down in gloom, instead of which you emerge braced and bolstered, as if by a cold shower and a cocktail. There are thirty-eight tales in all, composed over fifty-two years. Some will be familiar, having been corralled in *Work Suspended and Other Stories;* others, including a trove of juvenilia, were never easy to unearth, and it is gratifying to find them so readily to hand. The earliest effort, written in 1910 and new to me, is "The Curse of the Horse Race." It is thrilling stuff:

> On they went aintil they were face to face with each other. the peliesman lept from his horse only to be stabed to the hart by Rupert then Tom jumped down and got Rupert a smart blow on the cheak.

Not bad for a seven-year-old. Such boyish taste for Victorian melodrama was hardly uncommon; one surprising revelation of *The Com-*

plete Stories of Evelyn Waugh is that the adult storyteller never shook it out of his system. We are so accustomed to the legend of Waugh the patient craftsman—or, less happily, to the honeyed ruminations in which *Brideshead Revisited* gets stuck—that we tend to neglect his talent for whipping a tale along. There may be no unsung masterpieces in this latest volume, but nor is there the slightest temptation to skip, and some of Waugh's openings leave you ravenous for further particulars: "The marriage of Tom Watch and Angela Trench-Troubridge was, perhaps, as unimportant an event as has occurred within living memory." Or, "John Verney married Elizabeth in 1938, but it was not until the winter of 1945 that he came to hate her steadily and fiercely."

Marital friction, or the farce of wedded lethargy, was one of Waugh's enduring obsessions; he himself married a woman named Evelyn Gardner in 1928. They were known as He-Evelyn and She-Evelyn: the perfect couple, at least until the following year, when she fell in love with another man. Waugh filed a petition for divorce in September 1929, and it is a commonplace of Waugh criticism to point out that his fiction was henceforth stained by the rich mortification of the cuckold. Tom Watch and Angela Trench-Troubridge can't even make it through their honeymoon without adultery rearing its tousled head. Tom alights from their train ride to the country, gets left behind, meets an old school friend whose name he can't remember, drinks, hunts, and gets lost; Angela arrives too late to find him there, but thrives anyway. *("Quite all right,"* she cables. *"Your friend divine. Why not join us here.")* Nothing is stated, but we learn in passing that the young bride is thinking of taking a cottage out of town.

This sly history of betrayal, "Love in the Slump," was created in 1932, three years after Waugh's own downfall. The whole thing clips along with the curtness of a telegram; under the pressure of his own fury, the young writer had discovered a species of suffering that he could be funny about. Turn to the back of the book, however, and the chronology of humiliation hits a bump. There you will find a ragbag of fiction from Waugh's time at Oxford, including a cod-historical romance called "Antony, Who Sought Things That Were Lost." I naturally warmed to the title, but the story doesn't really come alive until the death rattle of the last page. Count Antony is imprisoned with his betrothed, the Lady Elizabeth: "And they made a bed of straw on the step and thus among the foul and creeping things was their marriage made." The lady soon tires of her paramour and looks for a replacement. The only candidate is the pockmarked jailer; she makes love to him in full view of the agued Antony, who then rises up in silence and throttles her. Five years *after* the creation of this cheerful scene, Waugh entered the holy estate of matrimony.

One should not read too much into the excesses of youth; it does seem, though, that Waugh the undergraduate was preparing himself, consciously or otherwise, for a lifelong scrutiny of bad faith. The whole point of excess was that it should be reported; if you indulged in it personally, good for you, but your pleasure still awaited the cool stroke of a pen and the careful coloring of exaggeration. The joys of *Decline and Fall*, as of the early stories and the barbarous deadpan of the letters, are those of drunkenness recollected in sobriety; even the perpetration of serious crimes seems to be leavened, if not pardoned, by the punctiliousness of the prose. In the 1923 story "Edward of Unique Achievement," an undergraduate murders his tutor for no better reason than that he dislikes him. The slaughter is blamed on a fellow-student, Lord Poxe, who is censured by the warden with the words "It was an act of wanton foolishness, but I do not wish to be hard on you. . . . Lady Emily Crane, your great aunt, you will remember, married a Mr Arthur Thorn, my grandfather. I feel that the College owes it to your position to treat this matter as discreetly as possible." Poxe is fined thirteen shillings.

All of Waugh is there in bud: the rude names, the wrongful accusation, the clashing rocks of good behavior and evil deeds, and the lunatic conviction that human worth can be measured by genealogy. (There are moments in *Brideshead* when Waugh, devoutly in love with the fine old Catholic name of Marchmain, veers ominously close to the warden.) Like Lord Poxe, the author himself never killed anyone, although he once made a hapless attempt on his own life, swimming out to sea from the Welsh coast; as he recalls in his autobiography, he met a shoal of jellyfish and turned back. (It's a fine joke against himself; only the thoroughly spineless would be deterred by invertebrates.) "All fates are 'worse than death,' " he noted in his diary in 1963, and he delighted in submitting his characters to unlikely varieties of doom and denouement. "The Balance" (1926) imagines its hero downing a blue bottle of poison; the aging Irish hostess of "Bella Fleace Gave a Party" (1932) expires a day after her extravagant but unattended ball, the invitations to which she forgot to put in the mail; the heroine of "On Guard" (1934) is guaranteed a dismal spinsterhood when her jealous poodle, Hector, in a bid to repel all suitors, bites off her ravishing nose.

Then there is McMaster, otherwise known as "The Man Who Liked Dickens." The story was written in 1933, but it had taken root the year before, when Waugh, who spent much of the 1930s in a punishing series of explorations, stumbled across a desolate Brazilian ranch and discovered Mr. Christie. With his loosely extended family, curious theories on the doctrine of the Trinity, and a winning way with rum and lime, Christie was a gift; he stewed in Waugh's mind and emerged as McMaster, who dopes an English visitor, Paul Henty, with strong brews and never lets him go. In reality, Waugh set out freely after a night in Christie's company; but reality was always too meagre for the writer's liking, and he made it the business of his fiction to think along paths not taken—to wonder just how infernally, with a little help from mischance and a touch of sunstruck malice, life might have turned out. And so "The Man Who Liked Dickens" underwent a final fermentation, and became the penultimate chapter of *A Handful of Dust*, with Henty becoming Tony Last—another dreamy cuckold on the run—and McMaster retransfigured into the morbidly named Mr. Todd, requesting one more recitation of *Little Dorrit* from his helpless guest.

It is as plausible a portrait of damnation as you could wish for; even now, however, we have not reached the end of the affair. *The Complete Stories of Evelyn Waugh* has an eight-page offering, "By Special Request," that was used as a quiet climax to the serialized version of *A Handful of Dust*. This time, there is no Brazil; no Christie, no McMaster, no Todd; merely the glum prospect of Tony returning to his errant wife, and the resumption of their stony existence. "All the old faces," she remarks as they sit down in a new restaurant, amid the tribal savagery of a London lunch. The story ends with Tony taking over the apartment that his wife had found so useful for infidelity. Again, we are left to fill in the details, but it is a good bet that the cycle of deceit will lurch into motion all over again. To the comfortless, Waugh offers little more than a choice of living death: malarial mire or furnished flat? A delicious story of 1932, "Incident in Azania," makes the parallel explicit, and sniggers at the blessings of civilization:

> Far away in the interior, in the sunless secret places, where a twisted stem across the jungle track, a rag fluttering to the bough of a tree, a fowl headless and full spread by an old stump marked the taboo where no man might cross, the Sakuya women chanted their primeval litany of initiation; here on the hillside the no less terrible ceremony was held over Mrs Lepperidge's tea table.

This balanced disdain must be kept in mind as we enter the treacherous terrain that is ruled by Waugh the snob. A skim through his journals will provide ample proof that he was a racist, anti-Semitic, misogynist reactionary; but that is the trouble with skimming. The deeper you plunge into him, the more you realize that no one was spared the knife. His novels rejoice in the fact that the sinned against are as open to the attentions of satire as the sinning. Having joined the Catholic Church in 1930, Waugh saw no reason to be softer on the shortcomings of others than he was on his own. The trouble with liberalism, for example—and one can hardly begin to imagine the fun that Waugh would have had with the political dispensations of today—was that it provided unfair exemptions to original sin. If he laughed at the mimicry of European customs which he saw at the coronation of Haile Selassie, and which found full expression in *Black Mischief,* how much harder he laughed at the inability of Europeans to unbend in the presence of the alien. Waugh is fond of Mr. Youkoumian, the Armenian fixer who pops up in "Incident in Azania" and, later, in the pages of *Black Mischief,* but his real venom is reserved for the English community: "It did them good to find a foreigner who so completely fulfilled their ideal of all that a foreigner should be."

As the years progressed, Waugh himself swelled into the sort of Englishman who fulfilled a foreigner's ideal of all that an Englishman, if left rank and unweeded, might become. It was a sight guaranteed (and probably designed) to perplex the 1950s: pink and apoplectic, armed with cigar and ear trumpet, Waugh laid into the decline of modern manners with ill-mannered contempt. No one who claimed to prefer his books to his children ("A child is easily replaced") can have been *that* easy to love, and his journal adds to the insult, describing his own brood—he had six children by his second wife, Laura—as "feckless, destructive, frivolous, sensual, humorless." All in all, the privilege of reading Waugh is rivalled only by the relief of never having had to encounter such a rare, irascible beast in person; the privilege is all the more acute because, with age, his fiction starts to shimmer with self-consciousness—a quickened Falstaffian shame, far beyond the reach of your average club bore—about the monstrous figure that he knows he must cut. That is why this volume contains no senilia. "Basil Seal Rides Again," written three years before Waugh's death, is crisp with mischief and suffused with wintry regret:

> His voice was not the same instrument as of old. He had first assumed it as a conscious imposture; it had become habitual to him; the antiquated, worldly-wise moralities which, using that voice, he had found himself obliged to utter, had become his settled opinions.

Reading this, you ask yourself what manner of fear and uncertainty could lead someone—especially so lithe a social animal as the young Waugh—to wall himself in against the assaults, real and imaginary, of a hostile world. Waugh's biographer Martin Stannard passes a particularly harsh sentence: "His art was a theatre of cruelty; his temperament instinctively uncharitable." That sounds decisive, but it drags Waugh toward the arena of Artaud and Genet, where he most definitely does not belong. For one thing, his unkindness is made compelling by the pitch and frequency of his jokes—seldom registered by Stannard, whose industry is untroubled by humor. Dip at random into the letters, some of which are right up there with the great wit-shows of Horace Walpole and Sydney Smith, and you will immediately stumble upon plain events blooming into the surreal. When Lady Mary Lygon was elected to the London Library in 1946 (not a major achievement), Waugh wrote to congratulate her:

> I hope you will always remember to behave yourself with suitable decorum in those grave precincts. Always go to the closet appointed for the purpose if you wish to make water. Far too many female members have lately taken to squatting behind the Genealogy section. Never write 'balls' with an indelible pencil on the margins of the books provided. Do not solicit the female librarians to acts of unnatural vice.

Is this "instinctively uncharitable"? I think I smell the milk of human kindness: faintly curdled, perhaps, but brimming with licentious glee. During the Second World War, the novelist was described by his commanding officer as "so unpopular as to be unemployable," yet he was also a byword for physical courage, and, in the years that followed, his cruelty began to be infiltrated, if not by charity, at least by a nagging sense of those occasions which would be improved by goodness and mercy. The *Sword of Honour* trilogy, published between 1952 and 1961, is a masterpiece of ruefulness; who but Waugh could have woven the surrender of spiritual hope into the winning of a global fight? The stories from that era are suffused with a similar disillusion; "Scott-King's Modern Europe," about an English schoolmaster adrift in a sunny totalitarian state, is written with the peculiar shade of purple that Waugh could summon at moments of high irony—Latinate, unglutinous, and so steeped in the mock-heroic that susceptible readers may be moved by its dust-covered grandeur. "No voluptuary surfeited by conquest, no colossus of the drama bruised and rent by doting adolescents, not Alexander, not Talleyrand, was more blasé than Scott-King." More mouse than man, Scott-King joins the caged, uncomplaining collection of Waugh protagonists: Paul Pennyfeather, in *Decline and Fall;* Adam Symes, in *Vile Bodies;* William Boot, in *Scoop;* Guy Crouchback, in *Sword of Honour*—mock heroes by any standard, each of them a blend of prig and punching bag. The *Complete Stories* has a roster of new recruits: the narrator of "Work Suspended," for instance, a writer of detective fiction who tucks himself away in a

Moroccan hotel, and Major Gordon, the stolid Scot at the center of "Compassion."

This last tale is reason enough to buy *The Complete Stories of Evelyn Waugh*. Unlike "Work Suspended," "Scott-King's Modern Europe," and ten others, it was tricky to find before the book came out. You could read it, more or less, in *Unconditional Surrender*, the last third of *Sword of Honour*, where it is split and scattered among other strands of plot; here it comes in concentrated form, tense with moral stupefaction. Major Gordon, like Waugh himself, is sent to wartime Yugoslavia—northern Croatia, to be exact, where Tito's partisans are filling the vacuum left by departing Nazis. Gordon, like everyone else, is fouled up in the political tangle, but there is one issue he needs to straighten out: a band of Jewish refugees, desperate to find a home. Nobody wants them, not least Gordon; his first instinct is to wash his hands of them, with "their remnants of bourgeois civility." Slowly, against all odds, this unimaginative man takes up their case, and then their cause; by the end, they are all that matters to him in a dishonored conflict. "He had seen something entirely new, which needed new eyes to see clearly: humanity in the depths, misery of quite another order from anything he had guessed before." Even then, by one of those stabs of lousy luck which Waugh likes to inflict, the major lets his charges down. He achieves almost nothing, and you could say the same of Waugh; how can all the casual anti-Semitism, the slangy thirties use of lower-case "jew" that darkens his letters and journals, possibly be redeemed by this one tale? I can only point to the drama of Gordon's conscience; if he had been tolerant to begin with, the story would be an easy read, but there is something overwhelming in the erosion of prejudice and the dawn of unlikely love:

> Major Gordon did not forget the Jews. Their plight oppressed him on his daily walks in the gardens, where the leaves were now falling fast and burning smokily in the misty air. . . . By such strange entrances does compassion sometimes slip, disguised, into the human heart.

I would not be so precipitate as to claim the discovery of a new and unsuspected creature: a nice Evelyn Waugh. For every Major Gordon, there are a dozen bigots and yellowbellies rustling in the background, and, without them, we would miss the extensive and brightly feathered range of mortal sinners that readers have always sought in Waugh's menagerie. If he had entertained a profound respect for the Welsh, we would have no *Decline and Fall*; without his unsqueamish autopsy of California culture, *The Loved One* could not exist. Waugh was well aware of the price that had to be paid by anatomists such as himself:

> Humility is not a virtue propitious to the artist. It is often pride, emulation, avarice, malice—all the odious qualities—which drive a man to complete, elaborate, refine, destroy, renew his work until he has made something that gratifies his pride and envy and greed. And in so doing he enriches the world more than the generous and good, though he may lose his own soul in the process. That is the paradox of artistic achievement.

With the publication of the *Complete Stories*, the paradox of Evelyn Waugh is given another twist. That he enriched us with the unalloyed gleam of his prose—far purer than any of his leaden imitators can manage—is now beyond debate. He could certainly be odious, even to those who found him amiable; many friends were shocked by the lashes that he meted out in the diaries. But who can tell whether a soul was lost? In his short novel *Helena*, underrated by all but the writer himself, the heroine offers a tremulous prayer to the magi: "How odd you looked on the road, attended by what outlandish liveries, laden with such preposterous gifts! . . . For His sake who did not always neglect your curious gifts, pray always for all the learned, the oblique, the delicate." Those who know only the Waugh of popular myth—the hard, the unhappy, the truculent—should prepare to be shocked by his delicacy. It may at times be the delicacy of the dagger, but, for all his preposterous opinions, there is not a thud of clumsiness in his work, and the figures who wander through it, grievously tricked or drunkenly dim, will continue to console us with their company. He recognized that the struggle between low brutish beings and what he called "an almost fatal hunger for permanence" was both too solemn and too hilarious ever to be resolved. Waugh himself died on Easter Sunday, 1966, after Mass, in the lavatory; he could not have dreamed of a more fitting passage to the life to come.

OCTOBER 4, 1999

W. G. SEBALD

The new book by W. G. Sebald, *Vertigo*, is also the oldest. It appeared in German in 1990; the English translation, by Michael Hulse, has arrived after a decade, during which two other, later books—first *The Emigrants* and then *The Rings of Saturn*—have made a name and a place for themselves. The confusion stems from nothing more than the strategies of publishers, and yet it feels gratifyingly true to the world of Sebald, where nothing can be trusted to cleave to its proper place. Sebald was born in Germany in 1944; in 1970, he moved to England for good, although, to read his collected works, which both unsettle the nerves and ponder the resettlement of displaced persons, you can hardly imagine him pausing to unpack, let alone putting down roots. Since 1987, he has been professor of European literature at the University of East Anglia, where, for five years, he was also the first director of the British Centre for Literary Translation; fluent to a fault in his adopted tongue, he chooses not to write in it, entrusting Hulse with the alchemical task. Yet there is barely a handful of English-speaking writers who can rival the reach and play of Sebald's three publications to date, and connoisseurs of national contention will note that, in literature as in soccer, German talent has once again beaten the English at their own game.

Vertigo begins like this: "In mid-May of the year 1800 Napoleon and a force of 36,000 men crossed the Great St. Bernard pass, an undertaking that had been regarded until that time as next to impossible." *The Rings of Saturn* began like this: "In August 1992, when the dog days were drawing to an end, I set off to walk the county of Suffolk, in the hope of dispelling the emptiness that takes hold of me whenever I have completed a long stint of work." And *The Emigrants* began like this: "At the end of September 1970, shortly before I took up my position in Norwich, I drove out to Hingham with Clara in search of somewhere to live."

In May 2000, I think I see a pattern. Sebald is a rare and elusive species, and the question of what his books are about makes him hard to capture and classify; yet what could be crisper or more amenable than those opening words, as plain as the entries in a journal? These particular events, we learn, happened in a determinable place at a given time; we also learn to be grateful for that giving, because, as the books proceed, we are reminded of all that time takes away. *The Rings of Saturn*, for instance, prides itself on a kind of diplomatic immunity; arising from a ramble through various backwaters of southeastern England, it crosses and recrosses the borders between genres, taking up temporary residence in fiction, autobiography, thumbnail biographies of other men, travellers' tales, and a prayerful rumination on the crumbling of livelihoods and lives. The personal histories within it ascend and decline as irreparably, and sometimes as nobly, as nation-states; it is as though we were all empires unto ourselves—each of us our own Napoleon.

Vertigo, which is even more prone to disorientation than its fellow-volumes, is divided into four parts: "Beyle, or Love Is a Madness Most Discreet," "All'Estero," "Dr. K. Takes the Waters at Riva," and "Il Ritorno in Patria." Prospective readers may be feeling seasick before the book is even under sail. To have your wits about you is one thing, but what about your multiple language skills, not to mention your easy familiarity with the full parade of European literature? Fear not: *Vertigo* is designed to provoke and perplex, but, barring an occasional trip to the dictionary, there is nothing here to put you off. Beyle is Marie-Henri Beyle, better known as Stendhal, and the first section recounts the time—or, at least, his memories of the time—that he spent as a cavalry lieutenant and then advances delicately to some of the manifold complications of his erotic life, before alighting on his death in Paris in 1842, "with the approach of spring already in the air." *All'estero* means "abroad" and refers to Sebald's peregrinations in Austria and Italy, including short disquisitions on Pisanello and Giotto (whose lamenting angels, Sebald brilliantly notes, are so deep-browed that "one might have supposed them blindfolded") and a long excursus into the vexing question of a lost passport. Dr. K. is Kafka, and the title delivers precisely what it promises: Kafka did indeed travel to Vienna, Trieste, Venice, and Riva in the autumn of 1913. The last section of the book, again, means what it sounds like: the return to the country—in this case, the place of Sebald's birth, in southwestern Germany. That *Vertigo* manages to close with a flickering reference to the Great Fire of London, in 1666, as described by Samuel Pepys, should come as no surprise. Such is the first rule of Sebaldry: there is a world elsewhere.

Those are the four limbs of which *Vertigo* is constituted, and they leave us with a mystery: are they made incorporate, and, if so, does the body breathe? What on earth does a French officer of dragoons, as yet uncorrupted by syphilis and novel-writing, have to do with the meanderings of a university professor, nearly two centuries later, picking his way through the attic of an arthritic friend and finding, among other things, a tuba, a goldfinch cage, an abandoned wasps' nest, and "a hairless china doll"? Well, for a start, among those other things is a tailor's dummy, wearing breeches, a jacket, and a plumed hat. "From what I have been able to discover since," Sebald writes, "that uniform, trimmed in the colors pike-gray and green, almost certainly belonged to one of the Austrian chasseurs who fought against the French as irregulars around 1800." Contact. The present brushes against the past, and look what happens: the narrator touches one of the hanging sleeves, and, "to my utter horror, it crumbled into dust." We can assume, I think, that it was once worn by a young man in love.

There are some, perhaps, who will choose not to accept that coincidence—who will claim that Sebald is fixing the evidence in order to stitch together his scraps of sensation. I would reply only that nowhere in Sebald will you find a declaration of infallibility; the fabric of memory may be strong and richly threaded, but it will not always be true. When someone as perceptive as Stendhal gets his facts mixed up with his legends, what hope is there for the rest of us? Stendhal claims to remember a certain General Marmont clad in the blue robes of state, although the general must have been wearing military uniform at the time; he also remembers the town of Ivrea in fading light, with the mountains in the background, although he later discovers that his recollection was culled from an engraving. And here is the crucial point: the error does not make his impressions any less strong. Memory, in short, is engraved not merely by the life we have led but by the life of the mind (books that we have studied or opened in passing, pictures glimpsed on a wall), by all the lives we so nearly led but missed by an inch, and—if we grant enough leeway to the imagination—by the lives of others, which can cut into ours every bit as sharply as our own experience.

If *The Emigrants*, which represented Sebald's first appearance in English, lay within a breath of greatness, that was because its author submitted himself so willingly to the motions of history. We somehow expect literary debutants, whatever their age, to press their case or show their tricks, yet here was a man who raised modesty to the brink of metaphysics. There were four emigrants in all, far-flung Jewish fugitives from oppression, and you could almost hear the rustling sigh of relief as Sebald moved aside and floated his voice into theirs. An account of the painter Max Ferber, for instance, whom Sebald first knew in England in the 1960s, elides into a diary kept by Ferber's mother, and from there into a memoir of Sebald's own visit—as good as a pilgrimage, like most of this writer's journeyings—to the German town where a tombstone, though not a tomb, testifies to the mother's unknown fate. It says simply that Luisa Ferber was deported in 1941, although Sebald has told us earlier that she was murdered in Riga, along with her husband, Fritz. The title of the book suddenly feels darker than ever. Sebald bends his whole being to the problem of reading and hearing one's way back into a past that is, to a terrible degree, beyond all of us, but there are moments when his effort serves only to remind you that by far the most populous migration, that of an entire race, was to an unfindable land.

It is not easy to arrive at *Vertigo* fresh from the travail of *The Emigrants*. Beside those devout intimations of a vast, engulfing tragedy, the problems of paying hotel bills in quiet Italian towns can hardly help seeming inessential. But there is nothing frivolous in *Vertigo*, and the more you pick at it the more tightly it weaves its unease. The narrator slips in and out of the story like a child squeezing through the railings of a park; the technique was obviously ideal preparation for the graver concerns of *The Emigrants*, but it also bestows benefits of its own, minutely shifting the scenery of the action and forcing you to wonder not only what is going on but whether something awful, or awfully funny, is about to occur. During a discussion of narrow Venetian streets, and of the fluid speed with which people enter and leave them, Sebald writes, "These brief exhibitions are of an almost theatrical obscenity and at the same time have an air of conspiracy about them, into which one is drawn against one's will. If you walk behind someone in a deserted alleyway, you only have to quicken your step slightly to instill a little fear into the person you are following." Asked once by a hotelkeeper what he was writing, he said, "I did not know for certain myself, but had a growing suspicion that it might turn into a crime story." The only question is whether he himself would be villain or victim. I am torn between demanding that W. G. Sebald be given the Nobel Prize and suggesting as politely as possible that he be locked up.

Of course, no attorney could prove that the "I" who wrote the book—prim, pensive, and lightly paranoid—bears more than an unfortunate resemblance to the urbane and, by all accounts, highly congenial professor of literature from East Anglia. Sebald himself plays a wicked game on this score. *Vertigo*, like all his books, is littered with photographs and occasional drawings, none of them captioned or attributed; they provide documentary evidence that his recollections are authentic and, as with Stendhal's engraving, also confirm how rapidly our certainties can warp and fade. When Sebald goes to an Italian police station to apply for a replacement passport, we see a shot of the application form, with his name filled in. Except that half of it is blacked out. Sebald himself has (and this may be a breach of the law) gone back and erased all but the first letter of his first name; like a captured airman, he will never give away his most defining secret. Similarly, ten careful minutes with a map of Germany will tell you that W., as he calls his birthplace, is Wertach im Allgäu (for he happily identifies the surrounding towns), yet he prefers to keep it encoded, or perhaps nudge it to the edge of the fictional. There was a point in *Vertigo* when all I could think of was that line of Woody Allen's: "Should I marry W? Not if she won't tell me the other letters in her name."

We know, in part, where Sebald picked up the habit. The tremulous "Dr. K." who inhabits the third portion of the book is the Kafka who equipped his most famous novel with a hero known only as Josef K. By now, perhaps, such truncation is dangerously close to a mannerism, but both writers are all too aware of the conditions—bureaucratic, murderous, or else insanely boring—under which human beings are reduced to lists and abbreviations. Many of the Kafka components in *Vertigo* are stolen, or brazenly borrowed, from Kafka's letters to Felice Bauer and from his 1916 story "The Hunter Gracchus," just as the opening segment trades heavily on *The Life of Henri Brulard*—the name with which Stendhal (who wasn't even called Stendhal) disguised himself, and fooled nobody, for the purposes of autobiography. All of which is enough to induce vertigo in anyone. I trawled through some of the source material and came away applauding Sebald's powers of précis as well as his tiny editorial twists. According to *Vertigo*, Kafka, when staying at the Hotel Sandwirth, in Venice, "exchanged not a word with a living soul excepting the hotel staff"; according to Kafka himself, he spoke with *almost* no one—"*rede fast mit keinem Menschen*"—except the staff, which is not quite the same thing. This is not to quibble with Sebald, who knows a hundred times more about Kafka than most of us, and who has never staked his claim as a biographer, but to note how he has subtly deepened the pit of his subject's solitude—made it, dare one say, more Kafkaesque.

The debt to Kafka does not end there. Sebald's shining, wary, unexcitable prose is unmistakably his own, and Michael Hulse works wonders to maintain the quiet flow; but it keeps reminding you of other writers, and it was not until I read *Vertigo* that the comparison with Kafka hit home. You would not know it from the anxious praise that has been lavished on Sebald, but here is the shocking truth: the guy is an easy read. Heaven knows, he is serious enough, and unblushingly bookish, and the difficulties—historical and philosophical—that he takes on are as tough to negotiate as those ill-lit backstreets of Venice. But still, he is an easy read, just as Kafka is. Sometimes you wish that they weren't—that the sentences didn't draw you on with such courteous grace toward the soft verges of dread. Kafka can be as straight-talking as a fairy tale: "As Gregor Samsa awoke one morning from uneasy dreams he found himself transformed in his bed into a gigantic insect." Thrown by such simplicity, we toss meanings at it like the Samsa family throwing fruit at their son's shell, until an apple sticks and rots. Sebald does not interpret Kafka; he revives him, and, like a director, positions him in a scene that turns your stomach. Kafka looks horribly at home here:

> In the tram, Dr. K. is suddenly convulsed by a violent aversion to Pick, because the latter has a small, unpleasant hole in his nature through which he sometimes creeps forth in his entirety, as Dr. K. now observes.

If this were put any more strongly, it would curdle into Guignol; when you are as easily nauseated by circumstance as Sebald and Kafka, you have to cultivate tact and taste. It is no accident that both men sidle inquisitively toward animal life, with its scurrying, subrational rites. I laughed out loud at Sebald's account of a dog "with a black mark like a patch over its left eye, that appeared like all stray dogs to run at an angle to the direction it was moving in," although I was more freaked by the "large black Newfoundland, its natural gentleness broken by ill-treatment, long confinement or even the crystal clarity of the autumn day." What is happening here? Why should a beautiful day reduce a dog to rage? How can anyone—man or beast—be kept in conditions so dank and dour that, in the end, even sunshine feels like an insult? *The Emigrants* knows all too well the cause of people's upheaval, but *Vertigo* likes to keep us guessing; we are shepherded through incidents that operate, as if masonically, on rules that we struggle to comprehend. Sebald and a friend enter a Viennese bar and find "a silent gathering, the shadow of the waitress threading among them, as if she were the bearer of secret messages between the several guests and the corpulent landlord." Even a photo booth pauses to "yield up" its strip of prints, as though withholding classified information. Having read the book two or three times, I still can't decide on the tone of these lurking events; they feel too perilous for a sacrament, yet too inconclusive to be a plot. What I do know is that, even though some of Sebald's sentences need to be solved as if you were cracking a case, the task of detection never sinks into a hardship. On the contrary, it's a pleasure. To the bookstore browser, Sebald must seem more daunting than any of his contemporaries; to his fans, he is an addiction, and, once buttonholed by his books, you have neither the wish nor the will to tear yourself away.

Sebald's *Vertigo* feels, in the end, consolingly close to Hitchcock's. The past yawns and stretches below this book, and, like the James Stewart character, Sebald, in his guise of timorous hero, seeks a strange cure for his ills by remodeling what already exists—Kafka instead of Kim Novak, it is true, but you can't have everything. There is even a sense that giddiness—*Schwindelgefühle*, the inability to plot one's coordinates on the map of the world—may be not so much an affliction as a fruitful fit. Anyone who remembers the dislocated souls who sauntered through the New German cinema of the 1970s—Bruno S., for example, the smiling, half-named idiot savant who played the leading man for Werner Herzog in *Stroszek* and *The Enigma of Kaspar Hauser*, or the entire cast of Alpine villagers whom Herzog is said to have hypnotized for their performance in *Heart of Glass*—will recognize this peculiarly Germanic strain of tolerance. It goes back at least as far as Georg Büchner, and an American reader will probably be more aroused than anyone else by its insistence that what propels the romantic imagination is not longing but risk; if you want the mind to slip its moorings, you have to be the one to loosen the rope and cast off.

"I take refuge in prose," another of Sebald's acquaintances says, "as one might in a boat," and *Vertigo* is among the most marine of works—calm as a lake, and worryingly turbid below. Like the flat coastal county that he tramped through in *The Rings of Saturn*, everything here is moist. A car: "Now and then some vehicle would crawl slowly along the gleaming black roads, the last of an amphibian species, retreating now to the deeper waters." A chapel: "In that walled cell I sat for a while. . . . The moist smell of lime became sea air; I could feel the spray on my forehead and the boards swaying beneath my feet." Even behind that forehead, an ache, allayed by aspirin, begins to ease, "like the darkness that drains from the sand as the water recedes after high tide." We are stuck fast inside the writer's brain, with its rich pickings of flotsam, and yet what is most endearing about Sebald is his startling lack of indulgence. He writes about himself at almost every turn, comparing notes with the dead and the forgotten, and yet he tells us next to nothing about himself; even more disarmingly, and most unmodishly, he seems not to be very interested in himself. He is a walking headache with a railroad ticket and a leaking memory, and that is all we know for sure. He once claimed, apparently, that what he would most like to have been is a ferry pilot on Lake Geneva. As the Charon of the overworld, W. G. Sebald should not be disappointed; his marvellous books do equally useful duty, ceaselessly bearing us toward the other shore.

MAY 29, 2000

JOHN RUSKIN

John Ruskin was a man of many parts. He wrote with unflagging passion on art, society, religion, rocks, clouds, economics, Egyptology, war, and women, with an instinctive grasp of all but the last. He was the most passionate proselytizer of the nineteenth century and, in the face of stiff competition, the least successful husband. Though unconvinced, like Thomas Carlyle, by the profits of democracy, Ruskin shared in the common resolve to see education trickle down through every class: "I am going to set myself up to tell people anything *in any way* that they want to know," he wrote in 1854. "I am rolling projects over and over in my head." Shortly afterward, he started lecturing at a Working Men's College, bringing in a Gothic missal or a Dürer woodcut from his own collection to illustrate his arguments: "Ruskin was as eloquent as ever, and wildly popular with the men," one observer reported. How tropically remote they seem—those days when a public lecturer like Ruskin could expect to feed hundreds of hungry minds, when his works would be distributed by the thousand as school prizes, and when a two-volume anthology of his writings would sell thirty-five thousand copies. Today's audience might reasonably ask, Why read Ruskin now? Well, this year marks the centenary of his death, which is as good a time as any to pay tribute. He may drive you crazy, as he drove himself, but he will never bore you, and, if your spirits are lowered and thinned by the trafficking of current opinion, there is surprising comfort to be derived from the old-fashioned perorations of a pedagogue.

Above all, Ruskin remains the greatest of art critics, not least because of his urge—as he saw it, a moral obligation—to extend his critical inquiries far beyond the borders of art. Young artists, he once said, "are to be the guides of the nation through its senses; and that is a very important means of guiding it." His first masterpiece, *Modern Painters*, began publication, anonymously, in 1843, when he was twenty-four, and did not reach its climax until 1860. What started out as a chastising of the shortsighted—those who had sneered at the work of Turner—gradually became an exercise in taking the long view, concluding in dark cogitations on classical myth. Ruskin was the first person to champion a living artist with such fire and certitude; it is hard to imagine Clement Greenberg, for instance, trumpeting the virtues of abstract expressionism without the steadfast example of Ruskin before him. *Modern Painters* is a Gothic pulpit, resounding with an unprecedented blast of hectoring and prophetic ecstasy; there are times when Ruskin all but forgets the business of painting, modern or otherwise, so urgent is his will to classify the particular species of cloud, or foliage, that the painter must try to seize. Such beautiful moments, when responsiveness dawns into responsibility, are one of the prime Victorian legacies; one thinks of Tennyson eagerly quizzing the explorer Alfred Wallace about the exact coloration of a forest canopy, and switching a word in one of his poems as a result. "You will never love art well, till you love what she mirrors better," Ruskin said in 1872, and it is the meeting—sometimes the battle—between those twin loves that comes to the fore in Tim Hilton's *John Ruskin: The Later Years.*

This is a companion volume to *The Early Years*, which appeared in 1985. Together, the two books run to almost a thousand pages, which, by Ruskinian standards, amounts to little more than a footnote. Though Ruskin, like Blake and others before him, deplored the industrial scarring of air and land, he himself had no hesitation in treating literature as heavy industry, churning out treatises on everything not only under the sun but under the earth as well. In 1875, for instance, two years after his book on birds, and one year after his book on Tuscan sculpture, the fifty-six-year-old Ruskin published the first installments of his book on Florence, while also finding time to produce *Proserpina*, a botanical study, and *Deucalion*, a further contribution to his lifelong fascination with geology. The annoying thing is that none of this can be discounted; Ruskin resembles nothing so much as an encyclopedia with sideburns, and you can never tell when his deep cast of mind is about to hit a rich vein. Life, surely, must be too short to sit and read a lecture on "The Work of Iron, in Nature, Art, and Policy," first delivered in 1858, and yet to skip it would be to miss out on one of Ruskin's homages to piebald landscape, on a typically wrathful slash at economic oppression ("There never lived Borgias such as live now in the midst of us"), and—always a relief in so voluble a soul—on a neat, epigrammatical glance at the paradox of blood. "Is it not strange to find this stern and strong metal mingled so delicately in our human life that we cannot even blush without its help?"

That reaction is purest Ruskin; for all his manic gathering of hard, metallic facts about the world, there is barely a moment when knowledge is not oxidized—tainted, perhaps, but also transmuted into new life—by its contact with the air of our emotions. Maybe that is why his books seem not just long but constitutionally unable to stop, like the beating of a healthy heart. The Library Edition of Ruskin's works runs to thirty-nine volumes, each about the size and weight of a VCR; I hunted for it online and found it for sale on Melrose Avenue in Los Angeles—yours for the picturesque, not to say Alpine, sum of $16,500. *Fors Clavigera,* the ninety-six letters that the older Ruskin addressed to the "Workmen and Labourers of Great Britain," and that Hilton regards as the unsung masterpiece of a highly vocal career, is 650,000 words long; I have an eight-volume first edition in front of me now, next to five chunky foolscap volumes of *Modern Painters,* frazzled and foxed after years in secondhand bookstores. In the preface to the first volume, Ruskin ventures an explanation: "It was intended to be a short pamphlet." Thanks a lot.

Ruskin was born in 1819, the only son of Margaret and John James Ruskin. The father was a wealthy sherry merchant, the mother a potent evangelical: a strong cocktail, rendered even stronger by the fact that they were first cousins. John James's own father, another John, suffered from a melancholy that eventually buckled into madness; in September 1817, he slit his throat. As often happens, with talents as much as vices, the insanity skipped a generation; his grandson, in possession of a mind that even by Victorian standards was freakishly fine and capacious, would lose it in the end.

In his autobiography, *Praeterita,* Ruskin claims, "I had nothing to love." This is, in part, the crotchety complaint of an older man, but it may also cast an exhausted glance at the love that was bestowed upon Ruskin by his parents—an attentiveness that bordered on the suffocating. He was taught largely at home; father and son studied Tacitus, Cicero, Johnson, and Hazlitt together, as well as a French translation of Homer. After a visit to the castle of Chillon, where one of Byron's fettered heroes had dreamed despairingly of freedom, John James wrote of his hopes for the young John, "May he be the opposite of his lordship in everything but his genius and generosity." Meanwhile, the boy's mother made it her custom and duty to read the Bible from beginning to end and then start all over again. The thirty-second chapter of Deuteronomy was, as her son noted, "worn dark" with overuse, like a favorite shoe. She forbade her son toys; in his earliest years, so he claimed, he had nothing but a set of keys to jangle, and spent long hours studying the pattern in the carpet and the knots of wood in the floor. When Ruskin was ten, he wrote a poem entitled "On the Appearance of a Sudden Cloud of Yellow Fog Covering Everything with Darkness," an early indication that he was a watcher of the skies. At eleven, under the influence of Wordsworth, he wrote more than two thousand lines of rhyming couplets on the subject of the Lake District; John James, proudest of fathers, never travelled without a copy of his son's verses.

In 1837, Ruskin went up to Christ Church, Oxford. It is unsurprising to learn that his parents went, too. His mother and his cousin Mary moved into lodgings in the town; his father came on weekends. Ruskin was not forged by Oxford, as other Victorians were. To read of his time there is to sense a spirit already set apart, armored by the carapace of his upbringing; at ease neither with the young bloods, far richer and heartier than himself, nor in the more rarefied reaches of classical scholarship (in his final exams, he took a Fourth, which means that he just scraped through). It would be stretching the evidence to call him a self-made man, but there have always been intellectual equivalents of the commercial adventurer, and the middle of the nineteenth century, in England as in America, was a heyday for those who sought to shape and hammer their minds from within. Those influences that did impress themselves on Ruskin were of the unorthodox kind: Dr. William Buckland, for instance, the geologist and mineralogist (Ruskin himself had begun a dictionary of mineralogy at the age of twelve), who is now most fondly remembered for the tolerance of his palate. As Hilton crisply puts it, "He kept a bear, jackals, snakes, and many other beasts and birds. These he ate." Ruskin himself refers to "a delicate toast of mice."

Understandably, Ruskin left the university in ill health and travelled abroad with his parents. Altogether, he would make twenty-six journeys to the Continent; like many who become impatient with the failings of their homeland and obsessed with the molding of its future, he spent much of his life directing his gaze elsewhere. Anyone who knows anything of Ruskin will connect him with Venice, and it is true that he single-handedly shifted Western perceptions of the city, supplementing the sensual morbidity of Byron and Shelley with a painstaking architectural inquest. "The Venice of modern fiction and drama is a thing of yesterday, a mere efflorescence of decay, a stage dream which the first ray of daylight must dissipate into dust," Ruskin wrote in *The Stones of Venice*, adding, "its wonderfulness cannot be grasped by the indolence of imagination, but only after frank inquiry into the true nature of that wild and solitary scene." Earlier this year, "Ruskin, Turner and the Pre-Raphaelites," a comprehensive show at the Tate Gallery, in London, included pages of his spidery

Venetian notebooks, which blend broken sketches of Gothic tracery with lists of mathematical measurements. No one, least of all the Venetians themselves, had ever paid the place such pointed homage, and the Englishman was duly outraged by their amateurish attempts at restoration; thanks to his drawings of the south side of St. Mark's, it is possible to prove that the restorers put back one of the marble columns upside down.

What was eating Ruskin, you may ask, as he watched the city melt away? "The rate at which Venice is going is about that of a lump of sugar in hot tea," he said, boiling down 450,000 words of analysis into a single, well-brewed phrase. One gets the disturbing, almost ghostly sense, as one glides through *The Stones of Venice*, or through any of his grander works, that, for all the intensity of description, there are other, secret subjects hidden away—skulking behind the encrusted façade of the prose or drowning in private shame. There is a deep current of self-persuasion in Ruskin that pulls him away from sunken thoughts. "Do not let us deceive ourselves in this important matter; it is *impossible*, as impossible as to raise the dead, to restore anything that has ever been great or beautiful in architecture." The passage comes from *The Seven Lamps of Architecture*, but the shudder of futility, and the quietly horrified acknowledgment of decay, spread far beyond the crumbling of plaster and brick. That book was written in the first year of Ruskin's marriage, and we are right at the heart of his thwartedness, of his fear that he might yet again have "nothing to love," or, even worse, that love would prove too much. We are in the land of Adèle Domecq, Effie Gray, and Rose La Touche.

Toward the end of the first volume of Tim Hilton's biography, there is a startling moment. "Ruskin's sexual maladjustment is not an uncommon one," Hilton writes. "He was a paedophile." That is to say, he loved girls. We have no evidence that he ever abused any of the numerous young women to whom he was drawn; Ruskin's recoiling from physical congress seems to have been absolute. That is not to say that he did not ruin lives other than his own; even from a safe distance, the pressure of his infatuation could be hard to bear. Which is worse: to be a Humbert Humbert who seduces an underage female, with or without her consent, but who at least comprehends what he has done; or to be a John Ruskin, who is guilty of no rape or ravishment, but who hardly begins to know his own depravity? Whatever the case, the alarming precision of Ruskin's memory is Nabokovian in the extreme: "She was lying with her arms thrown back over her head, all languid and lax, on an earth-heap by the river side (the softness of dust being the only softness she had ever known) . . . a few black rags about her loins, but her limbs nearly bare, and her little breasts, scarce dimpled yet,—white,—marble-like."

The "she" is an unnamed Italian, ten years old or so, whom Ruskin caught sight of in 1858; perhaps the most troublesome aspect of this stuff is that it was *published*, seven years later, with all those stammering commas and dashes—the gulps and palpitations of his need—left intact. She would reappear in the course of an Oxford lecture, nearly thirty years on. Not only could Ruskin voice his attraction with impunity but—by the Carroll-like logic of Victorian prudery, which admitted to so little and thus wound up licensing so much—his readers barely flinched to hear of it. Perhaps they were gulled by its scene-setting; Ruskin was the most eminent art critic of the age and, if you were too polite to entertain any personal suspicions, then his account of this slender, marmoreal figure posed artfully beside a river might, at a pinch, sound more like a don describing a Giorgione than a pervert airing his dreams. In a way, you would be right, for Ruskin most happily viewed his beloveds not as living beings but as unravishable brides of quietness: fixed in time, cast like sculptures, immune to Venetian deliquescence, and deathless in their perfection—which is, of course, as good as dead.

Long before the Italian girl, there was Adèle-Clotilde Domecq, the daughter of John James's business partner; one could think of her as the Ruskinian answer to Annabel, the ur-nymphet who dazzled Humbert on a beach, and who presaged all the misery to come. Ruskin fell for Adèle in 1836, when he was sixteen; she was a year younger, born in Spain, educated in France, and Roman Catholic, which to John's mother was pretty much like having Beelzebub in the house. John was badly burned by this first ardor, reduced by Adèle and her sisters to "a mere heap of white ashes in four days." When Adèle announced her engagement four years later, John James was concerned at the effect upon his son: "I trust my Dear Child will not suffer an Injury from the violence of feeling." This was shrewdly said; it finds an echo in Ruskin's own confession in *Praeterita* that, "when affection did come, it came with violence utterly rampant and unmanageable, at least by me." The landscape of Ruskin's life, with its mountainous achievements and pits of sad bafflement, may be too vast and varied to allow a commanding view, although Hilton, who has studied Ruskin for forty years, gives us the fullest prospect that we are likely to have. If there is a binding theme to his book, it is the managing of violence—the idea of Ruskin fighting to contain, whether in his prose or his conduct, the forces of the mad and the majestical. No wonder he was so fired up by the tale of Turner, who, in gauging the exact conditions that he wanted to paint in his *Snow Storm*, lashed himself to the mast of a ship as it rode a riotous sea.

Like Adèle, Euphemia Gray—Effie for short—was fifteen when she first encountered Ruskin. They married five years later, in April 1848. The marriage was never consummated: a fact that they bore in silence for six years, and that has now become the most open domestic secret of the Victorian age. (Imagine the mortification of the decorous Ruskin, let alone of his mother, had they foreseen our prurience.) It has passed into opera and drama; *The Countess*, Gregory Murphy's play on the wars of the Ruskins, is currently running at the Lamb's Theatre on Forty-fourth Street. Ruskin emerges as the helpless blackguard of the piece, and Effie's surviving correspondence offers little reprieve:

> John . . . avowed no intention of making me his Wife. He alleged various reasons, Hatred to children, religious motives, a desire to preserve my beauty, and finally this last year told me his true reason (and this to me is as villainous as all the rest), that he had imagined women were quite different to what he saw I was, and that the reason he did not make me his Wife was because he was disgusted with my person the first evening April 10th.

Legend has it that Ruskin, reared on painted smoothness, was aghast at the sight of pubic hair; we have no evidence for this, and Hilton suggests, instead, that Effie may have been menstruating. At all events, Ruskin's dictum that "a man should choose his wife as he does his destiny" was proved, with distressing irony, to be correct; his destiny was bitter with fear and loathing. The marriage was annulled, and Effie eloped with the Pre-Raphaelite prodigy John Everett Millais, who had previously spent three months in Scotland with the unhappy couple. More vehemently still, the whole saga was elided from *Praeterita*, which dismisses the decade from 1850 as "wasted in useless work." Mind you, *Praeterita* is a strange coda to a life: a blend of untrustable facts—as Hilton and other biographers have pointed out—and gently wishful thinking, all of it shaped into a marvellously malleable prose, which can twist in an instant from the stop-and-go brusqueness of Carlyle to an unimpeded bliss. The book was finished in 1889, when, as Hilton tells us, "Ruskin's hand shook too much to hold a pen," and it tends to seek out points of light in Ruskin's past experience, as if the army of his shadows could be beaten back; the last words summon a vision of fireflies on a starry Sienese night.

If the will to rhapsodize is almost out of control toward the end of *Praeterita*, we should not be surprised; for it is here that Rose La Touche makes her appearance. Rose was Irish, wild, unschooled, unhealthy, and fanatically pious. More to the point, she was nine years old, "rising towards ten," when Ruskin first met her, in 1858: "The eyes rather deep blue at that time, and fuller and softer than afterwards. Lips perfectly lovely in profile." His time with Effie—one trip abroad involved Ruskin spending his days making notes on Norman architecture, while Effie sat nearby on a stool—was merely an embarrassing failure, whereas his entanglement with Rose was a dream that laid siege to Ruskin for forty years. The penultimate paragraph of *Praeterita* dissolves, as if through tears, into a recollection, more biblical than erotic, of "Paradisiacal" walks with Rose, "under the peach-blossom branches by the little glittering stream which I had paved with crystal." As a devoted reader of Dante, Ruskin knew all too well that a girl of nine could transform another's life, yet his own experience was little more than infernal. He proposed to her, out of the blue, in 1866, when she had not yet come of age; she did not finally refuse him until 1872. His journal ached at all the occasions when he was denied permission to see her: "Bright morning. Deadly day." She died in 1875, "raving violently" at their last meeting. "My poor little Rose is gone where the hawthorn blossoms go," Ruskin wrote. Rose swelled into the core of Ruskin's mythology, and she bloomed even brighter after her death. The second volume of Hilton's book is suffused with her, and with awful gestures of commemoration; the year after Rose's death, Ruskin went to Venice and spent six months copying Carpaccio's *The Dream of St. Ursula*, in the Accademia. St. Ursula, who also died young, mingled with Rose in Ruskin's overgrown brain: "My head certainly does not serve me as it did once," he wrote. Whatever you think of the man, it is heartbreaking to watch him falter; by 1887, according to Hilton, "Ruskin could hardly walk, was intermittently deranged, was without money and alone." His creative powers ran dry, as did his inherited wealth, and his final decade passed in cloistral silence. His last, crumpled crush was on a young art student named Kathleen Olander. She kept his letters, but one can hardly bear to read them:

> —And you *will* be happy with me, while yet I live—for it was only love that I wanted to keep me sane—in all things—I am as pure—except in thought—as you are—but it is *terrible* for any creature of my temper to have no wife—one cannot but go mad—

After such knowledge, what forgiveness? Given Ruskin's own strictures on restoration, one is loath to talk of restoring his reputation. He himself, in a letter to his good friend Charles Eliot Norton, was scathing at the expense of his own worth: "I've written a few second-rate books which nobody minds;—I can't draw, I can't play nor sing, I can't ride, I walk worse and worse,—I can't digest. And I can't help it." This is mournfully unfair. To turn from the biographies to Ruskin's published work (far too little of which is in print) is somehow to reach past, or through, his faults and agonies, and to discover a man who, even though his nature forbade him to live in truth, was all the more determined to preach it. In *Modern Painters*, for example, he took irreverent issue with "the system of the old masters"—with their approach to the idealized landscape and their handling of detail and tone:

> It may be sublime, and affecting, and ideal, and intellectual, and a great deal more; but all I am concerned with at present is, that it is not *true*.

It was the quest for the real that he respected in Turner ("the only painter who has ever drawn a mountain, or a stone") and that so enamored him of the Pre-Raphaelites. "False things may be imagined, and false things composed," he wrote toward the end of *Modern Painters*, "but only truth can be invented." If you are a keen anti-Victorian, you will tar Ruskin with hypocrisy—with the crying up of values that he, within his own heart, was unable to pursue. But there is tragedy in the coils of that struggle, and there is genuine vigor and beneficence in the hopes that he held out for the happiness of the many, as if in atonement for the wretchedness of the one, and the hopelessness of the two.

No wonder Ruskin's life abounded with schemes. His yearning for communal contentment and utility, whatever its roots in self-contempt, or in the parched loneliness of his own youth, took many forms. It is a bold art critic who feels it his duty to protest the inadequate sanitation of slums, as Ruskin did in 1854—imagining cholera victims, "horrible in destitution, broken by despair," being brought into a London dinner party and "laid upon the soft carpet, one beside the chair of every guest." Rather less practical was the Guild of St. George, established in 1875 for the purpose of "cultivating pure land, and guiding of pure streams," whatever that meant, among a chivalric company of Ruskin's friends. His most lasting attachment was to Winnington Hall, the girls' school near Manchester, where he taught and lived, infrequently but assiduously, from 1859. There were about thirty-five girls in the school; they received instruction from Ruskin in several subjects, including art and Bible studies. From one of his pupils, we have a haunting picture of the critic at a school dance—"very thin, scarcely more than a black line, as he moved about amongst the white girls in his evening dress." Given the history of his appetites, we find it astounding that such a man could get such a job, let alone make a respectable success of it; but we are not Victorians. No whisper of scandal attaches to his time at Winnington Hall; he was happy and popular there, even if none of his charges could guess how intensely he prized any happiness at all, and to be taught to draw by the world's most fervent exponent of good draftsmanship is no mean thing. Only Ruskin's father, John James, failed to admire the setup, and his lugubrious diary entry, recording yet another visit from his son's admiring pupils, is the funniest moment in two long volumes of biography: "5 virgins to strawberries."

In fact, Ruskin emerges from Hilton's magnum opus as the ideal teacher: kindly, exacting, temperate, relying on an inexhaustible store of intellectual example. He was not all gentleman, but he was no snob, and politically he remains the most intriguing hybrid of the Victorian age. In the opening sentence of *Praeterita*, he labelled himself "a violent Tory of the old school," and he was more than capable of analyzing the layers of pigment in one of Turner's oils without bothering to point out that the picture showed a throng of dying slaves; far more ignominious was his public support of Edward Eyre, the governor of Jamaica, who in 1865 had so brutally suppressed a rebel uprising that he was threatened with prosecution. To have launched a campaign in Eyre's defense sounds reactionary to the point of heartlessness, but look at the list of Ruskin's fellow-signatories: Tennyson, Carlyle, and even Dickens. These are men whose fear of deep disorder outstripped their appreciation of liberty; at the same time, while they may have had no concept of conditions in the Caribbean, two of them—Ruskin and Dickens—thought and wrote with vehemence about the dignity that should attend the working men of England. One of Ruskin's books, *Unto This Last*, would inspire the proponents of socialism and change the life of the young Mahatma Gandhi. The book rings with loathing for the power of money, and money alone, to determine the social contract; as a conservative, Ruskin found no allure in the egalitarian dream, but he saw evil in the prospect of labor without pleasure—the hallmark of the industrial age, and one reason for his increasing (and sadly superfluous) fondness for medieval craft. It was not just that he had moved on from aesthetics but that he made the move inevitable: no one, reading Ruskin, can contemplate the justness of pictorial composition without standing back to survey the wider fields in which that balance should be allowed to flourish. The relations between master and servant, between merchant and buyer, or between sovereign and subject could never be called equal; but they could be honest and true, and Ruskin deplored the effects of mechanization on the human soul:

> If you will make a man of the working creature, you cannot make a tool. Let him but begin to imagine, to think, to try to do anything worth doing; and the engine-turned precision is lost at once. Out come all his roughness, all his dulness, all his incapability; shame upon shame, failure upon failure, pause after pause: but out comes the whole majesty of

him also; and we know the height of it only when we see the clouds settling upon him.

That comes from a discussion of Gothic style, but it could equally apply to the works of Shakespeare, or employment policy, or the life of John Ruskin. Indeed, there is a sombre, sweetish strain of Shakespeare in any account of that life—in the vast discrepancy between the reach of Ruskin's ambition and the desolation that lay at his feet. What transported him in the work of Turner was the effort to bridge that distance; the foreground of our being could somehow meet and merge with our hopes of what lay beyond, or, at least, could promise it in fragmentary hints. Ruskin, who, like many of the best critics, saw with sunlit clarity in others what was veiled and misted over in himself, commended the "decisive imperfection" of Turner—anything that could honor the "beautiful incomprehensibility" of the known, unknowable world.

According to Tim Hilton, who is inspired but rarely deceived by his hero, Ruskin was "half a creative artist," who valued modesty and correctness. Certainly, the careful loveliness of his ink-and-wash sketches was no match for what a view of mountains—"foundationless and inaccessible, their very bases vanishing in the insubstantial and mocking blue of the deep lake below"—could do to his prose. But he, too, was a minor master of "decisive imperfection"; what I like in his drawings is not merely the crisp rendering of architecture, often done as an aide-mémoire, but the nicety with which he knew when to leave well enough alone. His disastrous cravings went on forever, like journeys that permit no sight of land, and no one could regret the oceanic, unceasing sway of Ruskin's prose; only as an artist without pretension did he understand the potency of the blank sheet. "Left off tired. Venice 1876/J Ruskin," reads the inscription on a pencilled perspective of the Grand Canal, but the fatigue was exquisitely timed; the Palazzo Tron, high to Ruskin's right, hangs and dies in the air, as if it stood for a city—an entire civilization—that itself, long before, had left off tired. The procession of his drawings in the Tate Gallery tells the short story of a long-suffering man. At first, you find intricate studies of buildings, and deferential, though never slavish, copies of Turner. Then come Wordsworthian glances at rocks, and stones, and trees. Later still, there are drawings of Rose—from the life, and near death, though she never looks truly alive. There are late self-portraits: Ruskin's head, holding steady in his grief, gazing hard at us, like someone waiting for the answer to a question; but drawn small on the page, as if he were dwindling from sight. After that, it is nothing but clouds.

AUGUST 14, 2000

A. E. HOUSMAN

The most recent play by Sir Tom Stoppard, *The Invention of Love*, will shortly be unveiled on Broadway. Opening night is March 29. The subject of the work is A. E. Housman: poet, clerk, classical scholar, and gourmet, with a palate so fearless that he once dined on hedgehogs. If all goes according to plan, and if *The Invention of Love* hits the public nerve as sharply as Stoppard's *The Real Thing* did in revival last year, then, come spring, Housman should be back in leaf. He has never really wilted out of fashion; *A Shropshire Lad*, his first and most celebrated book of poems, has remained in print since it was published, in 1896. After a slow start, it found particular favor during the Boer War, in which Housman lost a brother, and especially during the First World War, in which everyone lost brothers and sons. Housman was never Poet Laureate—he turned down almost all honors that came his way, managing to appear both lofty and lowly—but, to more than one generation, his poetry became an unofficial well of consolation:

> Here dead lie we because we did not choose
> To live and shame the land from which we sprung.
> Life, to be sure, is nothing much to lose,
> But young men think it is, and we were young.

That is Housman for you: the more simple, even heroic, the note he sounds—and the words of the poem above are as plain as crotchets on a stave—the more you catch a strain of discord or unease beating time below. After all, how consoling *are* those lines? If you were the parent of a dead soldier, Housman would give you plenty to take pride in; on the other hand, the poem—this is all it consists of—is spoken not by the mourners but by those who are mourned, and the last line, if read out loud, could easily sound bitter at the premature dashing of hopes.

On occasion, his work has been the instrument less of succor than of practical help. A devotee of American humor, with an unlikely fondness for Anita Loos, Housman never came to America, but he was visited in 1927 by Clarence Darrow, who, Housman said, "often used my poems to rescue his clients from the electric chair." In particular, Darrow had, when defending Leopold and Loeb three years before, proclaimed the lines

> Oh let not man remember
>   The soul that God forgot,
> But fetch the county kerchief
>   And noose me in the knot,
>   And I will rot.

The Housman magic did the trick. (Imagine that hard final rhyme rebounding like the blow of a hammer off the courtroom walls.) The young murderers were spared execution, although a crime of almost equal magnitude was perpetrated in the process: Darrow had changed "county kerchief" to "county sheriff" for maximum effect. You do not emend Housman, perhaps the most forbidding textual commentator in the history of English-speaking scholarship, and get off lightly.

Do people still turn to Housman in their hour of need, or will it require Tom Stoppard, or another high-profile court case, to revive our fascination? To be sure, there is much in the poems that will ring awkwardly in the modern ear; most of us find it hard to muster an enthusiasm for "many a rose-lipt maiden / And many a lightfoot lad." But poetry survives the death of its diction, and there is a gentle yet insistent pressure in Housman's verse which cannot be ignored, like someone taking your arm and telling you to come for a walk. It is true that the ideal Housman reader would have the Authorized Version of the Bible, especially the Book of Isaiah, the Psalms, and Ecclesiastes, at his or her fingertips, plus a heavy grounding in Milton and, for good measure, all of Horace and Heine; but we regret that the ideal reader is unavailable at this time, and thus the field is left open to nonprofessionals—to those who have just enough time to wonder why a poem that appears, in paraphrase, to be full of the joys of spring should sound, with its long autumnal vowels, like a lament:

> When green buds hang in the elm like dust
>   And sprinkle the lime like rain,
> Forth I wander, forth I must
>   And drink of life again.
> Forth I must by hedgerow bowers

To look at the leaves uncurled
And stand in the fields where cuckoo-flowers
Are lying about the world.

As Housman said, in some annoyance, about a line of Milton's that made him weep, "What in the world is there to cry about?"

Alfred Edward Housman was born in 1859, in Fockbury, a hamlet not in Shropshire but in the adjacent county of Worcestershire. His father, Edward, was a solicitor, though not an industrious one, preferring, with the cushion of inherited income, the life of a country squire. So dumbly ingrained is our notion of the standard-issue Victorian father—the pious ogre with his whipping belts—that it is always a pleasure to meet his opposite. Edward Housman may have been devout, but his devotion was of the charitable sort; if he heard a commotion during nursery tea, he would not only refrain from chastising the offender but, in the words of one of his children, "come and without inquiry put sugar on our bread and butter." The sweetness persisted until 1871, when his wife, Sarah Jane, Alfred's adored mother, died of cancer. Edward took to drink, although he half restored himself with a sober second marriage; Alfred, as the eldest son, was forced in his early teens to assume the responsibilities of an adult, not least with regard to his siblings. "From that time he became his own counsellor, confiding to no one his mental troubles or ambitions," his sister Kate recalled, adding, "He was sensitive and easily wounded, but wounds he bore in silence." That last phrase could be a line from one of Housman's own poems. Looking down the vista of his existence, you get the impression of one door after another being shut.

Housman was educated not far away, at Bromsgrove School; he briefly became a boarder there, when there was scarlet fever at home, and confessed to his stepmother, Lucy, that he had returned to stare at the family house, and especially at her window, from the safety—so to speak—of the local graveyard. The main charge against Housman, as a writer, is that he never truly grew up, and that his verse is murky with prolonged adolescence. In a splendid diatribe, included in *The Triple Thinkers*, Edmund Wilson wrote that "Housman has managed to grow old without in a sense ever knowing maturity"; that he was one of those Englishmen who make "insane attempts to conceal their blazing lights under bushels"; and that, like Lewis Carroll or Edward FitzGerald, he seemed "checked at some early stage of growth, beyond which the sensibility and the intellect . . . may crystallize in marvellous forms, but after which there is no natural progress in the experience of human relationships." Wilson is overstating his case. There is something all too mature in the figure of the youthful Housman, standing for an hour among the graves on a winter's afternoon (you almost expect a Magwitch to grab him by the neck); he is putting away childish things with a vengeance, and to gaze toward your loved ones without being able to join them seems like early training for a life of emotional exile. Besides, to be afraid of death, and thus to clutch at ghosts of happiness, is hardly the prerogative of the teenager alone; let he who is without fear cast the first stone.

From Bromsgrove, Housman won a scholarship to St. John's College, Oxford, which is where Stoppard prefers to observe him. *The Invention of Love* is partly set on cropped croquet lawns; in a tribute to the many facets of his hero's career and temperament, Stoppard divides his time between the dead Housman, ferried by Charon over the river Styx, and Housman the living youth, boating with fellow-undergraduates along the Thames. (At one point, living and dead enjoy a pleasant conversation.) Broadway regulars whose most pressing decision, in recent years, has been to guess whether Annie will or will not Get Her Gun may be allowed a nervous gulp as they are introduced to such characters as Mark Pattison, rector of Lincoln College, and Benjamin Jowett, master of Balliol, translator of Plato, and, by Housman's reckoning, barely a scholar at all. (One Oxford wag reported that Jowett's lectures consisted of "getting up quietly and giving a few faint glimpses into the obvious." I bet Stoppard wishes he had thought of that.) The play plunges Housman into the Oxford of the 1880s and the modish iridescence of the aesthetic movement, with its worship of fleeting intensity, but I am not altogether convinced that he had the will (or the money) to breathe that precious, Paterian air. Housman himself was succinct on the matter: "Oxford had not much effect on me, except that I there met my greatest friend."

The major events of that period were, to be brutal, nonevents: he took his final exams, and he fell in love. He failed the exams, and thus wrecked—or so it seemed—his chances of an academic career. And he failed in love, although the love born in Oxford never failed him as a poet. The man he loved ("my greatest friend") was called Moses Jackson—a scientist and an athlete, a year his senior, who never knew or guessed the effect that he had had. To say that this arrangement suited Housman would be unfair, for nobody could wish such misery on another, but one wonders how he might have coped with requital. The times were against it; *A Shropshire Lad* came out during Oscar Wilde's imprisonment, and we know that, when Wilde was denied reading matter in jail, his friend

Robert Ross used to learn some of Housman's poems by heart and recite them during visits to the prisoner. Housman wrote a rattling allegory on the injustice of the case ("Oh they're taking him to prison for the colour of his hair"). Yet all his instincts—or, rather, the cautious channellings of instinct into art—were set against Wildean display, and his poetry shrinks from the ostentatious heart that is bared by "The Ballad of Reading Gaol." Only after Housman's death did various verses come to light in a memoir by his brother Laurence. Some are no longer than a quatrain:

He would not stay for me; and who can wonder?
He would not stay for me to stand and gaze.
I shook his hand and tore my heart in sunder
And went with half my life about my ways.

The rest of Housman's life was one of monastic triumph, rigid with a certain furtive pride, although no one studying Housman—and he draws obsessives to him, as if to challenge them with his own example—can ever quite miss the scent of shame. At school he had been nicknamed Mouse, and his chosen burrows were hardly freer than traps. W. H. Auden, in a poet-to-poet sonnet, chastised him lightly for this secrecy:

Deliberately he chose the dry-as-dust,
Kept tears like dirty postcards in a drawer.

To which Housman might reply, "Best place for them."

He took a London job in the Patent Office, where he worked conscientiously for a decade. His was a double existence; largely unsuspected by colleagues, he spent his free time in the British Museum, examining manuscripts by classical authors, and publishing his findings in learned journals. These were rated so highly that in 1892 he was offered the post of Professor of Latin at University College, London; for a man who had flunked his degree, this was extraordinary, but the appointments board had no doubts. He stayed at London for nineteen years, occasionally reducing his female students to tears by sheer steeliness of brain, compounded by an inability to remember their names, before becoming the Professor of Latin at Cambridge. He was made a fellow of Trinity College, and remained there until his death, in 1936. There was a misprint in the funeral service, which presumably means that Housman, like Turnus at the close of the *Aeneid*, fled groaning to the shades.

Virginia Woolf wrote that there were no lives more mysterious than those of the great scholars, and in Housman's case the plot undeniably thickened. In London and at Trinity, his labors intensified; his five-volume edition of Manilius, an astronomer-poet from the age of Augustus, consumed no fewer than thirty-four years of his professional life—if you include the addenda to the second edition of 1937, as Housman would wish you to. Yet these were also the decades during which he learned to allow himself what looks suspiciously like fun. One friend, A. C. Benson, said that Housman "appeared to be descended from a long succession of maiden aunts," although another, Grant Richards, used to invite him for holidays with the Richards family in Cornwall, and anyone who views Housman as gloom in a suit will be surprised to hear of him picnicking on a beach and running in bare feet to rescue a child from high rocks. There is also a perfect, apocryphal poem about a couple of Cambridge professors which manages, in four lines, to laugh at both yearning and pedantry—his abiding specialties. Rumor attributes it to Housman, and one prays that rumor is right:

> *First don:* O cuckoo, shall I call thee bird,
> Or but a wandering voice?
> *Second don:* State the alternative preferred,
> With reasons for your choice.

No wonder he needed to get out of college. Starting in 1897, the poet decided to travel during vacations; accompanied by friends, he would visit the Continent by car or, to his soaring joy, by airplane. When Housman decided to investigate a subject, it stayed investigated, and he was so terrifying a connoisseur of French cuisine and wine, especially Burgundy, that, to read his biographers, you get a slightly Feydeau-like sense of portly sommeliers running to do his bidding from every corner of the land. "To watch the poet dressing a crab was a revelation," one observer said. "I never knew poets ate such food." There were other, less public tastes. Richard Perceval Graves, the author of the most excitable account of the poet's life, spends pages on a Venetian gondolier named Andrea, with whom Housman is said (we have no direct evidence) to have had a long-standing affair. Graves also refers us to a small document belonging to Housman that lists "what would seem to be references to a number of male prostitutes, including sailors and ballet-dancers." Never did "seem" have such a load to bear.

It was back in his study, though, that Housman was most roused to action. This was of little concern to the world beyond, but it was highly disturbing if your name happened to be Owen, an editor of Persius and

Juvenal: “Mr. Owen’s innovations, so far as I can see, have only one merit, which certainly, in view of their character, is a merit of some magnitude: they are few.” Or poor Dr. Postgate, an editor of Phaedrus: “Dr Postgate’s notes on I 19 7, 28 5, IV 9 5, 17 8 and 10, 18 14, 20 15, V 51, *app.* 13 25, 14 10, 15 10, appear to have been written before he knew what his text was going to be, or after he had forgotten what it was.” Not even those who typeset a new edition of Martial are spared the rod: “The printers have indulged immoderately in their favourite sport of dropping letters on the floor and then leaving them to lie there or else putting them back in wrong places; and at the top of p. 113 of the text their merriment transgresses the bounds of decorum.” In the event that you ever come across the three volumes of Housman’s *Classical Papers* in a secondhand bookstore, grab them; even if you don’t have a word of Latin or Greek (and Housman convinces you that it is better to have no words than to have the wrong ones), his sense of passionate glee, as he whets his intellectual knives for the purposes of ritual disembowelment, offers the reader as unflagging a demonstration of native wit as can be found in English since the reign of Sydney Smith. Housman has none of Smith’s tolerance or Christian benignity, but this is the arena of pure scholarship, where slackness is a sin beyond purgation.

By now you could be forgiven for thinking that what Housman meant by classical studies had nothing to do with literature—or, at any rate, that he treated ancient texts not as founts of wisdom but as diseased bodies that required unflinching attention if they were to be made whole. He even dismissed Manilius, on whom he expended half his existence, as “facile and frivolous.” Some readers have found this attitude not merely perplexing but distressing, as if Housman were using his professional skills to deny himself the pleasures of the text—as if to admit that you were moved by Propertius, say, were somehow to admit failure. How could the author of *A Shropshire Lad*, a book that feels snowbound with sadness, inhabit the same body as the stone-hearted critic? I cannot see the clash; Housman loved Propertius from his years at Oxford, and, as a poet, and therefore as a card-carrying defender of the mot juste, he saw himself as honor-bound to discover if what he loved really *was* Propertius or merely inferior guesswork, either of an ancient scribe or of a well-meaning twentieth-century idiot. Just occasionally, despite himself, Housman showed his hand. After his death, a Mrs. Pym, formerly a pupil, wrote to the London *Times*, recalling a lecture that he had delivered in 1914, in the course of which he had recited Horace *Odes IV* 7. Earthly love, Horace regrets to inform us, is no more permanent than the thawing and refreezing of the seasons, and that, for Housman, was too much to bear:

> He read the ode aloud with deep emotion, first in Latin and then in an English translation of his own. "That," he said hurriedly, almost like a man betraying a secret, "I regard as the most beautiful poem in ancient literature," and walked quickly out of the room.

It is a scene of high drama, and I was sorry that Stoppard could not find room to embed it in his play, although he does have the young Housman refer in wounded awe to the poem in question: "*Diffugere nives* goes through me like a spear."

The Invention of Love, itself the invention of a smart romantic, proceeds on the assumption that the sharpest spear ever to transfix Housman was his love of Moses Jackson. The play is cold to alternatives—to the notion of Housman as rural elegist, for instance. Shropshire is dismissed by our hero, in the opening scene, as "a county where I never lived and seldom set foot," and, geographically, one cannot quibble. Housman once admitted visiting the Shropshire town of Bridgnorth "for several hours," for the gathering of "local colour." To those sturdy readers who like to know, and go, where literature is set, this must be a grave disappointment; imagine Thoreau saying that he once packed a bathing costume and stopped off at Walden Pond for a dip. But Shropshire is precisely *not* where most of *A Shropshire Lad* is set; it is a place to be looked at, or longed for, endlessly out of reach. When Housman was a boy, he used to climb a hill near his home and look westward, toward Shropshire:

> Into my heart an air that kills
> From yon far country blows:
> What are those blue remembered hills,
> What spires, what farms are those?
>
> That is the land of lost content,
> I see it shining plain,
> The happy highways where I went
> And cannot come again.

That "come" rings strangely on the ear; we are expecting "go," as the counterpart to "went," and "come" is like a tragic slip of the tongue. It suggests that, even if only for the duration of the poem, he has rejoined the highways—or, at any rate, fallen under the illusion that they still exist to be trod.

* * *

In recent years, the strongest aid to our grasp of Housman—at once the most exhaustive and the most suggestive—has been Archie Burnett's 1997 edition of the poems. Housman published only two volumes of verse in his lifetime; there is something very Eeyore-like in the way that he moved directly from *A Shropshire Lad*, in 1896, to *Last Poems*, in 1922, followed by the afterthought of *More Poems* shortly after his death, in 1936. It is the slimmest of outputs, yet Burnett, who deserves some sort of medal for having the valor to submit Housman, of all people, to editorial attention, has unearthed enough variations and allusions to fill 580 pages. There is nothing more beautiful in the Housman canon than " 'Tis time, I think, by Wenlock town," the thirty-ninth poem in *A Shropshire Lad*, and I like the salutary shock of checking the variant readings in Burnett and discovering that the word "Wenlock" in the glorious lines "Oh tarnish late on Wenlock Edge, / Gold that I never see" had once been "Kinver," which needs to be pronounced with a pursed, and meaner, mouth. Truth is all very well, but in the map of the mind every place has to sound ideal. To say that Housman's ear is impeccable need not imply that his other organs were defective; he had the exacting eye of a naturalist ("The plum broke forth in green, / The pear stood high and snowed"), and no poet except Keats has made stranger reference, more wincing than drooling, to the properties of taste:

> When the bells justle in the tower
> The hollow night amid,
> Then on my tongue the taste is sour
> Of all I ever did.

I taste blood, iron-rich, when I read that short poem, and I think at once of Housman's infamous statement, in his 1933 Cambridge lecture "The Name and Nature of Poetry," that "experience has taught me, when I am shaving of a morning, to keep watch over my thoughts, because, if a line of poetry strays into my memory, my skin bristles so that the razor ceases to act." The most donnish of poets turns out to be helplessly physical in his response to the stuff of which poetry is made; it gets to him like a horror movie, and, once you know that, you start to notice all those clipped, semi-slangy, monosyllabic phrases with which he likes, as it were, to wake himself up: "A dead man out of mind," "And God knows why," "Guts in the head." Sometimes a single word is enough to crack the mood, and to rescue the beautiful from the menace of the pretty:

> On russet floors, by waters idle,
> The pine lets fall its cone;

The cuckoo shouts all day at nothing
  In leafy dells alone;
And traveller's joy beguiles in autumn
  Hearts that have lost their own.

On acres of the seeded grasses
  The changing burnish heaves;
Or marshalled under moons of harvest
  Stand still all night the sheaves;
Or beeches strip in storms for winter
  And stain the wind with leaves.

Shout, heave, strip, stain: this was not a writer who turned up his nose or averted his gaze. (If I could sit him down to dinner with anyone, it would be Emily Dickinson: the master and mistress of the short line and the sensory jolt, each with immaculate manners. You never know; it might work.) The Housman mythology, with its lads outnumbering lasses, its redcoated soldiers, and its short-lived flowers, may seem to be drifting back into the Tennysonian age, or further, but *A Shropshire Lad* keeps snapping to attention with phrases like "Put the pistol to your head," as if to remind any antiquarian readers that they will shortly be arriving at the twentieth century. Even one of the most famous verses in the collection begins with the urgency of a potboiler: "On Wenlock Edge the wood's in trouble." We are supposed to be in deepest pastoral, but that sounds to me like someone running into a bar to report a nearby fight.

If anything, Broadway, far from being too rough for Housman, may turn out to be too tame. When I learned that the director of *The Invention of Love* would be Jack O'Brien, who was responsible for the stage version of *The Full Monty*, I was not *entirely* convinced. If there is any man in history who could not have been prevailed upon to strip in front of cheering women, that man is A. E. Housman. On reflection, though, he was not averse, in either poetry or prose, to the occasional half monty, the cunning flash of self-exposure. Lecturing for the first time before the august fellows of University College, the thirty-three-year-old Housman had the nerve to tell them how to live: "One lifetime, nine lifetimes are not long enough for the task of blocking every cranny through which calamity may enter. . . . A life spent, however victoriously, in securing the necessaries of life is no more than an elaborate furnishing and decoration of apartments for the reception of a guest who is never to come. Our business here is not to live, but to live happily." Housman's own business can hardly be said to have flourished, yet, as he went on to say, "we must make up our minds to risk something," and so he did, whatever his detractors may allege. He took a chance on love, and lost; versed in loss, he took a chance on immortality, and, although these are early days, I reckon that he will win.

FEBRUARY 19, 2001

Profiles

THE SOUND OF MUSIC

Let's start at the very beginning. (It's a very good place to start.) Maria Augusta Kutschera was born in 1905. As a young woman, she became a postulant at the Nonnberg Abbey, in Salzburg, Austria, but suffered from ill health. It was deemed beneficial that she should venture outside and adopt the post of governess in the home of a naval captain. She married him in 1927, which put an end to any postulating. The captain already had seven children; Maria bore him three more and formed a family musical group, whose success was cut short when Hitler invaded his native land. Even now, no historian has been able to ascertain if this was a genuine bid for power or the only possible means whereby the Führer could eradicate the threat of close-harmony singing.

Maria and her family fled to Italy, England, and, finally, the United States. The captain died in 1947; two years later, Maria published *The Story of the Trapp Family Singers*. In 1956, the book was turned into a hit German movie; theatrical producers began to sniff around, and in November 1959, *The Sound of Music*, with original songs by Rodgers and Hammerstein, opened on Broadway. Twentieth Century Fox soon acquired the movie rights, but the film proved hard to bring to birth. After nearly five years of wrangles and pangs, *The Sound of Music*, directed by Robert Wise and starring Julie Andrews, had its New York premiere, on March 2, 1965. To date, the picture has earned 160 million dollars. It remains the most popular musical film in history. One woman in Wales has seen it almost a thousand times. In Hong Kong, it is entitled *Fairy Music Blow Fragrant Place, Place Hear.*

All of which is how I came to be standing on a sidewalk on a dark December evening, waving a foam nun.

* * *

The Prince Charles Cinema sits in central London, a hundred yards east of Piccadilly, between the Notre Dame dance hall and a row of Chinese restaurants. When it opened, in 1991, the idea was that you could catch new and recent pictures for less than two dollars—a fraction of what they cost around the corner, in the plush movie theatres of Leicester Square. Even now, the Prince Charles has nobly resisted the urge to smarten up; the furnishings are a touching tribute to wartime brown, and the stalls, flouting a rule of theatrical design which has obtained since the fifth century B.C., appear to slope downward toward the back, so that customers in the rear seats can enjoy an uncluttered view of their own knees. The cinema shows three or four films a day; come the weekend, everything explodes. Since August, every Friday evening and Sunday afternoon the program has been the same: "Singalong-a-Sound-of-Music."

The idea is simple. You watch the film—uncut, as nature intended, in a scuzzy print, with alarming color shifts as the reels change. The only difference is the added subtitles, which come alive, like the hills, during every song. These enable viewers to join in, which they do with undisguised lustiness. The titling of *The Sound of Music* was prepared by Martin Wagner, for London's National Film Theatre, and it struck me as the one work of unquestionable genius that I encountered last year. I tend to be embarrassed by subtitles; their audacious efforts to snatch at foreign vernaculars end up stressing, rather than allaying, the alien qualities of the setting. With *The Sound of Music*, however, they bring home just how tightly, even soothingly, we are wrapped in this unignorable film. In a sense, Wagner had a head start; what was required was not translation from another tongue but the simple transcription, for karaoke purposes, of words that most of us know pretty well. (I was appalled to discover that, after a thirty-year break, I was close to word-perfect.) This, however, is where Wagner shows his hand; who else would have thought to include the *Latin chant* that rises from the abbey as we pan down from Julie Andrews on a hillside and get ready for "(How Do You Solve a Problem Like) Maria?" I had never noticed it before—no audience is meant to notice filler, the blah that keeps a soundtrack ticking along—but suddenly there it was at the bottom of the screen *("In saecula saeculorum")*. Things get even better halfway through the picture, as the children gather at the foot of the stairs to bid the party guests good night. Friedrich sings, and the titles follow him closely:

> So long, farewell, auf Wiedersehen, adieu,
> Adieu, adieu, to yieu and yieu and yieu.

That was it for me. For thirty years, I have wondered about this torturing little rhyme. It should have been easy to avoid; if you want "Adieu" to chime with "you," don't pronounce it in French—simply opt for the Anglicized version, "Adyoo," and take it from there. But no: *The Sound of Music* made a tragic move to sound classy, and it paid the price. As for the yodelling in the puppet scene, it inspires Wagner to his finest work—a cluster bomb of meaningless vowels. For anyone who believes that *The Sound of Music* shows Hollywood at its most hopelessly square, what could be more bracing than to see it reborn as a Dadaist art happening?

All nonsense is a pleasure, of course, from Lewis Carroll down to Alexander Haig, but what lends particular spice to *The Sound of Music* is that it is known nonsense, remembered and revered. And that is why the Prince Charles has become a place of pilgrimage. It occasionally screens *The Rocky Horror Picture Show*, too, to a gathering of addicts. But that film is already armored by a sense of camp; nothing you can throw at it will dent its knowingness, whereas *The Sound of Music*, the most unwitting of cults, is blissfully up for grabs.

When I arrived on a Friday night, an hour before the start, the area around the cinema was packed. To be specific, it was packed with nuns. Many of them bore guitars. I was one of the few pathetic creatures who had not made the effort to come in costume. There were Nazis, naturally, as in every major city, plus a load of people who looked like giant parcels. I didn't get it. "Who are they?" I said to a nun who was having a quick cigarette before the film. She looked at me with celestial pity and blew smoke. "Brown Paper Packages Tied Up with Strings," she replied. I am relieved, on the whole, that I missed the rugby team who piled into one screening as Girls in White Dresses with Blue Satin Sashes; on the other hand, it is a source of infinite sadness to me that I wasn't at the Prince Charles when a guy turned up in a skintight, all-over body costume in bright yellow; asked which character he was intended to represent, he explained that he was Ray, a Drop of Golden Sun. I have hung around the entrance a couple of times as showtime approached, just in case this heroic gentleman returns as Warm Woollen Mittens—or, more challenging still, as Tea, a Drink with Jam and Bread—but no luck so far.

The impressive thing about all this is the apostolic level of dedication. I sat in a whole row of nuns—nurses from a private hospital, as it happened, having a cheap night out. (One had lovingly constructed her wimple from black cloth and a rolled-up pair of white knickers.) During the screening, they drank beer in almost Austrian quantities; one of them kept jumping up and hurrying to the exit. "What's the matter with that nun?" I asked the beefy sister beside me. "Pregnant," she said.

Nominally a reserved people, the British like to bottle up their exhibitionist tendencies and then, at opportune moments, let them flood out in a rush; this is the basis of pantomime, for instance, with its flagrant worship of cross-dressing. Even now, there is almost certainly a quiet soul who is preparing to attend *The Sound of Music* as Schnitzel with Noodles. To brush yourself with egg and roll around in bread crumbs for a while requires a nerveless ingenuity; but to walk to the nearest tube trailing ribbons of buttered pasta, and to sit on the train with a dignified expression, in the thick of the Friday rush hour, argues a fortitude bordering on the superhuman. I couldn't do it, but somebody will, and I think I know who that somebody will be. "Singalong-a-Sound-of-Music" is currently starting a British national tour, and then, in April, it will hit America, where bottling is less of an issue. Twentieth Century Fox will not yet name the lucky cinemas where it will screen, but I can safely reveal that New York and San Francisco, among others, should be girding their loins for Schnitzel Time.

It goes without saying that "Singalong-a-Sound-of-Music" is now a compulsory fixture on the gay calendar; it began life, indeed, as a one-off special for the London Lesbian and Gay Film Festival. Every screening gets its own emcee, who oversees a Best Costume competition during the intermission. (One week, just to confuse the issue, the winner was a *real nun.* What did she think the other nuns were?) At my screening, there was Rhona Cameron, a cheery Scottish lesbian who hosts a gay show on British TV. Rhona checked that there were no children in the audience, and then issued instructions: "Don't worry if you can't sing; the gay men in the audience will carry you." Fragrant music blow fairy place, place go wild.

I usually loathe any hint of live entertainment at the movies, preferring to hibernate in peace and quiet; but "Singalong-a-Sound-of-Music" launches so frontal an assault on reticence that everyone caves in. It is a stout rebuke to the couch culture of "home cinema"—a contradiction in terms, if ever I heard one. The bloodless interaction promised by DVD technology, for instance, in which the lone viewer can pause *The Matrix* to command a reverse view of Keanu Reeves's butt, cannot hold a candle to the sight of two hundred people whistling at Christopher Plummer when he enters with a riding crop, and waving their lighters above their heads, like a rock crowd, during his rendition of "Edelweiss." For an extra five dollars, ticket-holders at the Prince Charles can buy a helpful gift pack that includes a fake edelweiss, a packet of cough drops for sore throats, a head scarf, and, yes, a small foam-rubber nun, in which you are urged to "stick your fingers" and "sway along."

The repartee at "Singalong-a-Sound-of-Music" is of the very highest order. "Free the nuns!" was the cry as the sisters clustered behind an iron grille during Maria's wedding. Some of the backchat involves a dexterous cross-reference to other works; when Maria, having been ticked off by the

Baroness (Eleanor Parker), packs her bag to leave, someone shouted, "Don't forget the hat stand!"—reminding us of a similar scene in *Mary Poppins*. And, as the Mother Abbess lingered in the shadows in preparation for "Climb Ev'ry Mountain," she was told in no uncertain terms, "Do not go into the light!"—the tag line from *Poltergeist*, if you please. The instructions issued to Rolf as he danced with Liesl in the gazebo came from somewhere behind my shoulder; they were explicit, and they were repeated with such urgency that, after a while, they acquired the pathos of a plea—as if it were in some way unsportsmanlike, even unromantic, for a seventeen-year-old Nazi not to deflower a motherless sixteen-year-old while he had the chance. "You need someone older and wiser telling you what to do," crooned Rolf, and we sniggered at his nerve.

The joke is, of course, that Charmian Carr, who plays Liesl, was already twenty-one when the film was made (she kept quiet at the audition), and thus in no need of tutelage from a mere boy; the deeper joke is that, in the history of blockbusting movies, nothing can touch *The Sound of Music* for sheer, blank indifference to the reproductive act. No wonder Heather Menzies, who played Louisa, answered the call to strip for *Playboy* in the 1970s; the pressure of untouchability must have felt like prison. Captain Von Trapp has seven children, but the enigma of his fertility remains as unplumbed as his willingness, as a serving naval officer, to play the guitar in public. The baroness, with her glinting coiffure and cinched suits, could be taken, in a certain light, for a woman of the world; yet the captain throws her over for the sake of a certifiable virgin with a boy's haircut. "For here you are, standing there, loving me," he and Maria sing to one another; love, in so immaculate a world, is pure abstraction, unruffled by the physical. In the intermission at the Prince Charles, Rhona Cameron asked one nun what she liked best about the film. Without hesitation, the nun replied, "The sex."

The Sound of Music is not a good film. It is blithe, efficient, and constructed with care; the songs are carolled con brio; but it is not a good film. Famously, it received some of the most noxious notices of its era. Steeped in the flow of the counterculture, American critics should have been ready for the sight of small children dressed in flowery curtains, but somehow the psychedelic properties of the film eluded them. In the *Herald Tribune*, Judith Crist called it "icky sticky," as if she'd needed to rinse her hands afterward. In *McCall's*, Pauline Kael continued the candy motif, trashing the movie as a "sugar-coated lie that people seem to want to eat"; her review so affronted readers that she was fired from her post and landed shortly afterward at this magazine. Here she reigned supreme for the next quarter of a century, thus proving that *The Sound of Music* is so saintly that it confers a happy ending on all who touch its hem, even those of little faith. The film did more than any other, perhaps, to widen the split between critics and public from crack to chasm; it encouraged producers, like political hopefuls, to reach out over the heads of professional carpers and appeal directly to popular taste. (That it collared the Academy Award for Best Picture in 1966 merely sealed the deal.) The way to solve a problem like Maria is to love her for what she is, with or without wimple, and the movie begs the same indulgence; by ignoring the mean of spirit, it wishes them away.

All of which serves only to confirm the Kael line, and to demonstrate that you can fool all of the people all of the time. The lies perpetuated by Wise's film range from the personal—the real Maria Von Trapp, for instance, looked nothing like Julie Andrews and an awful lot like Nice Guy Eddie from *Reservoir Dogs*—to the broadly historical. If the Nazis' worst crime had indeed been to hang swastikas over people's doorways, the twentieth century would have been somewhat easier to bear. I was a sucker for such untruths; my family even travelled to Salzburg in order to haunt the byways where Julie Andrews had made so ringingly clear what the first three notes just happened to be. Being below critical age, I did not yet grasp the criteria by which a film could be adjudged good or bad, much less the procedures by which it arrived onscreen. If you had explained that the screenplay for *The Sound of Music* came from the pen of one Ernest Lehman, who had written *North by Northwest* and *Sweet Smell of Success*, this bewildering detail would have been lost on me.

To be fair, even some of his friends had trouble taking it in. When Burt Lancaster ran into Lehman at the Fox commissary and learned what he was working on, he said, "Jesus, you must need the money." That story comes from Julia Antopol Hirsch's *The Sound of Music: The Making of America's Favorite Movie*, a loving compendium of arcana. Here we learn, for instance, that both Walter Matthau and Sean "Edelweish" Connery were considered for the role of the captain. A more damning fact is that some of the Osmond boys turned up to audition, thus demonstrating that, however much *The Sound of Music* makes your flesh crawl, it could have been so much worse.

You could argue that the triumphal saga of the Von Trapp family was so sweetly outlandish that any dramatic representation of it was doomed to rot the teeth. But consider another family, the Smiths of Missouri—equally close, no less pure of heart, and, like the Von Trapps, given to bursting into song at the slightest provocation. So why does *Meet Me in St.*

Louis maintain the status of a nimble masterpiece, while *The Sound of Music* limps along behind? Then again, how come Vincente Minnelli's picture of 1944 was reckoned merely a success, while Robert Wise's picture, made twenty years later, is a gold-plated phenomenon? The answer to both questions is the same: because Minnelli showed happiness to be the most fragile of possessions, whereas Wise backed it as a sure thing. For all the highs and lows of its melodrama, *The Sound of Music* never dreams that there is any way but up, whether you are ascending a scale or an alp; and that, today and forever, is what moviegoers want to hear. "From now on, our troubles will be out of sight," Judy Garland sings near the end of *Meet Me in St. Louis*, but the throb and catch in her voice give the lie to such game hope, and, by the penultimate line of the number, the message is decidedly mixed: "We'll have to muddle through somehow." Julie Andrews, by comparison, is a muddle-free zone: "I have confidence in confidence alone; Besides which, you see, I have confidence in me!"

Garland was singing during the Second World War, of course, when a certain lyrical worry was inevitable. Andrews hit her stride in the midst of the cold war; the whole of *The Sound of Music* can perhaps be read as the artistic equivalent of antifreeze. It offered one of the last breaths of innocence in American cinema—after all, the same year saw female nudity in *The Pawnbroker*, and *Bonnie and Clyde* was only two years away. That is why we go back to Wise's film; we all know better now, but most of us secretly wish that we didn't. The atmosphere at the Prince Charles, during "Singalong-a-Sound-of-Music," was strangely unmocking, even in its coarsest moments. We assume that deconstruction is a heartless business, in which the vengeful ironist strips the decorous past to its underclothes; but the hoarse crowd that streamed out into Leicester Square seemed to have drawn strength from a communal act of fond consolidation. When they cried at "Edelweiss," it was not because the song is, in itself, anything more than slush; it was because they had cried at it in 1965.

Film, in other words, has revivified the Proustian principle that memory is not ours to command; that, for all our searchings and suppressings, the past comes unbidden or not at all. If, for millions of people, that past consists of a lonely goatherd on strings, so be it. Proust himself was more fortunate; for him, a typical throwback consisted of tripping over a paving stone and suddenly recalling a similar stumble in Venice. Few of us can rely on such tasteful apparitions. It is generally agreed, for example, that the last Golden Age of cinema occurred in the mid-seventies—the epoch of *The Godfather*, *Chinatown*, and *McCabe and Mrs. Miller*. I feel privileged to have been there; unfortunately, I spent my pocket money on tickets for *Zeppelin*, *Earthquake*, and *Rollercoaster* (in Sensurround). I now realize that *Chinatown* is a great picture and that *The Towering Inferno* is dreck; but the sight of a weary, begrimed Steve McQueen emerging from the tower is burned into my mind with a fierceness that Jack Nicholson, with his nicked nostril, can never match. I missed the Golden Age; catching up later was an education, but nothing I can do will bring it back.

What we feel about a movie—or, indeed, about any work of art, high or low—matters less than the rise and fall of our feelings over time. The *King Lear* that we see as sons and daughters (of Cordelia's age, say) can never be the same play that we attend as parents; the sound of paternal fury, and of the mortal fears that echo beyond it, will knock ever more insistently at our hearts. Weekly critics cannot do justice to that process; when we are asked to nominate favorite films, all we can say is "Well, just now I quite like *Citizen Kane* or *Police Academy 4*, but ask me again next year." By then we will have grown, by a small but significant slippage, into someone else, and we have yet to know who that person will be, or what friable convictions he or she will hold. The revellers at the Prince Charles Cinema were all in their thirties and forties; no one younger than us would have had the remotest clue what we were doing there, or why we were having such fun. Even our younger selves, of ten years ago, would probably have been mystified, if not humiliated, by the air of semi-delirium that prevailed; how could consenting adults join forces to declare their love for a bad film? Time, as ever, has played its comic trick, and all I can do is adapt the words of Captain Von Trapp and his lovely governess: somewhere in our youth or childhood, we must have seen something good.

FEBRUARY 14, 2000

EUGÈNE ATGET

"Paris will no longer see that strange silhouette, that energetic face, that figure out of Balzac, always dressed in an immense threadbare overcoat, crowned with an old round hat, his hands eaten away by acids." Who is this decrepit character? To us he sounds like something out of Beckett rather than Balzac. He is in fact Eugène Atget, the French photographer, who died in 1927, at the age of seventy; those mournful words come from a letter by his friend André Calmettes. They sound suspiciously like mythmaking, born of love and loyalty, but in a way they don't go far enough. The real sadness was not that Paris would no longer see Atget but that, without Atget, nobody could really see Paris.

His life began in spirited fashion, and slowly descended into the uneventful and the quietly creative. Born in 1857, and orphaned young, he went to sea as a cabin boy, travelling as far as Uruguay; back in France, he was drafted into the Army, then took to the boards as a provincial player of bit parts. In 1886, he met an actress, Valentine Delafosse Compagnon, who was to become his lifelong mistress. In 1888, he started to take pictures; within ten years, he had settled on his lifework—to capture Paris in photographs. His prey was more elusive than you might expect—not the proud, orderly streets planned by Haussmann but all that was ignored in that grand design: the arcana of the old city, its brothels and doorways and dirty fountains, the stages on which its daily drama was played out. Atget stopped to absorb the detail that others failed to notice, but he couldn't have cared less about seeing the sights. Not once, in almost forty years behind a camera, did he point it at the Eiffel Tower.

In all, he took over ten thousand pictures. The best array of them can be found in the four-volume edition published between 1981 and 1985 by the Museum of Modern Art. Now there is another option, a single, softback, brick-thick volume entitled *Atget Paris*. There is a curious sense of relief, of being in civilized hands, as you open the book, but also a sense of excitement as you start to flick through, and 840 monochrome images whirr past your eyes to produce, if only for a few seconds, the juddering, crackly film of a lost yet living place. There is no mistaking an Atget photograph, but no easy means of describing it, either; he seems to impose no style, and yet no one else, faced with the same scene, could ever have arrived at the same likeness. He is known, sometimes dismissively, for his conjuring of atmosphere; this book directs you to his mastery of line as well. (It's worth recalling that Walker Evans and Ansel Adams were among Atget's earliest fans.) The edges of his buildings are pure and hard, unbothered by background fuss, but as you look into the distance the light relaxes into a feathery haze. You are left with the extraordinary sensation that perspective is a matter not only of space but of time: in front of your eyes it is high noon, but day seems to be breaking at the end of every street.

This is not simply a trick of exposure; in later life, Atget would rise and photograph at dawn, following in the peaceful footsteps of his countryman Corot. He was, by reputation, even less ostentatious than his subjects; according to Calmettes, he dined on milk, bread, and sugar lumps for twenty years. Ten thousand snaps would be easy for someone with a Nikon and a motor drive; harder for a small guy with a camera the size of a typewriter and a stack of glass-plate negatives, eighteen centimetres by twenty-four. Atget bore the whole burden, more than forty pounds of it, around on his back: deeper shades of Beckett. In 1927, the American photographer Berenice Abbott, who had befriended the aging Atget and did much to spread the news of his genius, persuaded him to sit for her: with fraying collar and absent stare, he looks like a weary undertaker, or a hobo just in off the street, resting awhile, maintaining the last of his dignity. No wonder he has come to stand for the artist as self-denying loner—a type that always reaches out to us with an urgency not shared by more socially stable contemporaries.

But we need to tread warily. Recent research has dented the legend of Atget the trampish hermit, preferring to stress the patient craftsman with a keen eye for business. Both versions, perhaps, are part of the truth, just as an Atget photograph is not only a private, plangent act of contemplation but also a product of the exhaustive French desire for encyclopedic record. He sold in bulk to public institutions, including the Monuments Historiques and the Bibliothèque Nationale. *Atget Paris* divides his work geographically, by *quartier;* he himself was even more practical, compiling his pictures of door knockers, shop signs, or wheeled vehicles into albums. People would buy them and copy the designs. One step up, artists such as

Derain, Utrillo, and Vlaminck would use his urban scenes for topographical purposes, as a prosaic takeoff point for their own flights of invention.

It is from here that the curious history of Atget's reputation really starts. He had few imitators but more interpreters than he would have cared to contemplate. His first and most fruitful contact—you could never call it a collaboration—was with the surrealists, notably with Man Ray, who lived down the street from Atget and would stop by to truffle for appropriate images. Ray was quick to notice how suggestive the photographs' tranquillity could be; when four of them were reproduced in *La Révolution Surréaliste*, in 1926, they looked perfectly at home. There is something tense and poised in the decorum of an Atget composition: the camera tends to be tucked down low on its tripod, affording a broad and vulnerable angle, rather than the tight command of a lofted viewpoint. It seems to be lying in wait for surprises, knowing that they will come but unsure of what form they will take. Atget prepares the ground, in other words, for De Chirico; both are obsessed with the dramatic promise of the underpopulated, although Atget holds off from the sharpened sidelighting with which De Chirico, the ultimate foreshadower, likes to set a scene. The paintings rumble with the thunder of coming catastrophe; the photographs feel more mildly fated, as if the worst that could possibly happen were a postman's tumble from his bicycle, or the baker dropping a loaf. Inside the houses, it is the same story, with echoing drawing rooms ready to receive: Atget gave one of his albums the snappy title *Artistic, Picturesque, and Bourgeois Parisian Interiors from the Beginning of the Twentieth Century.* Bourgeois life had an artistry all its own, delicate and unremarkable rather than grand; the photographer was democratic in his vision but far from revolutionary. He was there to commemorate, not to explode.

This spirit of acquiescence, however, can be taken too far. *A Vision of Paris*, for instance, a tasteful publication of 1963, coupled scenes by Atget with extracts from Proust. It was not the happy marriage you might expect; for one thing, it reminded you just how deeply *À la Recherche* breathed the air of the *beau monde*, whereas Atget was a man of the *monde*, pure and simple. But something else about the book was off key: the attempt to dress Atget up as an expert in nostalgia and, by printing the images in sepia, turn him into a kind of minor-league Proust who longed to clutch at the past. You can see the temptation: no one can look at his shots of the Tuileries, or the Arcadian vistas that he found at Versailles, without a sympathetic pang.

At the other extreme, there is Molly Nesbit's 1992 study, *Atget's Seven Albums*, which takes its epigraph from the second stanza of *The Waste Land:* "What are the roots that clutch, what branches grow / Out of this stony rubbish? Son of man, / You cannot say, or guess, for you know only / A heap of broken images . . ." It's a tall order. Can she really fasten that glimpse of desiccation and decay to Atget's placid portraits of Saint-Germain or the Quartier de Bonne-Nouvelle? His lens never flinched from clutter, of course—from the crust of grime on a stately façade, from unreadable posters peeling off a wall—but the gaze that he levelled at it was clean, wholly immune to the many-angled, tight-nerved scrutiny of the modernists. Molly Nesbit, however, is only just warming up. By page 99, she is giving those bourgeois interiors a piece of her mind: "The document was fetishized in the intermediate spaces that bound the signs together and held the functional ambiguity in place." We can only wonder what M. Atget, elderly resident of the Rue Campagne-Première, would have felt about being so efficiently deconstructed.

Proust or Eliot? Surrealism or fetishization? Atget the businessman or Atget the bum? Every cast of thought, every emotional strategy, it seems, has remade him in its own image. The man himself, when he was alive, was a magnet for rumor, and the work has been overrun ever since. We can't resist it; we dream of a life for ourselves on those wide boulevards. That is one reason his work has barely dated: you can fill it with Frenchness—any kind you like, from whatever period, according to taste. It beckons you into its unexceptional landscapes, its well-stocked but crowdless shops, and your gaze is free to wander, because there's no one else around. The later tradition of Cartier-Bresson and Doisneau, great photographers who caught their country on the wing, has somehow fared less well: the charm remains intact, but all those spontaneous gestures tend to crumble into snatches of social history. Atget, by contrast, knows all about the half-life of happiness and the forgettable crisis, so he doesn't run off to look for them. When Parisians do step into the light for him, it is never the limelight; they go about their business—the waiter, the Gypsy, people hawking baskets or looking at the newly constructed Métro—while he goes about his, and the photograph marks the point of intersection. The point often broadens into a blur, as the people waft like ghosts through his long, sunlit, tolerant exposures. The tail of a dog becomes more of an open fan than a straight line, showing the arc of its wag.

Compared with more luxurious editions, *Atget Paris* is flat and fuzzy in its standards of reproduction, but it is also blessed with one great advantage: you can pick it up and walk around Paris and see where Atget has been. The dog is long gone, but the tail never stops. What shocks the casual stroller these days is not so much what has changed in the course of a violent century as what has stayed the same: you can still buy wigs at the hairdresser on the Boulevard de Strasbourg, and the bones displayed in a shop front on the Rue de l'École-de-Médecine, recorded with morose wit by Atget in the last year of his life, remain there today, although the skeleton has dwindled to a pair of skulls. Someone must have changed that awning on the Rue de Buci a dozen times, but the scalloped fringe keeps the shape that it had in 1900. This may be the most lyrical city in the world, but the lyricism is resilient, neither vaporous nor flashy, and that is why Atget's views of it refuse to fade. He didn't pickle the city in formaldehyde or turn it into a museum; he became its guardian angel, sticking around to watch it grow. The Paris revealed here lies somewhere between Baedeker and Baudelaire, a guided tour to one man's imagination. You keep looking up from page to street, expecting to see that worn old coat pass by.

APRIL 25, 1994

JAN ŠVANKMAJER

Two people, a man and a woman, sit facing each other across a table. They have blank eyes and hairless, unblemished, gray-brown flesh. Suddenly they reach across the table and kiss. The flesh melts. The heads start to *ripple*, one flowing into the other, followed by their bodies, until it becomes impossible to tell them apart.

Sawdust spills out of a stuffed rabbit. The rabbit looks down in surprise, produces a safety pin, and closes himself up.

A man lies down on a bed and goes to sleep. Within seconds, the bed has peeled, rotted, and collapsed. He wakes up to find himself buried in a soft pile of wood shavings.

With infinite patience, a snail explores the eye socket of a skull.

Welcome to the world of Jan Švankmajer.

Over the centuries, Western etiquette has evolved into the most flexible of arts, but it has yet to come up with an attractive way to put the following question: "How about coming around to my place and watching a thirteen-minute Czech movie that contains no dialogue and a bunch of puppets?" I have tried it on friends, and they always manage to turn me down. Yet on the rare occasions when I physically take them hostage and make them watch, they get the point. "We see what you mean," they say, and stagger out into the dark, heading straight for a night of insomnia. And who would want to sleep after a dose of Švankmajer? His movies are so close to bad dreams—blood relations, you might say—that it takes very little to slip them under the door of our unconscious. Some people would balk at this invasion; others would like to risk it but have never had the chance. For the moviegoing world is split into two unequal camps: those who have never heard of Jan Švankmajer, and those who happen upon his work and know that they have come face to face with genius.

Švankmajer was born in Prague in 1934, and turned sixty on September 4th this year. He trained at the School of Applied Arts from 1950 to 1954 and then at the Academy of Performing Arts. He has studied puppetry and graphic design, and worked at various theatres, including the Laterna Magika and the Black Light Theatre of Prague, both of which specialize in objects—puppets, people, props—moving weightlessly against a backdrop of utter darkness. (A better night out than it sounds.) In 1964, he made his first film, *The Last Trick*, in which a pair of marionettes are locked in violent rivalry. His latest, a full-length movie entitled *Faust*, features—among other things—marionettes locked in violent rivalry. Altogether, he has made nearly thirty films, ranging from *Flora*, a twenty-second MTV promo, to *Alice*, a celebrated fantasia on Lewis Carroll, which runs for eighty-four minutes and is the movie for which he is generally known in America.

Švankmajer's life has been, to all appearances, a quiet one, and you catch a precision and a patience in him which hardly suggest that he has gone in search of a wild time. Instead, he has concentrated his energies on a body of work that combines animation, collage, live action, human figures, wooden figures, trick photography, a Bach fantasia, funfair music, and some horrible squelching sounds. There is more than enough wildness—social, political, architectural—in Prague itself to satisfy the most outlandish taste, which may explain why Švankmajer has taken such deep root there and seldom strayed. If you really want to distinguish the full flavors of his achievement, you need to go to his home town. "Prague does possess a certain quality of magic," Švankmajer says. "I tried to discover the last fragments of it in *Faust:* those catacombs, those archways . . ." Before you soak up the intangible weirdness of the place, however, there are more downbeat clues to be sought; the tendency to cannibalism in Švankmajer's work, for instance, so redolent of political rapacity, now strikes me as a purely practical measure. Given some of the dishes available in Prague, the idea of eating your neighbor seems like a tasty option. At lunch one day, I had something called a Farmer's Dream, from which I am still trying to awake; chewing on my fatty goose rump, I thought fondly of Švankmajer's 1992 film *Food*, where diners tuck into a meal of limbs. (The director told me that as a boy he was considered undernourished and was packed off to a special school for forced feeding, where they gave out prizes for weight gain.)

Švankmajer has labelled himself "a militant surrealist"—Czech surrealism has always been graver than its French counterpart, less shrill and capricious—and Prague is the place that pushed him onto the attack: the city that nourished the Jewish legend of the golem, a clay man who comes alive; the city where tree roots of carved stone writhe over a tomb in the cathedral; the city where Rudolf II, sixteenth-century Holy Roman Emperor and collector of oddities, encouraged both religious tolerance and alchemical fantasy, a potent mixture that has yet to simmer down. Rudolf also furthered the career of Arcimboldo, the painter best known for his portraits of human faces constructed from fruits and vegetables—faces that reappear in Švankmajer. Arcimboldo's visual puns are little more than technical tricks, however, and they fade fast, leaving nothing but cleverness behind. Švankmajer's version is much wittier and more suggestive: the edible head that moves, chafes, and decomposes, and is soon transformed into something else entirely.

In Prague, of course, it is impossible to speak of transformation without having your elbow nudged by the spirit of Franz Kafka. The suspicion that your fellow-creatures are not to be trusted, and that your physical surroundings are not much better; the collision (and sometimes collusion) between the man-made and the softer substances of which man himself is made; the profoundly amused yet wholly unshockable realization that the same things seem to be happening, with minor variations, again and again—all these great, if unenviable, gifts were handed down from Kafka to Jan Švankmajer. Both men are far less despairing than their critics (let alone their admirers) would like them to be; when Kafka describes the infernal machine of "In the Penal Colony"—which etches into the skin of condemned men the exact law that they have violated—he knows that the only way to meet such horror is to keep a level gaze. And so it is with Švankmajer: he is not one to brandish his camera in extravagant swoops and glides, preferring to hold steady and watch hostilities break out.

That equanimity has sustained him through the changes of the last five years, in which peace has broken out all over Eastern Europe. Liberated Prague is under siege; Kafka's small house in Golden Lane, where he lived from December 1916, to March 1917, is barely visible above the visiting crowd. Švankmajer stood firm against the forces of the old regime, but he hasn't been swept away by the new one. His city is uneasily balanced—prodded by the butt end of communism and the sharp end of capitalist initiative. One was despised and is now burned out, the other is largely welcomed and gleams more brightly every week, but both cultures arrived from beyond; they are essentially alien to Czech soil. Young Americans show up every month in search of the laid-back life, having read one too many articles extolling the city's civilizing pleasures—Prague is to the nineties, they are told, what Paris was to the twenties. One doesn't like to point out that Paris contained a tiny number of great artists, indelibly serious and industrious, plus a vast throng of hopeless hangers-on. They were the ones who had a fine time, and who were responsible for the now wearisome myth of that age. The process will presumably repeat itself: Prague in the nineties, Americans will confide to their grandchildren, was a dead ringer for Guangzhou in 2044.

Švankmajer lives on a steep slope, halfway up a quiet street below Prague Castle. (More of Prague lives below the castle than can possibly be good for the nerves. Only after coming here do you understand that Kafka's *The Castle* is less a parable than a guided tour.) The visitor is met at the door by the movie director—or, to be precise, by a melee of movie director and dogs. There are only two of them, but it feels like many more; they don't guard him, or guide him, or cozy up to him—they just hang out with him. As we talked, one of the pooches strolled in, nuzzled him, and then went out *backward*, sort of moonwalking. I half expected it to spin round and turn into a bowl of fruit.

You enter Švankmajer's house in a double dream. Nothing, you tell yourself, could be more homely than this, and yet nothing is more unsettling. He surrounds himself with books and objects, the flotsam of a life, as most people do; but there the resemblance ends. Most people would not pass you a book with a hand cut out of sandpaper on the cover and wool running down the spine. Touching it, I felt like Alice, and wondered if I was supposed to open the cover, climb in, and go to sleep. Around us were heads that looked like plaster busts of the Elephant Man but were in fact fashioned from shells. There was a butterfly turned miniature carpet-beater up on the wall, and a strange red flying pig, which looked at me as if to say, "You got a problem, kid?" I had no problem; I was content to sit and drink the wine brought in by Švankmajer's wife, Eva—herself a painter and poet—and to listen to her husband in full flow. Trim and restless, neat white beard, one hand gripping his spectacles, the other frantic with gestures, as if conducting the complex score of his thoughts, Švankmajer radiates a peculiar blend of wryness and passion—a blend that survives, perhaps, only in the cultures of Middle Europe, and dies away as you move farther west, into countries that have, happily, been denied the chance to reflect at length on the meaning of unhappiness.

When I met him, his worries were focussed on *Faust:* not on the movie itself but on all the gremlins that have attended it from birth. The film bristles with magic; when Faust wishes to summon Mephisto, for instance, he uses an old book of spells. The words that you hear contain original cabalistic incantations, whose effectiveness seems to be undimmed. To start with, there was the man who evicted the crew from the studio. Švankmajer's diary takes up the story: "He was walking down the road with his wife, when suddenly a strange man came up to him in broad daylight, shot him, and disappeared. The police haven't found anything yet." Then, there was the animator who slashed her wrists before the shoot even began; the carpenter, "our best technician," who went mad halfway through and was found the next day hanging in a barn; the cameraman who tripped "on completely flat ground," destroying five teeth and a camera; and poor old Jarømír Kallista, the producer. "Someone stole Kallista's car from outside his house in broad daylight. And ran over his dog. Let's be reasonable. We can't blame it all on Faust." Švankmajer may be superstitious, but he never relinquishes his gloomy good humor. It almost saw him through the crowning irony of the whole affair, the serious illness of Petr Čepek, a distinguished elder citizen of the Prague stage, and the film's leading man. "Čepek asked me why it was that Mephisto had planted himself in his stomach and left me alone. I replied, joking, that he was Faust, and not I—that I was only narrating it." Čepek died the week of the film's Prague release.

All of which is no reason to stay away from *Faust* when it comes to New York. It could easily freak you out, but its maker would probably feel hurt if it didn't. There are always moments in a Švankmajer movie when the wish to avert your gaze is only just overcome by the horrified need to see what happens next. The hero of *Faust*, for instance, is confronted by a clay homunculus whose head grows old—from baby face to jaw-clicking skull—within a matter of seconds. Nothing about it is quite as nasty as the wet, sticky sound you hear whenever it blinks. This is not most people's idea of animation. However much you admire the skill of the great Disney pictures, you can't miss their essential timidity—the way they engage (and flatter) half our faculties and leave the rest alone. The problem is not that they look cute, which is unavoidable, but that they are somehow *easy:* once the formula is in place, it can—like Aladdin's genie—conjure up almost anything you desire, with no hard reality to get in the way. Disney proves that, contrary to what you might expect, there is nothing duller than an unlicensed imagination, unless it's an imagination born of good taste. Švankmajer would probably agree. "Disney is one of the great liquidators of Western culture," he told me. "It destroys children's souls." There is something bracing in his willingness to come out with such grand pronouncements. "No art is unsuitable for children" is one of my favorites. Turn the Hays Code upside down but keep the tone of outrage, and you end up with Švankmajer.

Yet he himself is in the business of animation; how does he escape its kitschy conditions? The answer begins with technique. Disney is the home of cel animation—a sequence of two-dimensional images, drawn and colored by hand (or, increasingly, by computer). When run together, they deliver the impression of continuous action: the principle of the flip-book writ large. But Švankmajer deals almost exclusively in stop motion, using three-dimensional objects, puppets, and even—unbelievably—real people. These are photographed by a camera that advances frame by frame; after each advance, they are given minute physical adjustments. This process cannot be computerized, or even mechanized; it is the most laborious craft in cinema, and the end result is like no other. Depending on the number of frames per second, the motion of the objects can be anything from jerky to suave, but there is always something willful and driven about them, a sense of being possessed. When, in Disney's *Beauty and the Beast*, the candelabra and the cutlery start to sing and dance, the effect is charming and slightly fey; when, in Švankmajer's greatest film, *Dimensions of Dialogue*, a head made of similar materials—forks, pot lids, scissors—clanks and rattles toward its opposite number, an organic monstrosity with cabbage cheeks and a lemon for a nose, you feel amazed and destabilized. Yet, as when reading Lewis Carroll—"Mentally, we're on the same side of the river," Švankmajer once said—you accept the craziness straight off. The situation is perfectly clear: a known world has awakened, surging out of control and already waging its own wars. Švankmajer doesn't appear to be making anything up, merely kicking a kitchen into life. Other filmmakers have tried this method, but without success. Even *The Nightmare Before Christmas*, Tim Burton's valiant effort to bring stop motion into the mainstream, went only so far; it was lunatic enough, but not laconic. I remember coming out from an early showing of it last year, behind a couple of film buffs. "That was pretty good," said one of them. "Yeah, it was," said the other. He paused, then added, "But it wasn't as good as that Czech guy."

The best of Švankmajer reminds you, inescapably, of that Viennese guy. Watching a season of his films is like flipping through *The Interpretation of Dreams* but skipping the interpretations. Everything happens so fast that you have no time to let it settle in your brain. "Real time in the movement of a camera is very boring," Švankmajer says. "You move between two points, but between them is a dead area. What is important is where you want to get to." And what gets you there is a cut. Two of his finest films, *Jabberwocky* (1971) and *Punch and Judy* (1966), rise to a violent rhythm that is achieved almost entirely by editing. In both cases, we see walls lined with old newspapers and engravings (shades of Max Ernst), which come and go before us like flash memories of childhood, though whether scary or consoling it is hard to say. And what of those clay figures in *Dimensions of Dialogue*, who kiss and melt? Are they twin souls, merging into oneness, or opposing forces, each bent on suppression of the other? Is this a *Liebestod* or an *Anschluss*? It's both: a great image that draws us to the heart of Švankmajer's imagination, and to a suspicion that his imagination feeds off public life more eagerly than we can ever know. He was asked once whether the movie was "a synthesis of your own moral outlook," and calmly replied, "I don't think you should underestimate the film in this respect." In the space of a few minutes, he delves further into carnal possibilities than his more fashionable compatriot Milan Kundera has done in a shelf of books. Kundera seeks refuge in the bedroom; its exertions are a relief after the intolerable pressures of life outside, in the communist state. Švankmajer takes his camera closer, up against the tangle of limbs, and sees even there a desire to take control. Nowhere is safe.

To what extent, then, are the films of Jan Švankmajer political? The people best qualified to answer this are an extinct breed—the officials allotted the unhappy task of deciphering his work under communist rule. It is hard to conceive of a more infuriating job: a movie such as *Dimensions of Dialogue* certainly *feels* offensive in all sorts of ways, most of them having nothing to do with ideology, but if you tried to pin down where, precisely, the political danger lay, you would end up tearing your hair out—the ideal tribute to the movie, I guess, which is full of enraged domeheads. But somebody, in some graying office, plainly decided that enough was enough; that, even if the state didn't understand Jan Švankmajer, it didn't like what it saw; that anything so thoroughly incomprehensible, in fact, could only be an insult. And so from 1973 through 1980 Švankmajer "rested," or, more specifically, *was* rested, the way South American dissidents were disappeared. He spent part of his time making tactile objects, and playing games with them. For instance: cover an object in black velvet with a hole cut in the side, then have someone put his hand in and describe what he feels. Sooner or later, the feeler "starts talking like a poet—interpretational delirium," Švankmajer says. "Watch the guy when he's touching the object; the world ceases to exist at that moment. His eyes are open, he can't see anything." Sounds like a censor watching a Švankmajer film.

Sometimes the communists objected to particular images, like the footage of a hockey game that Švankmajer worked into his 1972 picture *Leonardo's Diary*, shortly after Czechoslovakia's team defeated the Soviet Union, 4–3, in the World Championships. He was forced to change it to a soccer game; even then, the movie was condemned as "ideologically confused." There were other times, after the ban was lifted, when the ill will grew vague and insistent; he was simply denied the materials and the space for making a movie. *Alice* was shot on film stock brought in from Switzerland and processed on the quiet by a state-owned company that usually dealt in slide shows for trade fairs. It was listed as "an audio-visual demonstration of the demystification of time and space," which, come to think of it, is a pretty fair account of the movie. The real trouble began at the sneak screening. Screenings need projectionists, and projectionists—in communist Czechoslovakia, at least—may not like what they see. According to Švankmajer's British producer, Keith Griffiths, "when we came out of the projection room, the film bosses were waiting for us, and immediately demanded that we go with them to discuss the making of this film, which they didn't even know was taking place." Lewis Carroll would have loved it. The situation was saved by one of the movie's backers, a Swiss, who threatened to withdraw funding. "The thought of the Czech economy losing Swiss francs was even worse than the thought of the movie going ahead," Griffiths says.

And so, by defiance or subterfuge, *Alice* and other films got made. This was mildly heroic, but Švankmajer is shrewd enough to unpack such courage and inspect its contents. Hence the need for *Faust*. Turn the movie so that it faces the past, and the Faustian dilemma runs as follows: Is it better to stay and work under repression, and risk the charge of complacency, or to flee the system (as Kundera did, when he left for Paris), and risk the charge of cowardice? Turn the movie toward the future, and the question becomes: Since the market is working, shall we sell ourselves? What have we to lose? And who is the real buyer? When Čepek Faust—a weary middle-aged man who wanders in off the street—succeeds in raising the devil, he sees a head with horns and horrible tusks curving up from the lower jaw. There is a brief flurry, and the head changes shape. The two of them look at each other again; this time, they are identical. It is the look that matters, the look that says, "Of course it's you. Who else could it be?"

The president of the Czech Republic, Václav Havel, wrote in a letter from prison in 1981, "I am not interested in why man commits evil; I want to know why he does good (here and there) or at least feels that he ought to. . . . It seems to me that even when no one is watching, and even when he is certain no one will ever find out about his behavior, there is something in man that compels him to behave (to a degree, at least) as though someone were constantly observing him." Here is the source of the intense watchfulness that prevails in Švankmajer's movies, a sort of resigned terror that lies beyond politics. "I select my actors not for how they play but for what their eyes look like," he says. When he was casting *Alice*, he tried out a lot of children before deciding on his perfect heroine. "She could have had a more interesting face, her front teeth were broken, she didn't have a nice mouth—the closeup is of another girl's mouth—but the *eyes!* She comes from a broken family, and so she has experienced things. The way the mother surrendered her to us, we could have done anything with her." It's a creepy way of putting it, and in fact the movie does quite a lot with her; but she sails through the strangeness like a miniature Hitchcock blonde. She could be a personal emissary from Švankmajer, sent into Wonderland not merely to report back but to convey the true qualities of her creator: inquisitive, headstrong, unfazed. (Švankmajer takes the illogical very seriously, and expects you to do the same. As I was leaving, he gave me five issues of a surrealist magazine that he edits. One was a special number on eroticism. I had to abandon it; you just can't take that much penetration through Heathrow.)

Jan Švankmajer is the last great obsessive in cinema—the end of a distinguished line that goes back to Orson Welles, Luis Buñuel, and Carl Theodor Dreyer. There are plenty of fanatical craftsmen still at work today (indeed, major studios are unlikely to hire anyone else), but those who use their craft to nag away at recurring themes—who are infected, so to speak, by the pleasures of the medium—are dying out fast. Perhaps they are considered untrustworthy; obsession, after all, is trailed by oddity and excess, and it is the mark of the true obsessive that, where calmer professionals stumble and recover, he will take a wrong turning that can last for an entire film. Watch more than a handful of Hitchcocks, and you start to hear the guilt and apprehension knocking inside the director's head. The same is true of Švankmajer: his movies return us time and again to questions of enmity and curiosity, of closeness so intimate that it turns into violence, and of violence so rabid that it turns into farce. There is immense integrity in the determination to confront what lies just out of reach or what others would prefer to shun. Whatever happens, he never blinks.

A young girl goes down to the basement to fetch a basket of potatoes. She looks through a slat. An old man is going to bed in a pile of coal, pulling black lumps over himself like a blanket. He turns and beckons her in. She backs away. A cat startles her with one bright eye. The lid of a chest swings down and cracks her on the head. She takes her basket and starts to climb the stairs. When she's halfway up, the potatoes spill and roll to the bottom. The girl pauses. Down there is everything she fears. The cellar door is still open.

She goes back down into the dark.

OCTOBER 31, 1994

KARL LAGERFELD

"Naomi! Trish! Helena! Brandi! Claudia!" Pause. "Trish? Treeesh!" It is Thursday, October 13. We are at the hub of Paris, underneath the Louvre, and the speaker is a young man named Arnaud. He is not, as you might think, sobbing out the lost loves of yesteryear but calling a bunch of girls into line before sending them out onto the runway. Trish arrives. She's cool. Brandi, however, does not. She is in full view, less than six yards away, but she is not *here*, where she ought to be. "Can someone please help me with these shoes?" she asks. Five helpers pounce on her simultaneously, which is no help at all. The helpers work at unbuckling the shoes, which aren't really shoes—more like Barbarella boots, banded by transparent straps right up to the knee. "Relax, or you're never going to get it off," Brandi says. This is good advice, and roundly ignored. Arnaud calls her name again, this time in the tone you might adopt if your only child had just slipped your grasp and fallen into a ravine. The boot comes off, and for some reason doesn't take Brandi's leg with it. She puts on the next pair of shoes. These have to be buckled *up*. "It's not important," Arnaud says. But everything is important: the helpers are determined to finish the job, so, as Brandi strolls toward her place in the line, they trot behind her in a running crouch, bent almost double, fussing at her heels. When she stops, they all cannon into her, like a train hitting the buffers. The panic level is rising, but Brandi is unmoved. She can cope with this. She's seen it all before. She's sixteen.

Brandi is the second-calmest person on the premises. The calmest person is a man in a baggy black suit and sunglasses, standing at the side of the queue. He will not be joining the girls on the catwalk, not just yet; like other designers, Karl Lagerfeld appears only at the finale. For the moment, he is busy talking to the girls, adding last-minute details, finding time to try new earrings on Kristen McMenamy—someone hands him a pair that don't match—and to fiddle with a neckband at Trish's throat. It sounds crazy, but, guess what, this guy is *enjoying* himself. There are many things to do at the Paris prêt-à-porter collections (shop, strut, smoke, drink, shout, smile, and shop again), and many things not to do (eat, sleep, save, think, read, or wrap up warm); but the idea that you could simply have a nice day never arises. Lagerfeld, however, spends most of his time obeying the old Noël Coward principle: Work is more fun than fun. He creates the clothes, he dreams up the joke handbags, he photographs the girls, he even writes rhyming couplets for the press release. Other designers come to Paris to put on a good show, but not Karl; he puts on three good shows. "I cannot be one," he announces with mystical defiance. On Tuesday, it was Chloé; today is Lagerfeld, his own label; and still to come, next Monday, is Chanel. Even by his standards, it's kind of a busy week.

Lagerfeld grew up in Germany, the only son of a German mother and a Swedish father; that, at least, is the official version of his provenance. To understand the man more fully, you need to go further back; after a week in his company, I became convinced that someone in the Lagerfeld line had married into a family of sharks. Basking sharks, probably, for Lagerfeld is not notably voracious; he just won't stop moving. If he did stop, he would sink and die. A friend of twenty years, Patrick Hourcade, calls him "a force of will," which is great for Lagerfeld, and exhausting for the rest of us. He designs seventeen collections a year, migrates between five homes, and is said to rise before six. Never having been awake at such an hour, I can't say what that's like, but it sounds pretty damn early. Only once did I see him tired, just before midnight on Wednesday, when he took off his shades and rubbed his eyes. We were sitting in the Lagerfeld offices, waiting for Kate Moss to arrive for a fitting. For a moment, his face looked gray and fallen. The moment passed. He brightened again. Kate turned up. "I've just flown in from Arizona," she said. "On Saturday, I'm going to Japan." The music for the next day's show pumped through the room: "Life is good," went the chorus, over and over again. When I crumbled and left at one in the morning, Karl was busy writing an article for German *Vogue*.

In Paris, the real test of stamina is not the shows themselves but the days that precede them, when Lagerfeld retreats to his three fashion houses and marshals his troops for combat. The models parade in front of him in the outfits they will wear on the catwalk. Accessories are added; hemlines are raised or, on rare occasions, lowered; Polaroid photographs are taken, pinned to a board, then bound into a precise order of battle. This requires total concentration, which makes it all the more impressive that Lagerfeld himself appears to pay no attention whatsoever. When Naomi Campbell turned up, much delayed, for a late-night fitting, he greeted her warmly, made sure that she was properly decked out in pink palazzo pants trimmed with black lace, then proceeded to tell me all about this terrific idea he had for a movie. Lagerfeld is surrounded by assistants, hangers-on, and droppers-in, some of whom interest him more than others ("People who work hate being visited by those who don't," he says), but all of whom are met with armfuls of charm and depart in the belief that *they* were the ones he really wanted to see. Only if you watch carefully do you notice his glance flicking up at each model, or a motion of his hand suggesting an alteration. Any further comment is concise: "That's vulgar," "Too *Cage aux Folles*," and, to some vain male posers, "No, no bedroom mood, please!" Lagerfeld has neither the time nor, I suspect, the inclination to pursue political correctness. When Stephanie Seymour, who recently gave birth to her second child, entered the room in a swimsuit, he turned to me. "Huge balloons, no?" he exclaimed. "With a cleavage like that, everything fits."

Last week's campaign began at Chloé, on the Rue Faubourg Saint-Honoré—the long, spotless street that has for decades been the Vatican of fashion, issuing all manner of earring encyclicals and heel edicts. Yards from the boutique, just over the way, are the British and American embassies, offering the prospect of a great Parisian day: Go and have a good cry about your lost passport, then nip across the road and cheer yourself up by buying a velvet evening bag with little bronze feet, for $1,680. Downstairs in Chloé, I watched a young woman emerge from a changing room in a wedding dress. "It's transparent," she said. "Not *too* transparent," cried the sales assistants. Well, up to a point. From ten paces I could read the labels on her underwear. One floor above, a middle-aged woman tried on a black chiffon two-piece. "I'm too old," she said to me. "I'm going to trip, right?" There was no polite answer to this. She was confronting the terrible truth that prêt-à-porter does not mean "ready to wear"; it means "ready to wear if you have legs as long as the Eiffel Tower." I left her to her sorrows, and ascended to the inner sanctum of Karl Lagerfeld.

He sat at his desk, surrounded by the tools of his trade: the full range of Caran d'Ache crayons, a fistful of green Pentel pens, writing paper, sketching paper, and a little basket of lemons. At first, I took the lemons to be a visual pun—something to fortify his acid tongue—but it turned out that Karl likes a dose of lemon in his Diet Coke. Food is a big deal around here: surprising, really, because the models themselves subsist on the traditional party-hermit diet of water and cigarettes, boosted occasionally by sugar-free gum and a shot of champagne. The creative types, however, function on a fairly intensive snack rhythm, to keep their energy up as the night grows long. Everything needs to be eaten with one hand, leaving the other free to wave hello and goodbye. Cheese, for instance, should come in tasteless slices or wax-wrapped balls, not in interesting fungoid pools. One of Lagerfeld's best clients, Susan Gutfreund, arrived with a bag of goodies from Debauve & Gallais, who make the kind of chocolates you dream about on your deathbed. She offered me one from a tin labelled Les Incroyables. It was unbelievable. Karl, meanwhile, made steady headway through a pile of frankfurters with a side dish of mustard. He might as well have hung a sign over his head saying "I'm still German."

Well, you do wonder. Lagerfeld speaks four languages: German, French, English, and Italian. This is five fewer than his father, a condensed-milk millionaire with a particular penchant for Russian, but Lagerfeld can still unnerve you, because he often appears to be speaking all four at the same time, roaming across the linguistic map within the course of a single exchange. As a boy, he says, he taught himself to read in order to follow the text of a favorite picture book. "Which book?" I asked him, trying hard to imagine the young Karl poring over Richard Scarry. He replied, "*Das Nibelungenlied.*" There is more than a dash of Nabokov in Lagerfeld: the classy solitude of his upbringing, the mental speed that is easily taken for arrogance, the restive obsession with detail that is bred by unending exile. "Where is home?" I asked him. "Wherever I am," he replied. He wrote the *Vogue* article with a French-German dictionary at his elbow, as if the finer points of his native language had grown blunt from lack of practice; but he certainly rattled it off with brio when talking to Claudia Schiffer. "Nobody else understands us," he said gleefully. I guess she loosens the tongue.

Claudia is, by all reports, the most wanted woman in the world. She stood in the middle of the room wearing a garment whose style could best be described as cling peach. Karl summed up its appeal: "How to look naked in a long dress." I asked Claudia if she had come straight to Paris from the Milan shows. "No, I went to Frankfurt, to the Book Fair. I was launching two books," she said. Was one of them, by any chance, a novel? "No, it's too early for that," she replied, which may or may not have been a dig at Naomi Campbell, whose own foray into fiction, *The Swan*, was published recently. And that was as sharp as Claudia ever got. Anyone who came to Paris hoping to find outrageous acts of bitchery among the stars—as recorded, or invented, by the tabloid press—would be badly disappointed; there is nothing backstage at a week of fashion shows to touch the meanness of spirit that you would have found at, say, a single soirée of the Bloomsbury Group. Not among the designers, at any rate, who are working flat out; or among the models, most of whom keep long hours (hair and makeup at six in the morning, two or three shows, a shoot, maybe a final fitting toward eleven at night) while maintaining a commendably even temper. True, one of them said that Brandi should be given a good slap, but that's just motherly advice. I watched Brandi playing air guitar to the soundtrack of *Pulp Fiction* and thought she could probably ride a slap as well as any other teenager. On the runway, she sashays with such a violent swing of the hips that I was worried she might swing too far and start walking backward.

The problem with fashion is not spoiled supermodels but supermodels' boyfriends. It is at this juncture that the whole business goes haywire. Watching Linda Evangelista as she chatted with Kyle MacLachlan in a foaming ring of camera crews (possibly the least spontaneous conversation in the history of human contact), or wandering backstage after a show and finding Karl in conversation with Claudia, David Copperfield, and David Copperfield's *father*, I thought: Is it worth it? Lagerfeld loves designing clothes, but can he really take the cloud of unknowing, the nimbus of bullshit, that surrounds it all? In the course of one evening, he talked about the novels of Maurice Barrès (author of *Le Culte du Moi*), early Kokoschka, Bresson's *Les Dames du Bois de Boulogne*, and the likelihood that the gardens of Versailles had been laid out with Ovid's *Metamorphoses* in mind. Still pondering this, I turned up at the show next day and watched the photographers swarming around the B-list celebs. Up went the cry "*Voilà Lennee Kraveetz!*" In front of me, a guy turned to his neighbor. "We had this genius time shopping," he told her. How do you get from Ovid to Lenny Kravitz? What links the distant boroughs of interest inside Karl Lagerfeld's brain? The answer, of course, is clothes.

Anyone who complains that high fashion offers nothing to the low tastes (and lower funds) of ordinary people is quite correct. But the grievance misses the point. A fashion show is not a practical guide; you are not supposed to wear that multicolored stretch dress in nylon, cotton, and Lycra, or even to want to wear it. And if you did buy it could you ease it on like a five-foot condom, as Kristen McMenamy does? What would happen if your dog started pulling from the other end? Be honest: a show is more like an exhibition of paintings, to be gazed at in respectful awe. The big fashion houses make heaps of money, mostly through perfume and accessories, but, unlike the film world, they never directly touch a broader public. "I don't buy. You don't buy. I propose," Karl said to me.

One afternoon, I went to the Hôtel George V and watched the collections being bought by the stores. The buyer for Bergdorf Goodman said she loved the plain black jersey dress. I asked her how many she would order. Hundreds? She laughed. How many, then? "I can't tell you that," she said. Fifteen? Twenty? "Maybe." (I sneaked a look at the Lagerfeld price list. A black jersey outfit would be purchased by the stores at $995 and sold to the client for $2,290. Nice work if you can get it.)

After the final show, I asked Patrick Hourcade to describe the three collections that Karl had unveiled in Paris. Chloé? "*Poétique.*" Lagerfeld? "*Laboratoire.*" Chanel? "*Opportuniste.*" Pretty shrewd, I thought: put the three together, and you get a rounded view of his old friend Karl. Chloé was fluid, mock-pastoral, full of lemon, lilac, and grass green; some girls promenaded in print skirts fanned out by an undercarriage of stiff tulle. They ended the show in an impossible shimmer, lace laid over cotton and beaded with sequins, an effect that you can easily create in your own home: just run a rainbow through your sewing machine. Two days later, the Lagerfeld show slapped you awake. It was like being mugged by a bunch of fuchsias. The lines had hardened since Chloé; some hats were no more than ovals of clear, crownless plastic; the jackets had a slight upward tilt at the shoulders, as if Lagerfeld had taken sartorial advice from George Raft. The girls marched down the runway to a dance remix of "Hello, Dolly!" and "Hawaii Five-O." Afterward, I asked Karl to sum up the look. "Femininity, mystique, glamour," he began. I braced myself for philosophy. "Let's not talk about those words," he said. "Let's talk about *impeccable grooming.*"

Finally, there is Chanel. They order these things differently at Chanel. There is a list of backstage visitors at the barrier; if you do not appear on it, there is nothing you can do except go away and come back ten minutes later in a state of intense fame. Even that may not be enough; rumors that Madonna would be attending proved unfounded, but it may be that she turned up, saw that she had slipped off the list, and spent the show sitting in the ladies' room crying quietly into a Kleenex. My name *was* on the list, and, trying to quell the sensation that I had become part of a giant video game, I proceeded to the backstage entrance and was handed a form to sign. It said: "I undertake: 1) Not to take picture or film Claudia Schiffer during her makeup. 2) Not to take picture or film models in the nude." This was fashion's answer to the McCarthy hearings: "Are you now, or have you ever been, a member of the Staring Party?" Sheepishly, I signed on the line, strengthened only by the knowledge that I had already committed a daringly double crime by remaining backstage during the Lagerfeld show, where an entirely nude Claudia was part of the scenery.

The truth is that a fashion show is the least sexy environment in the civilized world, nowhere near as arousing as, say, a bookstore. Even out on the catwalk, there is no languor, no subtlety of suggestion; the only desire is to change clothes as fast as possible in a given period, as in a Christmas party game. (I had clocked the Lagerfeld show at thirty-one minutes and thirty seconds; within that time the audience saw 226 separate outfits, which works out at a new look roughly every eight and a half seconds.) The atmosphere and the lighting remind you of a boxing match, but the sheer delight in surfeit—more than the eye can absorb at any one moment—is closer to the mood at a fireworks display. Everybody had fun at Chanel. We clapped a lot, and even wolf-whistled. We had a genius time. The models wore loud little tweed suits in pink and baby blue; the skirts were unzipped up the front to expose glittering G-strings. ("Not too porno for you?" Lagerfeld had asked his older assistants at the studio.) The jewelry, as in the other shows, appeared to be molded from candy. Marxist dialectic would dismiss all this as commodity fetishism, but the trouble with Karl Marx is that, through no fault of his own, he never saw Helena Christensen wearing a flame-colored, rhinestone-studded bikini thong.

It is commonly and breathlessly said that a Lagerfeld show is full of "ideas," but this is just the vanity of the fashion pack, who like to cry up the intellectual verve of their calling. Lagerfeld is a great designer precisely because he doesn't have ideas, because he refuses to share the eternal French appetite for conceptual order: he has whims, habits, and minor inspirations. He plays jokes. ("My small talk is low and dirty," he says, "but my morality is clean.") He puts a girl in a pure-white wasp-waisted dress, with straps that cross at the throat, then blows the purity by lacing her midriff into a corset of shiny scarlet leather. It's the classic modern tactic of playing off high against low, soft against tough, and it didn't need to be thought through; Lagerfeld just did it. He got an anguished letter the next day from Suzy Menkes, the fashion critic of the *International Herald Tribune*, complaining that he was producing fashion without roots; but fashion is not like poetry—it doesn't need roots. If you don't like them, you can chop them off. This was the lesson of the Chanel show, with its forties beachwear and its snowstorm of logos: parody will get you everywhere.

Karl Lagerfeld is lord of all he surveys; you suspect that he could give up his crown at a moment's notice, and you know that he never will. There is nothing wrong with the emperor's clothes; it is his subjects who are bare and don't know it. The fashion world is more rabid and self-involved than any other, because, in the end, none of it matters. At its core is an aesthetic high, spun around a delicate manual skill; for some people that is quite enough, but for Lagerfeld it offers dangerously easy pickings. After a week, I began to sense that somewhere, wrapped up inside his generosity and eagerness, is a tiny sliver of boredom. It is not inertia; it is the boredom of Wilde and Huysmans, the boredom of the man who is cleverer than the people around him, who has to keep his mind fresh with a flux of ever more startling sensations, and who knows that what he does with his life is at once thrilling and void. (Lagerfeld himself would deny this fiercely.) One evening at Chloé, he and I looked at a model in a thin silk pants suit—pajamas, almost—covered with falling leaves. "You can see through it from the sides but not from the front," he said. Sounds like fashion to me.

NOVEMBER 7, 1994

BUSTER KEATON

On a dark night, in a nameless town, a nameless man decides to end his life. He sees a pair of headlights approaching. Why not make it quick, step out in front of a car? He walks out into the road and goes into a half crouch, with hands on his knees and eyes squeezed tight like someone who can feel a sneeze coming on. The two headlights hurtle toward him and go on hurtling, passing harmlessly by on either side: two motorcycles. The man opens his eyes, straightens up, and walks off as if nothing had happened. That is his problem: he wants something to happen, but nothing keeps on happening, in a big way.

The scene comes from *Hard Luck*, a two-reel Buster Keaton movie made in 1921. The movie lasts twenty-two minutes, and was lost for more than sixty years. The final scene is still missing. The reconstructed film proved to be unreconstructed Keaton—a sequence of sight gags that would have little or no logical connection were it not for the man at the center of them. Whether he is suffering the impact of the gags or willing them into being is hard to tell, but they flock toward him as though his very nature were a kind of magnetic north. *Hard Luck* is dumbly plotted, cheaply shot, and drizzling with age; there is no reason it should do anything except stutter along. And yet it flows. Again and again, the hero tries to do away with himself—by swallowing a bottle of poison that turns out to be bootleg hooch, by lying in front of a tram that never reaches him—with a will that verges on the heroic. He courts death as if his life depended on it. Still, there is no despair on his face, not a whiff of melodrama. He seems to favor the minor-league emotions: determination, embarrassment, a gentle breeze of ennui. So what *is* it with this guy? Where does he fit in?

Nearing the millennium, we like to think that black comedy is our specialty, our big number—that, after all that's happened, we've earned it. But

Buster Keaton was there before us. If you're looking for irony and fatigue, high speed and hard luck, the strong toil of grace, then Keaton is your man.

Joseph Frank Keaton was born on October 4, 1895, in Piqua, Kansas. This year, therefore, we are celebrating two important anniversaries: Keaton was born a hundred years ago, and so was cinema. The more one thinks about this coincidence, the happier it seems. It has been agreed, for the sake of argument, that the images projected by the Lumière brothers in 1895 signalled the fact that pictures were now officially in motion. Since then, it's been a blast. No other medium has accelerated with such outrageous brio from a crude new technology to a fully expressive art form; on the other hand, many movie lovers fear that it may have stalled along the way and is currently heading with equal haste in the opposite direction.

In a sense, it's all Buster Keaton's fault. He was just too good, in too many ways, too soon. We call his films comedies, but the more closely you inspect them the more convincingly he seems to have invaded and mastered other genres. No action thriller of the last, blood-streaked decade has matched the kinetic violence at the end of *Steamboat Bill, Jr.*, in which a storm pulls Keaton through one random catastrophe after another. Anyone who thinks that the movie-within-a-movie is a recent conceit, the province of *The Purple Rose of Cairo* and *Last Action Hero*, should check out *Sherlock Jr.*, a film in which Keaton *dreams* himself into another film: he strolls up the aisle of the theatre, hops into the action, and fights to keep up with its breakneck changes of scene. As for *The General*, where do you start? It's a film about a train, but it's also a spirited romance, peppered with bickering and longing, and its evocation of the Civil War period has never been surpassed. Keaton's transformation from a hapless Ashley Wilkes type into a manly serial kisser—a Rhett without the bombast—is not something that he needs to sell us. We just believe it. He is the first action hero; to be precise, he is a small, pale-faced American who is startled, tripped, drenched, and inspired into *becoming* a hero.

These days, we look down on physical comedy; critics like to say that movies "descend" into slapstick. Physical comedy has gained a reputation for being cheap, an easy way out for directors and performers when their ideas run dry. The old skills seem to be fading: nobody knows how to take a fall anymore, and some of what we sit through is cruder than the antics of the Keystone Cops. When the cops pitched off trucks or bopped their adversaries over the head, the craziness was hardly sophisticated, but the energy felt appropriate to the spirit of a quickening industry: every frame was a space to be filled, like a shop window. Early movies didn't descend; they rose to the occasion of a speedy, febrile art that was itself founded on the spinning of a reel, whereas the physical gags of today (what you can find of them) come across as mean and tired.

We know that Buster Keaton entered the world in the fall of 1895. The exact point at which he entered the world of entertainment is harder to pin down, although there is a photograph that shows his father, Joseph Keaton, in blackface, with a baby Buster plumped down between his legs. Joe came from Quaker stock, but he grew up a drifter and a brawler, with a high kick that could break a man's jaw; he quit his home state of Indiana and wound up in Frank Cutler's Comedy Company, a troupe that worked the new small towns south of the Cherokee Strip. He also fell for Cutler's daughter, Myra; they married in 1894, and made a meagre living in travelling medicine shows. In 1899, they moved their act to New York to try their luck in vaudeville; within a year, "The Two Keatons" became "The Three Keatons"; soon after that, the billing changed to "*BUSTER*, assisted by Joe & Myra Keaton." The toddler had become a professional performer at an age when most people are still amateurs at going to the toilet. Buster was once sent to school, but the experiment lasted less than a day.

It was no surprise that he came to the attention of the Gerry Society, which fought against the injustices of child labor. As part of the act, his father would grab hold of a suitcase handle stitched to the back of Buster's jacket, swing him through the air, and let go. Sometimes the boy would be spread flat and pushed around the stage as if he were a mop: Joe wiped the floor with him. In an effort to deter the Gerry investigators, Joe took his son to the mayor of New York; Buster was stripped bare and inspected for bruises. No one believed that a youngster should be kicked and hurled for a living, let alone that he might *enjoy* the experience, and might relish the refinement of his skills. There is an argument that the famous Keaton expression is not just restrained but close to tears, that he is musing on miseries past and is bent on blanking them out, and that his screen persona was essentially rooted in a form of child abuse. The trouble with this theory is that the adult Buster was anything but blank: within the quietude of his gaze—backstage, behind the eyes—there is a chorus of emotions, many of them running close to eagerness and joy. In Keaton's universe, violence means no harm; the scene from *Battling Butler*, in which he pummels a guy into submission, is weirdly out of character and is difficult to watch. In any case, he revered his parents and learned almost everything he knew about comedy from their example. Joe Keaton was later employed in some of his son's movies, together with other cronies from vaudeville.

Slapstick toughened and seasoned the young Buster. The bruises mattered less than the muscles. Keaton's pictures often play on his shortness (he was five feet six) or play it up by casting him against men shaped like grain silos. The archetypal Buster plot—the one that fuels *College*, *Steamboat Bill, Jr.*, *The Navigator*, and a host of shorts—involves the weedy, hapless loner who slides into the jaws of fate, finds undreamed-of strength, and gets the girl. It is a measure of Keaton's delicacy as an actor that we can believe in this transformation, because he himself was a strongman from the start. When the shy scholar of *College*, taunted by his beloved, finally strips down to running gear and joins the other athletes, we notice just how sinewy and streamlined he really is. The shape never changed: from the time Buster was a boy, that amazing, rectangular head remained too big for the torso beneath it. The mismatch is just right: you feel sure that the body will never fly out of control while the mind is in command. No wonder Buster balked at doubles; it is just conceivable that another man, with similar training, might have survived the ordeals that assault a Keaton hero, but no one else could have borne them with such equanimity. As Buster explained, "stuntmen don't get laughs."

Keaton was not unbreakable. While working on *The Electric House*, in 1922, he smashed an ankle; two years later, in *Sherlock Jr.*, the gush from a water tank blew him off the top of a train. The impact knocked him out, and gave him gruesome headaches; in 1935, an X-ray showed that he had broken his neck. Having been reared as a human beach ball, Keaton was able to survive jolts that would have killed a normal, non-rubberized person. The weird thing is that, unlike Jerry Lewis or Jim Carrey, he never melts or weakens into bendiness. The traditional Buster stance demands that he remain upstanding, full of backbone, looking ahead. His moral attitude and his physical attitude are indistinguishable; where Lewis and Carrey cringe and swank, Keaton holds firm. Nothing is more exhilarating than the great sequence in *The General* in which he clambers onto the roof of his locomotive and leans gently forward to scan the terrain, with the breeze in his hair and adventure zipping toward him around the next bend. It is the *angle* that you remember: the figure perfectly straight but tilted forward, like the Spirit of Ecstasy on the hood of a Rolls-Royce.

The theatrical career went on until 1917. The Three Keatons found fame, toured England, and then broke up. And then: "I was walking down Broadway—down along Eighth or someplace—and I met an old vaudevillian, and he was with Roscoe Arbuckle. Roscoe asked me if I had ever been in a motion picture, and I said, 'No, I haven't even been in a studio.' And he said, 'Well, come on down to the studio Monday and do a scene or two with me and see how you like it.' "

That, at least, is the story that Keaton gave to an interviewer in 1958. His biographer Rudi Blesh makes it more prosaic: in *Keaton* (1966) Blesh writes that the vaudevillian took twenty-one-year-old Buster to visit the Colony Studio, on East Forty-eighth Street, where three pictures were being shot—one with Roscoe (Fatty) Arbuckle; one with Constance Talmadge, starring opposite the charmingly named Harrison Ford; and one with Norma Talmadge. (Luckily, no one told Buster that four years later he would marry the third Talmadge sister, Natalie, and that all three sisters *and their mother* would move in with him.) Buster started work with Arbuckle the next day.

It is typical of Keaton that his first instinct was to find out precisely what happened inside a camera. He was a gadget freak, stirred by his good fortune at being on hand for the youthful, exploratory years of a new mechanical medium; you sometimes feel that his movies' obsession with machines is a homage to that era. The guy who practically crawled into Arbuckle's camera is the same guy who stuffed his films with trains and boats and whiled away his later years by rigging up vast contraptions designed to pour a shot of bourbon or crack walnuts. One of the disappointments of Keaton's first full-length feature, *The Three Ages*, is that much of it is set in Stone Age and Roman times, both of which are sadly gizmo-free. He does his best, and piles up the chariot gags, but it isn't until he hits the modern era that you sense him relaxing into the chaos of mechanized society. He drives a low-grade automobile over a bump in the road, and the car just *crumbles* beneath him. Rerun it on video, in slow motion, and you can see Buster riding the collapse like a surfer, hanging on to the steering wheel, coming beautifully to rest as the wave of wreckage breaks.

None of this is an indictment of the industrial age. It is Chaplin who took that noble, simpleminded line: when he walked away from the conveyor belt in *Modern Times*, his hands still tightening an invisible bolt, the joke implied that the human soul was under threat from machinery, and that man must strive to escape its grip. Keaton, more thoughtfully, identifies an element of play: his work suggests that man and machine are a good match—that man, on occasion, can even come out on top. In *Sherlock Jr.* we see him perched precariously on the handlebars of a fast-moving police motorbike; far from panicking, he soon settles into this new arrangement, considers his options, crosses his legs as if he were perched on a sofa, and prattles amiably to the cop. In his coolness, his love of improvisation, his casual reluctance to be crushed, Keaton moves further away from the querulous, jumpy genius of Chaplin and closer to someone like Fred Astaire, who could come upon the chugging pistons of a ship's engines and hear within a matter of seconds the excitable rhythms of a new dance.

Buster worked with Arbuckle on and off for three years. Together, they made fifteen two-reelers, some of them disconcerting to watch. For one thing, Keaton was still in the process of paring down the smile. Most people think of him as the essence of deadpan; they should take a look at *Fatty at Coney Island* and catch the chirpy, shining grin that splits Buster's face. You can see a milder version of it in *The Saphead*, his first starring feature, when Buster's character reads his name in a newspaper. His smile is not unattractive; it just turns him into a different being. If, from 1920 on, Keaton chose not to beam at the surrounding world, it was not because he was privy to some unrelieved grimness but because a steady, tight-lipped expression is the only look that remains, like a good suit, appropriate for all occasions. It respects, even expects, catastrophe, but it also honors sweetness—especially when Keaton closes his eyes, as if to sniff an unseen rose.

The Saphead is about a wealthy idler who can barely summon the energy to become a profligate; *The High Sign*, made the same year, saw Keaton cast as a rootless bum. The opening title reads like Camus for cowboys: "Our Hero came from *Nowhere*—he wasn't going *Anywhere* and got kicked off *Somewhere*." Taken together, the two movies demonstrate Buster's enviable talent for playing every octave of the social scale. He didn't hate the rich, and he refused to rain pity on the poor. With mawkish cunning, Chaplin had turned the Little Tramp into a potent symbol of the downtrodden; Keaton, less consciously, embarked upon a decade of films that would range across the American experience, from the Wild West to the Stock Exchange. All he asks of his characters, whatever their status, is that they not spurn the opportunity for self-reliance. Rollo Treadway, the hero of *The Navigator*, numbed by his millions, drifts through the days like a sleepwalker and uses his chauffeur to get from one side of the street to the other; it is only when his yacht is set adrift, when he is all at sea, that he can wake himself up and function as a complete being. Chaplin would never have given Rollo the chance; he would have used the character in passing and knocked his hat off with a rock. Chaplin was reluctant to shake off his Englishness or his touchiness about class, and his work represents the last gasp of Victorian melodrama; Keaton drew the first breath of modernism in film, and was the first—Griffith notwithstanding—to show why America would be the movies' natural home.

By 1920, Keaton was making his own pictures, under the aegis of Arbuckle's producer, Joseph M. Schenck. Over the next eight years, they made nineteen shorts and ten full-length features together—from *The High Sign* to *Steamboat Bill, Jr.* Keaton is invariably listed as a codirector and, occasionally, as cowriter, with friends such as Eddie Cline and Clyde Bruckman. Bruckman told Rudi Blesh, "I was at Buster's house or he at mine four or five nights many a week—playing cards, horsing around, dodging the issue. Then, at midnight, to the kitchen, sit on the sink, eat hamburgers, and work on gags until three in the morning." The perfect life, surely: a utopia of creative brotherhood. But Bruckman added a twist. "Those wonderful stories were ninety percent Buster's," he said. Keaton tempts us toward the auteur theory but proves that it is not incompatible with a loose-limbed habit of collaboration. He reminds you of Orson Welles: whatever the movie, he spiced it with his own obsessions. Even the earliest shorts proceed on the understanding that tumult is all the wilder for being arrested in mid-flow, and that a concentration of closeups should be regularly dissolved by the discreet retreat of the camera. Keaton's long shots, in which a forlorn figure dashes through serene open spaces, are the deep breaths of an artist who knows the value of the long view.

Keaton's narrative beat was partly a matter of technique. Until he came along, cameras had been undercranked for slapstick, thus insuring that the projected image was twice as fast—and therefore, it was believed, twice as funny—as human activity in real time. Keaton saw neither the justice nor the logic of this practice, and he was the first, according to Bruckman, to shoot comedy at standard speed; the life that he saw around him didn't need whipping up—it was funny enough as it was. Moreover, it was funny even when it was boring; Keaton's real daring lies less in the technical advances he devised than in the moral progress he made with them. There is nothing more adventurous in the Keaton oeuvre than the low-key, unhurried opening of *The Goat*, a 1921 short, in which a starving Buster is sent to the back of a breadline, on the sidewalk outside a clothing store. Not realizing that the two men in front of him are mannequins, he stands and waits, and the camera waits with him. He shuffles his feet, leans against the wall, clasps his hands behind his back, and so on. This seems to me a moment of revolution: after the Keystone Cops, and after the universal truths, or truisms, that rang out so majestically from *Intolerance*, here is a guy doing zilch. The movies have learned to tolerate ordinary existence, and even to celebrate its paltry pleasures; Keaton practices what Griffith preached.

Nothing, I guess, is more ordinary than getting married and settling down. In *One Week* (1920), a strong candidate for the perfect short film, Keaton takes homemaking literally. Starting from a plain, gag-rich premise—a pair of newlyweds are given a house in kit form, but with the wrong set of instructions—he fashions a surreal nineteen-minute epic of trial and error, which also happens to be a touching portrait of a marriage. Some commentators think that Keaton's pictures are let down by the slenderness of female characterization; Daniel Moews, in his dogged 1977 study *Keaton: The Silent Features Close Up*, thinks that Buster's women are "late Victorian hangovers in the long tradition of medieval courtly romance" and that "the heroines, desirable though they may be, exist only as pretexts for initiating his adventures." No one could watch *One Week* and agree with Moews. The actress playing the bride, Sybil Seely, has that perky, outdoorsy, try-anything hardihood that separates the women of pre–Hays Code cinema from the lacquered, innuendo-bound creatures who arrived later. She is Buster's unquestioned equal in the film; they pull through together. In one extraordinary scene, Seely is in her bath, the tops of her breasts exposed; she drops the soap on the floor, grins at us, and reaches out for it. At this point, a hand covers the lens, although Seely doesn't look as if she would mind either way. So there you are: near-nudity and a self-conscious camera back in 1920. You wonder just how much Jean-Luc Godard had to invent.

If only Keaton's first marriage had been such bliss. In 1921, he married Natalie Talmadge, and three weeks after the wedding the happy couple posed for a publicity shot in *Photoplay*: Buster sits beside her sporting a ball and chain. They had two sons—Joseph, born in 1922, and Robert, born in 1924—and Natalie would pain Keaton deeply by changing the boys' surname to Talmadge after she divorced him, in 1932. If there was misery on both sides, Keaton, at least, knew better than to let it sour his movies. In *Seven Chances* (1925), the prospect of marriage becomes pure farce: Buster plays a man of such eligible wealth that the climax finds him running away from an entire churchful of wanna-be brides. When he finally gets the girl he really wants, his attempts to snatch a crowning kiss are blocked by the successful efforts of the minister, the bride's mother, the best man, and a pet Dalmatian. His frustration is a good joke, but its chief function is to deny us the comfort of a major chord—to scrub the last traces of sentimentality from what threatens to become a love story. Maybe this is why Keaton leaves some viewers cold: his pictures suggest that love, like courage, must be proved in action. Hearts are there to be won, not warmed. It was a tough job for any woman, romancing the stoneface.

* * *

In celebration of Buster's centennial, a New York company called Kino on Video has issued three boxed sets of Keaton videos: thirty silent films in all, freshly transferred to tape. The quickies are a revelation, and the full-length features reassert their power; viewers will be amazed at how little has dated. If we are honest, we should admit to ourselves that the acting styles of early Hollywood now look overheated—that some of Garbo's swoons, in short, can make us giggle. Even in a classic such as F. W. Murnau's *Sunrise* (1927), the hero is still indicating anguish by gripping the hair at the sides of his head and staring saucer-eyed at absolutely nothing. In Keaton's work there is none of this. He pioneered the art of underacting. Heaven knows, he gave his heroes plenty to react to; the fact that they chose to scoot away from trouble or else to face it with tranquillity was a sign that film was ceasing to be merely an extravaganza. Keaton's character is more interesting than his surroundings; whatever they toss at him, he doesn't rave or gape—he doesn't hype what movies can do. In the final scenes of *Steamboat Bill, Jr.*, what matters is not the ferocity of the wind: it is the tiny leap that Buster gives as he pushes into that wind—the endless, fruitless comedy of needing to press on. "Such frustration in that little body!" Louise Brooks once said.

After *The Navigator* became a smash hit, in 1924, Keaton was given a contract for six features: two a year, at twenty-seven thousand dollars per picture—serious money in those days. He built the Italian Villa, one of the grandest properties in Beverly Hills, and spent fourteen thousand dollars moving a line of trees from the front to the back. By the time filming began on *Steamboat Bill, Jr.*, in 1927, Buster's work was netting him an annual income of $200,000: nothing could go wrong. Needless to say, everything went wrong. *Steamboat Bill, Jr.*, his final masterpiece, foundered at the box office, as *The General* had done the year before. In 1928, Joe Schenck dissolved Buster Keaton Productions and handed the outfit over to his brother Nicholas, at MGM. There Irving Thalberg grasped the genius of Keaton straight off, but it flew right past Louis B. Mayer, who, true to form, failed to see what was so funny about the man. The well-oiled new mechanisms of the dream factory soon snagged on someone like Keaton, who hired people because they could bat ideas around instead of writing a script, because they were good at cards, and because they were his friends. According to Keaton's third wife, Eleanor, "His guys all played baseball, and if they'd be stuck for a gag or something, they would go out and play ball. And then somebody'd say, 'Oh, hey, I know how to do that,' and they'd go back to work. One of the first things Buster did was get a ball club together at MGM. And Louis B. Mayer wouldn't stand for that."

Keaton made one good movie for MGM, *The Cameraman*, and then began to slide. In 1930, he made his first starring talkie, *Free and Easy*. There was nothing wrong with what Eleanor Keaton calls "his bass-baritone gravelly voice"; he never shared the indignity of John Gilbert, the silent, smoldering Romeo who opened his mouth and instantly changed into Tweety Pie. Keaton didn't object to words; he just didn't *need* them. Unhindered by dialogue, he had floated movies to the limits of their form. Where could he go from there? Earthbound and unwanted, he became a serious drinker and then a complete joke; his last film for the studio before it fired him, in 1933, was the sadistically titled *What, No Beer?* Natalie filed for divorce; in 1934, just to round out the dreadful burlesque, Keaton was declared bankrupt. He entered a sanitarium and wound up marrying a nurse named Mae Scriven—"in an alcoholic stupor," according to the Keaton scholar Jim Kline, although the pair went on to live together for two years. In 1937, in a spasm of generosity, M-G-M took him on again—this time as a gag writer—on a starting salary of a hundred dollars a week. This was like hiring Shakespeare to paint scenery. It is upsetting to follow the chart of Keaton's decline, and difficult to fix its lowest trough; I would suggest the sight of Buster caught up in a pie fight during a 1939 comedy about the early days of movies, *Hollywood Cavalcade*. By that time, it was commonly thought that this was what silent stars had done: they had chucked custard pies. The truth, of course, was that not once in all the pictures that he made in the twenties had Buster Keaton thrown a single custard pie.

The rehabilitation came late, but not too late. In 1938, over a bridge table, he met a blonde. Eleanor Norris was nineteen at the time, a hoofer at MGM. She had never seen a Buster Keaton movie. They were married in 1940, and it was Eleanor who set Buster back on the track and saw it carry him to his final fame—to what he eloquently described as "that genius bullshit." These days, Eleanor Norris Keaton lives in a condo in North Hollywood, and I visited her there on a roasting August day. To knock at the door of her house is a curious sensation: you half expect the front of the building to swing down and fall on top of you, tugged by the spirit of slapstick past. But I made my way safely up the stairs, past Japanese posters of Buster's best-known films. At the top stood Mrs. Keaton, spry and immaculate at seventy-seven, and rightly protective of her husband's reputation.

She wasn't the first person to want to look after the guy. "He must have had fifteen or twenty mothers and fathers," she recalled. "I guess they'd seen this helpless creature on the screen, so everybody adopted him and set out to take care of him." No one understood more clearly than Eleanor Keaton, though, that the helplessness was an act. "He never played for sympathy. If they wanted to feel sorry for him, that was their problem, not his," she said, adding, "Chaplin was just the opposite." Yet, as we sat there drinking iced tea and talking about Buster Keaton, I found my take on the man beginning to shift and fray. Even if he wasn't vulnerable, there was still something disturbing in his eagerness to take the rap. The sequences in *Cops* and *Seven Chances* in which he was harried by howling mobs sprang directly from Keaton's own fear. "Couldn't stand crowds," his widow said, and she went on to recount a time when an aging Buster gave the slip to adoring fans at the Cinémathèque in Paris, ducked down an alley, and threw up with nerves. The all-American star was almost English, sometimes, in his desire to evade confrontation. "I guess he just didn't want to make waves," Mrs. Keaton said. "If somebody dropped a glass and broke it in the kitchen, you know, he'd figure out a way it would be his fault. He knew that he'd wrecked his own career with drink." It's a bizarre turnaround: involved in every minute of his movies, Keaton can take more solitary credit for his achievements than any other filmmaker, and yet he behaved as if everything were his fault—as if the thousands of pratfalls were a punishment for irredeemable crimes, most of which he had never committed. Keaton hated to make a scene, and out of that distaste rose some of the most elegant scenes ever filmed.

Buster cut back on the drink, but he kept on smoking two packs a day. The war years were among the leanest of his life; Marion Meade, in her new biography, *Buster Keaton: Cut to the Chase*, cites an MGM memo of 1942 that describes Buster as almost destitute. Not so, says Meade: Eleanor was still dancing for a living, after all, and Buster's principal daily duty was to drive his wife to the studios. After the war, he found a new career in Europe performing old vaudeville routines, and picked himself a few delicious minor roles: one of the bridge players in *Sunset Boulevard*, a sorrowful presence opposite Chaplin in *Limelight*. But true salvation arrived toward the end of the forties, in the squat shape of television; at the age of fifty-four, Buster refreshed some old slapstick for *The Ed Wynn Show*. On the strength of this, he was awarded his own program, which ran for four months at the start of 1950; for the rest of his life, he made good money from TV appearances (Ed Sullivan, Steve Allen, Johnny Carson) and commercials.

Keaton's late works are a mixed bag. On the one hand, there is his 1964 slot for Budweiser; on the other, there is the exotically titled *Film* (1965), the only movie written by Samuel Beckett. Buster plays the anonymous, self-haunting wreck who scuttles through the twenty-two minutes of action, or inaction. We do not see him head on until the closing frames; he seems to be summoning both the courage to look himself in the face and the almost irretrievable memory of what that face once was. *Film* is not widely liked, or widely seen, perhaps because it offers a frightening spectre. How often does cinema, our shrine to beautiful people, dare to reveal the unstoppable blighting of beauty, let alone reveal it to the blighted themselves?

Buster Keaton died on February 1, 1966, and was buried with a rosary and a deck of cards. It's the neatest possible combination—a little light sinning with built-in penance, and a guarantee of eternal good luck. Somewhere, high above the clouds, someone is getting skinned.

Keaton's great pictures are, in the best sense, feature films; they are meditations on a face. Those deep-lidded, dark-rimmed eyes, the carved prow of the profile—no living person has *ever* looked like Buster Keaton. Louise Brooks said he was the most beautiful man she ever saw, and she wasn't exactly a frump herself. Risking absurdity, every Buster fan longs to read a story, or a genealogy, or a philosophical position into Keaton's aspect. You can't help it; once you catch his eye, there's no looking away. Viewed from the side, he has always reminded me of the solemn, grieving figures in Giotto's frescoes. The critic Stanley Cavell tries a different tack. "I see the speculation of Heidegger exemplified in the countenance of Buster Keaton," he writes. This would have been news to Buster, who never tried to exemplify anything except the art of landing on your butt without jarring your spine.

But even if Keaton didn't exemplify intellectual theories—there is nothing abstract about being crunched between two carriages of a train—his movies nevertheless send you into the realm of idle perplexity that is traditionally prowled by the intellect. By his own admission, Keaton wanted nothing more than to raise a laugh. But the regularity with which he *gets* that laugh, and the fact that he refuses to join in it, force you to marvel at his struggle for happiness in the teeth of a ridiculous fate. "Be like the headland against which the waves break and break: it stands firm, until presently the watery tumult around it subsides once more to rest. . . . The thing could have happened to anyone, but not everyone would have emerged unembittered. . . . The mind can circumvent all obstacles to action, and turn them to the furtherance of its main purpose, so that any impediment to its work becomes instead an auxiliary, and the barriers in its path become aids to progress." Thus Marcus Aurelius, in his *Medita-*

tions. It seems as clear an account of Buster Keaton as you will find, and it restores him to his status as the leading stoic of cinema. As Marcus makes plain, stoicism involves not willful gloom but a temperate acceptance of the eternal Heraclitean flux. For instance, the hero of *The Three Ages* flees a police station, runs up a fire escape to the roof, leaps toward the next-door building, misses the parapet, drops three stories through canvas awnings, and catches hold of a drainpipe, which then swings around 180 degrees, rifling the hero through an open window and straight into a pole, down which he slides, coming to rest on the back of a fire engine, which moves off and hastens back to the very police station he started from. If that isn't eternal flux, I don't know what is.

The best comedy entails the near-avoidance of tragedy, a sidestep away from the cliff's edge. Buster Keaton knows where the edge is; in truth, he can't get it out of his mind. That is why his films give off such a weird, flexible maturity, a wisdom not set in its ways. Sitting through a score of them, I was left to wonder what kind of man would feel driven to create such a modest, ennobling body of work from close shaves. "A tremendously nice person, you know, but also a man of secrets," Orson Welles said of Keaton, adding, "I can't even imagine what they were." Keaton family legend had it that when Buster was nearly three years old a cyclone picked him up, blew him down a street, and deposited him gently four blocks away. The incident eventually wormed its way into *Steamboat Bill, Jr.*, but the cyclone twisted deeper still. It is Keaton's Rosebud, you might say: impossible to verify, probably a tall tale, and by no means an explanation of the man. Yet, for all that, it is an image that flowers perennially throughout his work. He launches himself into one whirlwind after another—into car wrecks, capsizings, wars, and marriages—not so much to test his nerve or his aptitude as to savor the primal shock of coming through unharmed. Buster Keaton sleeps through bedlam. His eyes are the heart of the storm.

OCTOBER 23, 1995

THE OSCARS

"Win or lose, who cares?" This bold and blatant lie was voiced by Mel Gibson on the evening of March 23. Two days later, in common with every other winner of an Academy Award, he looked as if he cared very much.

There is nothing new, let alone culpable, in such a change of heart; it is, indeed, strongly recommended under the rules of the emotional diplomacy by which Hollywood has long been governed. Anjelica Huston, whose dynastic pedigree is positively medieval by the standards of this town, explained how the system works. "Even those who don't care for competition find themselves getting involved, even if they don't want to, and end up getting whipped into a kind of frenzy," she said. She was speaking on Saturday night, with forty-eight hours to go before the announcement of Best Picture, and, looking round the room, you could tell that most people were still in the pre-whip stage. Our host was ICM's Ed Limato, who is a long-standing agent of so many stars that he was commonly believed to have signed up Hyakutake, the comet then heading for the Little Dipper, long before it swam into our ken. You don't make yourself visible to the naked eye without calling Ed.

When Ed decides to throw, or lightly toss, one of his pre-Oscar parties, the invitations—in this case, stiff cards dusted tastefully with pink spangles—are sent out only to those who can be relied upon not to look nervous about the forthcoming ceremony. The one scary thing about the whole evening was the bank of raw gray squid that lay waiting to be sizzled; it made you kind of glad that Sigourney Weaver, who has made three *Alien* pictures and is getting ready for a fourth, was not among those present. Also notable by its absence was the merest murmur of concern over the demonstration being threatened by the Reverend Jesse Jackson, who was indignant that only one of this year's 166 nominees was black. Questioned on the issue, Denzel Washington was supremely unfazed, but then Denzel Washington would remain cool if the French recommenced nuclear testing under his chair. "To protest an imbalance in the industry is one thing," he said. "To pinpoint a specific awards ceremony is another. People said to me, when I was nominated for *Malcolm X* and Al Pacino was up for *Scent of a Woman*, wouldn't it be a racial decision if he won and I didn't? And I said, 'Hey, the guy's been nominated eight times or whatever. I'd vote for him.' In fact, I *did* vote for him."

In the face of such gentlemanly conduct, you just knew that the reverend's protest would burn away like mist. The English director Mike Figgis had a better idea. At the Independent Spirit Awards, earlier the same day, he said the only group that was overrepresented in Los Angeles was the English.

Kevin Spacey leaned against the bar chez Limato and said, "Albino Alligator." The barman looked up with fear in his face. Was Spacey ordering a cocktail—something white with bite that tastes like a sewer? It's every barman's nightmare: the request for a drink that, until now, he wasn't even aware existed. The man's hand lifted toward the gin in despair—surely the thing had Tanqueray in it somewhere?—and then dropped in relief. Spacey was simply telling us about directing his first movie.

All actors yearn to direct—or, at any rate, they say they do. When Nicolas Cage declared, in accepting the award for Best Actor, "I know it's not hip to say it, but I just love acting," there were many in the audience who took this touching confession as a coded message to the industry, meaning, "As yet, I have not seen a script that I wish to direct, but packages may be messengered to my agent from eight o'clock tomorrow morning." In keeping his ambition tamped down, Cage was an exception. Tom Hanks, smarter than most, has already shown his hand: his first feature, *That Thing You Do!*, is a wrap. After winning the Oscar for Best Live Action Short, Christine Lahti remarked, "In directing, I found a newfound love; I'm hooked." She had just beaten off the challenge of four other directors, among them Griffin Dunne and Jeff Goldblum. Mel Gibson then turned the whole conceit briskly on its head when, holding his Best Director Oscar for *Braveheart*, he said, "Like most directors, what I suppose I really want to do is act."

If you needed a master class in Oscar technique, the man to consult was James Cromwell. Equitable and kindly, like an ambassador who happened to have strayed into the movie business, he sat beside the pool at the Bel-Air Hotel and disclosed his plans for the ceremony: "I intend to enjoy every minute of it that I can." He then proceeded to consume a Sunday lunch so resoundingly vegetarian (a yolk-free mushroom omelette, no less) that even passersby who failed to recognize him would have instinctively connected him with *Babe*. Cromwell—the son of the director John Cromwell, who himself once hosted the Oscars with Bob Hope—was nominated as Best Supporting Actor for his grizzled Farmer Hoggett. "It's not a leading role, but you have to carry the movie," he said. In a town where a liberal conscience involves little more than cracking Pat Buchanan jokes in public, Cromwell was one of the few stars prepared to go along with Jesse Jackson: "I have some sympathy for Jesse's protest, because it mirrors the larger problems of society."

The smaller problems of Hollywood, however, are never far away. Cromwell said that his stepdaughter, Rosemary, has an agent. "And her first audition is today," added the proud father. Rosemary is twelve.

Two days before the ceremony, Spacey was on his mettle. He couldn't quite get over the delicious, Keyser Söze–like coincidence that Mare Winningham, a fellow-nominee this year, for *Georgia*, was an old friend. "I wanted to change schools to be with her, *and I did*," Spacey said in triumph. He then proceeded, after a little light prompting, to reveal a flawless William Hurt impression that would have been hair-raising had it not consisted of one balding movie star playing another. Even this was trumped by Laura Dern, who sat there in shimmering silver-blue and, without any prompting whatsoever, interrupted her own serenity with a knockout impersonation of the young Muhammad Ali. What was going on here? Maybe it's a freak condition of the Oscar climate: just when the world congratulates them for being who they are, the beautiful people of Hollywood stay ahead of the game by pretending to be someone else.

Two hours after the ceremony, Spacey was himself again, but only just. He sat at a corner table in Mortons and clutched his Best Supporting Actor statuette, looking like the little boy that got the dog that got the cat that got the cream. "They're supposed to take it away to put my name on it, but they'll have to *tear* it away," he said. The ceremony had been a blur. "I don't have a clue what I said." He seemed reassured to learn that he had remembered: a) to thank his mom; and b) to hold back from attempting a Vanessa Williams impersonation. A disconcerting time, the Oscar season. Jim Carrey put it best: "There's something weird that happens to you when you're being watched by half a billion people." In Carrey's case, the weirdness never stops.

Rehearsal time at the Dorothy Chandler Pavilion: according to connoisseurs, the most authentic Oscar experience. The Sunday-afternoon run-through was such a rich and thronging shambles that you could hardly imagine a watchable show emerging, twenty-four hours later, from the mess. The celebrities sauntered on in jeans to practice their presentations; Sandra Bullock thought her contribution had gone pretty well. "I saw a couple of people getting a little teary up in the back," she said. "You know, a little moist." As late as Sunday, there was a plan to greet the hopefuls for Best Actor and Best Actress not just with clips from their nominated films but with a montage from their previous oeuvre. In the case of Elisabeth Shue, née *Cocktail*, this seemed downright discourteous: "I mean, thanks a lot," she said. "I want to put that lot behind me." In place of winners, selected stagehands trotted up, gathered the statuettes, and delivered ersatz acceptance speeches—"I'd like to thank my twelve and a half lovely children," and so on. A tip for the superstitious, or for anyone placing underhand bets: a winner's name read out at any given rehearsal bears no relation to the name of the eventual victor, and therefore cuts one horse out of the field. Someone was heard phoning Lindsay Doran, the producer of *Sense and Sensibility*, with the non-good news: "Just to let you know that you won."

On the morning of the Oscars, *Variety* reported that Mel Gibson would be wearing a waistcoat woven from his "family tartan," and also that he had been fitted out at Giorgio Armani on Rodeo Drive. The relation between these two facts was not explored. Gibson looked all right that night, but then the sixty-eighth Academy Awards ceremony was faintly disappointing to those of us who like to see famous people putting on clothes that make them look like an explosion at the Jelly Belly plant. We saw a fine parade of Empire lines and silk sheaths, and by far the most impressive array of natural greens since Linda Blair showed off the highlights of her supper in *The Exorcist*. There was peppermint, aquamarine, verdigris, iceberg, eau-de-nil, and a lemon-and-lime special from Mare Winningham. There were pinkish grays so soft and subtle that onlookers were reminded of the furring found in uncleaned kettles. Then there was Susan Sarandon's Dolce & Gabbana ball gown, a sort of one-night stand between chocolate and bronze; it exactly matched the hue of her hair, although which had come first was a matter of urgent debate.

She was accompanied by Tim Robbins, whose jacket was scaly, sharkish, and distressingly similar to what he wore last year. How can a guy of such evident sense, whose movies are a rebuff to bad glitz, opt on an annual basis for a garment that was apparently woven overnight from strands of crude oil? The men always let their ladies down on Oscar night. Hollywood is congenitally unable to grasp that the great advantage of a dinner jacket is that it is, in essence, a uniform. The basics are unwavering, the variations minimal. When you are asked to wear a black tie, do not take this as a concealed excuse not to wear a black tie. Do not be tempted by the current fad that omits the tie altogether in favor of a single black stud. You may find this sexy, but to the watching world it appears that you have leapt up from an emergency tracheotomy to attend the show.

If you must be a maverick, do it in spades. Again, Mike Figgis led the way. He strode around in a long black frock coat of rare magnificence. Topped with his imposing frizz of hair, it brought to mind a radical bishop from the pages of Trollope, pondering schism with solemn glee. "I intend to treat the whole thing as performance art," Figgis had declared. He was as good as his word.

Last year's Academy Awards had been billed as a straight fight between *Pulp Fiction* and *Forrest Gump:* dark versus light, stormy versus calm, McEnroe versus Edberg. This year, the only one-on-one took place Sunday at MGM/UA's party at Eclipse, on Melrose: fellow-nominees Nicolas Cage and Sean Penn broke off a friendly conversation to indulge in a brief bout of air-boxing.

The 1996 awards were supposed to be more open and unpredictable, but in the event Hollywood closed ranks. It dumped five awards into the kilted lap of *Braveheart*, a shaggy-Scot story that was made by an actor who looks cute with an Oscar in his fist. And the show itself? Well, it passed—quickly at first, but ending up at slug speed. Still, the percussion ensemble Stomp were a hit, and they confirmed Tom Hanks's view that "the big numbers look a lot cheesier on TV. When you see them live, they look kind of cool." This sounded highly unlikely but was, on closer inspection, quite true, especially if you were canny enough, or lowly enough, to get a seat near the back. Those of us in the stratosphere could both chew on the flavor of the live show and sneak out to the bar for regular transfusions of champagne, in the way that television viewers visit the fridge. One guy, an old Oscar hand, was snacking hard on chocolate bars to keep his strength up, like a mountaineer.

Sympathy peaked for Christopher Reeve and Kirk Douglas, and for Bryan Adams's endearing confidence in his own voice. Nobody seemed to mind the idea of treating Holocaust survivors with the same rapture that attends a comfortably paid performer. (Why does *applauding* Gerda

Weissmann Klein seem, in a curious way, the most embarrassing insult to her experience?) The major disappointment, apart from that of Elisabeth Shue, was that no one from the *Braveheart* team had the courage to mount the stage with a face half smothered in blue woad. Last Monday was all the brighter for Oprah Winfrey's blinding jewels, but, next year, how about upping the wattage even further—have the stars turn up in the guise of their most recent dramatic roles? It was soggy enough when Mira Sorvino reduced Paul Sorvino to tears, but just imagine: she could have made Henry Kissinger weep. You don't see that every day.

APRIL 8, 1996

SHAKESPEARE ON FILM

It was Rodney Dangerfield who got me thinking about Shakespeare. In *Back to School,* Dangerfield plays a businessman of surpassing wealth and vulgarity who for various reasons decides to become a student again. There follows a series of low gags—Dangerfield inviting a poetry-loving babe to help straighten out his Longfellow, that kind of thing. But what struck me most was the scene in which our hero goes on a buying spree at the campus store, unleashes one of his fat-frog grins, and exclaims, "Shakespeare for everyone!"

Whether he knew it or not, Rodney was voicing one of the great ambitions of the movies. From the very infancy of the medium, stars and directors have seen an opportunity to open Shakespeare up, not merely to bring him to the attention of the masses but to convince the masses that he is ready for immediate consumption—easy on the eye, sweet to the ear. In the days of silent movies, the ear had a particularly rough deal: you might suspect that Shakespeare without words was like flying without air, but this handicap counted for surprisingly little with stalwarts such as Herbert Beerbohm Tree, who in 1899 filmed a scene from his own production of *King John.* Last month, the American Film Institute festival showed a *Richard III* that was made in 1912 and had long been believed lost. The original publicity boasted of, among other things, "1500 People, 200 Horses, 5 Distinct Battle Scenes, A Three-Masted Warship, Crowded with Soldiers, on Real Water." Richard on Water sounds about as convincing as Timon on Ice, but already you can discern a two-way tug that will tauten the filming of Shakespeare for the rest of the century: for every elastic flourish of extravagance, there has been a countermove toward dramatic distillation. I like the sound, or the silence, of the 1907 French *Hamlet,* which ran for all of ten minutes: you get the dirt from the ghost, skip the arras, kick the skull out of the way, and head straight for your stepfather.

In *Reinventing Shakespeare*, a chronicle of the Shakespeare industry, Gary Taylor says that "in 1908 American studios alone produced ten Shakespeare films, more than in any subsequent year of the century." Taylor may have spoken too soon; the century is not dead yet, and there are signs that Hollywood may be limbering up to break the record. This past year has already seen a new *Richard III*, starring Ian McKellen, and a flabby *Othello*, stiffened only by Kenneth Branagh's Iago; last month saw the release of Trevor Nunn's disastrous *Twelfth Night*, of Al Pacino's provocative and entertaining *Looking for Richard*, and of a new *Romeo and Juliet*, from the director of *Strictly Ballroom*. Still to come are Adrian Noble's *A Midsummer Night's Dream* and Branagh's own version of *Hamlet*, which is scheduled to run at a cool four hours.

Why this sudden gush of interest? The most depressing answer came in a queue outside a movie theatre, where I overheard someone say, "Oh, Shakespeare is this season's Jane Austen." Never underestimate the sheer horsepower of the bandwagon; all it took, perhaps, was one brief kick of rumor, three or four years ago, about Branagh and his prospective *Hamlet* to make producers gallop around in search of the guy behind the script. Whether there are more brooding, subterranean reasons for the fad—whether the time is so out of joint, as far as Hollywood is concerned, that only Shakespeare can set it right—is open to question, and I tend to prefer the more prosaic motive offered by the makers of the latest *Romeo and Juliet*, who point out that, give or take a year, the play was written four centuries ago.

Anniversaries are cause for celebration, and the new *Romeo* certainly resembles nothing more than a humongous birthday party that spirals out of control. In the hands of the director Baz Luhrmann and his production designer, Catherine Martin, Verona has become modern-day Verona Beach, a lurid Latino dump patrolled by a pair of rival gangs. The opening prologue is intoned by a TV newscaster; Captain Prince rides around in a police helicopter; and a "sword" is now a make of handgun—a neat conceit that gets rid of any historical bumps in the verse ("Put up your Swords!"). For the first half hour or so, the joy of watching Luhrmann and his crew yanking every detail up to date is enough to set the audience fizzing, but gradually the inventiveness grows flat. So much energy is expended on preventing even one frame of the film from smelling of theatre, or of scholarly texts, that poor old Shakespeare—whose scholarship, whatever else you can prove about it, was quick and greedy, and whose love of theatricality extended far beyond his profession into a crystalline view of men and women as helplessly performative beings—is swept up in the druggy rush. The poetry is all but drowned out; music pumps over it as though to save the audience the constant grind and possible embarrassment of trying to follow the words. Some members of the cast, too, can do with all the drowning they can get; the howling intonations of Mercutio (Harold Perrineau) appear to be founded on the principle that if you rap and rant with sufficient brio the meaning will somehow be sprung loose, like a beast from its cage. The irony is rank: here is a movie that strains every fibre to prove to a young audience that Shakespeare consists of more than John Gielgud filling the aisle with noises, but the actors end up twice as stylized, and a tenth as intelligible, as the loftiest Gielgud performance. I don't mind if the film recruits Shakespeare to the banner of hip, but I resent the covert implication that Shakespeare still, to an extent, gets in the way of the hoopla, and that the language is more hindrance than help.

There has long been a curious unease in the treatment that moviemakers mete out to Shakespeare: most of them revere him, but they don't trust him. They believe that he lends automatic weight to a film, but, on the other hand, they don't want to be burdened, and every director likes to devise a patent method for lightening the load. There was a notorious and admirably up-front piece of work at United Artists in 1929, when *The Taming of the Shrew* was heralded by a credit that read "with additional dialogue by Sam Taylor." Why did the studio bosses bring in Sam? I guess they got exasperated when Will failed to show up on the lot. Maybe he was too busy picking up dark ladies on Sunset Strip. It's worth remembering that most of the plays are in any case cut-and-paste jobs, some of them patched with interpolations from the scripts of actors in Shakespeare's own company; in this light, anything that Hollywood can do to fatten or skin the lines is less a matter of sacrilege than the continuation of a long-established and rather messy practice. The best Shakespearean joke of the last few years came in *Last Action Hero*, when Schwarzenegger appeared without warning in heroic costume. "To be, or not to be," he said. There was a pause. "Not to be." And with that Elsinore was blown into the sky.

Arnie, in short, was rising to the challenge that confronts every Shakespeare adapter, which is not to preserve the virgin text but to ravish it without causing too blatant an uproar. You can always tell a pro in this game: he will be the one who is so at ease among the lines that he has no compunction about hacking them around at his own convenience. Zeffirelli's 1991 *Hamlet* is deadly with decent respect, whereas men like Laurence Olivier and Orson Welles know from long experience that Shakespeare is far stronger than anything they can inflict on him. They charge in with blue pencils flying: Olivier insures that *Richard III* hits the ground running by starting with a helpful scene taken from the end of *Henry VI, Part III,* and the film returns to that play to steal a moment of magnificent annoyance, when Richard—or, as he then was, Duke of Gloucester—ponders his own fixation:

> I'll make my heaven to dream upon the crown,
> And whiles I live, t'account this world but hell,
> Until this misshap'd trunk that bears this head
> Be round impaled with a glorious crown.
> And yet I know not how to get the crown.

Olivier is not showing off here, however large his acquaintance with Shakespeare; he is simply demonstrating that a great actor is more often than not a great thief and a great scavenger, too—grabbing his opportunities wherever he can. Once moviemakers grasp what is available to them, their rapport with Shakespeare is quickened by a kind of febrile excitement, as if they were reading the stuff for the first time. For one thing, they find themselves unencumbered by an intermission; none of that nonsense of leaving the Macbeths to strop their daggers while we go and jostle for warm Chardonnay. Within the text, moreover, some of the treacherous archaism drops away; the aside, for instance, can now be genuinely private and underhand, sparing us the trickiness of a bellowed whisper and a stageful of fellow-actors all pretending not to have overheard. The heart-to-heart, or the drunken gossip, or the murmured threat—any of the staples of Shakespearean conversation—can be pronounced and recorded at a natural level instead of being beefed up and thrown out into the auditorium. As for the soliloquy, what else was voice-over invented for? You could certainly argue that many of the monologues in the history plays, or those of Othello and Macbeth, demand to be voiced out loud; the need to set the record briskly straight, or the sinewy drive toward self-persuasion, is too forceful—too outspoken, you might say—to be holed up in the mind. Hamlet, however, is another matter: this guy, you feel, would happily order a drink inside his own head, and his preferred method for hearing the narration of his dead father would probably be through a Walkman. So it seems natural that Olivier's prince should deliver most of "O that this too too solid flesh . . ." in voice-over, occasionally interrupting himself, like a madman, with fragments of naked speech.

Grigory Kozintsev, in his 1964 Russian version, goes one better: again, Hamlet (played by the splendidly named Innokenty Smoktunovsky) intones the speech to himself, but this time he does so at a *party*—drifting through the crowd, setting his features in a mask of politesse, acting the dutiful son as he ponders self-slaughter. Kozintsev's movie is rather too artful for its own good, but this is a moment of genius, for it reminds us that Hamlet is, among other things, the first angry young student—hating his parents but doing what they say, and then hating himself for caving in so bonelessly. Kozintsev's hero has less to do with Elsinore, or with the Royal Shakespeare Company, than with Dustin Hoffman in *The Graduate*, fleeing the ghastliness of a poolside party for that dream-blue underwater peace: "Hello darkness, my old friend. . . ."

Many Shakespeare pictures leave you with this imponderable sense of regeneration—of Shakespeare's suddenly becoming both stranger and more familiar in front of your eyes. When you see *Hamlet* onstage, you come out discussing the acting, the pacing of the direction, where to go for dinner, and so forth, whereas movies return you sharply and unerringly to the text, to the whole landscape of felt argument which it reveals. Olivier's *Hamlet* film is not important, or even worth talking about, as an interpretation of the play; what it does is scrape the mold off your senses and press you up hard against the swords and stones of which Hamlet's world is composed. The air really is nipping and eager; the battlements on which the prince encounters the ghost seem to sweat with anticipation, or with the dirt and salt flung up by the sea. Everywhere looks primed for a haunting—the castle's warren of passages, the staircases that curl into gloom behind Hamlet as if to mock the baffled contortions of his will.

To view it another way: *Hamlet* is film noir. American audiences who had spent the previous decade in movie houses could count themselves fully prepared. Hamlet's shadow life, his pointed gibes, his appetite for the half-light, his tracking of a mystery that can never work out well: none of this would be news to anyone versed in *The Big Sleep*. And what of the astonishing shot that greets the start of his best-known soliloquy? The camera scurries through corridors and winds up at the back of Hamlet's head, as if preparing to bore into his skull and continue its quest within the matching labyrinth of his brain. "To be or not to be," he asks gently, overlooking a boiling sea: a tempting drop, and an echo, I suspect, of Hitchcock's *Rebecca*, in which Olivier had starred eight years before. Then, there is the sad sight of Ophelia, stranded with her prayers in a drafty hall while the prince on the stairs talks down to her; we could be watching Susan Alexander Kane and her jigsaw, and the looming figure of Charles Foster Kane. Far from dragging *Hamlet* down, these allusions excite the movie—they feed Shakespeare into a world of give-and-take, into the sort of image exchange in which he himself learned his trade. The play of *Hamlet* grew out of creaky, overheated revenge dramas by lesser talents, just as film noir bloomed from the rotten romance of pulp.

If we look back, the real surprise is that Olivier, lord of all theatre, should have not only filmed *Hamlet* but turned it into a movie about movies. His moment of revelation had come in 1944, with *Henry V*, when he unhesitatingly took his cue from the images of speed and flight that course through the text: the battle of Agincourt, parcelled out on the page between a few close encounters of friend and foe, is loosened into a flowing charge. Reading between the lines is no longer the prerogative of the prying editor but a hunt for concealed action; what remains most amazing about Olivier is that a man whose fame had been forged in the momentum of verse-speaking should realize when he came to make a movie that the combustible core of the drama lay in a dry scattering of stage directions—"Alarum. Excursions." His opening device for the picture—an aerial approach to the Globe Theatre, into an Elizabethan performance, then out into an unstaged world—is both homage and farewell to the arena that Olivier had previously made his own, as fraught a moment in the history of Shakespeare as the playwright's own move from Stratford to London. Henceforth the throng in the Globe's pit can be multiplied, and reproduced a thousand times over, in the movie houses of the world. Shakespeare for everyone!

Well, that's the idea, at any rate. *Looking for Richard*, which registers Al Pacino's long-nourished obsession with Shakespeare—and more particularly with *Richard III*—shows what happens to that idea in practice. The movie is split between excerpts from the play—staged with black-blooded gusto by actors like Kevin Spacey (Buckingham, of course), Alec Baldwin (Clarence), and Pacino himself as the King—and a shrugging, loose-limbed documentary about the problems inherent in getting people to watch Shakespeare at all. The early scenes are studded with moments of vox pop, as Pacino and his crew trawl the streets of New York asking passersby what they know of the Bard and what, if anything, they make of him. In a way, it's the least convincing part of the picture; this reaching out to an ideal public is bound to be a disappointment, because the majority of the population doesn't care a whit for Shakespeare and never will. You could argue that Pacino is putting the wrong question: Ask not what you know of Shakespeare but what Shakespeare knows of you.

It's no wonder that, as the movie proceeds, Pacino narrows his gaze and pulls the rest of the action tight around the play; he talks less with the common herd and turns to rarer species—actors, academics, those who can fix Richard to a particular patch of history and those who would drag him into line with modern concerns. *Looking for Richard* is in some ways a slender movie, but its very lack of portentousness is cheering; there is something sly and rather Richard-like in the throwaway glee with which it approaches matters of grave intent. It is, in short, a comedy about a tragedy—the first, perhaps, since Lubitsch's *To Be or Not to Be* of 1942, in which Jack Benny and company staged *Hamlet* in Warsaw on the brink of the Nazi invasion. Pacino's film is less bitter to the taste, but it still marks a distinct shift from the efforts of Olivier and Ian McKellen, both of whom have played Richard on the screen; in their versions, the comic and the tragic have been collapsed into a kind of vicious camp. Olivier's Richard enjoys himself hugely; his rapport with the other characters is as flat and flimsy as the sets, but he makes love to the camera, as if the true purpose of soliloquy were to strip the audience naked. It's fun to watch, but it's such a *performance*, and the film hasn't the strength to do anything but record it for posterity. Pacino, on the other hand, takes his evil neat; there are laughs to be had in circling around the role, but once he climbs into it and begins to speak the movie grows darker and more doomy than any stage production I've seen. The passage in which Richard must turn Lady Anne from enmity to love—by reputation, an almost impossible scene to bring off—is wonderfully played by Pacino and Winona Ryder, who seem to beckon us to draw close and join them in their hothouse mood. As Richard lauds Anne for her beauty

> that did haunt me in my sleep,
> To undertake the death of all the world,
> So I might live one hour in your sweet bosom,

his gaze flicks for half a second to her breasts, as if to check them one more time for sweetness. He is playing very dirty indeed, and she, despite her most honorable instincts, is getting into the game; and only the intimacy of the camera can catch them at it.

What's pushing Pacino here? Not, I would suggest, his credentials as a Shakespeare nut but his track record as a movie star. If his Richard is colder and more convincing than, say, Ian McKellen's—despite the fact that McKellen's feel for the swing and surge of the pentameter is infinitely more practiced—then the person to thank is Michael Corleone. Three *Godfather* movies do not merely prepare a man for the diplomatic savagery that is required to place him on the English throne; they also offer a fresh angle of approach to a tale grown musty with use. One thing I love about Shakespeare movies, even some of the lousy ones, is their tendency to induce a chronic allergy to greasepaint. Without really trying, they perplex a settled theatrical tradition, bending and breaking a long line of grand performing masters in favor of something not just more sneaky but also, in an odd way, more democratic; it is those who carry the least Shakespearean baggage who tend to step most lightly. I was not a fan of Branagh's *Much Ado About Nothing*, but I did relish the realization that, for all the long shadows of Burbage and Kean and Garrick and Irving, there are times when what you really want from Shakespeare is Denzel Washington in leather pants. The issue is not simply one of novelty or in-jokes; I have a particular horror of Zeffirelli's *Taming of the Shrew*, which traded with a nudge like a sledgehammer's on the celebrated courtship of Elizabeth Taylor and Richard Burton. Zeffirelli took pains to set the picture in period, but, sadly, the period in question, thanks to Miss Taylor's unique way with mascara, was unmistakably 1967.

Mind you, people often sneer with similar distaste at the remembrance of Marlon Brando playing Mark Antony for Joseph Mankiewicz's *Julius Caesar.* The implication is that here, too, was an actor way out of his depth—out of his ground, at any rate—and that the movie records his desperation to prove himself more than a Hollywood player. But Brando *was* more; he pushed his art beyond that of his peers, and the courteous, slightly leaden calm of *Julius Caesar* is ruffled and whipped into life by his appearance. Watching the elegies for Caesar, you are struck as never before by the obvious difference between Brutus and Antony: one speaks in prose, the other in verse. Antony is self-consciously raising the lyrical stakes. This is not to say that he fakes his grief for Caesar; he is genuinely moved. But not for an instant does he consider doing anything besides dramatizing that grief for the sake of worldly gain. He reaches into himself, inspects his feelings, and uses them; he is, in short, the Marlon Brando of his day. That is why the scene entangles us so tightly in the machinations of the original, and why it remains surprising that Hollywood has never made much of the other Roman plays, *Antony and Cleopatra* and *Coriolanus:* they are object lessons in Method politics, and Hollywood is still well stocked with actors, and even with a couple of directors, whose hearts are hard enough to make such armored poetry ring.

The most telling clue to what is going on in Brando's speech comes where he cracks (or feigns a fractured nerve) under the strain:

> Bear with me,
> My heart is in the coffin there with Caesar,
> And I must pause till it come back to me.

He throws in a caesura where none is expected—a sobbing stutter on the word "pause." The crowd begins to murmur its sympathy. Antony turns his back and walks up the steps of the Capitol; only the camera can watch him now, and it makes the most of that advantage. Brando's face spreads wide across the frame; he bows his head but stares up under his brows, like Schwarzenegger thwarted in mid-mayhem, and, just before we cut to the next shot, there is a ghost of a smile. As the people warm toward him, he is thinking, *Suckers.* The perfection of this deceit would be undetectable onstage; even if you could arrange for your Antony to swivel around and still face the audience, he would need a grin like a slice of watermelon to project his little secret to the back row.

Does one dare to claim that Shakespeare is better on film than onstage? Probably not; it is an unhelpful heresy, and there will always be millions who prefer the one-shot high of the stage. (There are even some of us who like nothing better than to stay home and *read* the stuff, but that is now the most underground heresy of all.) Suffice it to say that there are times when you can't help telling yourself that Shakespeare was waiting for movies to come along. What could be more rapturous, or less theatrical, than the smothering of Desdemona in Orson Welles's movie of *Othello*? No pillows required: he pulls a white bedsheet over her face and molds it tight like a death mask, as indeed it is. Then he kisses her—stops her mouth, as a Shakespearean lover would say, and thus takes her breath away.

This *Othello* is a mess; it was shot on the kind of budget that would just about cover the snack expenses on a Tom Cruise project; filming took place so erratically, and in so many locations, and over such a long period—from 1948 to 1952—that there is no sure way of telling whether characters engaged in conversation are actually standing in the same country, let alone in the same room. The text is in shreds—what you can hear of it, that is, since post-synching was one of the more common casualties of the Orson Welles Experience. And yet out of this farrago, this blur of bad business, came a work that delved more cleanly and swiftly into the essence of its original than any other Shakespeare movie. It reminds you that evil, like sugar, is best left unrefined. *Othello* the movie is not a version of *Othello* the play, nor is it a reading of it: it is a fantasia on the theme of Othello himself—and on that of Iago, too, for Welles found in the Irish actor Micheál MacLiammóir a villain so clearheaded, so capering, and so enamored of his own malice that the movie can hardly help being touched by his spirit.

In David Thomson's new biography, *Rosebud*, easily the best book on Orson Welles, he says of *Othello* that "the poetry hangs in the air, like sea mist or incense," and I suppose that is what I love about the film. Some of the action was shot in Venice, and I occasionally wonder what crept into the camera casing; the movie looks blackened and silvery, like an aged mirror, or as if the emulsion of the print were already poised to decay. You can't tell what is or isn't Shakespeare, where his influence begins and ends. There is fine acting, and yet the film hardly seems to be performed at all. It is as if the story were driven by a spell, or a premonition; this is *Othello* redrawn as a midsummer night's bad dream, and whether it passes muster as tragedy is a moot point. The wittiest shot in the film comes after a brawl around a fountain, when the characters depart and a little dog patters and splashes into view. The composition is born of the comic instinct—that is, of the need to hang back and wait for life to resume its normal service once the aberrant tumult has passed on. Comedy, like happiness, is a long shot.

So where are the comedies? What happened to the romances? Why, after a century of cinema, is there no enduring movie of *Love's Labor's Lost*, or *As You Like It*, or *The Winter's Tale*? Max Reinhardt's *A Midsummer Night's Dream*, of 1935 ("Three centuries in the making!" crowed Warner Bros.), manages the interesting feat of going heavy on the wispiness, with an Oberon who appears in black spangled catsuit and matching antlers. No movie director has ever worked out precisely, or even roughly, how much Shakespearean comedy is supposed to weigh. Trevor Nunn, in his new *Twelfth Night*, is no nearer to solving the conundrum. There are some dense, velvety interiors that suggest a sumptuous relish in Viola's mourning, and Nunn is rightly intrigued by the vengeful vows with which Malvolio gashes the happy ending; but the stateliness of the movie soon descends into the merely sluggish, and the efforts at farce are so unwatchable that I had to turn my face away from the screen. The last time this happened to me was during a screening of *Much Ado About Nothing*, as Branagh messed around with a deck chair, and as revellers gambolled happily in masks. Masks! Get me out of here!

Shakespearean roistering is notoriously hard to bring off—all that dreary raising of goblets—and the verbal knottiness of bawdy is almost impossible to unpick, but my heart still sinks at the thought of Michael Keaton and Ben Elton in *Much Ado*, as they carefully mangled the lines into gibberish. The slapstick in that film, as in *Twelfth Night*, is puppet-stiff, but then nobody has choreographed any decent slapstick since the death of Preston Sturges, so I guess we shouldn't complain. What I miss in such movies is any whisper of relaxation: the spats between Beatrice and Benedick are mentally hectic, as they should be, but even so you feel the movie pulling a muscle as it strains to make them hilarious. This is a common failing of Shakespearean comedy onscreen; the exact point at which Reinhardt's *Dream* finally lurches beyond the pale is the moment when Mickey Rooney, as a pubescent Puck, says "Lord, what fools these mortals be." Or, to be precise, when his spotty, half-broken voice yodels to the surrounding glade, "Looohhhrd! Haha! What foools these muttals behehe!" Rooney seems to think that Puck should laugh heartily, and indeed randomly, so as to indicate that we are in the blessed presence of comedy.

It could be argued that the finest comedy turns up in Shakespeare when you least expect it—that one of the problems with approaching his works is that they are awkwardly shovelled into holes where they don't belong. If *Pericles* is a romance, that is only because it swerves aside from tragedy; the final, exquisite reconciliation of father and daughter is barely an inch away from *King Lear.* Cinema, of all things, should be double-jointed enough to accommodate these near misses, these clashes of emotional color. As a tragedy, Luhrmann's *Romeo and Juliet* is nothing, and the climax left me as cold as if Friar Lawrence had slipped something nasty into my Coke; but to the film's credit it demonstrates how hugely untragic most of the original is. It is more of a sprinting, pun-packed, and fairly filthy comedy that breaks its head open in the final minute. Luhrmann is thirty-three, but Shakespeare was even younger when he wrote *Romeo and Juliet,* and both play and film have a just-you-look-at-this quality, easily read as young men's riffs. The one dab of brilliance in Luhrmann's picture is his notion that Romeo (Leonardo DiCaprio) does not speak his monologues on the topic of Juliet's perfection but jots them down in a journal. He is a poet—your basic horny teenager trying to collect and prettify his thoughts on paper—or, if you prefer, a Shakespeare in bud. This tallies beautifully with our apprehension of the play's youthfulness, of a poet who was still wrestling his own unnerving dexterity (*Venus and Adonis* and the Sonnets were already under his belt, as were the early Histories) into dramatic submission.

One of the lasting oddities of Shakespeare movies, in fact, is how frequently they turn to the earliest works. *Romeo and Juliet, Richard III,* most of the *Henry* plays, and *A Midsummer Night's Dream* are attributable to the playwright's salad days. Maybe directors warm to the green unsubtlety of that period, as they do to the big-name heroics of the major tragedies. Anyone running his eye down a list of Shakespearean cinema might find it dismal and cowardly, its preferences tied to the orthodoxy that is first encouraged in the classroom. You study *Julius Caesar,* for example, and along the way you watch the loyal movie version, and that's that. The glory of Shakespeare on film, however, rests in its leaning toward the inglorious; even the whistling arrows of Olivier's Agincourt strike the ear like a death hiss. Above all, there is Welles's *Chimes at Midnight,* which is liable to make most Shakespeare professors wake up in shock. Alternately wistful and savage, it is a stew of the *Henry IV* plays, with sprinklings of *Richard II*, *Henry V*, and *The Merry Wives of Windsor*, and yet a Shakespeare novice who drank in its wintry humor and floundering fights could be forgiven for concluding that it was based on the ripeness of late Shakespeare. Basically, the movie is potted Falstaff, although what Welles means to conjure up is not just historical continuity—the very best of Sir John—but a sense that the Complete Works of Shakespeare constitute, as it were, one vast poem, from which his devoted and audacious interpreters are free to quote. I watch *Chimes at Midnight* and see the canon beginning to slip its moorings and drift free; the picture both honors Shakespeare and spurns the industry, academic and theatrical, that has encrusted him over time. From here, it is but a short trip to Gus Van Sant's *My Own Private Idaho*, in which Prince Hal and his cronies have become gay hustlers on the streets of Seattle, overseen by the Falstaffian figure of Fat Bob. Shakespeare is all but banished from the dialogue, but he lingers like a drug in the rough, melancholic joys of the film's camaraderie; he gets into its bloodstream in ways that we can't directly trace, and at times when you think he is long gone.

So when will our revels end? Never mind the movies that will emerge as the Shakespeare sensation glows and burns itself out. What of the films that could yet be made? The ones that will *never* be made? The ones that could do delicious damage to the text, or could even—and this would be a faithful service—make audiences wonder whether Shakespeare was quite as heartening, or touching, as they had previously thought?

I have frequently pondered, for example, a version of *Troilus and Cressida*. The play is not much known and not remotely loved, and it is cussedly resistant to definition, but that very twitchiness would bring it profanely alive onscreen. It is a love story that skews out of control and crashes; it is an epic, set outside and within the walls of Troy, with plenty of dashing chaps in greaves and cuirasses; and it is a livid and scandalous comedy, in which the waxy hearts of Troilus and Cressida are melted together by Pandarus, a mock-sentimental Machiavel who has seen it all before, and are chipped away by Thersites, a pot of poison who squats in the fringes of the action and waits to feast upon the end of everything, not least the fall of Troy. Thersites has Steve Buscemi written all over him, but Pandarus? Could someone persuade Brando to drag himself back? Imagine his mirth and girth as he lumbers into the postcoital boudoir with an unromantic snigger—"How now, how now, how go maidenheads?" Ralph Fiennes could reprise the sleek and shattered Troilus that I saw him offer onstage, and there are any number of leading weirdos, starting with Christopher Walken, who would relish Achilles' metamorphosis from tented languor into homicidal rage. Cressida would be the toughest role to cast, for she is the most baffling of all Shakespearean heroines: she loves a Trojan in all sincerity, then swaps him for a Greek. Her lechery makes sense only in the way that Goneril's venality does: their betrayals must rise out of a moral miasma, an atmosphere of rot that creeps into the characters' eyes and ears like sand. The whole thing would make Polanski's blood-laced movie of *Macbeth* look like *Brigadoon.* How could a director say no?

It's not as if the contemporary audience would be taken aback by such goings on. *Troilus and Cressida* swerves back and forth between long paths of tortuous talk and sudden detonations of violence. Tarantino, anyone? For American viewers, too, schooled as they are in the Civil War and Vietnam, the prospect of Troy—of a conflict that seems to its participants as if it will never end, and whose ethical purpose has been all but mislaid in the bloodbath—would slide with ease into the guts of their imaginations. On the other hand, the Shakespeare critic Barbara Everett (who is, incidentally, one of the experts quoted to acute effect in *Looking for Richard*) did once draw attention, in an essay on *Troilus and Cressida,* to its stretches of "fascinating boringness," and something tells me that this might not wash too well with the moguls. It is a pleasing idyll—to sit by a pool in Santa Monica, with a script on one's knees and a trio of producers awaiting a verdict. "Bernie? Brian? Biff? You're going to *love* this, guys. It's so . . . fascinatingly *boring.*" For this reason, if for no other, *Troilus* will never see the light of a projector. But it is the duty of Shakespeare addicts—and, even more, of movie lovers—to follow the reveries that appear to unspool, with only the gentlest tug, from one's favorite plays. Orson Welles made Shakespeare for everyone, but only because of his arrogant and justified faith in wanting Shakespeare all for himself. Culturemongers may believe that we need Shakespeare, but reason not the need: it is enough to want him. No other writer has been so thoroughly filtered through other eyes and minds; he comes out differently every time, although it is we who are transformed as he passes through. Movies cannot put Shakespeare on a pedestal or a stage, although they are sometimes plucky enough to put him on hold; they plunge him into the dark, five fathoms down, and a few of them haul something rich and strange back into the light. As someone in *To Be or Not to Be* says to Jack Benny, "It's nothing alarming, it's only Shakespeare." And Benny replies, "That's what *you* think."

NOVEMBER 25, 1996

CANNES

This year, the Cannes Festival held its fiftieth anniversary. It was a fitting moment to take stock: to stand back and marvel at this luminous fortnight, as stars and stargazers came together to honor the greatest medium of mass communication that has ever existed. It was time, in short, to celebrate the cell phone.

True, there were ugly rumors flying around that some people were laying down their Motorolas and going to watch *films*. But the sombre silence of a movie theatre is hardly likely to deter the dedicated phoner; if anything, it's a good place to talk. As the lights went down on the first night, with an audience of thousands—among them Bruce Willis and Demi Moore—preparing to watch *The Fifth Element*, a public announcement asked us politely to switch our phones off for the duration of the screening. We nodded sagely, in communal disapproval of this shocking new trend. Then a phone rang. We giggled like convent girls. During the opening ceremony, Jeanne Moreau—the spirit of Cannes incarnate, with a voice that made you feel you were being seduced by a coffee grinder—had spoken of "*la solitude des hommes dans ce monde moderne.*" A nice idea, but there wasn't much solitude in the air at Cannes 1997, not with all the electronic messages crackling through the atmosphere. If you stood on the Croisette at noon and threw an egg into the sky, it would come down fried.

Jean-Luc Godard, who was in town to present two portions of his *Histoire(s) du Cinéma*, did his best to shield us from the blast. In the course of a witty and ruminative press conference, he berated the beeping generation. "I have never heard a real conversation on a mobile phone," he said. "It is always, 'See you in ten minutes.' " But that's just the point: the crucial thing in Cannes is never whom you saw ten minutes ago, or what happened yesterday, but what comes next.

Hence *The Fifth Element* and its ensuing jamboree: both were derided, but, in their blend of frenzy and dawdling, they set the tone for the whole festival. After the screening was over, we lined up to get out of the auditorium, then we lined up to get onto buses. It was a hell of a squeeze: movers, shakers, and the occasional star, all straphanging together. The buses drove us a few hundred yards toward a vast blue nipple-shaped tent that had been constructed—at a cost of more than three million dollars, it was said—solely as an arena for the *Fifth Element* party. That short trip was the highlight of my stay in Cannes; standing next to Greta Scacchi as you go over a speed bump is one of those things, I feel, that every man should try to do once in his life. Having reached the nipple, we hung around some more; I passed the time contemplating Demi Moore's dress, which looked as if she had tried to leave her airplane too quickly and taken the seat with her. Finally, on the stroke of midnight, we sat down to cold red mullet. An hour later, we watched a Jean-Paul Gaultier fashion show. And thirty minutes after *that*, they let the little people in.

Why had everyone waited so long in the cold? Simply because at Cannes, unlike anywhere else, the act of waiting justifies what you are waiting for, and deepens your need to get there. I wandered around town for two full days in a tuxedo, feeling like the world's most underused gigolo, for no other reason than to smooth my path into screenings of films from which I would normally run a mile. The festival is a mess, but its arousal of expectation approaches the status of high art. No movie is as good as the one showing tomorrow at eight-thirty in the morning, although by ten-thirty you'll be wondering why you bothered to wake up. This year, most of the interesting stuff—Atom Egoyan's *The Sweet Hereafter*, *L.A. Confidential*, with Kevin Spacey—was squashed into the second half of the festival, so that you could spend the first half getting itchy. The quintessential Cannes fortnight, indeed, would involve no films at all—just invitations to parties that never happen and rumors of films that will never be made. On the principle that foreplay sells better than sex, Miramax showed half an hour of *Copland*, starring Robert De Niro, Harvey Keitel, Ray Liotta, and—hang on—Sylvester Stallone. It looked great: better than most of what was shown in competition, and quite possibly better than the finished product, which is due to arrive in August. *Copland* was the cinematic equivalent of festival food, which not only leaves you hungry for more but is designed to prove that the human constitution can survive on a diet of pure canapé.

Socially, this unsatisfied craving translates into outright madness. If any party was hotter than the one to which you couldn't find an invitation, it was the party that you missed the night before. The latest twist, courtesy of the folks at MTV, was to issue an excess of tickets to their soirée, thus insuring the presence of a baying mob at the gates. On Monday night, I went to the New Line party for ten minutes, stepped out to make a phone call, and then spent an hour and a half trying to get back in. Unlike the rest of the throng, I knew what lay inside: a chance to sip warm wine from plastic cups and scream small talk over the sound of the Pimp Daddies. Yet still I stood in line, with a chunky German couple pressing lightly against my kidneys, and with no hope of getting a cab home, because that is what you do. Eventually, I hooked up with Nicholas Klein and Traci Lind, the writer and the supporting star, respectively, of the new Wim Wenders picture *The End of Violence*. They were gracious, good-looking, honest about the strengths and weaknesses of their movie, and, above all, they had a *car*. Later, over a drink at the bar in the Hotel Martinez, I asked Traci if she minded all the hoopla. "Not hoopla," she corrected me. "Turbo-hoopla."

This year saw the traditional Cannes balance of chaos and fun tip dangerously into the red—unless, of course, you were a seasoned enjoyer, like James Woods. "Even the chaos was fun for a while," he said cheerily as we trooped onto the Airbus at Nice. "See any movies?" I asked. "Oh, no," he said. That explains it. He should have tried one of the afternoon press screenings, when film companies juice up the desirability of their products by showing them in a theatre the size of a squash court. The crowd trying to get into the new Abel Ferrara movie, *The Blackout*, was more like an Abel Ferrara movie than the Abel Ferrara movie was. As the crush reached cattle-truck intensity, the woman in front of me fainted at my feet. It says a lot for my Cannes-contaminated soul that my first instinct was not to catch her as she dropped but to hail her genius at PR. "Blackout!" I said to the guy next to me. "*Love* it," he replied. I finally remembered my manners, knelt down, and adopted the Rhett Butler position, but even now I wonder whether she was starting a fad. After all, the Riviera skies grew suspiciously tempestuous for the screening of Ang Lee's *The Ice Storm*. As for the premiere of the Korean entry *Wind Echoing in My Being*, I don't even want to think about it.

By comparison with the main contenders, in fact, the Korean films sounded promising. I was particularly sorry to have missed *Crocodile*, from the director Kim Kee-Duck, in which "a woman wants to roll back her own history and an unknown man." What Kim didn't realize was: I am that man. At the Fiftieth Anniversary Gala, I was completely rolled back by the women who streamed up the red carpet, oozing history as if it were perfume. Just when you think you're immune to celebrity, along comes a genuine grande dame—Anouk Aimée, Claudia Cardinale, or Gina Lollobrigida—to lay you low. Gina, sadly, was without the fourteen chihuahuas who accompanied her to an earlier festival, but you can't have everything. It must be said that 1997, though a mixed year for films, was well over the limit on beauty. The president of the jury was Isabelle Adjani, who likes to lower her shades in the way that less retiring performers used to whip aside their tops on the beach. Among her fellow-jurors were Mira Sorvino and the radiant Chinese actress Gong Li; by way of compensation, there was also room for Tim Burton and Mike Leigh. I heard one French reporter refer to "*Gong et Mike Leigh.*" They would make a lovely couple. If any place can swing it for them, Cannes can.

MAY 26, 1997

LEGO

Take a brick. Look at it. Is it plastic? Does it have eight knobs on top and three tubular holes underneath? Is it, would you say, molded to a tolerance of five-thousandths of a millimetre? If so, you are probably holding a piece of Lego. If you're still not sure, gather five more bricks of the same design and start clicking them together. Take your time. If you discover that there are 102,981,500 ways in which those six pieces of plastic can possibly be combined, then Lego it is.

During the past forty years, some 300 million children have played with Lego, and it is estimated that in the course of a single year these children spend five billion hours amid the bricks. At last count, Lego had filled the world with a hundred and eighty-nine billion molded elements. Most of them, given the unbreakable longevity of the product, must still be in circulation. Half, as far as I can make out, are in my attic.

The rule that governs any self-respecting box of old Lego is that it should contain not just single bricks but the exciting debris of half-made projects: a three-wheeled chassis, a robot's lonely torso, a plastic Piranesi ruin. I find it heartbreaking to comb through the bricks of my childhood—not because the click of stud into hole promises a Proustian retrieval of lost bliss but simply because I am touched to discover that even when I was six my engineering concepts were crap. Lego posed a formidable challenge: being essentially curveless, it seldom bothered with anything as fancy as aerodynamics. That was how we liked it, of course. Roundness was for slackers.

These days, I gaze in disbelief at what Lego has become. There are currently 433 different Lego sets available, 207 of which came out this year. I recently spent a day cruising the Lego department of F. A. O. Schwarz, on Fifth Avenue, discovering such delights as the Riptide Racer, the Speed Splasher, and the Fright Knights. I could choose between Lego Primo, for infants; Duplo, for children one and a half and older; Technic, for those aged seven and up; and something called FreeStyle, which seemed to mean a load of Lego bits thrown into a bucket, like chicken wings. Even the basic backbone of the product line, Lego System, comprised a number of subsets, such as Aquazone, U.F.O., ResQ, Castle, Extreme Team, and the daringly antiquated Town and Boats.

All at sea, I enlisted the aid of Jason Bligen, F.A.O. Schwarz's eagerly clued-in Lego manager. I was tempted by the Dark Forest Fortress, but Bligen demurred. "Oh, that's really old stuff," he said.

"How old?"

"Year, year and a half."

Hotter by far was the new range of Adventurers, which was released in January. For forty dollars, I could have had the high-tech Mummy's Tomb, but it was clear that its designers were cashing in on *Stargate*, and I wasn't in the market for merchandising. After deep deliberation, I plumped for the Cyber Saucer—113 pieces, and mine for only $21.99.

Back in the safety of my bedroom, I made my Saucer. It took eighteen minutes. I encountered no major construction problems; Lego instructions, wordlessly international, are known to be among the clearest in the world. (The Swedish furniture manufacturer Ikea approached Lego for advice on this point.) And yet I can't say that I had any fun. The path from components to finished product was so smooth, and so hostile to improvisation, that I felt less like a child at play than like the last man on the assembly line.

This is the nub of the charge—half lament, half complaint—that older Lego lovers level at the company of today. It is voiced most ardently by Bug, a computer jock in Douglas Coupland's novel *Microserfs:*

> You know what really depresses the hell out of me? The way that kids nowadays don't have to use their imagination when they play with Lego. Say they buy a Lego car kit—in the old days you'd open the box and out tumbled sixty pieces you had to assemble to make the car. Nowadays, you open the box and a whole car, pre-fucking-built, pops out—the car itself is all one piece. Big woo.

I went back to my Saucer, took it apart, and stared at the pieces. An hour later, I had turned it, or tamed it, into a cat and a mouse. The pivoting antennae from the spaceship were now the cat's whiskers. My rodent had black radio-dish ears, like Mickey's, and a revolving abdomen. I had applied my imagination to New Age Lego, but I was still stranded with four large sloping panels of plastic. Plugged together, they had formed the body of the ship; unplugged, they were totally useless. Big woo.

One hardly needs to point out the steely commercial wisdom that underpins Lego's new marketing and design practices: ten or twenty years ago, a mother who gave her son or daughter a midsized, brick-based Lego kit could watch it go through countless transmutations without the need for further investment, whereas a mother who shelled out for a pair of green and purple Lego Technic Jaw-Tong Slammers last Christmas will have to reach Buddhist levels of quietude by August if she is not to cave in to raucous demands for the new Insectoids Arachno Base and Beetle Pod.

"The new stuff is a slap in the face for old Lego," I was told by an advertising executive who works on the Lego account. "What matters now," he said, "is not Lego the product but Lego the name—how to spread the brand."

Last year, for the first time, the Lego Group published "selected key figures." Its turnover in 1996 was 7,534 million Danish kroner ($1,267 million), which left a profit after tax of 470 million kroner ($79 million), or 6.2 percent of earnings, down 0.1 percent from the previous year. According to a company report, this just isn't good enough: although Lego is now sold in 138 countries, "earnings are not satisfactory in the light of our long-term objective to self-finance the operations and investments that we believe to be right and necessary." Lego is bigger and brighter than ever, but nobody can be sure that it's getting better; meanwhile, rivals such as the Pennsylvania-produced K'Nex are squaring up and watching their profits rise. In the moving words of the Lego catalogue: "Build the two opposing slammers and then prepare to compete."

Lego began life in 1932, in the workshop of a poor, God-fearing Danish carpenter. If that sounds like something out of Hans Christian Andersen, it may be because the woodworker in question, Ole Kirk Christiansen, lived in Billund, which is only a couple of hours' drive from Andersen's birthplace, on the island of Funen. Fly to Copenhagen and en route you will see a soft landscape dotted with neat villages that look oddly familiar; as I peered down at the red roofs of the notoriously pretty Ærøskøbing, my ideas about Lego turned gently upside down. I had always presumed that a brick is a brick is a brick. Lego seemed so anonymous and ubiquitous that it could have come from anywhere. But, in fact, it was, in its formative years, a distillation of Denmark: every time you got your bricks out, you were founding a miniature Northern European welfare state—bright of hue, placid of demeanor, basically solid but given to occasional disturbing creaks. To the rest of us, Lego looks like toytown. To the Danes, it must sometimes feel like home.

Ole Kirk Christiansen made wooden toys for a living. (He also made stepladders and ironing boards.) The Lego company started using plastic in 1947, and dealt in it exclusively after 1960, when its wooden-goods warehouse burned down. Part of Christiansen's genius was to make the new material feel almost as comforting, as domestically reliable, as wood itself. There was nothing very natural about cellulose acetate—or, later, about the more stable acrylonitrile butadiene styrene that replaced it—but until recently a certain folksiness still clung to the image of Lego.

Christiansen's other masterstroke came in 1934, when he held a competition among his employees to choose a company name, and won it himself. "Lego" is a contraction of the Danish "*leg godt*," or "play well," and it's one of those blessed names, like Coke or Kodak, that get their hooks in the auditory imagination and never let go. Rivals have failed to devise anything that can boast a fraction of this universal snappiness: the Lego headquarters, in Billund, sports a fabulous display of Lego ripoffs, including Bildo, Blocko, Loko, Moto, Klip, Polly Plus, Hobby Land, Playgo, LocBlocs, OK, NA, and the tragically unambitious Toy. There is even one product called Ego, which is presumably all stud and no hole.

The Christiansen dynasty still runs Lego. Ole Kirk died in 1958, the year that saw the patenting of the brick we know and love, and Godtfred, one of his four sons, took over; it is Godtfred's son Kjeld who runs the Lego Group today. In the same spirit, Billund remains the hub of the Lego universe. Since 1968, millions of people have come to this place, sometimes more than twenty-five thousand in a single day—for Billund is, among other things, home to Legoland, the original, hundred-thousand-square-metre theme park. Its main attraction is Miniland, where selected highlights of the known world are reproduced in Lego. When I toured the park on a forlorn and gusty day, Washington was in turmoil. Someone had lifted the lid off the Capitol. Same old story.

The Lego experience—three parts charming and inventive to one part creepy—starts the moment you touch down at Billund Airport. I collected my bag, walked over to the information bureau, and asked the woman in charge where I could catch the shuttle bus into Legoland. "The bus is waiting outside," she said. She paused, then added, "There will be small people on the bus." I gazed long and hard into her eyes for the tiniest sign of mockery, but they shone with clear, unsmiling innocence. I thanked her and went to meet my fate among the small people.

Ah! Cruel destiny! There were small people on the bus, but they were not, as I had fondly hoped, arrayed inside with fixed plastic smiles and their asses clipped to the seats. Instead, they were simply painted on the outside, and I travelled alone with my disappointment to Hotel Legoland. Nothing in Billund is more than a short haul from anything else; to get from the church to the supermarket to the civic center (endowed with Lego money) you drive at a sensible speed along ludicrously quiet streets, halting courteously at little roundabouts to allow other friendly drivers to pass by. At the side of the road, you keep seeing giant Lego bricks—perfect eight-studs, magnified a hundred times and piled up like Claes Oldenburgs. By the time you reach Hotel Legoland, the visual jokes have become addictive. But the most vertiginous moment of illusion, which would have reduced E. H. Gombrich himself to whimpers of satisfaction, came as I strolled into the bar and ordered a cocktail. In a pitiful attempt at Roger Moore–style sophistication, I turned to raise my glass to the man who was noodling away on a grand piano, then realized that he was made of Lego. Even the "Do Not Disturb" sign on the door of my room showed a grinning little Lego man lying wide awake in a single bed with two plastic hands peeking over the edge of the blanket—a tomb-like position that I dutifully assumed, and maintained, for an entire night.

Over at the modelling department the next morning, I stopped at the workbench of Malene Helbak. She was dressed in black, with an earring clipped to the upper rim of one ear. Music flowed from a boom box by her side, and she was being paid to play with Lego all day. I gazed at her and thought, *You have the best job in the world.*

Helbak was making a tall, plump bird.

"Penguin?" I asked.

"No, fanfare pigeon," she said. I asked what a fanfare pigeon was.

"A pigeon playing a fanfare," she replied, reducing me to Lego Primo with a single look.

Almost none of Helbak's work was done on a computer; she simply looked at the image of a pigeon, drew it by hand on Lego graph paper, and started building. Some Lego designers had been artists in a previous life; some had been architects; and one, Søren Lethin, had been a journalist. There is a God after all.

Lethin was a Lego nut as a kid, and nothing has changed. He is now a product consultant for Lego's Shows and Events section, where one-off company display models are invented. We inspected some of his achievements, including a grungy four-foot rock star complete with shades, goatee, and guitar. "Gibson Les Paul," said Lethin proudly. Press a knob and the rocker starts to play; for all I know, you could program him to throw televisions and to pee on your children's heads. The dexterity of such modelling is beyond belief. During the course of my trip I saw a dachshund, a lunar module, the Doges' Palace, the Holy Family at rest, and the rather Clinton-like spectacle of a happy yellow monster whose nose turns into a saxophone. Lethin told me that he had once worked on a Lego Michael Jackson. "It's fabulous what you can do with plastic," he said with a smile. What is required is a kind of modular alchemy. When would-be master builders audition for Lego, they are given a pile of bricks and asked to make a perfect sphere. Then they have to turn it into a head. One guy produced a flawless Teddy Roosevelt and was told to take it away, dismantle it, and come back with Carmen Miranda.

If this all sounds too much for mortals, consider the Lego World Cup, at which selected children are invited to Billund and allotted two hours and a stash of bricks to conjure a creation of their choice. One Italian girl produced a game of Lego Ping-Pong, and was asked how she had thought of it. "Well, I was planning to make a gondola," she confessed, "but there were no black bricks."

One reason that children have long treasured the order and flexibility of Lego is, perhaps, that the realm of play is one of the few areas of life where control has not become a dirty word. Among his or her bricks, the child is an absolute deity, forging coherence out of chaos and then reversing the process. If that omnipotence were to lurk and linger into adulthood, however, we would all be in trouble. Hence the nasty black comedy that hangs around the work of the Polish artist Zbigniew Libera.

In 1996, Libera was given a consignment of bricks by Lego distributors in Poland, which he used to construct a Lego concentration camp. The model was photographed, and its image was pasted onto a fake Lego box, with a fake Lego serial number, to give the impression that concentration camps were now part of the official Lego product line. When the boxes were exhibited in a Copenhagen art gallery, the Lego company understandably cried foul, but had the good sense not to sue. Libera's conceit is a respectable one, and, insofar as there is any sting to the work's satire, it comes from the sober (if unexceptional) fear that nothing—not even the Holocaust—is immune to our demand for entertainment.

In the end, Libera's Lego art seems too obvious to be shocking, and the company can count itself unlucky to have been singled out as a moral mercenary. Why mock the potential of Lego and leave the Power Rangers unscathed? In comparison with many other toy companies, Lego feels benevolent toward the aspirations of the creative, and tolerates what it calls "foreseeable misuse." Denmark, after all, favors freedom of expression as rampantly as the other countries in Northern Europe—perhaps on the understanding that only a minority of its citizens would even dream of abusing that liberty.

Legomakers everywhere have availed themselves of this opportunity. If you had to name one American, for instance, who clubbed together with a couple of friends in 1965 and spent more than three weeks building a futuristic seven-foot vertical city out of Lego, you might not immediately think of Norman Mailer. Thirty-three years later, however, the city still stands in Mailer's living room in Brooklyn Heights, and its creator remains enthusiastic about his project. "It was very much opposed to Le Corbusier. I kept thinking of Mont-Saint-Michel," he explains. "Each Lego brick represents an apartment. There'd be something like twelve thousand apartments. The philosophers would live at the top. The call girls would live in the white bricks, and the corporate executives would live in the black." The cloud-level towers, apparently, would be linked by looping wires. "Once it was cabled up, those who were adventurous could slide down. It would be great fun to start the day off. Put Starbucks out of business."

Just as I was about to suggest that Mailer fly to Billund and be elected honorary Master Builder—who better to relish the Ibsenite power of such a post?—he admitted that he didn't even like the stuff. "Lego's not perfect for it, because you have all those little, what can you call them, nipples, on top of each block, and they tend to spoil the line. I never enjoyed working with the plastic as such."

Mailer's metropolis, whether he likes it or not, would make a magnificent launchpad for Exploration Mars, one of three sets that supplement the new Lego Mindstorms Robotics Invention System, which will arrive on the market this fall. The heart of this system is a special Lego brick containing a microcomputer that you program from your PC and then incorporate into your Lego creation. I recently had a brief encounter with a Mindstorms car that came toward me, touched my finger with its front bumper, freaked out, turned around, and scooted off at ninety degrees. This struck me as authentic behavior.

Mindstorms is all part of the grand plan, as it was expounded in a 1997 Lego mission statement. Amid the usual nonsense about synergy and mind-sets, you hit this: "We want the LEGO brand to be the most powerful brand in the world among families with children. Our aim is to attain this objective no later than the year 2005." Bricks are clearly only a part of the deal. The new Lego kid will wear a Lego backpack to school, and shelter from the rain with a Lego umbrella and a pair of Lego rubber boots called Mudhoppers. When he gets home, he will lock himself in his room with the interactive building guide for his Lego Technic CyberMaster to make Stinger and Crusher. His only prayer will be that Mom and Dad won't try to come and help.

If there is a new dash of impatience, even of panic, in the soul of Lego, that is not the company's fault. The days when we could crouch down to play with Lego in the company of our kids—that wonderful sensation of joint solitude, both builders furrowing their brows over separate problems—were bound to be numbered. Childhood itself is reaching a pitch of knowledge and appetite that would flummox and exhaust your average Danish carpenter of 1932, and the temptation to move into Stingers and Crushers must be hard to resist.

The future belongs to such projects as Legoland California, which will open in spring 1999, in Carlsbad, near San Diego. The ideal to which it will aspire is not Billund but the British Legoland at Windsor, less than an hour west of London. I went there on March 14, the opening day of the season, and spent five delirious hours shooting waterjets at the open mouths of Lego crocodiles and spinning around in Lego helicopters. Any place where an eight-year-old can earn his Lego driver's license by driving a Lego car around a road system is an intrinsically good thing, as is any lunch that consists of elephant-shaped chicken nuggets, an apple, a Coke, and a free Lego racing car. This last detail, I thought, could easily be incorporated into more fashionable dining contexts: "Yes, I'll have the squash risotto, the guinea fowl with grilled endive, half a bottle of Calon-Ségur, and Big Chief Rattle Snake's Camp."

There was a line to get into the Legoland Mindstorms Center, so I sneaked next door and found myself standing beside a rubberized track that was four yards long with a gentle slope. At the top was a starting grid, with room for five vehicles. At the bottom was a mass of Lego bits. This was my chance. I scooped up an armful of bricks and retired to a corner. Five minutes later, I was back, sizing up the competition. The kid on my left had come up with a hybrid of dragster and dragonfly. The kid on my right, newly versed in the law that momentum equals mass times velocity, was cradling what appeared to be a wheel-based version of the Chrysler Building. As for the quiet, self-possessed girl at the far end, I didn't trust her an inch. I had met her type before. And what about the red-haired kid with a car the size of a vole? We jostled for position, placed our speed machines, and waited for the ramp to drop. It was over in seconds. The girl romped home. The vole failed to start. The Chrysler Building fell over. I came in third. Lego is the greatest toy in the world.

APRIL 27, 1998

OBITUARIES

When Antony died, Cleopatra was nice enough to claim that there was "nothing left remarkable beneath the visiting moon." She also pointed out that "the soldier's pole is fall'n." As a tribute, it all sounds magnificent; as an obituary, however, it's a nonstarter. We get the point that Antony was something special, but when was he born? Which school did he attend? At what stage did his pole begin to rise? Cleopatra, always a quick learner, could use some lessons from the obituarists of the *New York Times*. Compare her soaring style with this tough and rooted approach:

> Helen Bunce, who knitted so many mittens she didn't know what to do unless she was knitting more mittens, died at a nursing home in Watertown, New York, where she was known as the Mitten Lady. She was eighty-six and had been knitting mittens until a few days before her death.

There you go: crisp, compact, and free of moons, visiting or resident, yet not without its share of peculiar and woollen atmosphere. Helen Bunce is one of the blessed souls who appear in *The Last Word: "The New York Times" Book of Obituaries and Farewells—A Celebration of Unusual Lives*, which is a hell of a mouthful for such a simple idea. This weighty and enlightening volume, edited by Marvin Siegel, is nectar to those of us who consider the obituary to be not merely an art form but one of the few art forms that have remained coherent enough to demand any measure of obedience. Novelists can do more or less what they fancy to linear narrative without getting arrested, and no one turns a hair when Oliver Stone switches film stock every three seconds, but an obituarist who bends the rules does so at his peril: beware the ravening dead who rise from their graves, or, even worse, the vengeful blue of the editor's pencil. The fact that the obituary is unquestionably a minor form only strengthens one's desire both to take care of it and never to take it too seriously. It should be swiftly skimmed, or even left unread, with the sort of comfortable inattention that Victorian readers used to bring to light verse. Even someone who never studies the obituaries would feel cheated if they were to vanish from newspapers altogether.

The principles that govern the true obituary are as stringent (and therefore as likely to provoke silliness) as the metrical demands of a haiku. First, you must state the facts of the death; they need not be bald facts, nor should they be hairy with surplus detail or supposition. Thus, from the *Times* of September 20, 1995:

> Orville Redenbacher, the agricultural visionary who all but single-handedly revolutionized the American popcorn industry, died in his home in Coronado, California. He was found in a bathtub with a whirlpool in his condominium, where he drowned after a heart attack, the medical examiner's office said. He was eighty-eight.

By this time, seasoned obituary addicts will be wide awake and licking their lips. There is so much to savor in that opening paragraph alone: the pleasing thought that yet another great inventor was named Orville; the sick little chime of "Coronado" and "heart attack," which would not have disgraced the diary of Humbert Humbert; the promise of tussles, or even heartbreak, contained within the phrase "all but single-handedly"; and, last, the illogical but nagging connection between popcorn and whirlpool, which somehow suggests that this most useful of lives had reached its finale in a whirring, buttery blur.

Next, we backtrack to the high point—in this case, to 1965, when Mr. Redenbacher and a partner "came up with the first significant genetic improvement in popcorn in more than five thousand years." I'd love to have seen the obituarist trying to nail that one—combing the daubs on the walls of prehistoric caves in search of dim white fluff. The story then proceeds swiftly to the present day, only to halt and return once more, this time to the very beginning; not until we are two-thirds of the way through the obituary, for instance, do we learn that Redenbacher was born in Brazil, Indiana. After a quick spin through the family from which he sprang, we are led, with delicate symmetry, to the relatives from whom he has recently departed in peace. This can take up considerable space: there is barely a soul in the *Times* book who doesn't seem to leave behind a restless herd of grandchildren. America emerges from its pages as the most elastic, inventive, laudatory, and, let us say, seminal nation on earth.

To unpack an obituary like Orville Redenbacher's makes it sound choppy and shapeless; in fact, a good obituary will flow and accelerate as smartly as a sonata, or a movie. Anyone raised on the restive chronology of *Citizen Kane* will warm to the natural complexities of the form; if anything, it draws us closer to the imbalances of life, to the rise and fall of all our fortunes, than does the stern procedural plod of the full-length biography. The obituary likes to hint and nudge where the latter grandly expounds, and the demands of suggestive concision mean that obituarists bereft of wit are not worth reading at all. As professional journalists, they are spared the mournfulness of elegy, and eulogy, too, lies beyond their brief; instead of lifting up our eyes unto the hills, they induce the steady, semi-amused gaze into the middle distance.

It was not until the late 1980s that I became fully conscious of the wicked talents of obituarists. I was working on a British daily newspaper, and came to treasure the Monday-morning conferences at which the editor would quiz the heads of departments about their plans for the week. These were sullen and coffee-stained affairs, dreaded by hacks who were slightly put out at having to think aloud before noon, but there was invariably a final twist. The editor would start: "Home news?"

"Um, we've got new attacks on Tory spending plans. There's a rail strike set for Friday. And the IRA trial could possibly reach a verdict by the weekend."

"Good. Foreign?"

"Main story is Gorbachev hosting the summit. Official recognition of the African famine by the UN; we should have someone there by tomorrow. And far-right groups claiming a big turnout in the German elections."

"Fine. Sport?"

"Well, it's the second week of Wimbledon, so obviously all the British players are out. And the cricket's rained off. We may have to lead on yachting."

"Pity. Anyone else? Obituaries?"

A brief pause.

"Well, the bad news is that Mother Teresa's getting better."

"What? But you said . . ."

"I know, I did promise, but last week her cold really *was* getting worse, and I thought I could have her for you by Thursday. Sorry about that. Couple of good comas, though. . . ."

It is hardly surprising that the obituary, like the stubborn and time-wasting crossword, should have attained its singular place in British newspapers. You can tell just how securely it is ensconced in the national consciousness from all the crumbling apocrypha in which it has been enfolded. There is the instructive tale of the man who liked to begin his day by turning to the obituaries columns of the London *Times;* only when he had satisfied himself that his name was not featured there would he proceed with the rest of his day. There is even a Wildean sequel to that story—the occasion on which, thanks to a printer's confusion of names, a certain British peer really did open the newspaper and find himself confronted by his own obituary. In a rage of curiosity, he rang the obituaries editor and announced defiantly who he was. Without hesitation, the editor replied, "And where are you speaking from now, Your Lordship?" Or so the story goes.

This blend of absentmindedness and snobbery—not quite cruel, but certainly suspicious of excess warmth—could not have emerged from any country other than England. The estimable writers who contributed to *The Last Word* would, quite rightly, be wary of the tone that is set by some of their counterparts in London. Not for a moment would one suggest that English obituarists find themselves suppressing a laugh as the funeral procession passes; it would be fair to say, nevertheless, that they can hardly wait to get back to the pub and start mulling over the inhabitant of the coffin.

The clear leader in the field is the London *Daily Telegraph*, which in recent years has raised its obituaries page to such a pitch of eminence that one finds oneself ruffling briskly past the news pages in order to reach the real news of other people's demise. To be brutal about it, cold bodies are hot stuff, and yet to crave this regular fix is in no way a morbid preoccupation. The *Telegraph*, unlike most other newspapers, rarely provides the cause of death; when it does, the motive tends to be comic, as in the case of the sixties chanteuse Nico, purveyor of what the obituarist calls "depraved Germanic lullabies," who passed away in 1988. "In recent years," we are told, Nico "gave up heroin for bicycling, which was to turn out the more dangerous amusement—she died when she fell off a bicycle while on holiday." If you find such druggy tragedy to be no laughing matter, then the *Telegraph* is not for you; if, on the other hand, you like the sound of a courageous, cockeyed universe that was plainly invented by a feather-brained Supreme Being who mislaid the instruction manual, and is crammed with men and women of indomitable oddity, you should seek out the three books of *Telegraph* obituaries. These were collected and edited by Hugh Massingberd, who was the newspaper's obituaries editor from 1986 to 1994, and were published by Macmillan: the first, *A Celebration of Eccentric Lives*, in 1995; the second, *Heroes and Adventurers*, the following year; and the third, *Entertainers*, in 1997. A fourth volume, with the enticing subtitle of *Rogues*, is on the way.

Though the majority of the entries concern dead Brits, quite a few distinguished Americans—among them Liberace, Divine, and Jimmy Carter's brother—do make the cut, and there is a heartfelt tribute to the Toronto-born Beatrice Lillie:

> She had a reputation as a prankster and in 1951 ordered a live alligator from Harrods and sent it to Noël Coward with the message: "So what else is new?"

Nothing funnier or more stirring than these volumes has arrived in print for some time. The comedy is of an intricate variety, starting with the established rhetoric of euphemism: when an obituarist ends an article with the words "He never married" or "She was unmarried," this is and always has been acceptable shorthand for homosexuality, or occasionally—and this can be confusing—for a heterosexuality so all-embracing that the person concerned was physically unable to make it to the altar. The paper's obituaries have two further distinguishing features. First, unlike those in *The Last Word*, or those in some other British newspapers, they are always unsigned, leaving the reader to ruminate on the exact relationship between writer and subject. Second, they are aided by a subheading, which runs beneath the name of the deceased and is intended to sum up the principal landmarks of the life, as a taster for what follows. The *New York Times* has these, too, but somehow in England the results are more reliably surreal, either through majestic anachronism ("Colonial officer who, armed only with a walking-stick, quelled seething mobs in northern Nigeria") or through hideous juxtaposition: "Fervent supporter of capital punishment who detested dogs." He sounds nice.

If you had to make a distinction between *The Last Word* and its English equivalents, you might say that the American volume specializes in makers, whereas the *Telegraph* collections focus on doers—or, occasionally, on those who did absolutely nothing of any worth but did it with such verve and application that their very indolence makes for exhausting reading. The fine, sustained middle section of *The Last Word* includes the developer of artificial sweetener, the Belgian-born genius behind the classic Corvette, the best diamond-cutter in the world, and the man responsible for the zoot suit, whereas in the *Telegraph* books you will find the sort of obituary that begins, "Denisa Lady Newborough, who has died aged 79, was many things: wire-walker, nightclub girl, nude dancer, air-pilot." Not, one feels instinctively, a useful life; but not exactly colorless, either.

Two pages later, it all ends on a masterstroke of historical bathos: "She is survived by her daughter Juno, who is married to a dentist." Lady Newborough was unorthodox but far from atypical of her generation. A quick skim through the first book will soon lead you to alight upon such figures as Sir Atholl Oakeley:

> He started wrestling seriously after being beaten up by a gang of louts and built up his body by drinking eleven pints of milk a day for three years. This regimen had been recommended by the giant wrestler Hackenschmidt, who later told Oakeley that the quantity of milk prescribed had been a misprint.

Or Commander David Wemyss, scourge of submarines and connoisseur of siblings:

> In 1924 he married Edith La Touche, the middle one of three sisters. When she died in 1930, he married her elder sister, Avice, and when she died in 1961 he married Lynette, the youngest, who had earlier been bridesmaid to her two elder sisters.

Or John Bindon, a celebrated London villain:

> He was justly famed for a party trick which entailed the balancing of as many as six half-pint mugs on one part of his anatomy. . . . In 1982 he pleaded guilty to using a section of pavement as an offensive weapon against a "short and weedy" young man.

Or the fifth Duke of Portland:

> The staff at Welbeck were instructed to pay him no attention, but to pass him by "as they would a tree." He liked to stay in his bedroom, communicating through a letter-box in the door. Each day he would be posted a roast fowl; His Grace would lunch off one half of the bird and dine off the other.

Or the happily named philologist John Allegro:

> In a series of increasingly fantastical books he claimed that Christianity was a cryptic version of ancient sex-cults inspired by the hallucinogenic mushroom *Amanita muscaria* . . . and that most of [the Bible's] leading characters, including Moses, David, and Jesus, are in fact walking mushrooms.

To which the obituarist adds, "Such theories did not find favour with the academic establishment." As a crowning gag, that is unimprovable: quiet as smoke, and so vastly amused by the histrionics of others that its only option is to take the opposing tone—the starched and undemonstrative—and push it to extremes.

When it comes to the second volume, *Heroes and Adventurers*, such reticence goes beyond politesse, and acquires the flavor of lethal understatement. In an account of Lieutenant-Colonel Charles "The Boss" Tripp, whom the obituarist hails with disarming simplicity as "an altogether exceptional man," there is a passing reference to an encounter between Japanese forces and the 1st Commando Fiji Guerrillas, led by Tripp: "The ensuing conflict included numerous close-quarter fights at night. It was described as 'very personal.' " Tripp was later to call his guerrilla work "the best three years' holiday I ever had, and I got paid for it too." This makes him sound like the bluffest of Englishmen; the chastening fact is that he was a New Zealander. (Australasia also provided the Allies with some of their most skillful airmen; Sir Harold "Mickey" Martin, the acknowledged king of low-flying, once snagged his wing on a German balloon cable, which he eventually cleared "by diving to fifty feet and getting it caught in a tree." And we moan about the traffic.)

There is a simple reason for the presence of these steel-nerved types. Having been born in the first quarter of the century, and having spent many years skirting the Grim Reaper and leaving him thunderstruck and scytheless in their wake, they are finally going to their eternal rest. There are few remaining veterans of the First World War, who are mostly centenarians, and even the stock of those who saw active—and, in many cases, hyperactive—service in the Second is beginning to dwindle. Once it is exhausted, there will be no replenishment, and one shudders to think of those colossi who will bestride an updated *Heroes and Adventurers* in fifty years' time, after leading lives of barely interrupted peace: bungee-jumpers, stuntmen, rap artists, bank tellers who rescued mongrels from storm drains. In short, this is your last chance. Never again will you be introduced to "a well-dined major-general trying to light his cigar with a geranium," or to Keith Elliott, who, with a handful of men, "captured and destroyed five machine-guns, one anti-tank gun, killed a great number of the enemy, and captured 130 prisoners" in the North African desert, and who was ordained an Anglican priest five years later. Here, too, honor is justly paid to Xan Fielding—traveller, writer, fighter, and stalwart of SOE, or Special Operations Executive, which ran high-risk undercover missions in the Second World War. (Its American counterpart was the Office of Strategic Services.) In the helpful words of his *Telegraph* obituarist, "Fielding was the sort of man one would be happy to go into the jungle with":

When Crete fell, Fielding was interviewed in Egypt by SOE. He was asked: "Have you any personal objection to committing a murder?" His response being deemed acceptable, Fielding was put ashore in Crete with a load of weapons and explosives by Cdr "Crap" Miers, VC, skipper of the submarine *Torbay.*

Fielding, who had adopted the style and dress of a Greek highland peasant, was accompanied by a First World War veteran, who was inseparable from his solar topee and unrecognisable as the village schoolmaster he was supposed to impersonate.

What needs to be remembered about such an incident is that if the occupying German troops had seen through the veteran's unconvincing disguise they would have arrested both men as British spies, interrogated them, and most probably shot them. That underlay of seriousness, not to mention the larger strategic contribution of special forces in the Mediterranean, in no way contradicts the breezy near-farce of the telling; if anything, the two are intricately twinned, suggesting that the imminent prospect of losing one's life is, among other things, a matchless education in the art of treating it lightly. It is no insult to the dead, therefore, if we come to find this litany of courage not just inspiring but entertaining. The obvious (and socially sustaining) moral to be drawn from the second *Telegraph* book is that, having absorbed the sacrifices made by previous and better generations, we should lend fresh thought to our own existence and value it more; but we are also left with the sneakier feeling that to value it less—preferably while wearing a false mustache—is a more binding guarantee of good fun.

All of which makes me wonder about the pupils who studied French in the late 1970s at a rowdy London school. Could they possibly have guessed that Harry Rée, the sixty-five-year-old gentleman who was manfully attempting to teach them the future perfect, had a past as pluperfect as this?

Eventually rumbled, Rée hit the German military policeman sent to arrest him over the head with a bottle of Armagnac, but was shot in the process: one bullet penetrated a lung, another grazed his heart. After a twenty-minute struggle during which he bit off the German's nose, Rée escaped. He managed to cross a river and crawl several miles through the countryside to the Swiss border.

There *is* something comic about great lives, but the comedy does not diminish them; on the contrary, we are the ones who feel small. Our age is so resolutely unheroic, and the employment opportunities for registered demigods are now so scarce, that all we can do, in our enfeebled state, is laugh with envy and disbelief at the memory of those who still had the wit and the wherewithal to live large.

There are two objections to the view of the world that is offered by obituaries. The first accusation, which can be levelled not at *The Last Word* but at the three *Telegraph* books, is that they represent political incorrectness gone wild—that they perpetuate such an outlandish and dog-eared imperialism that, for all the incidental delight they provide, the joke is very much on them. Running down the roster of disreputable peers and double-barrelled wastrels, I find it hard to formulate a response to this charge. There is also the long list of men who were seldom, if ever, addressed by their full names, preferring to be called Crap, Rasher, Biffy, Brookie, Dixie, Braces, Weary, Stuffy, Buster, Boney, Blinker, and the unambiguous Monocle. What is it that draws us toward them but one-eyed nostalgia? Why, especially, should readers here feel any fondness for these leathery chaps who fought and played long ago in the name of another nation? The answer can only be that any closed world has its fascinations; the more defining its rhetoric, and the more subtly codified its conduct, the better. If the English can lap up Damon Runyon, then Americans should be suckers for Braces and Rasher.

The other and more incisive complaint levelled against obituaries is that they shrink our experience in the world to a smallness that is close to insulting. When we read, at the end of an obituary, "He was twice a widower, and had no children," we are getting a monstrously distilled version of what most of us, nowadays, would call life. What was the quality of distress that was visited upon the childless couple, or did they fulfill a plan to stay free? We take it for granted that our links with loved ones, and the severing of them, will clutter up our existence and lend it weight, and that our friends, if they talk about us, will talk of little else; so how can an obituary that harps on a few years (sometimes a few *minutes*) of unrepresentative violence be considered the adequate record of a character, let alone of a self?

Well, I suspect that a surprising number of readers will sigh with relief at having discovered that gemlike rarity: the Book Without Relationships. Most current publications, fiction or otherwise, involve nothing *but* relationships, so it is a pleasure to move from that warm emotional bath to the cold plunge of friendship circa 1918, and a certain Billy Stawell: "He met a sportsman by the name of Wingfield who convinced him that any animal, even a bird, was ridable if it was large enough." Stawell subsequently, though briefly, mounted both a bull and an ostrich. Whether Mrs. Stawell ever learned of this is unclear. Equally, we can never know what Billy himself dreamed of on his deathbed. Even as the obituarists sharpened their quills, did he muse on his loving wife and son, or on the refulgent life to come? Or is it just possible that his mind wandered back through the life just gone, and decided that, all things considered, the ostrich ride he took with old "Birdy" Wingfield back in '18 was the happiest moment of them all?

In the final section of *The Waste Land*, Eliot wrote of

> The awful daring of a moment's surrender
> Which an age of prudence can never retract
> By this, and this only, we have existed
> Which is not to be found in our obituaries

Until recently, I always took this truth to be self-evident. Can an obituary, even one that is fully equipped with certifiable fact, be anything other than an assemblage of true lies? Now I'm not so sure. Studying the best obituaries, I get the sense that bursts of awful daring—many of them virtuous, some foolhardy, and all committed in the public eye, though with no eye on public relations—mark precisely those times at which a few fortunate souls most thoroughly and lucidly exist. Of course, there are ill-lit crimes and flushes of shame, not to mention slides into sexual release, that will always go unmentioned by the obituarists, who know their job too well to stray into such ungallant areas; but it is safe to say that a single selfless action—or, indeed, one ridiculous pratfall, or an epiphany born of popcorn—can fix and define a man as honestly as his most scalding love affair. I never had the pleasure, for instance, of meeting the fourth Earl Russell, son of Bertrand Russell, but thanks to his obituary, from which I learned that he once rose to his feet in the House of Lords and confided to "startled" peers that Jimmy Carter and Leonid Brezhnev were one and the same person, I feel that I know the innermost secrets of the man. Visitors to his home were proudly shown a pair of pants hanging from a nail. His Lordship explained that he had crocheted them from string, adding, "I didn't have a pattern. I had to keep trying them on." May he rest in peace.

JULY 27, 1998

PRESTON STURGES

Preston Sturges was born a hundred years ago, on August 29, 1898. It is hard to figure how this important anniversary should be celebrated. In New York, Film Forum has screened a season of his movies, and crowned it by arranging for Eddie Bracken—one of Sturges's favorite leading men, and now a hale seventy-eight—to be interviewed onstage. The Los Angeles County Museum of Art has just finished its own Sturges festival. For movie buffs, then, the angles are pretty well covered. For ordinary and less pallid members of the population, however, the question of the centenary is compounded by a more basic inquiry: Who, exactly, is Preston Sturges?

Well, he was a big fellow with the build of a boxer and a high lock of hair that flopped over his face. It was one of those square, readily amused, and suspiciously reassuring faces that you hardly see in public life anymore; Gable had one, and so did Hemingway. By trade, Sturges was a screenwriter who became a director. To us, that seems old hat, one of the paths by which the ambitious get to run their own show, but back in 1940, when *The Great McGinty* came out, it was very new hat indeed; the opening credits proclaimed "Written and directed by Preston Sturges," and it was the first time in the history of talkies that the two passive verbs had appeared together onscreen. From that conjunction sprang a whole tradition of filmmaking: literate, spiky, defensive, markedly personal, and almost always funny. One cannot say that without his example there would have been no Billy Wilder or Woody Allen, but it was Sturges who made the breakthrough. The fact that all three men use movies to caution us against the perils of overestimating human nature is, needless to say, sheer coincidence.

In the course of an eight-year spree, Sturges directed eleven features; in the first five years, he set off one of the most deafening fusillades that moviegoers have ever had to face. *The Great McGinty* and *Christmas in July* came out in 1940, *The Lady Eve* in 1941, *Sullivan's Travels* and *The Palm Beach Story* the year after that, and *The Miracle of Morgan's Creek* and *Hail the Conquering Hero* in 1944. These works occupy a curious position in the pantheon of cinema, if there is such a place. To anyone who knows his movies, they are not just entertaining; they are so obviously entertaining that only some vast, subterranean conspiracy can have stopped them from becoming as undyingly popular as *Some Like It Hot* or *Diner*, or any of the other standbys that everyone has on video, and that are ideally watched on damp Sunday nights with a tub of Chunky Monkey. But the Sturges canon remains stubbornly half known; there are plenty of people who enjoy *The Lady Eve* without even realizing who made it.

Sturges's film stars Henry Fonda as Charles (Hopsie to his friends), a stiff-spined millionaire who fears women and collects snakes, and tries not to confuse the two. On board ship, Jean (Barbara Stanwyck), a professional cardsharp, slithers into his life and coils herself around his cash. The joke is that, against the form book, she finds herself falling for the sap. He discovers her true calling and spurns her, whereupon she retires hurt. Later, she returns to the fray, disguised as an English aristocrat named Eve, and humiliates Hopsie to such an excruciating extreme that, after a further switch of identity, she has no option but to fall for him all over again, and he for her. Put like that, it sounds muddled, not to say harebrained, but *The Lady Eve* is a model of clarity. What it happens to clarify is that people are liable to mislay their hearts as easily as their wallets, and—just in case you are tempted to construe such a loss as romantic—that both can be swiftly retrieved.

At one deep-breathing moment ("She fools with his ear," say the stage directions), Jean cuddles up to Charles and talks about her ideal man: "He's a little short guy with lots of money."

CHARLES: I shouldn't think that kind of ideal was so difficult to find.

JEAN: Oh, he isn't. . . . That's why he's my ideal . . . what's the sense of having one if you can't ever find him? Mine is a practical ideal you can find two or three of in every barber shop . . . getting the works.

CHARLES: Why don't you marry one of them?

JEAN *(almost indignantly):* Why should I marry anybody that looked like that?

And there, in a tough nutshell, you have Preston Sturges. Scenes like this are signed with his own verbal flourish, as easily recognized as a spat between Laurel and Hardy. It isn't just the way the lines knock back and forth, with each competitor trying to read the other's spin, or even Jean's mastery of the demotic, with its patina of homely detail. What singles it out as Sturges talk is the bewildering balance: on the one hand, a chin-up, all-American assumption that dreams are right there within reach, like apples; on the other, a slightly alien cynicism toward such rosiness, and a heavy hint that the fruit, once tasted, may prove not to have been worth the plucking. Capra comedies dwell on the gentle irony that the perfection you seek may have been sitting in your own home all along—and *that*, Sturges would contend, is the problem with perfection. His movies remain a bracing tonic against the sentimental; most of them were lapped up by audiences in the 1940s, yet modern viewers, unschooled in the lean lessons of the Depression, are more wary of such knowledgeable comedy, as if it cut too close to the bone.

The nearest relative of *The Lady Eve* is *Bringing Up Baby*, Howard Hawks's frontline report from the sex war. A number of props, narrative and physical, appear in both films: a large inheritance, a heroine who breaks a heel, a menace from the animal kingdom, desecrated evening wear, and, above all, a central clash between what Henry Adams used to call the virgin and the dynamo. This being screwball, of course, the virgin is a guy: tall, dark, handsome, and freeze-dried from the waist down. Fonda and Cary Grant are barely masculine until they mate with their respective predators—Stanwyck and Katharine Hepburn. Watch these two masterpieces side by side, and you feel that Hawks is summoning a dark fantasia, in which his creatures are touched (as if by a capricious moon) into the lunacy of love, whereas *The Lady Eve* is, even in its peaceable moments, knockabout stuff: like the rest of Sturges's movies, it acts on the assumption that people, as much as the objects around them, make excellent ninepins. Here is my rough list, in no particular order, of the things that Sturges found amusing:

1. Money.
2. Alcohol.
3. What you do with No. 1 when No. 2 gets hold of you.
4. And vice versa.
5. Running.
6. Falling over.
7. Fat people.
8. People in fancy clothes.
9. People who talk funny.
10. Politicians who get away with it.
11. Politicians who don't.
12. Prigs.

13. Patsies.
14. Coffee.
15. Marriage.
16. Gambling. (Note: Try not to confuse this with No. 15.)
17. Misunderstandings. (Note: Ditto.)
18. Mussolini.
19. Hitler.
20. A lion with its head in your lap.

Fired together, the prejudices of Preston Sturges constitute a broadside against the blandishments of an orderly life. It may be some comfort to learn that he practiced what he preached.

Sturges was born in Chicago, although, true to form, even his beginnings were misleading. He was christened Edmund Preston Biden. "Mr. Biden never sounded like much of a husband to me," Sturges wrote in his autobiography, "but it must be remembered that he was one of Mother's very first ones, and, like the celebrated Mrs. Simpson, she did better later." The marriage soon ended, and in 1901 his mother got married again—this time to a stockbroker called Solomon Sturges. One night in Illinois, when the boy was about eight, his parents woke him up and announced their separation. His mother asked which parent Preston would like to live with.

"I adored this big man," Sturges wrote. "The perfume of my father, a mixture of maleness and the best Havana cigars, was the breath of Araby to me. So without any hesitation at all I said, 'I want to stay here with Father.'

"And he said, 'I am not your father.' "

Whether the tale is true is beside the point. Sturges's memoirs—unfinished at his death, and smoothed into shape by his widow, Sandy—are so expert at socking us over the head with tall stories that to query their authenticity feels like an insult to the broad, boulevardier air with which Sturges passes himself off as a man of the world. No gust of bluffness, however, can disguise the fact that his films are peopled, to an alarming degree, by families that don't add up, and by couples who click together and then come apart like toys. The hero of *The Great McGinty* marries his secretary (who already has children of her own) purely because, as an aspirant political thug, he needs a mate. More startling is *The Palm Beach Story*, in which Claudette Colbert runs out on her husband (Joel McCrea) even though her toes go all funny whenever he kisses her; she simply needs more money in her life, and that means somebody else.

The movie starts and ends with the curlicued words "And they lived happily ever after" filling the screen, followed at once by the jaunty rider *"Or did they?"* At no point in a Sturges comedy does a happy family sit around being a happy family; you could read that as a psychotic reaction to his own precarious parentage, but I prefer to think that Sturges was so taken by the drama of his origins that he chose to milk it dry.

Mother and son were photographed together, rapturously manless, in 1899. She has a hand on her cocked hip, while Preston pulls her close; they grin and jut their matching chins, as if they had just signed a deal to map out the future of this one-year-old. When he grew up and wrote movies, he could barely stop himself from inventing characters whose prime desire was, in turn, to reinvent themselves, if necessary by pretending to be someone else. Whenever his plots needed a kick in the pants, Sturges could refer to the memory of his mother. Born Mary Dempsey, she considered the name cheap and became Mary d'Este Dempsey, in an effort, unusual among Chicago Catholics, to join the ranks of the Italian aristocracy. Later, she metamorphosed into Mary Desti and, lastly, into Madame Desti, which may have the aroma of a Coney Island palm reader but stood her in good stead when she grandly set up her own perfumery in Paris.

The main thing to know about Preston Sturges's mother is that she was best buddies with Isadora Duncan. She even gave Isadora the scarf that caught in the wheel of a car and snapped the famous neck. "When I look back over what I was exposed to as a child, I realize how extraordinarily lucky I was never to have become a (God forbid) male interpretive dancer with a wreath of gold laurel leaves around my head," Sturges wrote. It was not the most conventional of upbringings. Like a one-person demonstration of the complete works of Henry James, Sturges split his years, and his youthful consciousness, between Europe and America. Within a few pages, his memoirs lurch from sentences such as "Father is taking me to see Buffalo Bill and his Wonderful Wild West Show in the old Madison Square Garden" to a gruesome Wagnerfest in Bayreuth: "We also graced the lap of Frau Cosima, and the tenor Burgstaller's lap, and Humperdinck's lap, and Frau Thode's lap, and the laps of the King and Queen of Württemberg, and that of the Ab-Princess of Meiningen, the Kaiser's sister." If you ever wanted to know why Preston Sturges crammed his movies with folks named Bildocker, Hackensacker, Diddlebock, and Waggleberry, not to mention the beauteous Trudy Kockenlocker, there's your answer.

In 1944, James Agee wrote a fine essay, much mulled over by Sturges fans, on the divided soul of the director's films, which he described as "uncontrollably, almost proudly corrupt, vengeful, fearful of intactness and self-commitment . . . their mastering object, aside from success, seems to be to sail as steep into the wind as possible without for an instant incurring the disaster of becoming seriously, wholly acceptable as art. They seem to me, indeed, in much of their twisting, the elaborately counterpointed image of a neurosis." Agee makes you peer through Sturges's movies to the background beyond—to the steadying ethic of his stepfather and the dizzying pull of his mother, to the crazy conflict between Buffalo Bill and Bayreuth. Still, I don't understand why this should be plunged to the level of the neurotic; it is, after all, more than possible to lead—even to luxuriate in—a life of contradictions while retaining one's sanity, and anyone who isn't turned on by the sight of art sharing a bed with business shouldn't go into pictures. If you follow through the logic of Agee's claim, the Hollywood of the thirties and forties should have been so jagged with schizophrenia that nothing of value could conceivably have emerged. The fuel that drove Sturges was pretty much the mixture that swilled around inside Wilder and Lubitsch—a drop more Feydeau and a little less Schnitzler, presumably, but otherwise the same. When William Wyler (born in Alsace) and Sturges met at Universal in the thirties, they spoke in French.

It is true that Sturges wastes no opportunity, in his memoirs, to trash what he calls the "mandatory dose of exposure to great minds," but you can't sneer at the "allegedly hilarious comedies" of Molière without betraying the embarrassing fact that you are *au fait* with Molière. Men like Sturges, the sporty types who can read without moving their lips, have always played down the number of hours that they rack up in the library; how else can they expect to get the girls? The life of young Preston, as recounted by his biographers—among them James Curtis, Donald Spoto, and, the best and most recent, Diane Jacobs—seems to have covered an exhausting amount of ground. Educated in Paris and Lausanne, he was dispatched at fifteen to run a branch of Maison Desti at Deauville. With the outbreak of the First World War, he returned to America and another branch of the business; New Yorkers, like Parisians, flocked to buy his mother's celebrated Youth Lotion. (In Paris, home to every vice, it had been labelled Secret of the Harem.) Sturges went, in his own words, "*every* place: George Rector's, the Midnight Frolic over the Ziegfeld Follies, the Biltmore Roof, Delmonico's, Reisenweber's, Shanley's, and my favorite place of all, the Knickerbocker Grill." He joined the military, learned to fly (too late to see action), left as a second lieutenant in the Aviation Section of the Signal Corps, returned to New York, and invented the kissproof lipstick—Desti's Red Red Rouge.

This kind of life can easily continue, with minor detours, to the grave:

the wealthy swell has half a job, too much fun, too many lovers, and the occasional brainstorm—Sturges, according to Diane Jacobs, came up with an idea for "bottling concentrated clam broth as a cocktail drink and calling it 'Pepoclam.' " He fell in love with a married woman named Estelle Godfrey, who, after her divorce, became the first of his four wives. (The second was Eleanor Hutton, the breakfast-cereal heiress.) So what turned the listless Preston Sturges into a hectically industrious writer? Who threw the switch? By his own account, it was a burst appendix at Christmas, 1927; he scraped close enough to death to crank up his life again. That sounds pat, but the fact remains that on July 13 of the following year his first play, *The Guinea Pig*, opened at the Wharf Theatre, in Provincetown. His second, *Strictly Dishonorable*, ran for more than five hundred performances at the Avon, in New York; by 1929, he was tinkering with movie scripts, and three years later he left for California. In 1933, he delivered *The Power and the Glory* to Jesse Lasky, a producer at Fox. Lasky had asked for a treatment, but Sturges had refused. Instead, he simply sent the final shooting script, which caused no end of consternation. It was word-perfect. "Imagine a producer accepting a script from an author and not being able to make *one change*," Lasky said. The film practically made itself, and Sturges collared a percentage of the gross.

By now, he was flying up the ladder, and the next rung was obvious. He wanted to direct his own movie, but nobody else at Paramount, where he arrived in 1936, was so enthusiastic. In recognition of the risk, he agreed to accept a one-dollar fee for his pains; this was later upped to a munificent ten bucks, for which Paramount got *The Great McGinty*. McGinty is a bum who impresses the local boss by voting for him thirty-seven times in one evening; from there he ascends with Sturges-like ease and ends up governing the state; you could call it *Mr. Smith Screws Washington*. Whether the Academy noticed this outrage is uncertain, but it gave Sturges an Oscar for Best Original Screenplay—the first such award. Never a man to let the moment subside, he promptly opened the Players, a three-story restaurant on Sunset Boulevard, across from the Chateau Marmont. It had a drive-in at the bottom and a tony French restaurant on the top; it boasted good bouillabaisse and a revolving bandstand. Sturges would make movies all day and then hit his own joint in the evening, hanging out with big names into the small hours. He had a new wife, the smart and luscious Louise Tevis. It is hard to imagine a time when Hollywood was more tightly packed with talent, or more redolent of fun. The life of Preston Sturges was going nicely. It was even better than Pepoclam.

* * *

The films that Sturges made in the ensuing years are as classy as the milieux through which he strolled. Yet they are also roaringly unsnobbish; to Preston Sturges, the crucial thing about the class structure is not that it is morally offensive or, from the reactionary standpoint, a guarantee of social cohesion but precisely that it is a structure. You can clamber up and down it like a monkey in the rigging. "Don't I *look* like a picture director?" asks the imprisoned hero of *Sullivan's Travels.* "To me you look kinda more like a soda jerk," says the fellow-inmate by his side. What emerges from that movie is the unadorned proposition that poverty is no picnic, though it can have its dignities, and that wealth is delicious, though it can rot the brain. The most compelling shots in the film are those of faces: whether we gaze at Veronica Lake, with her filthy little smile and that waterfall of hair, or at the toothless mug of a hobo, we are seeing them through the eyes—or the camera—of a man who was obsessed by what damage, or what favors, the farce of fortune could do to the human expression. Sturges kept a company of stock actors, some of them relicts of the stage or of silent movies, who crop up like faithful hounds in one film after another. It hoists your spirits just to see them: the lisping and lubricious Franklin Pangborn, the Jeevesian Robert Greig, the flustered fidget Jimmy Conlin, and William Demarest, the two-legged bulldog. Who in Hollywood these days is interested in the elderly or the corpulent, or in the radical possibility that age makes us not sadder but more comic—brimming with the sour yeast of a silly world?

It is worth stressing the visual habits of Sturges the director because it is all too easy to be overwhelmed by Sturges the writer. No one has ever written better for the movies, but Sturges wanted his words to earn their keep, and that's why he had to direct. His educated fondness for the florid, and for the tumble that it takes when it bumps into slang, was there from his earliest stage plays, but onscreen it acquired a newly minted strangeness, as if there were secret rituals going on that the audience could only guess at. One of his later pictures, *The Sin of Harold Diddlebock*—made after Sturges had quit Paramount, in 1943, and teamed up with Howard Hughes—is a mixed bag, but it does sport one scene that rings with the old joy. Diddlebock (a born-again Harold Lloyd) is a teetotal clerk who loses his job, goes to a bar, and orders the first drink of his life. "You arouse the artist in me," declares the barman, scorning the suggestion of a Texas Tornado. "A Tornado is a perfectly reliable commercial drink," he says, "but *this* . . . this is almost . . . is the word *vestal*?" Well, if it wasn't the word before, it is now. Funnier if you did Latin in school, of course, but that's Sturges for you.

In my favorite part of my favorite Sturges film, *The Palm Beach Story*, the lines of dialogue come close to cracking up entirely. Claudette Colbert is fleeing New York for Florida, by railroad; she hitches a ride as the mascot of the Ale and Quail Club, a collection of dubious gentlemen whose idea of a quiet evening is to get out their shotguns, load, and tell the steward to throw crackers into the air, so they have something to aim at. If this is what James Agee meant by "fearful of intactness," I can't get enough of it. The club comes to sing good night to Colbert, who takes refuge in another berth, treading twice on Rudy Vallee's pince-nez as she climbs up. (Shades of *Some Like It Hot* and *Twentieth Century:* when train travel lapsed in America, something died in the national sense of humor.) And so the plot sprints on, as if to prove that when people talk about breakneck farce they mean it. Some viewers find Sturges's love of slapstick both juvenile and evasive, but its chronic intrusion is *meant* to disrupt the flow; I come away from *The Palm Beach Story* (whose Thurberish working titles were *Is That Bad?* and *Is Marriage Necessary?*) with the sense that nothing is to be trusted. The sole exception is sex, which is invariably the safest bet; as Colbert remarks, "You have no idea what a long-legged gal can do without doing anything."

Sturges made some of the best sex movies of all time, although practically no sex is on show. Even now, his gift for innuendo—and his ability to sneak all manner of dirt under the nose of a sniffy censor—is enough to snap your elastic. Size doesn't matter. There is the small innuendo, as when Henry Fonda invites Barbara Stanwyck into his cabin to inspect his snake. "Would you care to come in and see Emma?" he asks. "That's a new one, isn't it?" replies the dame. And there is the grand, slow-burning innuendo: the whole plot of *The Miracle of Morgan's Creek*, for instance, which finds Betty Hutton not only married to a man she can't recall but pregnant with six children after a night on the tiles with soldiers bound for war. The title points politely to an immaculate conception, but the awful likelihood that apple-pie Betty was cored and peeled more than was strictly good for her is not, I feel, a scenario that Sturges would have rejected outright. "You never think of anything but Topic A, do you?" Joel McCrea asks Mary Astor, in *The Palm Beach Story*. She replies, "Is there anything else?" In a letter, Sturges called sex "the Man Act," although if his movies bequeath us anything it is a stern belief that women belong on top. His men are more like Evelyn Waugh heroes: decent sorts, more often than not, on whom Fate, in a pair of high heels, likes to rehearse its fancy moves.

In the end, Fate got around to Sturges himself. By 1948, he was nearing the end of the ride. He made the sinister *Unfaithfully Yours*, with Rex Harrison, tried dinner theatre at the Players and writing for television, stumbled heavily into debt, and moved back to France. His own movies had laid bare the trickeries of luck: "It is quite natural for the dice to roll differently for a while," he wrote to Jimmy Conlin. Happily, his fourth and final marriage, to Sandy Nagle, was a double six. Sturges was miserable without her when, in 1958, he was summoned back to New York with an offer of work. He was sixty now, but as poor and hungry as a new kid in town: according to Diane Jacobs, he would deliberately choose bars where you got free dips and crackers with your drink. He died sad and gassy and alone, in the Algonquin Hotel, after too much coleslaw and beer.

Or did he? Certainly Sturges boarded the great sleeping car in the sky on August 6, 1959, but it is difficult to pin loneliness on a man who strained every muscle to push so many people, of all shapes and sizes, onto a movie screen. Sturges once went mad for a book called *Two Lifetimes in One: How Never to Be Tired*, and his work stands halfway between a bachelor party and a compression chamber, with all the lifetimes of his tireless characters rolled into one. Some critics find him hysterical, and his comedies may never be loved because they themselves find so little to love in the throng that they survey; but they are far more tolerant than cruel, and nobody of Sturges's learning and libido could consider it either his right or his duty to stitch together a world that is bursting at the seams. He is forever disdaining the sonorous call of solemnity, as if to tamp down any private yearning to answer it: "There's nothing like a deep-dish movie to drive you out in the open," in the words of *Sullivan's Travels.* But Sturges had nothing to apologize for: he saw life unsteadily and saw it whole, and that may be the deepest dish of all.

SEPTEMBER 14, 1998

ROBERT BRESSON

Who's afraid of Robert Bresson? Me, for a start. There are movie directors who are monsters on the set, and others who reserve their terrorizing for the screen. But Bresson is something else. He has made no scary movies; indeed, he might well consider the notion of a horror film to be beneath his consideration. Little is known of him personally, and even less is reported. One actress who worked closely with him described him as "implacable." Yet there is something about the very *idea* of Bresson that afflicts his admirers with a kind of dry-throated awe and his detractors with snorts of dismay. It's not that I don't look forward to a Bresson picture; it's just that as I shuffle into the theatre I feel like a pupil approaching the principal's door, wondering what crimes I may have committed and how I must answer for them.

In short, I feel like a character in Bresson. In the 1950s—the high-water mark of Bresson, the period of *Pickpocket*, *A Man Escaped*, and *Diary of a Country Priest*—moviegoers came to recognize the typical bearing of the Bresson hero, with his air of demure devastation. Like Raskolnikov in *Crime and Punishment*, Bresson's pickpocket lives alone. He endures difficult relations with his mother and scarcely knows how to respond to the tender advances of a young woman, and he seems to come alive only when his misdemeanors begin to obsess him. As he rehearses his moves with a friend, the camera cuts from lapel to button to a wallet dropped sweetly into a palm, while baroque music sings out on the soundtrack. If you had read your Dostoyevsky, the sight of this was not, perhaps, too traumatic, but it would be fair to say that neither here nor in Europe had ordinary viewers ever seen anything like it—nor, as it turned out, would they see anything like it again. Filmmakers remember Bresson by heart, and plunder him at will; few of us who watched *American Gigolo* realized that the closing sequence, with Lauren Hutton making eyes at Richard Gere, was a passionate homage to *Pickpocket.* But the age of Bresson himself, and of Bergman and Fellini in their prime—the age of moviegoing as a hallowed and improving habit—now feels more distant than the Berlin of Brecht and Weill.

Your chance to revisit history, and to wallow in the human condition, gets a big push this month when the Museum of Modern Art unveils a retrospective of Bresson's work. Since he has made a mere fourteen films, of which only one lasts more than a hundred minutes, you could sit down and run through the whole corpus in about twenty hours, with an eleven-minute break for lunch.

Bresson himself will not be attending. He is still alive, living an hour or so outside Paris with his second wife, Mylène. These days, he gives no interviews in person, and does not care to be photographed—a pity, for the few images that exist show a face that one would like to see more of. (That may sound prurient, but his own movies have taught us that it's never rude to stare.) The French cover of Bresson's book of aphorisms, *Notes on Cinematography,* shows a full lip, a fuller shock of hair, and eyes that turn down at the corners, as if the lids had, over a lifetime, drooped in sadness. The mixture of sensuality and disillusionment comes as no surprise; what takes you aback is the note of merriment tucked away in his steady gaze.

Robert Bresson was born in 1901. Or 1907. Or was it 1911? Bresson himself is unforthcoming on the matter. He studied classics and philosophy, and then decided to become a painter. That plan fell slowly away, to be replaced by a dedication to cinema. The funny thing is that his own debut was a comedy. For many years, *Public Affairs* (1934) was missing in action, presumed lost; then, in 1987, a substantial chunk was dug up at the Cinémathèque in Paris. The picture was described by its director as "*un comique fou,*" full of chorus lines, sinking ships, and yawning statues. It is set in an imaginary kingdom, like the Freedonia in which the Marx Brothers cut loose, and one is tempted to speculate that Bresson was using *Public Affairs* to flush all traces of frivolity out of his system. From here on, he would go private.

From 1940 to 1941, Bresson spent some nine months as a prisoner of war in Germany. He returned to France and made his first two full-length films: *Angels of Sin* (1943), which is set in a convent, and *The Ladies of the Bois de Boulogne* (1945), which would also be set in a convent if the characters knew what was good for them. *The Ladies* was poorly received at the time, but its classic status is now as solid as that of Cocteau's *Beauty and the Beast* or *Orphée.* Indeed, it was Cocteau who wrote the dialogue. In a sense, he had little to do; the film is adapted from an episode in Diderot's

Jacques the Fatalist, and some of the lines were transplanted with barely a scratch. But Diderot, ever the game player, kept interrupting his tale with boozy backchat; Cocteau and Bresson strip it down and leave us with the stony bones of the plot. A wealthy woman takes revenge on her lover, who has announced that his feelings for her have grown cold. Feigning a civilized friendship, she introduces him to a young ingenue, and only when the match is made and the wedding ceremony over does she reveal that he has ended up with damaged goods: the ingenue used to be a nightclub dancer, with a flurry of eager men at her bedroom door. In Diderot, the man forgives his wife, and they live happily ever after. In Bresson, she drops into a major swoon; whether this is death by shame or a touch of the vapors we cannot tell.

The story was a bit rich in the eighteenth century; by the time it hits modern Paris the whole thing should collapse under the weight of absurdity. Who gives a damn about the past of a loved one? But Bresson, with a deftness that would mark the remainder of his career, outwitted plausibility to arrive at a dream logic of his own. None of his movies could be called fantastical, not even *Lancelot of the Lake* (1974), which began with knights cantering through leafy Arthurian glades. Yet his entire oeuvre seems to move—to glide rather than labor—under a nameless spell, as if he had hypnotized his players before the cameras rolled. Cocteau, the addict of myth and fairy tale, helped to breed in Bresson a fascination with what is bound to happen—with acts for which we alone are responsible but which somehow remain beyond our control, and even beyond the grope of our understanding. By the time Bresson had finished with them, of course, they no longer looked like fairy tales; they looked like acts of God.

This is where Bresson, for many moviegoers, starts to get out of hand. He was a Catholic by birth, although he is since said to have labelled himself "a Christian atheist." To complicate matters further, the views that are most frequently ascribed to his work are Jansenist. Named after a seventeenth-century bishop of Ypres and condemned as heretical by the pope, Jansenism cleaved to a peculiarly bleak reading of human experience and its attendant follies; the only possibility of redemption lay in the mystery of God's grace. The most famous adherent of this mirthless creed was Pascal, although his worldliness made him, perhaps, less a convert than an interested party; his *Pensées* are twice quoted in *Notes on Cinematography*, and Bresson's 1950 movie, *Diary of a Country Priest*, which followed its lonely central figure through the agonies of stomach cancer, closed with the image of a cross and the murmured words "All is grace." Nine years later, *Pickpocket* ended with the shamed hero pressing against his girlfriend through prison bars and saying, "In order to reach you . . . what a strange way I had to take." Over the years, Bresson also planned a life of St. Ignatius of Loyola and an adaptation of the Book of Genesis, but neither was ever made.

The crucial thing, at this point, is to hold your nerve. The fact that Susan Sontag wrote an essay entitled "Spiritual Style in the Films of Robert Bresson" is no reason you shouldn't take a date to see *Pickpocket* at MoMA. At most, the film is what, following St. Ignatius, you might call a spiritual exercise; it is bracing stuff, and there are moments that are not simply exciting but engineer the excitement so beautifully that you feel like laughing with glee. The sequence that shows a trio of pickpockets working a rail station—brazenly plucking a woman's clutch bag, say, as she tucks it under her arm, and replacing it with a folded newspaper—is seamless enough to make you leave the theatre and turn immediately to a life of crime. This is not exactly what Pascal had in mind.

Rising from the works of Bresson, in fact, is the heartening suggestion that within the ranks of human venality crime is not much to write home about. There are sins more acute than filching a handbag, and more damnable even than murder; the mercy of the divine, for instance, is unlikely to descend upon those who are consumed with self-love. Given that film stars take their vanity freshly squeezed for breakfast, it is hard to see how Bresson could bring himself to work with them; in the most audacious move of his professional life, he solved this quandary by phasing out fellow-professionals altogether. No stars, no performers of any kind: in *Notes on Cinematography* Bresson even disdains the word "actor," preferring "model," as if he were a painter. "Most films appear to me as competitions in grimaces," he once said, and so, starting with *Diary of a Country Priest*, he hired a succession of gaunt, malnourished, non-grimacing nobodies to carry his movies. Each of them threatens to become a bore, and yet their pale, morose expressions grow on you, like the unsmiling faces of saints in Sienese paintings.

All this—the austere Bresson method, and the stunned but purposeful behavior of his protagonists—could have remained at the level of an intriguing experiment. He could have been a footnote in the history of cinema; instead, he became a headline, and what made the difference was a 1956 film called *A Man Escaped*, or, in its full and catchy French title, *Un Condamné à Mort S'est Échappé, ou Le Vent Souffle Où Il Veut*. That gives away the plot: we know from the opening credits that the imprisoned Fontaine—based on a wartime member of the French Resistance, and played by a Sorbonne philosophy student called François Leterrier—will succeed in his jailbreak. Such knowledge should render the action superfluous; instead, it frees Bresson up to insist upon the intricacies of liberation—to fix our gaze upon the hero as he sharpens the handle of a spoon into a makeshift chisel. The movie redefines suspense: the traditional question of whether something will or will not happen becomes infinitely less tense than the urge to discover *how* it comes about. If you have a taste for religious allegory, *A Man Escaped* can be viewed as an allegory of the soul's glorious flight from the body—or, better still, as a shapely dramatization of the ancient contest between predestination and free will. Fontaine is one of the chosen, but only the momentum of his own courage will earn him the benison of grace.

These pressing metaphysical matters hang around at the back of what is, by any reckoning, a great adventure story. Only thus can you account for the sheer, startling jubilation of the film's climax; people came out of *The Shawshank Redemption* looking satisfied, but I have seen them leave *A Man Escaped* as if they were walking on air—as if they had just scaled a couple of walls themselves. This reaction is all the odder because the film itself is a model of hushed restraint; Bresson has always been the master of ellipsis, but here he surpassed himself, with a flurry of quick, grave scenes that gently bounce the action on its way. Why the result should be all serenity and no haste is, frankly, beyond my comprehension, although I suspect that Mozart was a big help. Only one piece of music is used, a snatch of the Kyrie from the Mass in C Minor, and Bresson plays it at least seven times, most movingly when the men are emptying their slop pails in the prison yard. With its sacramental air, this sequence is the opposite of those endless shots in *Death in Venice* when Visconti forcibly sank us in a lagoon of Mahler's Fifth; he was covering his options, making the loveliness of the Lido lovelier still, whereas Bresson crisply conscripts a few phrases of Mozart to convince us that transcendence is available to even the most sordid of human acts. We are all in the shit, but some of us are looking at the stars.

If Bresson's taste in music is impeccable—the films resound not just with Mozart but with Lully, Bach, Schubert, and Monteverdi—it's nothing compared with his taste in silence. He once noted, with approval, Debussy's habit of playing the piano with the lid down. To anyone who staggered out of *Titanic* with busted eardrums, the Bresson season should come as a blessed relief. You leave his movies with senses peeled, your memory jangling with the keys that the Nazi guard rattles against the bannisters in *A Man Escaped* and with the harsh raking of the gravel in *Diary of a Country Priest*. The residue of those pictures, and of the three that followed *Pickpocket*—*The Trial of Joan of Arc* (1962), *Au Hasard Balthazar* (1966), and *Mouchette* (1967)—is a sense that the world revolves in an ominous quiet, and that we should prick up our ears, like dogs, to every rustle and scrape. There are countless books and articles linking Bresson to other directors of noted solemnity, but the man whom he most reminds me of is Jacques Tati. The trembling peace that envelops Monsieur Hulot has the same dire vulnerability as the hush in which Bresson's pickpocket reaches behind him for a wad of banknotes, or in which Mouchette, a teenage girl, rolls repeatedly down a riverbank. Tati punctures the silence with the *pock* of a tennis ball or the infuriating *boing* of a swing door, whereas Bresson appalls us with the offscreen splash of the girl who drowns, but the cloistral suspense is the same.

Maybe that is why the hero of *Au Hasard Balthazar* is a long-suffering donkey (in Bresson's eyes, presumably, the ideal performer). I admire the Bresson pictures of the sixties, but they are stringently unlovable works; at some point, Bresson's fondness for people who were both besieged and defiant subsided into a despairing predilection for pure victims. I wonder whether this was a straightforward issue of history: the further the Second World War receded into the distance, the sadder and more stranded Bresson's characters became. The fact is that he was a prisoner of war and then an inhabitant of Occupied France, and his best films are soaked through with the combative dread of those years. The nuns in *Angels of Sin* unwittingly conceal a killer in their midst, and the vengeful heroine of *The Ladies of the Bois de Boulogne* mocks the newly besotted lover with the line "So you spend your life waiting on stairs, in grottoes, at railway stations. . . ." He could be a member of the Resistance on the run. The whole movie, with its rapid changes of apartment and identity, and with its collars turned up against the rain, lends a thrilling furtiveness to the pursuit of love. For some twenty years, while the war was fresh in his mind, that fretting persisted; I smell fear even in *Diary of a Country Priest*. We watch the priest writing his journal and simultaneously hear his voice reading it—a strange doubling effect, as if he were huddling close to his own secrets, not wanting them to be glimpsed by God, or by someone worse.

Little of that consternation survives in the later films. They seem so sure of catastrophe that the possibility of eluding it, let alone fighting it off, hardly seems to arise. Sontag, in her acute 1964 essay on Bresson, wrote that "it is almost impossible to imagine a Bresson film in color." Five years later, we got a Bresson film in color. In all, we got *five* of them: *A Gentle Woman* (1969), *Four Nights of a Dreamer* (1971), *Lancelot of the*

Lake (1974), *The Devil Probably* (1977), and *Money* (1983). If you like to think that color means mellowing, think again: most of these movies are as hard as ice. Three of them are obsessed with suicide, and the two others concern multiple slaughter. Bresson retreats in part from his reliance on nonprofessionals—*A Gentle Woman* features the screen debut of Dominique Sanda—but there is no letup in the haunted automatism of the performances, and some of the line readings in *Four Nights of a Dreamer* sound as if they came from beyond the grave. It is touching to watch Bresson coming to grips with the modern world; there are hippies here, and sing-alongs by the banks of the Seine, and even a heroin junkie. But group behavior is not Bresson's forte; American audiences, weaned on Brando, were never going to be impressed by the weedy gang of bikers who menaced Mouchette, and I cannot watch these pictures of the seventies without feeling nostalgic for the glumly beatific loners of the fifties.

On the other hand, there is *Money*—the best film ever made by a senior citizen, not least because it has all the sprightly economy of youth. Adapted from a Tolstoy tale, *The Forged Coupon*, and set in present-day Paris, it centers on a counterfeit banknote that changes hands and besmirches all that it touches. One young man begins the film with a job, a wife, and a child, and ends it as a murderer. No one is spared the axe in this picture; like Flaubert or Maupassant, Bresson takes a clean swing at an entire society. And yet the film is not a downer; you feel spruced and vivified by the miraculous distilling of the narration and by the possibility that the sinner, in his last days and hours, has met with saintliness face to face. What is more, *Money* is a kind of ghost story: Bresson's patient camera treats the components of the visible world as if they were possessed. The wretched banknote itself, of course, crackles with the hint of evil, but the menace spreads—to a telephone that is crouched and ready to ring, to a food ladle that would make a useful weapon, and to the small shriek of a mug being scraped across the floor. Only a European, perhaps, could have arrived so naturally at this surreal reversal: men are dead souls, but the stuff that surrounds them is alive.

For many moviegoers, needless to say, Bresson's late masterpiece will confirm their worst fears. To American eyes, he is easily cast not just as a purveyor of hard-core art movies but as a parody of the type—dark, difficult, allergic to pleasure, and stubbornly Eurocentric. The roster of authors whom he has brought to the screen is unrepentantly highbrow, although one could argue that it demonstrates the perfect pitch of his taste: Diderot, Georges Bernanos, Tolstoy, and, time and again, Dostoyevsky. I count myself an ardent Bresson supporter, but even I laughed out loud when, cruising the aisles at Tower Video on Broadway, I found a tape of *Mouchette* and read this on the back of the box:

> Mouchette, a sensitive 14-year-old, lives amidst the peasant squalor of an isolated rural community. Her alcoholic father and terminally ill mother all but abandon her to become a child of the streets. Not surprisingly, her fate is sealed when she is abducted and raped by a half-witted game poacher.

That "not surprisingly" is a stroke of genius. Whoever wrote it was attuned to the doomy expectations of art-house fans, who would, one imagines, applaud Bresson's declaration that "there is nothing more stupid, more vulgar, than working for an audience." At his best, however, Bresson is anything but hostile; he has a matchless ability to work *with* an audience, and to wrap us in the skin of a film. His great achievement, in *A Man Escaped* and elsewhere, is to tear at the wall that exists between art cinema and commercial movies: there is nothing more visceral, even in Hitchcock, than Fontaine's lunge for freedom, just as there are moments in Hitchcock—or in Fred Astaire, for that matter—that provide exactly the perverse, half-dreamed, faintly cruel suspension of the ordinary which, for better or worse, we associate with the art house. Worshippers of Bresson, who use his work as a stick to punish lesser pictures, should be referred to an interview he gave in 1965, in which he rhapsodized over a single shot from *Goldfinger*. Contrary to his reputation, Bresson does not set his heart, or bang his head, against the joys of existence; he merely points out that they can be ferociously hard to come by, and all too easy to lose. More than ever, we need movies to remind us that life is not just a cabaret but a crucible. Robert Bresson made it his business to look coolly on the heat of the moment, and, if he has really given us his last movie, who will take up the burden of that task?

JANUARY 25, 1999

ERNEST SHACKLETON

If you happen to find yourself on the Upper West Side this month with an hour to kill, you should go and see a boat. She is called the *James Caird*, and she was built in 1914 of Baltic pine, American elm, and British oak—an unimprovably diplomatic combination. She measures twenty-three feet four inches from bow to stern and six feet nine inches across, and, believe me, the more you know about her the smaller that seems. The best way to describe her, perhaps, and the reason that she is now being accorded such glory, is that she is the antithesis of the *Titanic:* in place of that unwieldy leviathan, primped by human pride and brought low by a single berg, the *James Caird* was powered by little more than ingenuity and grit, and she resolutely refused to sink. The canvas that covered her makeshift deck had to be thawed over a fire of seal blubber before it could be stitched, and the needles could be pulled through only with pincers. In 1916, six men climbed into the boat and sailed eight hundred miles in sixteen days, through the worst seas in the world, "a seething chaos of tortured water," from Elephant Island, which lies off the tip of the Antarctic Peninsula, to the barren haven of South Georgia.

The *James Caird*, which began life as a whaler on the deck of the three-hundred-ton *Endurance*, is the centerpiece of an exhibition running at the American Museum of Natural History. The show is entitled *"The Endurance": Shackleton's Legendary Antarctic Expedition*, and it represents a further staging post on the startling progress of Sir Ernest Shackleton; seventy-seven years after his death, he is becoming almost as lionized as he was at the summit of his living fame. When he announced, in December 1913, that he would lead a team of men across the polar continent, the world was all ears. The South Pole had been reached by Roald Amundsen in 1911, and—more stirringly to British hearts, which always thump harder at the sight of romantic failure—had been reached too late by

Captain Robert Scott. But no one had travelled from sea to sea, and Shackleton's declaration of intent put him in the headlines. At the Scott Polar Research Institute, in Cambridge, England, a few weeks ago, I found the front page of the London *Daily Mirror*, dated the final day of 1913. Most of it consists of a photograph of Shackleton, alone in Oxford Street. Everyone else is wearing hats and carrying umbrellas; he stands coatless in the cold (close to tropical, by his standards) in the dying hours of the year, looking lost. That his mind must be elsewhere is obvious to the point of embarrassment. At the top, above the paper's masthead, a teaser directs us to a story on pages 8 and 9: "BIG GAME HUNTING TO CURE HEARTACHE." On the same day, across the Atlantic, the *Times* took the opportunity to wish Sir Ernest godspeed and to muse on the curious mentality of polar explorers: "Their very sufferings, apparently, are joys in memory, for they seek them again and again."

This was very acute, and it remains so. Even a cursory glide through the wide and growing literature of Antarctica should be enough to deafen you with the call of the wild, the unfailing two-tone protestation of the polar addict: It was the best of times, it was the worst of times, and you should have seen my toes. Seasoned armchair travellers can get much the same effect, without the bother of frostbite; sit down and open Shackleton's *South*—published in 1919, and still best read in the course of a single, stormy night—and you will be gripped both by an intense gratitude that you were not forced to experience what he did, and by a racking frustration that you will never get the chance to try. Next to the mountainous risks with which he lived, you tend to feel safe but dead.

There are few emotions more profitable than principled envy, and that may be why Caroline Alexander's *The Endurance* has been such a gratifying hit. Her brisk and well-turned account of Shackleton's voyage has been reprinted seven times and has sold close to 200,000 copies since it came out, suggesting a hitherto unsuspected desire on the part of ordinary Americans to eat dog food and fried seal just south of the sixty-sixth parallel. The onset of Shackleton fever was predicted in the *Wall Street Journal* last spring, but no one could have guessed precisely how infectious it would be; the epic of the *Endurance* is one that needs to be retold for every generation, but this generation, for reasons not altogether fathomable, has fallen for her with chronic neediness. Hollywood, of course, is on the case; it should be impossible to go wrong with a story of such natural shape and momentum, but I'm sure that the studio executives will spare no effort to mess things up. Even now, they must be fretting over the question of finding a part for Gwyneth Paltrow. It is true that the skipper of the *Endurance* noted what he called the "sex jealousy" of bull elephant seals, but that, I regret to announce, is the limit of the love interest. We will have to make do with courage, comradeship, snow blindness, and special effects.

The *Endurance* left England on August 8, 1914; the date insured, in more ways than one, that this would be the last adventure of its kind. War had been declared days before, and Shackleton, having immediately offered both his ship and his men for active service, was told to continue as he had planned. He himself joined the *Endurance* at Buenos Aires, and, with a complement of twenty-seven men and sixty-nine dogs under his command, he reached South Georgia on November 5. Along the way, the crew had grown by one—a Welsh stowaway named Perce Blackborow. Legend has it that Shackleton confronted him with this threat: "Do you know that on these expeditions we often get very hungry, and if there is a stowaway available he is the first to be eaten?" A photograph shows Blackborow with a toothy grin and the ship's cat—a male tabby named Mrs. Chippy—perched on his shoulder like a pirate's parrot.

On New Year's Eve, 1914, a year since he had stood bemused in Oxford Street, Shackleton entered the even less hospitable terrain of the Antarctic Circle. A little more than two weeks later, his ship was stuck fast among the floes of the Weddell Sea: she would never sail freely again. She was no longer a vessel but a floating home, and Shackleton's overriding duty was to make sure that she would not turn into a tomb. His quest to traverse the continent was abandoned. As the months of imprisonment wore on, and the men quit the ship to pitch camp nearby, the true thrust of Shackleton's character was revealed. According to his granddaughter, Alexandra Shackleton, he rated as the most necessary virtue neither dexterity nor bravado, nor even the endurance that was enshrined in his family motto and bestowed upon his ship, but optimism. "A man must shape himself to a new mark directly the old one goes to ground," he wrote in *South*. In this case, the ground was the ice that squeezed and crunched the *Endurance* and, on November 21, 1915, finally swallowed her. The prospects of survival were so slim that, in company at least, Shackleton gave himself no option but to ignore them entirely.

In April 1916, having shot the last of the dogs and eaten the more tender ones, Shackleton's men cast off in three small boats, among them the *James Caird*, in search of land. It is from this point that the story passes beyond our normal reckoning and heads for the improbability of myth. The journey to Elephant Island, their hastily agreed-upon destination outside the pack ice, took seven days. "Rest was not for us," wrote

Shackleton, whose tongue grew so swollen with thirst that his orders had to be whispered. Frank Worsley, formerly the captain of the *Endurance*, took the tiller of one boat, the *Dudley Docker*; by the time he was relieved, he had steered for eighteen hours and had not slept for ninety. Once on terra firma, which was little more than an inhospitable chunk of wasteland, the crew slept. "I decided not to share with the men the knowledge of the uncertainties of our situation until they had enjoyed the full sweetness of rest," Shackleton wrote. His next plan was ludicrous. He would leave his unflappable deputy, Frank Wild, in charge of a luxurious camp: twenty-two men huddled under a pair of upturned boats for four and a half months, wreathed in blubber soot, venturing forth occasionally to contend with flying sheets of ice the size of windowpanes. That was nothing: Shackleton himself would take five men in the *James Caird*, sail eight hundred miles, walk across an island that was universally hailed as impassable, get help, find another ship, break back through the ice to rescue his companions on Elephant Island, and return them all intact to England in time to go to war. And that is what he did.

We are fortunate to have a mass of evidence for the *Endurance* expedition, and for the progress of its fate, since without proper documentation the whole thing would have veered toward the tall tale. Many of the men kept journals, and Shackleton was not alone in working his memories up into a book; Frank Worsley's *Endurance: An Epic of Polar Adventure* is to be republished this month. Above all, there was the Australian photographer Frank Hurley, who captured so much of the action, and the eeriness of the inaction, on film. He was also the most professionally ambitious—as opposed to morally determined—member of the team. It was hoped that the rights to his work could redeem some of the expedition's costs; he shot movie footage as well as stills, and the resulting film was indeed screened to great acclaim on his return. Hurley was "a warrior with his camera," wrote one of the crew in a letter home, and the photographer was quick to see his chance when two men fell overboard into the Antarctic surf. Shackleton was not amused by such opportunism: "I firmly believe that he would have liked the two unfortunate men to remain in the water until he could get a 'snap' at close quarters."

To be fair, Hurley himself was bold and mulish enough to take a similar plunge. As her crew divested the sinking *Endurance* of all personal possessions, he stripped to the waist, dived into mushy ice, and retrieved his negatives, saving 120. Many of these were freshly printed for Caroline Alexander's book, and for the American Museum of Natural History; the crispness and clarity are like a sharp blast of polar air in your face. Most appear to have been taken last week rather than eighty-five years ago; the ice flowers that coat the Weddell Sea look as if you could reach out and pick them. Beyond their severe beauty, however, Hurley's images embody the essential balance of the story: against the melancholy sight of the *Endurance* keeling over and dwindling into a tangle of rigging, we can set his portraits of the men and see in their expressions the reason they did not go down with their ship. Look at the Churchillian jut of Shackleton's jaw and the unexpected mildness of his gaze; at the relaxed pose of the pipe-smoking Frank Wild and the boyish, bespectacled features of Jimmy James, the young Cambridge physicist; and, above all, at the deep-seamed face of Tom Crean, the Irishman who had already been south twice with Captain Scott. As Caroline Alexander neatly puts it, "Crean was perhaps as close as one can come to being indestructible." He is reported to have died in 1938, but that sounds unlikely.

It was Crean whom Shackleton picked to accompany him and Worsley across South Georgia. They left three rattled shipmates, with the *James Caird*, on the western coast of the island, and set off across "a chaos of crumpled ice," with neither tent nor sleeping bags. Each man kept his rations in a sock; screws were pulled from the boat and attached to the soles of their boots, for a better grip on the ice. These three were the last gasp, and the only hope, of the *Endurance* expedition. If they failed—and Shackleton, at one point, had to shake his two companions awake, "for sleep under such conditions merges into death"—none of their twenty-five companions, either from the *James Caird* or back on Elephant Island, would be found alive, or even found at all. On the first night of their thirty-six-hour march, they were struck silent upon a peak in South Georgia, in what even their leader admitted was a testing predicament. Behind them lay a bank of gathering sea fog; ahead and below was what Worsley called "impenetrable gloom." Shackleton said, "Let's slide." They sat on coiled rope, "locked together as one man," as if on a toboggan, and went "shooting down the side of an almost precipitous mountain at nearly a mile a minute." All three, despite their situation, found themselves yelling with glee; at the bottom, they shook hands. What matters here is not just the ability to have fun in the face of the frozen unknown but the fact that a knight of the realm, educated privately and toasted in London drawing rooms, should have held on for dear life to an Irish farmboy who never went beyond primary school. Shackleton was a firm leader, but there was not an ounce of snobbery in him; indeed, you almost sense that he sailed to the ends of the earth to escape the confines and fripperies of society. When it was discovered that not enough good sleeping bags had been rescued from the *Endurance* to go around, lots were drawn, but somehow Shackleton saw to it that the reindeer-fur ones went to the men and that the officers had to make do with wool. It was like Wellington worrying over the condition of his soldiers' boots.

This could explain some of America's fascination with the Shackleton legend. He may be an example of strong command—the chief global strategist of Morgan Stanley Dean Witter, Barton Biggs, recently likened him to "a good but manic investment manager who is bearish in a bull market"—but in historical terms he allows us the rare liberty of revering an imperial achievement without getting cluttered up by the impediments of imperial guilt. Not only did Shackleton fail to subdue any indigenous peoples; he even expressed remorse at having to kill young albatrosses for a stew: "Our hunger knew no law." He took with him a Bible inscribed on the flyleaf by Queen Alexandra, plus a copy of Browning; our tedious modern division between the tough guy and the sensitive soul was not yet in place. Shackleton—"the frustrated poet" to his biographer, "a born poet" in the eyes of Frank Hurley—wrote a fair amount of verse, and once declaimed some of it to a fellow-officer in Russia during the war, adding that it was by someone named Shackleton. "That explorer-man?" said the officer. "I never knew he was a poet!" Shackleton replied, "Then why the devil did you think he became an explorer?"

It is true that Shackleton claimed various featureless wastes for King and Country, but that counted for as much as the observation, by Leonard Hussey, his onboard meteorologist, that a bad winter in the Weddell Sea "is a sure precursor of a drought over the maize and cereal bearing area of Argentina three and a half years later." That's useful to know, but Shackleton's motives went even higher than maize, and his endeavors—his collected works, so to speak—offer a rebuke to virtually every standard by which we now choose to conduct our lives. In the words of his granddaughter, the story of the *Endurance* is a demonstration of "restful absolutes": instead of urban infestation, a thousand miles of pure nothingness; instead of solo self-advancement, a reflex attachment to those in your care; instead of rampant accumulation, the intricate art of making do. "Lamps were fashioned out of sardine tins, with bits of surgical bandage for wicks," Shackleton recalled. At his old school, Dulwich College, I came across a menu for his pre-expedition dinner, on March 31, 1914. It runs to twelve courses, including Mousse du Homard à la Shackleton and Cerises à l'Arctique. Two years later, he was sucking a lump of ice chipped from the *Dudley Docker.* At the moment when he finally hove in sight of

Elephant Island to help the stranded men, their commander, Frank Wild, was serving soup—"particularly good that day, consisting of boiled seals' backbone, limpets, and seaweed." Try asking for that at Balthazar.

There was one man who made a fuss about such privations. Captain Thomas Orde-Lees was the skiing expert and resident smart-ass: he resented the vulgar manners of the men, considered floor-scrubbing unfair "for people who have been brought up in refinement," and, worst of all, thought they were all going to die. His diary scorns the "fatuous optimists." According to Shackleton's biographer, Roland Huntford, there were serious discussions on Elephant Island as to who should be sacrificed and consumed when the food ran out: "Orde-Lees was first choice." The awful thing is that he sounds like most of us; we, too, would have been skinned and popped into the pot. His constant half smile infuriated the others, who were trying to subsist in one of the last irony-free zones of the twentieth century, and who preferred to challenge their predicament with the uncomplicated humor that accompanies—and assists—the will to live. It may sound ungracious for us to laugh at the extremity of their exploits, but it is worth recalling that, by and large, those performing the heroics had exactly the same reaction. When the *James Caird* landed on South Georgia, the sailors stumbled ashore and sought refuge in a cave, whose entrance was guarded by fifteen-foot icicles; just to add to the fun, these would drop at random during the night. The men were too enfeebled by the voyage to drag the boat from the water; finally, they renounced any hope of sleep and spent most of the night clinging to the painter, so that the *James Caird* would not be swept away. Worsley takes up the story:

> When our spirits were almost down to zero Shackleton got a laugh out of us by saying, with the most elegant formality, "I do hope that you are all enjoying my little party."

It would be simple to ascribe this nonchalance to a surplus of British backbone. Yet, as Caroline Alexander said to me, "those mannerisms were not affectations but survival tactics." To play the game and show good form were the only means by which any of Shackleton's men had a hope of pulling through. That handshake at the foot of the South Georgia slope was all the more potent because the ordeal was not yet done—the three men still had to hook a rope to the top of a freezing waterfall and lower themselves to the base. As they approached the Norwegian whalers' base at Stromness, they tried to smarten themselves up, in case there were women present. When they finally arrived, nobody recognized them.

Shackleton said, "My name is Shackleton." The manager shook hands and led them inside; that, at any rate, is the version of events in Shackleton's *South*. Another recollection comes from an elderly whaler standing nearby:

> Manager say: "Who the *hell* are you?" and terrible bearded man in the centre of the three say very quietly: "My name is Shackleton." Me—I turn away and weep.

In these two complementary accounts we touch the truth of the *Endurance* expedition. One looks back to the past, to a culture of restraint, and of feats so surreally impressive that they can be completed, and acknowledged, only in decorum; the other peers forward, to all the tears to come. Shackleton asked the manager when the war had ended. "The war is not over," came the reply. "Millions are being killed. Europe is mad. The world is mad." So much for the return to civilization. I am surprised that Shackleton didn't turn around and head back the way he had come.

The legacy of the terrible bearded man goes further than his writings, or his discoveries, or Hurley's visual records of the voyage; what Shackleton handed down was the urge to go south—to catch fire at a vision of the ice. The flame seems to be strengthening by the year; I went recently to a reception given by the James Caird Society in Dulwich, where the boat normally lives, and entered a room humming with explorers, amateur and professional, and polar converts. There, as elsewhere, I couldn't find anyone who had been to the Antarctic just once. If you go, it seems, you will go again, and you keep on going; think of a white, powdery drug stretching for five and a half million square miles. Even as a reader, you grow avid for anecdote; I myself am partial to the tale of the Russian doctor who was forced, in 1961, to remove his own appendix, there being no one else around in the Antarctic to do the job. Wherever you look, there are reports of sensory deprivation, vertiginous solitude, and rushes of wonder; unlike other outposts of the world, the poles have not substantially changed their story for a hundred years. It is easy to forget that the *Endurance* set sail within living memory, and I was introduced to James Blackborow—the son of Shackleton's stowaway, and a sailor himself. He seems to have inherited his father's taste for adventure: "I suffer," he announced, "from what I call youth deficiency."

Shackleton had the same complaint. After the war, in which he and many of his fellow-explorers saw action, his restlessness grew worse—

"Shackleton sitting still and doing nothing wasn't Shackleton at all," said one of his ship's surgeons—and in 1921 he issued a call to old companions from the *Endurance*. Eight heeded it, and the *Quest* headed off, with no particular purpose, for South Georgia. There is a wonderful photograph of Wild and Shackleton, taken on board. Wild has his jacket buttoned up, but the feet that he braces against the deck are bare, as if he were a child at play. Shackleton sits wearing one of his favorite slouch hats, wholly at ease; the deck tilts at an alarming angle, and you can see the muscled swell of the sea behind them, but the two men look more comfortable than most people do on dry land. Twelve days after the picture was taken, Ernest Shackleton died of a heart attack on the *Quest*; one contributing factor, in the words of the postmortem, was "overstrain during a period of debility." That's one way of looking at it. For him, there was no masochism in the urge to explore. Adventure had functioned neither as therapy nor as conquest, and no one who knows the tale of the *Endurance* could for a second accuse him of recklessness, let alone of a rage for honor; he simply upended our traditions of happiness. To relinquish the firm footing of home and the handholds of material possession—all the means by which we guarantee our capacity to prosper—was for him a chance to begin afresh on a tabula rasa, the endless white slate of the South. There he discovered not just friendships, and what we like to think of as management skills, but something far more primitive: the deep contentments of desolation. They carry only the barest message for modern minds; according to taste, you will either deem Shackleton's fixation perverse or, more charitably, pinpoint his enterprise within a breath of the spiritual. "We had pierced the veneer of outside things," he wrote. "We had seen God in His splendours, heard the text that Nature renders." He was buried, according to the wishes of his widow, on South Georgia. The ice had claimed him after all.

APRIL 12, 1999

ALFRED HITCHCOCK

A hundred years ago, on August 13, 1899, a boy was born. He was the son of a greengrocer from Leytonstone, a small town in Essex, which has since been swallowed by the sprawl of East London. Ten years earlier, another London boy was born; both would migrate, both would end up as knights of the realm they had vacated, and both would grow wealthy in the pleasurable purveying of their obsessions. Strangest of all, these two Englishmen would become the most recognized shapes in the history of cinema. The Essex boy would ripen swiftly in Falstaffian directions; the other would stay as trim and proud as a penguin. It is one thing to have your name known around the world, but to be identified by nothing more than your silhouette—well, that is an honor accorded to very few. If Alfred Hitchcock and Charles Chaplin have any peer in this regard, it is Mickey Mouse, who was hailed by Hitchcock as the most pliable of performers. "Mr. Disney has the right idea," he once said. "If he doesn't like them, he tears them up."

That is the chord that Hitchcock liked to strike, and one that his admirers—especially those who watched him fronting TV dramas in the fifties and sixties—came to expect: an easy fusion of the sadistic and the sardonic, delivered with such dead-eyed relish that, like an outrageous con trick, it could somehow be construed as benevolent. How on earth did we come to worship this portly and paranoid figure, this anti-Santa with his funereal suit and tie and his sack of vicious toys, who liked almost nothing about us except our need to give him money in return for the promise of temporary distress? The outward refinements of a Hitchcock picture may be a delight, but they are frayed by emotional wear and tear; when Grace Kelly, in *Rear Window*, is hunting for clues inside Raymond Burr's apartment, and Burr appears in the corridor outside, James Stewart, watching from across the courtyard, looks genuinely aghast, and for a minute we forget the harmless pleasure of watching Grace Kelly in a summer frock. Indeed, it is a rule of Hitchcock's cautionary tales that no pleasure can be wholly harmless—that the more needling the harm, the more pointedly the pleasure will be pricked into a thrill.

The Hitchcock centenary has been greeted with appropriate ceremony. Books such as *Hitchcock's Notebooks* and *Hitchcock's America* have directed our gaze to unconsidered corners of his work, while the Museum of Modern Art has organized a complete retrospective of his movies (fifty-three are extant), together with an exhibit of Hitchcockiana. Among the highlights is a 1962 written exchange between the director and Grace Kelly, whom Hitchcock wanted for the title role in *Marnie.* In the event, it was decided that a European princess was not quite right for the part of a frigid kleptomaniac. Hitch was unmoved. "Yes, it was sad, wasn't it?" he noted. "After all, it was only a movie." That shrugging dismissal is one that he tried on several occasions, but he could never make it ring true: movies were all he had.

The most suggestive commemoration I have found is the Hitchcock show at the Museum of Modern Art in Oxford, England. This includes a mockup of James Stewart's bedroom in *Vertigo*; a rear-projected, frame-by-frame screening of *Psycho*; and a beguiling series of looped montages by Christoph Girardet and Matthias Müller, entitled "The Phoenix Tapes." These are scraps of Hitchcock crammed with objects and actions that we have come to recognize as his imaginative property. One loop rifles through the following images: name cards, tiepins, monograms, letters, keys, locks, drains, the color red, spots, basins, washing, haircutting, hair-burning, fires, matchbooks, race cards, addresses, newspapers, music scores, telephone directories, phones, papers against a door, doorknobs, hands, cups, breakages, spills, rings on fingers, rosaries, handcuffs, bags, purses, guns, drawers, knives, forks, and back to name cards.

What struck me about these visual quotations is how much they reveal not about Hitchcock but about us; whatever the source of his undoubted fetishism, the more compelling fact is that he ended up making fetishists of us all. We come out of movies saying, "I liked that bit where. . . ," and Hitchcock's bits were simply neater than anyone else's. Moviegoers like that bit in *Notorious* where the camera glides down, as if in annunciation, to discover a stolen key in Ingrid Bergman's fist; I *really* like the bit just before that, when Claude Rains tries to kiss that hand, and she, thinking smartly, throws her arms around his neck, drops the key on the rug, and slides it aside with her foot. Critics like to damn the frenzied editing practices of current cinema, but Hitchcock reminds us that rapid cutting is not in itself a sin. There is a serenity in his speed; he is driving the action forward with such confidence that the emotional burden of the moment—which in Bergman's case could not be more fraught—comes to feel almost weightless. Only a man who took no exercise whatsoever, and who once ate three steaks in a single sitting at "21," could derive such bliss from the athletic possibilities of his art.

It is impossible to tell, with Hitchcock, where fear ends and fantasy begins; indeed, the two are twisted together for strength, like the cords of a rope. His cinema is one of compulsive repetition; from film to film, his characters are initiated afresh into rituals that Hitchcock alone can comprehend. If this was designed as a purgation, it failed beautifully; far from being broken, the spell of unease merely tightened its grip, as if the director were half in love not just with his actresses but with the perils they faced. He liked to claim, for instance, that he never drove a car—untrue, of course, like many of his claims, although he did employ a chauffeur in Hollywood. "If you don't drive a car, you can't get a ticket," he explained, and a ticket—the stub of authority, stamped with trouble—was what Hitchcock dreaded most. And how did he mold and decorate his dread? He lingered on the tight-gloved hands of Tippi Hedren as she rested them lightly on the steering wheel, in *The Birds*, and gunned her green Aston Martin up to Bodega Bay; he had Barbara Harris's brake cables comically snipped in *Family Plot*, with unstoppable consequences; and, best of all, in *To Catch a Thief* he had Grace Kelly drive Cary Grant around the bends until Grant was clutching his knees. Hitchcock's pleasure was to dip his performers into precisely the type of quicksand in which he himself would have sunk without a trace; the ingenious bravado with which they hauled themselves free not only tickled him, as it did his audiences, but offered the comforting thought that our treacherous world could sometimes, by a whisker, be put to rights.

It is the whisker, the humming wire of suspense, for which Hitchcock is still most highly honored. When Martin Balsam climbs the stairs in *Psycho*, we want the bedroom door to open, but only by a couple of inches; the waiting spices the agony. This practice of procrastination began early, one gathers, and it was indivisible from crime. At Hitchcock's school, St. Ignatius College, in Stamford Hill,

> The form master would tell the pupil of his wrongdoing and the pupil would have to go before the disciplining priest. It was left to the pupil to decide when he would go for the punishment, and of course he would keep putting it off.

That Hitchcock could recollect this torture so plainly in 1973, sixty years after the event, suggests that the pain of indecision was undimmed. Hitchcock commentators have traditionally made merry over the fact that young Alfred was a scion of the Catholic lower middle class and, as one schoolmate described him, "a lonely fat boy who smiled and looked at you as if he could see straight through you." On the other hand, we should beware the temptation to post-rationalize. The majority of boys who undergo a Jesuit education grow up as useful members of society, largely untroubled by the urgent desire to watch blond women in handcuffs. In tracing the trouble with Alfred, we require further particulars.

We know, for example, that as a boy, and even as a young man with a full-time job, Hitchcock would be summoned by his mother, Emma, to the foot of her bed and pressed for a litany of the day's events. "It was a ritual. I always remember the evening confession," he admitted to Tippi Hedren, who passed the information on to one of his biographers, Donald Spoto. According to Spoto, such maternal interest "inculcates guilt of a scrupulous and neurotic type." Hitchcock fans have learned to be cautious of Spoto, who is always ready to pass briskly over the fruits of Hitchcock's talent if there is a chance to check out the undergrowth; still, staring at the swarm of fearsome matriarchs who invade the Hitchcock corpus, you do wonder. There is the doting presence who files the nails of her wicked son, in *Strangers on a Train*; the entirely petrifying Nazi who cows Claude Rains in *Notorious*; the weariness of not loving that wears down the heroine's mother in *Marnie*; and the hawkish Lydia, of *The Birds*, who resents her son's billing and cooing with another woman. Lastly, there is old Mrs. Bates, a boy's best friend.

The other woman who oversaw Hitchcock's life was Alma Reville, who was one day younger than him, and whom he met in 1921 and married five years later. She was small and smart ("my severest critic," he said), and was already skilled in editing and continuity when Hitchcock entered the movie trade as a dogsbody. (Professional pride forbade him to wed until he rose to the rank of assistant director.) He had trained as an engineer and worked at a telegraph-and-cable company, where (helped by an evening course in painting) he had ended up in the advertising department; he now took a portfolio to the Famous Players-Lasky Corporation, an American film company that had arrived in London at the end of the First World War, and he was hired to design titles. "I'm American-trained," he said. "As soon as you entered the studio doors you were in an American atmosphere."

* * *

For the sake of convenience, Hitchcock-watchers like to split his career down the middle—between the English pictures, which began in 1925, with *The Pleasure Garden*, and ended in 1938, with *Jamaica Inn*, and the American period, which saw Hitch hit the ground running with *Rebecca*, and keep on running, with occasional stumbles, until *Family Plot* was released, in 1976. But the two halves of his achievement blur and bleed into one another. Hollywood allowed him to revisit and resuscitate performers and setups from his British days—and, in one case, to remake an entire movie, *The Man Who Knew Too Much*. Equally, the achievements of the young Hitchcock show an artist craning forward in excitement, as if from the prow of a ship. He was based in London, but his mind's eye was elsewhere. He visited the vast UFA studios in Berlin, learned German, and watched F. W. Murnau—who would also emigrate to Hollywood—shoot *The Last Laugh*. For decades, British cinema was little more than a bad hangover from a night at the theatre; the only way to get the taste of sawdust out of your mouth was to watch movies from Germany, the Soviet Union, and, above all, America. As Hitchcock himself wrote, "The Americans have shown themselves adept at this trick of switching from grave to gay. Why shouldn't we do the same?" And elsewhere: "They have learnt, as it were, to put the nouns, verbs, and adjectives of the film language together." The landscape of early Hitchcock could not be more British, from the Victorian fogs of *The Lodger* (1927), his first big hit, to the seaside dance hall of *Young and Innocent*, ten years on; but the grammar of these movies has lost any trace of starch. It is fluid, furtive, and as quick as a knife in the dark: *The Lodger* is silent, but, as the killer strikes, Hitch cuts away to a cat and a woman nearby, who whip around and listen to the soundless scream.

This takes us immediately not just to the heart of Hitchcock but to the vexed matter of film direction itself. It was the French—in the persons of François Truffaut, Claude Chabrol, and others, most of them critics who would later cross the river into creativity—who eagerly proclaimed their faith in the theory of the auteur, and it was Hitchcock whom they took as their model. On the face of it, auteurism—the notion that a film bears the mark of its maker, the director, as unmistakably as a novel bears that of its writer—is either a cracked fancy or a crummy joke. Anyone who has seen a film being shot will be richly amused by the possibility that one person could impose a signature style on such a throng of innumerable disciplines, let alone lord it over the bear pit of cinematic egos, each of them chafing at its chain. Yet the stubborn fact remains that for more than fifty years Hitchcock delivered work that—for all his intensive collaboration with producers such as Selznick, writers such as Ben Hecht and

Ernest Lehman, and composers such as Bernard Herrmann—could have bloomed from no other brain. Some of his easiest conquests are achieved by touches no heavier than the brush of wire on drumskin, and his effects kick in absurdly fast, without blare or buildup. I once asked a friend who had never seen *Marnie* to guess the director. Skipping the opening credits, I started a stopwatch on the first shot—Tippi Hedren's clutch bag under her arm as she walks along a station platform. "Hitchcock," he said, and I checked the watch. Twelve seconds.

Marnie is, of course, a late work, made in 1964. But even a brief stroll through the high-humored films of his youth demonstrates that most of them already reeked of Hitchcock; at any rate, they helped to nourish the look that soon became both mystery and giveaway, like a paragraph of Kafka. *Sabotage* (1936) begins with bewitching speed: within two minutes, we have seen the lights of London fail, we understand what caused the blackout, and we know the grim visage of Verloc, the saboteur. The film then fans out into the chatter and bustle of city life: the detective goes undercover as a greengrocer (Hitchcock paying homage to his own father), the heroine sells tickets at a movie theatre, and a bomb is taken blithely onto a bus. In short, the film honors the democratic principles that Hitchcock proclaimed the following year, in an article on the failings of British cinema:

> Forgotten are the men who leap on buses, the girls who pack into the Tube, the commercial travelers, the newspaper men, the girls who manicure your nails, the composers who write the dance numbers, the city clerk and his weekend Rugger, the stockbroker and his round of golf, the typist and her boyfriend, the cinema queues, the *palais de danse* crowds.

This is the Hitchcock who grew up reading Shaw and Wells, who inherited their hatred of snobbery and their penchant for unextraordinary souls—and for the mantrap into which such souls can step. That observant litany could have been written by the young John Betjeman, another tubby addict of the suburban; Betjeman would have applauded the tidy English habits that the Hitchcocks maintained in Hollywood—back from work at six, cocktails, dinner, reading, and bed by half past eight. I would place Hitchcock among that small band of artists—W. H. Auden being the most distinguished—who found a new way to frame the drama of ordinary people. If human curiosity obliged you to usher the masses into your fictions, it was not enough to let them wander through, as if they were milling on a stage; the world of clerks and crowds could be hooked into shocking affiliation with the abrupt and shadowy angles of modernism. That is why *Sabotage* eventually quietens to a terrifying scene at the dinner table where Verloc and his wife, who knows he is a killer, eye the carving knife with fearful symmetry. The camera lingers on Verloc's face while he walks around the table. "Instinctively," the director said, "the viewer should be pushing back slightly in his seat to allow Verloc to pass by." That is the essence of Hitchcock: nothing so drab as a meeting of form and content but, rather, a technical intensity so adamant that it forges fresh anxieties as it moves along, creating the need for a whole new etiquette of fear.

Whether England realized what it had on its hands is another matter. To Hitchcock, America was always more lucratively discerning; *The Lady Vanishes* won the New York Critics' Best Director Award in 1938. Such a prize may sound solemn for so watchable an entertainment, but that is precisely the point; there were people in America who understood the powers of visual persuasion which were required to make people watch. You cannot tune in to *The Lady Vanishes*—even on TV, and even if you happen upon it halfway through—and not stay with it to the end. No wonder David O. Selznick wanted Alfred Hitchcock for himself.

Otto Friedrich, in *City of Nets*, his study of the movie world in the 1940s, describes Hitchcock as "one of the few people in Hollywood who could out-Selznick Selznick." The producer, who signed him up in 1938, liked to keep tabs on his directors, and to cover his options by having them shoot each scene from numerous viewpoints, so that the ideal sequence could be pasted together in the editing suite. Hitch, on the other hand, framed only those shots that he knew he would need. He never looked through the viewfinder, and he definitely didn't want a producer breathing down his neck. When Selznick visited the set of *Spellbound*, the camera inexplicably malfunctioned, and then righted itself, by sheer coincidence, when the producer left.

Their first project was supposed to be something called *Titanic*, but Selznick pulled the plug. In the event, they made just three films together: *Rebecca*, which, in 1940, won the Academy Award for Best Picture; *Spellbound;* and *The Paradine Case*. Only one of these, the first, is an out-and-out masterpiece, and even that has a heavy dose of Selznick about it. It could have been worse: he wanted the smoke that rises from the burning Manderley to form a giant black "R" in the sky—although, to be fair, Hitchcock wanted the picture to open with Max and his new bride being seasick on their honeymoon (Hitchcock had a lifelong horror of vomiting), so producer and director probably served as a good check on each other's excesses. *Rebecca* introduced Hitchcock not just to the technical talent available in Hollywood but to the peculiar luster that Hollywood alone could bestow upon the skin of a film and to the fleshly assumptions that lay beneath. The British films have a larkiness that fades from view as America looms large; *The 39 Steps* and *North by Northwest* tell comparable tales, but there is a stealth and purpose—a barely explicable air of universal intimacy—in the later picture, which even Robert Donat, Hitchcock's most lovable leading man, could not have supplied.

Spellbound is an oddity, largely by comparison with *Notorious*, released a year later, in 1946. The two films share a director, a screenwriter (Ben Hecht), and a star (Ingrid Bergman). Both have a caressing texture, and I once heard an audience applaud Gregory Peck, on his first appearance, purely for being so good-looking. Yet *Spellbound* is a dud. Psychiatry was becoming chic toward the end of the war, and Selznick wanted to cash in on it; unfortunately, this meant involving Hitchcock in a Big Idea—never his happiest terrain. Hitchcock was not a thinker, and profundity is what we should prize most nervously in his work; the speech that he wrote for Joseph Cotten in *Shadow of a Doubt*, about the world's being a "foul sty," is little more than an adolescent rant. The moments where Hitchcock does graze the profound are those where he is least bothered with it; *Notorious*, which boasts a daft plot about a man who keeps radioactive soil in his wine cellar, is one of the most provocative films ever made. When Grant and Bergman, both of whom are on his trail, descend to the cellar to find out more, they are disturbed by Claude Rains, who is married to Bergman. "I am going to kiss you," Grant says, and Bergman obliges. Rains sees them, and his face falls with the sadness of betrayal; thanks to their pretense of passion, he does not yet suspect them of spying. But they *are* passionate; the deceit is true.

If I'm trapped at a party and asked to name my favorite films, I tend to duck under the drinks table, but I guess I would find life without *Notorious* unutterably bloodless and bleak. Come to that, Western civilization needs *Rear Window* just as badly as its heroine needs that pistachio suit with the pencil skirt and the halter-necked blouse. Then, there's *North by Northwest.* When, a couple of hundred years from now, an alien federation finally pulls in for gas on planet Earth and asks to see one of those things called "movies," we could do worse than offer it Cary Grant having cocktails on the train, or hanging off a ledge of presidential rock, as an unsurpassed demonstration of what we mean by film—what it's all about, what it can be made to do, what it is *for.* Hitchcock's movie is no more substantial than one of those dining-car martinis, yet there is something in its transparency and bite, something beyond the fumes of sophistication, that takes your breath away. When Grant stretches for Eva Marie Saint's hand, swings her up off the mountain and into his marital berth, you realize how tenderly, with what careful shades of chivalry, the whole enterprise has reached out toward height and depth. (How sharply we share the trepidation of Cary Grant in the clean, Frank Lloyd Wright spaces of the villain's hideaway, as opposed to the Gothic hoariness of the Bates house in *Psycho.*) *North by Northwest* is not a meditation on loneliness or madness (any more than it is a guide to smuggling microfilm), but it never ceases to gesture in their direction. Grant plays a man named Roger O. Thornhill, who is accused—falsely, of course, as is the rule in Hitchcock—of murder, and is forced to go on the run. At one point, he is asked what the "O" stands for. "Nothing," he says, with a snap of satisfaction. The most arousing sentiment that Hitchcock has ever induced—here, as in *Notorious*, and in countless other tales—is the suspicion that to slip from one identity to the next, with no more ado than a businessman changing his suit, will pull you farther away from your tailor-made role in society and closer, if you can handle the irony, to the truth of your desires.

What this tells us about Alfred Hitchcock is a matter of debate. A split has opened up in recent years as the films beloved of film buffs, of theorists and therapists, have drifted apart from the more cheerful popular hits. The later dreamscapes—*The Birds*, *Marnie*, and, above all, *Vertigo*—are now the prey of an analysis almost as obsessive as the mind that conceived them. If a film such as *Vertigo* disturbs us with its near-necrophilia, when James Stewart refashions a live woman in the image of a dead one, that is apparently because of similar storms within the humid mind of Hitchcock himself. As an adult, he said, he was too shy to walk across the lot at Paramount; and the man who found corpses funny also thought that the most horrible thing in the world was the smell of a hard-boiled egg.

It is tempting to read these manias as no more than foibles dressed up for the sake of PR—a vocation at which Hitchcock excelled even more than Cecil B. De Mille. He used eccentricity to deflect attention from what he considered his consuming concern: "pieces of film assembled," otherwise known as "pure cinema." This disdain for anything except style would be more convincing if it were not for the vampiric way in which he feasted on the same material over and over again. Or perhaps it was that very familiarity that allowed him to perfect his touch—perhaps the chase sequence was to Hitchcock what Mont Sainte-Victoire was to Cézanne. Hitch liked getting things right in advance, complete inside his head, and sitting with writers to iron out the wrinkles in the plot; he and Ernest Lehman spent a year on *North by Northwest* before filming began. But he saw the shoots themselves as a chore and a bore. Joel McCrea, the star of *Foreign Correspondent*, told Donald Spoto he was surprised to find his director (who had drunk a *pint* of champagne at lunchtime) nodding off during a take: "He had fallen asleep. So I said, 'Cut!' and he woke up and said, 'Was it any good?' I said, 'The best in the picture!' and he said, 'Print it!' "

Needless to say, all of this may have been one more mask. As eager as any murderer to conceal his motives, Hitchcock laid a maze of false trails to confound his trackers. There was the occasion when, at the age of five, he was locked up in a prison cell, on his father's orders, for being a naughty boy: a story that Hitchcock repeated with such wearisome regularity that it began to resemble the Rosebud of *Citizen Kane*—the clue that solves everything and means nothing. There was the director's curt reply to the fan who asked why he made movies: "Money." There was his puerile love of practical jokes: pretty funny when he sent sixty kippers around in a taxi to Robert Donat's house, or a dray horse to Peter Lorre (an act reciprocated with three hundred canaries, delivered at three o'clock in the morning); less so when he chained a man to a camera, gave him brandy laced with laxative, and left him in the studio all night.

The charge of sadism rang louder when it came to *The Birds*, and to Hitchcock's treatment of Tippi Hedren. For the attic scene, he put her through a week's torment that ended with a beak gashing her under the eye, and he took wax casts of her face, supposedly as part of the makeup process; for the filming of *Marnie*, he chose all her clothes and forbade her to go out without asking his permission. Finally, something buckled: Spoto says that Hitchcock made "an overt sexual proposition," which she rebuffed; another, less heat-seeking biographer, John Russell Taylor, says that Hedren called her mentor fat. Big mistake. Either way, they didn't speak to each other for the rest of the shoot; he referred to her as "that girl."

Everything about *The Birds* sounds cruel until you actually see the movie: it is gracious, shrewd, and sunlit, glinting with flirtatious backchat, and lulling itself gently toward the apocalyptic. Most remarkable of all, Tippi Hedren makes it her own. The good-time girl from San Francisco may be bandaged and traumatized by the end, but she puts up a hell of a fight; Camille Paglia, in her short book on the movie, compliments the character on her "mesmerizing narcissism." It would be easy to cast Hitchcock as the demon misogynist were it not for the nagging sense that women are the guiding spirits of his movies; resourceful and redoubtable, all smiles in their sexual self-possession, they take the male gaze and stare straight back. Fellini thought that *The Birds* was a lyric poem, and, as if in tribute to all those cunning gulls, it provides a bizarre sense of uplift; as with any good Hitchcock, from *The Lodger* onward, material that should leave you humbled and wrecked sends you out on a mystified high. Hitchcock was once asked why he had never made a comedy. "But every film I make *is* a comedy," he replied.

For once, I think Hitchcock was telling the truth. He did make an overt comedy—a screwball entitled *Mr. and Mrs. Smith*, with Carole Lombard, whom he liked for her filthy jokes—but it wasn't funny. What is funny is the enduring mismatch between what the world pitches at us and the way we choose to hit it—between the stranger on a train who wants to be rid of his wife, preferably in the divorce courts, and the stranger beside him, who takes this as an invitation to strangle her. On a less reckless level, you get seductive misunderstanding:

> "Do you want a leg or a breast?"
> "You make the choice."
>
> "Tell me, how long has it been?"
> "How long has what been?"
> "Since you were in America last."

That is Grace Kelly offering chicken, among other things, to Cary Grant in *To Catch a Thief.* Sex becomes a sort of animated suspension; lovers in Hitchcock circle warily around each other, more like predators than like dancers, and even when their lips meet, the camera is likely to continue the waltz. (In *Rear Window*, Hitchcock double-printed the closeup of Grace Kelly's face descending toward Jimmy Stewart, so that their kiss was self-shaking, with the orgasm built in.) Hitchcock is the only great director who mastered those elusive hybrids, the romantic comedy and the comedy thriller. In each instance, he sees that the comedy is not something you apply like lipstick, to brighten the tone, but something that is already there—a luminous natural coloring under the thrills, a blush in the very notion of romance. My favorite passage in Hitchcock begins with Kelly springing the catch on her dinky overnight bag in *Rear Window*. It's no bigger than a briefcase, but out of it froths a Botticellian spray of lingerie. Before leaving to put it on, she shows the contents to

Stewart, and says, "Preview of coming attractions." Movie love is so hot that it sounds like a movie.

Such elegant self-reference, of course, can border on artistic vanity. I am cautious of those who praise *Rear Window* and *Vertigo* as films that are primarily about watching films, if only because Hitchcock strove to ensnare as wide an audience as he could get. That is why we should be grateful for the presence of Thelma Ritter as the bloodthirsty masseuse in *Rear Window* and for that of Barbara Bel Geddes as the underwear designer in *Vertigo*; they are comic choruses, spry and unfazed, letting a touch of fresh air into pictures that could otherwise thicken into the delirious or the unbreathable. Such women are the proper inheritors of the typists and manicurists whom Hitchcock wanted to summon into the British cinema. He was never so at ease amid the American masses (even the townspeople in *Shadow of a Doubt*, one of his favorites, are on the stiff and stagy side), and so he diverted his sympathies into supporting roles. Hitch himself trundled or popped into all his films, like a Renaissance painter glimpsed in a row of heads on the fringes of a fresco, but, if you want his authentic voice, listen to Thelma Ritter as she gazes across the courtyard at Raymond Burr's apartment: "He better get that trunk outta there before it starts to leak."

What is at work here is something more intricate than comic relief; Hitchcock is not merely relaxing the viewers before he cranks them up again. One of the disarming morals of his movies—even of such a glum and hunted work as *The Wrong Man*—is that it's fun to be cranked; to watch someone take a wrong turn or to see Vera Miles glance curiously at the cellar door in *Psycho* is not to congratulate yourself on your own safe path but to get into your imaginative stride, to follow the victim or the sucker as far as you conceivably can. Film has eroded the stony Aristotelian principle that pity and terror become tolerable at a decent distance—say, at twenty yards from the stage. The movie screen flattens that aplomb and sucks the viewer in; what is more, as Hitchcock knew, we can even be invigorated by our helplessness. If Aristotle had ever checked into a motel and taken a shower, he would have felt the same.

Hitchcock himself was an inveterate traveller, and his movies take us along for the ride. He even maintained a sturdy devotion to the monumental (Mt. Rushmore, the Golden Gate Bridge, the Statue of Liberty, the British Museum), though whether that makes him a corny tourist or an imperturbable satirist is hard to tell. The finest way to travel in a Hitchcock picture, however, is not by car or plane, or even, as with Robert Donat, on the outside of a train, but by staircase. Stairs are a beginner's guide to vertigo; they lead to the nursery and the cellar alike, and they show how far the heart and the nerves can stretch within your own home. In Hitchcock's case, they lend grandeur to his fretful loftiness; his first film, *The Pleasure Garden*, kicked off with chorus girls descending a staircase, and his penultimate film, *Frenzy*, left a murderer at work and politely withdrew downstairs and out into the Chaplinish hubbub of London streets. Is that retreat an evasion of the tragic, or does it sport a sinister comedy of its own? Is a devotion to the cause of pure cinema a way to grace the world with order, or a flimsy front for the privately perverse? "Nothing leads more certainly to perfect barbarity," wrote the poet Paul Valéry, "than an exclusive attachment to the pure spirit." A hundred years after his birth, we have yet to decide whether Alfred Hitchcock held the sufferings of others in contempt or whether the amused cool of his gaze makes him as indispensable a modern artist as de Chirico, Bacon, or—the director's own favorite—Paul Klee. Our only reliable evidence is the movies; beyond that, the lonely fat boy disappears from sight.

AUGUST 16, 1999

MUSEUM OF SEX

Until last week, few New Yorkers were aware that the city is to be adorned with a Museum of Sex. It was perhaps unfortunate that they should learn of this project at a time when the temperature dropped to three degrees. Row upon row of icicles, pendant and forlorn, present a less than ideal backdrop for such a grand design, and a young man's fancy will not lightly turn to thoughts of love if he is unable to feel his own nose.

The new institution will be known, unofficially, as MoSex, which sounds like the better sort of Spike Lee film. It is slated to open in the fall, but only at temporary premises; as yet, its permanent home consists of no more than a tempting space on Fifth Avenue at Twenty-seventh Street. The plan has precedents in Europe, such as Copenhagen's Erotica Museum, which overlooks a downtown pedestrian mall. There, you start with two or three floors of history: a gathering of Greek vases, plus a room of those exquisite Indian miniatures in which the woman's calm, otherworldly gaze suggests not that she is nearing climax but that she is trying to remember where she put the keys to the elephant. After a while, though, the scholarship runs dry, and, by the time you reach the top, the museum has more or less thrown in the towel and given the punters what they came for: a wall of video screens, each of them crammed with unsmiling gymnastics. There is even a little movie theatre, behind a red curtain. From within, to the ears of this reporter, came a low but distinct neigh. Is this really what New Yorkers want when they drop into MoSex for a quick Danish on their way to the toy store?

If you believe Alison Maddex, the director of the new museum, the answer is no. What New Yorkers want—or, at least, what they're going to get—is nothing less than "the Smithsonian of Sex." Think of the air and space displays in Washington, and then replace that early biplane with Ms. Lewinsky's outstretched, unwashed dress, or that frail lunar module with

Monkey Business, the yacht in which Senator Hart ran aground. As yet, this is a pipe dream; we must wait four long years, hearts pounding, before MoSex is ready to welcome us in. Still, according to SHoP, the New York architecture firm behind its creation, the agony should be worthwhile. Layered panels will undulate and shimmer across it like skin; they will "blush" at different hours of the day and night; they will be nearly, but not entirely, see-through . . . Take me, Twenty-seventh Street, take me!

It is assumed, of course, that such transparency is a good thing. Freedom of information, and the visible workings of open government, are now such proud essentials of Western democracy that it has become almost vulgar—and hopelessly Victorian—to ask whether they should apply to private life. It may just be that shame and secrecy, not to mention the shamelessness that secrecy brings, are precisely what embellished the boudoir in the first place. That is why collections of erotica have traditionally been concealed behind the third oak panel on the right in the ducal library, and why they may seem slightly foolish when exposed to passersby on Fifth Avenue. Sex, at its best, is an in-joke; for once, we are defined not by what other people know of us but by what they would like to know—by what their gossip grabs at but misses. A meeting of two bodies, hoggish or sinuous, is no more penetrable than a meeting of two minds; the meeting of three bodies has its adherents, but it belongs less to the realms of pure pleasure than to those of geometry and backache. A meeting of a hundred thousand bodies—the number that MoSex hopes to greet every year—sounds like no fun at all.

The organizers of MoSex hope to dispel such gloom with novel varieties of interaction; at the merest brush of a knob, presumably, customers will be encouraged to riffle through a thousand years of rearing priapic imagery, much as their counterparts at the nearby Banana Republic burrow through cargo pants in search of an XXL. We wish Ms. Maddex and her colleagues well in their endeavors, but they should reflect that the city is not exactly low on sensual attractions. Forget the skin flicks; there are desserts on offer at Danube that would make our grandmothers fall off their chairs. If we go to MoSex, it will be for the reasons we go to any other museum: to find refuge and the balm of enlightenment. Even those New Yorkers with a Picasso over the fireplace make the pilgrimage to MoMA to check out the other Picassos, to see what they're missing. But will they really hand over six-fifty to enter the pellucid glories of MoSex? Why pay for art when you can make it in your own home?

JANUARY 31, 2000

THE NEW YORKER AT 75

Seventy-five years ago, under the midwifery of Harold Ross, *The New Yorker* came into being. Three-quarters of a century is not bad, although, by the latest standards of life expectancy, it counts as no more than a promising start. Our grandchildren, their genes tailored like suits, will reach 150 with ease; for them, seventy-five will be the peak and the prime—a midlife without the crisis. Even now, looking around, you wonder whether notable citizens have been receiving eternal youth through the mail and not letting on. Paul Newman turned seventy-five last month, and he still behaves like the new kid at the pool hall. *The New Yorker* has done well to keep pace with Mr. Newman, but, to be honest, until we start running an Indy-car team and selling our own spaghetti sauce, we should go easy on the hoopla.

There is, nevertheless, much to commemorate. The magazine has had five editors, four homes, one guy with a monocle, and such a plethora of cat cartoons that sensitive readers have been known to complain of hairballs. There has also been a steady flow of books relating to the magazine and to the lives of its begetters. When someone hands you a tradition, the crucial thing is not to ape it, still less to seize up with awe, but to ask yourself what, by way of homage, you can possibly bring to the party. A brisk flip through any history of *The New Yorker* will confirm one's suspicion that the leading lights of Forty-fifth Street burned so hard, and took their pleasures at such a tilt, that the worst favor we could do them now would be to agonize over their legacy. In the depths of Prohibition, Ross started up an office speakeasy in a nearby basement; one day, his managing editor, Ralph Ingersoll, walked in and found his star cartoonist, Peter Arno, and the "Tables for Two" columnist, Lois Long, lying naked together on a sofa. "Arno and I may have been married to one another by then; I can't remember," Long later said. "Maybe we began drinking and forgot that we were married and had an apartment to go to." Let us not forget the sacrifices these people made.

Before Ross launched his new publication, he sat with friends and mulled over possible titles. One of these—according to Jane Grant, his wife at the time—was *Truth*. Had that choice prevailed, the magazine would not be alive today. No printed product should be saddled with so terrible a burden of veracity. As it happens, *The New Yorker* has made matters of fact its business; sticklers for exactitude will agree that, when an employee is packed off to a movie theatre, bearing a copy of the week's film review, in order to check that the second shirt from the left in the casino scene is woven from purple plaid and not magenta velour, there is not much to stickle about. Yet the principle stands: it's not just the truth, it's the way that you tell it—the way that you hint at other, competing truths that are tucked away. This holds good even for those jagged areas of life where the room for maneuver seems minimal: murder, poverty, political infighting, or the threat of a mysterious disease that has already crossed from the Ivory Coast to the Upper West Side, and that you had never heard of before last Thursday. *The New Yorker*, in short, is at its best when conditions grow most chaotic; if you want the brute data of war, but you want them treated with nerveless aplomb, read A. J. Liebling's dispatches from North Africa. When the *Infantry Journal* commends you for accuracy, as it did *The New Yorker* in 1944, you know you're on the right track.

It is in seasons of peace, of course, that perplexity comes into full bloom. The time to catch an infantryman is when he puts down his rifle and picks up a guitar, or a skillet, or a librarian in pearls—when the need for prowess and the prospect of failure bring him nearer to our common comedy. The *New Yorker* tone is really a *New Yorker* chord, combining respect for human enterprise, and for the particulars of the case, with a deep delight in human bewilderment. Once your ear is attuned to it, you hear it everywhere: in a biographical sketch that James Thurber wrote of himself—"Two overcoats which he left in the *New Yorker* office last spring were stolen, or else he left them someplace else"—and again, decades later, in "The Talk of the Town," when Donald Barthelme explained how to cook dinner for sixty: "About twenty pounds of sliced onions would be a good addition, although they probably should have gone in earlier."

It is safe to say that no other magazine would have printed that. If the editors at *Gourmet* forgot an ingredient, they would be set upon by aproned subscribers and beaten into stiff peaks with whisks. The craving for crisp, instructive facts should not obscure the fuzzy, peccable realities that lie beyond the reach of the exposé and the problem page. A professor once sent E. B. White a questionnaire, which included the query "Does your periodical endeavor to render public service or to wage crusades?" White went to work. "We are on the side of snow, and against its removal," he replied. "We succeeded in getting the information booth at the Pennsylvania terminal moved out into the middle of the floor, and then discovered there was no information we needed." Americans, amid their genuine worries and their heavy civic tasks, have a duty to be irresponsible; if *The New Yorker* has ever inspired a group of upstanding citizens to sit down and finish their drinks, then a public service has been rendered. Such is the crusade we wage: we seek the truth, the whole truth, and any unsuitable friends with goatees who are riding in the back of truth's car. *The New Yorker* did not invent a world of its own; it stared and squinted at the existing one from unfamiliar angles. Seventy-five years on, the view is just as fine.

FEBRUARY 21, 2000

WALKER EVANS

The body of a child lies on a pair of thin pillows, which are laid on bare boards. The age, sex, and appearance of the child are uncertain. The trunk and head are covered with a flour sack, leaving one hand and the lower half of each leg exposed. The right foot is heavily bound with bandage; the left has a dark spot the size of a dime which could be either birthmark or sore. Such are the particulars of a photograph taken by Walker Evans in 1936. There is a surge of relief when you finally discover its title: *Squeekie Burroughs Asleep.* The moment I read that, I thought of Jairus's daughter in the Gospels—of Jesus entering a house of grief, where keening relatives mourn a child, and consoling them with the words "She is not dead, but sleeping." That cloth over Squeekie is no shroud but a simple guard against flies; by dinnertime, he will be awake. And yet, for all that, the afternoon stillness remains unsettled; there is something about the helpless figure, drifting on his soft white raft in the center of the frame, that whispers a fear of abandonment. He could be not sleeping but dead.

Squeekie Burroughs Asleep is a title soothingly appended by the Metropolitan Museum of Art for its Walker Evans retrospective—nearly two hundred images strong. When the picture first appeared, it bore no name at all; you just had to look and pray. It was one of a batch of thirty-one Evans stills, untitled and unadorned, that accompanied almost five hundred pages of prose by James Agee; the book was, of course, *Let Us Now Praise Famous Men*, their collaborative record of a summer stay among poor tenant farmers in Hale County, Alabama. The photographs stand proud at the head of the book; they do not illustrate so much as distill. They give you all you need and, at the same time, they make you want to know everything else—to get the lowdown on the Burroughs family, on the twin weathering of their faces and lodgings, on the hurt to Squeekie's foot. Calmness in art, from Piero della Francesca through Vermeer and on to Rothko, invariably has this effect: the more restful and reclusive the scene, the more we seek to fill it with our fears.

Interest in Evans has never sagged since his death, in 1975, and the full forces of biography and scholarship have been trained, like fire hoses, on this gratifyingly unknowable man. It is easy to be swept up in the fuss, and, if you are planning to attend the show at the Met, you should certainly go prepared. Evans was literate, difficult, and furtive, and you can hardly hope to scratch the surface of his achievement without steeping yourself in the following: upper-middle-class society in the Midwest at the turn of the century; the early technology of the penny picture and the Kodak folding camera; the development of French symbolism and nineteenth-century realism; the poetry of Hart Crane; Greek Revival architecture in (a) the eastern states and (b) New Orleans; the Civil War photographs of Mathew Brady; the history of the New Deal, with particular reference to the Resettlement Administration set up by the Department of Agriculture; the use of text and typography in modern painting; the life and death of James Agee; the career of Henry Luce, especially the design and editorial practices of *Life* and *Fortune;* the work of Alfred Stieglitz, Robert Frank, and Diane Arbus; the rise and fall of the American left; the American love of advertising; and the American working man. If you also understand the sharecropping system in the cotton industry, and the precise means of operating the tilt device on an eight-by-ten view camera, so much the better.

Just kidding. In fact, the procedure could not be simpler. You walk to the Met, pay your ten dollars, go to the second floor, and look at the photographs. Do not consult the catalogue first; it is lush and helpful, but no reproduction can do justice to the august glow of the prints. All photographs capture light; Evans managed to seal and store it so securely that, like a day remembered as endless, it may never run out. Also, these are small pictures; apart from magazine covers, only one image is more than a foot tall. When you leaf through a book of photographs—or, for that matter, of paintings—they tend to sit snugly within the confines of the page, and you have no true measure of their impact. I remember the shock of entering a gallery of Brueghels at the Kunsthistorisches Museum, in Vienna; some contained whole armies, surely enough to fill a wall, and yet here were these modest, implacably detailed canvases, a few no bigger than a blotter—great reckonings in a little room.

And so it is with Evans. Take *Mississippi Town Negro Quarter, 1936,* with its three men biding the hours—hours that stretch away like fields, you sense, from this fraction of a second—outside a barbershop. Look closer, and you find a fourth man: the ghostly white jacket of the barber himself, beyond the dim doorway. By the time you can read the signs for Coke and cigarettes or the sinister help that is offered to the sick ("666 FOR COLDS FEVER"), you will practically be breathing on the glass. As Evans saw, and as he wanted us to see, there is a world within this frame; and the frame itself is only three and three-eighths inches by five and three-eighths. If the exhibit is a workout for the eyes, it must be hell for the attendants; all along the walls of the Met, there are knots of visitors leaning with suspicious intent, as if they were not on the second floor but stalking the medieval section on the first, peering at a gilded panel to distinguish the sorrowing saints.

The Met makes majestic claims for the show, describing Evans as "among the most influential artists of the twentieth century." This may be true, although there is something in the temperance of his achievement that shrinks at flag-waving and chides our quest for the symbolic. Consider *Joe's Auto Graveyard*, taken outside Bethlehem, Pennsylvania, in 1935; some critics read it as an indictment of ecological waste, and I have also seen it analyzed as a deliberate tribute to those who fell at Gettysburg. Neither explanation is implausible, but we should be careful to note that it is primarily a picture of old cars in a field; Evans spent half a century taking samples of his country, as though of blood or skin, and, if we wish to grow them into an entire culture, that is up to us. His own mantra, like that of so many American artists and writers who pledge to grasp the roughness of the real, was frightening in its modesty: "If the thing is there, why, there it is."

Evans was born in St. Louis in 1903. His father was an advertising executive; a photograph taken in 1900 shows him wooing his bride, Jessie Beach Crane, by means of neatly parted hair, a seducer's wolfish grin, and a guitar. When Evans was about four, the family moved to the swish suburb of Kenilworth, Illinois; the Met exhibit has some snapshots—happy mug shots, mostly—from the end of their time there, including a ten-year-old Walker cocking his head in front of the Stars and Stripes. The Kodak slogan of the time was "You push the button. We do the rest." In the summer of 1916, Evans photographed a pair of pants hanging on a wall in Hamilton, Montana. Never fond of fancy talk, he labelled it "pair of pants." Twenty years later, the same creased honesty—and the same interest in walls, not to mention the stuff people hang on them—engendered some of the most celebrated images of the century.

The family moved around, and Evans's education was rocky. He attended public school in Toledo, Ohio; boarding school in Connecticut; Mercersburg Academy, in Pennsylvania; and Phillips Academy, in Andover, before landing up at Williams College, where he lasted a whole year. And then, just to be different, the sensitive young American sailed for Paris. The fact that Hemingway, Joyce, Gide, Fitzgerald, and William Carlos Williams were at large there has been ground to a fine dust by hordes of cultural historians; far more entertaining is the fact that the young Evans apparently failed to meet any of the above. (According to his most recent biographer, the late James R. Mellow, Evans was accompanied by his mother. So much for wild youth.) One would like to report that he came of age as a photographer in the City of Light, but it seems that all he did was read. Here are the first indications of his unerring taste; he didn't mess around, going straight for the major players—Baudelaire, Flaubert, Joyce. These are the people you have to read if you wish to develop your ruthlessness—the artistic answer to upper-body strength. It should not be confused with meanness; it entails no more than looking with a clear eye, unclouded by the trace of a tear, and rebuffing all blandishments—the need to please, say, or the cry for change—as you struggle to set down your observations. The beauty is in the beholding, not in the beheld. In short, by the time Walker Evans returned to New York, in 1927, he was ready to become a photographer. Instead, he went to work in a bookstore.

How did this man—to some, the greatest of American photographers—happen upon his art? He didn't plan it; it fulfilled no boyhood dream; he acquired no formal training. "I just caught it, like a disease," he said later. If so, he got it bad; inspect the walls of early work at the Met, and you soon realize that here was a chronic case, terminally gifted from the start. Evans lived down the street from Hart Crane—which, given the poet's incandescently awful behavior, was an act of courage in itself—and he was soon invited to supply images for an edition of *The Bridge.* Evans delivered a thick black arrowhead of steel, hammered down from the top of the frame, with a small Empire State Building, grayed by distance, jutting in the opposite direction; how could Crane match that?

> Under thy shadow by the piers I waited;
> Only in darkness is thy shadow clear.

Even now, "thy" is a nasty shock; it's like a hoopskirt in a Jimmy Cagney film. Crane was tuned in to grimy subway talk, and he knew all about the peeling romance of billboards, but he just couldn't bring himself to shake off the courtesies of the Old World—of the way poets, like lovers, were supposed to speak. You could argue that Evans was similarly trapped; after all, the tip of his Brooklyn Bridge is lost in curlicued smoke from the riverboats. Is that not a trace of nineteenth-century fog, lingering like the dreamy climate of an Edward Steichen, or the polite clouds that Evans so deplored in the work of Alfred Stieglitz?

If so, the fog was soon dispelled. To say that it's always fair weather in the world of Walker Evans would be pushing it; think of the rain-slicked diagonals of *Main Street, Saratoga Springs*, taken in 1931, with its ranks of hearse-black cars. But there is no doubt that he enjoyed a clear view. America was so various, so engrossingly cluttered, that to leave any nook or dent of it in deliberate obscurity, let alone in an artful mist, was tantamount to a lapse in democratic duty. Evans himself was not of the sunniest disposition, but the light that plays over *Tin Relic, 1930* so flatters a crumpled loop of architectural detail that it is somehow, without mockery, resurrected as a monument. He liked the curiosities, even the indecencies, of vernacular style: neoclassical columns stuck bravely on the faces of shy New Orleans houses, or a wooden awning, punched like lace, above a simple stand pump in Maine.

At the start of the 1930s, Evans travelled to the South Seas with wealthy acquaintances, and to Cuba on assignment. The pictures that he took on his return look freshly sharpened; you sense the zeal of impatience, and maybe a renewed determination to register the physical fallout of the Depression. By now, he was carrying a 35 mm Leica, sometimes fitting a right-angled viewfinder so that he could catch his subjects unawares; at the same time, he continued to use a heavier, large-format instrument for less fleeting studies. The alternating technique seems true to Evans's nature; he was restless, both in wanderlust and in other varieties of desire—in his sixties, he would sit and recite the names of girls on whom he currently had a crush—yet we honor him today for steadiness of intent. His famous shot of a barbershop in New Orleans, with its vorticist battle of stripes, is softened by the plump stare of the woman at the door; according to Mellow, she is not in the previous exposures—she must have suddenly appeared, although whether she was invited to strike a pose we will never know. Evans effortlessly asks the oldest question of all, the snapper's dilemma: Do you want to cage life, or catch it on the fly?

Evans was so decisively his own man that it's strange to realize how frequently his art belonged to others. His first commissions, in the early and middle 1930s, came from men like Lincoln Kirstein, his friend and promoter, who wanted records of Victorian architecture; in 1935, Evans was hired by the Department of the Interior to document a beaten-down mining area of West Virginia. Soon he took up with the Resettlement (later Farm Security) Administration, an agency of the New Deal. His brief broadened; he was sent south, "to execute photographic work for informational and publicity purposes." He performed his task conscientiously, as he did when compiling color portfolios for *Fortune*, in the 1950s; yet there is scarcely a single instant in the entire Met show when Walker Evans can be accused of executing photographic work for the purposes of anyone but Walker Evans.

This is true even of *Let Us Now Praise Famous Men*. The book has had a curious critical ride. It met with indifference when it appeared, in 1941, but came of age in the sixties, when its anthem to doomed workers struck a chord with the civil-rights movement. Agee toiled for four years on his prose, and you wish he hadn't. These days, the only parts that stay with you are his sturdy, delicate inventories of the sharecroppers' worldly goods: "A cracked roseflowered china shaving mug, broken along the edge . . . A pink crescent celluloid comb: twenty-seven teeth, of which three are missing." It could be a forensics report from a crime scene, and, from the point of view of Agee, a card-carrying communist, that was pretty much what it was. His torrid idealizing of manual labor, matched only by a guilt-scarred fretting over the intrusiveness of his presence, makes him sound like a more clotted version of Levin in *Anna Karenina*, cutting hay with peasants whom he will never resemble; the irony is that Agee's mission succeeds only when it starts to approach the condition of a Walker Evans photograph. I would swap all his swooning evocations of "the tragic land" for one shot of a local cabin—the crisp white wood of its walls, layered like geological strata, shining against the forest of foliage and the storm-dark backing of the sky.

From here, the irony deepens and spreads. The most persuasive visual renderings of the Depression were, it turns out, made by a man who, in 1935, wrote a memo to himself that declared, "NO POLITICS whatever." This means not that Evans the voter had no views but that he would under no circumstances allow them to color the monochrome precision of his prints. He himself was of a liberal cast, although, by the standard of his more fiery friends, he cut a conservative figure in his English tweeds and shoes. My favorite Evans anecdote concerns a trip to Georgia that he made with a friend named Gifford Cochran in 1935; if the 35 mm shots of roadside life seem a little blurred, that may be because Cochran's butler, James, was driving too fast. In one frame, the hood ornament in the foreground pokes at the black family walking by. Such condescension would be laughable were it not for the nagging fact that the photographs of the

Savannah docks, where James chauffeured Evans one afternoon, are as witty and respectful as you could wish for. It's the old Flaubert trick: compassion, like contempt, is all very well, but feelings cannot begin to warm up until the cold eye has done its duty. Although Evans pursued what he called "the art of seeing," at some indefinable point the art shades into morality: don't look up at people, and don't look down on them, either; just give them your level gaze.

That's why the most affecting pictures in the show come at you head on. When Evans points his lens skyward at a statue, it strikes a false note; when he sets up directly opposite a fruit store, or a movie poster, or one of those squat, heroic little churches which he sought and loved, his scrupulous record feels like a matter of honor. One of the advantages of a large-format camera, for all its bulk, is that the final image can be a contact print—the negative laid straight on the paper, with no enlargement to degrade the clarity. You might expect head-on shots to lack the dimension of depth, but it is there in the microscopic play of texture; consult the great Alabama townscapes of 1935–36, and you find yourself following every ridge and wrinkle in the tin façade of a contractor's store in Moundville, and thrilling to the angled sunlight that knifes in from the side of a Selma street. If you think you recognize that angle, you're right. The first Evans show—"Photographs of Nineteenth-Century Houses"—staged by Lincoln Kirstein, at the Museum of Modern Art in 1933, ran alongside an Edward Hopper exhibit. From this distance, the kinship looks intense; the Selma photograph is no homage, but the shadows (and the ominous silence) are as clean-cut as those of Hopper's *Early Sunday Morning*. Is it early morning in the Evans, too? Or is the day winding down in disappointment?

The most disquieting thing about the Met show is that, as it proceeds, you find yourself wondering just how interested Walker Evans was in people. The biographies present a dedicated, often unsympathetic figure. "I play tennis and drink iced tea in grateful seclusion," he wrote from Florida in 1934. If you want evidence of his casual anti-Semitism (Ralph Steiner, who gave him photography lessons, was "a bitter little Jew"), or of his even more startling misogyny, it is not hard to find. On the other hand, the list of things he held in contempt, typed out in 1937, begins with "men who try to fascinate women with their minds."

Evans married twice, and divorced twice, and strung women along; he was involved with Agee's sister, and then with Agee's first wife, and then, for good measure, he got into a threesome with Agee and his second wife. But the sense of try-anything boredom is more pressing than that of passion; his brio is reserved for his camera, and what matters is how insistently—and, if one is honest, how fruitfully—such diffidence leaks into the work. He was not a humanist like Henri Cartier-Bresson, or a sentimentalist like Robert Doisneau, and he lacks the nostalgic *douceur* of Eugène Atget, whom he much admired; Evans was a classicist, and, as such, he forced himself to acknowledge that the human spirit, like the bodies and rooms that house it, is stamped and flattened by the imprint of time. The way to trace the fortunes of the American people, as far as he could see, was to ponder the places where they had come and gone.

In 1938, Evans began to photograph what he called "the crashing non-euphoria of New York subway life." He would hide his Contax under his coat, with the lens peeking between two buttons, and shoot his unwitting subjects across the car. The results, collected under the title *Many Are Called*, had to wait a quarter of a century before they saw the light of day, in a MoMA exhibit—as if the souls enshrined by the camera were permanent residents, and had spent the intervening years in the dirty tunnels. There is a wondrous range of expression here, including an array of the expressionless—city dwellers, alone even when they squash together, weary to their bones. Evans labelled himself "a penitent spy" and "an apologetic voyeur," and *Many Are Called* will grip the psychologist and the sociologist alike; but although the pictures hit hard, the bruises fade with surprising speed. By Evans's own illimitable standards, the character study is never quite enough; even in the Alabama portrait of Floyd Burroughs, Squeekie's father, what one remembers is not just the look in the farmer's eyes but the fraying on the shoulder of his shirt. He is clothed in his own story, and, when the details start to smudge, as they do in the fug of the subway shots, the fullness of life drops away.

By 1940, whether he liked it or not, the master of incognito had become a public figure. "American Photographs," a major one-man exhibit, had shown at MoMA in 1938 to high acclaim. He had the first of two Guggenheim fellowships. By the mid-forties, he was on the staff of *Fortune*, where he later rejoiced in the title of Special Photographic Editor and made himself unpopular. All this might suggest a slackening of effort, or a dimming in the eye; such is the traditional price to pay when the loafing outsider is beckoned into the fold. But, as Mia Fineman points out in an instructive essay for the Met catalogue, "Evans spent most of his professional life lingering just inside the gates of the Establishment." It was a smart place to hang out; you got paid, but nobody would notice if you vanished for a while, and, like a court painter under the Medicis, Evans—the prickly artist as smooth operator—used someone else's money and space to air his lustrous obsessions. He began to shoot in color, but he made sure that it was nothing to shout about. "If you tone it all down," he said, "it's just about bearable." He also designed layouts and supplied short texts, offering further evidence of a lightly saddened wit:

> The methodical, almost loving destruction of a building seems to answer a deep human need that is surely akin to humor, to impudence, and to the balm of irreverence. Hence the rapt sidewalk attendance at spectacles of demolition. Who has not cheered the loosening of a dignified old cornice? Or glowed inwardly over the nicely calculated fall of a really solid brick wall?

That comes from 1951, when Evans was not yet fifty; he had the knack of appearing, or sounding, slightly older than he was. This was no deceit; his sympathy with the wrecking crew and his heartsick reveries on railroad trips across the American plains—where "the country is in semi-undress" and the traveller slides past "the classic barns and the battalions of cabbages"—tell of a genuine addiction to the fading and the failed. Evans hoarded stuff as a dragon gathers jewels into its lair; by the end of his life, he owned nine thousand picture postcards, and, according to his friend the artist William Christenberry, he would steal traffic signs with a tool kit and a can of Liquid Wrench. The Met has some of his junk—stolen goods or otherwise—mounted on a wall, plus some extraordinary Polaroids, taken when Evans was too infirm to handle a bigger camera. It is as though the manic compulsion to register experience—even in rusty scraps, the body parts of a civilization—had become the only surefire way to know that he was still living it. To the end, Evans gave it his best shot.

There is a simple Polaroid from 1973 or a year later. Again, the color is kept to a minimum—charcoal, dull brown, and cream. It shows a sign saying "OP," with a whorl in the wood as neat as a thumbprint. Evans, the sharpest cropper in the history of the medium, was up to his old tricks. As long ago as 1929, he had printed a tight, scumbled closeup of a roadside gas sign, with the scrawled word "Gas" and a large capital "A." It probably stood for "Air," but you never knew, and so it is with OP: STOP? OPEN? SHOP? We can be fairly sure that it is not a segment of POP ART; art historians may try to recruit Evans to the cause, but he lacks the gaudy graphic explosiveness, and his lettering is just too found, too stumbled-over, for the heavily worked numbers and targets of Jasper Johns. At most, Evans embarks on a kind of narrative tease, challenging us to guess what happens next—what lies over the threshold of the frame. "Paul Klee would have jumped out of his shoes had he come upon the green door below," he wrote of one of his color prints in *Architectural Forum*, and there are times when Evans's slow amassing of American things, whether on film or in his own overburdened kitchen, comes close to Klee's secret bestiary of doodles and directives.

Yet Evans the artist was not a keeper of secrets; as a private citizen, he remains self-guarding, but his work fans out into shared pleasures. His pictures are never in-jokes—never belittled by the amusing, look-at-this charm that is so lethal to photography. The crystalline rightness of his compositions makes you think not of days sweated out in the darkroom, let alone under studio lights, but of a guy going out on the road, like a hunter or a salesman, and gazing at places until they bequeath the beauty of their natural form—as if it were hidden there already, and needed only patience to flush it out. An Ansel Adams print leaves you wary of daring to take another photograph ever again, for fear of falling short; it would be like trying to cut your own diamonds. A Walker Evans, on the other hand, makes you want to grab your scabby old Olympus and head for the streets. It's not that you can do better—you would be lucky, in fact, to do a hundred times worse—but your eyes have been rinsed and descaled. The world out there suddenly feels like a movie show, and you don't want to miss it. "Stare," said Evans. "Pry, listen, eavesdrop. Die knowing something. You are not here long."

MARCH 13, 2000

ASTRONAUTS

Immanuel Kant said that two things gave him constant cause for wonder: the starry firmament above and the moral law within. Both are addressed at the Rose Center for Earth and Space, the new and resplendent appendage to the American Museum of Natural History. Drivers who turn off Central Park West onto Eighty-first Street and catch sight of the new planetarium can be forgiven for losing control of their rear ends; a silver-white sphere, eighty-seven feet in diameter, hung inside a glass cube like the desk toy of an executive giant, is hardly your standard roadside attraction, even in New York. Since it opened, visitors have been lining up to enter the sphere, like those hardy pioneers in red jumpsuits at the end of *Close Encounters of the Third Kind.* In the soft darkness, they sit and watch "Passport to the Universe," a thirty-minute virtual canter to the end zone of creation. After that, they are spoiled for choice: they can head for the Hall of the Universe, the Planet Zone, the Black Hole Theatre, and the Earth Event Wall, or simply cool off amid galactic merchandise. A day at the Rose Center is ample demonstration that Kant missed a trick. There are in fact three things to marvel at: the starry firmament above, the moral law within, and the specially designed bow-tie-and-cummerbund set available at the Planetarium Shop for $76.

So what happens to the moral law inside you as the show exerts its grip? How could your valuation of humanity not start to sink as the awful truth hits home? The bottom half of the sphere is filled with a brief demonstration of the big bang; as the aftershock fades, all you want is to lie back and light a cigarette, instead of which you are swiftly ushered out onto the Harriet and Robert Heilbrunn Cosmic Pathway. This spiralling ramp covers thirteen billion years of evolution; depending on your size and stride, it will take you about fifty million years to advance one step, a sensation familiar to anyone who has tried waiting for a cab outside the Port

Authority on a Monday morning. The luminaries who gathered on February 16 for the official dedication of the Rose Center made a credible case for the thrill and lustre that the new exhibit will add to the city, and a slightly less trenchant case for the improvement that it will bring to our interstellar ratings. New York, we were told, has long been "the capital of the world"; from here on, it would be "the capital of the universe." Bad news, ladies and gentlemen: as far as the cosmic map is concerned, we're somewhere in a chicken coop on the outskirts of a ruined village in Chad.

Yet there is hope. Like Mr. and Mrs. Heilbrunn, we march slowly and steadily upward. Not only have we evolved to a level at which we can nurture such majestic inventions as the Hayden Planetarium, the Hubble Space Telescope, and Cameron Diaz; not only have we peered into the farthest reaches of other solar systems and wondered if that faint, spectroscopic glow could be someone waving back at the camera and saying "Cheese!"; we have also, in the full courage of our cluelessness, stepped off the edge of the planet, held our breath, and taken the plunge. The space program gets a pretty bad press these days, and with some justice; it is generally agreed that, next time the boys at NASA land one of their hundred-million-dollar Lego sets on Mars, they should all try to work from the same slide rule. But there was a time—and some of us can't wait for it to come again—when breaking the surly bonds of Earth was the most pressing of scientific challenges, the sharpest spur to human enterprise, the coolest career choice, and the only way by which perfectly healthy citizens could get to suck lunch out of a tube. In retrospect, the space race was less about feeding an old spiritual hunger, let alone scoring political points, than about finding new and unsuspected hungers to sate. Reading Tom Wolfe's *The Right Stuff* or Andrew Chaikin's *A Man on the Moon*, you catch barely a whisper of atomic-age leeriness; what you hear, through the jockeying of the fliers and the word-clipping static of their exchanges with Mission Control, is more like the last hurrah of the Oklahoma land rush. As with any space museum, the Rose Center needs to honor the floating sweat and free-fall exultation of life in orbit, and so it is showing a selection of Apollo photographs entitled *Full Moon.* If your mind wilts at the thought of other people's vacation snaps, think again.

There were a dozen missions in all, starting with Apollo 1, which burned up during the launchpad test in January 1967, and closing with Apollo 17, which staggered back to Earth with 243 pounds of rocks and soil under its belt, in time for Christmas, 1972. In the intervening years, the astronauts found time—it's not as if they had anything else on their hands—to take roughly seventeen thousand photographs. A further fifteen thousand were taken automatically by mapping cameras installed on the spacecraft. The cream of the crop has been picked by the artist and photographer Michael Light; last year, he arranged them into *Full Moon*—a large, square volume that is almost comically beautiful. Now seventy-two of those images have found their way onto the walls of the Rose Center, where they split into three categories: the voyage to the moon, the trip around the moon, and the big stone ball in the sky that caused all the fuss.

When mankind first headed in that direction, nobody thought to preserve the trip for posterity; the dynamics of rocketry and orbital flight were so engrossing that poor old photography—an invention of the previous century—didn't stand a chance. As on every mission for the last forty years (most cleverly, and most fruitfully, *Apollo 13*), a textbook procedure needed a further touch of improvisation, of casual human marginalia; John Glenn had to go and buy himself a 35 mm Minolta over the counter, like a tourist hoping to catch the sunset in Hawaii. Even then, NASA didn't click until Wally Schirra followed suit in the fall of 1962; he went to a Houston camera store and came back with a basic Hasselblad 500C and an 80 mm lens, having presumably asked the salesman—as you do—what would work best in space.

He got the right answer. Hasselblads were already associated with flight; the earliest models were constructed for use by the Swedish Air Force. By the time the Apollo missions began, the NASA-Hasselblad connection was functioning smoothly; it continues to this day, and the near-mythical status of Hasselblad in medium format (the negatives are two and a quarter inches square), forever enhanced by the images from space, is rivalled only by that of Leica in 35 mm. The camera that Neil Armstrong and his team took to the moon was a customized but perfectly recognizable version of the commercial Hasselblad; the trim was stripped away, the controls were made chunkier for gloved hands, and any lubricants—not a good idea in zero gravity—had been replaced by graphite. Conspiracy nuts, inspecting the results, have declared that the lunar photographs are so good that they could never have been taken by amateurs under such testing conditions; they must therefore have been rigged under studio lights, probably by the same people who killed President Kennedy. One flaw in this argument is that astronauts are noted more for their flying skills than for their mendacity; had NASA wanted to maintain a deep pretense, it could have waited twenty years and hired Robert De Niro. The other objection is statistical; on Earth, pros will always hedge their bets by firing off multiple rolls of film in a session, and the same holds true in space. If you take thirty-two thousand photographs, some of them will come out pretty well.

They look even better these days. Michael Light has digitally scanned them, so that you can spot every wrinkle in the imprint of Buzz Aldrin's footstep. (That step, incidentally, could survive intact and uncorroded for as long as two million years, thanks to the lack of wind on the moon; if we blow ourselves up, it could be one of the few means by which other civilizations will be able to learn of our glorious existence, or, at least, of our average shoe size.) The folds and scoops of the lunar landscape, with their backdrop of permanent velvet, assume a strange, granular softness, as if they were etched in drypoint. Sometimes, the ridged tracks left by the lunar rover, dwindling toward the hills, offer the perspective you need; at other times, the reliability of the image begins to crumble. If you pride yourself on distinguishing telephoto shots, because of the way in which background and foreground squash together and shrink the depth of field, try to decipher the pictures that David Scott took of the Hadley Rille in the summer of 1971. Photographed through a 500 mm lens, the stone-strewn floor of the valley looks gentle and close—a bend to be rounded in a few minutes' walk. Only when you pull back, and observe it through Scott's standard 80 mm lens, does the curve resolve itself into the distant segment of a monumental canyon; the loose, kickable rocks ahead are actually boulders, up to forty-five feet wide. Kick one of those and your leg would fall off. On Earth, you would never be tricked like this; even on the most shining day, up in the mountains and away from the smog, remote objects will start to haze in the atmosphere. Such helpful gradations of tone are unknown in the airless clarity of the moon; the yonder may be far, but it is never blue.

So what color is the moon? What we stare at in the sky is a circle of pale gray, unevenly patched; but the astronauts saw a light tan that baffled them, and some of the individual samples broke all the rules. James Irwin and Scott, during Apollo 15, found lumps of what turned out to be green glass, as if young alien partygoers had left their empty bottles behind. On board the final mission was Harrison Schmitt—a geologist, and the first scientist in space. One of the creepiest passages in Andrew Chaikin's history of the Apollo program comes when Schmitt, staring at the dust disturbed by his boots, shouts into his microphone, "It's *orange.*" In the photograph taken that day, you can just make out the glow of this mystery substance—the vestige, like the glass, of ancient volcanic activity—a few yards on either side of him. The surprise is even greater because, apart from minuscule details like the wheel arches of the lunar rover and the lemony tinge of its radio dish, nothing else in this vast picture tells you that it is a color print. At first glance, you would swear that it was black-and-white. If the Apollo missions hadn't come to an end, maybe NASA would have run out of geologists and started sending up movie buffs; who better qualified to report back on a world made from film noir?

The scale of these photographs is a big issue. They were impressive enough on the page; at the Rose Center they are generously enlarged, with a corresponding increase in what astrophysicists term the Wow Factor. Some are composite images—single photographs joined at the hip, as it were, to form a linked panoramic sequence, not unlike the Polaroid constructions of David Hockney. Because of the time taken to frame each photograph, the same astronaut will sometimes appear twice, having walked, or lightly bounced, from one area of landscape to another. Then there is the jaw-dropper, the photograph that tells so dazzling or terrifying a story that you run around showing it to anyone who will look—Ken Mattingly's shot of the lunar module *Orion*, for instance, as it rises from the moon to dock with him in the orbiting *Casper.* The module is a speck, a scrap, a morsel of metal plankton, and the craters looming behind it are a thousand times bigger; you half expect them to pulsate, like jellyfish, and the idea that we dared to visit such monstrosities, let alone to depart in the assumption that we had prised open their secrets, feels impudent to the point of madness. Our relationship with unearthly things, and hence our precarious sense of self, is transformed by such grandeur; a moon the size of a mural somehow acquires a force so iconic that you wonder whether it belongs in a museum at all. You can picture it hung high in a temple, and you certainly understand the exalted place that it still holds in the religious imagination. Andrew Chaikin tells the story of Stu Roosa, the Command Module pilot for Apollo 14, who many years later visited Nepal with his wife. Some Nepalese believe that the moon is home to the spirits of their forefathers, and Joan Roosa was told, "You're married to a god."

The astronauts who appear in *Full Moon* do not look like gods. They look like coal miners hitting a rich seam. True, the visors on their helmets give off a heavenly golden glimmer, but everything else bears the scars of extraterrestrial graft. Once moondust works its way into the wrinkles of a costume, it's impossible to brush away, and if Eugene Cernan's mother could have seen him—happy but wrecked—posing for a colleague after three days on the lunar surface she would have told him to go and wash up before appearing in front of the camera. On Apollo 7, Walter Cunningham took a picture of his commander, Wally Schirra, who had a bad cold; sinuses don't drain well in space, and Schirra has the piggy eyes and puffed cheeks of a man in serious need of hot whiskey and lemon. Cunningham himself, snoozing in Earth's orbit, is hardly a pretty sight: with his rounded black shades, and his stubble even thicker than Schirra's, he makes all too clear the physical strains imposed by the Apollo enterprise. Nobly into the unknown goes the fine flower of American manhood, and back comes Lou Reed.

The most celebrated photograph—the full-length color portrait of Buzz Aldrin by Neil Armstrong—does not appear here, and you can see why. It has become the Mona Lisa of the moon gallery: repeated on a million posters, at once thinned and overburdened by familiarity. The lunar explorers were fed and sustained by fresh imagery as if it were oxygen, and the point of this exhibit is to recapture the shock of the new. So, instead of the Aldrin photograph, we get something altogether less posed and more pugnacious: Charles Conrad's head-on shot of Alan Bean, taken at Sharp Crater in 1969. Bean's arms are half splayed by the distended sleeves of his spacesuit, so that his hands hang wide of the hips; his own Hasselblad is mounted on a bracket at chest height, with a pistol grip screwed to the base. The total effect, with the lens jutting straight at us, is alarmingly close to the classic pose of the gunslinger. It suggests, with a vigor that I haven't seen since the movie of *The Right Stuff*, that the astronauts' professional curiosity was overlaid by something close to confrontation. The moon didn't go all the way and turn them into wolves, but you can see how the legend arose. When you read of Armstrong switching to semi-manual control on his final approach, landing the module with only twenty seconds' worth of fuel in the tank, or of John Glenn, in the hard infancy of the space program, wrestling his capsule down through the Earth's atmosphere, you can't help feeling the heat of life at full burn.

Needless to say, the fellows in white suits kept their cool. "You cats take it easy on the lunar surface," said Mike Collins to Armstrong and Aldrin, as he unhitched *Eagle* and sent them on their way to the moon. Two and a half hours later, he told Charlie Duke, down in Houston, "Listen, babe, everything's going just swimmingly." Some people—writers, mostly, who would have fainted with dismay after one day of basic training—lamented that the men whom America sent into space were not articulate or impassioned enough to register the enormity of their undertaking, but such an ungrateful complaint is wrong in every respect. The astronauts knew full well that they were pioneering on behalf of a planet, and it was in the very ordinariness of their reactions that they carried the human voice—always impressionable, never free from caution, resting on dependable words when fancy ones sound too rich—across 240,000 miles. "It's big, and bright, and beautiful," Neil Armstrong said as *Eagle* settled onto the surface. "Beautiful view," agreed Aldrin a while later, as he followed down the steps. "Isn't that something?" Armstrong said, as if they were stretching their legs at the end of an August picnic. When he went to the launchpad, Armstrong had in his pockets a roll of LifeSavers and a comb. After all, you never know whom you might meet.

Full Moon is true to this clash—the quotidian bumping gently into the unprecedented. A closer shot of *Orion* shows it battered and buckled by its adventures; how touching to be reminded of the lunar modules, and of the absurd, if correct, belief that human beings could be protected by metal sheeting 1/250th of an inch thick. Beyond its frailty, however, the module also delivered a stern rebuke to the imaginings of science fiction. Well before Flash Gordon, writers and designers had favored the sleek and the symmetrical, as if the sole concern of future societies would be to iron out anything that people could trip over; yet here was a small bundle of steel that, in all its crumpled pokiness, was an unsurpassed guide to the virtues of the race that made it—tenacity, teamwork, and the will to find use and even beauty in the graceless. Look at a flying saucer, on the other hand, zipping between galaxies with no more than a low hum, and you just know that the guys inside would be completely floored if you gave them a plate of ribs and no cutlery, or told them to change a flat.

It may sound odd that a tour of the Rose Center, with its clean lines and efficient sense of history, should make us proud of our shortcomings; but the effect of *Full Moon*, as of the other exhibits, is not merely to trumpet our scientific ability but to drive home our delightful inability to make sense of the universe. Listen to people walking around, and the word you will hear most frequently is "like." The moon shots were a flurry of experience for which we still have no adequate points of comparison, so we just toss up as many inadequate ones as we can think of and hope that some of them stick. My notes on *Full Moon* read like this: "Bullet holes." (Four shots of the Timocharis Crater.) "Icebox." (Clouds over the Pacific Ocean, viewed from 120 miles.) "Golf ball." (An especially pocked-looking moon; no wonder Alan Shepard packed a makeshift six-iron.) None of these are accurate, but they are as close as I can get. There is even "Vagina" (Messier Crater) next to "Sperm" (Hadley Rille); that smacks of perversity, of course, but the crater in question does lie in the Sea of Fertility, and Michael Light juxtaposes the two pictures in his book, so I guess I am not the first to see the joke. Whether Neil Armstrong would have got it is hard to say, although he and Aldrin, as they removed their helmets in the safety of the lunar module, happily traded similes over their day's work; one man thought that moondust smelled of "wet ashes in a fireplace," the other preferred "spent gunpowder." Both would be outdone by Clifford Frondell, the Harvard geologist who was present when the first box of moon rocks was opened on live television, in July 1969. "Holy shit!" he said. "It looks like a bunch of burnt potatoes."

When words fail us, we have to make them up, and I like the tale of Ken Mattingly, as he dropped his colleagues on the surface and began his lonely vigils—made companionable by Mahler and Berlioz—on the far side of the moon. Once back in radio contact, he said, to no one in particular, "There's old Mother Earth. Man, that's a beauty, too. Never get tired of watching earthrise." The rest of us will never see it. "Earthshine" and "earthrise" are not merely neologisms; they were coined to describe experiences that were themselves entirely new, at least to human eyes, and you wonder how far the vocabulary of a lunar community would stretch. Would moon dwellers spend their cold, lonely evenings reading *Earthraker* or sitting around a digitally enhanced fire singing "Earthlight Becomes You"? There are inchoate plans to revisit the place and add to the eternal footprints, but the dream of permanent bases, either as mineheads or as staging posts for further exploration, may be the purest moonshine.

One photograph from the Apollo days is even more solidly embedded in our culture than that of a triumphant Aldrin; it is the image of Earth from space—looking, as Armstrong would say, big, and bright, and beautiful. It single-handedly jolted the environmental movement into active life, and made everyone think twice about fouling our blue skies. There is, it turned out, no place like home; but why does that mean we have to stay put? There will be other places, somewhere over the rainbow, that look like nothing on Earth, and somebody—Hasselblad in hand—should go and check them out.

APRIL 10, 2000

JACQUES TATI

When people think of Jacques Tati, what do they think? They probably think of *Monsieur Hulot's Holiday,* which came out in 1953. They may not have seen it for many years, and it will thus have acquired the chafed and faded aspect of a picture postcard. Nothing could be more appropriate, for the film itself, even at first viewing, feels like a memory, reporting back from a past we never had—a string of delicious sensations, as tart and insubstantial as a sorbet. If you can't quite remember the story, that could be because there is none, or, at best, only a ghost of one: a man goes to the seaside, lunches, dines, plays an unwittingly vicious game of tennis, and so on. He converses with a young woman and arranges to go riding with her, but there are unforeseen horse problems, and he never shows. Between them is the merest glint of romance, not only unfulfilled but unbegun. Finally, none the wiser, the man takes his leave, though not before touching off a shackful of celebratory fireworks. There is little for him to celebrate, aside from the fact—we can't prove it, but we would be mortified to learn otherwise—that he has been to this place before and will come again. His brief summer, in all its sandy frustration, is the climax of a plotless life.

Hulot was devised and played by Tati, who directed all four films in which his creation appeared; after the nonadventure of Hulot's vacation, there were calls for *Hulot in London* or *Hulot Goes West,* but, as a man of infinite pains, Tati waited five years to create *Mon Oncle* and nine more before unveiling *Playtime,* the catastrophic crown of his career. *Traffic* followed in 1971, and for Hulot that was the end of the road. Like most serious artists, not least of the comic variety, Tati knew only one way to meet public demand, and that was to answer the needs of his own private imaginings, and then to cross his fingers and see if anyone out there was interested. His films don't look much like anyone else's—if you had seen nothing but *Monsieur Hulot's Holiday*, or even a few stills from it, you could come into a room where *Mon Oncle* was showing on TV and know within seconds whom you were looking at—and they sure as hell don't sound like anyone else's. Half the time, they don't even sound like films. They sound as though someone were holding a radio to your ear and slowly spinning the dial.

Tati was a career funnyman; whether he himself was a funny man is a moot point, but, once the cameras rolled, his dedication to the gag became that of the unappeasable, almost humorless purist. He arrived at simplicity—the visual punch line that gets you in the guts—by means of outrageous complication, and even his most basic jokes have the telling Tati slant. The sight of a man falling into water is unlikely to make you laugh, but Tati returned to it again and again, as if the very plainness of the action challenged his powers of elaborative wit. In *Jour de Fête*, his first masterpiece, he misses a turn and bicycles into a river. He is not looking where he is going because he is too busy imitating the head-down sprint technique of the professional cyclists he has just passed; even better, he finds time, while soaring through the air, to look sidewise with a whip of the head, as if trying to work out what happened to the road. In *Monsieur Hulot's Holiday*, he trips over a cable and flies off a wharf. We hear the immortal twang of the wire, we see him fly, but we do not see him hit the water; all we have is an exquisite, three-second silence as we wait for the offscreen splash. Finally, in *Mon Oncle*, Hulot steps blindly, if demurely, into an ornamental pond—not because he is carrying a chair on his head but because that particular chair has a tasselled fringe that, when inverted, is enough to hide his eyes. This is slapstick heaven, lovingly tricked out with wrong turns and spookily shorn of pain; the angel is in the details.

We do not know much about Hulot; he has no wife, no children, and our only glimpse of his house—a Rube Goldberg affair, overstocked with stairways, in *Mon Oncle*—is from the outside. In the first three Hulot films, he holds no discernible job, and his attempt to get one ends in disgrace, when a typical slither of misunderstandings, beginning with builder's plaster on the sole of his shoe, ends with the interviewer dismissing him for peeping into the women's lavatory. She is quite wrong, of course, not only in her construing of the evidence but in ascribing sexual curiosity of any kind to so scrupulously lustless a gentleman. Even if Hulot remains a cipher, however, his conduct—his physical strategy for the steeplechase of daily existence—has become as familiar as Chaplin's, and if he really is the alter ego of Jacques Tati then the urge to discover more of the ego in question is overwhelming. Enlightenment has now arrived, thanks to David

Bellos, whose *Jacques Tati: His Life and Art* is by far the most attentive biography to date.

For a start, Tati, born in 1907, was not Tati, any more than Walter Matthau was Matthau. Half the great movie personae started life as someone else and never let up; Matthau was a billboard-busting Matuschanskayasky, and Tati, more elegantly, was Tatischeff. His father was half Russian and half French, his mother half Italian and half Dutch; the exotic list of ingredients may help us understand why Hulot, the apotheosis of the Gallic, also leaves behind him, as if to mingle with his pipe smoke, a faint air of the self-effacing Everyman—hailing from anywhere and belonging nowhere in particular. Tati *père* went into the picture-framing business, following his father-in-law, and did very nicely; he was followed in turn by young Jacques, who did less well, although, given that his framing of cinematic compositions was to grow almost Kubrick-like in its obsessive caution, something must have stuck. What Tati excelled at, it turned out, was a range of less delicate skills: rugby, riding, and dancing the Charleston.

David Bellos previously wrote *Georges Perec: A Life in Words* and has translated many of the novelist's famously demanding works, including *Life: A User's Manual.* It is all the more creditable, then, that he should have turned for his next trick to a man who, by his own account, "hardly read anything." Nor, Bellos adds, "did he like writing things down." Tati was as ludic and precise as Perec, but in a medium shorn of verbal flourish; most Tati pictures feel far more heavily choreographed than scripted. He never hung with the intellectual circles of Paris, although his work was suspiciously to their taste; and, for all the rigor of his artistry, he was perhaps the least arty figure in French cinema. Bellos has a good chapter on Tati's military service, which the twenty-year-old beanpole spent with the Sixteenth Dragoons, a cavalry regiment stationed outside Paris. "For sheer comic effect," he recalled more than half a century later, "no clown, no supposedly amusing film, can match the first riding lesson of a squad of raw recruits."

What matters about Tati the rugby player, apart from the thought of that darting, long-boned figure bearing down on his terrified opponents, is what happened after each match: in the locker room, he would apparently replay the entire match for his own benefit—"in a kind of trance," as Bellos puts it. This knack was noticed, and Tati was asked to repeat the routine for an audience, at club dinners; it was soon worked up into an act entitled "Sporting Impressions," which an impoverished Tati then took to the boards of the music halls. The targets of his mime were a cyclist, a boxer, a goalkeeper in soccer, an angler, and a centaurish blend of horse and rider, and as Tati switched to film—he was infuriatingly vague about the transition, and Bellos, perhaps unavoidably, keeps pretty quiet about it—the action never stopped. The first film in which Tati appeared was a 1932 short about tennis; there was a boxing match in *Work on Your Left*, in 1936, and his first movie of any consequence, the fifteen-minute *L'École des Facteurs*, was about a cycling postman. The postman then got a whole film to himself, the glorious *Jour de Fête*, while both tennis and horseback-riding—or bridling horseplay, at any rate—made a comeback appearance in *Monsieur Hulot's Holiday*. In the last film that he directed, *Parade*, Tati performed, in refined but essentially unaltered form, his sporting impressions; he was back where he began. That was in 1974, and we gain a touching sense, as with Buster Keaton, of skills learned and burnished with such graceful application in an artist's springy youth that, like his best friends, they remain in service through the fall and winter of his career; the habits of the body are thankfully more ingrained than any ideas concocted by the mind, and always, in some mysterious way, more telling than the motions of the soul. The great cycle of life, for Jacques Tati, was not so much a matter of cosmic truth as something that you pedalled into a hedge. Both, of course, could be a pain in the ass.

Everyone loves *Jour de Fête*, just as everyone likes a certain idea of France. Finished in 1947 but not released until 1949, the film is set in a village named Follainville (in reality, Sainte-Sévère), embedded in deep country—so deep that you could be forgiven for treating it as timeless. In this malodorous Eden, the only serpent is progress. All the trappings are in place: skipping kids, foggy hangovers, and a scrunched old peasant with a goat. (She wanders around like a cackling chorus, commenting on her neighbors, including, at one vertiginous moment, "Old Godot." Beckett wrote his play between 1948 and 1949.) When Tati's character, François the mailman, comes to deliver a letter to the farrier, the guy is busy shoeing a horse, so François deftly flips up the animal's tail and tucks the letter underneath. We are so carefully cushioned with gentleness that it comes as quite a shock to see a couple of American servicemen lounging by the side of a road, next to a jeep marked "Military Police." The film was shot in the raddled aftermath of war, and Bellos is assiduous in reminding us of that weird proximity; the chugging tractor that hauls the components of a fun fair into the village square, passing gilded fields where the locals make hay, was borrowed from a farmer, because the waiting list for a new one would have been unending. "Less than three years before the shoot began," Bellos writes, "the Gestapo still had an office on the main square of Sainte-Sévère."

Jour de Fête was a great success; it won the prize for best screenplay at the Venice Film Festival—a notable achievement for a film that contains more chicken squawk than dialogue, but also a demonstration that viewers everywhere were thirsty for amnesiac art. Tati himself, after a brief spell in the defeated French Army, had spent the war playing the clubs and music halls of Paris; he had also performed in Berlin, although his judicious biographer points out that this was not uncommon, triggered more by penury and ethical slackness than by any will to collaborate. (Maurice Chevalier, for instance, did far worse, and was welcomed back to Hollywood.) According to Bellos, Tati "was neither a war hero, nor a member of the Resistance, nor an active collaborator. . . . In other words, he behaved like most French men and women." His genius for the ordinary, inherited from Chaplin, enabled Tati both to root his gags in common experience, lightly soiled and easily recognized, and to cultivate the sweet-smelling myth that a trauma of extraordinary proportions had been little more than a bad dream. The shell-shocked may well flee gratefully into the arms of an idyll, and there is little in *Jour de Fête* that would have troubled the senses of the Vichy regime; you half expect Captain Renault, on the run from Casablanca, to turn up as the village mayor.

Does this determination to look the other way, if not to wipe clean, persist into *Monsieur Hulot's Holiday*? Is there something more than an orderly aesthetic—something morally willed—in its tableaux of calculated whimsy? If so, Tati would hardly have been the first Frenchman to throw himself into the notation of noontide joy as a means of dismissing the shadows; Matisse retired to a tropical paradise inside his villa while his wife and daughter fought in the French Resistance, and, nearly 250 years earlier, some of Watteau's *fêtes galantes*, all fans and lutes, were painted when starving Parisians were feasting on the dead. Bellos doesn't labor the point, but it had never occurred to me that the summer of 1952, when the film was shot on location, "was the first in which holidays had once again become possible for the French middle classes." In other words, people in France rushed to the coast much as moviegoers around the world then lined up to see them rush; there is such balmy relief in watching the movie, which guides us through the jokes as if they were paintings in a gallery, that we may not notice the grit in its eye. Although Tati's gaze is benign—it would grow colder, if never caustic—he neatly dots the days with specks of the weary and the fractious. (This is, after all, a vacation.) Critics often chastise him for his pallid lack of interest in character, but *Monsieur Hulot's Holiday* provides a withering portrait of a marriage. A middle-aged British couple idle through the scenery, the broad-hatted wife exclaiming brightly, "Look! A boat!," the scolded husband not daring, or even bothering, to complain. As she hands him seashells, to be stored as mementos of this placid imprisonment, he glances at each one and tosses it away.

In person, the director was seldom lavish with his feelings, and Bellos offers many instances in which Tati's reserve—and, increasingly, a pride in his own inventive gifts—tightened and pursed into rudeness. Yet the movies, especially in the first half of his life, glitter with a kind of emotional pointillism; individual gags seem neutral, lit only by technical brilliance, but they accrue into a strange panorama of loss, inviting us to laugh with a clear conscience at the stunting of insignificant hopes. My two favorite sequences consist of Tati in solitude; he makes only loose connection with other folk, but, left to his own destructive devices, he allows the basic centrifuge of his nature to spin. On a moon-drenched night in *Jour de Fête*, the mailman—much the worse for drink, and all the better for it—tries to ride his bicycle next to a fence, and there is nothing lovelier in Tati than the *thud* of his front wheel meeting an apple tree and the mild, Hesperian rain of fruit upon his head. For his part, Hulot, in riding gear, goes to a boarding house on a date; he is seen to a living room and asked to wait. By the time the girl comes down, he has taken the place to the verge of chaos and steered it back again, the crisis deepening when the spur of his boot hooks the open mouth of a fox pelt on the floor. He is annoyed, but not unhappy, at this constant stream of mishaps, and Hulot would scarcely be himself if the flow dried up. Not since the perfecting of silent cinema had anyone nudged us so neatly toward the essential conundrum of comedy: do we make things happen or do they happen to us? If I find myself being chased around an empty room in Normandy by a fox, even a dead one, whose fault is that? Why was it so predictable that when Tati had the honor of an audience with the pope, in 1958, a mixup led to the Holy Father's addressing him on the subject of gas, electricity, and plumbing?

In the major works of Tati's maturity—*Mon Oncle* and *Playtime*—the balance undoubtedly tips. Not a whole lot happens in these movies, apart from Hulot's getting snarled up in unfamiliar settings, but, by any reckoning, they were grand designs; Tati's preparation for each movie, and his control on set, allowed almost no room for maneuver, and Bellos includes a photograph of the director showing one of his actors the precise way in which he should sweep the street. The centerpiece of *Mon Oncle* is a modern house in a Paris suburb: chalk-white and cuboid, marked by brief shrieks of color, tricked out with meaningless gadgets and, by way of a gushing centerpiece, a statue of a spewing fish in the garden. *Playtime* takes that idea and multiplies it a hundredfold. We are now in Tativille, as it came to be known: an actual conurbation that was constructed solely for the purposes of the movie, complete with soaring office blocks and functioning road systems. It stood in southeast Paris, and took six months to build, starting in September 1964; the film did not screen until 1967, and in the meantime Tati had mortgaged everything he owned. By the end, he had almost nothing; his own house was repossessed, and his life's work, including all rights, was sold off to an Italian banker with no interest in cinema. Tati was tided over, in part, with money raised from his fellow–rugby players; a loyal man, he had kept in touch for half a century. He died in 1982, after a decade of sporadic work that included a commercial for low-fat yogurt; according to some friends, he wanted his body to be taken out with the trash.

To this day, *Playtime* has never been properly released in America. Even the prints that screen elsewhere are disfigurements of the original; to hit the two-hour mark, Tati amputated twenty minutes that have not been seen since. *Playtime* was shot in 70 mm, which somehow magnifies the disaster; it becomes his *Heaven's Gate*, his *Apocalypse Now*, except that those pictures can boast the sprawl and strife, the sheer loudness of mouth that befit a broken epic, whereas what Tati ruined himself for was, when you come down to it, the chance to see a chair covered in black plastic make a funny sighing sound when he sat on it. Few of the gags are louder than that, and many of them, tucked away in remote corners of the screen, will pass you by until you see the film for the fourth time—itself an improbable event. As Bellos wrote of *Jour de Fête*, "Tati treats the dialogue track as if it consisted of background noise, and sets the background noise in forward perspective, as if that were where the story really lay." Tati is the only filmmaker I can think of who was brave enough, and mad enough, to suggest that we can operate without a center of attention—or, at any rate, that our attention tends to flicker and flip with such speed that we don't need a center. This theory (Tati labelled it "democratic") flies in the face of all aesthetic evidence; surely we yearn to focus on *something*. Tati would argue that he had life on his side; that in the echoing halls and airport lounges of *Playtime*, lightly peopled with stragglers we can't place and itchy with muttered conversations in tongues we half understand, we are getting, at long last, a simulacrum—a sporting impression—of being alive.

The reputation of Jacques Tati has itself suffered from slapstick. It slipped and fell well before his death, then sprang to its feet, only to sink once more; you rarely hear contemporary directors mention his name, and Bellos was bold to go public with his admiration. Most movie stars would beg for a biography like this; shy of dumb hero worship, stoutly defensive of genuine inspiration, it throws nothing more than polite glances at the personal life of its subject, preferring to unpick the stitching of his jokes, or to step back and stare at the society from which he emerged, and which he could never quite bring himself to flay.

By rights, *Mon Oncle*, *Playtime*, and *Traffic* should seethe and spit; they hold modern architecture, modern manners, and modern communications up to the light, and we expect the worst. Whereupon Tati comes to the conclusion that, far from being oppressed, mankind has done rather well to surmount these various innovations—which are, admittedly, good for a laugh. "All Tati's work . . . is essentially angled toward reconciliation, not revolt," Bellos says. "Tati was not out to change the world, but to help us look at it with less horror." There is less venom in the whole of *Traffic*, or, indeed, in the whole of Tati, than there is in a single tracking shot by Jean-Luc Godard: the slow, infamous procession, in *Weekend*, along a row of stalled or stuttering cars, with the camera gliding nervelessly past the fatal wreck that caused the gridlock and the corpses lying untended, as if awaiting vultures, by the side of the road. This is where you are heading, Godard says, eager to blow up the culture before it runs out of gas, whereas *Playtime* ends with the serene vision of a rotary system transformed into a carousel; the cars circle without haste or wrath, buoyed by a fluting score, and suddenly we feel ourselves back in the warm air of *Jour de Fête*. Tati's career is thus bracketed by fun fairs; against all the odds, the land of lost content is regained, the spirit of cornfields reborn amid glass and concrete. This is the sheerest fantasy, just as Godard has to overreach himself in the damning of bourgeois indifference. You can feel the drive, at once bullheaded and balletic, of both directors; both of them, impatient with the world as they find it, set about reorganizing it—Tati to his satisfaction, Godard to meet the high standard of his disgust.

Yet Godard was a Tati fan, and it is he who nailed, in a single sentence, the imperishable oddity of Tati's comic approach: "He looks for problems where there are none, and finds them." Just what manner of mind would dream of a circumstance in which the bulbous, old-style horn of a car would be stuck to the spare tire, which would fall off and rotate against the ground, which in turn would make the horn emit regular honks, which in turn would cause a nearby hunter to pause in mid-shoot, swivel, and fire at what he believes to be approaching ducks? That flirtation with the surreal, never quite yielding, keeps *Monsieur Hulot's Holiday*, like its elastic hero, on its toes. As the movies proceed, however, they harden up in a rage for exactitude, and the fullness of their curiosity dwindles as the ambition swells; *Playtime* is astounding, but to think back to *Jour de Fête* is to trace the arc of a man who began as a Brueghel and wound up as a Mondrian.

Late Tati discovers amusement not so much in things that he, or Hulot, happens to observe as in gags that have been primed like booby traps; if there are high, round windows in the house in *Mon Oncle*, for instance, it is because, when the lights come on at night, a figure can appear at each porthole and move from side to side, thus creating the illusion of huge, inquiring eyes. There is, I have to admit, nothing particularly funny about that, although everyone smiles at the cunning of the conceit. I sometimes have the sense, when stranded in deepest Tati, that I am watching a game of chess, or a puppetry demonstration, that was accidentally transferred to film.

There will always be those who don't get Tati—who are repelled by the chill patience of such manipulation, or who simply find Hulot an intrusive bore. Returning to the slender body of work, with its unexpected intensity, I found myself welcoming the intrusion, and looking forward to the arrival of that gangling shape, with its continual suggestion of a man about to morph into a cartoon. The props hardly vary: raincoat, pipe, umbrella, and pants just short enough to show a sticklike pair of ankles. There are no bends. If I could take anyone to a Tati retrospective, it would be Euclid; he alone, perhaps, would appreciate the stern mastery of unswerving line, and the implication that a human being can be measured by the angle at which he meets—and, more often than not, demolishes—his environment. Everything is Hulot's fault, and yet he is never to blame; when the swish, hushed restaurant falls apart in the climactic second act of *Playtime*, Hulot is merely lending a helping hand to the inevitable entropy of the modern age.

He does so, of course, with reflex, antiquated courtesy; I love Tati film posters, but they can never catch the stiff bob, the bounce on the balls of the feet, the tip of the hat to belles and bounders alike. Maybe our own time is too informal for great comedy; Tati was one of the last, lucky artists to operate on the Wildean principle that anarchy is best practiced within the confines of codified behavior. That he came to resemble Charles de Gaulle—increasingly so, as one movie succeeded another—merely completes the picture, with the savior of the nation meeting his mirror image in the man who, without really trying, kept tripping over selected areas of the nation and ripping them to bits. Mind you, all Frenchmen of distinction, even such arch anti-Gaullists as Mitterrand, seem to acquire the profile and demeanor of the general; let us call it the hauteur theory. David Bellos records the occasion when the two men—film director and president—came face to face. "Jacques Tati," murmured the president's secretary. There was a pause. "*Mon Oncle*," he added helpfully, whereupon de Gaulle congratulated a bemused Tati on his nephew. It sounds true, even if it isn't; the same can be said of Tati's unmistakable oeuvre, which shows us, in case we hadn't guessed, how much fun there is to be had in tinkering with the intricate mechanisms of the world. We can come together; all it takes is a little misunderstanding.

NOVEMBER 13, 2000

LUIS BUÑUEL

The first thing to say about Luis Buñuel, movie director and disturber of the peace, is that he looked the part. The great filmmakers, however rare their own appearances in front of the camera, almost always come to resemble their collected works. No one could sit through a Hitchcock season, for example, and imagine that its creator was a carefree and sexually contented beanpole. Godard is the mad professor, beloved of his students and nobody else; Howard Hawks is the sly jock with money and girls to burn; Billy Wilder grins like a miniature devil from the margins of a gilded manuscript—the imp who knows too much. Buñuel beats them hollow: that square, sawed-off head, the ripe, amusable mouth, the martial breadth of brow and chin. And, most of all, there are the eyes. Hooded above and pouched below, they shimmer with the virtues, or vices in disguise, of the Buñuelian gaze: dignity, lubricity, and doubt. You can easily picture yourself being hypnotized by this man; sit through a sample of his movies, and you will think you have been.

Your best chance is now available at the Museum of Modern Art, which has organized an overview of the Master's domain. The season includes a screwball comedy from 1949, adaptations of *Wuthering Heights* and *Robinson Crusoe*, and even the shortened version of Leni Riefenstahl's *Triumph of the Will* which Buñuel edited for MoMA during the Second World War. Then, there are the greatest hits: you can catch a fresh case of the jitters from *Un Chien Andalou* (1929), test the sincerity of your anarchist leanings against *L'Age d'Or* (1930), leer at Jeanne Moreau and her glittering little boots in *Diary of a Chambermaid* (1964), struggle vainly to pretend that you are not turned on by *Belle de Jour* (1967), and wonder if you are among those under suspicion in *The Discreet Charm of the Bourgeoisie* (1972). The most beguiling of his comedies, *Discreet Charm* was a hit; Buñuel's gaggle of well-dressed characters, continually meeting up for meals that are pulled or postponed at the last minute, may have been meant to indict the metronomic cravings of the middle class, but to anyone who has ever prowled the Upper East Side at nine o'clock with an empty stomach and no reservation the film feels like an authentic vote of sympathy.

Its success spoke of another possibility, one that is now almost unthinkable: moviegoers can be stretched, and they can learn to love it. Buñuel's movie is a picaresque, yet it never rambles; it asks you to keep up, to follow the leakage of one story into the next, and to join in the fun when the diners take their places at a table and find themselves on the stage of a theatre, with the curtain rising, and a prompter hissing their lines. Is Buñuel implying that the social round is no more than a bad charade? If so, he doesn't say as much, preferring to flatter us with an outrageous suggestion: work it out for yourselves.

Buñuel was born a century ago, in February 1900, the eldest of seven children. He came from Aragon, in the northeast of Spain; his birthplace, Calanda, was not far from that of Goya. In his delectable autobiography, *My Last Sigh*—published in 1982, the year before his death—Buñuel wrote of his home town, "The Middle Ages lasted until World War I. . . . The same gestures were repeated from father to son, mother to daughter. Progress, a word no one seemed to have heard, passed Calanda by, just like the rain clouds." The sounds that beat the time of Luis's childhood were those of bells and drums—the notorious drums of Calanda, which are pounded by the menfolk without cease for an entire day, beginning at noon on Good Friday. "By the early hours of Saturday morning, the skin of the drums is stained with blood," Buñuel wrote. He himself took part in the ceremony until well into adulthood, and the echo of that sound carries into his films; many of them are sparsely scored, requiring no lush tunes to make an emotional point but pitted instead with gunfire, drumrolls, and the ringing of the Angelus—the soundtrack of worship and war.

Buñuel's father cuts an admirable figure, especially for those of us who treasure the lazy and the lax. "The fact of the matter is that my father did absolutely nothing," his son says. In Zaragoza, where the family spent much of the year, Leonardo Buñuel's most demanding physical task, according to Luis, was to carry a jar of caviar down the street. There is something about the neatness of this image—the careful asceticism of the action, spiked with the luxury of the goods—that slots unmistakably into the Buñuel armory. It makes me think of all the little containers that litter his films, from the striped box that hangs around the neck of the bicycling man in *Un Chien Andalou* to the musical box in *The Criminal Life of Archibaldo de la Cruz* (1955), which the fantasy-fuelled hero believes to have murderous properties, and so to the fabulous, secretive casket in *Belle de Jour*, which buzzes like a delinquent bee and intrigues all those who peek inside.

Buñuel was educated in Zaragoza, first at the College of the Brothers of the Sacred Heart, then at the Jesuit College of the Saviour; he served at Mass, sang in the choir, and became, by his own account, fluent in Latin. It is a commonplace to regard Buñuel as the leading anticlerical light of the cinema, and to applaud him for the unstinting siege that he laid against religious hypocrisy. "He is a deeply Christian man, and he hates God as only a Christian can," Orson Welles said of him. You can only hate something that you know to exist; the Almighty is the cause of much defiance and disappointment in Buñuel's films, but nowhere could I find any denial of His presence. The extent of His efficacy, let alone that of the Church, is another matter. *Simon of the Desert* (1965) is the fable of an early hermit who lives atop a pillar, casting about for godly things to do. ("Who can I bless now?" he asks vaguely.) A man with stumps for arms prays to be healed, and Simon grants his wish, but the miracle backfires; the first thing that the man does with his restored hand is to cuff his small daughter over the head and tell her to shut up. That Buñuel lost his faith as a teenager seems to me less interesting than the tenacity with which the habits of faith—the rhythms of ritualistic behavior, the hallucinogenic draw of decorum—swung as smoothly as a censer through the calm of his career. His characters, left to their own devices, will invariably worship something, but it tends to be the shape of women's legs. Just to make the point, *Él* (1952) begins with the courtly Francisco falling in love with the devout Gloria—or, to be precise, with a glimpse of her feet and calves—right in the middle of the Mass. Buñuel was the first upstanding heretic in cinema, and the last.

At the age of seventeen, he went to Madrid, and moved into the Residencia de Estudiantes. There, among other things, he cultivated the banjo, the boxing ring, and the brothel; he also discovered a rare talent for putting people into a trance. His studies followed a patternless course, from agronomy to industrial engineering to entomology to philosophy; even when he wasn't sure where he was going, Buñuel could rely on his good taste—including, of course, a taste for the devilishly bad—and a surge of bullish momentum. That flirtation with entomology, for instance: did he know how useful it would be? Could he somehow foresee all the shiny automata that throng his early works: the ants that scurry over the palm in *Un Chien Andalou*, the fighting scorpions that herald *L'Age d'Or*, or the brief tutorial on the malarial mosquito in *Land Without Bread*? Even cooler than Buñuel the intellectual vagabond is Buñuel the picker of friends. His memories of that time brim with a host of Spanish artists and writers, including Lorca and Salvador Dali, and with an instructive lexicon of Spanish attitudes; it is worth acquainting oneself with the niceties of *chulería* ("virile insolence") and *morcillismo* ("a kind of manipulative humor"), because, although Buñuel spent decades in exile, much of it self-imposed, he always travelled with a store of these patriotic spices, adding a pinch of turn-of-the-century Calanda or a twist of twenties Madrid to even his most far-flung concoctions.

His itinerary, on leaving Spain in 1925, was a series of distinct chapters. He went to Paris, as you might expect, and made *Un Chien Andalou* and *L'Age d'Or*, loading his pockets with stones for the premiere of the latter, in case of trouble. A wise move, as it happened; when the movie turned out to be a rampant endorsement of sexual hunger, with musical soirées and government delegations alike being interrupted by the need for fornication, the cinema was stormed by the Anti-Jewish League and other furies of the right. To the ravenous Buñuel, this was easy meat; he later introduced a screening of the movie with the words "What I want is for you *not* to like the film, to protest. I would be sorry if it pleased you." In 1930, in the space of a few months he both received an invitation to attend the Second International Conference of Revolutionary Writers, in the Ukraine, and a call from MGM. As career choices go, it must be a world first, and Buñuel decided on Hollywood, where his proudest achievement was to be thrown off the set by Greta Garbo. With exquisite timing, he arrived back in Europe just after a socialist republic had been declared in his homeland. The climate of that era suited Buñuel, and the product of the ensuing years was his bone-dry documentary *Land Without Bread* (1933). For forty dumbstruck minutes, we are stranded in a forgotten, infertile region of Spain, where children die of throat infections in the street and the only smiles are those of the mentally handicapped. There have been complaints from modern residents that Buñuel faked or forced his evidence, but by the time of his visit he was a trained surrealist, guaranteed to focus on the object that compels and repels; what is more, he was on the side of the sufferers. *Land Without Bread*—no metaphor, in that wheatless place—is the tough link between a refined artistic movement and the rawness of political protest.

Buñuel was not a politician; his gifts lay elsewhere, in images that both slithered and snapped, like eels, and that would make any politician nervous. Even a polemic as direct as *Land Without Bread*, which should have lent weight to the left, was rejected by Republican authorities, who wanted their rustics to look happy. Buñuel befriended many communists but was never, as far as one can gather, an active member of the Communist Party. *Viridiana* (1961), the tale of a novice nun who inherits her uncle's estate, has an enviable reputation for blasphemy (one shot is an artful parody of Leonardo da Vinci's *Last Supper*), yet I find it no less merciless toward the notion of class solidarity. When the peasants finally take over their employer's house, they lurch headlong into gluttony and rape; no card-carrying communist, sworn to uphold the perfectibility of man, would have countenanced such a scene, and Buñuel had as little time for the sentimentalizing of the proletariat as he did for the glamorizing of its overlords. He may have described *Un Chien Andalou* as "an incitement to murder," but when it came to real bullets, in the Spanish Civil War, he was disgusted by the killing of priests. (One thinks of W. H. Auden, whose poem on the conflict made infamous reference to "the necessary murder," a phrase the poet later withdrew.) A Buñuel film bathes in anarchy, but real chaos—the splintering of the revolutionary left into factions—is bare of blitheness and poetry, and the war, far from hardening the director's political creeds, merely deepened what he called "my fundamental need for order and peace."

Buñuel spent much of the Second World War in Hollywood, which could never quite decide what to make of this singular figure. In 1946, he moved to Mexico, reforging his contact with Hispanic culture; the result was *Los Olvidados* (1950), as down and dirty a film as he would ever make. After a decade and a half of strongly brewed melodramas, few of them free of surrealist surfeit, he returned in triumph—or, to some onlookers, in disgrace, which was his preferred version of triumph—to the uncertain embrace of his homeland. *Viridiana* represented Spain at the Cannes Film Festival in 1961; the director insured that no one from the Franco government saw the film until after it screened, by which time all complaint was far too late. That it was then banned in Spain and condemned by the Vatican proved that the middle-aged revolutionary, the magician with the bomb under his hat, was still on active service. It was not until 1970, and the chill of *Tristana*, that he was able to work in Spain; the intervening years found Buñuel, a tireless bird of passage, shooting his most distinctive and finely feathered films, such as *The Exterminating Angel* (1962) and *Belle de Jour* (1967), in Mexico and France. Scorning any hint of a whimper, he finished off with a bang: the last image of his last movie, *That Obscure Object of Desire* (1977), is a loud explosion. Buñuel was back where he had begun.

* * *

Some months ago, I met a couple at a party. They were English but, until recently, had lived in France, where their first child, a daughter, was born. She arrived prematurely, and was delivered in a provincial hospital; there were no major problems, but her eyes were sticky and gummed shut. The medical staff took her to an adjoining room to clean her up, while the husband stayed to comfort his exhausted wife. Suddenly, he told me, "I had a terrible feeling that something was wrong. I pushed open the door, and there was this doctor, leaning over my newborn daughter, holding a scalpel to her eye."

The very thought of it makes you wince; the proximity of steely hardness to tender flesh—the just-made child confronted by its first man-made object—brushes against our most basic terror of vulnerability. Even as the father concluded his tale, drawing moans from those around, I was thinking: Buñuel. To be specific, I thought of *Un Chien Andalou*, the seventeen-minute assault that was launched upon Paris by Buñuel and his collaborator, Salvador Dali, in 1929. Less than two minutes into the picture, a man—played by the stocky, unmissable figure of Buñuel himself—stands on a balcony, gazing wolfishly at the moon. Cut to the face of a woman. Cut back to the moon; a thin slice of cloud drifts across its face. Cut to an eye; a razor blade knifes neatly and without hesitation across the eyeball, whose contents well and spill like an outsized tear. Cut.

At this point, if you are of a nervous disposition, you faint. (Similar reactions have greeted the blinding on the Odessa steps, in *Battleship Potemkin*, and the vacant iris of Janet Leigh, on the white bathroom floor of *Psycho*. Three of the most famous close-ups in cinema, in other words, are of eyes, either damaged or dead. This is no coincidence; what do you think we are watching with?) Even hardened horror fans, sanguine habitués of gash and gore, tend to flinch at these few seconds; film historians are less surprised, being aware that most of the strong jolts in cinema, like most of the best laughs, are to be found in the first third of its existence. It is an argument that spreads far beyond the movie theatres; one of the unfading signs—the birthmarks—of the major works of modernism is that they refuse to relinquish their power to shock. The first time you hear "The Rite of Spring," you take leave of your skin—not that you are transplanted back to 1913, but that 1913 keeps occurring over and over again, like a pagan liturgy, whenever the piece is played. Even long-term lovers of *Les Demoiselles d'Avignon* continue to bruise themselves on that armor-plated anvil of a face on the far right. And so it is with *Un Chien Andalou*, which is usually treated as a fusillade in the surrealists' noisy quarrel with civilization, yet which displays all the metallic intelligence and narrative rationing of high modernism, and almost none of the capering silliness that blights and dates so much of the surrealist melee. It was a film waiting to happen: not an artifact in the museum of culture but a pathological premiere, forever primed to open big.

Did Buñuel die down after this, even go a little soft? There are quiet patches in his output, to be sure, yet the more closely you look at the oeuvre, the more the chronology condenses. You can smile, or shudder, at something from a film of the 1970s, only to realize that the elderly prankster is revisiting a device of his youth. When a terrorist suspect in *The Discreet Charm of the Bourgeoisie* is wired to the strings of a grand piano, with an electric current running through them, the Buñuel enthusiast will be spirited back to the pair of grand pianos that are hauled into a room in *Un Chien Andalou*, with a rotting donkey's head protruding over the keys. (*The Godfather*, with its horse-head-in-the-bed trick, was not the first film to make use of decayed beast.) As for high-heeled shoes and stockings, the stock-in-trade of every proud pornographer, it is easier to list the few Buñuel films in which they do *not* appear than the many in which they do. The various tributaries of his obsessions streamed together, so that the light domestic madcap of *El Gran Cavalera* (1949) could mingle, in Buñuel's memory, with the erotic logic of *L'Age d'Or* to produce *The Phantom of Liberty* (1974), the most free-flowing of nightmares.

Everyone recalls the sequence, late in that picture, in which guests are politely ushered into a dining room; around the table are lavatories, where they perch, with skirts and pants lowered, to make conversation. Occasionally, someone excuses himself and retreats to a small room down the hall, where he eats a brief, lonely meal. It is a straight switch: the ingestion and expulsion of food have been reversed, allowing Buñuel to point out the arbitrary nature of our social arrangements. (Last month, a district health authority in northern England was condemned by an official report, which found that elderly patients had been strapped to commodes while they ate. Again, as with the razor and the eye, Buñuel was ahead of the case.) What matters in the movie is not the conceit itself but the stylish deadpan with which both the cast and the director carry it through. Even the priests who are interrupted in their boozy, smoke-filled card game by the sight of a hatmaker from Nîmes clinging to an adjoining bed and being whipped on the buttocks by his leather-clad Jewish assistant—not, in my experience, something you see every day—seem only mildly scandalized. I can take or leave the moment in *The Milky Way* (1969) when someone dreams of a pope being executed by a firing squad (by Buñuel's standards, it feels too blatant); what I love is the next line, as the fantasy ends and the man sitting next to the dreamer asks him, "Is there a shooting range nearby?" It is as if reverie worked by osmosis, seeping from one porous mind to another; there is a gentle telepathy in Buñuel, and he draws us into it like sleepwalkers. Only thus, I suppose, will we ever wake up to the fact that reality is mad.

The dream sequence is among the dustiest of devices to which directors resort. If you want it well done, you must turn to the old masters: to the moon-bright, featureless face that greets the aging hero of *Wild Strawberries* in the street, or to the buoyant ascent of *8½*, when Mastroianni, with a worrying lack of effort, floats upward from a traffic jam like a departed spirit or a child's balloon. Buñuel belongs in this company, with Bergman and Fellini; he specialized not just in dream sequences but in dream films. If there is a distinction between the actual and the imagined, you wouldn't put money on it, and Buñuel cuts between the two with disconcerting straightness—no wobbling or hazing of the screen. That is why *The Exterminating Angel*, his most beautiful film, can never be shaken off: it is obviously nonsensical, and it rings hideously true. The protagonists, rich and bored, gather at a town mansion for dinner and discover that they cannot leave the room they are in. They are free to go, but some nameless pressure—it could be politesse or politics, or any of the rules that we obey—keeps them penned in like sheep for weeks. They eat, rut, bicker, and sleep; a china closet, stacked with precious vases, makes do as a toilet. The ladies lining up outside to use it discuss what they have sighted within:

> "I saw a raging torrent."
> "As I sat down, an eagle flew by below."
> "The wind drifted dead leaves in my face."

This dark lyricism—anything but vulgar, despite the topic in question—spreads through *The Exterminating Angel*, and it is good to remind oneself that a Buñuel picture can be not just needle-sharp in conception but lovely to look upon. His militant stances, especially against the established Church, have caused fans and foes alike to think of him as a man with a message; the truth is that he was a man with a medium, and the message that emerged was given infinitely more poise and flavor—the antithesis of agitprop—by that mastery. There is no showiness in Buñuel, no need for visual gymnastics; why force your cameraman to race and swoop when your most special effect is a patient, Jeevesian *froideur*? Take *Diary of a Chambermaid*, with its wintry northern crispness. At one point, the libidinous cad (Michel Piccoli, with a Hitlerian dab of mustache) comes on to his scullery maid for want of anyone better. She is outside, boiling and hanging the laundry, and the combination of shrugging lust and the hot steam that rolls like breath into the frosted air, with the grace notes of chattering chickens and a thorn-crackling brazier, lends the whole scene an inescapable whiff of the medieval. It ends with a close-up, as the plump, placid maid ("I've worked all my life, sir") succumbs to his request; we see her slow tears, and Buñuel leaves us to wonder what upsets her more—these lewd advances or the rueful realization that they are the first she has ever had. All that, in a couple of minutes: so much for Buñuel's indifferent eye.

What will two months of MoMA do to our view of Buñuel? His work is so controlled that we have grown accustomed to the myth of Buñuel the serene and standoffish, hard to unearth from the stubborn ground of his movies. Working through the back catalogue and the biographies, though, I warmed to his presiding genius, and to the silvery editing that causes his films to whisk along, unburdened by indulgence. They are like murder mysteries without the denouement; the clues are left hanging in the air, and all the suspects stay tinged with guilt. When characters in a Bergman film check into a hotel, as they do in *The Silence*, they gradually accumulate a stifled agony; when Buñuel's creatures arrive at an *auberge*, as they do in *The Phantom of Liberty*, they wander in and out of one another's rooms, delighted to find them unlocked. Has any great director been so unabashed at the prospect of pleasure? We should not belittle Buñuel's fierceness; nevertheless, as his own title suggests, the bourgeoisie does at least have charm and discretion on its side, as he did himself. No character in his films, however imperturbable, could begin to approach the clockwork predictability of Buñuel's own days. His routine, at the age of sixty, is described by his biographer John Baxter: up at dawn, a walk, a morning's writing, first cocktail at noon, lunch at one, and so on. Bedtime was at nine. This is as it should be; the world was never changed by *poètes maudits*. If you seek the enemy of society, look for the quiet type in a suit, or the handsome one with a drink. Buñuel devotes a whole chapter of *My Last Sigh* to the importance of bars and to "the primordial role in my life played by the dry martini." He survived on six a day.

Buñuel did not make movies about himself, but he used movies to pursue passions that could belong to no one else. It may sound strange to connect him with love, yet hoards of love accrue throughout his work, and he never ceased to invest in its promise of release. You catch it in *L'Âge d'Or*, as the authorities try to tear apart the lovers who writhe in bliss on the ground; in *Belle de Jour*, in the slow, liquefied smile of Deneuve, raising her head from the sheets that have been rumpled by a giant foreign client; and again in the elderly landowners of *Viridiana* and *Diary of a Chambermaid*, who are felled by the onset of desire. I particularly admire the married couple in *The Discreet Charm of the Bourgeoisie* who, like first-timers or newlyweds, take every opportunity to rip each other's clothes off, even deserting their lunch guests to go and make out in the bushes. If you want to pay tribute to Buñuel at the close of MoMA's season, the most loyal gesture would be not to set fire to the Federal Reserve, or desecrate a church, but to have sex, as noisily as possible, in the foyer of the museum. It is a matter of great regret that no one, not even Warren Beatty, thought to offer such homage when the film won the Oscar for Best Foreign Language Film, in 1973.

The director, needless to say, did not attend—if you think that French high society is a smiling sham, Heaven knows what you make of the Academy of Motion Picture Arts and Sciences. Yet Buñuel did not refuse his golden statue; the thrill of smuggling his insubordination into the heart of the Hollywood beast was far too exquisite. Even if you don't buy the Buñuelian diagnosis of our common ills, you can't help pausing to acknowledge the honesty, clear as gin, with which he tells us how to behave. I like to think that it was in memory of his father, Leonardo, that Luis Buñuel strewed his fictions with fond variations on the *señorito*—the well-bred Spaniard, relaxing into age. The most dapper is Don Lope, of *Tristana*, guardian and later husband of Catherine Deneuve: fastidious, chivalrous, tacitly perverse; perfectly satisfied that humanity has fallen too far to meet his high ideals; a man of the world, yet lightly disconnected from its cares; a man of means rather than ends. How one longs for such a figure to stroll, cane in hand, into the frenzied arena of recent cinema; you can picture Don Lope raising a quizzical eyebrow at the Farrelly brothers and their flailing efforts to offend. The most accomplished *señorito* of all, and also the hardest to spot, was Buñuel himself: the gentleman joker, content to sit back and watch us make fools of ourselves, and to remind us that, as Don Lope says, "the dead don't dream." Hence the noble duty of the living, the one incontestable task that unites the poet, the political activist, the housewife, the sergeant, the saint, and the maître d': Dream on.

DECEMBER 18, 2000

JULIA ROBERTS

What will happen on March 25? A few months ago, moviegoers and studio executives alike were so dismayed by the quality of this year's films that it became possible, indeed fashionable, to fear for the very existence of the Academy Awards. As things turned out, we are facing, if not a feast, at least a decent meal. *Gladiator* will presumably slay all tigers, crouching or otherwise, although I for one would welcome a best-director nod for Ang Lee, largely because of a desire to see him run up the walls of the Shrine Auditorium, spin over Russell Crowe, and bounce lightly off Catherine Zeta-Jones. Amid a night of uncertainty, one sure thing shines out: the Oscar for best performance by an actress in a leading role will go to Julia Roberts. No offense to Juliette Binoche and the other players, but the contest really is no contest. Not just in the hive of Hollywood but in the minds of a hundred million drones around the world, Julia is Queen Bee.

This royal status was confirmed by the receipts for *The Mexican,* her latest picture. There was a distinct lack of rave in the reviews, but that didn't faze the fan base. You could argue that as many people lined up to see Brad Pitt, Roberts's costar, as they did for the lady herself, yet not even the most expert Bradologists would claim that he enjoys her crossover appeal. In short: men like watching Julia Roberts and women like watching Julia Roberts—or, at least, women don't mind watching Julia Roberts, and, even if they did mind, they could always pass the time by watching the men watch Julia Roberts. This is an entertaining, if not an edifying, sight: if you had knelt behind the screen at the premiere of *Pretty Woman* and peeked around the edge, you would have seen the menfolk sitting there, slack as puppies, waiting for Roberts to unleash her grin and wondering if they could climb into her mouth.

What matters about *The Mexican* is not that it collared $20.3 million in its first three days but that, in doing so, it completed a hat trick for the Roberts phenomenon: all three of her most recent movies have slid immediately into the top slot. *Runaway Bride* (1999) ran up $34.5 million over the same period, and *Erin Brockovich* (2000) took $28.1 million. Often a lonely figure, Roberts now has the box office to herself; no other female star comes close. Her male counterparts take home two or three times as much per picture, but that's Hollywood—liberal as you like, but with the crusty old inequalities, racial and sexual, still clinging on below the waterline. The two Toms, Hanks and Cruise, are Roberts's main contenders, but only Hanks seems able to match the progress of the new model Julia, all peaks and no trough. No *Eyes Wide Shut* for her, although it's a tempting thought, especially with those dinky black masks.

Turn back ten years, and the story was much the same. Julia Roberts, born in 1967, was finally living up to her genetic billing. She was a younger sister of Eric, the man who founded an entire movie career on the strength of his cheek muscles, and the daughter of two theatre-thirsty parents who had run the Actors and Writers Workshop in Atlanta. Now it was her turn. According to her biographer Frank Sanello, she had already been voted one of twelve finalists in her high school beauty pageant, which makes you wonder what the other eleven girls looked like, and had been described by her English teacher, following a class reading of *Julius Caesar*, as "a very emotional Brutus." Moving up a gear, she followed her brother to New York and then landed roles in *Mystic Pizza*, *Steel Magnolias*, and, after much lobbying, *Pretty Woman*, which went on to earn a very emotional 450 million dollars. All three films pulled the single whammy that Hollywood, in its sneaky heart, treasures above all else—not the critical and commercial hit but the commercial hit that outwits the critics and proves them superfluous, hooking up a direct feed into public taste. When the reviewers fawned over *Erin Brockovich* and—with more than a murmur of surprised condescension—over the rip and rancor of its leading lady, Roberts may have cast her mind back to the slush of yesteryear, which the same crowd could hardly wait to shake from its boots. Like many popular figures before her, she hitched a ride with Middle America and then waited a while—in her case, a decade—for her more fastidious viewers, the types who would rather die than cry, to catch up.

All of which is no reason to revise one's critical opinion. No amount of retrospection will transform *Mystic Pizza* into *Three Sisters*, although the plots are not that different, and none of us can say what would have happened if Chekhov had recovered from tuberculosis and gone into the pepperoni business. Yet the film works on its own terms, and, considering that it cost only six million dollars, which is what a Jerry Bruckheimer production spends on deep-pan specials to go, *Mystic Pizza* seems to have aged into the favorite movie of an awful lot of people. These are, admittedly, the same people whose notion of a good movie is one that enables them to lie on the couch and snuffle into their Cookie Dough Chip, but they still constitute an important fraction of the viewing audience, and Julia Roberts is mistress of their domain. One of her friends and confidantes has been Sally Field, another reflex tearjerker, who paired with Roberts on *Steel Magnolias*, in the company of Olympia Dukakis, Daryl Hannah, Dolly Parton, and Shirley MacLaine. The characters had names like Clairee, Truvy, and M'Lynn, the very sound of which, I recall, was enough to make me bring up m'lunch.

Steel Magnolias introduced a couple of themes that would echo through the Roberts career. One concerned the women around her; she was canny enough and, one suspects, effusive enough not to elbow other actresses out of her way, refusing to use her beauty, or the likelihood that she would be the Next Big Thing, to turn the picture into a showpiece. This generosity has seldom wavered; even in *Runaway Bride*, she is happy to let two funny women, Joan Cusack and an uncredited Laurie Metcalf, do their own running away with various scenes—a favor that is bound to play well with a female audience. Julia may get twenty million up front per picture, but look, she has difficulties with boys, and, on a good day, she is surely one of the girls.

The other strain was death. In a sense, *Pretty Woman* was an interruption; what flowed, with toxic logic, from *Steel Magnolias* was a stream of movies that began with *Flatliners* (1990) and *Dying Young* (1991), in which Roberts either succumbed to the Grim Reaper or made serious efforts to date him, and rolled straight through to *Mary Reilly* (1996), in which she wore the pallor of the permanent victim, and on to the gruesome *Stepmom*, of 1998. So ingrained is our expectation of Julia the nearly departed that I was convinced, thinking back to *Stepmom*, that it had been Roberts who contracted terminal cancer. Checking my notes, I learned that the sufferer was in fact Susan Sarandon, and that Julia's knit hats had thus been intended as a fashion statement rather than a polite signal of hair loss. Maybe that is why *Erin Brockovich* was such a blessing, such a clearing of the sky. Erin was not just full of life but specifically anti-death; people were falling all around her, as if on a battlefield, but she grabbed the flag and soldiered on. Did all this point to a new resolution and independence in Roberts's domestic setup, or should we thank Steven Soderbergh, who presumably instructed the caterers to slip something into her lunchbox? In many of her twentieth-century movies, Roberts had been led by her long-tressed, pre-Raphaelite looks (or misled by maudlin style merchants, such as Joel Schumacher) to come on like a nineteenth-century maiden in distress; now, in her first project of the new century, she has brought herself up to date.

Pretty Woman was not and will never be an interesting movie, but that doesn't matter; the saga of its success is lurid with all kinds of interest, whether your field is politics or shoulder pads. Garry Marshall's film had been kicking around for a while, initially as the tale of a drug-addicted hooker who sleeps with a rich guy and ends up back on the street. Then Disney bought it and painted it in Cinderella stripes. With this movie, the eighties delivered a bitter, all but unanswerable slap to the mantras of the sixties: money, contrary to what Paul McCartney had informed us, could buy you love.

The intercourse in *Pretty Woman* represented the first and, if my research is correct, the last occasion on which Julia Roberts consented to action in the sack. Though there are plenty of bedroom scenes in her career, she either lies there and nuzzles, as she did in *Mystic Pizza*, or she lies there waiting to expire; she half disrobed in *Flatliners*, but only so that the other medical students could clamp electrodes to her skin. The leading scholar of such niceties is Craig Hosoda, the author of *The Bare Facts Video Guide*. Hosoda doesn't do art; he fast-forwards his VCR to glimpses of nudity and labels them in crisp shorthand. His findings on Roberts are brief but forensically precise, consisting of one scene from *Pretty Woman:*

> Very, very brief tip of left breast, then right breast, then left breast seen through head board, in bed with Richard Gere. It's her—look especially at the vertical vein that pops out in the middle of her forehead whenever her blood pressure goes up.

This may be the most telling analysis of Julia Roberts that we possess. Hosoda, the guy who causes perspiring teenagers across America to hit the pause button, suddenly stops his exhaustive notation of "breasts" and "buns"—there are no other components—to talk about a vein. Roberts herself is on record as saying, "I'm really against nudity in movies. When you act with your clothes on, it's a performance. When you act with your clothes off, it's a documentary. I don't do documentaries." This is neatly put; it shows, incidentally, how remote she is from any European visions of cinema—not just from the relaxed, Old World attitude toward sex but from the European assumption (found lingering in the work of Americans like Robert Altman) that the scent of documentary can and should be allowed to flavor a fictional method.

It may sound mad, or cold, or downright blasphemous to claim that

Julia Roberts is not sexy. Any well-briefed attorney could proffer evidence to the contrary. What of those push-up bras in *Erin Brockovich*, say, that had steam venting from critics' ears? Well, for one thing, they were a prop; they were as awkward and distorting as the neck brace that Erin wears in the early scenes, after her car accident. She wasn't arousing in the movie; she was mock-arousing, poking her killer cleavage at the clerks from whom she required information, and therefore, by extension, at the lunks in the audience who could be expected to fall for the same trick.

So, if the underwear won't support the argument, how about the smile? If Julia Roberts doesn't rely on word of mouth, who does? As her movies remind us, the pathological gaze of the close-up, something that directors of photography share only with dental hygienists, allows the oral habits of life to be writ engulfingly large. Characters use their mouths to transmit reams of promise about their loves and leanings: they kiss, drink, smoke, and smile, and it is always something of a comedown—too low a reminder of bodily necessity—to see them eat. (That's why there are comparatively few chewing scenes in cinema, and hardly any that are non-comic; the most celebrated, such as the oyster-sucking in *Tom Jones*, are blatant stand-ins for lust.) Not that full-lipped stars are guaranteed to be loudmouths: Ava Gardner was no chatterbox, and Jeanne Moreau's superb sulk, with its downturned corners, was like a worldly, sex-heavy acknowledgment that all men are doomed to disappoint. If Roberts summons the ghost of anyone, it is an actress like Ann Sheridan: funny, busy, noisy, all-American, no-shit—hoping that her sensibility, however hyper, will lose out to her good sense.

The most common comparison, however, is with Audrey Hepburn; both women reign more serenely than the films that they crown, and the laughing Vivian of *Pretty Woman*, like the Holly Golightly of *Breakfast at Tiffany's*, switches to full beam with so little provocation that it feels ungallant to point out that in both cases—one is a pro, the other an eager amateur—their virtue is meant to be easy. They don't want to work on their backs; they want to be swept off their feet. But Audrey was tiny, Belgian-born, and never less than cosmopolitan, whereas the rangy Roberts is, in her own words, "just a girl from Smyrna, Georgia, who wanted to be in the movies and get some attention." She palpitates with worry and need; the famous upper lip, so hilariously unstiff that I am amazed she was allowed through British customs to shoot *Notting Hill*, spends more time in tremble mode than in any other, and she tends to throw herself hungrily at kisses, as if she hadn't had a square meal in weeks. Hannibal Lecter would describe her as tasty. The essence of Roberts's appeal—notably old-fashioned, if you think about it—is that she is more lovable than desirable, and that, even when love is off the menu, she cannot *not* be liked. There is no more flattering illusion in movies, none that we prefer to hear over and over again: here is a goddess, and she wants to be your friend.

It wasn't always like this. It wasn't like this in 1996, certainly, when Roberts was coming off *Mary Reilly* and heading into *Michael Collins.* Those are both interesting movies, although not as interesting as her decision to act in them, and the public shied away like a startled horse. Social historians broadly agree that while the mid-nineties were good for the economy and the New York transportation system, they were bad news for Julia Roberts. Her choice of titles is telling: anyone who voluntarily goes to work on a picture called *I Love Trouble* is asking for it, and her 1995 movie *Something to Talk About* was, in a word, not. The late Alan J. Pakula cast her in *The Pelican Brief* and refused to show her full-on smile until the final shot, which is like keeping Cyd Charisse in cargo pants. Roberts had already been miscast as Tinkerbell in Steven Spielberg's *Hook*, where both her hair and her shorts, cropped to a dandy boyishness, suggested that, in line with the androgynous tradition of the stage, she would have made a delectable Peter Pan.

A trace of childishness has glittered through the life and works of Julia Roberts; you can feel other actors responding to it—should they chide, indulge, or defend this singular creature? In *Something to Talk About*, a tale of a hobbled marriage, the confusion is rife; at one point, Robert Duvall, playing Julia's leathery father, says to her, "Now, look, child . . . you're a grown woman with responsibilities." Onscreen, she tends to register distress with the helpless speed of a hurt little girl; elsewhere, however sturdily she is castled in celebrity, legends of brittleness keep peeking through. It cannot be good for your conscience, let alone your equanimity, to know that half the country can recite a list of your lost loves: Liam Neeson, Dylan McDermott, Kiefer Sutherland (to whom Roberts was engaged), Jason Patric, Daniel Day-Lewis, and Matthew Perry. None of the above qualify as anonymous, and it comes as a pleasant shock to learn that, in 1996, Julia dated a personal trainer called Pat. Then there was the marriage to Lyle Lovett; many onlookers took it as a good omen, arguing with unkind logic that, if *she* was attracted to *him*, it must be love. The wedding took place in 1993, in Marion, Indiana, where the clerk of the local courthouse described them as "nice people," and went on to say, "I was very impressed but not awestruck. I was awestruck when I met Dan Quayle."

The marriage did not last. Lovett and Roberts split up two years later;

one can only imagine the pain of separation, what with Julia trying to yank her mane of ringlets away from the scary Velcro thatch of her beloved. Nobody, not even the *National Enquirer*, knows what goes on in the private life of Julia Roberts, but it is difficult not to watch the vulnerable performer of that period, alternately fractious and mousy, without asking yourself what, or whom, she had to go home to. The film that snapped her out of this slump was *My Best Friend's Wedding*—a graceless work, hardly stronger than some of her comedy flops, yet humming with enough high spirits to earn about $300 million, much of it in countries where they dub everything but the smiles. The film wakes up at the exact moment when Roberts, arriving at an airport, sees Cameron Diaz shimmying toward her—not just a blonde, and not just a blonde who has been vaccinated against all known neuroses, but a blonde with a smile as canyon-wide as her own. If this were a Chuck Jones cartoon, you would get a closeup of Julia's eyes, flashing bright red like the cherries on a slot machine—"Rival! Rival!" Forget love; this was war.

From then on, screenwriters and directors have followed suit; it is as though a memo had been circulated among the studios to the effect that the most lucrative Julia Roberts movies had to be parables on the theme of Julia Roberts. Hence, *My Best Friend's Wedding* is as much a catfight for the throne of Hollywood as a tussle over an inoffensive jock; *Conspiracy Theory* is a study of justified paranoia; *Notting Hill* is a headlight turned on the deerlike panic of its heroine, faced as she is with a nonfamous man from a foreign land; and, as for *Runaway Bride*, consider this conversation between the settled Peggy (Joan Cusack) and the itchy Maggie (Roberts), who just cannot decide on one man:

PEGGY: I think sometimes you just sort of . . . *spaz out* with excess flirtatious energy and it just . . . lands on anything male that moves.

MAGGIE: Anything male that moves? As opposed to anything male that doesn't?

PEGGY: Well, like certain kinds of coral.

MAGGIE: I'm definitely going to have to kill myself today.

PEGGY: Why?

MAGGIE: Because you think I'm all like, *Hey, man, check me out!*

PEGGY: No, I don't. I think you're like, *I'm charming and mysterious in a way that even I don't understand and something about me is crying out for protection from a big man like you.* It's very hard to compete with, specially for us married women who've lost our mystery.

MAGGIE: Lost? You haven't—you are *totally* mysterious.

PEGGY: No. I'm weird. Weird and mysterious are two very different things.

MAGGIE: I'm weird.
PEGGY: No. You're quirky. Quirky and weird are two very different things.
MAGGIE: Peggy, I think there is a distinct possibility that I am profoundly and irreversibly screwed up. Despite that, I love you.

And there the scene dies. Doesn't anybody in Hollywood know how to write zingers anymore—how to lead an audience on and then sock us in the jaw? Comedy, when it doesn't gross us out, has shrivelled into a prelude to sincerity: something to be hustled out of the way, almost with embarrassment, to allow warm feelings in. This is a dangerous practice, given that the best comedy, from Ben Jonson to Preston Sturges, was designed to strip our nobler nature down to its socks; but it is perfect for a star like Roberts, whose levity tends to darken, not dazzle, with the onset of perplexity.

That is the open secret of her success: she satisfies all the current requirements of an American star, being at once seductively outgoing in her wit, or in her rare flashes of wrath, and consolingly inward in her furrowed brow and her fondness for the homely. She looks luminous in jeans, T-shirts, and sweaters, and she looks tacky and trapped in posh frocks and wedding outfits—which is slightly unfortunate, given that so many of her movies seek to railroad her down the aisle. Indeed, with her endless limbs and uncool gait, the highest-paid actress in the world sometimes wanders through her movies like a stoned foal—one more instance, perhaps, of Roberts not wanting to frighten or freeze her average viewers, who must be thrilled to discover an ungainliness to match their own. Like both Hepburns, Audrey and Katharine, she cheers you up simply by walking into the frame; unlike them, she often seems to be casting around for reasons to be cheerful herself. Just now, she has plenty, with an Oscar in her sights and Benjamin Bratt, "my own golden man," in the palm of her hand. So, will Julia continue to be a Brockovich, or will she stumble into a rerun of the nineties? Will she get married again and raise a little Bratt pack? She ascended to fame during one Republican administration, and there is no telling how fruitfully Pretty Woman—or Lovely Older Woman—might thrive under another. It's asking a lot, but Julia Roberts could yet be as awesome as Dan Quayle.

MARCH 26, 2001

WILLIAM KLEIN

William Klein is an American photographer. One is tempted to say that he is *the* American photographer; among his coevals, only Richard Avedon can match him for stamina and range, and for a visual instinct so sure that you wonder whether both men had cameras implanted in their heads at birth. The difference is that Avedon operates out of New York City, whereas Klein, who will take any cliché you like and bust it wide open, is an American in Paris. One is tempted to say that he is *the* American in Paris: a more authentic example of the type than even Gene Kelly could pretend to be. Klein speaks English with a French trip of the tongue and French with a hefty American curve to his vowels. He arrived in Paris in the late 1940s and has stayed ever since, with regular, fruitful forays to other lands. On his second day in the city he met Jeanne, "the most beautiful woman in the world," who became his wife. They live in a fourth-floor apartment, once owned by Francis Poulenc, that overlooks a northern tip of the Luxembourg Gardens: hard-core Paris, as it were, and quite a switch from 108th Street and Amsterdam Avenue, in Manhattan, where Klein grew up.

He was born in 1928, but the thought that he is now in his seventies is a joke; threescore and ten may be the span of man, but no one has broken the news to Klein, who still behaves as if he were turning one score and five. There is a restlessness, even a sexiness, in Klein's longevity which can only infuriate those who purport to revel in their youth. He is a big, loping fellow with a mane of white hair swept back over his collar, a roaring laugh that hangs around in his throat, and a pair of Reebok ankle boots on his hind paws. Meeting him face to face, I realized that he belongs to a genus now so rare, so closely identified with another age, that you could be forgiven for thinking it extinct. William Klein is a *cat*. I am not so experienced a naturalist as to know whether he hails from the species *hep*, but, like anyone else, I know catness when I see it, and it is there in the Klein limbs, long and loose, in the rotating riffs of his storytelling, and in the peculiar cocktail of ardor and amusement—of engaging hotly with the troubles of the world and then standing back to lend them a cool eye—that instantly summons the scent of the 1950s.

Klein's father was in the clothing business; he was all but felled by the Crash, a year after his son was born. There was money and prestige in the family, but it lay with uncles and aunts. ("I can't say they did anything, *ever*, for me.") The young Klein attended the City College of New York, but left before graduating to take advantage of the GI Bill of Rights. He was dispatched by train to Fort Riley, Kansas. "For the first time, I saw America," he recalls. "I couldn't go to sleep." He joined the cavalry—as a radio operator on horseback, which sounds like a surrealist collage—and wound up in occupied Germany. "Someone looked through my record and found that I had got out of university at eighteen, that I spoke a little French, and they chose twenty-five soldiers to go to the Sorbonne," he says. He never saw action—not the military kind, at any rate. The Klein luck held, and he found himself taking art lessons from Fernand Léger. ("Léger was something else. He looked like Rocky Marciano. He looked like he could take them on. Lee Marvin, the French version.") Some of Klein's early paintings—I saw racks of them in one of his Paris studios—show a chunkiness that betrays the muscular presence of his master, although the young man's talent was always going to be more kinetic than Léger's, less embarrassed by the force of the fleeting. In 1952, some of Klein's murals were shown in Milan, where he took photographs of them; it was not the first time he had picked up a camera—in a myth that he confirmed to me as accurate, he had won a Rolleiflex in a poker game with other GIs—but it was only then that he understood the firepower of his new weapon.

From here, events moved fast. His abstract shots were featured on the cover of an architectural magazine called *Domus* and seen by a guy from a fashion magazine called *Vogue*. This was Alexander Liberman, no less, the art director who could spot talent an ocean away and bring it home. By 1954, the prodigal son was back in New York, on a five-month stay, with a dream brief: come and work for us, *carte blanche*, two hundred bucks a week, limitless photographic supplies, and while you're about it, shoot the city. "I approached New York like a fake anthropologist," Klein says, "treating New Yorkers like Zulus." He and Jeanne lived in a small hotel; "I would print like a maniac—fifty photos a night, washing them in a bathtub."

The result was *Life Is Good and Good for You in New York: Trance Witness*

Revels, which was published in 1956—published in France, that is, to instant acclaim. It did not appear in America, a laughable omission that remained uncorrected until the book was reprinted in 1995. New York publishers turned up their noses. "They would say, 'What kind of New York is this? It looks like a slum.' I said, 'Listen. New York *is* a slum. You live on Fifth Avenue, you come to your office on Madison Avenue—what do you know? You ever been to the Bronx?' " Not only did Klein design the book himself; he alerted readers—those who could get hold of the thing—to the possibility that a photography book, no less than a photograph itself, could be a work of art. "My first idea was to do a collection of the front pages of the New York *Daily News*." What emerged was hardly less alarming. There are no captions, and the rhythm of the layout keeps to no known beat: some shots are bordered in white, others leak across the central gutter or spill to the edge. At one point, Klein uses a spread to mount an all-out assault; each facing page shows the front of a movie theatre, ablaze with names of the period (Van Heflin, Cesar Romero, Leo Genn) and tilted so that the lights on the marquees bounce and gleam off the enamelled darkness of a car. The whole book ends with a bang: a sun raging low on the Manhattan skyline, printed with such rich pointillist grain that what was, presumably, a nice warm day is cranked up into an artist's impression of a nuclear firestorm. Just what America wanted in 1956.

A mint first edition of *Life Is Good and Good for You in New York* will set you back four thousand dollars or so; the same goes for its celebrated sequels, *Rome* (1958–59), *Moscow* (1964), and *Tokyo* (1964). In each case, Klein developed a style that was utterly his own while insuring that he answered the public demands of reportage; if you stare at the broad-boned, stoical features of his Muscovites, you feel yourself planted in a real place, and yet the elastic intensity of such portraits could have issued only from Klein. Much of this springs from technique; until he came along, the wide-angle lens was largely the preserve of landscape photographers, or a witty aid to social perspective. In his hands, it made the world fatten and bulge; nothing was safe from his reinvention, not even the fashion scene, to which he has continually cleaved, with a mixture of scorn and raucous glee. At *Vogue*, where the arrival of this strapping figure with his truncheon of lens must have struck the more delicate habitués as almost medievally rude, Klein was also the pioneer of the long shot. He liked to stick himself at a distance, or even at rooftop level, and let his models roam the streets, so that no one else realized they were being snapped; in Rome, of course, the passerby assumed that the girls, in their pristine hats and coats, had to be high-class hookers, thus risking a minor riot, although what stays with you from the shoot is the zebra stripes of the road crossing, flattened by the telephoto into a patch of instant Jasper Johns. Even a road can be à la mode.

Klein is a one-man band, and it is hard to think of any instrument into which he has not tootled or brayed. Although the four great city books are all in black-and-white, he could convert to color without a hitch or a wince, especially when there was a ketchup-red coat to be shot beside a yellow cab. He would swipe the camera through long exposures and let off a flash in the middle, leaving a flare that, at first glance, could be mistaken for a battlefield; he would refocus the enlarger *as he printed*, causing the black tiles on a New York washroom wall to blur and breathe, like something at the ragged end of a dream. In April 1955, both he and Robert Frank were sent to cover the same society event, Elsa Maxwell's Toy Ball, and the results bear lasting comparison. Frank's image, published in *The Americans*, has a pearly wistfulness that fits the occasion, as if he himself were sporting a tuxedo; Klein's, a violent, semi-abstract haze, could have been taken by an intruder in blue jeans. ("Open at f/2. Fifteenth of a second . . . an eighth, one fourth, I didn't give a shit," he says. "That was really a night. I went to town.") Neither picture is a truer record than the other, and *The Americans*, which came out in 1958, is like a sad, consumptive cousin to the hearty, sarcastic braggadocio of *Life Is Good and Good for You in New York*. Frank was a native of Switzerland, quietly weighing a brave new world; Klein was back, for a while, where he belonged.

Just now it is Klein time in New York. The Howard Greenberg Gallery, on Wooster Street, is running a formidable exhibit of Klein's work, including vintage prints from his city books; visitors will be able to catch such treasures as the fat, happy Roman seated beside a lithe classical sculpture, with a Vespa showing its own curves on the curb. Ancient and modern compete, and the honors are even. At the same time, the Charles Cowles Gallery is tracing a more recent departure, Klein's painted contact sheets. These are startling constructions: blown-up strips of negatives, bathed and looped in bright paint, as if the photographer, gambling on the standoff between chance and control, wanted to up the stakes. The unavoidable lesson of all this work—old and new, old slamming into the side of the new—is that Klein is on a roll. Oh, and one other thing: his latest movie is coming out.

Klein has made more than twenty films. He began in 1958, with *Broadway by Light*, and over the years he has turned his hand to such scattered subjects as the French Open, Eldridge Cleaver, and Little Richard. In

1965, if you can believe it, he actually gave up photography for cinema, and didn't return to the fray until the start of the 1980s. It's not that the break wasn't therapeutic, or that the films weren't worth the effort; it's just that fifteen years on the wagon, for a man who seemed drunk on the frozen look of things, is a long haul. He had always felt the magnetism of a righteous cause—he spoke to me of heading down south in 1963, when he was "hassled by the police just for talking to a black person on the street"—and in 1967 he split from *Vogue*, where the fierceness of his political stance, especially his contribution to the portmanteau picture *Far from Vietnam*, along with those of directors like Alain Resnais and Jean-Luc Godard, had ruffled fur and feathers. *Women's Wear Daily* ran the unusual headline "FAMOUS VOGUE PHOTOGRAPHER DOING ANTI-AMERICAN FILM," as if Klein's convictions were an insult to the rise of the hemline. There were other, more pleasing pressures on his time, as he casually recalls. "Louis Malle called me up one day and said, 'I would love you to codirect *Zazie in the Métro*.' " On his own initiative, Klein went to introduce himself to Federico Fellini, who was staying at a Paris hotel. "I gave him a copy of my New York book, and he said, 'Oh, I already have a copy next to my bed. Look, why don't you come to Rome and be assistant director on *Nights of Cabiria*?' So I went."

Most of Klein's own movies are documentaries, but there are digressions into fiction, too, as with his wicked poke at the fashion industry, *Who Are You, Polly Maggoo?* (1965–66), and *The Model Couple* (1975–76), in which a pair of humans are watched and measured like lab rats. It comes across as a cheaper, hipper *Clockwork Orange*, with less pith and a lot more juice; there is no Klein movie, not even *Mister Freedom* (1967–68), an irate expressionist broadside starring Donald Pleasence and Delphine Seyrig, that does not share the essential good humor of its creator. Not many people have seen this stuff, but you should at least try to track down Klein's two boxing pictures, *Cassius the Great* (1964–65) and its expanded reissue, *Muhammad Ali the Greatest* (1974), which adds footage of the Ali-Foreman rumble in Zaire. Klein is a fountain of opinion, but in Ali—"the heavyweight champion of *everything*"—he finally met his match. "You know what he called me?" Klein said in Paris recently. "He made a point of not knowing people's names, the way that white people used to call black people 'boy.' He knew I came from Europe, so he used to call me England. 'Hey, England!' It's the only place he knew of in Europe."

There's a great still of Klein watching his hero's triumphal procession from the ring in Miami after the Sonny Liston bout of 1964. On the flight down to Florida, he had sat next to Malcolm X, and now he was right there in the heart of the Clay camp: "Nowadays you wouldn't get five hundred yards away." The fight has not gone out of Klein, but I suspect that the world has grown too fenced and managed for his liking; certainly his new movie, *Messiah*, has a restraint, almost a diffidence, that would have surprised the streetwise Klein of earlier years. *Messiah* takes Handel's score and carries it around the world; different sections are performed by different choirs—mainly by a professional outfit dressed in black, but also by prison inmates in Texas, who slap hands to congratulate themselves on making it through the tricky warbles of "For Unto Us a Child Is Born," and by the police choir of Dallas, with sirens flashing and the city's towers shining in the distance. There is a stream of visual wit here, but no sneering; everyone has his say, or his sing, and thus the original fire of the narrative is kindled afresh. It is the first truly Christian film I have seen in a long while; needless to say, only a Jewish-American exile could have made it.

"Jewish kids are not supposed to be technically handy," Klein told me, hovering as usual between principle and jest. "If you want to talk about one of my theories, I think there are two kinds of photography—Jewish photography and goyish photography. If you look at modern photography, you find, on the one hand, the Weegees, the Diane Arbuses, the Robert Franks—funky photographs. And then you have the people who go out in the woods. Ansel Adams, Weston. It's like black and white jazz." The theory is so contentious that you expect to find a whole army of exceptions, but the rule holds surprisingly firm. If anything, you want to send it out into the world of modern art and see how it fares. One of the few people keeping pace with *Life Is Good and Good for You in New York* was Robert Rauschenberg, who was putting together his first "combines" in 1954, at the same moment that Klein and Frank were branding American energies onto film. The bursting red surface of a typical combine, a grand abstraction made concrete by the addition of newsprint and metal and slivers of mirror, seems in retrospect less like a deliberate campaign of shock and more like a Kleinian refusal to exclude anything that caught the eye. Is it too fanciful to find something specifically Jewish in this comic-ironic embrace, this appetite that grew into a tolerance? Think of Saul Bellow: *The Adventures of Augie March*, a wide-aperture book if ever there was one, had come out the year before.

When Klein came back to photography, in 1980, he found plenty to shoot. ("Of course, I never really stopped completely. Nobody does.") His published work of the last couple of decades, in books such as *Close Up* (1989), *In and Out of Fashion* (1994), and *Films* (1998), has been jumpier than ever, the camera so keen to get in your face that in some cases it's halfway up your nose. *In and Out of Fashion*, for example, is a vibrant album of fads, freak shows, and the beautiful people, plus a handful of those determined to steal beauty for themselves. Read the captions at the back of the book: "Soho, London, 1980," "Fake Dolly Parton, Hollywood, 1985," "Gay Parade, Hollywood, 1980," "Oktoberfest, Munich, 1980."

These suggest a man doing homage to honest vulgarity, yet, unlike many of his peers, Klein never strays into the deeper vulgarity of passing sentence on what he observes. At the center of the Soho shot, for instance, we have a couple of punks: batwing eyeliner, a Mohican strip of rosy, matted hair as thin as a toothbrush. Klein was hardly alone in his appreciation of such exotica; by 1980, three years into the monarchy of punk, the process of domestication was well under way, and any London tourist could buy postcards of Sid Vicious clones to amuse the folks back home. What no one but Klein could see, or bothered to notice, is the figure standing on the left-hand verge of the frame: glasses, mustache, windbreaker, turtleneck sweater as beige as bread, one hand gripping a can of lager, and eyes glazing over at the Technicolor popinjays before him. Most photographers, and all fashion editors, would have cropped him out, embarrassed by his utter want of style—which is, of course, precisely why Klein counts him in. The man's presence is a rebuke not just to the loud, lunging fashion needs of the punks but also to our romantic notion that a country is defined by its convulsions; British social historians will mark down the late 1970s and early 80s as a period of high-energy change, whereas the truth is that most people, as is always the case all over the world, were content to watch these small explosions of revolt from the safety of the sidelines and carry on drinking their beer.

You can leaf through any of Klein's books, or scan his New York shows, and suddenly realize that what you are inspecting is less a sheaf of images—heaven knows, you can find those on any newsstand—than a sort of chemical reaction. Turn back a page from Soho and you find yourself in Clermont-Ferrand, with a bevy of priests resplendent in caps and capes. Your eye is drawn at once to the elaborate geometry of their lace sleeves; frankly, the fathers put the punks to shame, though whether that makes the picture irreverent, pious, or plain funny is hard to decide. The curse of photography books is to be left in artless array on coffee tables, as talismans of our taste; and it is the duty of William Klein to disturb that peace. Why else would he keep reproducing his contact sheets, which resemble nothing so much as clips of abandoned movies, if not to demonstrate the tide of life that flowed on either side of his chosen snap? He doesn't want your friends to leaf idly through *Life Is Good and Good for You in New York* while discussing schools or tickets for the Met; he wants your friends to pick it up, flinch, and wish they had worn oven mitts. He wants them to wonder if life is still good, and whether, to their secret annoyance, it might once have been better. In the Charles Cowles show, one of the most famous New York images—a kid pointing a toy gun at the camera, the barrel out of focus and a mock-mean snarl on his face—is splashed with paint the color of movie blood. You look at it and think: These days, forty-six years on, the gun would not be a toy.

Maybe the best is yet to come. Down in Montparnasse, a ten-minute drive from his apartment, Klein has a small complex of studios on either side of a mews; there he showed me the proofs of a book, as thick as a shoebox, tentatively titled "KLEIN + PARIS." If it honors his abrasive devotion to the place, it should be quite an event. He once made a documentary about the rebellious spring of 1968, *Maydays*, but I have seen single Klein photographs of Paris that are themselves movielike in their tense and thronging dynamic. One of them, in particular, is a landscape hung with portraits. In the foreground, there is the leading couple—well matched, though too cool and frowning to give off discernible signs of love. Then, there are the supporting players: the second-string sweethearts, the woman whispering in the man's ear; funereal groupings on the far balconies, perched as precariously as pigeons; the hit man at the far right, a trenchcoated Charles Aznavour figure who knows too much. You can read the picture like a novel, forested with subplots; or you can chop it into abstract components and whittle it down to the thin white line of the lover's Gitane; or you can play the historian and ponder the fact that it was taken in 1968—during Armistice Day ("probably the last armistice for de Gaulle's regime," Klein writes in a note) rather than the delirium of May, although you can't help feeling a hangover of unrest. Are these citizens watching the parade, or has it already gone by?

"A lot of French people resent me," Klein says. "I'm still considered a foreigner." But it is equally hard to imagine so peregrine a spirit ever settling again in America; his achievements, closer to those of a war reporter than to the homelier virtues of someone like Cartier-Bresson, are those of a man who belongs and does not belong. "I'm such a loner," he told me. "My dream always, when I was a kid, was Cézanne, who nobody paid attention to, who was out in the fucking country. He was there, painting his fucking mountain, day in, day out, and that's the sort of life I lead." Yet Klein is so naturally given to the dramatic gesture that he is never going to be one of life's invisible men. Spending a few hours in his company is like hanging out with Tristram Shandy. Even the prose that accompanies his photographs, when he supplies it, bears the reek of the flashlight and the front page. Here is Klein at Madison Square Garden, in 1989, watching the Knicks play the Phoenix Suns. Five minutes to go: "Time out. The sweaty supermen, heads hanging, cluster around the coach, half their size, sharp in a grey business suit and in a very bad mood. You're surrendering, he rasps. What's the matter, you gonna give it to them? Hell no. Boom. Ten points in two minutes. Ewing gets forty for the game. The Suns go out. The Garden goes wild. Whaddya mean."

Now turn to the shot he took that night. Not a glimpse of the court; he was too busy facing the other way, drinking in the crowd. No supermen to be seen; just a cross-section of ordinary men and women, hands in a blur of applause, fists in mid-pump. William Klein's big moment was theirs, too. Whaddya expect. Fifty years in the business, and curiosity is still driving the cat.

MAY 21, 2001

BILLY WILDER

One morning in the summer of 1950, Billy Wilder was sitting alone, eating breakfast and reading the *Hollywood Reporter.* His wife, Audrey, came into the room and asked:

"Do you know what day this is, dear?"

"June 30th."

"It's our anniversary."

"Please," Wilder said, "not while I'm eating."

And there you have him. Like most Wilder anecdotes, this tale has been told many times, and we have gone beyond the point of being able to ascertain whether it might actually be true. I guess you could ask the man himself, who is still alive at the age of ninety-five, but that would be no help; when it comes to spinning webs of Wilder mythology, he is by far the worst and most enjoyable offender. (Who else, reliving his career as a cub reporter in Vienna, would claim to have interviewed Richard Strauss, Arthur Schnitzler, and Sigmund Freud on a single day?) Still, if the facts don't fit the legend, print the legend and to hell with it; what matters about the breakfast story is that it *sounds* right—the wisecrack zipping across the room and drowning the crunch of toast.

And so the rumors accrue, hardening the image of Wilder the cynic, Wilder the man-hater and woman-scorner. Who else would bother to assert that his bad back, which has plagued him throughout his career, was brought on by an urge to make love in Viennese doorways, standing up? More to the point, who else would say so in front of his wife? Wilder was one of those steely souls, forged in the Hollywood of the thirties and forties, who were even tougher than the actors they were slated to direct. In 1960, the year of *The Apartment,* he looked back on the duties of his chosen profession: "A director must be a policeman, a midwife, a psychoanalyst, a sycophant, and a bastard." It's not affection that Wilder minds, I would imagine, but the fuss that is made of it—the anniversaries, the flowers, the song and dance. "Did you hear what I said, Miss Kubelik? I absolutely adore you," Jack Lemmon says, soft as a puppy, in the closing moments of *The Apartment.* But Shirley MacLaine is having none of it: "Shut up and deal," she replies, addressing herself to the more pressing matter of gin rummy. She adores the guy, of course, and she has just run uptown to tell him so, but, still, there are limits. You have to keep the puppy on a leash.

There is only one catch in the Wilder world—not even a catch, perhaps, but an irony that is strong enough to crack his cool. People love his movies. Needless to say, Wilder himself had an explanation for this, as he did for everything else. "You know how it is," he told reporters in London in 1961. "You hate your dentist while he's pulling your teeth out, but the next week you're playing golf with him." Over and over, Wilder shows us mankind behaving badly, or using one another as props and pawns, or racing into follies from which there is no escape, and still, like sheep to the shearer, we come back for more. *Double Indemnity, The Seven Year Itch, Sunset Boulevard, The Apartment:* these are part of the basic lexicon of moviegoing. One picture, in particular, has become an icon. Last year, the American Film Institute invited its members to vote on the hundred best comedies ever made. The top spot went to Billy Wilder's *Some Like It Hot* (1959).

Everyone knows that these hundred-best lists are a bore. Not a fix, exactly, although the film crowd, like all social groups who are presented with a questionnaire, tends to repeat the conventional wisdom without troubling to think it through. Still, it would take a brave critic to dispute the status of *Some Like It Hot*, just as it would take a historian of the highest subtlety and resourcefulness to explain, before a tribunal of his peers, why the most entertaining cultural spectacle of the last hundred years has been, by common consent, a pair of full-grown American males wearing falsies.

Falsehood, it must be said, is the fuel of this famous movie. It is rabid with deception, and all attempts to summarize the plot tend to skip one of the changes of costume, or of heart; not until I saw the film again recently, perhaps for the tenth time, did I notice that Jack Lemmon turns briefly into a bellhop. The roughest of outlines would go as follows: A pair of small-time jazz musicians—Joe, a tenor-sax player (Tony Curtis), and Jerry, a bassist (Lemmon)—are accidental witnesses to the St. Valentine's Day Massacre. Pursued by a big-time gangster (George Raft) and his hoods, they dress as women and join an all-girl band on a train to Florida. There Joe, who has become Josephine, makes one more switch, pretending to be an oil baron in order to woo the band's singer, Sugar Cane (Marilyn Monroe), née Kowalczyk. And Jerry, who has become Daphne, draws the attention of the insatiable Osgood (Joe E. Brown), a bona fide millionaire with a mouth like a mailbox. It all ends well, with both couples heading for a moonlit yacht.

What more is there to say? Many filmgoers can recite lines from this picture more fluently than they can tell a story from their own past. The closing zinger has Daphne yanking off her wig and declaring herself to be a man, and Osgood replying, "Nobody's perfect," his beatific randiness intact. Meanwhile, the traditional Wilder mischief has calcified into received opinion; when he said that Marilyn Monroe had breasts like granite and a brain like Swiss cheese, he must have realized that the line—one part idolatry to three parts slur—was here to stay, and it is true that Monroe's bosom, thrust in and out of the spotlight as she sings "I Wanna Be Loved by You" and "I'm Through with Love," has become as proud a feature of the American landscape as Mt. Rushmore. In fact, the whole film is a national treasure; you can look at it, but you can't touch.

Now a new angle has opened up. Just one warning: it'll cost you. A hundred and fifty dollars, to be precise, for which you get a book. *Billy Wilder's Some Like It Hot* is the size of an old electric typewriter, and it weighs more than many common domestic animals. Spookier still, it is furrier than many common domestic animals, being covered in a lightly padded velvet the color of *crème pâtissière.* The title is picked out in orange leather lettering, as bold as a billboard, on the front cover; inside, you get colored production stills, dripping with Florida sunshine, plus full-page blowups of pencilled lines from the screenplay, and the effect is to seize an unsuspecting black-and-white comedy and propel it toward the status of Pop Art. There are many books devoted to single films, but they tend to be unsmiling monographs, neatly nailing the work in question to the social history of its era; this book, by contrast, is more like one of Osgood's laughs—sinful, delirious, and loaded.

The publisher of this unusual volume is Taschen, which explains a lot. Benedikt Taschen is an outspoken German who started producing books in 1981, and who has since built up a catalogue so hip, so huge, and so hungry for taboo that you see people in Barnes & Noble make a beeline for the Taschen table and then sneak a glance around the store to make sure that nobody is looking. It goes without saying that you can't open a work entitled *1000 Dessous: A History of Lingerie* without being tapped on the shoulder by your fourth-grade teacher, whom you haven't seen in thirty years, and who once taught you the names of her favorite flowers. The thing about Taschen is that even the books that *are* about flowers bear a distinct fragrance of perversion; this fall sees the publication of *A Garden Eden: Masterpieces of Botanical Illustration*, and a brief glance suggests that all those thrusting pistils should give the antique girdles and stockings a run for their money.

The Wilder book is split into three acts. The first section delves into the making of the movie and contains a facsimile of the final script, on aging buff paper, complete with holes punched at the edge. The second section is a sheaf of interviews with, among others, Wilder, Curtis, Lemmon, and Barbara Diamond, the widow of I. A. L. Diamond—Iz to his friends, and the cowriter on the movie. Diamond had no better friend than Wilder, nobody better qualified to match his smarts; as a team, they wrote a dozen films. ("Never a harsh word, twenty-five years of working together," Wilder once said, at a lecture. "We were like bank tellers." They finished the screenplay of *Some Like It Hot* four days before the end of the shoot.) The interviews are new, conducted over the last couple of years. This doesn't mean that the material itself is new—all concerned have taken the opportunity to buff their anecdotes, like silver, over time—but it's useful to find it packaged together, and even Wilder scholars should rejoice to find Tony Curtis, especially, in such brazen form. You can hear the wide Brooklyn bark as he remembers, only too vividly, the professional drag queen whom Wilder flew in from Berlin to act as tutor to his leads:

> This guy told us to keep the cheeks of your ass tight. You tighten up—which you did if you were in the Navy anyway—and make one step good before the other. So when we started to put it together, it all became a very charming manner. I loved it . . . Jack was outrageous as a girl, he couldn't wait to go tromping out. I was more hesitant, I was more like Grace Kelly than like my mother. I was on track.

What's sweet about these recollections is that Curtis plainly took a genuine pride in his womanly appearance; even now, the wording ("a very charming manner") retains a feminine correctness that borders on the prim. Or at least it does until he gets to Marilyn's door, and to the little tailor who was busy with his tape measure, checking the statistics of the stars:

> Anyway, he measured me, 16, 34, 43, 18, 19, 18 . . . and then he goes to Marilyn, this is all in the same day and this is the truth . . . He comes in to Marilyn's room and Marilyn had on a pair of panties and a white

blouse and that's all. He put the tape around her legs, looked up at Marilyn and said, "You know, Tony Curtis has got a better-looking ass than you." She was standing there, she unbuttoned her blouse and said, "He doesn't have tits like these."

For once, I think we need these salty stories, because Monroe needs all the salt she can get. The Marilyn industry is so deeply soaked in her crackups—shaking the poor woman until we can hear the slosh of booze and the rattle of pills—that it's sobering to get back to the floozie with the forked tongue. If *Some Like It Hot* remains her best as well as her most celebrated film, that is because Wilder was lucky enough, and perceptive enough, to catch Marilyn when her balance was still intact. Wilder knew precisely how good a comedian she was, he knew the ratio of bite to fluff, and he saw that her pathos—which the public, avid for the crash of failing marriages, was increasingly keen to ascribe to her—wasn't worth a damn unless it came wrapped in shining lines. "That's the story of my life: I always get the fuzzy end of the lollipop" is dangerously close to one of Marilyn's private confessions, but Wilder and Diamond give the image such a lick and a twist that it slots quite happily into the given scene—Sugar Cane chatting to the new girls on the train heading south, and taking a slug from the flask of bourbon that she keeps tucked into her garter. Shortly afterward, she jumps into bed with Jack Lemmon, just for comfort. Both are in nightgowns:

SUGAR: When I was a little girl, on cold nights like this, I used to crawl into bed with my sister. We'd cuddle up under the covers, and pretend we were lost in a dark cave, and were trying to find our way out.
JERRY: (mopping his brow) Interesting.

It's only when you read this in the Taschen book, as part of the printed screenplay, that you realize how fantastically dirty it is. (Dirtier, indeed, than it plays onscreen, where Lemmon adds a "very" and froths the line up with a giggle.) Somehow, under the camouflage of a joke, Wilder got that dark-cave stuff past the censors; if challenged, presumably, he could always claim to be unwise in the ways of symbolism. A lollipop was just a thing you sucked.

Taschen saves the best for last. The third section is a roundup of the global reaction to the movie, including a Mexican poster for *Una Eva y Dos Adanes* and a newspaper clipping announcing that, whatever some might like, it was too damn hot for the state of Kansas. (The authorities wanted to cut the smooch on the yacht between Curtis and Monroe, in which he feigns impotence and invites her to cure it, but United Artists said no.) Finally, tucked into the inside of the back cover is a scrappy-looking notebook: an exact reproduction of Marilyn's own shooting script. It is not very long—it contains only her lines, with the ends of the lines that precede them, so as not to confound her—and scrawled here and there are her frazzled, misspelled comments and jabs of self-persuasion: "*what* am I doing," "inocent," "Acting being private in public to be Brave." On the front, she put her name and address—"MARiLYN MONROE, GoLdWyN Studios, N. FORMOSA," in case the book got lost. Or, more likely, in case *she* got lost. Once, when filming *The Seven Year Itch*, she arrived at eleven o'clock for an eight-thirty start; when Wilder wanted to know what had happened, she replied that she couldn't find the studio. "She'd only been under contract for six years," Wilder said later, with one of his dry grins. A particular line reading for *Some Like It Hot* required eighty-three takes, at the end of which he told Marilyn not to worry. "Worry about what?" she asked.

That sublime question hovers in the air, whenever *Some Like It Hot* is showing, as blithely as a bird. It's as if Wilder were daring us to give him a list of things—the dreadful evidence of the world—that are worthy of significant worry, and then swatting them aside. Remember, this is a film that looks on as a line of thugs commit multiple murder in a Chicago garage; Wilder shows only the thugs, however, not the jerking bodies, and thus gives us leave to laugh. The picture begins in death, with a respectful shot of a hearse, and ends in a double helping of love. Ed Sikov, in his clever, compendious biography of Wilder, quotes the director in one of his milder moods: "Movies should be like amusement parks. People should go to them to have fun."

The fun in Billy Wilder feels like an attack; sleeping around the office was never quite the same after *The Apartment*, which—contrary to the charges of misogyny that have been laid at Wilder's door—passes much harder sentence on the guys than on the dolls. Yet, the more you learn of Wilder, the more you wonder whether his dialogue, as black and gleaming as wet ink, might not have been his first line of defense. Like half the great American directors, he was the pure product of Europe. Humphrey Bogart, who didn't take to Wilder on the set of *Sabrina*, labelled him a "Prussian German." Even by Bogie's standards, this was wide of the mark, since Wilder was born a Polish Jew. He lived in Krakow, Vienna, and Berlin, where he made his name writing screenplays. In 1933, when Hitler came to power, Wilder moved to Paris: "It seemed the wise thing for a Jew to do." Less than a year later, as if the needle of his talent were seeking magnetic north, he came to America, bearing, according to Ed Sikov, copies of *Babbitt*, *A Farewell to Arms*, and *Look Homeward, Angel*, and the sum of eleven dollars.

In 1945, he returned to Europe, in the uniform of a colonel; he was working for the Psychological Warfare Division, and one of his duties was to view and cut the footage that was coming in from the concentration camps. This was then shown to German audiences. As far as Billy Wilder knows, his mother, stepfather, and grandmother died at Auschwitz, and nobody can tell such a man how he should or should not respond. If his first film after the war, a Tyrolean fantasy called *The Emperor Waltz*, starring Bing Crosby in lederhosen, seems almost pathological in its urge to ignore suffering, so be it. With time, it seems that Wilder has returned to the scene of those crimes: he tried to buy the rights to the Thomas Keneally novel *Schindler's Ark*, and there was even talk of his emerging from retirement to direct. When Spielberg's film was released, Wilder approved, and he used the occasion to write an article for a German newspaper, posing a quiet, unanswerable question to those who were tempted to doubt the existence of the Holocaust: "If the concentration camps and the gas chambers were all imaginary, then please tell me—where is my mother?"

For fans of his work, it is legitimate to ask whether Wilder's restive habits—the migrations of an orphaned cosmopolitan—somehow find their way into the movies. The heroes and heroines in his films may not go in for many changes of scenery, but is there not something obsessive in the ease, or the eagerness, with which they shift the landscape of their own lives, as if preparing at any instant to flee? First up is Ginger Rogers, who adopts the not altogether credible disguise of a twelve-year-old girl in *The Major and the Minor* (1942), Wilder's first film as an American director. Then we have Franchot Tone in *Five Graves to Cairo* (1943), pretending to be a waiter and being mistaken for a spy; Audrey Hepburn in *Love in the Afternoon* (1957), the ingenue who poses as a fur-lined sophisticate in the hope of snaring Gary Cooper; virtually the entire cast of *The Apartment* (1960), followed by Jack Lemmon again, in *Irma La Douce* (1963), playing a lowly French cop who passes himself off as an English lord. Finally, and most acridly, there is Kim Novak in *Kiss Me, Stupid* (1964), the hooker who becomes a temporary wife.

Wilder is not the first person to connect comedy with a taste for subterfuge, as anyone familiar with *Twelfth Night* can confirm. And Shakespeare has nothing to brag about, either, given that he lifted half the plot of *The Comedy of Errors* from a play by Plautus written in around 200 B.C.

All we can say is that, if Wilder had a vested interest in shape-shifting, *Some Like It Hot* brings that interest to the boil. Joe and Jerry are not so much characters as quick-change artists with good musical technique, and the fluidity of their self-invention, like their sense of rhythm, confronts our feelings of dullness and stolidity and merrily blows them away. When they first decide to dress as women, the camera honors the outrageousness of the plan: no kooky shots of waxing and padding, no close-ups of wig tape and tweezers, just a straight, no-bullshit cut to the railroad station and a hearty couple of broads. Wilder has always scorned what he calls the "fancy-schmancy," and *Some Like It Hot* takes a convoluted problem and lays it on us straight.

That is why all efforts to tease a deeper entanglement from Wilder's manic film are fated to fail. I looked up *Some Like It Hot* in a chunky, five-volume work entitled *International Dictionary of Films and Film-Makers*, and came across these words:

> When Joe tries to assert his masculinity with Sugar, Jerry insists he maintain his female identity. Aware of their dilemma, our pleasure becomes dependent on the ramifications of gender identification and sexual exposure.

As Osgood would say, "Zowie!" In fact, *Some Like It Hot* has almost nothing to tell us about transvestism, and surprisingly few suggestions on the topic of homosexuality. It really is about two men who put on women's clothes to save their skins, and it was part of Wilder's genius that he encouraged his leading men to push their faux girlishness in opposite directions—Curtis toward the demure, Lemmon headfirst into the lubricious and the loud. That way, we get no single statement on the pathology of cross-dressing, and we soon realize that we don't need one. Remember their heated exchange after Jerry gets engaged to Osgood:

> JOE: Why would a guy want to marry a guy?
> JERRY: *Security.*

Lemmon really whacks that second syllable, and backs it up with a sharp shiver of his maracas. (Wilder devised them as a prop; he needed something for Lemmon to be doing while the audience laughed, so that Curtis's next straight line would not get buried. Get that for confidence.) Jerry isn't lying, but he's not gay, either; strangely, *Some Like It Hot* only becomes truly fraught with sexual confusion if you try to decide what will happen after the end of the picture. Imagine all four of them chasing each other around the fo'c'sle.

So where does that leave Osgood's final, contented dictum: "Nobody's perfect"? As a universal truth, a withering Wilder glance at life beyond the movie theatre, it remains unimpeachable. As a wrap-up for *Some Like It Hot*, however, it's less of a sure thing. Inside this picture, everybody *is* perfect. It goes without saying that nobody is good or morally deserving, unless you count the crumbling Sugar, yet all the dizzy men and women on display are allowed to fulfill the essential duties of their nature, to act as we would want them to act, and more than that we surely cannot ask. Wilder has often been disdained by critics for his misanthropy, a complaint that strikes me as absurd; if we were to start striking artists off the list because of the attitudes they happen to hold toward humanity, we would be left with very few. For one thing, there would be piles of Flaubert burning in the street. More pertinent is the question of what Wilder does with this narrow-eyed suspicion of his fellow men, and the most vigorous reply is made by *Some Like It Hot.* The movie holds itself between a sober recognition that none of us can be trusted and the more spirited, even stirring sight of lovers straining every sinew to break the cycle of disenchantment and keep their ridiculous promises. If that sounds tricky, you try straining a sinew in heels.

All of which means that *Some Like It Hot* is an object of beauty. Comedies, under Hollywood law, are not supposed to be beautiful, but Wilder's film, like *Sunset Boulevard* and *The Apartment*, finds a balance between hope and despair, and that in turn translates into a Viennese play of shadow and gleam. ("I hate color," Wilder said, adding, "Even words sound phony when the picture is in color.") When the upright citizens of Kansas tried to ban *Some Like It Hot* because of the scene on the yacht, they didn't know what they were missing: not merely Monroe's astounding backless dress but the enticing glitter when she turns off the lamp—a thousand points of light, reflecting off the dress and the shelf of sporting trophies at the side. She is a trophy, too, but the gorgeousness of the scene makes her momentarily more precious than even Joe, with his fogged spectacles, could possibly know. Likewise, when Sugar thinks she has lost her millionaire, she takes her sadness out on a song, "I'm Through with Love," and Wilder lets her long vibrato—"For I must have *you-oo-oo* or no one"—ring and ripple around the movie, as if it could halt the merry-go-round of constant pursuit, and as if her yearning were more than a silly crush. The happy endings of *Some Like It Hot* and *The Apartment* are not tacked on as an afterthought or a sop; they inform us that good fortune, including the luck of requited love, cannot be relied upon to arrive like a train. It can only be grabbed in passing, at the last gasp.

Billy Wilder knows what happiness is; he once defined it as having a doctor who smokes four packs a day. When the profits of *Some Like It Hot* came in, he himself was handed $1.2 million, which in 1960 was a lot of dough. He bought himself two Paul Klees, an Egon Schiele, and a couple of Braques, to go with his Balthus and his Matisse: happiness you can stare at. Almost three decades later, he was asked, in all seriousness, whether he would have made movies if he hadn't been paid to do so. And Wilder, the man who has told more cold truths than many of us would care to hear, didn't hesitate for a second: "What do you think, I'm a sucker?"

OCTOBER 22, 2001

ACKNOWLEDGMENTS

I must first thank Tina Brown and David Remnick, the two editors of *The New Yorker* under whom it has been such a pleasure to work. Then, there are those who have been assigned the terrible burden of editing my prose on a regular basis; nobody, surely, deserves such a fate, and yet all of them—Charles McGrath, Hal Espen, Deborah Garrison, Alice Quinn, and Virginia Cannon—have borne up bravely, even cheerfully, under circumstances that would have broken lesser souls. Mind you, it is notable that none of the above (apart from Virginia, who is still on active service) was able to take the punishment indefinitely; after a year or two, each editor chose quietly to move on, sometimes to other departments, often to other organizations, and in one case to another state, many time zones away, where the warmer climate might help to heal his wounds. I wonder if the Federal Government should consider starting up a Witness Protection Program for textual editors, who could thus be guaranteed immunity from any writers who might try to ring them up at two in the morning and ask if they could change "subtle" to "overwrought" at the top of the second paragraph.

I should take this opportunity to offer particular thanks to Charles McGrath; he was put on my case when I first arrived, and no writer could ask for a more discerning guide. The courtesy with which he amputated my opening paragraphs could itself be viewed as one of the fine arts, and his silences, as I was throwing lame rephrasings into the air, were more acute than most people's interrogatory rants. I like to think of Chip as the John Robie of editing; Robie, you will recall, was the Cary Grant character in *To Catch a Thief*, and the finest cat burglar on the Côte D'Azur. And so it was with Chip; I could hardly tell that he had broken into my reviews, and there was certainly not a fraction of fingerprint to show where he had been, but the evidence—the sudden arrival of coherence—was there for all to see. Any improvements, it is fair to say, were his alone.

I am immensely grateful to Sally Ann Mock and Michael Agger, of the "Goings on About Town" department, without whom any hope of a schedule would have vanished utterly from my life; they have made it their business to get me to the film on time. That I am nevertheless late for almost every screening, running in scarlet and winded halfway through the pre-credit sequence, has nothing to do with their respective efforts and everything to do with the fact that the grid of New York, designed to be idiot-proof, has finally found the idiot against whom there can be no proof. If you ever see a feverish Brit hopping up and down in a Korean drugstore on Fifty-third Street and asking loudly where the Nutty Professor is, that'll be me.

I am indebted to the patience and industry of the fact-checking department, and especially to Martin Baron, Patricia Brown, Peter Canby, Susan Choi, Gita Daneshjoo (who also helped generously with this book), John Dorfman, Emily Eakin, Blake Eskin, Erin Ferguson, Marina Harss, Nandi Rodrigo, Liesl Schillinger, Caitlin Shetterly, Sarah Smith, and Bill Vourvoulias. My gratitude, for all manner of kindness and advice, goes also to Roger Angell, Elisabeth Biondi, Bill Buford, Justine Cook, Chris Curry, David Denby, Perri Dorset, Henry Finder, Ann Goldstein, Brendan Lemon, Amy Loyd, Susan Morrison, Elizabeth Pearson-Griffiths, Brenda Phipps, Rhonda Sherman, Deborah Treisman, and Dorothy Wickenden.

Beyond the confines of the magazine, many thanks are due to Gerd Grace, and to Ben Macintyre and Kate Muir, for their genial hospitality; also to Anthony Quinn, and, as ever, to Giles Smith, Dermot Clinch, and Roland Philipps. Adam Gopnik and Martha Parker were wonderful friends and guides, both in Paris and New York. It goes without saying that were it not for the love and support of Allison Pearson, and for the tirelessly creative interruptions of Eveline and Thomas Lane, this book would not exist.

I am aware of the distinguished custom which states that, as an author, one should go in awe of one's publisher and in mortal fear of one's agent. Sadly, in the case of Jordan Pavlin, my editor at Knopf, and of Sloan Harris, my agent at ICM, companionship kept getting in the way. Still, Sloan has promised me a ride in his pickup, so maybe fear will yet carry the day. His assistants, Teri Steinberg, Pamela Schein, and Katharine Cluverius, have been models of forbearance, as have Alexis Gargagliano and Sophie Fels at Knopf.

Finally, I must thank the many readers who have written to me at *The New Yorker*. At a rough guess, I would say that bursts of wrath and exasperation have outweighed any sporadic gestures of approval by nine to one. That is at it should be; there is no opinion I hold so ferociously that I would expect, or even want, a majority of people to agree with it. Also, as regards the quality of correspondence, contumely seems to breed a concision denied to more benevolent pens. As one reader wrote some years ago, in response to a piece of mine: "With this review, you have joined the legions of those who would rather be right than happy. And you're not even right." Perfect.

INDEX

ABOUT THE AUTHOR

Anthony Lane was born in 1962. He has been a film critic for The New Yorker *since 1993.*

A NOTE ON THE TYPE

This book was set in Janson, a typeface long thought to have been made by the Dutchman Anton Janson, who was a practicing typefounder in Leipzig during the years 1668–1687. However, it has been conclusively demonstrated that these types are actually the work of Nicholas Kis (1650–1702), a Hungarian, who most probably learned his trade from the master Dutch typefounder Dirk Voskens. The type is an excellent example of the influential and sturdy Dutch types that prevailed in England up to the time William Caslon (1692–1766) developed his own incomparable designs from them.

Composed by Creative Graphics, Allentown, Pennsylvania

Printed and bound by Berryville Graphics, Berryville, Virginia

Designed by Iris Weinstein